'One of our finest medieval historians . . . a sound, lively and engagingly detailed book about the individuals who fought in that war, of knights, chivalry, fashion, literature and the enduringly fascinating private lives of everyone from queens to freebooters. It will satisfy academics and history buffs alike. I cannot praise it highly enough' Alison Weir, *BBC History Magazine*

'In this, his latest and most ambitious book, Barber offers a major reassessment of the battle of Crécy, its sequel in the foundation of the Order of the Garter, and the Order's place in the history of English knighthood . . . He argues his case powerfully . . . his achievement in this book is a very considerable one' Nigel Saul, *History*

'A valuable and thorough addition to the body of work on this most impressive of English monarchs' Dan Jones, *Sunday Times*

'This absorbing book is layered rather than linear, sifting with uncommon sensitivity through challenging sources to test the boundaries of what we can and cannot know . . . We discover the complexity of the world in which Edward and his commanders lived – the relationships between the brutal realities of war and the elegant codes of chivalry, between realpolitik and deeply held faith – and find that the Company of the Garter, as it was known to its founding members, was less an Arthurian tournament team than a religious confraternity intended to remember the souls lost on the killing field at Crécy' Helen Castor, *The Times*

'Barber has brought together old and new research to forge an important new account of Edward III's remarkable career as king. His analysis of the Order of the Garter reveals that any true understanding of modern British institutions relies on a proper appreciation of the Middle Ages' Mark Ormrod, *Independent*

04405725

Richard Barber has had a huge influence on the study of medieval history and literature, both as a writer and as a publisher. His major works include *The Knight and Chivalry* (winner of the Somerset Maugham Award), *Edward, Prince of Wales and Aquitaine*, *The Penguin Guide to Medieval Europe* and *The Holy Grail: The History of a Legend*. He lives in East Anglia.

RICHARD BARBER

Edward III and the Triumph of England

The Battle of Crécy and the Company of the Garter

PENGUIN BOOKS

PENGUIN BOOKS

Published by the Penguin Group
Penguin Books Ltd, 80 Strand, London WC2R ORL, England
Penguin Group (USA) Inc., 375 Hudson Street, New York, New York 10014, USA
Penguin Group (Canada), 90 Eglinton Avenue East, Suite 700, Toronto, Ontario, Canada M4P 2Y3
(a division of Pearson Penguin Canada Inc.)
Penguin Ireland, 25 St Stephen's Green, Dublin 2, Ireland (a division of Penguin Books Ltd)
Penguin Group (Australia), 707 Collins Street, Melbourne, Victoria 3008, Australia
(a division of Pearson Australia Group Pty Ltd)
Penguin Books India Pvt Ltd, 11 Community Centre, Panchsheel Park, New Delhi – 110 017, India
Penguin Group (NZ), 67 Apollo Drive, Rosedale, Auckland 0632, New Zealand
(a division of Pearson New Zealand Ltd)
Penguin Books (South Africa) (Pty) Ltd, Block D, Rosebank Office Park,
181 Jan Smuts Avenue, Parktown North, Gauteng 2193, South Africa

Penguin Books Ltd, Registered Offices: 80 Strand, London WC2R ORL, England

www.penguin.com

First published in Great Britain by Allen Lane 2013
Published in Penguin Books 2014
002

Typeset by Jouve (UK), Milton Keynes

Printed in Great Britain by Clays Ltd, St Ives plc

A CIP catalogue record for this book is available from the British Library

ISBN: 978-0-141-02067-9

www.greenpenguin.co.uk

For Helen
16 August 1942–17 February 2013

Contents

PART THREE
The World of the Garter Companions

PART FOUR
A Question of Honour

List of Illustrations

Maps and Diagrams

Maps

Diagrams

A Note on Terms

Writing about medieval history always poses problems of terminology, and there are two particularly difficult concepts at the heart of the present book. The first is that of knighthood and chivalry, for which we have two words in English; in all other European languages there is only one, and the subtle distinction between the status of being a knight and the ideology of that status is lost. I have used knighthood for both, as chivalry has – thanks to Sir Walter Scott and the Victorians – acquired romantic overtones which are only occasionally appropriate.

'Man at arms' presents another problem; it is a term used generally and quite vaguely in medieval texts. I have used it to denote any soldier wearing metal armour, which means that they could be armoured infantry or the most heavily armed knights; it is not a rank but a classification. It excludes archers, who would have been lightly armed, and infantry with short lances or daggers who might have leather armour or heavy quilted jerkins as protection.

For reasons which will appear in the course of the book, I have followed the usage of the royal accountants of Edward III, and called what we know today as 'the Order of the Garter' 'the Company of the Garter', except for references to the body of Garter knights after 1415, when the contemporary sources begin to use the word 'Order'.

In order not to confuse the reader, I have used what might be called the personal name for nobility: Henry of Grosmont is successively earl of Derby, earl of Lancaster and duke of Lancaster, for example, and I have simply called him Henry of Grosmont throughout. Full titles can be found in the index.

Countries and regions are generally given their modern names; in some cases this is anachronistic or slightly misleading, but, again, it simplifies an already complicated text.

Currency is normally in sterling, as pounds, shillings (20 to the pound) and pence (12 to the shilling); the mark is two-thirds of a pound, or 13*s*. 4*d*. The French *livres tournois* were usually exchanged at five to the pound.

All unattributed translations are by the author. In these cases, the original source is cited for reference.

Companions of the
Garter Elected 1349–1361

This list covers all the traditional founding knights listed in the statutes, together with those appointed subsequently, again according to the traditional lists, down to 1361. The uncertainities and problems surrounding these lists are discussed on pp. 299–300.

Edward III
Edward prince of Wales

Henry of Grosmont, earl of Derby and Leicester, later duke of Lancaster
Thomas Beauchamp, earl of Warwick
Roger Mortimer, later earl of March
William Montagu, second earl of Salisbury
Thomas Holland, later earl of Kent
Robert Ufford, earl of Suffolk
William Bohun, earl of Northampton
Jean de Grailly, captal de Buch

Ralph Stafford, later earl of Stafford
John, Lord Lisle, of Rougemont
John, Lord Beauchamp
John, Lord Mohun
John, Lord Grey, of Rotherfield
Reginald, Lord Cobham
Thomas, Lord Ughtred

Bartholomew Burghersh the younger
Hugh Courtenay
Richard Fitzsimon
Miles Stapleton, of Bedale
Thomas Wale
Hugh Wrottesley

Nigel Loring
John Chandos
James Audley
Otho Holland
Henry Eam (Oem)
Eustace ('Sanchet') d'Auberchicourt
Walter Pavely
William Fitzwarin
Walter Mauny
Frank van Hale
Richard de la Vache
Thomas Ufford
Edward, Lord Despenser
John Sully

In addition, the king's three sons, Lionel, John and Edmund, were appointed in April 1361.

Preface and Acknowledgements

This book arose out of a conversation with Henry Summerson, medieval editor for the *Oxford Dictionary of National Biography*, for whom I had written a number of entries on the knights of the Garter. At that point, the first group biographies were being added to *ODNB*, and my offer of an article on the original knights of the Garter was warmly accepted. However, I was not entirely happy with the result, which summarized existing scholarship; I felt there was more to be discovered, and my suggestion for a full-scale book on the question was encouraged by Simon Winder at Allen Lane. What follows is not what I expected to write, and has taken much longer into the bargain; I hope Simon feels that his patience has been rewarded. It has been a particularly difficult book to structure, tracing as it does the careers of individual knights as well as the world in which 'the Company of the Garter' came into being and the events which shaped it, and his advice has been particularly welcome. I also owe a great debt to Fionnuala Jervis, who read the text with particular attention to non sequiturs and obscurities, and to Lisa Barber, who challenged me on numerous points of scholarship from her considerable expertise on the early documents concerning the Company of the Garter: in both cases, the book was considerably improved.

In the narrative which follows, I have tried to avoid the temptation to speculate, the great lure of writing medieval history. There are therefore two discussions which I have put into appendices. These are both fascinating and potentially controversial questions. The nature of the English battle formation at Crécy will aways be a hypothesis, and in order to present the evidence as clearly as possible, I have tried to restrict the account of the battle in the main text to an analysis of the varied versions offered by the chroniclers. However, that analysis also points to a possible solution to the problem of how Edward drew up his army, and it is this which forms Appendix 1. I am deeply indebted to Sir Philip Preston for his contribution to the result, since he knows the topography of Crécy and the theories about the battlefield far better than I do, and he can also draw much better plans than I.

Appendix 2 discusses the identity of the mysterious 'Sanchet d'Auberchicourt' among the early knights of the Garter. Here I am grateful for the comments and references of Professor Michael Jones and Professor Michael Prestwich, and particularly for the sustained criticism of my argument by Lisa Barber; we have agreed to differ, but the argument has much improved my presentation of the case.

The other people to whom I owe a great debt are Mark Ormrod, who knows far more about Edward III than I do, for his encouragement and help, and for reading the draft version; and Paul Dryburgh and Jonathan Mackman, who have patiently hunted down references in the National Archives, and sent transcriptions and photographs, from which much of the detail in the book derives. Andrew Ayton helped to point me in the right direction at an early stage, and has also kindly read a draft version. Adrian Ailes greatly improved Chapter 14 on the evolution of the office of herald.

I have shamelessly questioned other scholars about specific points, and doubtless bored them with my latest speculations on obscure details. I am grateful to those who have listened patiently and read parts of the book, particularly Jonathan Boulton, Michael Jones, Chris Given-Wilson, Christopher Allmand and Kelly DeVries. Maurizio Campanelli, whose paper at the Leeds Conference some years ago led me to the dramatic account of the battle of Crécy in an anonymous Roman chronicle which had been overlooked by historians for more than two centuries since it was first printed, has been generous in letting me publish before his own account has appeared in print. Others who have helped on linguistic matters are Michael Lapidge and Bart Besamusca, while Werner Paravicini, whose account of the Prussian crusaders has been a basic text, has also contributed his extensive knowledge of Continental heraldry. Linne Mooney, when the book was almost complete, explained that the poem about the Garter knights which was attributed to Chaucer was in fact by Thomas Hoccleve. My thanks go also to Elizabeth Archibald, Christopher Berard and Nigel Saul for discussions on points ranging from heralds in fifteenth-century plays to the relationship between Arthurian romance and chronicles and the early form of the company itself.

I discussed modern military matters with Jamie Lowther-Pinkerton, and medieval seamanship with the late Alan Gurney, whose friendship and nautical knowledge are sorely missed. My sister Philippa Lane shared her knowledge of harvests, chalky soil and the decreasing height of corn. On more obviously relevant topics, I am grateful to Thomas Woodcock and Hubert Chesshyre at the College of Arms, and particularly to Tim Tatton-Brown on Windsor Castle: it was his knowledge of the building accounts there which inspired the book on Edward III's Round Table building while we worked with Time Team on its excavation in August 2006.

As to books, the London Library's resources account for most of the titles quoted in the bibliography: their staff as always have responded impeccably to innumerable requests. Cambridge University Library provided many of the remainder, together with the British Library, the Society of Antiquaries and the Bodleian Library. Finally, I am grateful for the help of Clare Rider, archivist of St George's Windsor; Robert Yorke, librarian at the College of Arms, and to Elisabeth A. Stuart at the Duchy of Cornwall office for the loan of a manuscript translation of Henxteworth's journal.

I am grateful to the copy-editor, Elizabeth Stratford, for her close reading of the text, and particularly for detecting the points where I had contradicted myself over dates and facts; and to the proofreader, Stephen Ryan, for his thorough work. Similarly, the work of the indexer, Auriol Griffith–Jones, helped to uncover problems over the treatment of names and a number of actual errors. Keeping control of often very disparate material is always difficult, and their work has eliminated most, if not all, of the resulting vagaries.

I am aware that, despite all this expert advice, errors and omissions undoubtedly remain, for which I am unwittingly responsible. I am, however, entirely aware of my responsibility for the revisionist view both of the tactics of the battle of Crécy and of the nature of the Company of the Garter itself, and regard this simply as a contribution to an ongoing scholarly debate. I may well be wrong on both counts, but would be disappointed if I have not made at least a reasonable case to be answered, and encouraged other scholars to look again at the evidence.

Since the hardback edition appeared in 2013, a new site for the battle of Crécy has been proposed by Dr Michael Livingston of The Citadel and Dr Kelly DeVries of Loyola University Maryland. The location that they have identified between Crécy and Abbeville is an area that would easily be large enough for the fortification of carts proposed in Appendix I, and it corresponds to many details mentioned in the chronicles. Furthermore, they report that there is a deep man-made ditch which runs for roughly a hundred yards in a direction which would imply that it was a defensive obstacle created by Edward III, though archaeological investigation will be needed to confirm this. This discovery, presented at a conference in Swansea in June 2014, will appear in a casebook on the battle edited by them to be published in 2015 by Liverpool University Press. Since the projections in Appendix I do not depend on a specific site for the battle, it does not invalidate them, but rather tends to support the idea, and Dr DeVries confirms that several neglected sources, which will appear in the casebook, also provide additional evidence in its favour.

EDWARD III AND THE TRIUMPH OF ENGLAND

Different Voices: Reading the Evidence

Only twice in English history has a full-scale seaborne invasion of France been attempted. On both occasions, at the height of summer, a huge invasion fleet appeared off the Normandy coast south-west of Cherbourg. D-Day in 1944 was an unparalleled operation, with a huge range of ships of all sizes, and involved landings on a wide front along the Baie de la Seine. Six hundred years earlier, Edward III's fleet in 1346 landed from ships more similar in size to those of the armada of 'little ships' that rescued the survivors of Dunkirk in 1940. They moored in the anchorage of the Grande Rade off St Vaast-la-Hougue, close to Cherbourg itself, the safest place in the Baie, which offers shelter from the prevailing south-westerlies that blow up the Channel.[1]

Edward had led armies into France before, and would do so again, in pursuit of his claim to the French crown. Since the twelfth century, English expeditions which had been sent to Gascony had landed at the port of Bordeaux, held by Gascons loyal to their English masters. The estuary of the Gironde offered safe harbour for hundreds of ships; on the north coast of France, by contrast, there was little choice. The Breton ports, sometimes but by no means always in friendly hands, were far too small for a naval force of more than 1,200 ships. To the east of Cherbourg, all the ports were securely in French hands, and the only possible landing places were well defended.

Like D-Day, Edward's invasion in 1346 was shrouded in secrecy. The French were aware of his intentions, but had little hard information about his plans, with the result that the landing was unopposed. The campaign which followed was to lead to the first great victory of the English army over French forces, and to the capture of the key port of Calais, the most desirable foothold for the English on the north coast of France, with ready communication with Dover. It gave plausibility to

Edward III's dream of enforcing his claim to the French crown, and transformed England's reputation from that of an unimportant offshore island to that of a major military power with new methods of fighting which aroused dread and admiration among Continental princes.

This book examines the men to whom this achievement can be attributed. The central figure is of course Edward III, but it is his comrades in arms who were the crucial element in the English success, seasoned campaigners who had a decade and more of experience in the harshest kind of warfare, and who had learnt the lesson which so often evaded medieval commanders, that of a genuine comradeship and *esprit de corps*. It is a study of a group of men and their culture – culture in the widest sense, from their places in society and politics to their attitudes and beliefs, their dynastic ambitions and their role models and ideals.

Edward III achieved the almost unique feat of retaining the loyalty of the great lords of England throughout his long reign from 1327 to 1377. There were of course doubtful moments, and times when relations between king and magnates were uneasy, but by and large it was an era of exceptional loyalty to the sovereign. Many of Edward's comrades in arms fought at his side for thirty years or more, and his most intimate friends were a close-knit group. The ties that bound them were a critical element in Edward's success, and found their outward expression in the creation of the Company of the Garter, which we know today as the Order of the Garter. The nature of that company, and the way in which it attained its unparalleled reputation in the world of knighthood, are central to the theme of this book.

Who were the original members of the Company of the Garter? First and foremost, they were the men who led the expedition of 1346, the men who changed England's military reputation with their victory at Crécy, and took the town of Calais in the following year. We know the names of forty-nine of the commanders of Edward's army, and of these fourteen were to become knights of the Company of the Garter. A further seven individual knights who fought on the campaign were also among the probable founder members. It is for this reason that the Crécy campaign is crucial to our understanding of the company. Although the common military experience of the earliest Garter companions was much wider than this one expedition, it was in Normandy in 1346 that the bonds between them were fully forged.

There is a basic assumption behind the study of a group of this kind

4

which also needs to be declared. This book starts from the idea that individuals can make a very considerable difference to the course of history, and that economic and social movements are only part of the story. Edward III is a supreme example of this: his political skills and his relations with the men around him largely account for the exceptional degree of co-operation between crown and magnates during his reign. The men he selected as companions of the Garter shared his ideals and tastes, and, although their personal history is often fragmentary and disjointed, we can in most cases form a good idea of their different characters and origins.

A great deal has been written about the military history of the year 1346, and the outlines of what happened are well established. But as soon as we begin to ask more detailed questions, it becomes clear that, behind the confident narratives of the nineteenth-century historians and the more critical commentaries of recent writers, there is a basic issue which is rarely addressed, and problems which need to be declared before we investigate this small group of men and their individual biographies, let alone try to assess them as a group.

My starting point is therefore the question 'How do we know what we think we know?', and I begin by looking at the writers and sources who can shed light on the history of England and France in the mid-fourteenth century. It produces important and sometimes surprising results; and the question of evidence is a theme which recurs throughout the book. This is particularly true in relation to the early history of the Company of the Garter itself; despite its subsequent fame, we cannot even be sure of the names of the original knights. To listen carefully to these different voices and what they have to tell us, we must first discover who they were, and what lies behind the documents they have left for us.

The medieval past comes down to us through a range of different voices, and the nature of these is an essential part of our story. It is possible to write the history of the fourteenth century from the dry entries in the public records; or it can be done from the vivid story-telling of Jean Froissart, whose highly individual view of the warfare of the period was the chief source for historians until the twentieth century. Neither of these sources is quite what it seems, and between the two extremes is a whole range of further texts and documents.

Before the fourteenth century, chronicles had largely been created by monks or clergy as a record of institutional and national history, and secular writers were very unusual. For Edward III's reign we have a much wider range of authors, writing out of personal enthusiasm and sometimes personal involvement in the events they describe. Their immediacy is gained at the expense of the measured consideration of the cloistered chronicler, but it is unjust to dismiss the majority of them as 'episodic, prejudiced, inaccurate and late'.[2] The public records can give us dates, names and places, but little of what people thought and felt. The chronicles may fall down on precise details; yet they alone can give us the material to understand something of the times. Precisely because they are 'different voices', however, we need to have a sense of the original audience for each text if we are to understand what it is telling us, and how we can use it to assemble the evidence.

Let us begin with the dramatic and picturesque. Jean Froissart's chronicles, written from the viewpoint of someone who travelled between the English and French courts and owed allegiance to both (or neither) at different times, should be a wonderful resource. However, although historians have been admirers of his work for centuries, they have also been baffled and infuriated by it: we have to confront its origins and nature and try to understand this essential text which has so dominated the history of Edward III and the exploits of his knights. Even a historian as rigorous as Jonathan Sumption has to refer to Froissart frequently in his magisterial work on the Hundred Years War, but we have to remember that Froissart was writing towards the end of the fourteenth century, as much as fifty years after the events he describes. For the early years of his chronicle, with which we are largely concerned, he too was listening to the same voices as us and interpreting them as best he could.

Froissart's model, as he himself tells us, was the chronicle of Jean le Bel, canon of Liège, who had written his work at the request of Jean de Hainault, uncle of Edward's wife Philippa.[3] We have a pen-portrait of Le Bel by a man who knew him personally, Jacques d'Hemricourt: tall and handsome, he dressed in rich knightly clothing, and was attended by a following of sixteen to twenty people when he went to church on weekdays. On Sundays and festivals, his entourage, fifty strong, was as grand as that of the bishop himself: and the bishop of Liège was a prince who ruled his own diocese as a state within the Holy Roman Empire. Le Bel's men dined at his table and received robes from him annually, forty sets for his squires, three for his canons and two for his knights. He himself had been trained as a knight in his youth, had fought in tournaments and had been in the household of Jean de Hainault. Jean de Hainault accompanied Edward III on his Scottish expedition in 1327, and Le Bel served under him. He had twin sons by his mistress, one of whom became a knight and the other followed him as a canon at St Martin's.[4]

Writing chronicles was essentially a literary occupation; the idea of a professional historian does not appear until much later, and all the histories, chronicles and annals on which we shall draw have a strong literary background, whether secular or religious. Le Bel's approach is distinctly on the secular side: he 'knew how to write songs and *virelais*', according to Hemricourt. However, he makes no pretensions to a high style: his great virtues as a writer are directness and clarity, and he is an accomplished and orderly narrator.[5] His account of the warfare in Scotland is exceptionally vivid, and makes him one of the very few writers of the period who actually experienced a campaign.[6] He wrote the chronicle in stages: the first part, covering up to 1340, was written some time between 1352 and 1356; the second part, to 1358, was finished that year, and the final chapters are contemporary with the events they record.[7]

Le Bel sets out his objectives in the prologue to his chronicle, chiefly in terms of presenting a riposte in plain prose to the puffery of a large book in verse which has lately appeared claiming to present the history of the recent wars between the French and English kings. He will offer a short, accurate account of events – though the result is far from brief – and he is particularly concerned to do justice to all those who took part in 'such cruel and dangerous battles' without exaggeration or 'attributing to someone incredible prowess which the human body could not achieve'. It should be enough to say that a particular knight had performed best in such and such a battle, and that other knights had done well, 'and to name the knight and the battle'. But he acknowledges that he is partisan: Edward III is his hero, and it is the story of the 'gallant and noble king' that he sets out to tell.[8] His hero has one fatal flaw; Le Bel is reluctant to believe the story which shames the king, but, because he believes it to be true, he resolves to include it. This is the legend of Edward III's rape of the countess of Salisbury, which almost certainly originated in French propaganda designed to defame the king's knightly reputation.[9]

The events which particularly interest him are the knightly episodes, within the context of a narrative which is very much focused on personalities rather than the details of diplomatic documents. And his only possible source for these knightly deeds is the knights themselves and their personal memories. Jean de Hainault himself was a prime source, and Le Bel therefore has a first-hand account of the battle of Crécy from the French side, which he must have recorded no later than nine years after the event (Jean died early in 1356); he had information not only from Jean himself but also from ten or twelve of his household knights, and from several English and German knights who were present.[10] The romantic account which he gives of Walter Mauny, a knight from Jean de Hainault's circle, at the siege of Hennebon in Brittany was also first-hand, though very different in tone. Mauny was with an English force to help Jeanne de Montfort, countess of Brittany, and when they landed she entertained them lavishly. After the entertainment he looked out of the window, and swore he would destroy the huge siege machine which was pounding the town. Taking 300 men, he destroyed it and retreated, pursued by the enemy: he turned and faced them, crying, 'May I never be embraced by my dear love if I return to the fortress without unhorsing one of these attackers, or being unhorsed by them.' This is warfare overlaid by knightly convention: the countess, an accomplished military leader herself, as a lady in distress; an encounter with the enemy as a knightly adventure complete with knightly vow.[11] The truth, as we shall see, was probably much more prosaic, but this was how Mauny wanted the event to be remembered; it may well be how he did indeed recall it after the event.

Jacques d'Hemricourt records that Le Bel's squires were under instructions to invite any 'valiant stranger' to dine with their master, so that he could talk with him. But Le Bel was quick to admit when he was unable to find an informant. He writes in his account of the year 1340 that he has not described the conflict between the English and the Scots at that time because he does not know enough about it. 'And certainly in what I have written above, I have kept as close to the truth as I could, according to what I personally have seen and remembered, and also what I have heard from those who were there, telling me what they really knew, when I was not present; and if I am mistaken about anything, may I be forgiven for it.'[12] More than any other chronicler of the period, he admits openly to his ignorance, refuses to write about matters of which he knows nothing, and tries to distinguish between rumours and information of which he is sure.[13]

Le Bel's presentation of what he has learnt, observed and researched remains literary; he is writing history with heroes and villains, with moral lessons in mind. This may influence his selection of facts, yet he tries to be a conscientious recorder, and largely succeeds in his aim of writing a 'true history'.

Another writer with even closer links to the court of Hainault was Jean Bernier, the provost of Hainault and one of William I of Hainault's most trusted officials. His memoirs are not really a chronicle, as they open with a series of episodes from his career, and other notable events from the history of Valenciennes, where he lived. What he offers is a wonderful insight into the life of wealthy Flemish merchants and their peers, and a rather less important narrative of the history of Flanders, which was evidently continued by other members of his family. In 1334, at his house near the St Pol bridge in Valenciennes, he gave a feast for about seventy people, including the kings of Bohemia and Navarre, the count of Flanders and the bishop of Liège, as well as his master William I and Jean de Hainault. He gives us the seating plan, the menu and the wines they drank; he even tells us that the lampreys came from the royal fishmonger in Paris.[14] Like Le Bel, he was in a position to learn a great deal at first hand from the nobility of Flanders, but only occasional insights appear in the chronicle which follows. The impulse to write history is secondary to his (and his descendants') desire to justify his career, particularly as he was in disgrace after William I's death, and only exonerated some time later.

Le Bel's follower Jean Froissart was of humbler origins; like Jean Bernier, he seems to have been from Valenciennes, but his life before his departure for England in 1361 is obscure. Nor do we know how he managed to get an introduction to Queen Philippa, and to present her with a chronicle of the Anglo-French wars of the previous decade. This sudden appearance at the heart of the English court must have been due to an introduction from someone in Hainault of knightly rank who knew Philippa well, and it was probably due to his literary genius that he obtained this introduction. For we may remember Froissart as a chronicler today, but he had a reputation as a poet and writer of romances before he turned his hand to history. He was famous for his lyrics, and, while he was writing the first version of his chronicles, he was also composing a long Arthurian romance, *Meliador*. For much of his life, he was more famous as a poet than as a historian; and, just as episodes in *Meliador* are drawn from real life, so there is a strong element of knightly romance in his history. He may not have aspired to the knightly lifestyle of Le Bel, but he certainly felt that he belonged to the same knightly milieu.

Froissart sets out a grander scheme at the beginning of his chronicle:

> In order that the great deeds of arms which have come about through the wars of France and England may be suitably recorded and held in perpetual remembrance so that good men may take them as an example, I wish to undertake to set them down in prose. Indeed Sir Jehan le Bel, formerly canon of Saint Lambert at Liège chronicled in his time something of these matters. Now I have augmented this book and this history by careful enquiry as I travelled throughout the world, asking the valiant men and knights, and the squires who helped them, to add to the truth of what happened; and also asking several kings of arms and their marshals, both in France and England, in order to establish the truth of the matter. For such men are rightly the investigators and reporters of such affairs, and I believe that their honour is such that they would not dare to lie.[15]

For the events of this book, Froissart is a second-generation historian. He was probably not yet twenty when the battle of Poitiers was fought in 1356; his information is not contemporary with the events, which means that, were he an ordinary chronicler, he would be piecing together his story from earlier writers. Instead, Froissart tries to discover the truth largely through oral evidence from the participants. While a modern historian will be much more sceptical than he is about their veracity, there are two very valuable elements in his work. Firstly, like Le Bel, he offers us a direct insight into the attitudes of these participants, and sometimes into their individual character. Talking to Froissart, who was known as a chronicler from his earliest days at the English court, the knights could ensure that their version of events was recorded, even if their voices come down to us with a literary veneer added by the writer rather than a verbally accurate report. Froissart often tells us, unconsciously, how such men wished to be remembered. Secondly, this is an age when personal memory was much more highly regarded than it is today: we demand written records or eyewitness accounts contemporary with the event in question. But in the fourteenth century an entire lawsuit could be built round the memory of knights, squires and clergymen: the case of Scrope versus Grosvenor in the Court of Chivalry in 1386 consists solely of the sworn statements of men who had seen one or other of the knights in question bearing the arms which were in dispute. Memory is of course fallible, but Froissart sometimes manages to be surprisingly accurate with very little apparent recourse to written documents. For instance, describing the English naval campaign of 1387, he notes the part played by Piers du Bois of Ghent; this man's presence on the expedition is confirmed by the official records, and makes it likely that Froissart's account of his influence on strategy is probably correct.[16]

Froissart has been called 'the ancestor of our great reporters ... in whose investigations the sensational and the unusual have pride of place'.[17] His work is closer to that of a journalist than of an orthodox historian of the period, and we can watch him at work on his journey to Foix in the winter of 1388–9, where he was anxious to find out more about one of the most famous princes of the age, Gaston III, lord of Foix-Béarn in the Pyrenees, nicknamed Phoebus. He also hoped for news of the affairs of Spain and Portugal from members of his court, 'since there had been no great deeds of arms in Picardy or Flanders for a long time'. On the last stage of his journey, he spent three days at Pamiers waiting for someone else who was going to Béarn and knew the roads, because a lone traveller was very much at risk. He found a talkative Gascon squire in the service of Gaston, Espan du Lion, who was the ideal companion, and also very knowledgeable about the count's affairs. Froissart's account of their conversations on the way show him using sophisticated interviewing techniques, gaining the confidence of his fellow-traveller and offering his own news stories in return for the information he obtains from him. He finds knights from Aragon and members of the household of John of Gaunt from England, and gets the latest situation in Castile, Navarre and Portugal from them; and he manages to learn a good deal about Gaston Phoebus himself from Espan du Lion, who talks with some hesitation about Gaston's murder of his only son and of his cousin. It is brilliant journalism, vivid and racily told; but Froissart was never one to check his facts, and the cousin in question was actually very much alive when Espan told his story.[18] In contrast, the Bascot de Mauleon, a Gascon knight whom he met on the same journey, provided him with what seems to be a straightforward and factual account of his career: where he first fought a battle, and his campaigns thereafter, all described in considerable detail.[19] Much of what he says is supported by other evidence, and, apart from the story of how he and his men captured the castle of Thurie disguised as women, the tone of the narrative is realistic.

Froissart is a man with a mission, and he is not afraid of revising his work. There are at least four versions of the first book of his history, and he returned to it again and again throughout his life in order to recast it and get closer to what he believed to be the truth. The version written in the last years of his life, after his visit to England in 1395, is the considered work of a man who has spent nearly fifty years in search of his vision of a true account of the events of Edward III's reign, when 'prowess reigned for a long time in England, through the deeds of King Edward III and of the prince of Wales, his son'.[20] The earliest versions are largely reworkings of Le Bel's chronicle. To these Froissart adds details from his frequent conversations with the knights who had taken part in the Crécy and Poitiers campaigns, expanding the text very considerably.

At the very end of his life, however, he set down a shorter version of these stories, as if he was attempting a real overview of the events which had fascinated him for so long. This version survives in just one manuscript, now in Rome. Here he showed that he could do more than tell a good story; his reflections and revisions produced a work which takes a much more thoughtful and sometimes philosophical view than his exuberant first attempts. And Froissart is distinctly less romantic about knighthood: there is a new cynicism about the kings and nobles and their politics which balances his account of their heroic deeds.[21] He had always adopted something of the high moral tone of the monastic chroniclers in his treatment of the three kings of England about whose reigns he writes: returning in 1395 from an England in the throes of a political crisis pitting the king against the nobility, he remembered the disasters of Edward II's reign seventy years earlier, and, by the time he finished the longest version of his chronicle, Richard II had met the same fate as his grandfather. In this last, short, version, Froissart reassesses Edward III in the light of experience, and, instead of treating him – as Le Bel had done – as a heroic figure from the start, tries to give some account of how he came to learn statesmanship. At the end of the book, Edward III and Philippa are presented as the most glorious sovereigns in the world; but they have earned this place by the king's wisdom, the queen's devotion and the wise counsel of men such as Walter Mauny.[22]

The Rome manuscript shows how Edward was remembered thirty years after his death; in terms of actual new evidence, there is very little, and it is sometimes most interesting for what it omits rather than for what it includes. We can test Froissart's own opinion of his earlier account against this text; obviously, the rejected stories have to be treated with more scepticism than those he repeats in his final, considered version.

Where we have to be cautious from the historical point of view is in respect of Froissart's literary quality. Froissart writes for effect, and his effects can be striking; when his material falls into a recognized literary pattern, he cannot resist moulding it to fit that formula. He may write pure fiction at times, and if we rely on Froissart for facts it can be very dangerous. His account of the treachery of Robert d'Artois is largely imaginary in terms of times and places.[23] Yet by using his superb literary skills, he can draw out Robert's motives and character by using this combination of a well-organized and integrated, if fictional, narrative. If we read him first and foremost for the mindset of the princes and magnates of the period, he is invaluable.

In the later middle ages Froissart was read as much for entertainment as for instruction, and in the sixteenth century his work was regarded as an adventure story like the romances. When the French translator of the hugely popular Spanish romance *Amadis de Gaula*, Herberay des Essarts, published the fourth volume of the work, he included a puff for his work from an anonymous poet which claimed that, now *Amadis* was available in French, there was no need for the 'Lancelots, Tristans and Froissarts'.[24]

As an antidote to Froissart, we turn to another canon, Gilles li Muisit of Tournai. Like Le Bel, he was a canon for most of his life, while Froissart's post as canon of Chimay was probably a reward for good service in the secular world. Like Le Bel and Froissart, he wrote poetry, much of which survives. But Li Muisit was a regular canon, that is, he was a monk subject to the Benedictine rule, and hence he was a less worldly figure than the other two. He lived within the monastery at Tournai for most of his life, apart from three years studying in Paris, and was abbot from 1331 until his death in 1352. His poems are moral and religious, and he wrote on the history of his abbey. The original manuscript of this survives, and at the end of it is Li Muisit's chronicle, his last work. In Paris, he had been nicknamed 'Pluma', quill pen, and it seems that for much of his life he noted down important events and information.[25]

In 1345 he began to go blind, and it was at this point that he started to write, unable to lead his previously active life. The notes he had accumulated over the years were read to him; he dictated a text based on them to his scribe, but was unable to read the result and correct it. Even though he recovered his sight in 1352 after an operation, he never revised the text, because he died soon afterwards. He completed the chronicle proper in 1348; this he then continued in what he called annals, and both these and the later years of the chronicle are therefore more or less contemporary with the events of Edward III's reign, which makes him a valuable source. His style is dry, and there are none of the picturesque details found in Froissart and Le Bel, but he is well informed and thoughtful. In particular, he is very cautious about figures, and tries to give accurate estimates wherever he can, perhaps because he had an interest in mathematics and in astronomy.[26]

Li Muisit does use written sources quite extensively, but only names one or two. Likewise, he draws on oral testimony, but reveals the identity of just two of his informants, a papal chaplain with much experience of the papal court at Avignon, and his cousin, a councillor in the French parlement. Tournai, although almost surrounded by Flemish territory, was an important French stronghold, besieged by Edward III in 1340, and Li Muisit is, like the inhabitants in general, very much pro-French. He describes how, during the siege of Tournai, the French forces defending the town managed their relations with the inhabitants so well that 'there was never a disagreement or strife between them; but they were like blood brothers together'.[27] His abbey received many distinguished guests, and it is from them that much of his information must have come. But he protests that he is a severe critic of what he hears: 'People in general believe easily, and even more easily repeat and spread what they have heard, so that what they say is partly false, partly true: I do not approve of such talk and put no trust in it, particularly because if I write down things about which I may not be certain, my whole work will be in disrepute, and I will not be believed in other matters.'[28] This leads him to give an account of the outcome of the battle of Crécy very different from that of other chroniclers. Yet for all his protestations, he is happy to repeat horror stories of the atrocities of English troops in 1338,[29] while the French forces can do no wrong. He is a dour but largely realistic counterweight to the narratives of chivalrous exploits in Le Bel and Froissart. And his voice speaks not for the nobility, for whom war represented glory and profit, but for the defenceless and weak who were the main sufferers.

Jean de Venette was, like Gilles li Muisit, a highly placed cleric, prior of the Paris convent of Carmelite friars, and eventually head of the order in France.[30] The work of the Carmelites put them in close touch with the lay world; Venette himself was of peasant origin. He was very probably writing as events happened from 1360 onwards, and has much detail of the disasters which overtook ordinary citizens and countrymen after the battle of Poitiers, in the time of the popular uprising known as the *Jacquerie*, a violent reaction to the failure of government after the capture of John II of France. He is less inclined to blame the English exclusively for the horrors of war, and sees events from the standpoint of the classic definition of the orders of society: for the well-being of all, the peasant should work, the clergy should pray and labour at spiritual matters, and the knight should defend all three orders. His theme is that the knights have failed in their duty, and that the disturbances are the result of this failure, particularly as they now extort payments in return for this non-existent protection. Jean de Venette is another voice to set against those of the aristocratic chroniclers. He, like Gilles li Muisit, is moved to set down what he has seen and heard as a record of the disasters of the times.

Le Bel, Li Muisit and Venette all seem to have been stimulated to write their histories because of their own personal experience of the war and its consequences. In England, there is only one comparable author, Thomas Gray, whose background, like Le Bel's, was the Scottish wars.[31] His family came from near Berwick, where an ancestor had been mayor in 1253. Thomas was probably born soon after 1310, and first appears in the records in 1331 accused of poaching, and in 1332 he was involved in the abduction and ransom of a citizen of Berwick. His first experience of warfare may have been at the battle of Dupplin Moor in the same year; six years later he was certainly in the retinue of William Montagu, first earl of Salisbury, when Edward III sailed for Flanders. He returned from Flanders in 1340, possibly after Montagu had been captured by the French, and his movements thereafter are not clear. He may well have been the Thomas Gray, 'knight of the prince's household', who was presented with £20 when he was given leave to go to visit his friends in 1344–5.[32] This was about the time his father died, and his career henceforth was in the north: he inherited his father's estates and played an increasingly important military role. He was at the battle of Neville's Cross in 1346, when the Scottish king David II was captured, but he himself was captured by a Franco-Scottish force in 1355, and found himself in prison for a year. Here, like the more famous knight-prisoner Thomas Malory, he occupied his enforced leisure by starting his chronicle. He was released by autumn 1356, and continued to write until 1362, seven years before his death.

Gray's chronicle is therefore largely the work of a contemporary, often an eyewitness, and of a man highly experienced in war. Le Bel's brief service as a squire gave him something of the same authority, but his is a more literary creation. Gray is practical, direct and independent: he is openly critical of William Montagu, his leader in Flanders, saying that he was captured due to his own folly in undertaking 'a foolhardy *chevauchée*'* and he accuses him and Edward III of wasting the army's time for fifteen months, jousting and devoting himself to pleasure, after they arrived at Antwerp in 1338. He has little time for the niceties of knighthood: warfare on the Scottish border was a harsher and more brutal affair altogether. He began his work by drawing on two chronicles written in the north, and on the popular history of the time, the so-called *Brut*,[33] and used these to bring his work up to the point where his own career began. His style is straightforward but often vivid in its descriptions, and it is a great pity that his account of the years 1340 to 1356 is missing from the unique manuscript.[34]

There is another knightly chronicle, which is the work of someone who was an eyewitness of the Spanish campaign of 1366–7. This is *The Life of the Black Prince*, by the herald of John Chandos:[35] a personal herald was known by his master's name, so he names himself 'Chandos Herald'. We know nothing about him apart from the evidence of his work: the language reveals that he was probably from Hainault, like Froissart, and indeed Froissart obtained much information from him.

---

* A *chevauchée* is an expedition on horseback, usually a raid into enemy territory.

Chandos Herald was a participant in many of the episodes he describes. He was probably the man who carried money to John Chandos from the king of Navarre in 1363.[36] However, his description of the battle of Poitiers implies that he was not in John's service at that time, and therefore was not an eyewitness, since he says at one point, 'The book and the story tell . . .'[37]

Chandos Herald writes in verse, perhaps because this was the traditional way of memorizing history in an oral culture; there are accounts of tournaments by heralds in the thirteenth century which use similar verse forms. It is an awkward form for a factual history such as his and was old-fashioned even when he composed his poem, and he admits as much in the opening lines. However, 'people . . . should not give up writing poems about good deeds, if they know how to, but should write them in a book, so that when they are dead there is an honest record'.[38] As to his purpose, he wishes to record the names of the participants and the feats of arms which they accomplished; shameful deeds are not on the agenda, and he pointedly refuses to list the French knights who fled from the field of Crécy: 'three kings left the field, many others fled – how many I do not know, and it is not right to count them.'[39]

Nearly half his chronicle is taken up by the Spanish campaign of 1367, at which he was present, and his role as a herald shapes his account: his lists of names can be checked against record sources and are very accurate, and he is our best source for the sequence of military events. Yet this factual record is overlaid with some of the conventions of romance, such as the scene of Edward prince of Wales's parting from his wife. And warfare is a matter for his heroes: when the Spanish ambush the army, they send 'men at arms riding mules and other ruffians to attack them'. The hardships of the crossing of the Pyrenees and the horrors of war are glossed over.[40] If, as is possible, the poem was written for Richard II in the 1380s, this is how a knightly audience wished to see itself reflected in the mirror of history.

The battle of Nájera is the only occasion when we have a detailed eyewitness account from the other side. Pero López de Ayala was definitely a grandee, and he writes in the same vein as Froissart. Born into the Castilian aristocracy, he had a distinguished career as a soldier, diplomat and finally grand chancellor of Castile. He fought at Nájera, and was captured by the English forces, becoming a prisoner of the prince of Wales. He was also a poet and a writer; his *Rhyme of the Palace* is both a satire on the life of the royal court and a confessional.[41] The foreword to his history of Pedro's reign declares:

> The memory of men is weak and they cannot recall everything that happened in the past. For this reason, the wise men of ancient times invented letters and ways of writing so that the sciences and great deeds of the world were recorded and kept so that men knew of them, and learnt from them to do good and to avoid evil, and to keep them in lasting remembrance. And books were later made in which such things were written and recorded ... And thence it became the custom that princes and kings should order that books be made, called chronicles and histories, where deeds of knighthood and any other actions of the princes of old were recorded, so that those who came after them, when they read of their deeds, would make greater efforts to do good and to avoid doing evil ...
>
> And therefore from now on I, Pero López de Ayala, with God's help, intend to continue recording, as truthfully as possible, what I have seen, and I intend to tell nothing but the truth; with all possible diligence I will also record other events which happen in my age and time in places where I was not present, if I hear of them by truthful report and witness from gentlemen and others worthy of belief.[42]

López sees history as an example to his contemporaries, reflecting his unusually intellectual education under his uncle, Cardinal Gómez Barroso; and he insists on the veracity of his sources. He sees the 'truthful report and witness' of reliable informants as the key to writing his chronicle, echoing the approach of Le Bel and Froissart: history should be reported by those who were present, and deeds are the mainspring of the action.

The insistence on reportage and eyewitness evidence does not surprise us today; indeed, it seems entirely normal. But the writers we have met so far are outside the tradition of the historians of the early middle ages. Since, before the fourteenth century, chroniclers were generally members of the clergy, and most commonly monks who were technically confined to their monasteries, they were entirely reliant on second-hand reports of events outside their walls. However, the great monasteries often had good contacts with the royal court: in England, this was true of St Albans in the thirteenth century. In France, the great French official chronicle, the *Grandes chroniques*, was the work of the monks of St Denis, the royal monastery to the north of Paris where the kings of France were buried and the *oriflamme* or banner of France was kept. This was both a history of the reigns of each king and also a general history of France. The continuation of this, dealing with John II and Charles V,[43] begins in the monastic style, but seems to have been written from 1350 onwards by someone close to Charles V. It is not far from being propaganda, and is much more interested in putting across official business and the official viewpoint on current affairs than in the details of campaigns, let alone of knightly exploits. But it is important for our understanding of the French side and of the king whose new tactics effectively held the English at bay throughout his reign.

Paris never became a great centre for the recording of history; London, by contrast, had a number of important authors in the mid-fourteenth century.[44] These men, like Le Bel and Froissart, were secular clerics, usually canons; they went about the king's business or the business of their cathedral or church among the populace at large, and had the opportunity of seeing events at first hand as well as access to official records and men of standing who could give them information. The canons of St Paul's were frequently also royal officials, and three sets of annals written at or near St Paul's in the early years of Edward III's reign give us a view of the king and his business from the heart of the capital.[45] The anonymous author of the first annals (up to 1337) gives us vivid descriptions of Edward's early royal tournaments in London, and details of government activity in the city. He was followed by Adam Murimuth, a diplomat who carried out a number of missions for Edward II to the papal court. His work is relatively brief and selective – he often comments that nothing important happened in a particular year – and it ends in 1347. His approach is unusual for the time, but also what one might expect from a senior government official. Much of what he tells us has to do with diplomatic work; his experiences make him anti-papal and anti-French. He gives us in great detail an assessment of Edward III's claim to the French crown, and information about several attempts to negotiate peace between the two kingdoms. But for our purposes the most valuable part is the descriptions of the skirmishes and battles, by land and sea, of the early years of the Hundred Years War. In some cases he summarizes what may have been a written report, but he also preserves the full text of several documents which were effectively royal circulars on the progress of the campaigns in France.[46] And he shows us government propaganda at work during the Crécy campaign, in the sermon of Archbishop Stratford in August 1346 at St Paul's, at which the archbishop read out a French plan for the conquest of England which had been found when the city of Caen was captured. He was not an unstinting admirer of Edward, however, and criticized his conduct of the war in Flanders. Like Thomas Gray, he attacked William Montagu for the 'senseless audacity' which led to his capture. On the other hand, he gives an admiring account of the great festival at Windsor in 1344, which he either witnessed or heard about from one of the many citizens of London invited to the occasion by the king.[47]

Robert of Avesbury was a legal official serving the archbishop of Canterbury, and lived near St Paul's. His chronicle is boldly entitled 'The wonderful deeds of the magnificent king of England ... and his peers'.[48] When Edward shakes off the rule of Isabella and Mortimer, Avesbury declares that 'from henceforth the said lord Edward the Third held the sun of his majesty and reigned as a magnificent king, wishing to exercise himself and his men in deeds of arms'.[49] The 'wonderful deeds' alert us to expect a narrative which sees Edward in knightly terms, and this is indeed what we get. However, Avesbury's sources, like Murimuth's, are the official reports of the fighting in France, many of which he quotes, including two from the St Paul's archives: others come from the Canterbury archives. Almost half his text is taken up with copies of such documents, which he obviously took great pains to collect: he is able to quote a letter to the king of France from the captain of Calais found in a ship captured by the English during the siege of 1347. Occasionally he finds an eyewitness who has a tale to tell, as in the episode at Calais in 1350 when Edward and the prince of Wales personally fought off a surprise attack by French forces: this was related to him by one of the captured French knights. This episode becomes a set piece in several chronicles, and, if there is an element of hero-worship in all this, it gives us a good idea of how the first half of Edward's reign was viewed by his supporters.[50]

The untitled chronicle written in French in London in the 1330s offers a very different perspective on the events of the time. It is much more direct, as if we were listening to someone telling of his experiences, though the stories may well have been at second or third hand. The chronicle is sometimes cast in a conventional literary style: Edward is made to voice remarks such as 'Because Christ died for us on a Friday, we will not attack the enemy today', or to exhort his troops with: 'Fair lords and my brothers, do not be dismayed, but be of good comfort, and he who enters the battle for me today and fights for the good cause will have God's blessing.'[51] Edward is called 'our king', alongside 'our archers' and 'our engineers', which implies that an oral narrative underlies the text: and episodes such as that of Edward's sudden return in 1340 to chastise the officials at home for their failure to send money to him in Flanders seem to be told by eyewitnesses of scenes in London and at St Albans. This is the talk of the London merchants, deeply concerned about the troubled times in which they lived, and eager for news.

Men were just as avid for news outside London, even if it was scarcer and less reliable than in the capital. One chronicle stands out as a history with many different continuations, rather like the *Anglo-Saxon Chronicle* four centuries earlier. This is the *Brut*, so called from Brutus, the supposed founder of Britain, with whose exploits it begins. It survives in French, Latin and English versions, in more than 300 manuscripts, and was aimed particularly at a knightly readership. The material on Edward II and Edward III in the original French version is often very vivid and evidently well informed, particularly about the events from Isabella's landing in England to the battle of Halidon Hill in 1333. This part of it (and perhaps the earlier sections as well) was written at the behest of two particular families of powerful magnates, the earls of Lancaster and the Bohuns; it certainly represents a view of England different from that of the capital. For these years, it has a vivid directness that implies that the author had access to good oral sources, for example for Edward III's coup against Mortimer in 1330.[52] Although the original version ended in 1333, it was continued by other hands. Most of these continuations are brief and rather dull; just occasionally we encounter a well-informed writer who has original material not found elsewhere.[53]

The best of the chroniclers outside London is Geoffrey le Baker, who was in a way a country equivalent of Adam Murimuth; although the latter's career was largely in London, the two men probably knew each other, and Baker started his chronicle using Murimuth as a basis.[54] He seems to have had connections in Oxford, possibly through the house of

Carmelite friars there, and came from nearby Swinbrook. One of his sources of information, and perhaps his patron, was Thomas de la More, a local magnate and member of parliament for Oxfordshire between 1340 and 1351, who was also nephew of Archbishop John Stratford, who played a central part in the government up to 1341. Baker also seems to have had a connection to the Bohun family, the king's cousins, earls of Hereford and Northampton. He must have been friendly with men who had seen service in Edward III's campaigns, both as soldiers and as clerks, because he has eyewitness accounts of the fighting as well as detailed notes of the routes taken by the armies which must come from official records. He gives a view of the war as seen by the provincial knights who were the backbone of the royal armies. As his chronicle ends in 1356, it was almost certainly written very shortly after this and is therefore a contemporary voice.

The chronicles from France which cover this period are largely written, like Froissart's final version, with hindsight. The best of them is the *Chronicle of the First Four Valois Kings*, whose author may have been a cleric in the Norman administration at Rouen, and which dates from the 1380s; it takes a strongly nationalist view, and reflects the changing attitudes at the end of the century, when the divisions of nationality outweighed the old common culture of knightly aristocracy. In some ways, it is the French equivalent of Geoffrey le Baker, a provincial voice; it gives a different, local perspective on many events: we hear of the heroic resistance of the Normans at the battle of Sluys, which appears in the earlier chronicles as a much more one-sided affair; and the English are very clearly the enemy. But accounts of deeds of arms and knightly episodes persist, such as that of the invasion of Guernsey, when the local girls gave chaplets of flowers and violets to their admirers, telling the men that with such lovers they should fight for them all the harder.[55] The author is also, like his predecessors in monasteries who wrote chronicles, partial to gossip which must have come from passing travellers. Examples are the story of the man who was commanded by a voice from the air to go and tell Charles V that he was not fighting hard enough against his enemies, and the rumours about the marriage of Edward prince of Wales and Joan of Kent, which was said to have roused Edward III to fury, because his son might have made a brilliant alliance with a foreign princess.[56] The myths are beginning to accumulate: this is not Froissart's measured reconsideration of the history of the English years of triumph. Instead, it looks forward to a world where there is a black and white contrast between English and French, and national identity is the overriding force.

The same is true of the *Norman Chronicle*, written in Normandy between 1369 and 1372 by a fierce supporter of Charles V just at the point where events were turning in favour of the Valois kings.[57] It is markedly different from most of our sources in being generally unenthusiastic about warfare, accepting it wearily as a fact of life rather than condemning it passionately. The author is difficult to place, but may have been a town-dweller: he is a record-keeper rather than a chronicler, and his work reads as a series of disjointed episodes. There are no heroes here, and he is more taken by a story of how a garrison was nearly lured out of a town when their herd of pigs was let loose by the enemy than by any knightly exploits. It is a different, rather incoherent view of the war, and where the author gained his information is unclear; perhaps from other towns, as we know that towns corresponded with each other during this period, sending warnings of imminent attack and other vital information on a regular basis.[58] Rodez in central France communicated with nearly sixty other towns in the period 1358–86, and recorded the costs in its accounts under 'Messengers and Spies'. If this suggestion is correct, the *Norman Chronicle* may preserve firsthand accounts of the events of the late 1360s; for the earlier years, it may tell us something of the resigned weariness of the citizens of France in the face of disaster.

We still have original copies of some of the town letters, and letters in general, whether original or, as so often, copied into chronicles or into official records, are a vital source of our knowledge of events. The French and English letters that survive are very different in character, but almost all of them are factual records which tell us little about the men who wrote them, reflecting only their immediate preoccupations. The purposes of the letters diverge sharply. The English letters are for the most part propaganda designed to encourage the war effort at home, while the French correspondence is part of a network of self-help against the unpredictable marauders at large in the countryside, whether it is an English army on a raid or freebooting adventurers in search of plunder – not that there was always much of a distinction between the two.

Communication between English forces on the Continent and the government at home must have been a problem from the campaigns of Henry II in the twelfth century onwards. The important messages may often have been oral, but from the late thirteenth century there are surviving letters about the progress of the English armies. Letters were often sent out before a campaign to the archbishops and bishops of England and Wales requesting prayers, masses, sermons and processions in support of the king and his army, and these letters usually included a brief statement of the reasons for the king's actions.[59] Other letters are formal government documents, and really belong with the official records: the most important example is a letter sent by Edward III to his council in London on 29 July 1346, just after he had taken the city of Caen on his campaign in Normandy. He relates the fortunes of the campaign, giving details of the castles and towns taken, and requests that letters be sent to the prelates and clergy, and to the City of London, telling them of these events, so that they are reassured, and so that prayers may be said for his future success. Then he turns to practical matters, requests for money and supplies, particularly bows, arrows and bowstrings. Other letters are sent with this one, to be forwarded to his allies in Flanders and to the archbishop of York and the lords in the north of England: these were presumably about military affairs, as he planned to join up with the Flemish army, and there was a threat of Scottish invasion.[60]

At the next level, there were semi-official communiqués which reported a victory. After the sea-fight at Sluys, Edward sent out a letter ordering public thanksgiving for the victory, but the details of the battle were very brief.[61] The short chronicle known as *The Acts of War of Edward III* may have been prepared for Bartholomew Burghersh the elder to read to parliament in late 1346;[62] its style is not unlike that of Edward's own letter, but it is much more extensive and detailed. For the battle of Poitiers, we have the letters of Edward prince of Wales: that describing the Poitiers campaign was taken by the prince's chamberlain, Nigel Loring, to the mayor and officials of London, and clearly had some status as an official document.[63]

There are also a large number of letters which are highly personal, but were clearly intended to be shared as widely as possible or summarized for other readers. The most personal of these is Edward prince of Wales's letter to Joan of Kent after the battle of Nájera: Joan had given birth to their first son, Edward, while he was away on campaign, and he writes to reassure her that all is well; he begins: 'My dearest and truest sweetheart and beloved companion, as to news,' and concludes after giving his account of the victory, 'You will be glad to know, dearest companion, that we, our brother Lancaster and all the nobles of our army are well, thank God, except only Sir John Ferrers, who did much fighting.'[64] This is the only time that we get any glimpse of the prince's character from his own hand, and is clearly written in the heat of the moment. If there were other official letters, they have not survived, but the news of the victory would have been copied and passed on.

The same is true of the much larger number of campaign letters which were sent by members of the army to their friends and contacts at home. Many of them are from the clerks who were responsible for the administration of the army, and therefore had writing materials to hand. Such letters often went from one royal official to another, but not as a formal report; Adam Murimuth and Robert of Avesbury, because they were part of this circle, copied a dozen or so of these documents into their chronicles. Indeed, it is possible that two letters from a clerk with the royal army, Michael Northburgh, may have actually been addressed to them; these cover the whole of the campaign, with a gap of about seventeen days between the events in the first and second letters, perhaps because a third letter is lost. This is real reporting, an attempt to give a systematic account of events.[65]

Other letters are more personal: the best example of this is a letter to Richard Stafford, who had been sent back to England from Gascony in 1355, from his friend and colleague John Wingfield, bringing him up to date with events in Gascony early in 1356. He reassures Stafford that his men, who are with John Chandos and James Audley, are at Castel-sagrat, 'and have enough of all kinds of supplies to last until midsummer, except only for fresh fish and greens, according to their letters'. He adds that a strong French contingent under Marshal Boucicaut has arrived nearby, and that 'there will be a good company there for each to try his comrades' worth'.[66] It is a rare glimpse of the concern of commanders for their men.

The reports sent home at the time of the campaign often resurface in a number of fourteenth-century chronicles which describe the king's march in some detail. Northburgh's letters and *The Acts of War of Edward III* are among half a dozen such documents which seem to have existed for the events of 1346, and by analysing the details which the chroniclers give we can see which 'campaign diary' they used. Similarly, two campaign reports survive for the Poitiers campaign, one of them apparently quoted verbatim by Geoffrey le Baker. Sometimes these diaries are simply a list of places at which the army halted, copied out as a separate text. In one instance, the so-called 'Kitchen Journal', the diary is part of a set of accounts kept by Walter Wetewang, in charge of the army's finances, which notes this information at the end of each day's entries.

The existence of other letters, now lost, can be detected in passages from the English chronicles which are clearly paraphrases of them. These represent one 'news network'; but there were other networks beyond that of the English government's propaganda. Across Europe, the great Italian trading companies maintained a detailed correspondence, for the latest and most accurate information was vital to their business; and mercenaries and knights fighting far from home also passed on news of their military adventures.

The Italian companies based in Florence were so deeply involved in the financing of the wars and commerce of the first half of the fourteenth century that by 1350 the major lenders, Bardi, Peruzzi and Acciaioli, had all been bankrupted. They were remarkably like modern firms, with shareholders and speculative capital, but because they did not operate for long, and had no direct successors, very little of their archives has survived.[67] We can only guess at the extent of their correspondence from chance survivals of later merchants' letters, such as those of the Datini company used by Iris Origo in *The Merchant of Prato*, which gives an extraordinary picture of one merchant's network. Up to 1357, each of the Italian companies seems to have run its own, highly expensive couriers; the need for retrenchment meant that in that year seventeen companies co-operated to set up a common service. The Datini records show the dispatch and receipt of 320,000 items over two decades, averaging almost fifty items a day. Much of this was purely commercial, bills and financial documents, but there was also vital market intelligence, which included political reports.

Giovanni Villani, who was still writing his *New Chronicle* when he died of the plague in 1348, was at the heart of this commercial world.[68] In 1324 he was head of the international company of the Buonaccorsi, while his brothers worked for the Peruzzi. The Buonaccorsi were a second-rank company, but nonetheless were active in England, and employed a former agent of the Bardi. They were soon involved in banking in France and Flanders as well, with branches in Bruges, Antwerp, London, Paris, Reims and Laon, all with agents who would report regularly on current affairs to the head office in Florence. The company failed in 1341, brought down like the others by huge loans to sovereigns – in effect, government bonds – and speculation in commercial activities. Both these activities required fast and accurate intelligence; for the last twenty years of his life Villani assembled the political information from his records into his chronicle day by day. He used both oral reports from Florentines returning from foreign countries, and above all the mercantile letters which flowed into Florence; sometimes he writes as if he is an eyewitness, but he is in fact quoting from a letter, while the final chapter is a letter on an earthquake in the Alps, copied verbatim. This final chapter provides extremely accurate information, confirmed by other accounts of the earthquake, and shows how the merchants' news network was generally very reliable.[69] Villani's evidence is therefore of prime importance, often less biased and sometimes better informed than that of English and French records.[70] His brother Matteo, who continued the chronicle down to 1363, is less well informed about English affairs, perhaps reflecting the declining commercial contacts between Florence and England after the Black Death.[71]

As to men who actually fought in the battles, their experiences usually come down to us at second hand in chronicles such as those of Jean le Bel and Geoffrey le Baker; and when we do have their own words, as in the case of a German knight writing to his lord about his part in the battle of Crécy,[72] they are often very general. The question of how much we can ever know, even from eyewitnesses, of what went on in a battle, is one to which we shall return. The English victories at Crécy, Poitiers and to a lesser extent Najéra, resounded across Europe, and we can watch the way in which the reports of these events changed over the years. After Poitiers, first news of the battle claimed that King John himself had been killed by a Navarrese squire, while other letters related accurately that he had been captured; the French emphasized the bravery of the king and his youngest son, while the English had only to underline the scale of their victory. By the end of the century, chroniclers are diligently sifting through the varying stories to try to arrive at a considered view of what had happened.[73] And they embellish their accounts:

Geoffrey le Baker and Matteo Villani give the prince of Wales a speech in which he rallies his men; Baker's is an exercise in rhetoric, while Villani uses it to outline the prince's dire straits, unable to escape and vastly outnumbered by the enemy.

There is one chronicle which seems to preserve in passing eyewitness accounts of the battle of Crécy from two viewpoints. One is that of a Genoese crossbowman hired by the French, who may be the source for parts of Giovanni Villani's story; the other view of the battle is very probably from a Bohemian or German knight in the company of King John. The combined description is preserved in an anonymous Roman chronicle which gives a dramatic account of the republican politics of Rome in the 1350s, and the information on Crécy was not of interest to the Italian historians who originally edited it.[74] It is a difficult text to analyse: written by a well-educated author, it is in a broad Roman dialect, and has many aspects of popular oral literature, particularly the repetition of key phrases, in the manner of a ballad singer. The content, however, is another matter. The striking aspect of this account is that it is in parts very detailed, in a way that would be difficult to invent. To take a single instance: the attack by the crossbowmen failed, and Villani attributes this to the crossbow strings being wet. He is right about the battle being fought in showery weather, but the Roman chronicle tells us that the rain had made the ground so slippery that the crossbowmen could not draw their bows, because when they put their foot in the stirrup, which had to be planted firmly on the ground so that the string could be wound upwards and tensioned, it was impossible to hold the bow still. Now, the land at Crécy is chalk, with a thin covering of topsoil, and, like all chalk hills, is 'slick as silk' after rain.[75] There are other aspects of the Roman account which are wildly off the mark, but these concern matters which a member of the army would only have known by hearsay. I believe this is one of those moments when, for once, we can actually see the reality of medieval battle: a man at arms struggling with his weapon in adverse conditions.

At the other extreme from this dramatic silhouette of the reality of battle lies the sophisticated art of propaganda, all too familiar today, but equally one of the weapons in the armoury of medieval kings. One of the greatest financial and military powers in Europe had been destroyed only decades earlier by skilful propaganda on the part of the French kings. The Order of Knights Templar, the bankers of Europe, had been brought down by Philip the Fair, who was seeking an excuse to confiscate their vast wealth, by accusations of heresy and black magic. Indirectly, this contributed to the emergence of the secular orders of knighthood; but the skills learnt during this episode were deployed by the French in the early years of the war between France and England. It is possible that the belief that Edward II escaped to the Continent rather than being murdered at Berkeley Castle originated in documents forged in France, reported to Edward III by his agent at the papal court. At a critical juncture in Edward's relations with his nobles, he was accused of raping the wife of his closest friend, a story which only appears in French chronicles. A satirical poem attributing the beginning of the war to a dissatisfied French nobleman who goads Edward into action at a feast to which he brings a heron, a symbol of cowardice, was another example of the attempts to undermine Edward's reputation. The English riposte was far less subtle: the mocking poems of Laurence Minot are little more than invective, and the whole emphasis of English propaganda efforts is directed at maintaining public support for the war. Edward was assiduous in reporting his successes back to the administration in England; the letters he wrote also went to the English bishops, bailiffs and sheriffs, and the clergy were urgently requested to pray for success.[76] The knights of England and Hainault were also expert at telling their stories to chroniclers such as Jean le Bel and Froissart, and building up their image as knightly heroes. The result is war, not as reality, but as heroic autobiography.

This, then, is the material from which the picture which follows is built up: hugely variable in origin and quality, often a minefield of contradictions, a range of voices so different that it is hard to weigh one against another. Sometimes the focus eludes us altogether, and then suddenly the picture is sharp and clear for a moment. We can usually map out the sequence of events, but, as we shall see, character and motive are much more speculative. By looking in detail at the 'Company of the Garter', a group of men with close ties to each other and similar backgrounds, there is perhaps a chance that their lives will illuminate each other, and that their communal activity will emerge more clearly.

PART ONE

The Rise of English Power

Prologue: The Political Background

When Edward came to the throne of England in 1327 at the age of fourteen, he faced three major issues. The most immediate was the war with Scotland, which had begun at the end of his grandfather Edward I's reign. The second was the political legacy of his father, Edward II, which had left the magnates deeply divided and power in the hands of Queen Isabella and her close adviser and probable lover, Roger Mortimer. Furthermore, the dramatic events surrounding his father's deposition and death were far from resolved. And thirdly, after the accession of Philip of Valois, Edward's cousin, to the French throne in 1328, Edward had a strong claim to be the rightful heir to the French crown.

The rivalry between the kings of England and France was an ancient one. When the forebears of the English kings, Viking raiders from Norway led by Rollo, invaded France at the beginning of the tenth century, the French were unable to drive them out, and attempted to restrain them by granting them the land around Rouen in 911. By 933 the Vikings had pressured the French king Raoul into conceding almost all the territory that became the medieval duchy of Normandy.

Much of medieval history is concerned with the tension between kings and their great vassals, and the duke of Normandy was to prove the most troublesome of all the lords who owed homage to the French king. With Duke William's conquest of England, the Norman dukes commanded resources at least equal to those of the French king, whose own domains were centred round Paris, and whose control over the more distant lordships such as Aquitaine was often tenuous. When, in 1137, Louis VII of France married Eleanor, who was duchess of Aquitaine in her own right, the problem of Aquitaine seemed to have been resolved: it was a huge territory, stretching from Poitiers to the Pyrenees, but intrinsically weak, since the ducal government at Poitiers had in turn little control over its own distant vassals. However, Eleanor failed to bear Louis a son, and, desperate for an heir, he divorced her in 1152, only to see the duke of Normandy and future King Henry II of England carry her off within a few weeks. Henry and Eleanor's marriage created a network of vassal territories far more powerful than that of the kings of France, since Henry had inherited Anjou and Maine from his father, and his lands now extended from the Channel continuously down almost to the Mediterranean. In addition, he was of course the king of England. Historians often refer to it as the 'Angevin empire', but it would be more truthful to call it 'Henry II's empire'; it was he who was its linchpin, and it was very much his personal creation.

But the contest was not as unequal as it might have seemed, since Louis VII was king of the Franks, and could use his status as overlord to restrain his overmighty vassal. Henry's position, as sovereign in his own right in England and vassal of another sovereign for much of his territory, was a complete anomaly in the feudal system, which needed a strictly pyramidal structure to function effectively. Henry was on the second tier of the French feudal pyramid, and at the head of the English feudal pyramid. As far as French affairs were concerned, however, he was simply a 'tenant-in-chief' holding his lands directly from Louis.

Henry II held his 'empire' together largely by the force of his personality and the effectiveness of the Norman administration. He fought not only the French kings, the Scots, Welsh and Irish, and the unruly barons of the south of France, but his own sons, all of whom in turn rebelled against him. It was therefore no surprise that after his death in 1189, the temporary union of these lands quickly unravelled, but what was unexpected was that the heartland from which the Norman expansion had begun, Normandy itself, was lost within fifteen years in the face of a determined onslaught from Louis VII's successor, Philip Augustus.

Kingship at this period was an institution in process of evolution. In the seventh and eighth centuries, kings were often elected, and not always formally crowned in a religious ceremony. Election by acclamation remained, if only as a formality, as part of the English medieval coronation ceremony. In the ninth century Charlemagne had replaced kingship in France with a revival of Roman imperial authority, and, when his empire broke up in the century after his death, the French lands became a kingdom once more. The crucial difference was that it became a feudal kingdom, in which the great lords held their lands from the king in return for military service in his army; they were also his councillors and his means of government in their respective regions. Furthermore, from 816 onwards the sacred nature of kingship was underlined by the use of a coronation ceremony which included both the crowning and anointing with holy oil; and this consecration came to be carried out in a specific place by the spiritual leader of the nation – Reims in France, Canterbury in England and Cologne for Germany.

Philip Augustus and his successors were able to challenge the Angevin threat by emphasizing their royal status, which gave them an authority outside that of the feudal system. In the tenth century, kings were generally described as leaders of a people, rather than rulers of a territory: Athelstan was the first ruler in the west to change his title, partly because he claimed overlordship of several nations as 'king of all Britain'. Philip Augustus styled himself 'king of France', though he continued to use the title 'king of the Franks' as well. Kingship was an important propaganda weapon in the struggle against over-mighty subjects; but, in the case of France, it was also to be an Achilles heel.

Under the leadership of Philip Augustus, the French held their own against the Angevins, fomenting rebellion among Henry II's ambitious sons. When Richard I, the most able of them, was mortally wounded in Poitou trying to bring one of his own fractious lords to heel, his younger brother John was no match for Philip, and a combination of manoeuvres under feudal law and force of arms led to the loss of Normandy to the French in 1204. Over the next century, particularly during the reign of Henry III, other Angevin territories fell away, until only the duchy of Aquitaine itself was left, an area which in itself was often ill-defined and subject to the wavering allegiances of local lords; it included not only Gascony to the south-west, but also provinces nearer Paris such as Poitou and the Limousin. The French kings were always on the alert for reasons to intervene, and in 1293–4 a feud between the sailors of England and Gascony and those of Normandy developed into a full-scale naval war. The fact that Edward I tried to stop his subjects from attacking the French was ignored, Philip IV declared that the breach of feudal loyalty warranted the confiscation of the duchy and war ensued. The French were able to seize large parts of Gascony, and Edward was only able to force Philip IV to negotiate by creating a large and expensive, but ultimately effective, alliance with the princes on France's eastern border. Threatened with a joint Anglo-Flemish attack, Philip agreed to mediation by the pope.

The papal settlement of this dispute, intended to reconcile the two kingdoms, was to have wholly unexpected consequences. One of its chief features was a proposed marriage alliance between the French and English royal families: Edward I's only surviving son, Edward of Caernarvon, was to marry Philip's daughter Isabella. Edward of Caernarvon was to become duke of Aquitaine.

The war with France was always in a sense a personal one, waged in the name of the English king as duke of Normandy or of Aquitaine. The English possessions in France did not belong to the realm of England, but to the king of England as an individual. How then did the English nobility and gentry regard their king's involvement in French affairs? Edward I had been forced to fight to defend his rights in Gascony back in 1294 by the French king's refusal to negotiate seriously. To raise an army, he issued a feudal summons to the great lords of England to send troops to Portsmouth with orders to embark for France. Their response seems to have been that war overseas, which was patently not in defence of the realm of England, could not be the reason for such a summons: it was above and beyond the duty they owed to the king as their feudal lord. The army that eventually sailed did not contain any contingents serving on feudal terms. The following year, Edward tried a different tactic, and offered wages to the magnates he asked to accompany him, but this was still unattractive. It was only by reminding the lords of their unpaid debts at the exchequer, and ordering his officials to collect these immediately, that he obtained the troops he needed. In the end, the expedition of 1295 took so long to organize that it never left England.[1] Yet in the end – and despite heavy taxation – Edward seemed to have carried public opinion with him, and the war with France was not openly opposed. Careful propaganda, portraying the French as a threat to England itself and even bent on destroying the English nation, may have helped.

The problem was not resolved, however, as the much more dramatic reaction in 1297 was to show. Personal grievances on the part of men such as Roger Bigod, earl of Norfolk, and Humphrey Bohun, earl of Hereford, combined with resistance from the clergy to the payment of

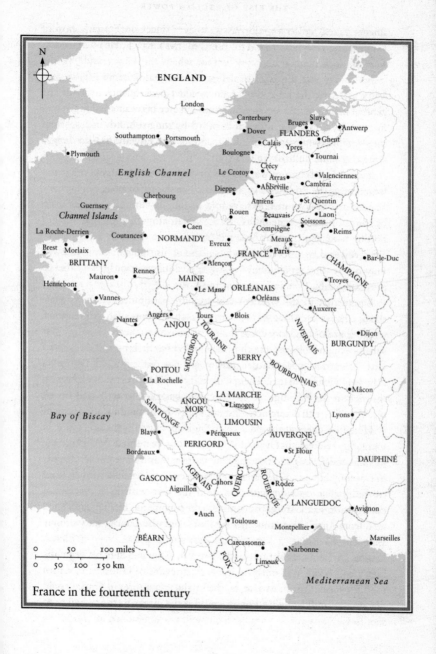

France in the fourteenth century

further taxes, led to a major crisis. Robert Winchelsey, archbishop of Canterbury, saw the demand for funds for the king's French war as outside the legitimate framework within which the king could tax the clergy; it was not a matter of defence of the realm, or an urgent situation affecting the kingdom which would permit him to override the general principle that the clergy should not pay taxes to secular governments. The same view was put forward by the magnates in respect of their requirement to serve the king, adding that England was in danger from the Scots and that it was folly to send men overseas in such circumstances. One chronicler has a story which may be apocryphal but which sums up the heated confrontation in the parliament of February 1297. Edward is reputed to have told Bigod: 'By God, sir earl, either go or hang,' only to get the retort, 'By the same oath, O king, I shall neither go nor hang.' In the end, Edward had to make do with a very small army, fewer than 1,000 mounted men and around 8,000 infantry. It was only by creating an expensive network of alliances that he was able to persuade Philip IV to negotiate a truce.

Opposition to the war was real enough among the men who mattered, and who provided the most resources for such expeditions, whether in men or money. But there was no overall motive for their dissatisfaction, which was often as much to do with their personal relations with Edward as with broader principles. Essentially, it was a failure on Edward I's part to manage them with sufficient skill, even though he won through in the end. But the element that was decided once and for all was that the feudal summons did not apply to the king's war in France.

Hostilities between France and England broke out once more in 1324, largely because Edward II had prevaricated about doing homage to Charles IV, who had become king two years earlier. A border dispute in Gascony in 1323 in which a French official was lynched by men loyal to the English crown triggered a swift reaction leading to the formal confiscation of the duchy of Aquitaine in June 1324. By September, the area from Agen, where the lynching had taken place, along the Garonne valley to La Réole, a key fortress outside Bordeaux, was in French hands; La Réole itself was surrendered by Edmund earl of Kent, the king's half brother, recently appointed lieutenant of Gascony, in return for a six-month truce. As always, the English territories in France could not be defended by relying on the local levies, and no troops had been sent to Gascony yet. In October a council was summoned in London to discuss the situation, with a view to raising an army to be led by Edward himself for the following summer. Edward was careful to act in conjunction with a small group of advisers selected by the council, and a date of March 1325 was set for the expedition's departure, to be led by the king himself. However, there was a change of plan at the last minute, and the earl of Surrey led this force; the king was to follow in May.

There was little opposition to this plan, though the advisers warned that its departure might leave the kingdom without sufficient defences. It was not Edward's handling of the recruitment of the Gascon expedition that led to his downfall, but the continuing anger aroused by his attitude towards the magnates, exemplified by his blatant favouritism. Early in his reign, Piers Gaveston had been showered with honours and had appalled the rest of the court by his arrogant behaviour. Edward ignored this, and a civil war ensued, in the course of which Gaveston was seized by the magnates and executed. Edward did not learn his lesson: he seemed to have a need for a close confidant, and within a few years Hugh Despenser the younger occupied the same position. Neither of these relationships was necessarily, on the evidence we have, homosexual; they were, however, friendships intense enough to blind the king to the enmity that such favouritism aroused. Both favourites were described by contemporary chroniclers as 'second kings'.[2] Edward was victorious in a second civil war in 1321–2, and set out to crush his opponents by confiscating their lands and imprisoning or executing them. One of them, Roger Mortimer, whose lordship was centred on Wigmore on the Welsh borders, escaped from prison in 1323 and fled to France, where he acted as a focus for the opposition to the king.

The reaction of Edward and his council to the military situation in 1324 was hesitant, and their diplomatic efforts were little better. Charles IV was in no hurry to reach a settlement, and, when English envoys arrived in Paris in December, the French raised new objections, accusing the English of treason and now rejecting the truce arranged by the earl of Kent. They did however propose that Queen Isabella and her son the young Prince Edward should come to Paris, and that Prince Edward should perform the homage which was the prime cause of the stand-off. In a sense, this was part of what the marriage alliance between the two royal families was intended to do: to create an atmosphere where personal relations might overcome diplomatic disagreements. Charles's motives, however, were probably more devious: he was on good terms with his sister, and knew of her intense dislike of Despenser; she had also been offended at being treated as a potential enemy alien, as her estates and household had been taken into the king's hands at the outbreak of war.

Edward and his council were aware of the potential conflict of loyalties if they allowed Isabella to go, but they had no obvious alternatives: they could not raise a new army for Aquitaine quickly enough to prevent the French making new conquests if the truce was not renewed, and there was no obvious way out of the diplomatic impasse. On 9 March 1325 Isabella left England, without her son; she was to return under very different circumstances. At first, matters went reasonably smoothly, though the new truce drawn up on 13 June was on harsh terms; there was now an additional threat, that a French army would be sent to Scotland to assist the Scottish king in an attack on England's northern border. Edward was therefore highly reluctant to leave England in order to perform homage for Aquitaine, and on 5 July he and his council proposed to the French that the duchy should be granted to Prince Edward, who would then be able to carry out the necessary ceremony on his own account.

This proposal was not immediately set in motion. Edward decided, despite all his reservations, to go to Beauvais on 29 August for the ceremony of homage, but then had second thoughts. The official version was that he was taken ill on his journey near Dover; in fact, a council seems to have been hastily assembled there on 15 August, at which he finally abandoned the idea. Instead, the alternative plan was quickly put in place: Prince Edward was granted Aquitaine on 10 September, and crossed the Channel two days later. He joined his mother in Paris, and performed homage at the French royal palace of Vincennes on 24 September. The prince was twelve, and this was his first major political act.

Edward and his council now expected Isabella and the prince to return to England, but they obviously doubted that this would happen without some persuasion. Walter Stapledon, bishop of Exeter, was given this task, but Isabella is said to have openly declared that she would only return when the person who was trying to break the bond between her and her husband – meaning Hugh Despenser the younger – was removed from the scene. Stapledon was so dismayed that he fled back to England at the first opportunity. About this time, it seems that Isabella first made contact with Roger Mortimer, whom she would have known at least slightly since her arrival in England. If Edward would not get rid of Despenser, she was now determined to do so herself. Her relationship with Mortimer at this point was probably simply a question of making common cause against a hated enemy. Early in 1326 the archbishop of Canterbury wrote to reassure her that Hugh Despenser bore no ill will against her; she replied that she was astonished he could say this, because it was for this reason that she had left Edward, since he had entire control over the king and kingdom; she protested her love for and loyalty to her husband, but declared that she was in danger of her life because of Despenser.[3]

Isabella and Mortimer were not alone in their opposition to Despenser; indeed, Mortimer may not necessarily have been the ringleader, though it was Mortimer's activities which were of the greatest interest to the English government. Edmund earl of Kent, the earl of Richmond and the bishop of Norwich were all part of the group, in self-imposed exile. Their activities, and particularly those of Isabella, became a diplomatic embarrassment to Charles IV; by June 1326 she was using the revenues from Ponthieu, of which Prince Edward was count,[4] to hire an invasion fleet to be supplied by the count of Hainault, William I. Rumours of an alliance between Isabella and the count had been circulating in England since the beginning of the year, and it was said that Charles IV was behind this. The French king may well have suggested Isabella's next move, which was a marriage alliance between Hainault and England; Prince Edward would marry one of the count's daughters. On 27 August 1326 the prince was formally betrothed to Philippa, William's third daughter.

Isabella, the earl of Kent and Roger Mortimer now moved the centre of their operations to Holland, also ruled by the counts of Hainault, where Jean de Hainault, the count's younger brother, joined them in their plans to invade England. Within a month, Jean had raised a force of 700 mercenaries, and the English exiles probably contributed a similar number of men. They were all, however, experienced soldiers, and the majority were mounted troops: it was a small but formidable army. They sailed in ninety-five ships to the haven of the river Orwell, and landed on the north bank, in Colneis hundred, on 24 September. By the time they had marched across Suffolk and Cambridgeshire, and had halted at Dunstable in Bedfordshire, they had gathered many supporters, including the earl of Norfolk, Thomas of Brotherton. At Dunstable, they were met by Henry earl of Lancaster, Prince Edward's distant cousin, and at least four of the bishops. How far this was due to contacts before the invasion took place, and how far to a simple dissatisfaction with the king's conduct which only needed a spark to transform it into open rebellion, is hard to say. The hostility to the king was such that he abandoned London just over a week later, and headed for Wales, where he hoped to find men who were prepared to rally to his cause.

Edward II's efforts to raise an army in the Welsh borders came to nothing. Because he was so uncertain of the response to his summons, he moved on from Gloucester, the mustering place for his forces, before the date when they were due to appear. He very quickly found himself moving from place to place with no real plan, and sought refuge on Lundy Island, accompanied by Hugh Despenser and a handful of men. He may have intended to retreat to Ireland, where the administration would have been sympathetic, but in the event contrary winds drove the ships back to Cardiff. He retreated to Despenser's fortress at Caerphilly, and once again tried to summon a non-existent army; even though the fortress could have resisted a long siege, he moved on at the beginning of November, since without support outside the walls his fate would have been sealed anyway. A fortnight later, after seemingly aimless wanderings in south Wales, he was betrayed and captured, and taken to Henry of Lancaster, while his followers were imprisoned at Hereford. Kenilworth, Henry of Lancaster's strongest castle, was to be Edward II's place of imprisonment.

On 13 January, a carefully orchestrated council at Westminster heard Roger Mortimer and Thomas Wake, Lancaster's son-in-law, speak for the magnates, giving reasons why Edward II should be replaced by his son. The bishop of Hereford described a recent interview with Edward II at Kenilworth, in which he claimed that Edward had annulled the oaths of loyalty sworn to him by the great lords; and the bishop of Winchester preached on the theme that the weakness of the kingdom was caused by the king's own weakness. Then the proposal that Prince Edward should replace his father was put to the assembly, and acclaimed by all present. Finally, Edward III was presented as king with the words 'Behold your king'.

The actions of the assembly were duly reported to Edward II at Kenilworth, and, according to those present, he abdicated in favour of his son. The whole business of deposing an English monarch was such a novelty that there were inevitable doubts and obscurities about procedures and about the validity of the deposition and abdication. The fact of the matter was that Edward III was nominal head of the new government, and his father was a prisoner. But there were men who still supported Edward II, and plots were made to free him. Who was behind these plots is hard to tell, as the actual participants seem to have been mainly a group of Dominican friars who 'had little or no idea of what they expected to happen if they succeeded in freeing Edward'.[5] As a security measure, Edward II was moved from place to place, ending up in Berkeley Castle, which belonged to Thomas, Lord Berkeley, a close ally of Mortimer.

It was here that the last act of the drama was played out. A further conspiracy, said to have the backing of the Welsh prince Rhys ap Gruffudd, was discovered in September, possibly by Mortimer himself, who was in Wales at the time. It seems to have been his personal decision to eliminate Edward II, and, although we cannot be completely certain of what happened, he died on 21 September, probably at the hands of Thomas Gurney and William Ockley and their men, who were his guards at Berkeley. Gruesome tales of his treatment circulated in later years, possibly with some truth; equally, and, much less reliably, he was said to have escaped and survived on the Continent until the middle of the following decade. It is of course possible that this story derives from the rumours spread by Mortimer to entrap the earl of Kent in 1330, which could have been picked up in France. Whatever the exact circumstances, Edward III was now undoubted king of England, but its real rulers were Isabella and Mortimer.

I

Edward, Philippa and their Comrades 1327–1330

We know remarkably little about the early years of Edward III's life. Apart from the occasional appearance at a great occasion of state, there are few records of his activities.[1] He did not even play a nominal part in the government, and was never named as keeper of the realm if his father was absent abroad, as was customary for the heir to the throne. He does appear once, in September 1322, presiding at a royal feast at York in honour of a visiting French nobleman while his father was in Scotland; but this is virtually the only mention of state duties.

As heir to the throne, he had his own household establishment from the outset, and this is where we can see a little of the men who looked after his affairs and the first companions of his own age. Richard Damory was 'keeper of the body' of the young prince by 1318, but he is the only figure we can name from these early years. By 1320, his household included his younger brother John and his sisters Eleanor and Joan; in that year, John in turn was given his own household, and one of the queen's ladies was appointed to look after his sisters, with a separate establishment. From 1323 onwards, William of Cusance, who had been clerk to the Despensers, was keeper of Prince Edward's household, and other Despenser retainers were placed in the queen's household and that of John of Eltham, evidence of the family's ambition to control all aspects of the king's life, and of the king's acquiescence in their domination. In 1324, John and Eleanor were placed in the care of Hugh Despenser's wife Eleanor; Prince Edward does not seem to have been so closely controlled. There are very few records of the prince and his father being in the same place, and this is underlined by the survival of letters which show him communicating with his father by letter rather than in person.[2] He was nominally required to attend the king as part of his duties as a peer of the realm, as in formal summonses to parliament, and the personal writ to him to serve with the army in August 1322. However, it is unlikely that he attended such occasions, or, if he did, he would have appeared at the ceremonial opening of parliament but not at the business sessions.

It is possible that Isabella succeeded in keeping him out of the inner circle of the court after Hugh Despenser became the king's favourite and her estrangement from her husband began. After the feast in York in September 1322, the king's Scottish campaign had ended disastrously: the king was nearly captured by a Scottish raiding party in north Yorkshire, well south of the border, and the queen had to escape from Tynemouth by sea. Prince Edward was, if only for a few days, in serious danger at York, with few if any troops present. After this, apart from a single account entry which shows him dining at the Tower of London with his mother in February 1323, the trail goes cold.

It is only through a fragment of his accounts used as part of the binding of a later manuscript that we get a glimpse of his household just before he left for France in August 1325.[3] Perhaps the most important figure is that of Henry of Beaumont. Five entries record Prince Edward gambling at dice with Henry, evidently losing as much as four shillings on one occasion. Henry of Beaumont was in fact a French nobleman whose grandfather had become emperor of Constantinople after crusaders seized the city in 1204. His sister had married an English lord in 1279, possibly because she was a distant cousin of Eleanor of Castile, then queen of England, and Henry may have come to England as a result. At the age of seventeen, he was one of Edward I's household knights, and was close to Edward II, who made him joint warden of Scotland in 1308, and gave him the Isle of Man, then a separate kingdom. He married the heiress of the earldom of Buchan in 1310. He had fought with Edward I in Flanders in 1297, and had been on the disastrous 1322 campaign in Scotland, and was a highly experienced soldier. On 2 September, as the process of granting Prince Edward the duchy of Aquitaine began, Beaumont was formally appointed his guardian, with Walter Stapledon, the bishop of Exeter. Unlike Stapledon, Beaumont joined Isabella in her opposition to Edward, and was with the prince during the whole of the period in exile and during the invasion of 1326.

Apart from Beaumont, a few other names appear, but none of them are the close knightly associates of the king who emerge in the course of the next five years. Gilbert Talbot, his chamberlain from 1327 to 1334, appears as a banneret in 1325, and Thomas Lucy rises from squire in 1325 to knight of the household in 1334.[4]

Just as the Despensers had placed their men in Prince Edward's household, so Mortimer ensured that the new king's rather larger household contained men who owed loyalty to him rather than to the royal family. Edward was still only fourteen at the time of his accession, and does not appear to have had any young men of his own age who were consistently with him during the upheavals of the last years of his father's reign. At his coronation on 1 February 1327, after he himself received knighthood from his cousin Henry earl of Lancaster,[5] Edward knighted Edward Chandos, who may have been the father of one of his closest friends of later years, John Chandos. Three years later, Chandos was further rewarded specifically for his loyalty, having stayed with the king 'continually by his side' without pay.[6] Edward also dubbed a number of other knights, some from his household; but most of these do not reappear in the records, with the single exception of Ralph Stafford.[7] Lancaster also knighted Edward Bohun and the three sons of Roger Mortimer. It was in Roger Mortimer's circle that he was to receive his first experiences of knighthood, and perhaps also to show the first signs of rebellion.

Within three months of Edward's crowning, preparations for war were under way. There had been an uneasy truce with Scotland since 1323, and this was now breaking down. Isabella and Mortimer, anxious to strengthen the alliance against Edward II, had made vague promises that Scotland should be independent if they succeeded. In January 1327, however, one of the reasons given for Edward II's deposition had been that he had lost Scotland through default of good governance, and this was taken by the Scots as an indication that attempts were going to be made to reimpose English overlordship. A renewal of the 1323 truce in March was little more than cover for military preparations on both sides, and by 18 May an English army was supposed to have gathered at Newcastle. As usual, the troops were not there on the appointed day, and the king himself did not arrive until the end of June.

Much of the army assembled at York before going north, and among the contingents were a group of men from Hainault, led by Jean de Hainault, who had played such an important part in the invasion of

1326. Among them was Jean le Bel, who later described the campaign in his chronicle. The venture started badly, with a quarrel between English archers and the Hainaulters over a game of dice, during a royal feast to celebrate Trinity Sunday. It was the knights of Hainault who quelled the riot, which left scores of English dead. From then on there was a persistent tension between the two groups in the camp, but interestingly, given that the episode occurred so early in the reign, any potential xenophobia did not recur once the campaign was over.

Le Bel gives a vivid portrait of the discomforts of the army in the field in the weeks that followed, unable to keep up with the highly mobile Scottish troops. They were often bewildered as to their whereabouts, while suffering from shortages of provisions and torrential rain. The armies spent days drawn up in battle order at a place called Stanhope Park on either side of the swollen river Wear, made impassable by huge rocks and raging waters. And he gives us an equally striking portrait of Edward himself. Edward was Le Bel's hero; how much of this is the chronicler seeing him in the golden light of his subsequent reputation, and how much is his genuine admiration at the time which fired his enthusiasm for Edward, is difficult to say. It does seem to be the case that this was a formative experience for the fourteen-year-old king. It is quite possible that the exclusive use of the cross of St George on this campaign for the pennons and banners of the army was his own idea: as far as we know, his father and grandfather had always carried the arms of St Edmund and St Edward as well.[8]

The leaders of the army were three earls: Edward named as captain in July his cousin, Henry of Lancaster, aged about forty-six, the most experienced soldier of the three, who had fought in Flanders, Wales and Scotland. The other two were much younger: his uncles Edmund of Woodstock, aged twenty-five, and Thomas of Brotherton, aged twenty-seven. Mortimer, their senior by more than a decade, held no official command, but was generally blamed for the failure of the campaign.[9] Mortimer and the three earls seem to have disagreed about tactics: one chronicler says that Thomas of Brotherton, as marshal, forbade Lancaster to attack, acting on Mortimer's instructions. Edward was little more than a figurehead, as a complete novice in the art of war. When the Scottish army was first sighted, and the English had formed up in battle order, 'some of the English lords led the young king to ride along our lines, to hearten the troops; he graciously appealed to each man to strive to fight well and preserve his honour; and he gave orders that no one, on pain of death, should go ahead of the banners or make any move until the command was given'.[10] But instead of a glorious victory, the encounter at Stanhope Park was nearly a disaster: the Scots under James Douglas made a surprise night attack on the English camp and rode through it in bright moonlight 'until they came to the king's pavilion and killed the men in their beds, crying "Douglas! Douglas!", at which the king, who was in his pavilion, and many other people were very frightened; but – blessed be Almighty God! – the king was not captured; and the realm of England was in great peril'. The Scots retreated, but it was a humiliating episode.

Edward returned to York, the temporary centre of government, by way of Durham, reaching the city on 13 August. His first experience of warfare had been harsh and frustrating; he himself was still inexperienced in the use of arms. At the end of the year, after his father's funeral on 20 December, he held a series of tournaments in a chain of festivities which lasted from Christmas until after his marriage to Philippa of Hainault at the end of January.[11] These began at Worcester on 23 December, continued with events at the royal hunting lodges at Clipstone in Sherwood Forest and ended at Rothwell in Yorkshire in mid-January, before the festivities at York on 25–8 January. This was the first series of the magnificent court occasions which were to be a major feature of Edward's reign.

Tournaments, since their inception in the twelfth century, had been both a serious method of training knights in the skills of handling their horses and weapons, particularly the specialized expertise with the lance, and important festivals, social gatherings which brought together many of the great nobles and their retinues. In peaceable times, such gatherings posed no danger to the kingdom at large; but if the nobles were disaffected with royal government, the tournament could either be deliberate cover for the assembly of an army, or could develop spontaneously into an armed rebellion. Tourneying had been subject to royal control since 1194, when Richard I restricted tournaments to just five sites in the whole of England, the reason being that such occasions, which were after all gatherings of armed men, could lead to rebellion and civil war. It was therefore rare for the ruler himself to enter the lists. Richard I and Edward I had jousted in their youth, but ceased once they came to the throne.

A series of English tournaments in the mid-thirteenth century which led to violence underlined the need for regulation, and in 1292, at the request of the magnates of the realm, Edward I ratified a code of conduct for tourneyers, which effectively limited full participation to great lords. Even in this legislation, the tournament was still a rough-and-tumble affair: each lord was allowed three squires, who could legitimately enter the fray and pull another participant from his horse, which then became their prize.[12] Both the lord's squires and his other attendants could wear only partial armour, and they and the onlookers were forbidden on pain of imprisonment to carry arms. Even in peace-time, there was always a danger that personal feuds could be settled under cover of a tournament.

At the beginning of Edward II's reign, Piers Gaveston had held a tournament at Wallingford in December 1307 to celebrate his marriage. He appeared with three times the number of knights he had said he would bring, and thus had roundly defeated the earls who attended. He also defeated them at a tournament at Faversham in honour of Edward's marriage to Isabella, and aroused such hatred that he himself asked the king to cancel a third tournament at Stepney planned as part of the coronation festivities.[13] Edward II held only one tournament during his reign, which he personally organized, at Kennington in September 1308. Despite lavish expenditure, memories of the troubles earlier in the year led the barons to stay away – 'wisely', adds the chronicler – and an unknown knight knocked down the tentpoles of several of the pavilions under cover of darkness.[14] Thereafter Edward II issued a series of edicts banning tournaments, and there are few instances of licensed tourna-ments: that at Northampton in 1323, at which the king was present, is a rare example, and was at one of the five sites named in Richard I's statute. The effectiveness of royal control is underlined by the fact that most important tournaments were fought at these places until the mid-fourteenth century, with the one exception of London.

The prohibitions continued during Edward III's minority, since at times of crisis Mortimer and Isabella were well aware of the dangers of armed assemblies, however apparently sportsmanlike. In 1328 a pro-posed tournament at Northampton was prohibited on the grounds that magnates might go to the tournament rather than to the parliament sum-moned in the same place, but the underlying purpose was to prevent a possible assembly of armed men who might disrupt the proceedings.

At the local level, prohibitions were designed to deal with the kind of local disturbance which is reflected in the activities of John Daniers, one of the prince of Wales's knights, in 1352. In the course of a feud with the local parson, he proclaimed a tournament at Warrington, near the parish, and seized the torches from the parson's house to burn 'at his revelry there'; the stands were built using the parson's timber stored in the church.[15]

For an example of a serious challenge to royal authority there is the tournament at Toulouse in 1343. Here, the king of Majorca, who claimed the county of Toulouse, entered the town in the absence of the French royal officials, and held a tournament in defiance of a ban in force in French territories, as a way of marking his right to hold Toulouse as an independent principality. To make matters worse, his knights entered the lists shouting the English war cry of 'Guyenne, St George'.[16]

The difference between the early tournaments of Edward II and those of Edward III could not be more marked. Instead of a king at loggerheads with his nobles, and a reluctant participant in tournaments, Edward III's enthusiasm, fostered by Isabella and Mortimer, was shared by his nobles, and his investment in rich displays of armour and clothing was far from wasted, since it created a new comradeship between the king and his lords. We have the detailed accounts for some of his equipment, such as the two suits of armour covered in purple velvet made for the Clipstone tournament, embroidered with 21,800 gold threads in a pattern of crowns and oak leaves at a cost of £8 3s. 4d. Clipstone is the first recorded instance of the very rare practice of jousting at night; there is one other known example in England, later in Edward's reign, at Bristol on New Year's Day 1358.[17] The image of the young king riding out into the night, the torchlight glinting on the gold of his armour, is a harbinger of the highly visual nature of Edward's later knightly celebrations.

The series of four tournaments in quick succession leading up to Edward's marriage to Philippa in January 1328, which seem to have passed off without any political repercussions, was unprecedented in England. Tourneying activity continued at a very high level for the next three years. In 1328 Roger Mortimer gave two great tournaments. His family had a long tradition of enthusiasm for tournaments: as long ago as 1195, the Mortimer of the day had had his lands confiscated for tourneying without licence;[18] and his grandfather had held a round table of 100 knights and 100 ladies at Kenilworth in 1279, partly paid for by wine barrels filled with gold presented to him by Blanche queen of Navarre, wife of Edmund of Lancaster, the lord of Kenilworth. Roger Mortimer's first tournament was at Hereford in June, to celebrate the marriage of his two daughters, and was attended by the king and Isabella.[19] This was followed in the autumn by tournaments at Wigmore to commemorate his creation as earl of March in the parliament of October 1328, an extraordinary title since it did not correspond to any territorial boundaries. The display he put on there, and the title he had assumed, was one of the reasons that led one chronicler to comment that Mortimer and Isabella had usurped royal power and had gathered up the contents of the royal treasury.[20] The chronicle of Wigmore priory had a different take on it: the king had swept into Mortimer's domains, and had spent a fortune at his castles and in his parks on tournaments and other entertainments, handing out generous presents – all at Mortimer's expense, since (so rumour had it) the king did not repay him.[21] If this was so, Mortimer was probably spending the king's own money in any case.

There is a very curious entry in the royal accounts for this period which may hint at a distinct coolness between Edward and his mother, the result of the affair between her and Mortimer. One of the entitlements of members of the king's household was a new suit of summer and winter clothing each year. Among the entries for the summer of 1328 are three entries that are not concerned with the regular issue of livery, which read as follows:

> ... red cloth for the king and his 12 knights for the performance of a game which is called the game of the society of Craddok, and coloured cloth for half-tunics for 14 valets, servants to the knights at the said game.

> ... for lining 13 tunics for the king and 12 knights of the society of Craddok ...

The date would seem to connect it with the festivities at Hereford at the end of May 1328. But 'Craddok' has a peculiar relevance to the situation. It is probably a reference to the Arthurian story of Caradoc, an episode attacking the morals of Arthur's court, which first appears around 1300. In the *Lay of Mantel*, Arthur is holding a high festival, and tradition demands that he does not dine until some new adventure has happened at court. A young man appears and produces a splendid mantle, which will detect any ladies who have been unfaithful. He asks the king to get the ladies of the court to try it on without saying what the results will show. Guinevere, told that the mantle will be hers, tries it on, but it is too short; and all the other ladies of the court try and fail, finding it too long or shrinking revealingly until they are almost naked. Finally, Caradoc's lady, who was absent at the beginning, comes in, and the mantle fits her perfectly. The original seems to have been a Welsh tale, and the story was certainly known on the English border with Wales in the fourteenth century; it was incorporated into a continuation of the romance of *Perceval* by Chrétien de Troyes, where a drinking horn rather than a mantle is the test.

It is not unreasonable to assume that this little episode is related to the increasingly scandalous relationship between Mortimer and Isabella. A later report claims that there was a rumour that 'the Queen Mother was pregnant, and Lord Mortimer more than anyone else was suspected of being the father. The rumour spread like wildfire until the young king was made fully aware of it . . .'[23] Was the 'game of Craddok' a re-enactment of the romance episode aimed at the lovers? If so, was it performed in front of them, or was it a private affair between the king and the twelve knights for whom costumes were made?[24]

Whatever this was about, it is the first instance of a theme which was to recur throughout Edward's reign: the team or group of knights led by the king in tournaments or games. At this stage, the twelve knights were very probably drawn from the king's household bannerets, knights and squires. The bannerets were knights who would have had retinues of their own and ranked above the ordinary knights, and it was they who were most likely to have been part of such a group. Of the names we have from 1328, there are men who either were related to the king, or were later among his confidants: Edward Bohun, his cousin, William Clinton, later earl of Huntingdon, Walter Mauny, who came over from Hainault with Queen Philippa,[25] and William Montagu, later first earl of Salisbury. Ralph Stafford, who had fought in Scotland the previous year, was probably also there, but whether Mortimer's three sons were with the king is harder to say. That their friendship with Edward survived their father's disgrace we do know, from Roger Mortimer the younger's subsequent career.[26]

We have left until last the queen and her entourage, a vital element in the culture of the Edwardian court in general, and important in the history of the Garter. Philippa came from a family whose cultivation of dynastic history and enthusiasm for chivalrous sports were as strong as those of Edward. Her entourage included a handful of knights from Hainault, and the Hainault connection remained an important one until her death in 1369, not least because she had a good claim to be countess of Hainault. Edward, preoccupied with his own claim to France, was not in a position to pursue this seriously; it was consistently opposed by a large section of the Hainault nobility, who, like the French with regard to Edward, saw Philippa's rule as leading to domination by a foreign power. In 1362 a scheme was put forward for a marriage between Edmund of Langley, their fourth son, and the daughter of the count of Flanders, the idea being that Edmund would inherit the claim to Hainault and the count would support him in enforcing it. This came to nothing because the pope refused to allow the marriage, on the grounds of consanguinity, though papal officials admitted that it was in fact because it would give Edward a dominant position against France.

When English kings had married abroad in the past, the influence of their wives' fellow-countrymen at court had often been a serious problem, most notably under Henry III. In Philippa's case, the Hainault contingent seem to have merged into the English court without difficulty, apart from the problems at York on the Scottish campaign of 1327, which had no later repercussions.

This absence of friction was probably due to Philippa's personal popularity. Thomas Walsingham remembered her in the 1390s as 'a most noble woman and a most constant lover of the English people'.[27] She emerges from both chronicles and records as a compassionate and warm-hearted person; when in 1331 she narrowly escaped death or injury in the collapse of a stand at a tournament in Cheapside, she asked for mercy for the carpenters whose negligence had caused the accident.[28] The scene in Froissart where she begs for mercy for the six citizens of Calais after the town's surrender in 1347 has passed into legend; it is entirely in harmony with what we know of her character, and there are several petitions in the English records where her intervention on behalf of young girls or pregnant women secured a pardon for them.[29]

Her father, William I of Hainault, and her brother, later William II, were also welcome visitors at court, and participated in Edward's tournaments.[30] Jean de Hainault, who had accompanied her to England when she went there to be married, returned several times; his military support, both in the invasion of 1326 and in the Scottish campaign of 1327, was much valued by Edward, but was also quite expensive: his full claim was for more than £14,000 in wages, though he settled for rather less.[31] It is perhaps precisely because he had been welcome at Edward's court that when Jean de Hainault fought on the French side at Crécy, the Rochester chronicler calls him 'traitor to the king of England'. Philippa was also in constant touch with her mother, who paid several visits to England in the 1330s: in 1333, Philippa paid for seven ships to bring her mother and her companions and 250 horses from Wissant to Dover on 23 September, returning the same way on 13 October.[32] During Edward's wars in Flanders she was with him for much of the time. However, after hostilities resumed in 1342, visits from Philippa's family became less frequent, particularly since William II was absent from Hainault for much of the time from 1342 until his death at the battle of Staveren in 1345.

The connection with Hainault seems to have been an influential one in knightly terms. William I jousted at the tournament held for Philippa's wedding to Edward in 1328, and the Hainault knights were also present at a tournament held by Edward in Brussels in 1339. Walter Mauny figures largely in the pages of his fellow-Hainaulter Jean le Bel, while Jean Froissart, also from Hainault, was in England in Philippa's household in the 1360s.

William II seems to have been almost obsessed by knightly ideals. At the beginning of his career, there had been a round table at Haarlem on the occasion when he was created titular count of Zeeland on 28 September 1333. He was the official sponsor of the event, at which his father gave a supper for the 'knights of the round table'[33] and their ladies, on the evening before the ceremony.[34] There were other jousts immediately afterwards, at 's-Gravenzande.[35]

In 1343–5 his career seems to have been almost exclusively concerned with such matters. In 1343 he went to Prussia, to crusade with the Teutonic Knights against the heathen, and was still there in early 1344.[36] He returned to Holland on 8 April, and almost immediately set in hand preparations for a lavish round table at The Hague. This was held, from Sunday to Thursday, and was on a considerable scale; the count's officers referred to it as the 'great feast' in their accounts:[37] the total expenditure came to £791 11s. 8½d., a very substantial sum.[38] The count rode straight from The Hague on the Thursday to another tournament. Tournaments, combined with another journey to Prussia, seem to have occupied most of his time in the years 1344–5.[39] In the spring and summer of 1344 he took part in 'festivals' involving jousting on seven occasions, beginning with the events at The Hague and Beauvais. In June he fought at Brussels; in July he was at Bergen, Laon and Gertuidenberg; and in September he was at Metz. The following year there were two tournaments in April, at Nijvel and Mechelen, and in August he returned to the favourite tourneying site of Haarlem. His death at the battle of Staveren in the following month brought to an end a knightly career which surpassed in enthusiasm even Edward's most spectacular efforts.

On William II's death, it appears that two of his squires made their way to the English court rather than risk the uncertainties following the loss of not only the count but many of the nobility of Hainault. Besides these two, Henry Eam and Eustace d'Auberchicourt, there may well have been others. Auberchicourt's father had received Edward and his mother in 1326 on their way to invade England, and had served Edward in Scotland, so he was assured of a warm welcome. The links with Hainault were also extremely useful in terms of providing a bridge to the politics of the Low Countries; the death of William I in 1337 was a major blow to Edward, as he was an astute, if not always predictable, politician, and his son was not in the same mould. William II joined Edward's alliance against France in 1338, but went over to the French side in 1343–4. On a different scale, the presence of the Hainault contingent in the English army, and especially that of Walter Mauny, seems to have smoothed the way for negotiations with the besieged inhabitants of Calais in 1347, who would have been more likely to trust them rather than the English invaders.

Philippa came from a family which included a number of women who had been patrons of the arts and particularly of literature. She ordered two books of hours for herself in 1331 from Robert of Oxford, 'with diverse images and large and small letters of gold', one of which may be the volume known as the Taymouth Hours; and she later had an illuminator called Master Robert.[40] Her wedding present to Edward was a lavishly presented manuscript, on whose opening page a young woman holds a book, evidently the volume itself, which she presents to the figure on the far side of the text, a young man with a surcoat embroidered with the arms of England. It seems to have been written in Flanders and illuminated by an English artist (Plate 3). This manuscript, like those presented to the king by one of his clerks, Walter Milemete,[41] concentrates on good advice for a future king, and indeed contains a French text, *The Secret of Secrets*, which was also presented by Milemete. Besides this, Philippa's manuscript includes an encyclopedia, *The Book of Treasures*, which ranges across world history, natural sciences, rhetoric and statesmanship. And there is a satirical poem on the ways of the world, the *Romance of Fauveyn* or *Fauvel*, a moral tale on the treachery of mankind. The hero is the horse Fauvel, who personifies deceit; the text is short and heavily illustrated in the manner of a comic strip. Illustrations also abound in *The Book of Treasures*; this is clearly a volume designed to entice the viewer, through its visual splendour, into reading the improving tales it contains; as such it does not reflect Philippa's own personal tastes, but has been designed as an appropriate formal gift for the occasion.[42]

Last but by no means least, the marriage of Philippa and Edward seems to have been one of enduring affection. There are hints of an affair in 1347 at Calais, and of some kind of attempt by John Stratford, archbishop of Canterbury, to stir up trouble between the king and his wife in 1340. The first depends on the interpretation of an obscure allegorical commentary on Edward's reign by a Yorkshire friar, which speaks of a lecherous 'Diana' who tempts Edward; Edward neglects the war with France as a result, and England is punished with the Black Death.[43] All this reads like the kind of monastic reasoning which later attributed the great storm of 1362 to plans for a tournament in which the knights would be disguised as the seven deadly sins; it is difficult to take it seriously, particularly as Philippa was present at the siege for at least part of the time. The second occurs in a letter to the pope which was written by Edward when he was furious with the archbishop over his political opposition to Edward's wishes.[44] Neither of these is a substantial charge, and it is only at the end of the marriage, when Philippa was ailing, that Edward took a mistress, the notorious Alice Perrers. Perrers was one of Philippa's attendants, ambitious and a shrewd businesswoman, who was determined to use her charms on the elderly king and to make her fortune. Although she bore Edward a son in 1364, it was not until after Philippa's death in 1369 that she played a major part in the court. But her activities in the last years of Edward's reign were to be remembered, and were to give Edward a lascivious reputation at odds with that of his prime.[45] For most of his reign, the image of the royal marriage was one of happiness and prosperity; his insistence on spending long periods with Philippa during her first pregnancies speaks of his devotion. And their sons, healthy and energetic warriors, outshone their French counterparts. Philip's only son, John, suffered serious illness in his youth, and his life was in danger in one of these episodes.

Since June 1328, Henry of Lancaster had taken offence at Roger Mortimer's control of the king, and his increasing usurpation of royal powers. The stand-off came to a head after Mortimer's creation as earl of March at Salisbury the following October, and armed conflict was narrowly avoided at Winchester in November 1328 and again at Bedford in January 1329. Henry of Lancaster and his followers submitted to arbitration, but they were forced to give sureties for the future, and a number of leading lords were excluded from the agreement. These included Henry of Beaumont, Edward's guardian in 1325, who with several other magnates went into exile. Nonetheless, perhaps to distract the king from Mortimer's secure hold over the government, tournaments continued throughout 1329; and the king was not the only promoter of such occasions, because the records of Thomas, Lord Berkeley note a number of occasions when he was jousting and the king is known to have been elsewhere. These were usually local affairs in the west country, at Bristol and Exeter for example, and on a much smaller scale; the fact that they were not prohibited says something for Mortimer's confidence in his control of this region, since, in the days of Gaveston and the Despensers, such events had been focal points for the opposition.

Berkeley was present at some royal tournaments, at Coventry on 2 January and Guildford on 6 March (with Thomas Bradeston, one of his retainers), where another of Mortimer's supporters, Geoffrey Scrope, was also a participant.[46] This was a court festival, because 7 March was Shrovetide, a day of carnival before the Lenten fast began, and 'false visages' or masks were provided for the occasion. In June, when Edward went to Amiens to perform homage to Philip of Valois for Aquitaine and Ponthieu, a tournament was on the agenda;[47] and it is possible that both kings entered the lists. There was more jousting on the return journey, at Canterbury and Dartford:[48] at Canterbury the king evidently fought fiercely, as an armourer had to be summoned to mend his armour on the spot, before the Dartford tournament a few days later.[49]

Mortimer then organized a series of tournaments to entertain the king on the Welsh borders, and perhaps to keep him out of the increasingly threatening political scene. These began with an event at Gloucester at the end of August, and then another at Hereford in September. There were jousts at both Hereford and Wigmore, but the king appears to have stayed at Hereford, and avoided Mortimer's home ground. The jousting fraternity then moved on to Worcester;[50] ailettes or shoulderplates were made for this occasion quartered with the arms of William Montagu and Bartholomew Burghersh the elder, probably because they were the leaders of the king's tournament team. Geoffrey Mortimer, Roger Mortimer's eldest son, was given a suit of armour. The grand finale of the season was at Dunstable on 12 October; witnesses in two different cases in the Court of Chivalry in Richard II's reign still remembered it, and one of them, William Penbrugge, had taken part as one of Robert Morley's squires.[51] No fewer than 400 pairs of shoulder-plates were made for the Dunstable tournament, 200 with the arms of Maurice Berkeley and John Neville quartered and 200 with the arms of St George.

We have detailed records for these tournaments, from which we can build something of a picture of the proceedings; the style of Edward's jousts varied little for the rest of the reign, even if they were not always as visually striking as in the early years. These were occasions in splendid style; Mortimer and Isabella were renowned for their extravagance, and they held the purse-strings. Philippa, whose love of clothes was later to lead to serious financial problems with her household, was allowed to place her own orders, and Edward was doubtless delighted with what his armourers and clothiers produced. He evidently loved the Hainault fashions: there was a suit of armour with blue angels and gold letters 'in the style of a suit of armour given to the king by the count of Hainault' and saddles 'decorated with various beasts and images in the style of Hainault' in honour of Edward's bride and her entourage. Letters, whose meaning we can rarely guess at, figure prominently: crowned silver letters P, I and E on costumes probably made for Dunstable stood for Philippa, Isabella and Edward, but the silver-crowned Ms at Guildford, and twelve tunics with the letters K and E at Worcester, are a mystery. The latter, which had silver chains as well as the letters, required 400 peacock feathers, and, with four tunics for the king's squires decorated with eagles' heads, caused so much work for the painter Francolin of Murkirk and his men who were employed to make them that large quantities of candles had to be bought so that they could work on them at night to get them ready in time. The Wigmore accoutrements included two sets of armour patterned with gold and quartered with silver, decorated with birds and beasts, and a banner to match, with birds and 'babbewyns' or grotesques. Highly decorated lances were made by Peter of Bruges: an order for twelve lances, 'well ornamented', ranged from blue lances with green rosebushes and red roses, to black lances with silver pommels and green lances with silver shields and red vamplates. At Worcester, an eagle crest was supplied, almost certainly for the king, matching the eagles on the squires' tunics. Masks are recorded for the same tournament. The joust at Dartford seems to have been on the theme of Richard the Lionheart's famous encounter (*passus*) with Saladin, an image found on medieval English tiles and embroideries, and taken from the romance written about him in the thirteenth century: there is a hat for the king with the 'passus Saladin' embroidered on it, and thirteen lances and swords finished in silver for the knights of 'the same passus Saladin'.[52] One of the royal treasures was a Saracen helmet 'lately of the Sultan Saladin' complete with silver-gilt circlet recorded on 30 April 1327, just three months after Edward came to the throne; and images of the encounter recur throughout his reign, ending with the will of Edward prince of Wales in 1376.[53]

By the end of 1329, it was generally known at court that Philippa was expecting her first child. Yet her status as queen had not been officially recognized, since she had not been crowned. Arrangements for her coronation were made in some haste, and the ceremony was carried out on 18 February. There seems to have been a major tournament in connection with the celebrations; according to Jean le Bel, the contingent from Hainault was led by her brother Jean de Hainault.[54] Once again, Hainault fashion was the favoured style: in the bills from the king's armourer, Thomas Copham, among the standard pieces of armour and tunics, there are items for decorating 'tunics in the Hainault and other fashions'.[55] Philippa's household may well have contributed a number of jousters at this time. We only know for certain at this point that Walter

Mauny, who came over with Philippa, was a squire in the royal household.

In the spring of 1330 the ominous political atmosphere precluded such lightweight events as tournaments. Despite the official announcement of Edward II's death, and his state funeral at Gloucester, rumours now began to circulate about his survival. Mortimer, aiming to consolidate his control of Edward III and therefore of the government, seems to have been behind these rumours as a means of ensnaring his enemies. He succeeded in deceiving such high-ranking men as William Melton, archbishop of York, and even Edward II's half-brother, Edmund earl of Kent. Edmund and the king's other uncle Thomas of Brotherton, earl of Norfolk, had kept a wary distance from the court since Mortimer was created earl of March, but they had also dissociated themselves from Henry of Lancaster's rebellion. Mortimer regarded the earl of Kent as an opponent and feared that he might gain the young king's confidence and turn him against Mortimer. It seems that his machinations successfully ensnared the unwary Edmund into a plot to restore the king's father, said to be imprisoned at Corfe. Mortimer was already highly unpopular because of the treaty made with Scotland in 1328 after the debacle at Stanhope Park.

At a parliament at Winchester in March 1330, Mortimer was also blamed for the inability of the government to pay for the sending of troops to defend Gascony, which was once more under threat from the French because Edward had only partially performed homage for the duchy at Amiens in 1329. The royal treasury was known to have been well funded before Edward II abdicated, and the suspicion was that Mortimer (and Isabella) had appropriated the money to pay for their extravagant lifestyle and to reward their followers lavishly. Mortimer distracted attention from these complaints by having the earl of Kent arrested on charges of treason, a turn of events which was completely unexpected by the king. The charge was supported by a letter from Edmund to the keeper of Corfe Castle, encouraging an attempt to place Edward II on the throne again. Kent was found guilty; and, according to the *Brut* chronicle, Mortimer went at once to the king, whom he found at dinner, and told him of the verdict. But Mortimer feared that the king would pardon his uncle, and arranged for Kent's immediate death; it was Isabella who ordered the bailiffs of Winchester to have him executed. 'And when the king learnt of it, he was exceedingly sorry, and had his body buried at the Greyfriars church at Winchester.'[56] The earl's estates were treated by Mortimer as his personal spoils and given to his eldest son, Geoffrey, and several of the leading knights who were loyal to him.

Edward retreated into his personal affairs; he went to Woodstock within a week of the end of the parliament, and spent the next three months there, awaiting the birth of Philippa's first child and hunting in the neighbouring forests. His son Edward, later famous as 'the Black Prince', was born on 15 June, and a few days later the king left the palace, returning at intervals during July and holding a tournament there for Philippa's 'churching', the service at which the medieval Church exorcized the superstitious taboos surrounding female fertility and readmitted the mother of the newborn child to its rituals. Such 'churching' festivals were to be a regular part of the life of the royal court.[57] As befitted such an occasion, the queen was provided with the most magnificent of robes, in purple velvet embroidered with golden squirrels – perhaps a reference to her favourite pet – at a cost of just over £200; a third of the cost was for the embroiderers' work.[58]

Quite apart from Edward's revulsion at the judicial murder of the earl of Kent, there were strong signs that he was chafing under the hold which Mortimer had over him through the liaison with his mother. It was now no longer a matter for satire, as in the episode of the 'society of Craddok' (if we have read that rightly), but of his own self-preservation. His friends among his household knights and fellow-tourneyers had little experience of politics, and his household was partly staffed by Mortimer's henchmen. John Maltravers, an associate of Mortimer's since 1322, was appointed steward of the king's household in February 1328, despite the fact that he was widely said to have been one of the men responsible for the death of Edward II. In May 1330 he was among a group of knights loyal to Mortimer who were to be 'always with the king'; the others provided a bodyguard of 230 men at arms, of whom the vast majority were under the command of Simon Bereford.[59] Edward Bohun, though a supporter of Mortimer, was also the king's cousin, while Maurice Berkeley was a tournament companion of the prince. The Berkeleys were relatives of Mortimer, and Thomas Berkeley, lord of Berkeley Castle, was Mortimer's brother-in-law, part of the west-country network which was Mortimer's power base. And Mortimer also had his spies in place: 'he put John Wyard and others around the king to spy on his actions and words, so that he was unable to do as he wished, so that he was like a man in custody.'[60]

Nonetheless, Edward had found means to circumvent Mortimer's attempts to prevent him from independent action. Richard of Bury, later bishop of Durham, had been chamberlain of his earldom of Chester from 1320 to 1323, and was later constable of Bordeaux when Edward was created duke of Aquitaine in 1326: in 1328–9 he was keeper of the king's wardrobe, and then keeper of the privy seal, the office responsible for the king's private correspondence. At the time when Mortimer was encircling Edward with his own men, it was Richard of Bury who helped to arrange for a secret sign by which the pope could distinguish those messages which were genuinely from the king personally from official messages, the implication being that the latter would be dictated by Mortimer. The king's personal letters were to bear the words 'pater sancte', 'Holy Father', written in the king's own hand. This scheme had been set in motion by William Montagu, one of Edward's household knights, during an embassy to Avignon in late 1329. He had explained to the pope Edward's frustration with his inability to act on his own account, and his wish to throw off the dominance of Mortimer. The original letter was carefully filed in the Vatican archives, with the specimen of the king's handwriting: but no other letters to the pope from Edward have come to light. The existence of this one letter, however, tells us that Edward was building a network of his own to counter Mortimer's ambitions as early as September 1329, when Montagu left England.

Mortimer's reputed involvement in the death of Edward II, his certain role in the execution of the earl of Kent, and his imperious manner – he always walked beside the king or in front of him, never behind him[61] – made it seem that he was bent on seizing the throne for himself and Isabella. Years later, Jean le Bel recorded a rumour that Isabella was pregnant by him, though it does not seem to have been current at the time.[62] Even without this, Mortimer had put himself in the same position as the ill-famed favourites of Edward II. But he was only the favourite of the queen regent, not of the king himself: and therein lay his weakness.

The spy Wyard did his job well, and got wind of a conspiracy. Mortimer knew that he was up against formidable problems, and when he and Isabella went to Nottingham in October 1330 for a great council (ostensibly to discuss the crisis in Gascony) he betrayed his nervousness.

He and Isabella arrived first, and Isabella took personal possession of the keys of the castle. The king arrived in the town, to be told that if he wanted to enter the castle he could only do so with three or four servants; his household knights and companions would have to lodge elsewhere.

What we know about the events that followed comes not from the chronicles of officials like Adam Murimuth, but from the anonymous writer of the *Brut* chronicle and from Thomas Gray's *Scalacronica*. Gray, as we have seen, was a member of Montagu's retinue in 1338, eight years later, and probably heard his version from Montagu himself: but he was writing thirty years after the events. We know less about the sources of the *Brut*, but the style in which the episode is told also implies eyewitness information, and was probably written around 1334, very shortly after the event.[63] The *Brut* names the ringleaders of Edward's party as William Montagu, Humphrey Bohun, William his brother,[64] Ralph Stafford, Robert Ufford, William Clinton and John Neville, 'and many others who agreed with them'. Thomas Gray says that the plot was discovered, and they were examined by Mortimer and the ruling council: all of them denied it, and Montagu openly defied the council to say that he had done anything improper, with the result that they only replied in general terms. Once the council was over, Montagu 'said to the king that it was better to eat the dog than to let the dog eat them',[65] and advised him to send someone to speak to the constable of the castle, telling him to keep the plan secret, and leave a postern gate* open that night. According to Thomas Gray, most of the conspirators missed their rendezvous in the castle park that night, and only Montagu and John Neville went in through the gate, with twenty-four men. The constable met them and led them through an underground passage into the castle. When they made their way to the chamber where Mortimer and the queen were discussing what to do next, the steward of the household, Hugh Turplington, saw them as they approached the room, and cried: 'Traitors! You have come here for nothing. You will all die a foul death!' He was killed at once, stabbed by Neville. Mortimer pulled on his armour at the door of the tower, but was seized, and Isabella cried out, 'Fair sirs, I beg you not to hurt him: he is a worthy knight, our

---

* A 'postern gate' often meant an escape route, and therefore does not contradict the story of the underground tunnels.

well-beloved friend and dear cousin!'[66] Mortimer was taken to the king, and orders were given for his close confinement; the king made arrangements for Isabella's safety, in reality a guarded exile from court that was to last until her death in 1358. Mortimer's supporters fled for their lives, and Edward's companions took charge of the government in his name. Mortimer's crimes were declared 'notorious' at a parliament in London in November, and he was therefore condemned without being allowed to defend himself. He was executed on 29 November at Tyburn, 'the common gallows of thieves'.[67]

In all, we have the names of sixteen men who were definitely involved in the attack at Nottingham, because they were specifically given pardons for the murder or rewarded for their actions that night. Seven of the knights are named in the *Brut*, as well as William Eland, keeper of the castle; in addition to these, there are eight other men. Three were knights, Thomas West, William Latimer and Thomas Thornham.[68] West and John Molyns, a squire at the time, were close companions of Montagu. Latimer's father and grandfather had distinguished themselves in royal service; his father had died three years earlier, and he became a knight of the king's household around the time of the coup. This promising career was cut short when he died in 1335, aged about thirty-five. Latimer brought at least four retainers with him, including one man, John Maunsell, who was a squire in the king's household. Finally, two other men about whom we know very little, Robert Walkefare and John Crombek, were also pardoned.

The men named are associates of Montagu and Neville, and this implies that Thomas Gray's statement that only Montagu and Neville and their retinues actually entered the castle is correct. It follows that Edward himself, who is usually said to have been present, is unlikely to have been there, particularly as the *Brut* tells us that those who seized Mortimer 'went thence', i.e. out of the chamber, 'and brought the Mortimer and presented him to King Edward'.[69] Thomas Gray makes no mention of Edward during the entry to the castle and the attack on Mortimer. The traditional scene of Isabella pleading with her son for Mortimer's life which Baker portrays so dramatically is therefore untrue; and he admits that Isabella could not in fact see the king.[70]

The moving spirit behind the plot was William Montagu, but he was acting with the king's full confidence. Edward was still learning the craft of managing men, and Montagu seems to have been an excellent tutor. In the parliament held a month later at Westminster, the bishops and magnates present asked the king to reward him because 'the said William had worked nobly concerning the arrest of the said Roger and his accomplices, for the peace and quiet of all the people of the realm'; and he was duly showered with lands and honours, much of it Mortimer's own territory.

Edward was fully aware of his powers as king, but, perhaps all too mindful of his father's disastrous handling of his favourites, seems instinctively to have regarded himself as first among equals, part of a group or team, rather than insisting on his superior rank. Montagu may have been his closest companion, and even his brother in arms;[71] but he never became more than that in the world at large, and his political influence was limited to advising Edward confidentially on government business. His seal might be used on royal letters, and he might convey the decisions of the royal council to the clerks in chancery, but Edward never went so far as to let him exercise power on his own, as the Despensers and Mortimer had done. Equally, Montagu was not ambitious: he never tried to outshine the other magnates, the fatal flaw which had led to Gaveston's downfall.

The social culture of the court continued to revolve around tournaments and festivals, and in both the king appears as one of the participants, sometimes dazzlingly arrayed as the sovereign, but at other times clothed in a team uniform. We have already met such uniforms in the case of the 'society of Craddok'; there is a particularly splendid set recorded in 1330, which has been associated with the coup of that year. These are aketons, which were basically padded jackets which went under armour to prevent chain mail or plates from chafing: they were worn over a linen shirt. In principle, they were invisible, since they were designed as an under-garment, but during a tournament there would be times when a knight would not be wearing his armour, and his quilted cotton jacket would be visible. The aketon replaced the heavier woollen or linen gambeson in the early fourteenth century, and first appears in Edward II's specifications for the arms to be borne by the wealthier members of the troops levied in the 1320s for feudal service.[72] The king and William Montagu had jackets of this kind made in the summer of 1330, and a further seven were made in November 1330; the materials were velvet, silk and linen, the colours purple, green and red, and the embroidery silver and gold. However, it is difficult to fathom the choice of the men who went resplendent in this costume. It has been suggested that they were all participants in the coup of October 1330, and the timing would certainly suggest this, as would the presence of John Neville, Robert Ufford and William Clinton, whom we know to have been involved. Thomas Bradeston and Maurice Berkeley are highly likely candidates for involvement. But the addition of the king's physician, Master Pancio, and the bishop of Salisbury means that this is not just a group of knights. Indeed, the bishop, Robert Wyville, is a real puzzle. He had been made bishop only months before, and the chronicler Adam Murimuth gives a hostile account of him: 'he wrote the queen's special letters, an illiterate and uncouth personage, whom, had the pope seen him, I believe he would never have promoted to such heights'. He had been arrested at Nottingham as one of Mortimer's supporters, but was soon released.[73]

This kind of puzzle is typical of the problems we face when trying to get closer to the men among whom the king was at ease and who shared his courtly life. Even if they were all involved in the coup, what did the wearing of these gaudy costumes convey, unless it was perhaps a whim of princely magnificence to a random group of followers? Where the same names recur as the recipients of magnificent costumes, we can be more certain that these are the king's intimates: Montagu, Ufford, the Bohun twins and Ralph Neville, John Neville's nephew. On one occasion Montagu and the king appeared in identical red surcoats embroidered with birds and mottoes.[74] But this apparently frivolous context was an important part of the life of the court, and can tell us much about the king and his relationship with his courtiers. It is a theme which tends to be submerged in the politics and military history of Edward's reign, appearing intermittently in the intervals of peace. Yet it probably occupied, together with hunting, as much time in Edward's life as the great affairs of state.

2

'A jolly young life': Tournaments, Festivals, Display

Thomas Gray tells us that, once the king had removed the controlling hand of Mortimer, he embarked on his favourite pleasures, and that it was William Montagu who aided and abetted him: 'At this time and for a long while after, the king was advised by William de Montague, who always encouraged him to virtue and honour, and to a love of arms, and they led a jolly young life, awaiting a greater season for greater affairs.'[1] A list of armour issued to the king for tournaments for 1330–31, ending on 24 January, shows four tournaments, beginning at Clarendon on 13 November, moving to Westminster later that month and then to Guildford for the beginning of the Christmas festivities, and Westminster again on 20 January.[2]

Edward III took to jousting with immense enthusiasm. What had once been a subversive activity, tolerated rather than encouraged, and rarely patronized by the crown, became the official sport of the English court. We have seen how Edward learnt to love tournaments and festivals while he was under the tutelage of Isabella and Mortimer, yet he was shrewd enough to see that such display could arouse enmity as well as admiration. By his extravagant display on these occasions, Mortimer was declaring himself as the dominant player in the English political scene, with power and wealth to rival the king. There is only a handful of tournaments in 1330 before Mortimer's arrest and execution in November of that year. Once Edward had dispatched his erstwhile master and mentor, he gathered round him a group of magnates and knights who were to be the core of his administration and household. These men were at the heart of the renewed festivities of the winter of 1330–31, and William Montagu, leader of the coup against Mortimer, was Edward's new fellow-enthusiast. The king, however, was now in charge, and Montagu was no more than an adviser.

The attitude towards tournaments was changing, perhaps because of the king's personal enjoyment of them. In 1331 three general prohibitions were issued, an indication that the political situation was still volatile. But in later years such bans were rare and were usually put in place when the king was going abroad or there was a military campaign in progress. Compared with France, where royal bans were largely directed at gatherings of great lords whose relations with the king were often hostile, the English magnates were now generally allowed to hold jousts in the king's absence. Few of their household accounts survive; most of the records of local jousts that survive come from the fourteenth-century accounts of Thomas, Lord Berkeley, which have remained at Berkeley Castle since they were written. And chroniclers from the religious houses of which the magnates were patrons took an interest in their lords' doings: the priory at Wigmore described the tournaments of the earls of March, and Henry Knighton at Leicester kept track of the activities of Henry of Grosmont, the king's cousin and heir to the earldom of Leicester. The king might also use a prohibition to eliminate events which clashed with his own: a royal ban was issued in February 1341 to the sheriff of Kent because the king was holding jousts at Norwich and did not want local competition which might reduce the attendance at his festival.

The distinction between *hastiludium*, literally 'game with the spear', usually translated as joust, and *torneamentum*, 'tournament', a word whose origins and meaning are less obvious, is difficult to define, but in the records of Edward's reign it is reasonably clear that *hastiludia* usually take place in a confined space, and are therefore more likely to have been single combats, while the tournament was the traditional mock-warfare (*mêlée*) as practised since the early twelfth century, which required open spaces and a large area for an encounter between groups of knights (Plate 25).[3] The French word *joute*, which is the equivalent of *hastiludia*, also appears in the Latin records as *justa*, and there is also the *burdeicium* (*bohort* in French, 'burdis' in English), which was usually a kind of practice tournament restricted to squires. A major event could include all three forms of fighting; the *bohort* is usually only mentioned in the chronicles when there is an accident or a disturbance, and is almost totally absent from the exchequer records.

In April 1331 Edward travelled secretly to France to swear conditional fealty to Philip, who was pressing for a complete oath of fealty to
complete the homage made in 1329. It was a move which could have
caused problems at home if it had become public. As if to mask his brief
absence, he celebrated a tournament at Dartford as soon as he returned.
The writer of the St Paul's chronicle evidently had an eyewitness account
of this occasion: the defending team, including the king, fought under
the banner of William Clinton, and the king, 'though he was of a tender
age, performed very well, battered by heavy blows and enduring them
strongly'. At the end of the tournament, his horse played up, and he
called for a palfrey* to be brought; but one of his knights protested that
it was not fitting for him to change horses on the field. The king ignored
this and rode safely back to his lodgings; meanwhile, the first horse
bolted with his new rider, and plunged into the river, nearly drowning
the knight: 'the horse was so overheated by the tournament that it
wanted to bathe in the water'. If the fully armed king had been riding it,
he would almost certainly have perished.[4]

The king, undeterred, spent much of the spring and summer jousting.
In early May, there was a tournament at Havering, a royal manor
belonging to the queen which had been remodelled on a lavish scale
under Henry III, with a chamber, chapel and two wardrobes for Eleanor
of Provence.[5] The event seems to have had an Arthurian theme, since the
king had a suit of armour decorated with 'a castle with the flags of the
arms of Lancelot issuing from it' made for the occasion.[6] The tourneyers
moved on to Newmarket at the end of the month; Walter Mauny was
present on both occasions, and suits of armour were bought for eight of
the king's household knights. Two further jousts were held, at Lichfield
and Bedford, some time during the summer and autumn.[7]

The major events, however, were held in the capital. The Dartford
jousts were the first of three which attracted the attention of the London
chroniclers in 1331. Edward had held tournaments at Westminster, but
not in and around the City until this year. Perhaps the memory of the
disaster of Gaveston's cancelled Stepney jousts in 1309 still lingered:
if so, it was a memory triumphantly expunged at the same place in June.
This was as much festival as tournament, showing off the regal style
of the new regime as if to counter any possible rumours of the king's

* An ordinary riding horse, as opposed to the larger tournament charger.

submission to France. The organizer was ostensibly Robert Morley, a member of the king's inner circle; it was paid for by the king, and marked the first birthday of his son Edward. The king fought under Morley's banner, together with his uncle, Thomas of Brotherton, and twenty-three other knights. The event began with a procession to St Paul's, where they all made offerings at the high altar. The knights were in uniform costumes of green tunics and mantles with red hoods, the mantles embroidered with golden arrows; their fifty squires were dressed in white with green right sleeves also with golden arrows, and green hoods. To conceal the king's identity, they were all masked.[8]

William Montagu was the leader in the even more splendid occasion held within the City itself , in Cheapside from 22 to 25 September. The writer of the St Paul's chronicle watched the event:

The whole market area, between the conduit and the cross of the queen [Eleanor] where they were to ride was enclosed with stout timber and planks, and the whole pavement was strewn with sand. At the bishop's palace, where William was the host, there was great plenty of provisions and many marvellous things. At the time for which the tournament was arranged, the king, earls and barons and all the knights in the kingdom gathered in London, and on the Sunday, the eve of St Matthew the apostle, William, who was captain of this solemn occasion, appeared with the king and other chosen knights in splendid clothing, with masks like Tartars. There came with them the same number of the most noble and beautiful ladies of the kingdom, all wearing red velvet tunics and caps of white camel's hair cloth; and each knight had on his right-hand side a lady whom he led with a silver chain. The king had at his side the lady Eleanor his sister, a most beautiful girl. All of them, both knights and ladies, came at the hour of vespers, riding in pairs down the middle of Cheapside, preceded by more than sixty squires all dressed in the same uniform; and they were followed by their jousting horses covered with fine horsecloths; and thus, to the sound of trumpets and a variety of other instruments, they rode to their lodgings. On the following days, that is, Monday, Tuesday and Wednesday, the sixteen knights who were the keepers defended themselves from early morning to evening against all comers, both native and foreign. On the first day of the jousts there was an extraordinary accident: the balcony which ran across the street, in which the queen and all the other ladies were sitting to watch the spectacle, suddenly collapsed; and many ladies as well as knights were seriously hurt, and scarcely escaped with their lives.[9]

The citizens were duly impressed: 'never were such solemn jousts seen in England', noted one of them.[10] The king's armourer, John of Cologne, was paid the huge sum of £356 3s. 7d. for his work on costumes, saddles and suits of armour supplied for these occasions.[11]

Behind the games and the spectacle, the apparent indulgence in idle pursuits and lavish expenditure, there was a deeper purpose. These events brought the aristocratic world of the court and the equally rich world of the City together, and we shall see how this is one of the key elements of Edward's success. The court moved round the country from one royal residence to another, and could seem remote to the citizens of London. Even when the king was at Westminster, this was outside the city walls, and except for the rare occasions when he was at the Tower of London, a fortress rather than a place for courtly pageant, he was not seen in London itself. The ties between court and the City could be of great political importance, and we shall find a consistent pattern of jousts in London and even invitations to the citizens to attend jousts elsewhere that seem to indicate that the king was using these occasions as a way of forging a relationship between the two.[12] This is knightly prowess as visual entertainment, even theatre, of a kind which was to become very familiar down to the seventeenth century; it is the direct ancestor of the 'magnificence' of Renaissance princes.[13] The Stepney and Cheapside jousts of 1331 are among the earliest known examples of the tournament as royal pageant, though Philip of Valois had staged jousts on his formal entry into Paris in 1328 which may have been in the same vein.[14] There were similar occasions in Flanders: it is possible that jousts at Tournai in 1331, for which we have a detailed record of the jousters' performance, included a parade of knights through the streets and possibly a dramatic scenario, though no record of this part of the proceedings survives.[15]

A grand occasion like the Cheapside 'tournament' in 1331 would begin with the traditional *mêlée*, in which all the knights took part. In the *mêlée*, the knights would fight as teams, and the same teams, usually called 'those inside' (*intrinseci*) or defenders and 'those outside' (*extrinseci*) or challengers, would then fight individual jousts against all members of the opposing team. Performance in the *mêlée* was hard to judge, though the romances of the period make great play of the heroic feats of individual knights in such combats, one of whom is then acclaimed by the heralds and the assembled company as the victor. What actually went on in the *mêlée* was hard to describe; even the writers of romances found it difficult to invent a detailed account of their imaginary tournaments, and are very vague as to the details of what was happening: 'Then Sir Gawain and his brother Sir Gaheriet began to perform such splendid feats of arms that anyone who saw them would have deemed them the best knights in the world: they spurred up the field and down, felling knights and horses, and doing so much by their valor that their enemies were defeated by their might . . .'[16]

Minstrels or public criers, the forerunners of heralds, provided a commentary on the action in twelfth-century tournaments so that spectators could identify the knights and understand what was happening. By the fourteenth century it is more likely that some kind of scoring system, such as is found on Tudor jousting 'cheques', was emerging, and that a knight such as Thomas Beauchamp, the victor of the jousts at Smithfield in 1343, was the winner of the largest number of individual jousts. The other problem with the *mêlée* was that most accidents in the sport happened in this type of combat: although tournaments were probably no more dangerous than rugby or American football today, there were some spectacular fatalities, including John of Beaumont, brother-in-law of Henry of Grosmont, at Northampton in 1342.

A knight who excelled in the lists was the equivalent of a modern sporting hero, and the small group of tourneyers whose names appear alongside that of the king himself were made up of such star performers. As with all tourneying records, the details are very sketchy – there is no equivalent to the lists of knights in a lord's retinue when he went on campaign – but certain names stand out. First and foremost is Henry of Grosmont, whose close friendship with his cousin Edward was partly based on their shared enthusiasm for jousting. Henry was responsible for the grant of a licence in 1344 to a company of knights at Lincoln who proposed to hold an annual tournament, of which he was to be the captain in perpetuity. In the charter Edward declares that he has made the grant because of Henry's 'delight in warlike deeds', and 'having studied the deeds of our forefathers, and bearing in mind how much the practice of knightly skills and the love of arms exalts the name and glory of men, and how much the royal throne is strengthened by the number of men expert in arms, as well as the confusion and danger which often arises from laziness'.[17]

The role of captain appears in other tournament records. William Montagu, the nearest to a favourite in Edward's court, was another, and Edward fought under his leadership as *capitaneus* at the tournament at Cheapside in 1331; in the same year he also appeared under William Clinton, at Dartford, and Robert Morley, at Stepney. Morley was certainly one of the most experienced jousters, as he was present on at least ten occasions over a twenty-year period. Twelve years later, in 1343, the king was again in the lists with Morley as captain. He also fought as a 'simple knight' at Dunstable in 1342, and in 1348 wore the arms of Thomas Bradeston, who was evidently captain for the occasion, at Lichfield. Such occasions must have created a strong sense of fellowship, yet none of these captains were to become companions of the Garter.

Jousts and tournaments took place almost entirely in peacetime. The records of such occasions show a clear pattern which confirms this. There are jousts in 1328–9, 1331–2, 1334, 1339–40, a major series in 1341–4, and another in 1348.[18] In the 1350s there were only brief intervals when there was no threat of hostilities or actual war, and, by the end of the decade, Edward was fifty, and his enthusiasm for the sport was diminishing. The Garter companions would therefore have experienced a court culture in which the art of performance was a major factor, very much in contrast with the opening and closing decades of the century. The younger knights, such as Edward prince of Wales, would have regarded tournaments and festive jousts as a natural and integral part of their lives; the older knights were among those who helped Edward III to revive and develop his grandfather's traditions.

Knightly gatherings may have fulfilled another function. Jousts were usually court events, and would have had an important influence on creating an *esprit de corps* among the household knights and those usually in attendance on the king. The degree to which the knights who took part in tournaments overlapped with those who served on royal campaigns is well illustrated by the event at Dunstable in 1334,[19] for which we have a list of 134 knights who took part. Of these, 89 can be identified as members of the household in the 1330s and/or participants in the campaign of 1346 which culminated in the battle of Crécy.

Tournaments held outside the capital were very probably useful to the king as a way of sounding out local opinion and impressing his subjects with his 'magnificence'. The series of tournaments held in 1328–9 looks very much like a royal tour by the new king, doing the equivalent of the later royal progress; just as Elizabeth I paraded herself and her court before her subjects, so Edward may have used these events both to introduce himself to his people, and to impress them with his martial skills, particularly as his father was said to have had a very unregal love of 'the art of rowing and driving carts, of digging ditches and thatching houses'.[20] The king also used such tours to celebrate his military successes, and his return from a campaign would often be marked with a tournament, as in 1334, at the end of the Scottish expedition which included the victory at Halidon Hill. The tournaments of 1348 are similar, in that they mark – on a much grander scale – the victories at Crécy and Calais. There were also tournaments at the end of rather less successful military activities: in Flanders in 1339–40, the first foray into France and the unsuccessful siege of Tournai, which ended in the truce of Esplechin, were celebrated with jousts, perhaps as a distraction from pressing problems of finance and as a way of raising the army's morale.

During a campaign, even if the king was not present, there was a continual flow of communication with important magnates and the captains of the army. In peacetime, there was no mechanism for discovering the mood of the nobility outside the court, other than through the formal summoning of a parliament – which was, as its name (from *parler*, to talk) implies, a place where discussion took place. The tournaments from 1341 to 1344 look like an informal way of keeping in touch with local magnates, particularly since they correspond to the low point of Edward's rule, following the opposition to his policies in the spring of 1341 after which he had had to accept terms imposed by Archbishop Stratford and his allies. This was possibly a deliberate way of regaining the confidence of the disaffected shire knights.

From the outset, the tournament had been governed by rules, designed to prevent injuries as far as possible and the degeneration of such events into private warfare. The nearest contemporary set of jousting regulations are those issued by Alfonso XI of Castile for the knights of the Sash, founded in 1330, and thus exactly contemporary with Edward III's tourneying activities. This is a severely practical document, which is concerned to prevent accidents or outright cheating, and to restrict any possibility that quarrels might arise, or be settled, in the thick of the fight. For the mass combat of the tournament proper, bugles and kettle-drums signalled the start of the fighting, as well as its ending. Swords were to be blunted, and armour should not have any sharpened points. A blow with the point of a sword, or with the flat of the blade in the face, was prohibited. If a knight lost his helmet or fell to the ground, he was not to be attacked or trampled on. If knights lost their horses, they were to be impounded until the fighting finished; but they were then returned to their owners. In the twelfth and thirteenth centuries it had been possible to make a fortune by capturing horses in tournaments, as if in war itself; but this no longer held good. The prizes were to be awarded to the knights who had performed best in each team: a large tournament of fifty knights on either side would have twelve judges for each side, and the judges would confer with the squires and ladies present before coming to a decision.

For single combat, which seems at this period to have been almost exclusively a contest with lances, the critical objective was to break a lance on the body of the opposing knight. A specified number of courses were to be run, and the winner was the knight who had broken most lances. If a knight succeeded in unhorsing his opponent, that counted for two lances. If two knights unseated each other, a knight whose horse fell with him was declared the winner of that course, on the grounds that his fall was the fault of his horse. If a knight dropped his lance, his opponent was to raise his lance and not strike him.[21]

The actual combats were only part of the tournament. From their inception in the twelfth century tournaments were major social occasions. It is possible that the rapid development of heraldry was due to the spectators' interest in the individual knights and their exploits, for which clear visual identification was required; and the mystique of the early heralds depended on the knowledge and skill with which they were able to pick out the champions of the day. As the tournament moved away from mass encounters to the joust between two participants, so the length of the proceedings increased: fifteenth-century descriptions make them sound rather less exciting than the most protracted of cricket matches, with only one or two encounters an hour. This in turn increased their potential as social occasions, combined with the opportunity for display, not only of horsemanship and knightly skills, but also of opulent costume and elaborate heraldic trappings.

Tournaments were held entirely at the king's will, though there were certain royal occasions where a tournament became part of the ritual of the royal court. There is a consistent series for the baptism of royal children and the churching of the queen: of Philippa's twelve children, on only one occasion can we be certain that there was no baptismal tournament, because Margaret of Windsor was born on 20 July 1346, a week after Edward had landed in France. Otherwise there are definite or possible records for all of the others. Betrothals and marriages of royal children were also occasions for tournaments: Lionel's betrothal in 1342, John of Gaunt's marriage, held at the same time as that of his sister Margaret in 1359, and Mary's wedding to the earl of Richmond in 1361, were all accompanied by jousting. However, the wedding which should have been the grandest of all, that of Edward prince of Wales to Joan of Kent, was treated as a largely private affair;[22] and that of his younger brother Edmund, marrying his sister-in-law's half-sister in 1372, also seems to have been low key, though jousts had by then faded from the court's rituals.

There was a widespread tradition of tournaments at Shrovetide and on Midsummer Day throughout Europe, but these are almost entirely absent from the records of Edward's tournaments. The major feast of the year was Christmas and Epiphany, a time of year generally unsuitable for the sport. By far the greatest number of tournaments after Edward threw off the tutelage of his mother and Mortimer, and after the halcyon interlude of his 'jolly young life', have to do with recent victories, or with political campaigns to rally public opinion. We have already looked at the jousts on his return from doing homage in France in 1331 up to the beginning of the Scottish campaigns. The jousts in 1334 were a celebration of Edward's first great military success; during the Flemish campaigns, the brief periods of military action were followed by jousts in Brussels and Ghent. The great tournament at Dunstable was definitely for the betrothal of Lionel; how far it was also a celebration of the recent Anglo-Scots truce as well is doubtful. Subsequent tournaments in 1342–3 seem to revolve round the political and military problems of renewing the war in France as Edward's grand alliance gradually dissolved and he determined to rely in future on his own military resources, a process which culminated in the tournament at which the Round Table was announced in January 1344. The jousts of 1348 were undoubtedly a kind of Roman triumph, proclaiming the king as victor of Crécy and Calais. These were in the same style as those of the early 1330s, with Edward jousting in the arms of Thomas Bradeston and Stephen Cosington to emphasize his role as fellow-knight rather than sovereign, and with highly decorative costumes throughout. Thereafter the list of tournaments is sparse: on average, we have definite knowledge of only one a year until 1363, and only two in the last fourteen years of the reign. This is partly because the highly informative and detailed chronicles available for the early years peter out in the early 1350s and partly because the royal accounts which tell us so much about the king's activities in the lists are missing. Such glimpses as we have fail to reveal any sustained periods of jousting, and offer instead only the ceremonial marriage tournaments or political spectacles, such as the occasion in 1358 when three kings were present at Windsor for St George's Day.

THE KING'S GAMES

Tournaments were not only occasions for the display of royal splendour. Equally important were the royal entertainments at great court festivals. Jousting is recorded in the official records as *hastiludia*; it is almost as if the clerks wished to classify it with the other royal frivolities, called simply *ludi*, the king's games. Jousts had military and political overtones; the royal games were pure entertainment, overlaid only by a deliberate display of splendour and an often elaborate – and now usually indecipherable – use of images and mottoes. The games were almost always associated with Christmas or with baptisms and weddings; they included music, dancing and the use of masks and disguises, possibly with some dramatic theme or simple play-acting, though this has left no positive traces. The word *ludi* covered a wide range of activities, from gambling through entertainments to actual plays; even the religious mystery plays were called *ludi*.

Ludi and *hastiludia* could overlap: there are several occasions when a joust had a theme, and the participants were disguised, or where masks were used. The costumes were used on these occasions for the preliminary parade, not in the jousting itself: the account of the 1331 tournament at Cheapside gives a very clear picture of the proceedings, and specifies that in this case the participants were *ad similitudinem Tartarorum larvati*, 'masked like Tartars'. *Larvati* is a word generally associated with hideous or devilish masks; the Tartars were obviously represented as nightmarish figures of pagans. It is difficult to associate the use of this disguise with an obvious political event, but the Tartars were a powerful and menacing force on the borders of Christendom at this period, raiding the Byzantine Empire and controlling Russian affairs. Masks ('false faces') were also used at Worcester, Guildford, Canterbury, Reigate and Hereford in 1329.[23] Fourteen years later at Smithfield, Edward's team appeared dressed as the pope and twelve cardinals, an allusion to the dispute over the use of papal taxes raised in England to help the French cause, about which Edward was protesting at the time.[24] In 1359, again at Smithfield, both teams, including the king and four of his sons, dressed as the mayor of London and the twenty-four aldermen of the City; in this case, it was probably a compliment to their hosts.

In 1362 a tournament was planned in Cheapside to mark the wedding of Edward prince of Wales. Two days before the event, one of the greatest storms ever to occur in England in recorded times struck, cutting a devastating swathe across the country: the unfinished choir of Vale Royal Abbey in Cheshire was blown down, and London was a scene of havoc and devastation. The tournament did not take place, but monks at Reading and Canterbury recorded that the prince and his knights had planned to dress as the seven deadly sins, and the hurricane was a divine judgement on this blasphemy. Reading between the lines, it seems more likely that the extreme violence of the storm demanded an exceptional act of impiety to explain it, and that the idea of this disguise was a figment of the imagination on the part of one or other of the monks.[25] Tournaments with religious disguises were not unknown, and in Spain in 1428 the king of Castile and his knights dressed as God and the twelve apostles:[26] but no dire consequences followed on this occasion.

Masks and costumes were an essential part of the king's Christmas entertainments. There are numerous records of expenditure on 'vizors' and on 'heads', and for two occasions we have detailed descriptions of what was ordered. For the king's revels at Guildford in 1347, the original bill from John of Cologne survives, giving more detail than the summary on the annual account roll. This battered sheet of parchment lists a series of different disguises: fourteen heads and busts of girls, fourteen heads of bearded men, fourteen silver angels' heads with curly hair, fourteen silver-plated dragons' heads with a black mane, fourteen heads of swans. To go with these there are tunics decorated with the eyes of peacocks and gleaming with stars.[27] At Otford the following year, there are twelve heads each of lion cubs, elephants, men with bats' wings, wild men and twenty-seven heads of virgins. The inclusion of busts and bats' wings implies that the 'heads' covered the upper part of the body, and were not simply masks, but something nearer to hoods, which came down over the shoulders. In some cases, there are tunics associated with the heads. Usually the disguises are decorative or fabulous, and no theme emerges: for Christmas games at Merton in 1349, there were simply masks of dragons' heads and crowned heads of men. At Windsor in 1352, however, we find thirteen devils and thirteen friars in black with white scapulars, a clear reference to the Dominicans.[28] This must refer to some contemporary event or dispute; but whether the Dominicans drove off the devils, or the Dominicans themselves were demonized, we cannot tell. Sadly, no actual costumes or even fragments of costumes survive (Plate 15).

Scenery was certainly used on these occasions, but is rarely specified: there are often extensive entries for payments to painters, but we are not told what they were doing. One exception is the Christmas feast in 1337, at Guildford, for which timber and canvas were provided and painted to resemble 'a wood with various trees', seemingly inhabited by the fifteen baboons for whom heads, tunics, hose and gloves were made.*[29] In 1331, canvas and wool were used to make hides for both wild men and deer, implying an overall costume.[30]

The puzzling thing about these entries is the consistent numbers, usually twelve, thirteen or fourteen (and sometimes multiples of this, for instance forty-two), for the quantity of heads or tunics or other items which are ordered. We have no account of a royal entertainment which would begin to explain this. The only reasonable assumptions are that we are looking at either some form of team game, or some form of dance. If the entertainments were in the context of a tournament, the teams might have been the two sides in the jousting, the defenders and

---

* The king kept real baboons: in May 1340, Hugh, 'keeper of the king's baboons', received a gift from the king.

attackers. But they are consistently called *ludi*, not *hastiludi*, so the most likely explanation is some kind of dance. This is supported by images in two illuminated manuscripts, the *Romance of Fauvel* and the *Romance of Alexander*.[31] In the *Romance of Fauvel*, a wide-ranging satire on Church and State written about 1314, there is a theatrical interlude at Fauvel's wedding in which actors appear with both masks and heads. The *Romance of Alexander*, written in Tournai in 1344 and therefore exactly contemporary with Edward's festivals, has an illustration which shows exactly what we are looking for: courtiers – identifiable by their expensive parti-coloured clothes – dancing in animal heads. A few pages earlier, there is a similar group with extravagant beards, unlike the neat beards which Edward III and the prince of Wales wear in surviving miniatures and effigies. These are probably examples of the fourteen bearded men's heads provided for the Guildford entertainment in 1347.

We are still left with the problem of why groups of about a dozen are evidently a key element in the proceedings. This is not an idle question, because when we come to the Company of the Garter, it is made up of two sides, the king's side and the prince's side, each with twelve knights. Most of the orders for sets of twelve items relate to tournaments, though at one point, in 1334, William Standerwyk provided twelve standards and banners with the king's arms, and twelve with the arms of St George and St Edmund for the Scottish wars, which might imply that the army was organized into twelve units of some kind; but the figure does not reappear. Twelve and thirteen are standard numbers in tourneying terms, with either the king in different clothing and his knights dressed alike, or both king and knights in one style. The idea of a uniform was relatively new in medieval armies: the earliest English records come from the mid-thirteenth century. Guilds in London adopted specific costumes by 1347, when Henry Knighton notes that, when David II of Scotland was brought to the Tower as a prisoner, the guilds paraded, each 'honourably arrayed in its own distinctive livery'.[32]

Edward's use of livery to mark out a smaller group may have been something of an innovation, and it appears at the very beginning of his reign, specifically in the context of a *ludus* or game, the 'game of the society of Craddok' which we have already looked at, and which seems to have a specific political context. Here we have both the figure of twelve costumes for the knights 'of the same pattern', and a further fourteen for the squires. Furthermore, the meaning of *ludus* here is not simply that of dancing, which seems to be one of the contexts for the use of masks and heads. Something is being acted out, which is neither a joust nor a dance; but beyond this we have little idea. We can only point to rare episodes which are reflected in the accounts: two squires compensated for the burns they suffered while 'playing' before Edward II in 1325, or Bernard the fool and fifty-four of his fellows dancing naked for him in 1313.[33]

An episode from the French court in 1393 is perhaps the best indication of how the masks and disguises were used. Charles VI and a group of nobles dressed as wodewoses or wild men, and danced at a court festival; an inquisitive onlooker (said by Froissart to be the duke of Orléans, the king's brother) put a torch too close to their costumes, which contained pitch, and several of them were burnt to death. The king himself was not with the dancers at the time, and this stroke of luck saved his life. The monk of St Denis who recorded this tragedy waxed eloquent on the iniquities of such wanton revelries.[34] However, the accounts of the so-called 'Bal des ardents' are clear evidence that it was not necessarily actors or minstrels who used these elaborate and expensive costumes, but that the performers and dancers could be the courtiers themselves.

The masks and costumes ordered by the king often seem to have some specific meaning in mind, as if there is a kind of programme behind both these and the decoration of the clothing. Occasionally, we also have mottoes, and the Garter motto itself may well have originated in the context of an entertainment. There are only three recorded mottoes which appear in the accounts: 'It is as it is', 'Sure as the woodbine' and 'Hey, hey, the white swan, by God I am the king's man'. Two mottoes appear for Philippa, 'Ich wrude muche' and 'Myn biddenye'.[35]

We may be able to decipher these mottoes, although with some hesitation. The woodbine is the modern honeysuckle,[36] and this is an old motif in Arthurian romance: in the twelfth century, Marie de France wrote a poem of Tristan and Iseult meeting in the forest, beneath a hazel branch along which honeysuckle was entwined, symbolizing the inseparable nature of their love. The most likely explanation is that this was a declaration of Edward's love for Philippa. Philippa's mottoes appear to be in a dialect of medieval German. 'Ich wrude' might be 'ich vreude', 'I rejoice', and the first motto could be 'I rejoice greatly'. 'Myn biddenye' is connected to 'beten' or praying, perhaps 'the answer to my prayer'. 'It is as it is' appears in 1342 in conjunction with the Dunstable tournament in honour of the wedding of the king's second son, Lionel. It was used on the white borders of a set of twelve green doublets, embroidered with the motto in jewels and pearls and with clouds and vines in gold. It also appeared prominently on the lavish hangings and resplendent state bed made for Edward on this occasion. Twelve hangings six yards long and three yards wide were made up, embroidered with the king's words 'It is as it is'. These presumably lined the walls of the room where the state bed was set up, and the top sheet of the bed was worked with a pattern of five circlets: the four corner circlets contained angels, and the central circlet the royal helmet and crest. The background was embroidered with the repeated motto, as on the hangings. Lionel was also provided with a similar state bed, without the motto and to a different design. In 1349, for the king's Epiphany games at Merton, a single doublet was made up, in white with a green border, which seems to indicate that it was more than an ephemeral choice of motto. It is a curiously stoical statement and is no clearer to us today than Philippa's mottoes.[37]

As to the swan motto, there are even wider possibilities. The legend of the Swan knight, made familiar to us by the story of Lohengrin, was known on the Continent, and various English families could claim descent from this hero of romance. The knighting of Edward II in 1306 was followed by the 'feast of the swans', at which the king and others swore oaths on the swans connected with the imminent campaign in Scotland. The swan badge was later to be associated particularly with Thomas of Woodstock, Edward's youngest son.[38]

At the end of it all, however, we are no nearer the meaning of the figures and mottoes: as the Elizabethan courtier Sir Henry Wotton said of the *imprese* or visual mottoes of Gloriana's tournaments, 'some were so dark that their meaning is not yet understood, unless perchance that were their meaning, not to be understood'.[39]

Occasionally, we get a glimpse of increasingly elaborate scenarios based loosely on the characters of Arthur's court rather than on the actual events of the romances. Both at a tournament at Le Hem in 1278 and in a Dutch account of an undated round table of Edward I, the emphasis is on role-playing. The characters are limited to the central figures of Arthur's court; at least, there is no mention of minor roles: we have evidence for knights playing Lancelot, Tristan, Palamedes, Yvain, Gawain, Kay, Perceval, Agravain, Gareth, Bors and even Arthur's treacherous nephew, Mordred. Ladies played Guinevere and Soredamors. There appear to have been scripts written for the occasion, with a reasonable amount of detail in them, and evidence from the century following the Windsor festival of 1344 shows an increasing literary element in later tournaments, often departing entirely from an Arthurian framework.

If play-acting seems an unexpected activity for a fourteenth-century royal court, we have only to turn to a contemporary historian's description of the elaborate theatrical staging at a French royal feast in Paris in 1378 (Plate 20).[40] The theme was probably inspired by Charles V's interest in leading a new crusade, and centred on the story of Godefroi de Bouillon and the conquest of Jerusalem in 1099. The first scene represented a ship carrying Godfrey to Palestine, which was moved by men inside it in such a way that 'it seemed like a ship floating on the water'; this was followed by a representation of Jerusalem itself, including the lifelike touch of 'a Saracen making the call to prayers, in the Arabic tongue'. Chaucer describes such an occasion in 'The Franklin's Tale', apparently the work of specialists in this kind of entertainment, whom he calls 'tregetours', and whose skills seem to have included the use of candles and glasses filled with water to create illusions.

These *ludi* or knightly charades took place within the framework of a great feast. In the romances, Arthur traditionally refused to dine on high days and holidays until some adventure had taken place, such as the arrival of a mysterious messenger asking for help or offering a challenge. Imitating this in real life would give the perfect cue for an Arthurian interlude to become part of the occasion. This line of thought leads us to the opening of the greatest of all English Arthurian poems, *Sir Gawain and the Green Knight*, written towards the end of Edward's reign or early in that of Richard II:

> This king lay at Camelot one Christmastide
> With many mighty lords, manly liegemen,

> Members rightly reckoned of the Round Table,
> In splendid celebration, seemly and carefree.
> There tussling in tournament time and again
> Jousted in jollity these gentle knights,
> Then in court carnival sang catches and danced;
> For fifteen days the feasting there was full in like measure
> With all the meat and merry-making men could devise,
> Gladly ringing glee, glorious to hear,
> A noble din by day, dancing at night![41]

The poet goes on to describe the richness of the setting, the courtesy of knights and ladies, and the character of Arthur himself, who announced

> that he never would eat
> On such a fair feast-day till informed in full
> Of some unusual adventure, as yet untold,
> Of some momentous marvel that he might believe,
> About ancestors, or arms or other high theme;
> Or till a stranger should seek out a strong knight of his,
> To join with him in jousting, in jeopardy to lay
> Life against life . . .[42]

The stranger who arrives to lay life against life is hardly what Arthur expects: a knight green from head to foot, bearing a great axe and a holly branch, a warrior as courteous as any of his knights but carrying the symbols of an earlier age. The Green Knight offers not a joust, but a bargain: one of Arthur's knights is to behead him, and must seek him out in a year's time to stand a return blow. All that he proposes, says the Green Knight, is an entertainment:

> So I crave in this court a Christmas game,
> For it is Yuletide and New Year, and young men abound here.[43]

It is not difficult to imagine this scene being acted out at Edward's court; indeed, a 'head' with a special framework could easily be constructed which would allow the Green Knight to be decapitated in full view of the audience. The poem is generally dated to after 1360, although its authorship and origins have been much debated. But its cultural context is firmly within the milieu of Edwardian court life, and the unique manuscript ends with a version of the Garter motto, 'Hony soyt qui mal pence', though the reason for its presence here is unexplained.

The results of the massive expenditure recorded so carefully by the clerks of the exchequer must have been an extraordinary splendour. Sadly, little of the opulent fabrics and costumes survives, and we have to rely on illuminations in manuscripts. The most vivid pictures of jousting costume are from Germany, in the famous Manesse manuscript of the love songs of the thirteenth century. The fashions may be different to those of Edward's court, but the ideas are the same. The fantastic heraldic crests, figures or emblems surmounting the helmets, shown on the stall plates of the Garter companions in the 1420s, appear in even more extravagant form in the Manesse miniatures. Whereas the Garter heraldry confines itself to the more orthodox heraldic bestiary, heads of boars, lions and so on, the Manesse images include such strange sights as the inverted legs and claws of an eagle, a pair of hunting horns forming a crescent, Venus goddess of love, two battleaxes trimmed with peacock feathers, and a pair of carp trimmed with black cock's feathers.[44] The knights wear long surcoats, matching their horses' trappings, which are patterned or emblazoned with their arms. The manuscript was probably completed in the first years of the fourteenth century, two decades before Edward III's first appearance in the lists.[45] The style of armour had changed in the intervening years, and the chain mail shown in the German miniatures had been replaced by plate armour. Numerous entries in the accounts refer to 'pairs' of plates (breastplate and backplate) being covered with material: usually this is velvet, as in the prince of Wales's list of items given to his friends in the years up to 1358. Interestingly, three of the pairs of plates are covered with black velvet, one 'powdered with feathers', the prince's ostrich feather badge;[46] others are in blue or red velvet. For a grand occasion, the richest cloth was used: Edward III, presiding over a meeting with King Peter of Cyprus at which David Bruce, king of Scotland, was also present, ordered a complete suit of armour covered in gold 'baldekyn of Lucca', as well as a set of clothes in the same material.[47]

A sumptuous appearance in the lists, where all eyes were on the individual knights, was highly important, but the real splendours were reserved for the social occasions, feasting, dancing and games, which formed the setting of the tournament. Edward III was spending lavishly at the beginning of his reign. The 'great wardrobe' which dealt with his personal and household expenses had outgoings of £2,427 in the last year of his father's reign. This immediately doubled to £4,574, partly because of administrative changes, but five years later, in 1332–3, it had risen to £10,083.[48] A fair proportion of this was going on clothing, and this was to increase to the point where 'the Great Wardrobe was almost certainly the major purchaser and employer in the City of London'.[49]

There were four elements in the richness and splendour of the clothing: the materials from which it was made, the embroidery, the pictorial designs on it, and the fashionable style. Merchants from Flanders, Paris and Italy provided an immense range of fabrics, both the cloths woven from English wool and more exotic materials in silk and linen traded by merchants from throughout Europe and from the near east. They acted as wholesalers, and supplied most of the expensive materials used in England. The best cloth was woven at Brussels; light and of a fine weave, it was dyed using highly expensive ingredients: scarlet dye came from the Mediterranean, and was such a byword for luxury that any costly cloth was known as a 'scarlet' cloth, and 'scarlets' ranging from black to peacock blue are entered in the accounts. Linen came from Paris and Reims, and, most costly of all, velvet and silk were imported from Italy and the east. Chinese damask has been found in London in a context which dates it to 1325–50; it exemplifies the culture of luxury represented by Edward's court.[50] Silk was also imported as thread for weaving and embroidery, and some plain silk cloth was brought in for dyeing. Patterned velvet was the most expensive of the fabrics, to be used without the addition of embroidery. In 1343 the accounts give prices for a wide range of materials. (As a measure of relative values, the annual wage for William Fitzwarin as knight of the queen's chamber in 1333 was £6 13s. 4d.)[51] Velvet with gold stripes bought in Bruges cost about £7 for a piece nine yards long, while other velvets bought in London were never less than half that price. Cloth of gold silks cost the same as ordinary velvet, and plain silks went for £1 for nine yards; interestingly, good quality woollen cloth was much the same price. Silks were usually patterned, and occasionally the design was so impressive that it was specified in the bill, as with the cloth of gold on which dragons and serpents writhed on a blue background provided for the marriage of

Edward's daughter Joan in 1348.[52] And still the search for even richer effects went on: the finishing touch might be gold leaf stamped onto the garments, which could be used to pattern them with heraldic arms. Finally, gold could be hammered into thin pieces to be sewn onto the material; we find examples of besants (gold coins) or even the badge of the Garter itself being added in this way.

For winter clothing, furs were needed, sometimes to make whole garments, but more often to trim the clothes, and sourced from the Baltic and from Russia. Miniver, made from the winter belly-fur of red squirrels, trimmed down so that only the white was used, and sewn together into large pieces, was bought in large quantities, while the most luxurious fur was ermine, the white winter fur of the stoat with a black tip to the tail. Furs supplied by the royal tailor in 1347–8 included more than 20,000 pieces of miniver, but only 20 of ermine: it was in effect reserved for the king and queen.

Many of the costumes described above would have looked very like the famous medieval embroidery known as *opus anglicanum*, 'English work', which was in great demand for religious apparel from the thirteenth century onwards: the best examples often survive in the treasuries of churches and cathedrals (Plate 16). John of Cologne, the most important of Edward's armourers, had a workshop with a large number of embroiderers; he is sometimes described as working in the Tower, but the armourers in the Tower actually date from the beginning of Richard II's reign.[53] Rather, he would have been an independent merchant with a large establishment, possibly in the Steelyard, the home of the north German merchants from the towns of the Hanseatic league. It is his bills submitted to the king's great wardrobe which are the main source of information about royal expenditure on clothing. Designs were probably drawn up by the king's painters, and sketched by draughtsmen on the linen base for the embroiderers to start work.

The king's tailor was responsible for the less elaborate clothing, and for the provision of the 'livery' provided in summer and winter for members of the household. His team was also involved in the manufacture of clothes for special events, notably for the Round Table festivities in 1344.[54] In 1352, the wages for the workers employed to make garments for the king's daughter Isabella for St George's Day and for her forthcoming wedding show that the draughtsmen were paid twelve pence a day, and the most skilled embroiderers nine pence a day, for a total of eighty-four working days. The bills for the court's ceremonial clothes were now on a par with those for the king's armour.

Banners, tents and standards were also needed for jousts and out-door events. The simpler banners, such as those with the cross of St George, were produced by appliqué sewing. If detailed heraldry or other patterns were involved, draughtsmen would need to be employed. In 1351, one draughtsman appears to have spent six days supervising the manufacture of twenty-four clouds of gold, silver and silk, made by six men and two women, and using an ounce of gold. These were evidently exceptional decorations on a large scale, rather than items to be sewn on a costume. Streamers, the huge masthead flags with bold heraldic or figurative devices designed to be visible from a distance to identify the king's ships, were produced in relatively small quantities; manuscript illuminations give some idea of how impressive they must have been.

For tents in the same period, draughtsmen were employed for a total of 158 working days: the most spectacular of these were a round blue linen tent with stars on the outside and crowns on the inside, and a green tent whose interior had gold eagles on a red buckram lining. In the inventory of the keeper of the Tower in 1341, the clerks note 'two houses of canvas, called pavilions', and although there do not seem to be detailed accounts from Edward III's tentmaker, we have an idea of the scale of such royal tents from those taken by Edward I on campaign in Scotland in 1303.[55] These included what we would call a marquee, 'a great hall with six posts'. Tents were certainly used at tournaments and ceremonial occasions such as coronations; the usual term for them, pavilions, is derived from the Latin *papilio*, a butterfly, which implies that they were highly coloured, as much for display as for practical use (Plate 7). This may have been in contrast to the leather tents used for the royal chambers and the financial office. Canvas tents had to be dried at intervals, as they were only moderately waterproof. The scale of the tents was substantial: the 1303 inventory for the siege of Berwick describes an ensemble of tents with two halls, ten chambers, four chap-els, and forty-nine 'houses', about half of them round tents. One of the halls was 140 feet long, and the king's chamber was 80 feet long.

Other technical processes included staining and painting: both were the province of the painter-stainers of London, who first appear as a company in 1268. Painting was used for scenery and hangings for the royal festivals as well as for military equipment.[56] Hugh of St Albans, in charge of the murals at St Stephen's Chapel, Westminster, also worked on the streamers of the royal ships, which were sealed with wax to make them waterproof. He was doubtless responsible for designs for clothing and for the king's entertainments, though we have no specific evidence of payments to him in this respect.

One of the most dramatic manuscript images of the period is the illustration of a royal carriage in the famous Luttrell Psalter (Plate 24).[57] A number of such carriages were probably made for Philippa and other members of the royal household: it is possible that the Luttrell picture actually represents Philippa, as the figure at the front is crowned and holding a squirrel: Philippa is known to have had these as pets. There is a detailed account of the cloth used for the carriage made for Edward's sister Eleanor in 1332, when she left England for her marriage to Reginald count of Guelders. The outer canvas had two alternative covers, one green and one scarlet; inside there was a purple velvet cloth studded with glass stars, as a canopy inside the canvas. Pillows and mattresses in red and green offered some comfort to the occupants, and there were silk loops to hold on to when the roads were particularly rough. The outside of the carriage was a display of heraldry, presumably of the arms of England and Guelders, which also appeared on the saddles of the horses. Similar details are visible in the Luttrell Psalter, and five horses were evidently the norm for such a vehicle, as the illustration corresponds to the accounts, which specify that number.[58]

FASHION

When Philippa and her entourage came to the English court in 1328, they brought with them fashions in dress and armour sufficiently distinctive to be noted by the king's armourer and tailor; we have already noted entries for armour and saddles in the Hainault style, and, in an entry under the year 1344, the *Brut* and John of Reading's chronicle both record that

> At this time, Englishmen so followed and clung to the madness and folly of foreigners, that from the time of the arrival of the Hainaulters some eighteen years before, they changed the shape and style of their clothing every year, abandoning the old honest and good style of large, long and

wide clothes, in favour of short, narrow-waisted clothes, cut with jagged edges, slit and buttoned, with sleeves and tippets on the surcoats, and great long hoods which hung down too far. To tell the truth, they looked more like tormentors and devils in their clothes and appearance than men. And the women copied the men in even more curious ways: for their clothes were so tight that they sewed foxtails beneath their clothes to hang down and protect and hide their arses . . .[59]

The period between 1330 and 1365 was a time when fashions changed substantially and rapidly. The novelties were such that a number of monastic chroniclers attacked the new fashions as immoral and described them as the cause of various natural disasters visited on the people at large because of the wantonness and decadence of the ruling class.[60] Although such tirades against court fashions can be found as far back as the reign of William Rufus in the eleventh century, the detailed descriptions given in the fourteenth-century chronicles are evidence that a real change was afoot.

Thirteenth-century clothes were loose-fitting, and the way in which they hung on the body was the most important element in tailoring them. The cloth was used economically, in long lengths, and the desired effect was a restrained elegance; the fastenings were girdles and strips of tied cloth. The outer clothes were loose, cloaks and gowns, while the tunic beneath consisted of two T-shaped pieces sewn back to back.

Early in the fourteenth century, dress became much more complex in structure. The T-shaped tunic gave way to a garment with armholes and sleeves, and the sleeves in turn could be loose or tight-fitting. It has been suggested that this style was following the development in armour at the time, the change from chain mail to the new plate armour which fitted the body more closely. Buttons are first mentioned in the early fourteenth century as an important feature of dress, and with them came the need for carefully stitched buttonholes. Tailoring became a highly specialized, and highly paid, skill; and where the splendour of the material – rich silks rather than woollen cloth, perhaps – had earlier been the only thing that distinguished the wealth and prestige of the wearer, the new style depended on the skill of the cutting and sewing.

Once the idea of designing clothes to fit the body had been accepted, tailors were quick to see that a huge range of variations was possible, and from 1330 onwards 'high fashion' began to develop. John of Reading's dating of the new style to around 1328 is supported by evidence from manuscripts from Paris and Tournai which can be dated to around 1330. In one, a man is shown wearing a buttoned tunic with inset sleeves, and in the other a lover wears buttoned sleeves (Plates 17–19).[61]

From a simple attempt to follow the natural lines of the body, features were unnaturally exaggerated: the low-slung waist of the 1330s, with a hipster belt and close-fitting doublet, the conspicuous waste of cutting clothes with jagged edges, and the visual distraction of parti-coloured garments were just a few of the variations that rapidly developed. Jean de Venette, writing in 1359–60, remembers 1340 as the year when appearances changed:

> Men were now beginning to wear disfiguring costumes. This was especially true of noblemen, knights, squires and their followers; but it was true in some measure of burgesses and of almost all servants. Garments were short to the point of indecency, which was surprising in a people who had up to this time conducted themselves becomingly. Everyone also began to grow long beards. This fashion which nearly everyone in France, except those of royal blood, adopted gave rise to no little mockery on the part of the common people.[62]

The new ideas travelled rapidly, because fashion was international, and the dress of the aristocracy was broadly similar throughout western Europe. Attitudes of moralizing monks were also similar: French chroniclers saw the military disaster at Crécy as punishment for the equally extravagant dress of the French nobility. According to them, short clothing was again at the root of the problem, and many of the details they give are the same. Some tunics, however, were gathered at the back like women's dresses, while others were so tight that the wearer had to be peeled rather than undressed. Giovanni Villani makes similar comments about the dress of the French companions of Walter de Brienne, who was appointed commander of the Florentine armies in 1342. The French and Italians seem to have loved magnificent hats: two extreme examples are the symbolic headgear worn by the republican Cola di Rienzo in Rome in 1347, on which a silver sword cut a golden coronet in half, and the 'parade' hat made for John II of France for the wedding of his daughter Blanche de Bourbon in 1352, on which gold figures of children keeping pigs under oak-trees 'as if they were alive' formed the main theme, with flowers, pearls and other ornaments.[63] The English milliners were much more sober, judging by the surviving records of simple beaver hats with the occasional jewel.

The best visual evidence for the new fashions is from a wonderful illuminated version of the romance account of the life of Alexander the Great, now in the Bodleian Library. Just as Arthur, a warrior king, became the focal point of romances from the twelfth century onwards, so the great conqueror of antiquity re-emerged in the guise of a medieval king, surrounded by a court with contemporary ceremonials and costumes. We know that this manuscript of the *Romance of Alexander* was made in Tournai in 1344. There has been much debate about the patron for whom it was made, as such a hugely expensive volume would not have been created without a commission. Tournai was fiercely loyal to the French during the warfare of the late 1330s, and this has been put forward as the reason why Philip VI is the most likely patron.[64] On the other hand, it was a trading city, with strong links to the other towns in the Low Countries, and lay between Hainault and Flanders. Edward's youngest son, Thomas duke of Gloucester, probably owned the manuscript in the latter half of the fourteenth century; it corresponds to a book described in the inventory of his goods after his death. There can be no definitive answer to the puzzle, but I would suggest that it was commissioned by Philippa; we have already seen that she is believed to have had other manuscripts made for Edward. The commission must have been placed by the beginning of 1338, as the scribe finished work on 18 December of that year. The work of illuminating the text was not completed until April 1344, and even allowing for the amazing array of pictures which are the book's glory, it implies that there was a considerable pause in the production process. If the *Romance of Alexander* was being produced for Philippa, work may have been suspended when Tournai was besieged by Edward and his allies in 1339; hostilities only ended with the switch of the theatre of war to Brittany in 1341.

Furthermore, the romances contained in the book include Jacques de Longuyon's *The Vows of the Peacock*, probably written about 1310 for the bishop of Liège. This was a highly popular work, which formed a self-contained episode within the framework of the Alexander story; it related the adventures which followed vows made by knights on a peacock at a feast. *The Vows of the Peacock* is itself continued in *The Restoration of the Peacock* of around 1335 by Jean Brisebarre and Jean de la Mote's *Perfection of the Peacock* of 1340.[65] For the counts of

Hainault, Alexander seems to be their specific hero, just as Arthur occupied the same place in the dynastic mythology of the later Plantagenets, particularly Edward I, Edward III and Edward IV. Just as Edward I had a personal interest in Arthurian legend, William I of Hainault was evidently an Alexander enthusiast. In 1319, Watriquet de Couvin wrote of him, 'As long as the count lives, Alexander will not come to an end,' and in 1330 his provost, Jean Bernier, provided a peacock for a civic festival at which the winning entry was twenty-two men bearing the shields of 'the most valiant of King Alexander's followers'.[66] After William I's death, Jean de la Mote compared him at length to Alexander, in an elegy addressed to his daughter Philippa.[67] The *Romance of Alexander* manuscript is the only one to contain the music for a poem in *The Restoration of the Peacock*, which would imply a close connection to Hainault where the text originated. It links, too, with the romance of *Perceforest*, a work which is presented as being 'found' by William I himself, and which was certainly written either in Hainault or in England.

Whether or not the manuscript was destined for England or France, artists working in Tournai, on the borders of Hainault and distant from Paris, would in any case be more likely to reflect the dress of Hainault. As with most medieval manuscripts, the pictures consist of large formal full pages or half pages and marginal decorations, usually at the foot of the page. Here we meet the world of Edward's court face to face. For the *Peacock* poems celebrate Alexander not simply as a conqueror, but as a model of princely courtesy. Their authors draw on a wide range of sources to transform Alexander from a great military leader into the leader of a cultured and resplendent court, the model which the counts of Hainault and Edward III all aspired to. The pages containing the *Peacock* poems present illuminations which are the nearest we shall get to a vision of Edward's court. A feast is held in honour of the peacock and the visual narrative in the bottom margin shows the feast being prepared, the queen going to the feast with her attendants and musicians, ladies dancing with a bearded man and others, ladies dancing a carol or round dance, and a whole orchestra of musicians. In another dance, six ladies face six knights before they start; this is repeated with five men in 'heads' and six women. The opening of *The Vows of the Peacock* is marked by ladies dancing with men in 'heads'. The margins only fill with dancers when court festivities are described in the text. These figures are small: to get a better idea of the costume and fabrics, in fabulous

museum at Lyons belonged to Charles de Blois; it is cut from six pieces of silk brocaded with gold, with twenty-four buttons, and is very much a tailored and designed garment, the sharpest possible contrast to the draped clothing of the beginning of the century. These exaggerated figure-hugging garments were for men only; women's clothing was generally more modest, hence the scandal caused by the amazons described by Knighton.

The abiding image of Edward's court, reading the accounts and these outsiders' views of it, is of a society with a fondness for splendour and display as a mark of rank and as a way of impressing the onlookers, and also of a world where that display could be competitive, in terms both of richness and of style. It was another area where knights would strive to excel, and where the king could use his patronage to single out his favourite companions. We begin with the king and William Montagu in the same costume and progress through the aketons given to the conspirators, to the appearance of teams with heraldic epaulettes or even heraldic suits of armour who take part in the king's games.

The members of the household and court of these first years of Edward's personal rule were of course beneficiaries of royal largesse, particularly those involved in the coup of 1330. The 'new men' who had in effect brought Edward to power were given considerable estates in the course of the next seven years, and, if Montagu was the most prominent among them, it was a broad group whose only allegiance was to the new king. Edward was careful to present these grants as the results of deliberations with his advisers and even with parliament, so that they were not seen as arbitrary awards made on a personal whim to favourites: the writs in favour of Ufford, Clinton and Montagu emphasize their part in Mortimer's overthrow, and other writs were made out with the agreement of parliament.[70] Edward was fortunate in that there was no obvious focal point for political dissent; he was on good terms with Henry of Lancaster, the only powerful nobleman surviving from his father's generation, who was in any case blind and prematurely aged. Lancaster's son, Henry of Grosmont, two years older than the king, was rapidly becoming one of Edward's closest friends.[71]

Edward, however, was careful not to be vengeful against those who had supported Mortimer and Isabella; if he kept them at arm's length for a time, this was a sensible precaution, but he was astute in not creating the kind of resentment which had been his father's downfall. Mortimer was the only great lord to be executed throughout his entire reign, and the nobility in general remained loyal to the king for the next half-century. This was in stark contrast to the relations of his father and grandson with their nobility. Edward retained many of his existing officers and household; this was not unusual, but those who had served Mortimer rather than him in the preceding three years were only briefly in disgrace, and figures such as Henry Burghersh, bishop of Lincoln, quickly returned to favour and played a vital part in the new administration. Lands and moveable property including jewels, which were in fact a form of cash rather than for pure ornament and display, were confiscated. The jewels would be retained by the treasury, but personal belongings, even in Mortimer's case, were soon returned to the heirs: Edmund Mortimer got back his father's armour and items which may have been his own property from the castle at Wigmore, including white hangings showing small children chasing butterflies, a year after his father's execution.[72] The lands might be granted to other lords, but usually on the basis that tenure was for a limited term, or was revocable at the king's will if he provided an alternative source of income, and in any case would revert to the king on the death of the holder. It was through measures like these that he was able to reinstate such men as Mortimer's grandson, also called Roger, and give them back their ancestral estates, if he deemed them worthy of it. When the younger Roger rose to prominence in the wars in France in the 1340s and 1350s, Edward rewarded him with the return of his ancestral lands and the revival of the title of earl of March which had caused such consternation when it was given to his grandfather. By such means, Edward ensured that his court was remarkably free of factions until the very last years of his reign.

3

Apprenticeship in War: Scotland and Flanders 1332–1340

By the end of 1331, the series of tournaments had drawn to a close, and the 'greater season for greater affairs' had come. The priority was the situation in Scotland, where the uneasy relationship between the two kingdoms – a close parallel to the problems of feudal lordship between France and England – had once more come to a head. Robert Bruce had died in 1329, having secured a treaty with Isabella and Mortimer at Northampton in 1328 which was regarded by the English nobles as a shameful surrender, and which contributed greatly to the couple's unpopularity. He was succeeded by his son David II, a five-year-old, who was married to Edward's seven-year-old sister Joan under the terms of the Northampton treaty. Another clause in the treaty had agreed that three English lords should have their lands in Scotland restored.

Among these lords was the man who had been Edward's informal guardian in 1325–7, Henry of Beaumont. He had gone into exile in 1329, in protest at Mortimer's behaviour, and returned in 1330. His claim was to the earldom of Buchan; and he and the other lords petitioned Edward for help in recovering their inheritance. Edward and his advisers, unwilling to mount a full-scale royal campaign against the Scots after the stalemate of 1327, instead turned a blind eye to a private invasion which the 'disinherited' organized. Edward was careful to denounce it in public; it is one of a series of unofficial or unexpected 'adventures' which recur during the first two decades of Edward's reign. No documents survive, but the military preparations went ahead despite writs to the contrary sent to the sheriffs. Thomas Gray has a curious story that Edward actually sent the petition to the earl of Moray, who was guardian of Scotland during David II's minority, for his reaction, and received the reply that he should 'let the ball roll'.[1]

The ball rolled with deadly effect. Henry of Beaumont strengthened his cause by enlisting the support of Edward Balliol, who was the son of the king whom Edward I had placed on the Scottish throne thirty years earlier. Several of Edward's household joined him, including Ralph Stafford and Walter Mauny, as well as veterans of Edward II's Scottish campaigns such as Thomas Ughtred, who had fought at Bannockburn with Beaumont. They landed with 400 men at arms in Fife at the beginning of August 1332, and were almost immediately confronted by the Scots, who could see how small the force was. The earl of Mar, commanding half of the Scottish army, surrounded them, and Beaumont decided on a bold night attack to escape from a desperate situation. His men succeeded in overrunning the Scottish footsoldiers, but when they regrouped they realized that not only were the mounted troops unscathed, but the other half of the Scottish army, led by the earl of Dunbar,[2] was only a short distance away. Beaumont seems to have been responsible for the disposition of the English, at the head of a narrow glen; he placed archers on each flank, and ordered his men at arms to dismount.[3] The Scottish leaders quarrelled as the battle began, because the earl of Mar was accused by one of the Bruce clan of being in league with the enemy. Bruce swore to be the first to attack, and led a disorganized charge against the English. The Scots, despite heavy losses due to the English archers, came up against the English spearmen, and were gaining the upper hand when, according to a Scottish chronicler, Ralph Stafford shouted 'Shoulders to your lances, not your chests', in other words, to stand sideways so that they presented a smaller target to the enemy; and the English line held.[4] The Scots broke up in confusion, only to become entangled with the troops led by Mar trying to force their way up the glen. In such circumstances, the archery fire was deadly, and the Scottish casualties included most of the leading nobles; Mar, Bruce and Moray all perished.[5]

Although the army of the earl of Dunbar was at large, and at one point besieged Balliol and Beaumont in Perth, Balliol succeeded in having himself crowned at the abbey of Scone as tradition demanded. But his triumph was brief, and at the year's end, lulled into a false sense of security, he went with only a small guard to his castle at Annan to celebrate Christmas. There he was surprised in a sudden attack by his enemies, and he and his supporters, including Beaumont, were once more driven out of Scotland.

Edward himself had spent May and June at Woodstock, where Philippa gave birth to her first daughter, Isabella, on 16 June. A tournament was held for her churching in mid-July. Henry of Grosmont was present, as were the king's household knights, including Gilbert Talbot and Thomas Bradeston.[6] The king's household accounts for 19 July record an expenditure of £292 3s. 11¾d., evidence of a major celebration.[7]

By the beginning of 1333, Edward and his advisers had decided to make a major attempt to settle the Scottish problem, and the centre of government had been moved to York, as it had been during his grandfather's wars in the north. The 'disinherited' returned, with the formal backing of the king, in March 1333, and proceeded to besiege the one Scottish stronghold on the border, the port of Berwick, which was also the wealthiest town in Scotland. This small force under Edward Balliol and Henry of Beaumont included William Montagu, John Neville[8] and Henry of Grosmont. Edward himself joined them on 17 May. When the army was fully assembled, it contained a number of familiar faces from the halcyon tournament days of 1330–31: William Clinton, the twins Edward and William Bohun, Thomas and Maurice Berkeley, Reginald Cobham, William Fitzwarin and Thomas Ughtred.[9]

The Scots, led by Archibald Douglas, tried to distract the English army from the siege by a series of raids; but forces from Carlisle won several small victories, and the raids merely gave Edward the formal pretext for declaring that the treaty of 1328 had been broken, and he was now free to make war on Scotland in person. By the end of June, Alexander Seton, the warden of Berwick, was forced to agree to a fifteen-day truce, at the end of which, if the town had not been relieved by a Scottish army, the inhabitants would surrender. This forced Douglas to do what he least wished: to confront the English directly, and abandon his tactic of drawing them away from the town. On the last day of the truce, a Scottish raiding party crossed into English territory and attempted to enter the town from the south: William Montagu intercepted them with a small band of English cavalry, but failed to prevent William Keith from getting into Berwick. Keith took over as warden, and claimed that the town had been relieved. Edward, however, had laid down precise terms for the relief of Berwick: the Scots had to approach from the north. He refused to acknowledge the relief, and hanged two of the hostages whom he held as guarantees for the truce. The Scots were in no position to rescue the remaining hostages, and swiftly agreed to a new truce, set out in writing and sealed, which gave them a further five days before they surrendered: if they did so, their lives and property would be safe.

The Scottish army was forty miles away; it was much larger than the English forces, but much of it was a crowd of infantry, better adapted for raids than for pitched battles. And since Edward knew the army could not reach him in less than two days, he had time to select the ground on which to fight. He chose Halidon Hill, high ground to the south of the town, which could be reached only across marshes and a steep valley, and positioned his men so that the covering fire of the archers would reach the enemy as they struggled across these obstacles. His men were rested and in good order, while the Scots had had three hard days' march. Henry of Beaumont was the commander of the first of the three divisions into which the army was organized, and may have been Edward's chief adviser as to tactics, given his victory of the previous year. The other two divisions were led by Edward himself and by Edward Balliol, each consisting of men at arms in the centre and archers on either flank.

The Scots advanced, a huge host that dismayed the English at first; but as soon as they came within range of the archers, it was clear where the advantage lay. When the Scottish schiltrons, squadrons of spearmen in close order, reached the English line, they were already decimated and in some disorder, and the battle was remarkably brief. Two of the three schiltrons turned and fled soon after they engaged the English men at arms; the third, which consisted of men whose job was to break the siege of Berwick once the English were defeated, was locked in combat with Henry of Beaumont's division for much longer, but in the end gave way. By this time, the rest of the English army was in pursuit of the fleeing Scots; it was during this part of the engagement that the majority of the Scottish casualties occurred.

Halidon Hill was the battle which founded the reputation of Edward as a commander, and of the English army as a formidable, if not invincible, body of men. The key elements recur in the later English triumphs: a well-chosen defensive position, established in good time, usually on a hill and preferably with physical obstacles which the enemy had to surmount; the use of flanking fire from the English archers, who were the only troops at this period to use the longbow; and a well-ordered and well-disciplined body of men at arms commanded by men who were less concerned with personal glory than with working together to achieve victory. Edward himself seems to have had one particular virtue as a commander, and the same applies to his son: because he was working with men whom he knew well and respected, he listened to their views and acted on their advice. We have little direct evidence about the English councils of war; all that can be said is that, in all the battles the English fought, there is no trace of the violent disagreements that afflicted the Scots at Dupplin Moor and the French at Crécy and Poitiers.

The threat to Berwick had been averted, and the Scottish defeat meant that, for the moment, Scotland seemed secure, and Edward returned south in September. He spent the autumn at leisure, hunting in Savernake forest near Marlborough in November and December, going on pilgrimage, visiting his mother at Castle Rising. A tournament was held at Dunstable in January 1334, about the time that the queen gave birth to her second daughter, Joan.[10] It is possible that this was one of the jousts organized by another member of the king's entourage, as the timing is improbable if Edward was responsible for it. There is a roll of arms listing the knights at the tournament which does not include him as one of the participants. However, next to the name of William Montagu is an entry for 'monsieur Lionel'. The arms are given as *argent a quarter gules*, in other words, white and red. We can be sure that this was the king, because a suit of white armour quartered in red was made for him for this occasion.[11] In addition, four horse-trappers in the same colours were provided, as well as one great 'harness for the joust' and four smaller harnesses with the same arms and pennants for lances; the king evidently had four attendants in matching livery. Eight years later, again at Dunstable, Edward was to fight as a 'simple knight'; but by then he had named his third son Lionel, and, once again, a suit of armour with Lionel's arms was made for him.[12]

Why should Edward wish to identify himself as 'Lionel'? The usual reaction from scholars has been to refer to the Arthurian legends: Lionel is the cousin of Lancelot, the supreme hero of Arthur's court, and his chief function in the *Prose Lancelot* is to search for Lancelot, whose endless adventures always mean that he disappears just as Lionel is about to find him. He acts as go-between for Lancelot and Queen Guinevere, and his chief characteristic is an impulsive and disobedient nature:

his nickname is 'Unbridled Heart'.[13] All in all, he is not a figure to be emulated. In the *Quest of the Holy Grail*, he attempts to kill his saintly brother Bors, in a test of Bors' character: will Bors lift his sword against his brother or not? He will not, even when Lionel slaughters a hermit who tries to restrain him. This is not a model for a would-be knightly king.[14]

The best answer comes from the heraldic world: Edward is playing the part of 'England's little lion', as his most recent biographer puts it.[15] 'Leonellus' is used in heraldry, and the 'lion shield', *l'écu lionel*, is referred to in twelfth-century poems.[16] The identification of Edward as the 'little lion' may go back to a nickname given to him by Mortimer and Isabella: at the tournament at Wigmore on 6 September 1329 he was given a golden goblet with 'four escutcheons bearing the arms of *leonell*'', and for the Dunstable tournament the following month, October 1329, he was provided with a suit of armour covered in white muslin and red velvet: this ties in with the arms of Lionel as specified in the tournament roll for Dunstable in 1334.

The arms of 'Lionel' are in fact those of the earl of Chester, Edward III's title before he came to the throne; although they now technically belonged to his eldest son, created earl in March 1333, the combination of 'leonellus', his nickname, and these youthful arms takes us back to Edward's boyhood: there are no specific records of his jousting in the royal arms before this date, so it could simply be that he continued to use the Chester 'badge', as the heralds called it, after he became king. 'Lionel' is simply an earlier avatar of Edward himself, not a pale imitation of a hero of romance.[17]

The arms of '*leonell*'', little lions, are therefore different from the arms of Lionel, but both refer to the same person, the king himself. And why should it be tournaments at Dunstable which centre on Lionel? Three major assemblies took place there – in 1334 there were 135 knights, in 1342 around 230 knights – and on each occasion the king is disguised in the same way. It is a nice puzzle, but not one that we can ever hope to solve exactly.

The 'four entire suits of armour' were evidently well used in the following months. Edward's tournaments tend to be grouped within short periods, and 1334 was typical: three, at Dunstable, Woodstock and Newmarket between 16 January and 9 February; two in summer, at Burstwick and Nottingham; and two in September, at Guildford and

Smithfield. The whole year could be read as a celebration of the battle at Halidon Hill, Edward's first great victory: this was the equivalent of the Roman triumph accorded to a victorious general. And it cemented the bonds between Edward and his commanders.

It was one thing to win such a victory as Halidon Hill, and quite another to follow up the advantage and secure the long-term objective of conquest or control. This again was to be the pattern of the English campaigns, as Edward learnt for the first time in Scotland in 1334–6. The apparent disappearance of opposition in Scotland had enabled Edward Balliol to reinstate himself as king, but the English government seriously underestimated the forces required to support the new administration. By the end of July 1334 Balliol had fled back to England, betrayed by even his closest supporters and robbed of his treasure. Even then, it was not until September that serious preparations were made for a new invasion of Scotland on the requisite scale. The army that marched north to Roxburgh in December 1334 was a mixture ranging from two companies of a hundred pardoned felons to the king's household knights and the retinues of the magnates; there were archers from Cheshire and south Wales, but the bulk of the army came from Yorkshire, Lancashire, Cumberland and Westmorland. This was normal practice, since the summoning of large bodies of troops from the distant south would take time and would be much more costly, as they would have to be paid on the march to Scotland. Because Edward himself was leading the expedition, the household knights and magnates were drawn from throughout the kingdom. In later years, however, when war could break out either in Scotland or France, or indeed in both simultaneously, a distinctive group of northern knights and magnates emerged who served as the commanders of the northern army; few of them appear in the court records or as household knights. Only two of these northern lords became members of the Company of the Garter in Edward's reign, Henry Percy in about 1365, and John Neville of Raby in 1369.

For the 1334 campaign, Edward had the same familiar group with him, since the composition of his household knights changed relatively slowly. The bannerets included Thomas Beauchamp, Henry of Grosmont, John Grey of Rotherfield and Thomas Ughtred, while among the household knights were William Montagu, William Bohun, William Clinton, Robert Ufford and William Fitzwarin, as well as Thomas

Bradeston, Maurice Berkeley and Reginald Cobham.[18] The campaign was not a success: a winter expedition was always hazardous, and the Scots were elusive. The Rochester chronicler recorded that

> Other than the youths of the realm and the magnates, he [i.e. Edward] had few people with him. No one bore the hardships and the harshness [of the winter] or laboured more willingly than he; and all the time he greatly comforted his army by words, gifts and deeds, saying that they would all drink from the same cup. And thus he inspired their resolve.[19]

What victories there were went to the Scots, and minor sieges and skirmishes often had a serious impact, such as the capture of Henry of Beaumont at Dundarg in late December. All that the English army could do was to ravage the Scottish territories; the savagery of these activities merely drove the inhabitants into the arms of the nationalists. Furthermore, the contracts for service were only for three months, and expired in February 1335, at the height of the hard weather. Few men chose to stay on, and new recruits were scarce, so Edward's army was effectively disbanded. Edward moved south, leaving only a handful of men under his brother John of Eltham and under Maurice Berkeley to counter any Scottish activity.

To make matters worse, there were new diplomatic complications. Since 1326 there had been an alliance between France and Scotland, which up till now had been of little practical effect; but in the course of the usual tortuous attempts to settle the dispute over Aquitaine, Philip VI had decided to use the Scottish situation to bring further pressure to bear on Edward. He had given refuge to David II in May 1334, and made it clear that any settlement would have to include the Scots. Negotiations moved very slowly, complicated by Philip's long-standing wish to go on a crusade in which Edward would participate. The ambitions of Philip and Edward were in a sense very similar: Edward admitted that Scotland was a kingdom in its own right, but claimed that it was held as a fief of the English king, while Philip equally admitted that Aquitaine was a duchy in its own right, and wished to enforce the homage of the English king in the latter's capacity of duke of Aquitaine.

On the ground in Scotland, a brief truce followed, which expired at midsummer. This suited Edward, who used the interval to raise a much larger army, which was to divide into two to invade Scotland, Edward taking the western route while Balliol moved up the east coast. The same group of men who had been on the winter campaign reassembled; there were more household knights than before, and, in response to the appeal for more troops, William Montagu distinguished himself by raising a very large retinue and appearing – unusually – at the appointed rendezvous at Newcastle on the day arranged, 11 June 1335. Soon after the campaign began, Edward honoured him by granting him the right to bear the eagle crest which was his own personal symbol, and giving him a charger with the Montagu arms on its trappings.

The two armies swept unopposed through Scotland, and met at Perth in mid-August, having laid waste much of the country, sparing only the lands loyal to Edward Balliol in Galloway. By the end of the month, Edward told Philip that the war in Scotland was over.[20] He seems to have believed that, faced with the military reality of the English domination of Scotland, Philip's desire for a crusade would outweigh his loyalty to David II. In this, Edward misjudged Philip; and Philip in turn misjudged Edward's determination to reach a settlement with the Scots on his own terms. Balliol's opponents had had a minor victory at Culblean in September, when the earl of Atholl, an ally of Balliol, was killed. This boosted their morale, and was later remembered as the turning point in the war; but the real turning point was the result of the diplomatic impasse early in 1336. Edward had named his closest confidants among his household, William Montagu, Robert Ufford and Ralph Neville, to negotiate a peace settlement with the French and the supporters of David II, with the help of mediators sent by the pope. Following meetings at Newcastle in January 1336, a draft treaty was agreed, and was sent to the Scots for ratification. The idea was that the difference in age between Edward Balliol and David II could form the basis for peace, David becoming Balliol's successor since the latter had no heir. But under this arrangement, Scotland would remain an English fief, subject to Edward III; and the Bruce party rejected the terms outright.

For the first time, serious French intervention in the Scottish war now seemed possible. Philip made major preparations to invade England in support of David II, and Edward sent another army to Scotland under Henry of Grosmont. Edward Balliol covered the lowlands, while Henry was to operate in the Highlands against a guerrilla force led by William Douglas. It proved a fast-moving campaign, not least for the king himself. The objective, as always, was to bring the main body of the Scottish forces to battle; but, in imitation of Scottish tactics, isolated fortresses were relieved by bold and decisive strikes, and even the main army moved extremely rapidly. The commander of Edinburgh Castle took thirty-two small boats across the Firth of Forth to Cupar Castle in Stirling, under siege from a strong Scottish contingent led by three earls, and with 200 men panicked them into flight and the abandonment of the siege along with all their equipment. Edward himself was at Northampton, for the approaching opening of a great council. On 6 June he left on a wild ride north with just fifty men at arms, reaching Newcastle five days later and Perth a week after that. Here he found the two armies, who had just rebuilt the town's defences, recently destroyed by the Scots. They were astonished by the king's sudden appearance, and greatly encouraged: 'seeing the king, they were amazed at his boldness, and wept for joy'.[21] Among the knights there were Henry of Beaumont, Thomas Beauchamp, William Montagu, Robert Ufford, Thomas Ughtred and William Bohun.[22]

Since the battle of Culblean the previous year, Henry of Beaumont's daughter Catherine, countess of Atholl, had been at Lochindorb Castle, unable to escape and now besieged by Andrew Murray, guardian of Scotland, and his men. They were seventy miles away, and Edward saw a chance of forcing a battle, as well as a splendid knightly rescue of a damsel in distress. He selected a highly mobile force, probably consisting of 500 men at arms and knights, and set out to challenge the besiegers. It was a calculated risk, since others had suffered on similar bold forays into enemy territory. Guy count of Namur had been captured on a raid the previous year, with a smaller escort, when he had been forced to take refuge in the ruins of Edinburgh Castle.

Edward covered the seventy miles and confronted the Scots in four days. He found the main army before he reached the castle and very nearly succeeded in surprising his enemy. Andrew Murray was at mass when his scouts recognized the English army, but none of them dared interrupt him. When the English came up, the Scots were just in formation, and had to retreat: one of them knew a rocky side path down which they were able to escape successfully. Baulked of his prey at the last minute, Edward was nonetheless able to ride on and lift the siege of Lochindorb, in itself an important strategic fortress, and release his old mentor's daughter.

This might be the knightly and romantic side of warfare; Edward sent a letter back to Philippa at the end of the campaign. It described his heroic exploits at Lochindorb but went on to outline the second part of the operations, a black devastation of the east coast of Scotland, where the French fleet was expected to land. Aberdeen, the largest port available to the fleet, was left in ashes, and the lands around were reduced to a desert. The king returned south in September, though various alarms in the autumn brought him temporarily back to Berwick and the lowlands.

Although Edward returned to Scotland at intervals until 1345, none of these occasions were major campaigns. In the autumn of 1336 much work was done on the defences of various castles, and this might have been a prelude to the creation of the kind of network of fortresses which had enabled his grandfather to subdue the Welsh. But the Welsh castles formed much more of an interlocking pattern, particularly the compact group along the north coast, and even the most isolated castle was not more than a few days' march from the English border. The Scottish castles were another matter: it is impossible to imagine a pattern of fortresses which would be viable in terms of supply and mutual support, and Edward never seems to have seriously envisaged such a plan. Without it, however, he had to reach a political settlement, and this was to elude him for another ten years. In the end, the fate of Scotland was determined by the chances of war, as, in a sense, he had always hoped it would be.

For the moment, he had to leave the defence of the English interest in Scotland to the lords of the north of England. The 'disinherited' remained disinherited. Henry of Beaumont abandoned his claim to the earldom of Buchan, and followed Edward on his French expeditions, as did William Montagu. Montagu had been promised considerable lands in Scotland at the beginning of the Scottish wars, and during the time in Scotland had been given the Isle of Man, the one conquest from the Scots which was to prove permanent; with it he acquired the title of king of Man. Thomas Gray has a curious story that Montagu, 'one of the most intimate of the king's council at that time', left Flanders when he 'realized that their support for their German alliance did not seem to be drawing to a profitable conclusion' and 'put his complaint before parliament rather than the king and took himself to Scotland', to the siege of Dunbar.[23] The chronology does not work, as the unsuccessful English siege of Dunbar, led by Montagu and the earl of Arundel, ended before the Flanders expedition left; but it is probably a rare glimpse into the attitudes of Edward's councillors at this period, as well as Montagu's relationship with Edward. The Scottish wars were not necessarily seen as a less important challenge than the coming war with France.

The most powerful card in Philip VI's hand in the Scottish negotiations was Edward's status as duke of Aquitaine. The exact terms of Edward's personal status as the liege man of Philip, the ruler who was potentially his greatest enemy, had not been resolved, either at Amiens in 1329, or after the secret and conditional homage of 1331. It would in any case have been difficult for Philip to claim that Edward was bound by the terms of any homage not to attack a king who was linked to Philip by a treaty of allegiance, but there were other ways in which the French could cause problems for Edward. When Edward offered Philip's enemy Robert d'Artois refuge in England in 1334, he unintentionally played into Philip's hands. Robert d'Artois had supported Philip's accession to the French throne, and in return expected the king's support over his claim to inherit his grandfather's territory, the county of Artois. However, Philip refused to back him, and, after an episode in which Robert tried to forge a letter to prove his claim, he fled France in 1332 to avoid trial and probable execution. He went first to Namur and then to Brabant, but both were fiefs of the French king, and Philip threatened to invade in order to seize Robert.[24] By seeking refuge in England, he placed himself beyond Philip's reach. On the other hand, this gave Philip the chance to use Edward's harbouring of a criminal as a new reason to confiscate the duchy of Aquitaine.

A series of diplomatic missions had failed to make any headway with Philip. Philip, for his part, was eager to go on crusade: but he could not go while hostilities with England were a real possibility, and needed Edward's participation to guarantee peace. If both kings were absent, there could be no war. When Geoffrey Scrope, an experienced lawyer, returned from France in July 1334, he had met such obstructive tactics from the French that he demanded that he should not be sent on any further such missions,[25] and his instinct was correct: when William Montagu and William Clinton, accompanying the new archbishop of Canterbury, John Stratford, went the following winter, they were treated to a lecture from Philip which ended with the declaration that peace 'will never be established among Christians until the king of France sits on the judgment seat in the middle of England and is judge and ruler over the kingdoms of France, England and Scotland'.[26] Two years later, Philip seized on Edward's protection of Robert d'Artois as the reason for the formal confiscation of Aquitaine, and proclaimed the territory forfeit on 24 May 1337.

When in February 1337 Edward created six new earldoms, four of which went to the comrades who had helped him to carry out his coup, he was careful to justify his action as being for the good of the nation as a whole:

> Among the signs of royalty we considered it to be the most important that, through a suitable distribution of ranks, dignities and offices, the king is sustained by the wise counsels and protected by the many powers of formidable men. Yet because the hereditary ranks in our king-dom . . . through a failure of issue and various other events have returned into the hand of the king, this realm has experienced for a long time a sub-stantial loss in the names, honours and ranks of dignity.[27]

The new earls were William Montagu, first earl of Salisbury, William Clinton, earl of Huntingdon, Robert Ufford, earl of Suffolk, William Bohun, earl of Northampton, participants in the events of October 1330; and Henry of Grosmont, earl of Derby, and Hugh Audley, earl of Gloucester. Not everyone agreed that the nation benefited from these promotions: Thomas Gray once more gives a dissident view, looking back on the distribution of lands following the creation of the new earl-doms as the cause of the king's heavy taxation in later years: 'So generously did the king distribute his estates to these earls and to his other favourites, that he scarcely retained for himself any of the lands pertaining to his crown, and was obliged to live off windfalls and sub-sidies at great cost to people.'[28] But there were few such dissenting voices, and in fact many of the grants were made from estates forfeited to the crown by nobles condemned as a result of the disturbances of the first years of Edward's reign up to 1330, notably the lands of the Despensers and Mortimers. And no one could deny the earls' excep-tional service to the king at the most critical juncture of his reign; if this was favouritism, it was in return for favours received. Furthermore, by increasing the number of great lords, Edward was avoiding the situ-ation that had prevailed in his father's reign, where one or two families wielded exceptional influence. And as in the first years of his personal rule, he was careful not to grant the lands in perpetuity, but either for a term of years or under conditions which meant that there was the possibility of reversion – a reversion which he might want to grant back to the original family if they were restored to favour, as happened with Roger Mortimer's grandson.

There was a further motive in the creation of new earls in 1337: a war was in the offing, and the earls were the traditional leaders of the army. Throughout the previous year, war of some kind had been regarded as inevitable, and the appointment of the new earls should be seen in the context of a council of the great lords at Nottingham in January 1337, when preparations for a campaign against the French began in earnest. Such a war was not a novelty. Over the past two centuries, the pattern had been that after a brief spell of open warfare, the two sides would come to a new compromise. The English had generally come off worse, because the resources to fight a war across the Channel were difficult to muster, and their kings could no longer draw on the resources of the vast domains bequeathed by Henry II. Normandy, homeland of the English dynasty and the most accessible point for an invasion, was now the fiefdom of the eldest son of the king of France, while Aquitaine barely had the resources to keep its turbulent lords loyal and obedient to the English crown, let alone contribute to an attack on the ruler of France.

Edward's remarks about the diminishing numbers of great lords when he justified his creation of the new earls were entirely true. Three of the existing earls died in the years 1336–8, and had either no successors or heirs who were not fit for military service.[29] Two others were invalids: the earl of Lancaster had been blind since 1328, and the earl of Devon, restored to his title in 1335, was elderly and seems to have confined his soldiering after this date to the defence of Devon and Cornwall. This left just three active earls, rather than the dozen or more who might usually be expected to lead the king's armies, and by creating the additional earls he was doing no more than making good the losses. For example, Humphrey Bohun, earl of Hereford, was one of the heirs who was an invalid, and in 1338 he transferred his hereditary office of constable of the royal army to his brother William, newly created earl of Northampton.[30] These men would serve with substantial retinues: the nine earls who took part in the Brittany campaigns in 1342–3 raised about 900 men at arms between them, against about 1,100 from all other sources.[31]

Edward saw the interest of king and magnates as essentially one and the same in this pronouncement. The highly structured state created by the Normans in the eleventh century had been modified gradually over the succeeding three hundred years, but it was still recognizably a unified system, in which the barons had a crucial role. The 'magnates' were a relatively small group,[32] ranging from figures such as Richard Fitzalan, earl of Arundel, capable of lending huge sums to his fellow-lords, to knights banneret who had made their way up the social ladder in the king's service, and who owed their status to grants made by their master. Like the king, the greatest of them lived off their estates, and maintained splendid households; and their power, if united against the king, could be fatal to royal ambitions, as Henry III and Edward II had discovered to their cost. In peace, they looked to the king to govern justly and maintain a suitably magnificent court; in war, they wanted a leader who would bring military success and the enrichment that went with the spoils of war. As K. B. McFarlane puts it,

> the real politics of the reign were not confined to the short if frequent parliaments; they were inherent rather in Edward's daily personal relations with his magnates. The king's service was profitable . . . men went to court and to the royal camp, not to express unacceptable views, but for what they could get. Under a ruler who knew his job they were amply rewarded.[33]

Among the magnates there were smaller groups, the knights of the royal household who (as we have already seen) were most closely associated with the king and were under his personal command, and the earls and barons who frequented the court in various official and unofficial roles. The knights of the household were hugely important in Edward's wars, and provided a large proportion of the troops who sailed for Flanders in 1338. Because this was not an army assembled for duty under a feudal summons, Edward was free to choose his followers more widely, and the result was a very varied group, including minor nobility from old families, newcomers to England – often from his father-in-law's county of Hainault – and professional soldiers of obscure origin who had won their place by their military skills. This harked back to his grandfather's days, when the household knights played a similar role in Edward I's

Scottish campaigns, and it was a commonplace that warfare should be waged by a group of men close to the king, an idea that had its origins in the war-bands of Celtic and Germanic tribal society. A 'household knight' was retained by the king, and would receive robes at the new year. The list of the distribution of robes, given the often erratic payment of fees to royal retainers, is perhaps the best way of identifying the household. They in turn would recruit men to serve in the royal army, so that sixty such knights in Flanders in 1338 had almost 800 men at arms in their own retinues.[34] In peacetime, the household knights had been as prominent in royal tournaments as the great magnates.

Other magnates, such as the marcher lords of the north, rarely came to court, and lived largely in their own country, preoccupied with their own interests. However, if the king's rule started to falter, they were often the first to show signs of rebellion, being independent-minded and wary of the central powers. A successful king had therefore to balance the aspirations of these different groups against his own ambitions; Edward I had done so with great skill for much of his reign, appearing at various times as a knightly hero and as a great lawgiver. Edward II's failure was a stark warning to his son.

Edward believed that England alone could not take on the armies of the vastly wealthier kingdom of France. So in 1337–8 he set about constructing a grand alliance based on Flanders, where Philip had been trying to enforce his rights over the Flemish towns and where there was considerable hostility to the French. In this he was imitating his grandfather, who had built a great alliance in very similar circumstances in 1297, when the English possession of Gascony was threatened. Edward's diplomacy was apparently successful, and, during the next three years, he established a substantial power base in north-western Europe: the count of Flanders, an ally of Philip, was forced out, and Edward was given authority over Germany and the Low Countries as the deputy of the German emperor. The new earls and members of his household were prominent in the negotiations for these alliances. Typically, a diplomatic mission would consist of an experienced royal official and his secretariat alongside a member of court who in a sense represented the king, and was assumed to have his confidence. William Clinton went on such missions to France in 1332 and 1334, and, at the beginning of the Flemish project of 1337, we find Montagu and Clinton sent with Henry

Burghersh, bishop of Lincoln, in April 1337 to negotiate the necessary treaties; they were in many ways the chief architects of the scheme. However, in order to achieve an active military alliance, Edward's negotiators had to adopt a policy of promising huge sums to his allies for the costs of bringing their troops to join his army. This in turn meant that the king would have to show quick results in order to balance his books. In November 1337, Walter Mauny provided him with a brief success; as admiral of the north, he escorted the English fleet taking wool to Flanders and on the way launched an attack on the Flemish port of Sluys, since the count of Flanders was a vassal of Philip VI. He was repulsed, but in an ensuing battle on the neighbouring island of Cadsand he captured the count's half-brother, and was able to sell his prisoner to the king for £8,000. The only long-term effect of this episode, however, was to give Mauny the foundation of his subsequent fortune.

In the midst of this vastly ambitious financial and political scheme, and at a time when the king was trying to raise huge sums of money, Edward typically put on a magnificent display at his Christmas feast at Guildford in 1337. Against a canvas background painted with a rabbit warren and a wood, a pillory and ducking stool were set up; fifteen baboons were the centrepiece of the action, while other actors wore white surcoats with red sleeves decorated with gold leaves. The king himself appeared in a dramatic piece of headgear, a hood covered in gold and silver ornaments, embroidered with 'tigers holding court made from pearls and embossed with silver and gold, and decorated on another edge with the image of a certain castle made of pearls with a mounted man riding towards the castle on a horse made of pearls, and, moreover, between each tiger a tree of pearls and a tree of gold ...'[35] Eight pairs of shields were made of gold and silver and varicoloured silk, for the king, Henry of Grosmont, Richard Fitzalan, William Montagu, Henry Ferrers, Thomas Poynings and the newly rich Walter Mauny. Seven less elaborate pairs were given to the Beauchamp brothers, Maurice Berkeley, Thomas Bradeston, John Molyns, and the Ufford brothers, Robert and Ralph. And three fantastic costumes were provided for the king, Henry of Grosmont and William Montagu,

> decorated with the image of a castle made of silk and trimmed with gold, displaying towers, halls, chambers, walls and other pertinent things around it, and within the walls divers trees of gold, while on the breast of

each tunic an embroidered figure in gold standing under a canopy on the battlements, whereas the hems of these tunics are designed in such a way in green cloth as to resemble the moats and ditches of this castle surrounded by a green field.[36]

The tunics and mantles of the king and queen and of William Montagu were trimmed with 228 golden clouds. If splendour equalled power, Edward was staking his claim to be one of the most powerful rulers in Europe.

Time was not on Edward's side, and as a result the grand alliance proved to be no more real than the golden clouds. His allies were more than happy to take his money, but much less happy about actually providing the resources for the kind of campaign that Edward had in mind. Other than the financial rewards, the rulers whom Edward had signed up – the lords of the various counties and duchies in the Low Countries and the German emperor, Louis IV – had little real interest in taking the war into France; the lords of the Netherlands were chiefly concerned to keep Philip out of their affairs, while Edward needed a considerable military victory if he was to enforce the restitution of the duchy of Aquitaine. Moreover, the allies knew that Edward was thinking of making public his claim to the French throne, at which point the rights of the French king would pass to him, and they would merely have exchanged the threat which Philip posed for a vastly more powerful ruler of France.

Edward arrived in Antwerp in July 1338. This was to be his base, and, just as when he had moved his court to York for the duration of the Scottish wars, Philippa and his two daughters accompanied him: the eight-year-old prince of Wales was left in England as regent, the nominal head of a regency council which included William Clinton. But the administration had to remain in England, whereas for the Scottish wars it too had moved north. Communication across the Channel was not always easy, and the king's plans were putting enormous strains on the government, with repeated demands for large sums of money. The allies were slow to commit troops to the planned campaign against France, while demanding the payments they had been promised, and Edward spent a frustrating year trying to bring them together as an army. He had a moment of diplomatic triumph at Koblenz on 5 September, when he was appointed as imperial vicar-general in a magnificent ceremony, for which Edward had fifteen tunics and mantles made in red and gold

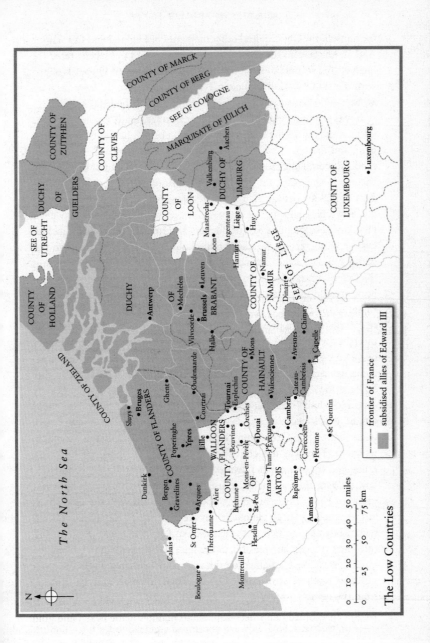

The Low Countries

for himself, the emperor and other magnates of England and Germany.[37] And at Antwerp in the second week of January 1339 he celebrated the birth of his second son, Lionel, and the churching of Queen Philippa with the traditional tournament. The participants would have been his household knights, the earls and possibly some of the local knights.

It was not until September 1339 that Edward finally cajoled his allies into joining him in the field; the promised subsidies had only been partly paid, and there was little money coming from England. He had to persuade his companions to sign a document by which eight of them would become hostages for the payment of the sums due to the duke of Brabant if the king defaulted. The document survives, signed and sealed by the king and twenty-five of his magnates: all the English earls, as well as Henry of Beaumont as earl of Buchan, and thirteen other lords, including the bannerets of the king's household.[38] After which – though not without some further hesitation until Edward himself set out with just the English army – the allies invaded the territory of the bishop of Cambrai, outside the borders of France, but like the count of Flanders a vassal of the French king. The object was to force Philip to come to the rescue of the bishop; he did so grudgingly, at first pretending that he thought the English king was still at Antwerp. We have a detailed diary of the campaign, which notes the raids carried out during the next fortnight, devastating the lands round Cambrai: William Montagu's brother Edward took two castles in a raid on 10 October, and Walter Mauny captured Thun l'Évêque, while Thomas Poynings, another household knight, was killed trying to take the castle at Honicourt. A larger raid, under Henry of Grosmont, William Bohun and William Montagu, followed. This was not enough to force Philip to challenge Edward's army, and on 9 October Edward invaded France itself. His brother-in-law, William II of Hainault, refused to accompany him, since he was a vassal of King Philip; but many of his men stayed with the English, as did his uncle, Jean de Hainault. On the first day of the invasion, Laurence Hastings, the heir to the earldom of Pembroke, was given his full title even though he was still under age; sixty-seven squires from the English army were knighted on the same and following days.

Philip had at last responded to the English threat, and was not far from the invading army. For the first time since the reign of Richard I, there was a real likelihood that the kings of France and England would meet on the battlefield. Edward encamped eighteen miles from Philip's position, at Péronne on the Somme, and his raiders burnt a village only two miles from the French camp; Walter Mauny and Wulfart Ghistels, a Flemish knight from Ostend, actually raided the outposts of the French position. Philip still refused to move, and appeared to be prepared to sit out the invasion until the English were forced to retreat for want of money and supplies. But the French lords with him were eager to engage, and he sent a challenge to Edward naming a day for the battle, with the result that the two armies came face to face at Buironfosse, on the border with Hainault, on 21 October. Edward followed the pattern of Halidon Hill in drawing up the army, dismounting his knights and men at arms, and placing archers, guarded by Welsh spearmen, on the flanks. The king's battalion formed the vanguard, and included Henry Burghersh, bishop of Lincoln, and Jean de Hainault, with Thomas Bradeston, William Fitzwarin, Reginald Cobham, Walter Mauny, Thomas Holland and Maurice Berkeley among the household knights. The right wing was under Henry of Grosmont and Robert Ufford, and the left under William Bohun and William Montagu, as well as Laurence Hastings taking his first command.[39] Edward's Continental allies were in the centre, with Robert Ufford's brother William evidently as a liaison officer. Almost all the English commanders were veterans of the Scottish wars, and had been comrades in arms on numerous occasions over the previous six years. The English army was a much smaller force than that commanded by Philip; yet when Philip came in sight of the enemy battle array, he ordered the vanguard to halt, and a defensive position to be prepared.

A fierce argument broke out among the French lords. Some argued that the king would be disgraced if he did not attack the enemy – exactly the reaction that Edward wished to provoke. Others urged caution, partly because of a fear of treachery on their own side, and partly because they were uncertain of the outcome of a battle with the English and their allies.[40] If Edward was unsure of his allies, he was at least confident that the English magnates would never betray him; Philip was in a worse position, because it was his own lords who were the source of his problems. Both sides withdrew after facing each other for a day; Edward could not afford to stay in a position where he had no supplies, Philip because he did not want to risk a battle. In terms of reputation, Edward had enhanced his fame: not only had he defeated the Scots in the open field, but the French had not dared to take him on. Philip was seen as having retreated out of fear or cowardice, although some French chroniclers tried to claim that it was the English who had withdrawn silently in the night when they saw the size of the French army. Philip had done the right thing in tactical terms, but that did not stop his nobles from wearing fox-fur hats mocking Philip's cowardly behaviour, like the fox in folklore.

But Edward had nonetheless failed in his objective. Military failure meant that the costs of maintaining the alliance could not be defrayed by the spoils of war, and what had been intended as a swift campaign dragged on with no end in sight. This war had to be financed out of taxation: and the result was one of the heaviest periods of taxation ever seen in England. In the spring of 1340 he had to return home to use such persuasion as he could muster on an increasingly recalcitrant country, and to explain that he had now declared his hand and had, in a ceremony in the marketplace at Ghent on 8 January, publicly laid claim to the French throne by assuming the title 'king of England and France'. The announcement was followed by jousts in celebration the occassion.[41]

In his absence, William Montagu and Robert Ufford mounted an expedition with the aim of capturing Lille, in advance of a major campaign planned for the summer. Three divisions, two from Flanders and one from Hainault, were to join forces for the siege; Montagu and Ufford, in charge of one of the Flemish divisions, seem to have ridden forward with no more than forty men at arms to reconnoitre the defences of Lille, and were captured when the French garrison sallied out against them. According to Le Bel, they found themselves trapped in the earthworks outside the town; another French chronicle says that Montagu was seriously wounded. The English chroniclers blamed them for their 'foolish audacity', and this was probably correct: overconfidence in the superiority of the mounted horseman over infantry was more often the downfall of the French, and, combined with Montagu's evident liking for bold action, proved disastrous in this instance.[42] News of Montagu and Ufford's capture reached the king at Windsor in early April, where he was holding an Easter tournament,[43] and must have cast a shadow over proceedings. It was the most serious loss that the English had suffered since the beginning of Edward's reign: Philip, triumphant, put them in a cart like ordinary criminals and locked them up in the Châtelet, a common prison in Paris, rather than in the honourable captivity which they might have expected. Montagu had already lost an eye in a skirmish in Scotland in 1337, and it is possible that his health was now permanently impaired.

The sheer power of the French military machine was now at its most daunting, even though Philip's counter-raid into Hainault achieved relatively little. At the same time as mustering a substantial army for this purpose, Philip also threatened to cut communications between England and Flanders by assembling a powerful fleet of 202 ships, which arrived in the Swijn estuary controlling the entrance to the port of Sluys about 8 June. Word of this quickly reached England. If Edward wanted to continue his French campaigns, he had to destroy the French fleet, but the stakes were high: defeat and the loss of his army would leave England open to French invasion. Archbishop Stratford, as head of the regency council, advised him not to go, and, when he appealed to the commanders of his fleet, both highly experienced seamen, they supported the archbishop. Robert of Avesbury, who was close to Stratford, claims that Edward declared: 'I will cross the sea in spite of you. You are frightened when there is nothing to be afraid of, and can stay at home.'[44] He continued to recruit men and ships with renewed energy.

Edward's fleet sailed from the Orwell estuary in Suffolk on 22 June, with a fleet slightly smaller than the French armada, but with more fighting men and smaller crews. They reached the Flemish coast near Sluys on the evening of 23 June, and Reginald Cobham was sent ashore to report on the French positions; Walter Mauny knew the area, and was able to provide additional intelligence. The French ships had been idle for a fortnight, and their captains were quarrelling; the vessels were chained together to prevent the English breaking through the line, but in so doing lost all means of control. The next day, early in the day, the English fleet set out to fight. The English were good seamen, and it is probable that they manoeuvred so that they approached the French from the south, anchoring once they were in sight of the fleet to wait for the tide. Once it had turned, about midday, the three admirals in charge of the fleet, Robert Morley, admiral of the north, William Clinton, admiral of the west, and John Crabbe, once admiral of Flanders and since 1333 employed by the English, hoisted anchor and moved towards the French, and then changed tack as if they were about to retreat. The French hastily broke their chains, and tried to pursue them.

At this point both fleets were attempting to sail into the wind, moving very slowly: when the English turned to attack, they had the impetus of both wind and tide with them. The first shots were from siege engines mounted on the ships, followed by the classic English use of archers. As on land, they had a deadly effect, driving the enemy from the decks of the ships. As the ships closed, the English men at arms clambered onto the French vessels, where their superior numbers made short work of the few French troops and of the crossbowmen and sailors. Edward himself was wounded in the thigh, but there were almost no English casualties, and a horrific slaughter of the French which shocked contemporaries. A contingent of Genoese galleys escaped in the early evening, but more than 150 French ships were taken back to England. The real heroes of the hour were the naval commanders, whose skilful handling of their squadrons had been crucial to the victory. Edward, however, claimed the victory as his personally; and in a sense it was, because he knew that he was not an expert in war at sea, and was prepared to hand over the fleet to those who were. Once again, the contrast is between collaboration and common sense among Edward and his men, and pride, distrust and quarrels among their adversaries.[45] However, the French still had considerable naval resources, including the Genoese galleys that had escaped at Sluys and which were often used to raid English ports, and they were accustomed to hiring their ships from Genoa and Castile, whereas Edward had to rely on English resources only.

Edward, as always desperate for money to pay his allies, turned his victory to good use. A parliament was hastily convened to hear the news of the king's great victory, and in the general enthusiasm the taxes voted for the next two years were converted into an immediate lump sum. With this reassurance, he embarked on his planned campaign: Tournai, the most important French fortress near the Flemish border, was to be besieged. If it was taken, it would be a major achievement; but the real objective was to try once more to lure Philip to the battlefield. In the event, Tournai held out, and there was no battle. When the two armies were apparently on the point of engaging in early September, Jeanne, dowager countess of Hainault, mother of Queen Philippa and sister of Philip of Valois, emerged from the convent where she was living in retirement to plead for a truce. With a suitable show of reluctance, Philip agreed to negotiate; and the duke of Brabant, Edward's most important ally, forced Edward, who was still hoping for a quick victory, to send Henry Burghersh, William Clinton and Geoffrey Scrope to open the talks. Within two days, a truce was agreed at Esplechin on 25 September 1340. One of its provisions was that Montagu and Ufford should be released on parole, though the ransoms were heavy. Philip VI was fully aware of Edward's close dependence on Montagu, and made it a condition of his parole that he would never fight in France again. However, in June 1342 this condition was removed in exchange for the release of two important French prisoners.[46] But he only fought briefly in Brittany late in 1342, and possibly at the siege of Algeciras in 1343, and his capture outside Lille effectively marked the end of Montagu's career as Edward's right-hand man in the English command.

Although the usual jousts were held to celebrate the end of the campaign, the absence of military victory was a disaster for Edward, who blamed his failure on the administration in England. The new taxation he had been granted by parliament in June yielded only 15 per cent of what had been expected. His closest advisers in England were now thoroughly opposed to the war, and at the end of November Edward sailed back to London, furious with what he saw as their lack of support, and suspicious that their reports were false. His response to the situation was to attempt to repeat the coup with which his personal rule had begun in 1330. His action was as dramatic as it had been at Northampton: he arrived secretly by night

> and entered the Tower of London by torchlight, and no one knew he had come. He at once asked for Sir Nicholas de la Beche, the constable of the Tower and guardian of the duke, son of the king of England. And the under-constable fell on his knees at the king's feet, and said, 'Sire, he is out of the town.' This put the king into a rage and he ordered all the chests to be opened for him so that he could see for himself what was in the Tower. And when he had looked at these, he sent urgently for Andrew Aubrey, then mayor of London.[47]

Aubrey was ordered to arrest leading members of the administration, even though he had no official post, and despite the fact that William Bohun and Walter Mauny were with the king. Even the official records note the king's midnight arrival,[48] but, despite the surprise, the results were not what he had hoped. The king had had secret information that the administration were cheating him: yet the truth was that his demands had been excessive in the extreme. Archbishop Stratford, who had been president of the regency council since 1330, withdrew to Canterbury, and waged an effective propaganda war against the king, knowing that right was on his side; he refused to answer for his actions except before parliament. When parliament met in April 1341, Edward tried to exclude him, but the other lords forced him to admit the archbishop and to come to terms with him. It was a tremendous blow for a king who had hoped to avoid the troubles of his father's reign; echoes of the fall of Edward II were particularly strong, since Stratford had been a leader of the opposition in the 1320s. The king had to agree to legislation which gave parliament a large role in selecting the royal officials, and to an audit of his finances; and the lords insisted that none of them should be imprisoned without a trial before his peers in parliament. Edward was perilously close to the kind of political crisis that had repeatedly marred his father's reign.

4

The Kingdom of France

If we are to understand the history of Edward's wars against France, we have to define the enemy – the king, nobles and people of the kingdom of France. They were Edward's opponents, and their strengths and weaknesses were as critical to the events which followed Edward III's declaration of war on France in 1337 as were those of the English leaders. Furthermore, the relationship between the kingdoms of France and England and the kings of the two countries were different in nature. The two kingdoms were separate political entities: there was no question of an English claim to France because that kingdom was a vassal state (or vice versa). It was the kings personally who were at war, rival claimants to the French throne. On Philip V's death in 1328 without direct male heirs, the law on the succession was not clear, since the last time that this situation had arisen was three centuries earlier, in 987. Philip VI claimed the throne as the nearest male descendant of Philip V's grandfather, Philip III, through a male line. Edward III claimed the throne as the nearest male relative of the late king through the female line, because his mother was the daughter of Philip IV. The question as to whether a claim to the throne could be inherited through a daughter was put to the lawyers of the university of Paris, who declared that such a claim was not valid; but there was enough doubt about the matter for Edward III to play the ultimate card in the rivalry between the French and English kings, and declare himself king of France as grandson of Philip IV. Edward's view of the matter is neatly demonstrated in a family tree, carefully laid out in the 1350s to show why his was the best claim.

The rival claimants to the French throne: a family tree from Geoffrey le Baker's chronicler, set out in such a way that Edward appears visually as the first claimant.

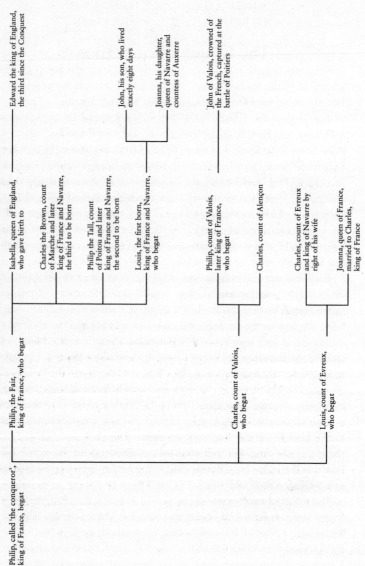

LANGUAGE, CULTURE AND
ANGLO-FRENCH RELATIONS

Edward's decision to make war had been entirely personal, in pursuit of his personal right to the French throne. Behind it lay the legacy of the ambitions of the Angevin kings. The two countries were Siamese twins, joined and yet separate; the English kings had at times ruled more land in France than the French kings themselves. Edward III himself was more than half French, since Henry III and Edward II had both married French wives. So there was an element of civil war about the conflict; the enemy were the inhabitants of a country with which the English aristocracy had close links, personal, cultural and historical. Only six generations separated them from forebears who had held lands in both Normandy and England, and there were continuing administrative links with Aquitaine and north-eastern France: Bartholomew Burghersh the elder had served as seneschal of Ponthieu in the early years of Edward's reign.

But the dreams of empire and memories of the former greatness of the English kings remained. The English nobility, many of whom retained lands in France, regarded the English presence across the Channel as part of their birthright. The kings of France and England might be at loggerheads over territorial claims; on the other hand, England and France were intertwined in ways which would seem unimaginable to us today. First and foremost, they shared a common language. Until the mid-fourteenth century, all those educated in England spoke French, not as an alternative language, but as their native tongue. They would probably know a little Latin, for the purposes of royal business. And they would also speak English if necessary. That it was not familiar is shown by the Anglo-French glossary compiled by Walter of Bibbesworth in the 1250s for the use of local gentry in managing their estates and talking to their stewards.[1]

The whole of north-west Europe was French-speaking to a greater or lesser degree as far as the landowning knightly classes were concerned. There was a shared body of literature, particularly in terms of the romances, which also reflected a shared ethos among the knights. Knighthood had always been an international movement, from the early tournaments of the twelfth century onwards, and knights continued to travel long distances in pursuit of their favourite sport. From this came a set of ideals broadly accepted by knights throughout Europe: the most popular book on knighthood, Ramon Llull's *Book of the Order of Knighthood*, was written in Catalan at the end of the thirteenth century, but was translated into Spanish, and into French in the fourteenth century; Caxton made an English version in 1484. The language of heraldry, too, was international; pride in ancestry was not merely a local affair, but something to be paraded abroad. We shall come across knights who left their coats of arms in churches they visited in the near east as a memento of their crusading journeys there.

The merchants were likewise an international community, though French was less of a unifying factor, since many of them came from German-speaking countries. The Hansa, the great league of north German traders, had a massive presence in London at the Steelyard, its fortified warehouse on the north bank of the Thames. And a succession of Italian bankers sought their fortune in England by lending to the king, only to be ruined by him. Their network of mercantile and political intelligence was highly sophisticated, and the great events of European affairs were swiftly reported to their headquarters in Italy. English merchants in the fourteenth century were rapidly growing in wealth and status; the prime example is William de la Pole of Hull, who replaced the Italian bankers as the leading creditor of the king in the 1340s, and whose son became earl of Suffolk in 1370. London merchants such as Andrew Aubrey and John Pountney were similarly wealthy. Their world overlapped with that of the royal court in many ways: they were its chief suppliers, especially of the hugely expensive textiles produced in Flanders, which cost the king as much as his purchases of jewels. Within London they played a sometimes crucial political role. We have seen how, in the most serious crisis of his reign, in 1340/41, Edward had to call on Andrew Aubrey to get his opponents arrested. Equally, merchants and their wives were spectators – though never participants – at the great displays of jousting in the City and at Windsor. They read much of the same literature, and shared the social values of the knights. And through their international contacts they were in touch with the latest fashions in the arts and particularly in clothing.

In terms of trade and business, there were of course numerous Englishmen working as administrators in the English-held territories, who would not necessarily return home when these lands were taken over by the French. Perhaps the most famous example of this is the man who guided Edward III across a crucial ford over the Somme in 1346; the abbot of Meaux near Beverley in Yorkshire records that he was 'an Englishman born at Ruston near Nafferton, who had lived in those parts for sixteen years'.[2] In 1330 this part of France, known as Ponthieu, had been under English control, and it changed hands during the war of 1338–40. So he had been there for almost as long under French rule as he had been under English rule, and there must have been many with similar experiences.

The clergy were international in a different way. Most of the English clergy were born in England, younger sons of noble families, who had entered the Church because the family lands were inherited by the eldest son; or they were the clever children of tradesmen or of the English managers of great estates. A few of the great princes of the Church were foreign, 'provided' to their bishoprics by the pope: the right to do this was fiercely resisted by the English kings, who wanted to place their own men in positions which were as much about secular power as religious devotion. All clergy, however, were acutely conscious of their loyalty to the pope, and many of the senior clergy had direct knowledge of the papal court at Avignon, because this was where appeals in cases involving Church law were determined, and there was a constant stream of English travellers to and from the city. During the whole of Edward III's reign, the papacy was here, in exile from Rome, and often heavily biased towards the French view of politics.

But for the bulk of the population, the native English speakers of the villages and small towns, the world of the wealthy was alien, not only in lifestyle, but in language and customs. England was still to some extent an occupied country. Although the Anglo-Norman nobility occasionally intermarried with their Anglo-Saxon predecessors, it was primarily a case of Norman lords marrying Englishwomen. The English rarely appear as more than freemen, with modest estates, parish priests and small traders, though able Englishmen might well rise to high rank within the Church. English was the language of communication for the parish priest teaching his parishioners and for the bailiff giving orders to the men in the fields. It survived as a literary language in monasteries, since entering a monastic order was an attractive prospect for a talented Englishman; alongside the manuals for preachers produced in

English, a handful of writers continued the literary tradition of the Anglo-Saxons.

When ordinary English soldiers went to France they did not find any points of cultural contact: this was a strange land, and a strange language. For most of the thirteenth century, there had been little military action, and it was only in the last years of Edward I that the English sent troops to Aquitaine in any numbers. The Flemish campaign was the first time that a major English force had ever engaged with the French on French soil; and the invasion of 1346 was the first time that an army almost entirely composed of English troops had campaigned there. It was here that the common soldiers discovered an alien enemy, with whom they could not communicate, a very different view of the world to that of their commanders.

PHILIP OF VALOIS

When Philip of Valois confiscated Aquitaine in 1337, he was venturing into territory which had never in practice been directly ruled from Paris, unlike Normandy, where there had been a full-blown French administration since the early thirteenth century.[3] Loyalty to the English as heirs to the dukes of Aquitaine was strong, at least in part because the fiercely independent local lords preferred a distant king in London to one whose army was only a few days' march away.

Edward faced three kings of France during his reign, three very different characters, with different political backgrounds. His quarrel was personal, and only indirectly a matter for the English state: the French territories under English rule were his personal fiefs, not land conquered by the English. His claim to the French throne was entirely personal, through his mother Isabella, and the personal enmity between him and Philip of Valois was reflected in the diplomatic insults in their correspondence after 1337: 'you who call yourself king of France' is a favourite line of Edward's, and it is interesting that he never uses this epithet to either of Philip's successors.[4]

Philip, unlike Edward, had never expected to be king. Edward himself had been heir to the English throne since his birth in 1312. Philip, nineteen years older than Edward, was no more than a first cousin of Louis X, some way down the line of succession. When Louis X died in

1316, he had no surviving sons, but his wife was pregnant, and another son was born two months later; but he lived for only a few days, and Louis's brother claimed the throne as Philip V. Louis had a daughter, Jeanne, but no woman had ever succeeded to the French throne, and Philip was crowned. A challenge to this on behalf of Jeanne was over-ruled by an assembly of lords, clergy and citizens in Paris, advised by the lawyers of the university, which declared that women could not succeed to the French throne.

Philip of Valois was brought up simply as heir to the county of Val-ois, son of a royal peer of France, no more than the eldest of a string of distant relatives of the king. Philip V's son Philip was born in 1313, and it was only on his death in 1321 that the twenty-eight-year old Philip of Valois became second in line to the succession. Philip V died in 1322, again without an heir; his younger brother Charles IV died in 1328, leaving his wife pregnant: the child proved to be a daughter, and only at that point did Philip of Valois become a claimant to the French throne. He rested his claim on the idea that a woman could inherit private prop-erty but not public office, which had emerged in discussions on the conflict between Roman law and the teaching of the Church.[5] But it was not clear whether despite this a claim could still pass down through the female side, as Edward argued. To make sure of his title, Philip was chosen as king by a council of the French magnates, the 'twelve peers' of France: outside the council, he was supported by other important lords, including Robert d'Artois, Guy count of Blois and William I of Hainault.[6] The leading royal officials, anxious for continuity, supported Philip's claim.

Philip of Valois's upbringing had therefore never been that of the confirmed heir to the throne; furthermore, he had been largely over-shadowed by his father, who died in 1325, and he had only been lord of Valois for three years. He was merely a member of the French peerage, whereas Edward had been at the centre of the English royal household since his birth. Moreover, the troubled history of the French monarchy since 1316 meant that there was a great deal of political manoeuvring in the uncertain situation, and Philip had no personal entourage among the men at the centre of power. On the other hand, he had at his disposal a well-organized administration, developed since the late thirteenth century under Philip IV and Philip V. One of the aims of these kings had been to continue the attack on English power in France that had begun in the late twelfth century under Philip Augustus. Philip of Valois continued this process, with the added incentive that by so doing he was weakening his rival for the throne.

However, because to some extent he owed his throne to the other princes and prelates, Philip was restricted in his ability to impose his power in the same way as his predecessors had done. The French kingship had tended to be more absolutist than that in England, with less reference to the consensus of the nobility which in England developed into a parliamentary structure. Philip admitted in negotiations with Edward in 1329 that, even if he wanted to restore all Edward's estates in France, he was not in a position to make sure that such an order would be carried out.[7] In the early years of his reign, while Edward was under the tutelage of Isabella and Mortimer, their personal relations seem to have been cordial, and they may have jousted together when Edward performed homage at Amiens in 1329. Once Edward was free of his mother's influence, however, the good relationship quickly evaporated.

Philip was an experienced soldier, having campaigned in Italy in 1320 and in Aquitaine with his father and brother in 1324,[8] and early in his reign had won a crushing victory against the Flemish, who were resisting his claims to be their overlord, at Cassel in 1328. It was a victory that had nearly been a disastrous defeat: there had been a stand-off between the two armies for three days, as Philip rightly refused to attack the Flemish, who had a strong position on a hilltop. Instead, he besieged them, and tried to provoke them into an attack by burning the surrounding countryside. The Flemish finally decided to attempt a surprise onslaught in the heat of the day; one chronicler says that the king was taking his accustomed nap.[9] Gilles li Muisit claims that the Flemish were aiming to kill the king himself, and they certainly reached his part of the encampment.[10] But the French rallied just in time, the king was armed and part of the French army quickly regrouped. Once the royal banners were raised, and the king appeared with the host, the Flemish footsoldiers, who had broken ranks to infiltrate the French camp, were driven out; they made a last stand on unfavourable ground and were overwhelmed by the French cavalry.

Despite the narrow escape, Philip's strategy, in not attacking an infantry force entrenched on a powerful defensive site, had been entirely correct. His subsequent tactics at Buironfosse in 1339 and outside Calais in 1347 were exactly the same, attempting to persuade his enemy to attack; but Edward was a different sort of opponent, as calculating as Philip, and even more disciplined. The decision to attack at Crécy was not characteristic of Philip – if it was indeed a conscious decision. The problem was that a defensive policy, which was eventually to break the English power later in the century, was not what the knightly attitude to war encouraged: and the knightly ideals of the time were an essentially French construct, even more powerful in the mindset of French leaders than in that of the English army. Furthermore, the French armies were consistently larger, grander and more confident of victory.

Philip does not come across as a sharply defined character. His father, Charles of Valois, had been a distinguished soldier, but Philip, despite his victory over the Flemish at Cassel in 1328, was not a natural commander. His weakness was his inability to surround himself with sound advisers; he himself was serious and committed, but the men he chose to serve him were often of a very different calibre. He seems to have been indecisive on the battlefield, but he was a determined opponent on the diplomatic front. He had none of Edward's panache, and contemporary poets and writers blamed him severely for his failure to attack Edward in Flanders in 1338, and equally severely for doing so at Crécy in 1346 and suffering a catastrophic defeat. And he did not get on with his fellow-lords.

TREACHERY

Philip's greatest difficulty, which was to remain a major problem for the next two decades, was that of maintaining the loyalty of his subjects. Partly because he himself had not been a particularly prominent member of the nobility before his accession, and partly through bad luck, he suffered from the kind of baronial rebellions that had brought down Edward II, though these arose less out of supposed favouritism and maladministration than out of the pursuit of claims to great principalities. Robert d'Artois, who was reported as saying that Philip 'was made king by me', felt that he was rightfully count of Artois on the death of his aunt, Mahaut; it was another claim involving rights through the female line, but complicated by the fact that Philip was married to Jeanne d'Artois, whose title to the county was probably better than Robert's.

There were now two claimants to the kingdom of France. The solution for peers of France discontented with Philip was simply to switch sides. In the French king's view, this was treason; in Edward's view, recognition of his just cause. Treason was the nightmare of the French monarchy, and is a recurrent theme in the reigns of Philip and of his son. Robert d'Artois was the most influential figure to change sides, and was seen by some chroniclers as the prime mover of Edward's war against France. A French poem satirizing Edward's claim to France, *The Vows of the Heron*, casts Robert in this role.[11] Robert is at Edward's court and goes hawking; he returns with a heron, which is served at a feast. Now, the heron was regarded as the most cowardly of birds, and Robert accuses Edward of cowardice because he will not attack the French to enforce his claim to the throne. Stung by his reproaches, the king and the assembled company take increasingly absurd vows to fight. By mocking the knightly idea of vowing to pursue a quest, the poet puts Edward's pursuit of his title into the same potentially ridiculous category. Furthermore, from the French standpoint, the accusation of faint-heartedness was made by a man who was himself a traitor, branding Edward's whole enterprise with both treachery and cowardice, the two cardinal sins of the knightly world.

But treachery was a real and present danger to Philip and his successors. Once Robert d'Artois had defected, traitors might be lurking anywhere. Le Bel says that at Buironfosse in 1339, when Philip and his advisers discussed whether or not to attack the English,

> there was much debate and quarrelling over this: some of the French lords said it would be a great disgrace and dishonour if the king didn't fight when he knew that his enemies, who'd been burning and ravaging his kingdom before his very eyes, were now so near and still in his own land; but others declared that on the contrary it would be a great folly to do battle, for there was no way of knowing what everyone was thinking and if there was any danger of betrayal . . .[12]

In 1342 there was a dispute over the inheritance of another great fief of the French crown, the duchy of Brittany. The rivals were Charles de Blois, son of another of Philip's supporters at his accession, and the English claimant, Jean de Montfort. One of the great Breton lords, Olivier Clisson, decided that it would be to his advantage to change sides; he was close to the French court and had indeed been with Philip in Italy and had been knighted by him. In the autumn of 1342 he made a secret treaty with Edward which seems to have included recognition of his title to France, and fought briefly on the English side before a truce was proclaimed in January 1343.[13] The following July, during another truce in the fighting in Brittany, he rashly attended a tournament in Paris, perhaps relying on the terms of the truce for immunity. He was arrested by Philip's officers, charged with dealings with the king's enemies – which he seems to have admitted – and executed as a traitor, with all the attendant spectacle of horrors.

Clisson was a man of considerable influence, and his continuing presence on the English side would have changed the balance of power in Brittany. In his wake, and before his downfall, other, lesser lords followed, notably Godefroy d'Harcourt, who was to become Edward's adviser on the Crécy campaign. He was lord of the great castle at St Sauveur-le-Vicomte, south of Cherbourg, which was to pass to two Garter companions in succession twenty years later,[14] and his defection arose out of a purely local quarrel with a neighbouring lord, Robert Bertrand, over the marriage of a heiress. Bertrand, however, was a royal servant, and was both wealthy and powerful. When Harcourt and Bertrand drew their swords over the quarrel in the king's presence, they were both summoned before the parlement in Paris. Harcourt, realizing that Bertrand was much more influential, refused to appear and began a private war against Bertrand and his brother, the bishop of Bayeux, which he comprehensively lost: St Sauveur was taken and razed to the ground, and Harcourt fled the country, eventually finding his way to England.

If the actual damage done by this treachery was relatively limited, the author of the *Grandes chroniques*, writing only a few years later, points to the psychological effect on the king:

> The king, seeing so many treacherous acts done by so many people in so many parts of his kingdom, was greatly troubled, and began to consider and wonder – not without good cause – how such things might be happening; because he saw that almost everyone in the duchies of Brittany and Normandy was in revolt, especially the very noblemen who had promised to serve him loyally until their dying day. He therefore summoned an assembly of the princes and barons of his kingdom to consider how he could avoid such great fraud and inquity, and how this enmity could be entirely removed from his kingdom, so that it was once more a reliable and loyal country.[15]

Treachery was not yet widespread, as the author claims, but related much more to local opportunism in the wake of the English involvement in Brittany. After the campaign of 1346 this was to change for the worse.

At Crécy itself, divided loyalties meant that the shadow of treachery was present. In many cases, there were genuine difficulties: the Rochester chronicler calls Jean de Hainault 'a traitor to the king of England',[16] even though he owed no formal allegiance to Edward, and the only tie was that he was uncle of Queen Philippa. The story in the anonymous Roman chronicle of the capture of the prince of Wales at Crécy may have some ground in fact;[17] the aftermath, however, in which the prince is set free by Philip's brother, Louis count of Alençon, is not really credible:

> Louis count of Flanders saw all this [i.e. the capture of Edward]; he had been chased out of his county and had been in Paris in the pay of the French king for a long time. He was an old man, a good and honest person. He loved King Philip and the king's honour. He saw this treachery in the midst of the French lords. He raised his voice and said: 'Ah, count of Alençon, this is not the loyalty and faithfulness with which you should serve the crown. The war was won and you have lost it.' When the count of Alençon heard this, he did not want to hear any more. He turned the head of his destrier and with the same mace gave the old count of Flanders such a blow that he killed him. What an evil thing that leads to a man being killed for telling the truth and reproving the wicked! Not one of the company of the count of Flanders was moved to do something about this deed. Only a close member of his household, a servant and footsoldier of common lineage, seeing such cruelty, unsheathed his dagger and ran it right through the count of Alençon's belly, so that the count of Alençon, who had betrayed his brother [i.e. Philip], died on the spot. This servant who killed the count of Alençon then went to King Philip and told him he had killed his brother to avenge his master, and proved this by good witnesses. When King Philip heard this he pardoned him and did not take vengeance on him.[18]

This picturesque episode, like many of Froissart's little set pieces, may have no real basis in fact, but it gives a vivid impression of the confusion of the battle, the claims of different loyalties and the possibility of betrayal for whatever reason.

Edward's victory at Crécy meant that there was a real possibility in men's minds that the English might become, if not rulers of France, then a major political and military force throughout French lands. The effect was immediate. Edward marched from Crécy to lay siege to Calais, and, as Jonathan Sumption says, 'Edward III had never received as many offers of support from well-placed French noblemen as he did during the eleven months when his army stood immobile outside Calais.'[19] Rebels from Burgundy came to him for help, and were given a generous subsidy; in consequence, the forces of the duke of Burgundy, Philip's brother-in-law, were tied up for most of 1347 dealing with the uprising. Opportunists tried to seize towns and go over to the English side; the most notable case was at Laon, on the edge of the county of Champagne, an area which a decade later was to fall into anarchy.

The most dramatic case of an accusation of treachery occurred in the first weeks of the reign of John II, Philip's successor, in November 1350. Raoul count of Eu, who had been constable of France in 1346 and was captured by Thomas Holland at Caen, came to Paris on parole to raise his ransom. Jean le Bel captures the mood of the events which followed, a bolt from the blue which no one seemed to understand:

> When he arrived back in France he went to see King John, expecting a fond welcome – he'd loved the count well enough before he became king. The count bowed to him in humble greeting, and expected to be warmly and joyfully received after five years as a prisoner in exile. King John led him into a chamber alone and said:
>
> 'Look at this letter. Familiar, is it?'
>
> They say the Constable was utterly dumbstruck when he saw it; and seeing his shock, the king cried:
>
> 'Ah, wicked traitor! Death is what you deserve, and you'll have it, by my father's soul!'
>
> And he ordered his guards to seize him there and then and imprison him in the tower at the Louvre in Paris, where the Count of Montfort had been held – and had died, so it's said. Everyone was distressed that the worthy Constable should be so treated, for he was much loved, and no one could understand the king's motives. And next day the king swore to all the Constable's friends who were pleading on his behalf that before he ever slept again he would have him beheaded, and no one would persuade him otherwise. And indeed it was done that very night, in the tower

of the Louvre,[20] without any trial or judgement, much to the grief and anger of everyone, and it earned the king great reproach and cost him much love. No one but the king's innermost circle knew why it had happened, but some guessed that the king had been informed of some liaison that had either occurred or been planned between his wife the lady Bonne and the worthy Constable. I don't know if there was any truth in this, but the way in which it happened made many people suspect it.[21]

The wild rumours were probably very wide of the mark: Matteo Villani reports a violent argument between the English and French ambassadors at the papal court a little later, in which it emerged that the count of Eu had arranged to sell the castle of Guines near Calais to Edward to settle his ransom, which he was otherwise unable to pay. It was his property, but it was also a French fief, and a key fortress on the French border. It was almost certainly this that John II regarded as treachery; the King's fury meant that there was no trial and a summary execution.[22]

It was a disastrous move, and one which unsettled and alienated his supporters. The morale of the French nobility, already damaged by Crécy, was now further lowered by this arbitrary act of tyranny. John was widely condemned, and it is possible that Edward may have enacted the Statute of Treasons in the parliament of 1352 partly in response to this dramatic episode. The statute strictly defined treason and limited it to physical attacks on the royal family or plots against them, making war against the king or helping his enemies, forgery of royal documents or counterfeiting money or killing senior royal officials. As in France, treason had begun to mean in English law an infringement of the king's rights as well as the direct actions defined in the statute. The charge of treason had also been widely – and often, but not always, correctly – used in his father's reign. The 1352 statute reassured the English nobility that they were not going to be exposed to the instant and unjust judgement of a furious king, as seemed to be the case in France, and reinforced the trust between Edward III and his magnates.[23]

The case of the count of Eu is made all the more dramatic because John II was much admired by his contemporaries; he is generally portrayed as benevolent and merciful. However, he was subject to sudden rages, and the extremely sensitive threat of treachery evidently roused this devastating anger. Petrarch admired him, and he is described as dignified and intelligent, a lover of luxury (though too liberal in his gifts) and a great hunter, an enthusiasm which Petrarch counts as one of his faults. His health was not good, and he was seriously ill in 1335 and 1344; doctors and surgeons were always near at hand. Perhaps because of this, he was not skilful with weapons: at the marriage feast of his younger brother, Philip duke of Orléans, he was unseated in the first joust by the lord of St Venant. His courage at Poitiers was perhaps unexpected: he was a relatively seasoned campaigner, but had never fought in a major battle. He was intellectually curious, a great reader and very interested in music: it was he who was the real founder of the great royal library usually connected with his son Charles V.[24]

John II was not the only man in France to mete out summary justice – or perhaps injustice. French politics, already complicated enough by Edward III's challenge to the throne, were made even more fraught by the activities of Charles king of Navarre, who (as if by contrast to John II, nicknamed 'the Good') has gone down in history as 'the Bad'. He too had a claim to the French throne. He had inherited the kingdom of Navarre through his mother, who was the daughter of Louis X. As daughter of the eldest son, if the French throne too could pass through the female line as Edward argued, she gave Charles a better claim than Edward. But the resources of Navarre were nothing like those of England, and Charles vented his frustration by muddying the turbulent waters of French politics throughout his lifetime. Unfortunately for John II, he inherited the kingdom of Navarre a year before John himself came to the throne, along with a handful of fiefs in Normandy. His mother should have inherited Champagne while she was still a child, a huge territory in eastern France, but her uncle, Philip V, had deprived her of it, and the Norman estates were a poor compensation.

None of this would have been serious had not Charles been the ultimate self-seeking politician, charming, witty and eloquent, a small, highly ambitious man, with the ability to win over great nobles or the common people to his cause. Soon after inheriting Navarre, he married John II's daughter and thus became part of the inner circle of John's court. But he had no great estates to keep him occupied – he visited Navarre only for his coronation, and thereafter avoided it for the next decade – and neither power nor position at court. His mother's loss of Champagne still rankled, and he was too ambitious to be content with anything less than a major and powerful role in French political life.

John was generous, to the despair of his treasury, but not always in the right way. Charles desperately needed money and estates and was promised both by John; but neither the lordships which were rightfully his nor the cash was forthcoming.

Furthermore, John was lavishing gifts on his favourite, a Spaniard called Charles de la Cerda, great-grandson of Alfonso X of Castile. His father had been the rightful heir to the Spanish throne, but had never been able to make good his claim against his brother, Sancho IV. Charles himself was a good soldier, and was making his way in the world as a commander: he seems to have been in charge of the Castilian galleys at the battle off Winchelsea in 1350. In 1352, among John's lavish gifts to him was the county of Angoulême, which had been exchanged by Charles of Navarre's mother for the lands they had never received in Normandy. Charles of Navarre's quarrel with Charles de la Cerda dates from this point; these two proud and arrogant characters were obvious rivals. The court quickly divided into two factions, and Charles of Navarre began to bring in Navarrese troops: if Navarre was poor in revenues, it had a high population, and was a natural source of hardy soldiers, who sought their fortunes elsewhere. He was intent on recovering the Norman lands to which he was entitled, and by 1353 there was a serious threat of civil war. But Charles of Navarre's first objective was to remove the man he saw as the obstacle to his advancement, and his brother Philip deliberately picked a quarrel with de la Cerda at the royal court at Christmas, during which weapons were drawn and insults exchanged. Barely two weeks later, Charles de la Cerda was assassinated by mercenaries led by Philip of Navarre, who trapped him in his bedroom in an inn in southern Normandy.

It was the beginning of a career of treachery, double-crossing and alliances and treaties made and broken which was to last for thirty years. Charles of Navarre seriously damaged John II's ability to rebuild the French military effort in the years before Poitiers; the exasperated king finally seized him in April 1356, and he was held in prison until he escaped in the chaos after the defeat at Poitiers. Once again his activities undermined attempts to restore some sort of order to the French kingdom. He was still actively scheming during the prince of Wales's expedition to Spain in 1367.

THE FRENCH ROYAL COUNCIL AND THE KING'S ADMINISTRATION

Charles of Navarre in himself would have been a serious obstacle to French success, but he was a symbol of the deeper weakness of the French kings. The emergence of a strong administration led by a council largely drawn from its ranks was theoretically an ideal structure for supporting the French royal power; but it largely sidelined the aristocracy who had until then been the king's advisers, separated the military and civil leadership, and meant that the court had become a largely ceremonial affair. In the face of defeat, it was the nobles who were blamed for military disaster, not only by the populace at large, but also by the civil servants in Paris. The atmosphere surrounding John II was poisoned with accusations and suspicions, and the king himself was far from immune from them.

When John II was captured at Poitiers, the dauphin Charles attempted to act as regent in the turbulent aftermath. He faced the hostility of the citizens of Paris during three years of violence in which the city fell variously under the control of the reforming 'Council of Eighty', the partisans of the king of Navarre, and the provost, Étienne Marcel. After the latter's death at the hands of the mob he had once encouraged, Charles managed to rebuild, slowly, a semblance of orderly governance; but he himself was tainted by his flight from the battlefield at Poitiers. Just as he was beginning the work of reconstruction, he was taken ill, an illness which left him too weak to wield a weapon; ten years later he was unable to ride a horse, and the sickness recurred at intervals for the rest of his life. But he was far more astute than his father and grandfather, and had one great ambition: to drive the English out of France. He pursued this single-mindedly for the whole of his reign, ignoring all the tenets of knightly superiority, and recruiting like-minded advisers, shrewd political operators who formed the new administration. Soon after he came to the throne, he sent one of his council to the count of Foix. They met at a small village on the northern border of the count's territories, and talked privately in a garden by the river. It so happened that one of the prince of Wales's agents was in the neighbouring garden, and overheard the entire conversation, which set out Charles's strategy in detail, and wrote at once to report it to his master. In summary, the councillor declared, Charles would respond favourably to English proposals until he had recovered all the hostages for John's ransom who were still in England, and then 'he would make war everywhere on the English and on the principality [of Aquitaine], because ... King Charles will be emperor and will recover everything lost to the English and finally he will destroy them'.[25]

In England, Edward's inner circle of advisers was consistent throughout his reign, the only dramatic changes being in the crisis of 1340/41; even then, Archbishop Stratford, who was dismissed as leader of the regency council, was on good terms with the king two years later, and there was an orderly succession to the great offices of state. In France, the king's council and the great officers of state who might have provided some degree of continuity between the reigns of Philip, John and Charles failed to do so. A handful of loyal servants remained in office for long periods, but the membership of the council was often as much a political plaything as the composition of the royal court.

Part of the problem was that the French royal family was much more numerous. Edward III had only one brother, John of Eltham, who died without children in 1336, and two sisters, both of whom married abroad. By 1340, his only surviving cousins were the Bohun brothers Humphrey and William, the earls of Hereford and Northampton, both good friends of the king and staunchly loyal to him. By contrast, the French king had numerous close relatives, as we have seen in the convoluted history of the claims to the French throne. Even if they were not in a position to claim the throne, the royal peers pursued their own agenda. On a personal level, they regarded Philip VI as 'first among equals'; he had been one of them before he became king, whereas Edward had always been heir to the throne, and thus set apart. Geographically, the problems of ruling distant provinces were obviously much greater in France, and the structure of the kingdom was that of a tightly held centre, the ancient royal domains around Paris, with a loose ring of semi-independent territories extending outwards from that centre.

The twelve peerages of France went back to Charlemagne's time, and the 'twelve peers' appear in the epic *Song of Roland* as the leaders of his army and his councillors. When Louis X had died in 1316, there were six ecclesiastical peers, and six dukes and counts who were lay peers, holding the great fiefs of Burgundy, Aquitaine, Flanders, Brittany, Artois and Anjou. In the troubled succession of the next decade, a further eight peerages were created, and this process continued until 1360, when the total of lay peerages reached twenty-four. Many of these peerages were territorially as large as or larger than the duchy of Lancaster, the greatest of the English lordships, and far more independent.

The leading figures in the French royal council under Philip were, at the outset, those peers who had backed his claim to the throne together with the leading crown servants from his predecessor's day, who included Pierre Roger, later to become Pope Clement VI. By 1335, the dominant figure was Mile de Noyers, an elder statesman among the French administrators. Born in 1270, he had a distinguished military career, and had fought in the Flemish wars from 1302 onwards: he was marshal of France from 1303 onwards. At Mons-en-Pévèle, he had saved the sacred French standard, the *oriflamme*, and it was he who alerted Philip to the surprise attack by the Flemish at Cassel in 1328. He was one of Louis X's executors, and a valued councillor under his two successors. Charles de la Cerda had been brought up under his tutelage. He was from northern Burgundy, and was close to the duke, Eudes IV; the Burgundian influence on Philip's council was resented by the other peers, but Noyers was astute enough to keep a relatively low profile, and never to appear to be the sole author of royal policy, though at times this was in fact true. He is said to have warned Philip against engaging the English at Crécy. Noyers was one of the very few figures in the administration who offered some kind of continuity.

After the disaster at Crécy, the royal council began to meet with much greater frequency, and there was an attempt to set up a commission of reform to deal with the causes of the defeat and the weakness of the government. However, after the fall of Calais, the three abbots who had been charged with this task were replaced by career civil servants, because the reforms had not produced results quickly enough to avert Philip's humiliating withdrawal. The council continued to meet very regularly, and from 1348 onwards John II, then duke of Normandy, was in effective charge of the government. It was at this point that Charles de la Cerda first appears as John's closest confidant. However, the council was to prove a weakness rather than a strength: it was more powerful than the informal English council, and nearer to those in Castile and Hungary, ruled by French dynasties.[26]

THE FRENCH COMMANDERS
AND THE FRENCH ARMY

In England, the royal household knights formed an influential group, not because of their specific office, but because they were the close companions of the king and were, so to speak, the pool of talent from which his commanders (and councillors) were drawn. In France, the *chevaliers du roi* were much less important, and were simply a royal bodyguard. This was mainly due to the far greater number of high-ranking magnates in France, who expected to hold high office under the king. Edward, on the other hand, had to create magnates in order to lead his armies. However, military offices were often held by lesser lords: the counts of Eu, both named Raoul, constables in succession from 1329 to 1350, had relatively modest estates in north-eastern France, and the large ransom demanded for the second of them after he was captured at Caen in 1346 reflected his military importance rather than his wealth. Charles de la Cerda and Jacques de Bourbon, their successors, were both members of the royal family, but were able commanders who had earned a good reputation before their appointment. Neither had had experience of a major campaign or a major battle. After Poitiers, where Walter de Brienne, appointed constable earlier that year, was killed, the post went to Robert Moreau de Fiennes, about whom relatively little is known, other than a minor role in the counter-attacks on Calais in 1347. He held the post until 1370, when he resigned in favour of Bertrand du Guesclin, the nemesis of the English armies in the last years of Edward III.

Bertrand du Guesclin is the most successful figure among the French commanders, accorded heroic status in the epic poem written about him by Cuvelier shortly after his death in 1380. He came from the kind of family which, on both sides of the Channel, often produced distinguished soldiers: a knightly family of small resources, where an ambitious young man could only make his way in the world by winning a reputation in the field. His forebears played their part in local politics and local campaigns, and most of them were knights: Bertrand himself was knighted at the relatively advanced age of thirty-four. The first trace of his military career is only a year earlier, in the Breton war between Charles de Blois and Jean de Montfort, but it was he who in 1356 inflicted a major defeat on Henry of Grosmont by his successful defence of the city of Rennes, the first reverse that the English commander had ever suffered. It was this that made his reputation: rewarded with £200 for his 'loyal and profitable services to the king in the war and in the defence of Rennes',[27] he was made captain of Mont-Saint-Michel. He fought against the English in the Reims campaign of 1359–60, and then returned to his home territory as the king's lieutenant in southern Normandy; in 1364 he defeated the English at Cocherel, taking the Anglo-Gascon leader the captal de Buch prisoner: the French fought with the war cry 'Notre-Dame, Guesclin',[28] the count of Auxerre's son, who was nominally in charge, having declined the honour. The tables were turned in the autumn of 1364, when he was defeated, and Charles de Blois killed, at the battle of Auray. Here he was taken prisoner for the third time by the English. He was leader of the free companies who deposed Pedro in 1366, and fought against the prince of Wales and Pedro the following year at Najéra, where he was taken prisoner for the fourth time. In 1370 he became constable, and took charge of the war of attrition which was to lead to serious losses on the part of the English; at his death he was accorded the honour of burial in St Denis near Paris, alongside the French kings.

The constable was overall commander; below him were the marshals; there were four at the time of both Crécy and Poitiers, but there were sometimes as many as six. They often acted as leaders of a campaign or of local forces: Robert Bertrand, who was in charge of the militia who briefly opposed the English landing at La Hogue in 1346, had been deputed to guard the Norman coast, with wholly inadequate resources. His campaigning experience was limited to the French manoeuvres in response to Edward's attack on the Flemish border in 1339–40, but he had commanded successful raids in the Channel, and had taken Guernsey in 1338; he was given the lordship of the Channel Islands, and returned to attempt to take Jersey in 1339. The galleys he was employing were needed for a raid on Gascony, and he had to withdraw in the face of a very small English garrison.

Three marshals stand out: Arnoul d'Audrehem, Jean de Clermont and Jean le Meingre, known as Boucicaut. Audrehem was marshal from 1351 to 1370, and fought at both Poitiers and Najéra. Froissart describes him as serving in Scotland with a contingent sent to reinforce the Scots under the count of Eu in 1332, and returning there in 1340 and 1341.

He fought in Brittany in 1342, and in Aquitaine with John II when he was duke of Normandy in 1346. He became the royal captain at Angoulême in 1349, and was captured in a skirmish with the English in 1351. He was appointed marshal in that year, and played a very active role in the next five years, firstly in the south-west and then in Normandy, where du Guesclin served under him, and was knighted in his presence; but he was also among the party who arrested Charles of Navarre in April 1356. He was given custody of him, and rewarded with an annual income of 1,000 *livres tournois*.

Poitiers was his first major battle, and the disagreement between him and Jean de Clermont, the other marshal, was one of the major factors in the French defeat. Clermont argued for caution, realizing that, if the English were prevented from moving south towards their own territory, shortage of supplies might force them to surrender. Audrehem's wish for an immediate attack was fulfilled, and he was captured, while Clermont fought to the death. Audrehem remained for the most part in England until agreement was reached on his ransom, which was to be paid by John II, in 1362; Edward evidently admired him, since he was granted a pension on his departure. He spent the next five years trying to control the free companies in Languedoc, but became commander, with du Guesclin, of these very same men on the Spanish expedition of 1366 in support of Henry of Trastamara.

Jean le Meingre also had experience of English captivity; he was taken prisoner three times, the third being at Romorantin in the month before the battle of Poitiers, in the year that he was appointed marshal. He had fought in Gascony from 1349 to 1352, and had been captured in minor engagements at Lusignan and Agen. In 1355 he was still on parole for ransom, and was unable to take up arms against Edward when the king made a foray from Calais in November of that year, but he was able to enter the English camp freely, and to report on the strength of the English army. Neither side, however, was strong enough to risk a battle. Despite a great reputation for prowess and knightly exploits, his military record lacks any notable campaigns or successes.

The French constables and marshals were not without experience in the field; indeed, they were often under arms for long periods, but they had never had the chance to learn hard lessons on the battlefield similar to Edward's ventures in Scotland in the 1330s, and, because few of them fought more than once in a formal battle, they failed to get the measure of the English tactics. John II used the technique of dismounting his knights at Poitiers on the advice of the Scottish knight William Douglas, but that in itself was not enough: the English commanders in a similar situation would have known that to attack an army which had entrenched itself in a reasonably strong position on a hillside was to invite disaster, particularly with knights unused to entering the action on foot. By comparison with the English leaders, those in charge of the French army were mostly – through no fault of their own – lacking in military skills.

The English army after 1342 had a strong and resilient structure, based on the recruitment of retinues by the knights, bannerets and lords who were to fight with them. In effect, the leaders of the units of the army were able to choose their men. The French still relied heavily on the *arrière-ban*, a summons invoking the general duty of all able-bodied men to fight in the defence of the kingdom: it was proclaimed seven times between 1338 and 1356. (It is fair to say, that in the same circumstances, faced with an invading French army, the English kings might also have used the feudal summons.) The problem was that these generalized summonses were much less effective: the structure of the army was much looser, and with the *arrière-ban* it was more difficult to exercise control over the disparate levies that arrived in response to the summons. For a start, service could be commuted by payment of what was a kind of war tax; this was particularly true of the non-noble participants, who would be assessed at so many men at arms for a number of hearths. They could – but rarely did – recruit the men at arms themselves and send them off to the army; or they could pay a set rate per man at arms. The results of the *arrière-ban* were therefore to some extent unpredictable, and matters were further complicated by those communities which chose to send their own men. The militia from the towns were unreliable into the bargain: at Crécy, only the men from Orléans stayed with the army for the actual battle. The towns also had their own crossbowmen, for the purposes of defence; these troops were much more valuable than the infantry, and continued to be sent once the attempt to get some military value out of the town militias had been abandoned.

It was primarily on the great nobles – as in England – that the core of recruitment depended. The use of the *arrière-ban* did not cover the feudal obligations of the nobles, but the feudal summons was always used alongside it. The system of written contracts (letters of retinue) was used in France in similar form to that in England, but because the French were fighting a defensive war, it was rare for the length of service to be specified: there was a period for which a first payment was made (the *prêt*) followed by an indefinite time served for wages (*caissement*). The actual rates of pay were not dissimilar, but the *prêt* was less generous than the *regard* paid in England. Furthermore, wages in France were not payable by the leader of a retinue or company, but were left to the king's war treasurers, who were renowned for the slowness of their payments;[29] the English system meant that the war was funded by a number of relatively wealthy individuals, who were either able to use their influence to get payment, or could afford to help the king by waiting for settlement.

In England, the recruitment areas were a very simple division between north and south, those who fought in Scotland and those who fought on the Continent. The French had a number of fronts on which they might be fighting, and recruited accordingly. In 1340 Philip had three theatres of war: Flanders, the Norman coast and Gascony, and later in the reign Brittany became another area of engagement. Recruitment was much more local, and even in the main army that assembled at Bouvines in 1340, the majority of the French contingent, 60 per cent of the troops, were from the north of the Loire. What was more striking was that one-third of the whole army consisted of knights from outside France – mostly from the borders of the German-speaking lands nearest to France. The French were used to using mercenaries, and had done regularly since the twelfth century: the large groups of Genoese crossbowmen and galley crews were the most prominent of these. The lords and the knights of the Holy Roman Empire came in smaller groups, but some of these came from families with a long tradition of service in France.

The cohesion of the French armies was undoubtedly weaker than that of the English in the two major battles of the period. The French army that fought at Crécy in 1346 consisted of four elements: the French feudal nobility and their retinues, the troops from the Holy Roman Empire, including Philip's allies and the traditional hired knights, the infantry from the towns summoned under the *arrière-ban*, and the Genoese crossbowmen. Philip had gathered his forces as best he could on hearing of the English landing, but there seems to have been little organization beforehand. The first gathering point was Rouen at the end of July, by which time the English had been in the field for three weeks; one of the reasons that Philip was not prepared to give battle in early August was that his full complement of men had not yet arrived, and some had come reluctantly, 'amazingly ill-armed'.[30] When Philip withdrew towards Paris, he was still receiving reinforcements, and the final rendezvous point was on the march north, at Amiens. Even so, large contingents had not reached the army by the time of the battle; they arrived in disorderly fashion on the day after the main action and were in turn overcome by superior English forces.

The leaders of the French army were the king and three great lords, his brother Charles d'Alençon, his nephew Louis de Blois and his cousin Louis de Nevers, count of Flanders. The largest foreign contingent was led by King John of Bohemia and his son Charles. The constable of France, Raoul count of Eu, who should have been the overall commander of the army, was not present for the simple reason that he had been captured earlier in the campaign. In his absence, his duties on the field were fulfilled by the marshals, of whom there were four at the time: Robert Bertrand, the commander who had failed to prevent the English landing at La Hogue, and three others, who may or may not have been there: Charles de Montmorency, Robert de Waurin and Guy de Nesle. The core of the French army had gathered in Paris about three weeks earlier, but the bulk of the army that arrived on the battlefield had only been together since Amiens, which it had left on 23 August, and reinforcements had probably arrived during the march. There had been no time for proper organization, or for an array of troops on the day of the battle itself, and the undisciplined nature of the French attack implies that this was not a coherent fighting force, but a loosely grouped set of units. The size of the French armies, consistently larger than the English, and the fact that there were ten separate battalions to control, required a far stronger command structure and left little room for improvisation if matters were not to get out of hand. The issue was further complicated by the way in which men were allocated to the different battalions: on arrival at the assembly point for the army, their mounts and equipment would be inspected, and they would then be told which battalion to join. As the bulk of the army were often individual knights, there were none of the links that existed within an English retinue, and very little *esprit de corps*.

At Poitiers a decade later, the problems were of a different nature. The large size of the army was possibly less of a disadvantage, but the army had again assembled in an ad hoc fashion, and only moved as a body on 6 September, when the king left Chartres. The results of three months of effort, with the *arrière-ban* proclaimed no less than three times, were unimpressive; the treasury was empty, and the knights knew that they might well serve for a very delayed reward. The shortage of money also meant that there was little hope of attracting the imperial knights who had been present in large numbers at Crécy. There were far too many infantry, largely of poor quality, and not enough mounted troops. A planned campaign in Gascony against the prince of Wales by the count of Poitiers had been cancelled, and his army, such as it was, was instructed to move northwards to hold the Loire against the prince until such time as the king's army could join it. The two armies met on 10 September, and therefore fought the battle only nine days after they had first come together, and only a fortnight after the royal army had moved off from Chartres. The morale of the French was an important factor in the battle; most of the troops led by Philip duke of Orléans and other battalions left the field without striking a blow, perhaps because they had seen the dauphin Charles being escorted to safety. An army with better cohesion would not have done this.

The English army had become skilled on the battlefield, and the lessons learnt at Crécy and Poitiers would be remembered at Agincourt; but battles alone did not win wars, and the English triumphs were countered, after terrible civil disturbances, by a system which used the vast resources of the French monarchy to deploy proper defences and to ensure good government. The English were unable to follow up their great victories in 1346 and 1356 by establishing themselves across wide areas in France which would recognize Edward's rule. The Reims campaign of 1359–60 was intended to produce a *coup d'état*, the coronation of Edward III as king of France, rather than a conquest, but the French defeated Edward by strengthening their towns and stubbornly refusing the lure of knightly glory on the battlefield.

5

'As it was in the days of King Arthur'

We left Edward at the low point of his career in the spring of 1341, his unjustified attacks on the regency administration set aside, and apparently facing serious resistance to his plans. However, by the autumn of that year all the restrictions imposed by parliament had been reversed. On 1 October Edward boldly annulled the legislation, on the grounds that he had been coerced into signing it. Behind this lay a swift personal campaign by Edward to regain the allegiance of the great magnates who had ranged themselves against him. It says much for his personality that he was able to do this, in the face of the record of military failure over the previous three years.

An element in this, which has not previously been noted, seems to have been a series of tournaments held during 1341; the records are almost certainly incomplete, but at least four tournaments are known to have taken place. They began shortly after Edward's return, before the crisis had come to a head. The king celebrated Christmas at Guildford, in Henry III's palace, which had belonged to the queens of England since 1273, and had reverted to the crown after 1330. It was still magnificent, though in need of repairs, with elaborate decoration and glazed windows, and a series of separate apartments for the king, the queen and their son; many rooms had fireplaces, and there were two chapels and a garden with a cloister.[1] He then held a tournament at Reading, followed by another at King's Langley on 2 February, where he knighted a number of Gascon nobles, who had probably come over with Oliver Ingham, the seneschal of Aquitaine, at the end of January. The next tournament was planned while Edward was at King's Langley, and was the traditional Shrovetide occasion to mark the beginning of Lent; it was to be held at Norwich on 20 February and no other tournaments were to be fought in the mean while.[2] The tournament was fought outside the gates of Norwich priory, and Robert Morley, who has contributed so much to the victory at Sluys, was among the participants. The parson of Scole remembered half a century later that he had seen the hero of the hour at those jousts.[3] And another traditional joust was held to mark the churching of Queen Philippa at King's Langley, after the birth of Edmund, her fifth son. This may well have been the first occasion on which William Montagu and Robert Ufford reappeared in the lists after their captivity in France, since the king's team fought bearing shields with the arms of Montagu and Ufford quartered.[4] The king was frequently at King's Langley during the year, and it is difficult to pinpoint the exact date, particularly as he seems to have been hunting there and at Woodstock as well as jousting. The accounts for the year record magnificent hunting costumes, all of green or mulberry Turkish cloth. These were seemingly for just one occasion, the 'king's hunting expedition', on which Edward was accompanied by eleven earls and knights, fifteen royal squires, Queen Isabella, Queen Philippa and four countesses.[5]

The following year, 1342, saw three major festivals.[6] The first was held at Dunstable at Shrovetide, and was specifically to mark the betrothal of Lionel of Antwerp, Edward's third son (at the tender age of three), to the heiress of the earl of Ulster. It may also have been intended to celebrate the recent truce with the Scots, as it was announced as soon as the truce was agreed. The king fought as a simple knight, alongside 'all the younger earls of the kingdom'. The earls of Gloucester, Devon and Surrey excused themselves on the grounds of age, while Richard Fitzalan and William Clinton were ill. Knights came from not only the south, but all parts of England, though no foreign knights were present; the total was more than 200, which was probably why proceedings did not start until it was almost nightfall, 'hindering the whole business so that ten horses were killed or injured'. [7]

This was followed two months later by an event at Northampton on 10 April. The tournament was on a smaller scale, but was marred by the death of John, Lord Beaumont, brother-in-law of Henry of Grosmont; fatalities in Edward's tournaments were rare, but something evidently went badly wrong, since many other nobles were seriously injured and maimed, and many horses were lost. Two months later, in July, the visit to England of Edward's brother-in-law, William II, count of Hainault, was marked by a tournament at Eltham Palace near London. Unfortunately, it was William himself who was injured on this occasion, breaking his arm.[8]

All these tournaments were good publicity, a means of rallying the great lords and the wealthy citizens behind him; and this harmony between the king and his magnates was to last until the very end of his reign. Edward's frequent appearances as *miles simplex*, a simple knight, emphasized his solidarity with the leading lords of the kingdom, fighting alongside them on equal terms. The king had not only made himself the chief promoter of the sport of jousting, once a potential rallying point for dissenting barons, but had made it one of his best methods of keeping the nobles on his side. And there was now the prospect of a new and more promising strategy in France. Instead of a full-scale invasion of France, Edward preferred for the moment to achieve his ends by stirring up trouble between Philip VI and his vassals. In a sense, this had already begun when Edward sheltered Robert d'Artois; Edward's proclamation of himself as rightful king of France meant that anyone who went over to his side was simply recognizing his claim. Any disgruntled vassal could offer his allegiance to Edward if he felt it was worth his while.

Although the truce of Esplechin was extended until June 1342, Edward was not going to miss any opportunities, and Adam Murimuth noted that, at the same time as the extension was negotiated, 'Edward and some of his earls were nonetheless making great arrangements for ships and victuals for an overseas expedition'.[9] Edward, acting in his right as king of France, backed the young heir of Brittany, Jean de Montfort, in his claim to the duchy, in opposition to Philip's candidate, his nephew Charles de Blois. There was little to choose between the rivals, because the previous duke of Brittany, Jean III, had tried to disinherit Jean de Montfort, who was his half-brother, in favour of his niece Jeanne, married to Philip's nephew, only to change his mind shortly before he died. Philip regarded this as an internal affair, though he knew that military action would provoke English intervention, and undeclared war followed in Brittany in 1341. Philip did all he could to prise Brittany from the English grasp without actually mounting a campaign. Edward recruited important allies among the French nobility, Olivier Clisson and Godefroy d'Harcourt, and was able to recruit disaffected nobles in Gascony, while his Breton allies continued a guerrilla war against the French. Jean de Montfort was himself an English magnate, since he was heir to the earldom of Richmond.

Although military aid was agreed in the autumn of 1341, Jean de Montfort himself was captured in late November, and it was left to the countess, his wife Jeanne de Montfort, to rally his supporters. It was the following year before a small force under Walter Mauny sailed to support the Montfortists, with instructions to secure the westernmost ports for the two expeditions which were to follow later in the year. He landed at Brest; his troops consisted of 128 knights and squires, and 200 mounted archers,[10] while Charles de Blois had a substantial army in the field, and had already taken the eastern cities of Nantes and Rennes. The countess had established her headquarters at Hennebont, and shortly after Mauny's arrival was besieged by the French army. The French started to skirmish with the garrison, but were driven back, at which point a full-scale, disorderly assault on the town was ordered. This ended with a counter-attack by the garrison, who burnt the French camp, but the French returned soon afterwards. The siege became a series of intermittent attacks and eventually simply an attempt to starve out the defenders. Jean le Bel (and Froissart after him) devotes his account of the campaign of 1342 largely to an account of Walter Mauny's exploits. These are certainly splendid embroideries of the real facts: while there is no evidence to counter the idea that he appeared at Hennebont to encourage the countess in her resistance, it is unlikely that he got into the castle and led sorties against the French as a kind of pre-dinner entertainment, as Le Bel would have us believe. His activities were low key, given his small resources, but did include an enterprising raid to capture one of the leading French supporters of Charles de Blois, Hervé lord of Léon. Mauny handed him over to Edward III, who gave him to Montagu to guard, and then used him, along with the captured Scottish regent, Andrew Murray, to secure Montagu's release from his oath never to fight again in France.

Mauny returned home in July to report that the Montfortist cause was in serious trouble. Charles de Blois had recruited reinforcements, who reached Brittany early in July, and forced the countess to abandon Hennebont and flee to Brest, where she was besieged by them from mid-August onwards. She had some English soldiers with her, led by Hugh Despenser (son of Edward II's notorious favourite), who had come into one of the Breton ports on his way to Gascony with Oliver Ingham, and had found the situation so desperate that he decided to stay. A month later, a second, much-delayed English expedition under William Bohun,

Ralph Stafford and Robert d'Artois sailed into the great harbour at Brest and surprised the fourteen Genoese galleys at anchor there. Eleven were burnt, and three escaped upstream where the English ships could not follow.[11] Bohun's fleet was large for the number of men it carried: almost half the ships were intended for naval actions. So the French grossly overestimated the army he led, and at once raised the siege, retreating to the north and east, and leaving the Montfort party in control of western Brittany.

It was the only real success of the year. Bohun attempted to follow it up by securing a port which would be more accessible from England, on the northern coast of Brittany: to reach Brest, the fleet had had to round cape Finisterre, heading south into the Atlantic and then east into the harbour. Morlaix, thirty miles away, could be reached without this difficult passage, as it lay north-east of the cape. But the defenders were on the alert by the time Bohun moved against the town, and he had to settle down to a long siege while he waited for the third expedition, under Edward himself, to arrive.

On 29 September Bohun's scouts reported the arrival of a French army. Charles de Blois had come to raise the siege, and Bohun risked being caught between troops sallying out of the town and the advancing enemy. That night, he moved his men to a site near a wood. His men dismounted, and fought in a solid phalanx with their backs to the trees. Bohun, a veteran of the Scottish wars, does not seem to have used the usual tactic of placing archers on the flanks, as he had too few men; instead, he dug pits in front of the line, and camouflaged them with greenery from the woods behind his position. The French vanguard, led by Geoffroy de Charny, were unable to reach the English line in good order because of these traps, and were thrown back; a second charge met with the same fate, and the French fled. Fifty French knights were killed, and about 150 captured. The fight at Morlaix was the fiercest encounter with the French before the battle of Poitiers, according to Geoffrey le Baker.[12] The result was indecisive: although the French cavalry were driven off, the English had to take refuge in the forest to avoid the large numbers of enemy troops in the area.

There had been huge problems in gathering the fleet for the king's expedition, and Edward had been at Sandwich since the end of August. He was hoping to employ the ships that had returned from transporting

Bohun's army, but half of these deserted, and a desperate search for boats, even small ones, ensued. When Edward finally sailed on 3 October, his luck in crossing the Channel for once deserted him. He later claimed that whenever he sailed for his kingdom of France the wind was always with him; it was only when he tried to return that he met storms and gales. But this time it took him three weeks, and some of his troops had to be marched to Portsmouth to embark.[13]

When he at last reached Brittany at the end of October, his plan was to retake Vannes, on the south coast of Brittany, which, like Brest, had a good harbour, and was in the centre of the territories where support for the Montforts was strong. Walter Mauny was sent to reconnoitre, and reported that there were potential faults in the defences which looked promising. However, by the time Edward arrived in late November, the defenders were very much on the alert. Edward had left the English fleet under the command of Robert d'Artois, the man who had been one of the key factors in triggering the Anglo-French war. He took the ships south, sailing past Vannes, and attacked the galleys from Castile and Genoa whose services the French had engaged. He was driven off, losing both large numbers of ships and many of his men; but undeterred he headed back to Vannes and, again entirely on his own initiative, attempted a surprise attack, which proved fatal both to him and to Edward's plans. At first it almost succeeded, but he did not have enough men to follow up his advantage, and was wounded in the fray. He encamped nearby, caught dysentery and died, cursed by the French and not greatly loved by the English.

The foray by Artois meant that any hope of surprising Vannes was lost, and Edward had to settle in for a winter siege. The small size of his force, no more than 5,000 men, meant that his options were limited, but Bohun's men operated as raiders and attacked Nantes itself with the help of Thomas Beauchamp and his retinue in December, while Montagu led a handful of men to raid the area round Dinan in the north-east. The English had made their presence felt the length and breadth of Brittany, but desperately needed reinforcements if they were to hold their gains, since a French army under John duke of Normandy was on its way. But the bad weather and difficulties of recruitment which had hampered the year's operations continued: the army which was meant to leave Plymouth on 3 November failed to do so because of a lack of ships, and was then driven ashore on the Scilly Isles. Hugh Audley and

Laurence Hastings managed to cross with their personal retinues, but in the interval 400 Welsh troops had come to the end of their contracted term and had returned home.

When the French forces eventually reached Brittany in January 1343, they came within twenty miles of Edward's army, but then refused to commit themselves to a battle. The pope had sent two cardinals to Brittany the previous summer in an attempt to secure a truce, and both sides were now prepared to talk to them. Edward was able to conceal the weakness of his position, and managed to retain all the lands he had taken during the year; Vannes was to be neutral for the duration of the truce; and Jean de Montfort was to be released by the French. The truce was intended to last until 29 September 1346.

Edward never returned to Brittany, and the war there was largely carried on by a series of commanders of lesser rank, who became specialists in Breton affairs, men such as John Hardreshull, William Latimer and Thomas Dagworth; William Bohun was to return in the summer of 1345, and in 1354–58 Thomas Holland and Henry of Grosmont were named as the king's lieutenants in Brittany. It remained an important but rather separate theatre of war, and after the war of 1341–3 the only other member of Edward's inner circle of commanders to appear there was John Chandos.

Edward did not take seriously the avowed reason for the truce, which was to enable a peace conference to take place at Avignon. At the end of 1343, although there were no specific plans for a campaign in France, Edward was anticipating renewed fighting; he refused to take the peace talks seriously, sending junior government clerks to meet the French princes of the realm, while supporting the partisans in Brittany. He sent Bartholomew Burghersh the elder to the parliament of May 1343 to explain the situation: and when parliament reconvened in June, the grant of a subsidy specifically stated that 'the many things attempted on the part of the enemy ... were declared in full parliament: and how his said enemy strives as much as he can to destroy our said lord the king, his allies and subjects, lands and places, and the English language'. Edward had neatly extended what was once a dispute over rival claims to the throne of France to cover the very existence of Englishness itself.[14]

Although the next two years brought very mixed success, the effect on French politics was considerable. Philip's relations with his great lords were much less congenial than Edward's; and he reacted violently.

It was at this point that Olivier Clisson was seized on a visit to Paris and summarily executed. His execution may have been politically expedient, but the manner in which it was carried out sent the wrong message to other French nobles who might have a quarrel with Philip: the king was not to be trusted. By 1343, Edward could see the prospect of being able to renew the French war with the aid of disaffected French lords rather than expensive, non-committal foreign allies.

It was clear that the task of gathering an army would not be easy. He had to persuade parliament to vote yet another tax for the purposes of the war, and he had only Flanders on his side on the Continent, which meant that his army would have to be raised almost entirely from within England. The Breton situation was too confused to expect any substantial force from his supporters there, and Gascony needed all the troops he could spare, whether local or English. A measure of the problems he faced is that in 1345, when the Crécy campaign was being planned, he introduced a special bonus for the English men at arms who fought overseas, while on the other hand he introduced a new method of assessing the military liabilities of landowners by relating it to their income.

All this implies deep concern about the levels of recruiting, and Edward enlisted knightly ideals as a means of solving the problem, announcing a great tournament at Windsor in January 1344. At the end of the festival, he declared that he would create a new knightly institution on the model of King Arthur's Round Table, which would also serve as a body of knights personally loyal to him, just as the members of the legendary order owed loyalty to Arthur. This was a strikingly original move, since the idea of a permanent association of knights was almost unknown, and Edward himself had not sought to identify himself with the legendary king until this point.

Contrary to general belief, there is little in the early part of Edward's reign to indicate that he was deeply interested in the Arthurian legend. His grandfather, Edward I, has been described as an 'Arthurian enthusiast',[15] and his involvement in the conquest of Wales was the driving force behind this idea. His Arthurian tournaments and the creation of the Round Table at Winchester all date from the period when he finally defeated Llywelyn the Great. The knighting ceremonies and tournament at Winchester in September 1285, which were the occasion for the making of the Round Table which still hangs in the castle hall, were a direct response to the aftermath of the Welsh wars, designed to impress his subjects and justify the heavy taxes they had paid to support the king's armies.[16] (Ironically, it was on this occasion that Hugh Despenser, the bane of Edward III's youth, was knighted.) After an earlier victory over Llywelyn in 1278, he went to Glastonbury and had the supposed remains of Arthur and Guinevere reinterred before the high altar, 'while the heads and knee-joints of both were kept out for the people's devotion'.[17] In 1284, before his return to England after the final conquest of Wales, he had held a tournament at Nefyn, once a court of the Welsh princes, where the prophecies of Merlin were said to have been found. In 1285, he presented Arthur's crown, which had been surrendered to him by the Welsh when they submitted to him, to Westminster abbey.[18] And he had used Arthur's supposed overlordship of Scotland when arguing his claim for sovereignty over the Scots in a personal letter to the pope in 1301.[19]

Edward III's association with Arthur is much slighter. He went to Glastonbury in 1331, accompanied by Philippa: we have two eyewitness accounts of their visit, but neither makes any mention of the relics of Arthur. He was there again in May 1344; although a royal writ was issued a year later for a certain John Blome of London to search at Glastonbury for the remains of Joseph of Arimathea, there is no evidence to connect the licence with the king's visit to Glastonbury.[20] And he seems to have played no part in the repositioning of Arthur's tomb by Abbot Monington in 1368.[21] Indeed, the supposed Arthurian enthusiasms of Edward III fit better, for the most part, into an effort to emulate his grandfather rather than something he himself felt keenly. It was the chroniclers who were eager to see him as the reincarnation of King Arthur: Jean le Bel compares him to Arthur at the end of the Scottish wars, not because of his military achievements but for the social life he led: 'these great feasts and tourneys and jousts and assemblies of ladies earned him such universal esteem that everyone said he was the second King Arthur.' And he repeats this a few lines below: 'he was so loved and honoured by all his people, great and small alike, for the high nobility of his deeds and words and for his great heart and glorious festivities and assemblies of ladies and damsels, that everyone said he was King Arthur.'[22]

Edward III is assumed to have been a great enthusiast for all things Arthurian, largely on the strength of references to him as the 'new Arthur', and his foundation of a Round Table in 1344. However, what interested him was the Arthur of history portrayed in the chronicles, not the heroes of the Arthurian romances. When we look carefully at the evidence for ownership and readership of Arthurian romances at Edward III's court, it is his mother Isabella who is the most enthusiastic collector and reader of such books.[23] There is a list of issues and receipts from the privy wardrobe during the keepership of John Flete, from 1322 to 1341, including many loans of books.[24] Nine books were issued to Isabella on 5 March 1327; of these, one is a copy of the romance of Perceval. At her death in 1358, Isabella possessed books in French on the deeds of Arthur, on Tristan and Iseult, on Perceval and Gawain, and on the Holy Grail (mistranslated as *de sanguine regali*, 'on the royal blood', because the clerk, unfamiliar with the book, read its title as *sang real*).[25] She also borrowed Arthurian romances from John II of France when he was a captive in England in 1357. Thomas of Woodstock, duke of Gloucester, whose huge collection of books is well documented, possessed two romances of the history of Troy, two of that of Alexander (including the copy written in Tournai in 1344 discussed above), a *Merlin*, a *Lancelot* and a book '*of the Tretys of king Arthur*'.[26] This is a relatively modest element in his collection. It has been argued that John Flete's list, which notes a stock of fifty-nine *libri de romanciis*, indicates widespread reading of romances at Edward's court in his youth and in the early years of his reign.[27] However, *romancia* means a book in a romance language, typically French,[28] as well as what we would now call a romance, and, looking at some of the surviving titles, this figure clearly includes histories in French, French versions of Latin treatises and even a 'romance' Old Testament. The only book of romances actually identifiable as Arthurian is the romance of Perceval. It is suggested that the 160 'various books' in John Flete's accounts represent a royal library, but, remembering that this account covers nearly twenty years, this is too small a number. Furthermore, there is very little evidence that books were sent out and returned; in only one case are books delivered into the great wardrobe, by the keeper of the king's chamber, as part of a miscellaneous collection of items.[29] The list is an incidental accumulation of items which have passed through the hands of the keeper of the great wardrobe, not an organized collection of any kind. Many of the Arthurian books can be connected to Isabella, whose interest in Arthurian romance may have been purely personal, and part of her French cultural background.

The second important list which could be evidence for Edward's reading is a list of books which apparently belonged to him at his death, which were in the care of John Bacon, commissioned to deal with his personal property.[30] Isabella's books officially passed to the king, but he gave away at least one to his sister Joan, queen of Scotland, and Bacon's list includes just three Arthurian books, one of which is probably Isabella's romance of Perceval, described as a romance of Perceval and Gawain.[31] Another is a romance of King Arthur, which could be her French prose romance of the death of Arthur, but equally might be a retelling of the historical story of Arthur in French; and the third is 'a book called Galaath [Galahad]', probably the Grail book belonging to Isabella mistitled '*de sanguine regali*'. Of the remaining nine books, two definitely appear on Isabella's list. Edward's interest in Arthurian romance, such as it was, does not seem to have extended to buying or commissioning manuscripts for his own use.

While Arthurian stories and heroes were very much part of Edward's cultural background, they are not a prominent part of the books that he or his descendants owned. Furthermore, ownership of such books is found mainly among the ladies of the court; the Arthurian romances are specifically part of the cultural heritage of his mother and of his wife. Philippa gave him in 1333 as a new year's gift a ewer with figures of heroes: Julius Caesar, Judas Maccabeus, Charlemagne (with Roland and Oliver) and Arthur, Gawain and Lancelot du Lac. And two items in an inventory of 1369 may have come from her household after her death, a cup with Tristan apparently in the forest, and a ewer decorated with the knights of the Round Table.[32]

Edward need not have owned or even read the romances of Arthur to have learnt about the Round Table and its reputation. There is still much debate as to how common what we would call 'reading' today was in the middle ages. Reading silently to oneself in private may have been the least common way in which manuscripts were used. There is a famous miniature of Chaucer reading his poetry to the court of Richard II, and a century earlier Alfonso X of Castile had prescribed that books of knightly deeds should be read aloud at meals at his court, to encourage the practice of arms and knighthood.[33] Such readings, to larger or smaller groups, would have been the most likely source of Edward's knowledge of the romances. Many more general books on history or on the heroes of the past would mention Arthur in passing, as part of the cultural background of the period. Only once do we find evidence of a more particular interest in Arthur on Edward's part, and we have already discussed it: the curious episode of the 'society of Craddok'. Nor were his tournaments Arthurian, in the way that his grandfather's tournaments appear to have been. There are two occasions when we know that Edward's tournaments had themes: in 1343 he and his knights fought disguised as the pope and twelve cardinals; in 1359 they appeared as the mayor and aldermen.[34] Masks were also frequently provided, though whether these were worn in the lists or at the festivities surrounding the jousting is not clear. There is no sign of Arthurian disguises, only the usual exotic figures such as Tartars and wild men.

This does not mean that Arthurian romances and heroes were absent from Edward's cultural background, but there is no question that they figure only occasionally after he became king. His direct knowledge of Arthur was almost certainly very different. In the romances, Arthur is portrayed as a grand but inert figure, who presides over the court but does not take part in the adventures. For most educated men in the fourteenth century he was quite simply the greatest of the kings of Britain. Edward's image of Arthur was that created by Geoffrey of Monmouth in the first part of the twelfth century, a fiction cheerfully copied into sober histories by chroniclers during the intervening period, and very rarely questioned by other scholars. The closest literary representation of Edward's image of Arthur is that of the alliterative *Morte Arthure*, written in the late fourteenth century when memories of his victories and of the bloody slaughter at Crécy were still fresh. It echoes episodes from his wars, but is by no means a *roman-à-clef*. Arthur's campaigns are not modelled on Edward's – or indeed on anyone else's; its real value is in the very different view of the nature of war from that found in the *Lancelot-Grail* and the romances based on it. War is bloodthirsty, and a means to political ambitions which hardly figure in the world of fiction. Edward would also have been aware at second hand of the Arthurian romances, and of the great Arthurian characters such as Lancelot and Guinevere, perhaps through hearing the stories read or told; this aspect of the Arthurian story, however, was something for a disguise at a tournament or a passing reference in one of his *ludi* at court, not for the serious matter of the king's royal image.

Beyond the specific records of book ownership, we can point to a long family tradition of involvement with Arthurian romance before his grandfather's day, stretching back to the first appearance of the stories in the twelfth century. Henry II was said to have been involved in the discovery of Arthur's tomb at Glastonbury in 1189; Richard I gave a sword said to be Excalibur to Tancred of Sicily in 1191.[35] Edward I, according to Rusticiano of Pisa, who wrote an Italian version of the story of Tristan, took a volume of Arthurian romance to Palestine with him when he went on crusade, and it was from this copy that Rusticiano made his translation.[36] And romances could be heirlooms: Edward II rewarded a minstrel who brought him a book of romance which had belonged to Eleanor of Provence, his grandmother, and had been bequeathed by her to Edward I.[37]

We are fortunate in having what may be a first-hand account of the great festival at Windsor in January 1344. Edward deliberately invited not only knights, but also wealthy citizens from London. It is Adam Murimuth who describes the occasion for us; he was probably either one of the London contingent, or heard about it from a friend who had been there. What he has to say is this:

> In this year the lord king ordered a most noble tournament or joust to be held in his birthplace, that is, at Windsor Castle, on 19 January, which he caused to be announced a suitable time in advance both abroad and in England. He sent invitations to all the ladies of the southern part of England and to the wives of the citizens of London. When the earls, barons, knights and a great number of ladies had gathered on the Sunday, 19 January, the king gave a solemn feast, and the great hall of the castle was filled by the ladies, with just two knights among them, the only ones to have come from France to the occasion. At this gathering there were two queens, nine countesses, the wives of the barons, knights and citizens, whom they could not easily count, and to whom the king himself personally allocated their seats according to their rank. The prince of Wales, duke of Cornwall, earls, barons and knights ate with all the other people in tents and other places, where food and all other necessities had been prepared; everything was on a generous scale and served unstintingly. In the evening dancing and various entertainments were laid on in a magnificent fashion. For the three days following, the king with nineteen other knights held jousts against all comers; and the king himself, not because of his kingly rank but because of his great exertions and the good fortune

that he had during the three days, was held to be the best of the defenders. Of the challengers, Sir Miles Stapleton on the first day, Sir Philip Despenser on the second, and Sir John Blount on the third, were awarded the prize.

Another writer, using Murimuth's account as his base, continues with a detailed description of the elaborate founding ceremony for the Round Table:

This feast lasted from Sunday to Wednesday. That night, after the end of the jousts, the king had it proclaimed that no lord or lady should presume to depart, but should stay until morning, to learn the king's pleasure. When the morning of Thursday came, at about nine o'clock the king caused himself to be solemnly arrayed in his most royal and festive attire; his outer mantle was of very precious velvet and the royal crown was placed upon his head. The queen was likewise dressed in most noble fashion. The earls and barons, and the rest of the lords and ladies, prepared themselves in appropriate fashion to go with the king to the chapel in the castle of Windsor and hear mass, as he commanded them to do. When mass had been celebrated, the king left the chapel; Henry earl of Derby, as steward of England, and William earl of Salisbury, as marshal of England, went before him, each carrying the staff of his office in his hand, and the king himself holding the royal sceptre in his hand. There followed him the young queen, and the queen-mother, the prince of Wales, the earls, barons, knights and nobles, with the ladies and all the people flocking to see such an extraordinary spectacle, to the place appointed for the assembly. There the king and all the others at the same time stood up. The king was presented with the Bible, and laying his hand on the Gospels, swore a solemn oath that he himself at a certain time, provided that he had the necessary means, would begin a Round Table, in the same manner and condition as Arthur, formerly king of England, established it, namely to the number of 300 knights, and would cherish it and maintain it according to his power, always adding to the number of knights. The earls of Derby, Salisbury, Warwick, Arundel, Pembroke and Suffolk, the other barons and very many praiseworthy knights of probity and renown likewise made an oath to observe, sustain, and promote the Round Table with all its appendages. When this was done, trumpets and drums sounded together, and the guests hastened to a feast . . .[38]

The spectacular nature of this occasion was duly relayed to Edward's arch-enemy, Philip of France, and a continuation of the official chronicle of the French court gives us the reaction to it. This ends in 1348, so it is almost contemporary with the event:

> When the king was in England again, he proclaimed very great jousts at a castle of his named Windsor. Knights came from all countries to win praise there. He commanded that the Round Table and the adventures of chivalry which had ceased since the days of King Arthur should be revived; but in his heart he was thinking of very different things, which he did not show outwardly. For all this time he was preparing great ships and gathering great provisions at a port of his called Portsmouth.[39]

For the French, this knightly gathering was simply a smokescreen for Edward's active preparation for the renewal of war, though in fact it was not until March that any active steps were taken towards a new campaign.

Most of the other chroniclers who report the event do so much more briefly, and give us only a few additional details. The author of the English version of the *Brut* chronicle, who like Murimuth had London connections, claims that 'of divers lands beyond the sea, were many strangers'. Edward's letter of protection issued before the feasts and addressed to his officials throughout the kingdom makes no mention of overseas participants, referring only to knights and others 'of whatever region or place', but it does seem from the evidence of the *Brut* and St Omer chronicles that there was a large contingent of visitors from the Continent. Few other chroniclers mention the event; only those close to the court would have regarded it as special, more than just another lavish court spectacle.[40]

A much more valuable source of information is the royal accounts. There is relatively little in the records about the preparation for this great gathering, but two telling details do emerge from the archives. Edward had pawned his great crown, his second crown and Queen Philippa's crown in 1339 when he was desperate for money to pay his allies in Flanders. Such transactions were not uncommon, as jewellery was a form of ready cash or security, but to pawn the great crown as well as two others indicates the seriousness of his situation. In 1343 negotiations had begun for its redemption from the archbishop of Treves and Edward's son-in-law the duke of Guelders, although the principal finance had actually been provided by Vivelin Rufus, a Jew from Strasbourg. It seems to have cost around £8,000 to redeem them all.[41] At the end of 1343 the great crown was still in pawn, but by 16 January of the new year Edward had his second crown back, just in time to wear it at the festivities at Windsor, and he paid the negotiators handsomely for their efforts.

It seems that the preparations for the festival were also made in a hurry, as if the decision to hold the festival had been made on the spur of the moment. Major tournaments usually involved lavish expenditure on costumes designed for the occasion, as well as gifts of robes. However, special costumes are not mentioned in the accounts, and any gifts of robes were probably included in the traditional Christmas handout of robes to courtiers a week or two earlier. We do learn that Edward wore two very expensive suits of red velvet, an exotic import, one long and one short, and consisting of six garments in all. An ermine cloak, for which 369 skins were used, and a smaller mantle of 67 skins, may also have been made for the occasion. At the same time as the suits, 118 tunics for the king's squires, men at arms and minstrels were made. The accountants note that seven furriers worked at great speed for three days to complete these.[42]

Despite the haste, these sound like clothes designed to present an image of majesty rather than the theatricality of earlier tournament clothes, embroidered with mottoes and elaborate pictorial designs. Edward was no longer playing the knight errant but was staking his claim to be regarded as a knightly monarch on a par with Arthur himself. And he proposed to create a building of unparalleled size as the home for his new institution. Thomas Walsingham, writing forty years later at St Albans, a monastery which kept a kind of official royal chronicle in the thirteenth and fourteenth centuries, does not actually mention the festival, although he knows the exact dimension of the house of the Round Table:

> In the year of grace 1344, which is the eighteenth year of Edward's reign, King Edward summoned many workers to Windsor Castle and began to build a house which was called 'The Round Table'. Its size from the centre to the circumference, the radius, was 100 feet, and its diameter was therefore 200 feet. The weekly expenses were at first £100, but afterwards, because of news which the king received from France, this was cut back to £9 because he needed a great deal of money for other business.

At the same time, Philip of Valois, king of France, spurred on by what the king of England had done, began to build a round table in his own country, in order to attract the knights of Germany and Italy, in case they set out for the table of the king of England.[43]

What exactly did Edward have in mind when he proclaimed his Round Table in imitation of King Arthur's original? One possibility is that he was thinking of the Arthurian tournaments of his grandfather, such as the Winchester tournament of 1285, which were called 'round tables'. These may have involved some kind of ceremonial and the formation of a temporary society for the purposes of the jousts. These were relatively common from 1220 to 1330, but rare thereafter, perhaps because they were too closely associated with the Mortimer family for comfort, and indeed the antics of Geoffrey Mortimer just after Edward came to the throne may have brought them into disrepute. The author of the *Brut* chronicle writes:

> And about the same time, Sir Geoffrey Mortimer the younger, Mortimer's son, called himself the King of Folly; and he did indeed become the king of folly afterwards, for he was so full of pride and evil ways that he held a round table in Wales for all comers, and imitated the manner and customs of King Arthur's table, but totally failed in his intention, for the noble king Arthur (unlike him) was the most worthy and famous lord in the whole world in his day.[44]

As to the original Round Table, it is so inseparably linked to Arthur in our ideas about the Arthurian legend today that it comes as a surprise to find that the Round Table is not part of the earliest accounts of Arthur. It does not appear in the Welsh stories, nor in Geoffrey of Monmouth, whose *History of the Kings of Britain* created an international audience for Arthur. Geoffrey's Arthur is the archetypal king as conqueror, who wins an empire for himself, and was immediately seen as the greatest figure in the line of British kings: but he has no Round Table of knights.

The Round Table is first mentioned in about 1155 in a free translation of Geoffrey of Monmouth's work into Norman French, some twenty years after the original had appeared. The poet, Robert Wace, came from the Channel Islands, and wrote the *Romance of Brut* for Henry II's court. Wace tells us how Arthur established a new type of seating arrangement at his court which was intended to avoid the

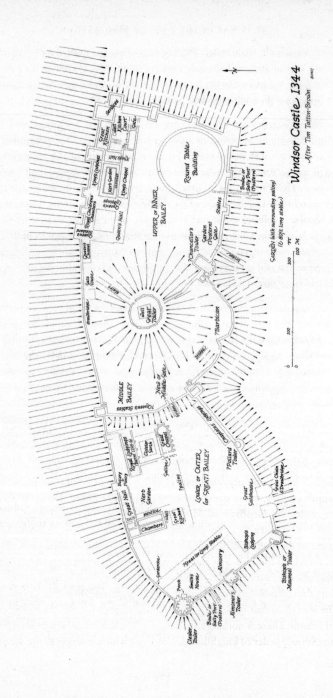

Windsor Castle 1344
After Tim Tatton-Brown

UPPER or INNER BAILEY

Round Table Building

Bomba or Sally Port (Postern)
Stables
Garden (Postern) Gate
Garden (with surrounding paling)
(c.80ft long stable)

Strapping
Great Kitchen
Kitchen Court
Wall Gate
Xmas Hall
Kings Lodgings
Herb Garden
Larder
Kings Chapel
Kings Children's Lodgings
Lodgings
Queens Hall
Queens Chapel
Queens Chamber

?Chancellor's Tower
Bell Tower

GREAT Tower

MIDDLE BAILEY

Store House
Broadbridge

Queens Stables
New or Middle Gate
?Barbican
Chapel Steps

Cloister
Royal Lodgings Berner Cross
Cloister Steps
Great Chapel
Swallow
Pavilion

LOWER or OUTER (or GREAT) BAILEY

Pollard Tower
Chaplains Lodgings
Great Chain & Drawbridge
Great Gatehouse
Bishop's Lodging

Bakery
Great Hall
Herb Garden
Pentice
Great Kitchen
Chambers
Garderobe
Spens
Smiths House
Bomba or Sally Port (Postern)

Spens
Spens (or Long) Stable
Almonry

Clewer Tower
Almoner's Tower
Bishops or Maunsel Tower

100 200 300 FT
0   100 300 M

quarrels which arose when there was a clear place of honour, at the king's right hand, and the status of an individual was judged by how closely he was placed to the king. Arthur withdraws from the main table in his own hall, and replaces it by the Round Table:

Never did one hear of a knight who was in any way considered to be praiseworthy, who would not belong to his household, if it were possible to have him. If he wished to serve for recompense, nonetheless he never left to gain recompense. For the noble barons he had, each of whom felt that he was superior [to the rest] – each one believed himself to be the best, and nobody could tell the worst – King Arthur, of whom the Britons tell many stories, established the Round Table. There sat the vassals, all of them at the head of the table, and all equal. They took their places at the table as equals. None of them could boast that he was seated higher than his peer. All were seated in the place of honour, and none was at the far end. At this table sat Britons, Frenchmen, Normans, men from Anjou, Flanders, Burgundy and Lorraine. There were knights who held land of the king, from the furthest marches of the west to the hill of St Bernard.[45]

At the outset, the Round Table was therefore the answer to a political problem, and Wace's depiction of it reflected the difficulties that Henry II had had at the beginning of his reign. He had inherited a kingdom torn apart by civil war and the rivalry of great lords, and had imposed order on it.

It is easy for us to forget that Arthur's fame in the middle ages took two distinct forms. Wace was writing a chronicle in verse, and thought of himself as a historian. Despite the severe doubts about Arthur's place in history expressed by some sceptical writers in the twelfth century, Arthur became an accepted part of the history of Britain until the sixteenth century, when questions were once more raised about the story presented by Geoffrey of Monmouth. We cannot read Edward III's mind in January 1344 to discover what he intended by the establishment of the Round Table, but I believe that the weight of the evidence is in favour of the idea that this was all part of his campaign to establish his rights in France, and that, just as his grandfather had used Arthur in support of his claim to overlordship of Scotland, so Edward was invoking the idea of Arthur to be found in the chronicles of the time as conqueror of France. There is nothing to indicate that at this stage he was founding any formal order of knighthood, a concept which emerges in the second half of the fourteenth century. The king says nothing about the formal constitution of the Round Table in his announcement; in the chronicles it is simply an alliance or fraternity of knights under the king.

Arthur's fame came in the end, not from his place in the supposed history of Britain, but from his image as a paragon of the new ideas of knighthood, and the Round Table too was transformed into the home of the best knights in the world. It is mentioned by all the early writers of romance; it begins as an incidental part of Arthur's court, as in the writings of Chrétien de Troyes, where Arthur is the central but rather nebulous figure around whom the world of his heroes revolves. Here, as in Wace's *Brut*, the knights of Arthur's court are referred to as 'ces de la Table Reonde' – those of the Round Table – on three occasions, and there is a similar reference in the poems of Marie de France, a contemporary of Chrétien. In these early romances, the Round Table is no more than a synonym for Arthur's court, with no idea of specific membership or specific rules; it is Arthur's court, rather than the Round Table itself, which is home to the best knights in the world.

As the Arthurian romances were expanded and grew more complex, the Round Table becomes a society or company with a limited and defined membership and at the same time the physical object where those members assemble. The number of knights is repeatedly given as 150, and they are called members or companions of the Round Table.[46] They are bound to each other by certain conditions; there is evidently an oath which they swear on admission to the company, though the terms of it are never precisely spelled out, and we only gather from passing references what these conditions might be. They seem incidental beside the much more prominent insistence on the importance of the relations between the members of the Round Table. First and foremost, the companions are bound by oath to help each other. When Gawain is fighting Hector, another knight reproaches him fiercely for attacking a fellow-member of the Round Table, and succeeds in stopping the combat: 'As for Sir Hector, your companion, by the oath of the Round Table you are bound to him and to all the others who are companions of the Round Table, so that you can't kill them except in self-defence without becoming the falsest and most foresworn knight of all.'[47]

Indeed, the members of the Round Table are bound to help each other, to the extent of avenging any defeat suffered by another of the companions: 'the custom of the Round Table is such that if I see my companion defeated or killed, I must avenge him before I leave and must kill with my own hands the man who fought him, unless both are companions of the Round Table.'[48] This became more than a mere custom: it appears that there was now an oath which all knights had to swear, though we never learn its exact wording. By the late thirteenth century, writers thought of it as involving an oath of brotherhood ('Remember the oath and pledge of the Round Table, in which we are brothers and companions . . .'[49]), and it also included an oath of obedience to the king.

Some of these ideas could have been part of Edward's thinking, but it was not the prime reason for his appeal to the past: he was staking a claim to the identity which he had already been given by the more enthusiastic chroniclers, a reincarnation of Arthur as ruler of Europe, and more specifically of France.

Let us look again at Murimuth's account and see what the details tell about Edward's agenda in making his announcement in January 1344, ignoring all the splendour surrounding the occasion and concentrating on what the king had in mind for the future.

First of all, the founding of the Round Table is not part of the festival itself, but a separate occasion after the jousts and feasting had concluded. The ceremony takes place with all the formal pomp that can be mustered, and Edward wears his crown, a symbolic act which normally happened only on certain specified occasions. He also carries the royal sceptre, which would indeed have been a highly unusual act even at a major court feast, and the chief royal officers of the court, the steward and marshal, also carry their ceremonial staffs. The assembly takes place, not in the chapel as might be expected, but in what appears to have been an outdoor environment. The staging of the occasion, as we have seen from the accounts, was carefully choreographed. The king had one of his most splendid sets of robes made for the occasion, an item which stands out even among the vast sums recorded in his accounts with his tailor. The crown, even though it was only his second-best crown, was also highly symbolic, since it had been in pawn for the previous four years. This may well have been the first time since 1337 that Edward appeared in full state regalia; it is likely that he did so in that year when his eldest son was created duke of Cornwall, and six of his closest associates were raised to the rank of earl. If so, it implies that the founding of the Round Table was intended, not as a simple adjunct to a joust, but as a moment of great political significance.

Perhaps the most curious aspect of this is the opening of the solemn oath sworn by the king. Instead of declaring outright his intention to found the Round Table, Edward prefaces his words with 'provided that he had the means'. In 1344 these words would have had a very specific resonance. The greatest crisis of Edward's reign had been three years earlier, when his extravagant plans for buying himself an alliance of German princes for his campaign against France had led him to near-bankruptcy and to a rift with the council charged with ruling England in his absence. The royal finances were only just on the mend, as witnessed by the recent redemption of the crown, and this was an undertaking that was likely to cost a great deal. Already the expenditure on feasting alone for this week amounted to £1,954 18s. 3¼d.[50] To put this in perspective, without attempting a false analogy with modern currency, it was approximately three months of normal kitchen expenditure for the king's household, and, although the feast in 1337 when the duke and earls were created cost £439 2s. 8¼d., there were no other festivities at that time. In comparison with the costs of mounting a military campaign, the kitchen expenditure for the Windsor festival would have paid the wages for Edward's army on the Crécy campaign two years later for seventeen days. Obviously the inaugural occasion was a special one, but to provide for an assembly of 300 knights on a regular annual basis was not going to be cheap if it was to be done in high royal style.

This number is the next detail which the writer gives us. The way in which he explains the membership of the Round Table is not entirely clear: I read it to mean that the total number of knights was to be 300, but that it would begin with a smaller number, and that Edward undertook to continually recruit knights until it reached that number. Otherwise, the membership would effectively have no limit. An institution as large as this would have been something quite exceptional, in terms of the size of the group, the scale of the building and the scale of expenditure on the inauguration. As a one-off event, it was manageable, but with the costs of providing a building for it and with annual gatherings, even Edward seems to have realized that this was going to stretch his resources.

Immediately after the feast, Edward gave his instructions for the building works to begin. Thomas Walsingham's account of the dimensions proved exactly right when excavations took place in the upper ward at Windsor Castle in 2006, and the foundations of the house of the Round Table were uncovered. It was a huge undertaking, and the number of men required for the workforce meant that building work on sites throughout south-east England came to a halt. At its peak, in the first week of March 1344, 720 men were employed. However, by April there was a real prospect of a renewal of open war with France, and the work almost ceased after this one month of hectic activity. The king's means were insufficient to support the anticipated building expenses, which amounted to £509 12s. 11¾d. by the time work stopped altogether at the end of the year. The peak rate of monthly expenditure was four times as much as the average for the whole of the work done when Windsor Castle was remodelled by William of Wykeham in 1356–61.[51] Wykeham's work was funded by the profits of the war with France; in 1344 there were no profits as yet, and a huge debit in prospect for the costs of the new campaign.

Given the lavish scale of the inaugural feast, what was Edward's objective in all this? The nearest we can get to Edward's intentions in this respect is from the response of the barons to Edward's promise to 'begin a Round Table, in the same manner and condition as Arthur, formerly king of England, established it'. The barons reply by swearing to 'observe, sustain and promote' the new institution. This implies that there was to be something which had to be 'observed'; but do we have any idea what this might have been? In the chronicles, and in particular in the poem *Morte Arthure*, which is almost entirely based on the supposed history of the real Arthur, the Round Table takes on a different aspect, and becomes the equivalent of the group of knights at the English royal court known as the household knights. The *Morte Arthure*, which is entirely concerned with Arthur's French wars, and was written around the end of Edward III's reign, depicts the Round Table as follows:

> . . . I'll tell you a tale both noble and true
> of the royal ranks of the Round Table
> who were champion knights and chivalrous chieftains,
> both worldly wise and brave in battle,
> daring in their deeds, always dreading shame,
> kind, courteous men, courtly in their manners.
> How they won in war the worship of many . . .[52]

It is conceivable, given the large membership proposed by Edward, that the Round Table was to be an extension of the institution of household knights, providing the king with even larger resources of manpower under his own direct control. The pomp and ceremony attached to it would then have been largely aimed at recruiting additional knights; if the core was to be the existing knights of the household, Edward's remarks about continually adding to the number make sense. There may be an echo of Edward's ideas in John Lydgate, writing eighty years later about the institution of the Round Table, who makes one of its roles a 'martial academy' where young knights could learn to bear arms, and avoid 'the idleness of youth'.

If this view is possible, the Round Table becomes both a training ground and a serious military grouping. Such an organization might justify the creation of a *domus*, but what we know of the building indicates that it was intended not as the headquarters of a permanently staffed organization, but as a place for feasting and knightly ceremony. A large enclosed space open to the sky – if that was indeed what the *domus* was to have been – would have its uses as a training ground, but few advantages over the usual jousting areas annexed to castles. We know that the upper ward was used for jousting, as there is a reference in the accounts to the special chamber provided for the king when he armed himself for jousts there.[53] Huge though the building was, the space outside it in the upper ward would still have been larger and better able to accommodate the lists. However, it is worth pointing out that the area required for lists was specified by Thomas duke of Gloucester in the fifteenth century as '60 pace long and 40 pace broad . . . and that the listes be strongly barred about'. A pace is about three feet, perhaps slightly less, so this area would just fit within the Round Table building with its diameter of 200 feet, even allowing for seats, table and arcade around the outside. The problem is that Gloucester is discussing trial by combat, which was usually on foot, and this specification would not therefore allow for jousting. And the shape of the building would be wrong for a jousting arena, even though an Elizabethan writer, John Ferne, in *The Blazon of Gentrie*, talks of lists as 'a place circular and rounde, compassed in with lowe rayles or pales of wood, painted with red'.[54] There are no surviving documents which give the measurements for a fourteenth-century jousting arena, and the style of fighting at tournaments was in the process of changing from the old-fashioned *mêlée* involving a large number of knights, to the joust in which one knight challenged a single opponent.

This may lead to one possible explanation of the function of the Round Table building. In the magnificent treatise on tournaments by René of Anjou, king of Naples, in the mid-fifteenth century, he illustrates the start of a *mêlée*. The opening ceremony takes place within a set of barriers, where the two sides are ranged against each other, with banners displayed. At a signal from the heralds, the barriers are opened, the knights ride out into an open space and the fighting starts, using swords only. Given the disposition of the House of the Round Table in the upper ward, we could envisage the knights assembling within the open space at the centre of the building for the opening ceremony. At the signal from the heralds, the great doors would be opened, and the fighting would continue in the larger space of the upper ward. This can only be a hypothesis, but it fits well with what we know of the organization of the events known as 'Round Tables'.

There is a second possible use for an arena of this size. Any discussion of the fourteenth-century concept of an Arthurian Round Table leads us back to the series of festivals called 'round tables' which are documented from 1232 onwards, when Henry III refers in an official document to knights assembling *ad rotundam tabulam*, 'for a round table'.[55] At the knighting of the sons of John of Ibelin in Cyprus in 1223 the chronicler records that the knights imitated 'the adventures of Britain and the Round Table'.[56] There are a number of events across Europe in the thirteenth century which are recorded as 'round tables', usually with no further information. The *domus* could have been the setting for the king's *ludi*, and these could have been re-enactments of the romances of the Round Table. Because we know so little about the content and context of the *ludi*, this can only be a speculation.

The Round Table building at Windsor does seem to have inspired the author of an Arthurian romance, the mysterious and dramatic *Perceforest*, which appears to be from these years, even though the version that has come down to us is definitely from the fifteenth century. *Perceforest* tells the pagan prehistory of the Round Table, and unites the legends of Alexander, much admired by the counts of Hainault, with the legend of Arthur. One of the central scenes is the moment when Perceforest, to whom Alexander has given the land of Britain, discovers a tower which has magically appeared in his castle. Within is a vast hall, with seats for 300 knights. When Perceforest sees the hall of the Franc-Palais for the first time, there are only twelve shields hanging on the walls, those of the band of knights who have undertaken a vow which provides the main framework of the action. The next day, when they re-enter the hall, the king's shield is above his seat at the high table; and next to it, in the place of honour on his right, 'there hung a golden shield with a red lion, and it belonged to Lyonnel du Glat'.[57] I believe this is a flattering reference to Edward in his character of Lionel; and the hall is modelled on the Round Table *domus*. Its dimensions are exactly those specified by Thomas Walsingham and confirmed by the 2006 excavations, a diameter of 200 feet. No other circular building of this period approached this size, and it seems highly unlikely that the measurement is a coincidence.[58]

The Round Table project looks backwards to a golden age of knighthood, and romanticizes the present by attempting to revive the ancient glories of Arthur's court. It is, however, typical of the time: Jean Froissart, whose imaginative version of the Hundred Years War still colours our vision of the harsh warfare of the times, makes ordinary knights and mercenary captains into men governed by knightly ideals. The patronage of knightly ideals by the courts of Europe, which had made them a kind of lingua franca of the knightly class, reached its apogee in the late fourteenth and early fifteenth centuries; but it was patronage with a purpose. The Emperor Frederick II had built great castles to impress his subjects with their power, castles which were not always strategically necessary but were highly visible, as at Enna in Sicily and Castel del Monte in Apulia; and Edward I's Welsh castles fulfilled the same role, and also evoked Britain's imperial past as recorded in Welsh legend.[59] Now monarchs turned to knightly festivals for the same purpose. It is the beginning of a tradition which led to the great pageants of the Renaissance and to the court entertainments of the Italian princes, the age when 'the art of festival was harnessed to the emergent modern state as an instrument of rule'.[60] I would argue that this process first emerges much earlier than has usually been acknowledged, particularly as we find one of the first examples of a 'royal entry' with a symbolic programme in London in 1357, when the prince of Wales brought King John of France to the city as a captive after Poitiers. Edward III's agenda at Windsor had moved beyond the conspicuous consumption enjoined by the romantic virtue of *largesse* to a novel use of knighthood. Note that the ceremony of inauguration of the Round Table was carefully orchestrated, and that Murimuth records that all the people flocked to see the spectacle. This is knightly display as public relations.

The Round Table failed, however. It was too ambitious, too extravagant. There was no intrinsic obstacle to its revival in 1347; the half-finished buildings were still in place. But the events of the ensuing months had dramatically changed the king's priorities. If the Round Table was to be a new focus for recruiting the king's armies for overseas campaigns, Edward had effectively solved that problem in 1344–6, and the system of raising an army by means of commanders with individual contracts and special payments of bonuses to captains and common soldiers alike was to remain in place for the rest of his reign.

Although the breakdown of the 1343 truce was expected as early as April 1344, it was a long time before the storm actually broke. Half-hearted peace talks at Avignon meandered on for twelve months. Edward wanted Jean de Montfort released from French custody before negotiating seriously, and in any case he was absolutely determined to pursue his claim to the throne of France. The pomp and ceremony of the Round Table festival was only one aspect of a propaganda campaign to present Edward as a monarch of the first rank: a new gold coinage was issued within weeks of the ceremony, and Edward made a point of using it when presenting the traditional Maundy money at Marlborough at Easter 1344. Documents given to the negotiators at Avignon contained the idea that 'since the king of France was sovereign in his lands, no earthly authority was empowered to arbitrate upon the title', which could be decided only by the divine judgement implicit in the outcome of war.[61] Since this blatantly ran contrary to the pope's claim to be God's vicar on earth, there was not the remotest possibility of the talks succeeding if this approach was mentioned. It can only have been a counter in the diplomatic dealings: there are hints that Edward would have settled for an independent Aquitaine and the restoration of the lands lost since the settlement of 1259.

About the time that the talks collapsed, Edward had formulated the strategy for his next move against France. The moribund Flemish alliance had collapsed, and even his brother-in-law William II of Hainault had gone over to the French side: only the Flemish towns led by Jacob van Artevelde remained loyal to the English alliance. William II's French allegiance was relatively brief, as he was killed in an abortive attempt to put down a revolt by the independent-minded Frisians at Staveren in 1345.[62]

Edward was seeking an alliance with Castile to secure the seas against the Castilian ships, which had fought on the French side, but, in terms of an attack on France, he was now going to rely on his own resources, and on his allies in Brittany and western Normandy. Fortunately for him, Jean de Montfort escaped from Paris and reached England in March 1345, and both local quarrels and the French nobility's fear of Philip after the summary execution of Olivier Clisson played into his hands: his most useful new ally in this area was Godefroy d'Harcourt, whose lordship lay in the Cotentin peninsula, south of Cherbourg.

Edward's plans for the campaign of 1345 were on a grand scale. William Bohun would go to Brittany, Henry of Grosmont to Gascony, and he himself would invade French territory somewhere on the Channel coast. In June Bohun arrived in Brittany, and by August Henry of Grosmont was in Bordeaux: at the end of that month he, Walter Mauny and Ralph Stafford, together with Laurence Hastings, earl of Pembroke, had taken Bergerac, a key stronghold on the Dordogne fifty miles east of Bordeaux, and with it important hostages and much of the wealth of the town. Henry then advanced south-east to La Réole in Périgord, having defeated the French at Auberoche in October, and taken prisoners estimated by Villani to be worth £50,000.[63] He recaptured the town in January 1346, and this success was followed up by Stafford's capture of Aiguillon, south-east of Bordeaux. But this was not much to set against the problems in Brittany. Jean de Montfort died on 26 September 1345, leaving his five-year-old son as heir to his cause, and all that Bohun could do was ensure that as many of Montfort's supporters as possible remained loyal. Edward himself had to make a hasty voyage to Flanders to salvage his alliance with the towns when the Flemish leader van Artevelde was assassinated in July. When he was finally able to set sail with his army, one of the most violent storms he ever encountered in the Channel blew his fleet apart, some of them limping back from the North Sea once it was all over. The army was in no fit state to re-embark and undertake a campaign, and he reluctantly called off the expedition. The invasion fleet was to reconvene at Portsmouth on 15 May 1346.

6

The Crécy Campaign

The fleet which assembled at Portsmouth in May and June of 1346 had long been planned. Its destination was secret, and precautions were taken to prevent any information about its objective from reaching the French. Yet the new expedition could only have been intended for Brittany or Normandy. The reason that we know the destination of any given expedition from England is simple. Medieval ships could not sail to windward, that is, into the prevailing wind. If the wind was south-westerly – and south-west is the prevailing wind direction in the English Channel – they can head north-west, through north and east, to south-east. Their range, so to speak, is only 180° or half of the compass. By contrast, a modern yacht, under the same conditions, can head within 30° of the wind direction and use 300°, five-sixths of the compass, from south of west through north, east and south to west of south. So expeditions for Gascony left from Plymouth, in the hope of catching at least a north-westerly wind; even so, they would need a wind in the east to clear the Breton peninsula. To get to Brittany from Portsmouth a westerly or north-westerly was needed, and Normandy could just about be reached in a westerly. Anything from the north or east made these journeys easy, but these are not the usual Channel winds. Because the timing of the crossing was so uncertain, tides could be used to certain advantage only at the outset of the voyage: going to Normandy from the Solent, to get as far to windward as possible. This would mean leaving at the beginning of the ebb for a west wind, the beginning of the flood for an east wind, since the tides flood towards Dover and ebb away from it.

Assembling a fleet was an elaborate operation, because there was no permanent royal navy.[1] The king owned a number of ships, but they were not organized in any way. At the beginning of his reign, Edward had only two ships of his own, and this number was not increased for a decade, because his chief preoccupation was with the wars in Scotland. As soon as France became the target, he set about building ships, and by 1342 there were ten available for an expedition to Brittany. The next four years saw a major effort to improve the situation, and twenty-five royal vessels were among those at Portsmouth. Technically, the men of the Cinque Ports, the five ports on the south coast which enjoyed special privileges in return for providing fifty-seven vessels for the king when he went to war, should have been the next major source of ships, but just as feudal service was commuted to money payments in the 1340s, so this obligation had become obsolete. The bulk of the fleet was therefore created by summoning ordinary trading and fishing vessels from the ports around the country, to serve at the king's wages. The total for the 1346 flotilla was more than 1,000 ships, the largest seen in England before the sixteenth century.[2]

In the absence of a royal navy, there was instead an admiralty, a highly efficient government department whose task it was to gather this enormous quantity of shipping. There were usually two admirals, and the country was divided into the admiralty of the north and the admiralty of the west; the dividing line was Dover, so the admiral of the north was in effect in charge of the ports on the east coast, and the admiral of the west covered everything from London round to Cornwall. These posts had largely been in abeyance up to 1335; thereafter, Robert Morley was admiral of the north until 1360, except in the decade after 1344, when he was replaced by leading military commanders. In 1344-7, the admiral of the north was Robert Ufford.[3] The admiralty of the west changed more frequently, and names such as Bartholomew Burghersh the elder and William Clinton appear up to 1344; from 1344 to 1347, Robert Ufford's colleague was Richard Fitzalan.

The admirals had overall responsibility for the operation: their lieutenants oversaw a substantial staff devoted to the task of organizing the requisition of ships, and the coast was subdivided into smaller sections for this purpose. Officials would be sent to individual ports to 'arrest' ships for the king's service, and to contract the shipmaster to be at Portsmouth at the agreed time. The pay offered was obviously acceptable, as we do not hear of the refusals to serve which had plagued the efforts to raise fleets under Edward II. Substantial payments were made in advance once the ships reached the appointed rendezvous: one official paid out more than £1,600 in two months.[4] The names of the shipmaster and crew, and the name of the ship, would be recorded and sent to Westminster, and we have full payrolls for several of Edward III's campaigns, though unfortunately not for the 1346 fleet.[5] However, contracting for a ship to be at Portsmouth was one thing; getting it there, particularly from the admiralty of the north, was another matter. The prevailing westerly winds meant that the voyage from major ports north of Dover through the straits of Dover was likely to be much slower than a voyage from the south-western ports, and distances were greater.

Despite generally excellent organization, there was an inevitable delay in assembling the ships. The summons for the fleet was issued rather hopefully for the end of February, and then postponed to the end of March. The equinoctial gales, usual at that time of year, again forced a delay, and it was the end of April before the first ships began to appear in the Solent. Once they arrived at Portsmouth, they were under the admiral's command, and they were provisioned and allocated a mooring, while they waited for the rest of the fleet to assemble. The process of gathering the ships was as usual a long affair; the king would have known that the earliest that he could expect to sail would be in April, in time for a spring campaign. In the event, it was the end of June before the ships were ready.

An even more formidable bureaucratic effort had been in process on land, to assemble the troops and to purchase the necessary provisions and cart them to Portsmouth. If we have little detail for the naval accounts[6] we have a great deal for the provisioning and supplies, the army retinues and the actual accounts for the king's kitchen during the months in Portsmouth and in France. Tantalizingly, the rolls for the army retinues probably survived until the early eighteenth century, when they were destroyed along with other papers after the death of a scholar who was working on them.[7]

Edward was setting out to fight a campaign where he would have no territories of his own to draw on, as would have been the case in Gascony, and no allies, however unreliable, as in the earlier expeditions to Flanders. In his Scottish wars he could call on supplies to be brought up overland, and he was not totally dependent on his fleet. In the summer of 1346, everything had to be loaded onto the ships, and he was relying on the same ships to bring him back, whatever the outcome of the fighting. Weapons and horses formed the bulk of the military supplies, but in addition the necessary equipment for the army's engineers was part of the freight, and even items such as coracles for the king's fishermen are to be found in the accounts.

First and foremost, huge numbers of bows and arrows were needed. Although numerous orders to the local sheriffs survive, we lack any secure idea of what sort of total number was involved. We can work backwards from the figure of about 7,500 archers in the army to arrive at a figure; one suggestion is that at the rate of seventy per man, half a million arrows weighing four ounces each would be the kind of quantity involved, and that they would weigh fifty-five tons, which in turn required fifty to sixty carts to carry them – and the carts also had to be shipped from England. Orders for 5,500 sheaves, or 132,000 arrows, are known to have been issued, along with 2,100 bows, giving a ratio of sixty arrows per bow.[8] Such huge quantities had to be divided out among the shires which were skilled in making them, and even then they were often delivered in stages, and there were often considerable shortfalls on the numbers requested: sometimes only a third of the order was supplied by the sheriff responsible. At the end of the day the archers in the field would be permanently reliant on being able to retrieve spent shafts, and on a regular further supply of arrows made en route. Each man would have his own bow, but reserve bowstaves and stores of bowstrings would be needed. Spare arrowheads and finished bows corded in bundles were shipped in barrels, as staves could be cut when the army was in the field: it was harder to set up forges, but there were undoubtedly a number of portable smithies with the army, essential for reshoeing horses and repairing armour and swords, as well as making arrowheads.

The other field weapons were the swords and lances of the mounted knights and men at arms, and the smaller swords and knives carried by the archers and other footsoldiers. These were not issued by the king, but were the responsibility of the individuals. There was one innovation in terms of weapons: the use of guns. The treatise which Walter Milemete presented to Edward at the beginning of his reign illustrates a simple bombard, a bulbous cannon about three or four feet long; the guns at Crécy are likely to have been smaller, since bombards were heavy and unreliable, and mostly used in sieges (Plate 6). It is possible that sieges were what the Crécy guns were intended for, and they were brought into play only as a means of terrorizing the enemy, and particularly their horses. Instructions were sent to the head of the Tower armouries in 1345 to supply a hundred 'ribalds', small multi-barrelled guns firing lead shot. These were experimental weapons, at the cutting edge of a new technology: even so, Edward seems to have had with him some 'guns', i.e. cannons, and as much as 2,000 pounds of gunpowder, a substantial amount.[9] Edward might love the antique trappings of knightly display, but he was also an innovator, interested in new techniques and ingenious devices, as illustrated by the great clock he had installed at Windsor, a novelty in England at the time. The guns might have been bought in Flanders or made at the armouries in the Tower of London. The Tower served as a collection centre for many of the military stores, and for naval supplies such as ropes and sailcloth. It was also a major factory for all kinds of weapons, and the shortfall in arrows supplied by the shires was usually made up by employing extra workmen at the Tower.

Alongside the archers and the handful of gunners there were forty carpenters, the engineers of the army, led by William of Winchelsea. Although there is no surviving record of what materials were supplied for their use, in Brittany three years earlier enough timber for three complete bridges had been shipped, the medieval equivalent of the Bailey Bridge of the Second World War. The engineers played a vital role in the progress of the army when they succeeded in repairing the bridge at Poissy near Paris, which had been deliberately broken. The gap was sixty feet, and they threw a single beam, a foot wide, across it. This was sufficient for enough archers and men at arms to cross and drive off the enemy harassing from the other side. They then used the beam as a base from which to build up a roadway strong enough for the rest of the army to cross to the north bank of the Seine.[10]

Another vital element in the army's composition does not appear separately in the accounts. A huge number of carts must have been needed to convey the stores overland once the army reached Normandy.[11] Quite apart from the fifty or sixty carts carrying bows and arrows, there were the vital provisions which the army needed to supplement what it could find by foraging. A medieval army on the march did not consist of serried ranks of horsemen and footsoldiers marching in tight formation: it was more like a huge straggling merchant caravanserai (Plate 9). It included live beasts and birds, who were slaughtered for food en route. The kitchen accounts differentiate between beasts taken from the stock brought from England and those captured in foraging raids. The latter are listed as 'kept from spoils'; if the accounts are right, there were still cattle listed as simply 'kept' as late as 30 August, as if they had been brought from England.[12] Relatively exotic birds as well as ordinary poultry were brought for the king's table, probably in cages on the carts, and there are regular entries for food for them throughout the campaign; the stocks of poultry were evidently replenished by the foragers.[13]

When the army encamped for the night, the image that immediately comes to mind is of a busy scene of pitching tents, organizing the camp, lighting fires and settling down to a night under canvas. There is actually little trace of this in the accounts, and we know very little about the art of the medieval tent-maker. That there were tents for the king, and that some were mended for the expedition, is about all that can be said.[14] If we trace the army's progress, there are many occasions when quarters for the king and magnates were requisitioned in a town or monastery. Encampment was an emergency procedure at best, and the army would often split up in order to find sufficient shelter. Between leaving La Hogue on 18 July and the encounter with the French army on 26 August, a total of thirty-nine nights, the halts were in small towns or villages on twenty-five occasions, in cities (Caen and Lisieux) for seven nights, and at abbeys for three nights, leaving four occasions when the army was almost certainly under canvas for lack of a suitable settlement nearby, as on the day when they laboriously crossed the marshes to the east of Caen. On five occasions, usually when the king was staying at an abbey, the forces were split, and the prince of Wales found lodging elsewhere. Some of the troops would have found shelter in these settlements as well; despite the king's initial proclamation that the inhabitants of his new kingdom were to be spared, what normally seems to have happened is that the local population were driven out – if they had not already fled – and the troops took over the houses before burning them as they left.[15]

Feeding the army was probably the greatest concern after the levying of the troops. The operation to provision the forces on this campaign was huge, on an unprecedented scale, because, once the army was on French soil, opportunities for sending further provisions would depend on the weather and the whereabouts of the king and his men, and would therefore be highly unreliable. When Edward's armies fought in Scotland, provisioning by land was possible, and the initial supplies were therefore less crucial. In effect, an English force fighting in France had to take as large a supply as it could, because the availability of local provisions was uncertain in the extreme. Foraging was a constant preoccupation, but deliberate burning of crops and slaughter of cattle was a recognized defensive technique for starving out a raiding force and ensuring that it would not remain in the area for long.

The system of obtaining the necessary food depended heavily on the royal purveyancers, who had the power to seize food and buy it at fixed, but not necessarily fair, prices. Not surprisingly, they were extremely unpopular, but it is possibly an indication of popular support for the campaign that in this case not only did the raising of supplies pass off relatively peacefully, but the required stocks were also raised. Getting provisions to Portsmouth was the most elaborate of all the bureaucratic operations for the expedition. We have the full receipts for some counties which detail all the stages involved.[16] Firstly, empty barrels had to be bought, usually tuns, which stood about six feet high and three feet in diameter. The flour sent from Yorkshire required eighty of these, and there were about forty more for oats, pork, peas and beans. Ten men had ridden round the country for a fortnight purchasing and arranging for the transport of these supplies, paying for them with wooden tallies which could be redeemed at the exchequer later. Boats and carts were requisitioned, and the supplies were taken by road and river to seven depots. They were then shipped to Hull, where the corn was ground. It took seven men a week to unload the wheat and reload the flour. At all stages, clerks had to record the transactions, and men were appointed to guard the goods. Everyone in the county must have been aware of the king's men at work, and the aftermath would be shortages and rising prices because of the extra demand.

The provisions raised in this way tell us what the army lived on. The common soldiers ate very much what they were accustomed to at home, mainly peas and beans or oats made into pottage with such meat and other vegetables as were available. The royal kitchen accounts are at the other extreme, and show the royal household also enjoying its customary, but much more luxurious, diet. The households of the great magnates would have eaten in a similar, but less elaborate style; there might have been between five and seventeen such groups within the army, each with their own supplies.[17] The menu for the king and his immediate companions was very varied. Mutton, pork and beef were all provided, but much of it was salted or cured, so it is not surprising to find a large expenditure on the ingredients for sauces: verjuice,* vinegar, mustard, garlic, onions and parsley. Fresh meat, as we have seen, was derived partly from the small herd that travelled with the army, and partly from the results of foraging. There are regular payments through-out the journey to the kitchen boys who 'pursue and kill oxen and sheep'.[18] Poultry came from stock, and was almost certainly foraged as well. Rabbit was also on the menu, as the king's ferreters were in the contingent. More important were the fishermen, since fish was regularly eaten on Friday, as prescribed by the medieval Church. The range of fish is surprising: in addition to the salt cod, or stockfish, which was a staple of medieval diet for Fridays, there was salmon, which must have been dried or even cured, rather like smoked salmon,[19] eels of varying sizes, spiced herring (the rollmops of today). The lamprey, a parasitic eel-like creature, was a great delicacy in the middle ages, since it tastes more like meat than any other fish: four were served on 12 July at a cost of sixteen shillings.[20] Again, fish from the original provisions, fish bought in the market and fish caught by the king's fishermen are sometimes noted sep-arately. Other items include carp, pike and crayfish: the king at least enjoyed a rich and varied menu. Wine was also supplied in large quanti-ties: nearly 300 tuns, or 130,000 gallons; but before we think of this in modern terms, wine and ale were the customary drinks, because of the poor quality of the water available. It was simply not advisable to drink water unless absolutely necessary, so this was no luxury, but an essential part of the supplies.

The provisioning and shipping of an expedition was a mammoth task even without the raising of the army itself. Edward had a great deal of experience of bringing together an army, but an invasion of the kind that he now had in mind was a novelty. In Scotland in the 1330s he had used tried and trusted methods of recruitment, which harked back to the old duties of defence of the realm, part of the duties of all who held land by feudal service. In the campaigns in Flanders and Brittany from 1337 to 1342, he had relied heavily on local allies, particularly in Flan-ders, which had not served him well. He had tried to recruit princes like mercenaries, for pay, and they had failed to deliver when their political interests outweighed the money on offer.

* Sour fruit juice, often used instead of the more expensive vinegar.

By 1346, Edward had determined to rely exclusively on his own resources. To do this, he had begun to move towards a new system, since the traditional feudal service did not carry the obligation to serve outside England. We have seen how the Round Table could have been part of an exploration of new methods of recruiting an army. The deliberations which may have been going on in early 1344 resulted in a royal commission, for which Edward did not have the specific agreement of parliament, but which he justified on the basis that parliament had given general assent to the war, and he was merely exercising his executive prerogative and responding to a threat of invasion. The commission was asked to provide a list of everyone in the country with an annual income of 100s. up to £1,000, and to assess how many troops they should provide on a scale related to their income from lands. However, the data provided were used by Edward to order a muster of troops at Portsmouth by Easter 1346, with the purpose of taking them abroad to serve at the king's wages. Because the operation had a financial basis, the obligation to provide troops was quickly commuted in many cases to a money payment, effectively a tax to subsidize the war in France. The rates were set by the rank of soldier to be provided. An income of 100s. meant that a mounted archer had to be sent; twice that, and a hobelar or lightly armed horseman was required. Over £25, a man at arms was to be provided and from then on the scale was in proportion to income: a lord with an income of £1,000 would provide forty men at arms. The cost to the landowners was either that of hiring men to serve, or losing the value of their own men's labour for the duration of the campaign. The men themselves would be paid the king's wages, and would either be led by their lord or attached to another lord's retinue if their own lord was not serving in person.

In addition to the men serving because of the military assessments, there were commissions of array, the traditional method of raising foot-soldiers.[21] The commissions were sent to the local officials, and requested specific numbers of archers or spearmen. They in turn would raise these troops from local towns and landowners. For example, on 10 February 1346 orders for the array of troops went to 142 towns in the southern half of England, requesting just under 2,000 men. We know how many men were requested under these commissions, but it was unusual for such requests to be fulfilled completely, and we do not have the necessary records to tell us the result. So we have to rely on estimates, and the best guess from a recent study of the problem is a total of 8,000 men, of whom 5,000 were archers.[22]

We then have to add to these the great lords and their retinues, which consisted in broad terms of equal numbers of men at arms and knights, and mounted and foot archers. Again, we have to use estimates, and the best guess is 2,800 men at arms and knights, and the same number of archers. If this is correct, we are looking at a total of 13,600 men who boarded ship at Portsmouth. The driving force behind this army was the retinues raised by the king himself, his great magnates and the lesser barons and bannerets. It was around these retinues that the three divisions of the army were arranged, and they were in effect the building blocks of the force.

The records of wages for the campaign do not define the king's retinue, which is listed as separate retinues for his household knights and officers; Walter Wetewang, the treasurer, whose accounts tell us so much about the personnel, was a banneret and had his own retinue of three knights, twenty-five squires and thirty-five archers.[23] The largest single retinue was that of the prince of Wales, with 11 bannerets, 102 knights, 264 esquires, 384 mounted archers and 69 archers on foot. He also had more than 500 Welsh infantry, organized under five standard bearers and twenty-five vintenars (commanders of units of twenty men), with their own chaplain and doctor, and a 'proclamator' or crier. Elsewhere we learn that the prince's Welshmen had their own green-and-white uniform, 'a short coat and a hat of both colours', which had its origins in the wars of the prince's great-grandfather.[24] This was normal for companies of archers, as the troops raised by array were to be clothed 'all in the same cloth'.

Next in rank below the prince were the earls, whose military function dated back to Anglo-Saxon times. They were crucial to the organization of any English army, and Edward had created six new earls in 1337, with the specific objective of strengthening the military structure of his kingdom. Three of these new earls were on the campaign: at the end of it (when Edward was besieging Calais), Huntingdon, Northampton and Suffolk brought 685 men between them, while the four hereditary earls, Arundel, Oxford, Warwick and Pembroke, provided almost double that number, 1,140 men. The new earls were not as rich as the established families, relying largely for their income on lands granted to them by the king since their promotion. Henry of Grosmont, who was in Gascony and only joined the army at the siege of Calais, had a retinue even larger than that of the prince of Wales.

A group of seven great lords each raised retinues of between 100 and 300 men, of whom about a third were archers. In total, these lords' retinues were almost as great as those of the seven earls. Below them were a large number of bannerets with around fifty to sixty men, and then knights who were not attached to a larger retinue.

This last group of men were largely raised from the estates of their lords, and therefore shared the same background and loyalty. In modern terms, the nearest equivalent would be the private regiments raised in the First World War, such as the Lovat Scouts, which came from the estates of one particular landowner, Lord Lovat, or the Sandringham company of the Royal Norfolk Regiment, recruited from the royal estate. It is a commonplace of military psychology that the soldier does not fight for the abstract 'king and country' but for his comrades and friends, and local groupings of this kind contributed greatly to the morale of the army as a whole.

The earl of Northampton's retinue has been studied in detail, and a further important factor in the shaping of these bodies of men emerges. This was not an ad hoc collection of soldiers who happened to be available in 1346, but a group who had fought alongside their lord for as much as a decade, going back to the Scottish campaign of 1336, and the days before he had become an earl. In the 1340s Northampton had fought at Sluys and in Brittany, and there is good evidence that the majority of his men had already been through a full-scale battle under his command.[25] There were of course men who many years later remembered that they had been 'first armed' when they landed in Normandy in 1346, and others who joined different retinues for this campaign, but there is a remarkable degree of cohesion and stability in this sample.

A 'retinue' was after all a group of 'retained' men, bound by a specific contract to serve their lord, and this core, who would in turn have their own loyal servants, is at the heart of the system. The knights and squires relate to the lord in terms of long service just as their lord relates to the king himself. A good example of such contracts is that between the prince of Wales and Henry Eam in January 1348:

Grant for life to Sir Henry Eam of a yearly rent of 100 marks payable by equal portions at Easter and Michaelmas out of the prince's manor of

Bradenash, co. Devon, with power of distraint in the manor if the rent be in arrear: as the said Sir Henry, when he received the order of knighthood from the prince's hands, freely offered and promised to be attentive to the prince's service for life, and to go with him on sufficient warning wherever he might wish, whether for peace or for war, and to be with him armed against all manner of persons, except only the duke of Brabant, his liege lord, when fighting in defence of his own lands; and the prince wishes to grant him such a reward as will bind him the more to his service, and enable him the better to support the advancement of his estate.[26]

Eam does not hold land of the prince as a reward for his service, but is paid in cash from a specified source so that he can maintain himself in suitable style. More particularly, the yearly rent of 100 marks is intended to cover the cost of maintaining horses, armour, squires and other followers needed to make him an effective warrior and contributor to the prince's retinue. On Eam's death in 1353, he was replaced by John Sully, who was retained by the prince of Wales on slightly more generous terms (£40 instead of £33 13s. 4d. from the revenues of the same manor), but he was required to provide the services of one esquire as well.[27]

Indentures 'for peace or war' applied only to a small number of retainers, the leading figures in the household of a magnate.[28] We have only chance survivals of the original documents, and the overall composition of the household retinue is difficult to assess. In the case of Henry of Grosmont, there are five surviving indentures, of which the most important is with Edmund Ufford (younger brother of Robert Ufford, earl of Suffolk). Edmund was steward of one of Henry of Grosmont's major estates, and he would have been expected to be on hand to deal with his lord's business and act as escort when required; he would almost certainly have been a member of Grosmont's household council. Edmund was to provide three men at arms in war; they were to wear the earl's livery. He was also required to have ten horses and pages to look after them, and a chamberlain; all his men were to dine in the earl's hall. In peace, the numbers were reduced by more than half.[29] In the case of another of Henry of Grosmont's retainers, Ralph Hastings, there is a document relating to one of his followers, John Kirkby, retained for life in 1362, which deals with the conditions under which Kirkby can be dismissed – the nearest we come to a modern contract of employment. Duties in peacetime in older contracts had often included attendance at tournaments, but this ceases to appear after about 1340. The commonest type of contract of retinue was an agreement for service either for a specified length of time or for the duration of a campaign. It was a system which was highly flexible, and which could apply to the greatest lords as well as to individual knights. In the largest contracts of this kind, the king agreed terms with his commanders which covered the numbers of troops they were to provide, the conditions on which they would serve and the division of any spoils or 'profits of war'. Since the king himself was the commander of the expedition of 1346, much of this did not apply, and we do not have surviving documents which tell us what the arrangements were. At the next level were the contracts directly between the king and individual lords, which set out rates of pay and expenses, and when payments would be made. It became the practice in the 1340s to pay *regard* to the captains of retinues, a sum additional to the customary rate of pay, which was related to the number of men they actually had serving under them at the beginning of the campaign and was designed to encourage them to produce the number of troops they had contracted for.[30] There would be a further series of contracts between the captain and his men, so that the whole system would form a legal basis for the recruitment and payment of the retained troops. Similar arrangements were made with the masters of the ships involved in the campaign.

This elaborate administrative edifice evolved as the solution to a problem which had dogged the English kings ever since their French domains had come under attack in the early thirteenth century. While they were in control of these domains, they could raise men and money for their defence in the territory in question; but once they had been lost to the French crown, the problem was one of reconquering them, and they had to use resources from England or from other parts of France. The war was no longer defensive in the eyes of those whom the English king wanted to fight for him, and there was therefore no obligation to serve, their argument ran. In the thirteenth and early fourteenth centuries, a series of uneasy compromises resulted, and Edward's solution was to prove strikingly successful in the short term.

However, not all the soldiers were covered by contracts or by the summons of array. A large number of them seem to have served for simple pay, without specific contracts, but with the hope of additional rewards if the expedition was a success. Taking Henry of Grosmont as an example once more, among the men named as serving him on military expeditions and diplomatic business abroad, about 10 per cent received grants of lands or annuities. Sometimes these were rewards for individual actions in war; on other occasions they could be a kind of pension for long service; and they might also be for 'past and future good service', both reward and retainer at the same time.

One factor which did not play any great part in the calculations of men who signed up for the Crécy expedition was that of the 'profits of war'. Apart from Henry of Grosmont's victory at Auberoche, previous English expeditions abroad had not produced any notable spoils, and there was no reason to think that this occasion would be any different. One view of the situation was that Edward was attempting to establish his right to France, and this was not therefore a war of conquest, but a question of winning over the inhabitants to support his cause. The proclamation made at the beginning of hostilities in France emphasizes this:

> the English king, feeling for the sufferings of the poor people of the coun-
> try, issued an edict . . . that no house or manor was to be burnt, no church
> or holy place sacked, and no old people, children or women in his king-
> dom of France were to be harmed or molested; nor were they to threaten
> any other people except men who resisted them, or do any kind of wrong,
> on pain of life or limb.[31]

If there was resistance, there might be spoils of war and ransoms. Anyone who captured and ransomed important prisoners was obliged to pay a substantial proportion of the money he received to his commanding officer or to the king; but such ransoms were always few and far between, a lottery win rather than a regular source of wartime income. Profits of war, ranging from casual trophies taken from a farm or village to the sacking of a rich town, hardly figured in the mindset of the ordinary knight in the early wars of Edward's reign. Scotland was a poor country, and the towns small and few. When Edward declared in 1327 and again in 1334 that anyone setting out to fight the Scots could keep any booty he gained, it looks more like revenge for the Scottish raids on the English border counties than a serious prospective source of income.[32] The campaigns in the Low Countries had been largely a stalemate, and little had been captured, while in Brittany the English forces were supporting the claimant to the duchy, and opportunities for plunder were entirely unofficial. The campaign of 1346 marks a watershed, as we shall see. The 'profits of war' were such that they became a regular part of the contracts for service, and after 1350 the pattern of granting the one-third of both booty and ransoms appears to be well established. Before that, the only evidence for a system of this kind is in the warfare on the borders of Wales and Scotland, though much older laws in Wales reserved one-third of all plunder to the king.[33] At sea, however, the rule seems to have been that income from ransoms and sale of plundered goods was to be divided equally between the crown and the master and crew.[34] The reason for this was that compensation was not paid for loss of ships in the royal service; and, interestingly, as the king began to claim a similar share in land warfare, the elaborate system for paying compensation for lost or injured horses to knights and men at arms was gradually abandoned.[35]

What is less easy to see is how this huge disparate mass of men was organized, both on the march and on the battlefield. There were three divisions in the army, and it seems that these may have been used as an organizational scheme from the start of the journey. The problem was that there was no clear chain of command. At one extreme, men from the towns were under the command of a relatively humble leader, whose authority was probably not very strong; at the other, there were the battle-hardened and reliable men at the heart of the noblemen's retinues. How all these were welded into an effective fighting force is also something we know almost nothing about. The *Acts of War of Edward III* tells us that, as the army was disembarking at St Vaast-la-Hougue, 'the English king appointed the earl of Northampton constable, and the earl of Warwick marshal of the army, to check the rashness of the troops. Then they divided the army into three divisions: the vanguard under the prince of Wales, the centre under the king, and the rearguard under the bishop of Durham.'[36] The author goes on to name the leaders of retinues who 'raised their banners' in each division, so we have a picture of three separate bodies of men with the banners as visual rallying points and rendezvous for the members of the retinues within each division. 'With the army divided in this way by the king's counsel, and with everything prepared in the correct fashion', they were able to set out. Discipline was in the hands of the leaders of the retinues, but ultimately lay with the constable of the army, while the marshal was responsible for assembling the army in good order, and organizing its encampment at night, whether in lodgings or under canvas.

All of these troops brought their own weapons, armour and personal equipment, but the men at arms and knights also brought horses; many knights would have two or more horses, so the total was probably well over 5,000 for these two elements of the army. We have to add another 3,000 or so for mounted archers, so something in the region of 10,000 horses would have needed transport. Shipping horses presented a huge number of problems, from getting them on board ship to making sure that they were rested after the voyage and in good condition for the arduous life of the campaign. The ships which had been collected were similar in type, but each would have to be adapted individually for transporting horses. The hold was divided into stalls by hurdles, and thousands of these were ordered as part of the supplies, as well as feed racks and barrels of water. It seems that relatively small ships were used: we have detailed specifications for the building of horse-transports used in the kingdom of Sicily in the late thirteenth century, which carried thirty horses each in specially constructed stalls.

Moving horses by sea was a skilled and specialist operation, commensurate with the value of the horses and the vital role they played in the expedition.[37] Obviously the adaptation of existing ships was a less satisfactory method, but the Channel crossing was usually quite rapid. When in 1344 Reginald Cobham raised a fleet for an expedition to Brittany, the smaller ships were specifically reserved for horse-transport. In similar circumstances in 1303, the number of horses ranged from ten to thirty-two per ship; if we allow twenty horses on average per ship, this would mean that there were 500 ships to be loaded and unloaded, an immensely slow process even when each of the great warhorses might have its own groom.[38] Methods of loading were cumbersome: each horse had to be led up a gangplank, either over the full height of the side of the ship or through a loading door specially cut in the stern, which would then be sealed for the voyage. Sometimes the horses had to be put in a sling and winched aboard using a crane.[39] Once the horse was on board, it would have to be manoeuvred in a confined space into its stall.

Fortunately, the voyage in 1346 was relatively brief, though even the horses were on board for a week or more from loading to unloading. Often horses had to be rested for several days before the army could begin its march: when Richard I landed in Cyprus in 1190, 'the horses were walked about, because they were all stiff and lame and dazed after being at a sea for a month, standing the whole time, unable to lie down. The next day, without giving them any more rest than they had had (although they deserved more), the king ... mounted.'[40]

The fleet was ready to sail on 5 July, and got as far as the Needles, off the western end of the Isle of Wight, but contrary winds made it impossible to proceed further, and the king ordered the ships back to Portsmouth. He said in a letter of 7 July from Yarmouth to John Offord, his chancellor, and William Edington, his treasurer, that he and his companions had agreed to set out on the next tide, and to go wherever the wind took them; but the second half of the letter warns against spies in London, and the vagueness may have been a precaution in case the letter fell into their hands.[41] Bartholomew Burghersh the elder, writing ten days later, was positive that the king had intended to go to Gascony. It is difficult to gainsay this first-hand evidence, particularly when the information was no longer of use as a deception, but the difficulties of a passage from Portsmouth to Gascony and the king's apparent indecision ten days earlier must count against it.[42] The weather changed for the better by 10 July, and on 11 July the expedition set sail for Normandy.

On Edward's arrival off the Norman coast on 12 July the length of time it took to unload the ships seems to have been determined by the sheer amount of material that was involved. The day-by-day diaries of the clerks of the army all agree that five nights were spent at La Hogue, which would mean that around 200 ships were unloaded each day. It is unlikely that they were all taken into the small harbour at St Vaast-la-Hougue for the purpose, which even today is about 550 yards by 220 yards overall. In the medieval period there would probably have been little more than a small jetty, to allow four or five ships at most to moor alongside. The shallowness of the bays to the north and south of St Vaast, protected from the westerly wind which had probably brought the fleet across, meant that a good number of ships could be moored so that they dried out at low tide. High water was at about 11 a.m. on 12 July, and the first ships would have been moored inshore at that point, and unloaded in the afternoon. The same pattern would apply to the following days, with the time of high tide moving on by about an hour

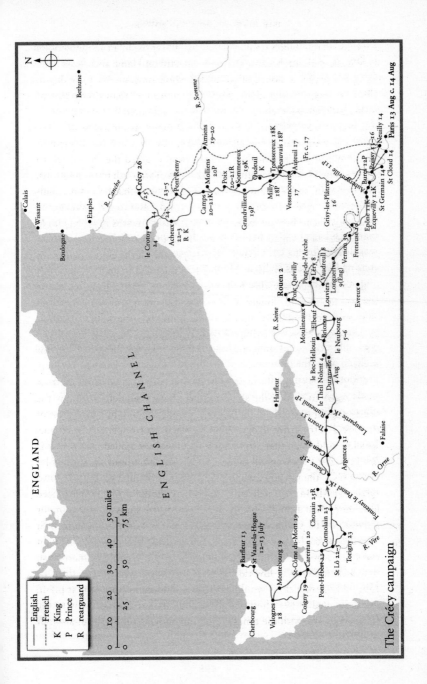

The Crécy campaign

ENGLAND

ENGLISH CHANNEL

Legend:
— English
--- French
K King
P Prince
R rearguard

Cherbourg

Barfleur 13
St Vaast-la-Hogue 12–13 July
Montebourg 19
St-Côme-du-Mont 19
Valognes 18
Coigny 19
Carentan 20
Pont-Hébert 21
St Lô 22–3
Chouain 25R
Cormolain 23
Torigny 23

Harfleur

Fontenay le Pesnel 1K
Cheux 25P
Caen 26–30
Argences 31
Falaise

R. Vire
R. Orne

Evreux

Troarn 31
Lisieux 1P
Rumesnil 1P
Léaupartie 1K
le Theil Nolent 4
Durand ... 4 Aug
le Bec-Hellouin
Brionne
le Neubourg 5–6
Elbeuf
Moulineaux
Louviers
Vaudreuil 8
Léry 8
Pont-de-l'Arche
Pont Quévilly
Rouen 2
Longueville
Vernon 3
Freneuse
Épône 11P

R. Seine

Grisy-les-Plâtres 16
Aubergenville 11P
Épône 11P
Ecqueville 12K
St Germain 14
St Cloud 14
Neuilly 14
Paris 13 Aug c. 14 Aug
Meulan 12K
Bures 12P
Poissy 13–16
Fr. c. 17
Auteuil 17
Vessencourt 17
Beauvais 18P
Troissereux 18K
Mille 18P
Grandvilliers 19P
Poix 20–21R
Sommereux 19K
Oudeuil K
Molliens 20P
Camps 20–21K
Amiens 19–20
Acheux 22–3 R K
le Crotoy 24
Crécy 26
Pont-Remy 23–5
25
24

R. Somme
R. Canche
R. Authie

Calais
Wissant
Boulogne
Etaples
Bethune

Scale:
0   10   20   30   40   50 miles
0   25   50   75 km

N

a day.[43] The tidal range is on average around sixteen feet, and the beach is largely sand with smooth rocks. Unloading could then have been done across the beach, with plenty of space to work on a number of ships at the same time. The selection of this landing place, ideal for a large fleet, points to good local knowledge, and thus almost certainly to the advice of Godefroy d'Harcourt and his companions, since the Harcourt lands lay only a short distance away: his base was the great castle at St Sauveur-le-Vicomte.

The English fleet came into the bay in the morning, at low water, and the leaders of the army only disembarked when the tide was nearly high, at noon. The first action of the campaign was a traditional ceremony: in anticipation of battle, it was customary to create new knights, and to mark the beginning of the invasion the prince of Wales, aged sixteen, was dubbed by his father, together with several of his companions. The *Acts of War* names William Montagu, heir to the earldom of Salisbury and son of the king's closest friend, as well as Roger Mortimer, son of the earl of March, William le Ros, Roger de la Warre and Richard de Vere 'and various others'. Other nobles knighted men in their retinues.

The expedition had achieved its first objective: complete surprise. It was only at the end of June that the French government in Paris had realized what the destination of the English force was likely to be. Preparations for raising a fleet to challenge any seaborne invasion had been made as early as March, but this relied on hiring galleys from Genoa, which had to make the long Atlantic sea voyage to reach the Channel: in early July they had got as far as Lisbon, and there was no French force at sea because the local shipping (including seventy-eight galleys built in Normandy) was to be under the command of the absent Genoese.[44] The French should have been able to deduce that the only likely objectives were Brittany or Normandy, since the fleet had assembled at Portsmouth, but no real provision had been made for the defence of the north. This was because the French armies were fully occupied elsewhere: in Brittany, Thomas Dagworth had defeated the troops of Charles de Blois on 9 June, and Henry of Grosmont was harassing the French besiegers of the great fortress at Aiguillon on the river Lot. As soon as it became apparent that the English fleet was ready to move, the constable of France, Raoul count of Eu, was ordered to return from the army in Gascony to take command of Harfleur, the port at the mouth of the Seine.[45] The garrisons along the coast to the north of Harfleur were reinforced; from all this, it is clear that the French believed that the landing would take place in the Seine estuary. The Cherbourg peninsula, more than 100 miles away, was defended only by local militias and a handful of mercenaries. At St Vaast itself, the only troops in the neighbourhood, 500 Genoese crossbowmen, had withdrawn because they had not been paid. A handful of local men attempted to ambush Thomas Beauchamp and his party, but were quickly driven off. Robert Bertrand, one of the two marshals of France, who had summoned the militia to resist the English landing, withdrew once he saw the overwhelming size of the English force. He must have done so reluctantly, because it was a personal quarrel between him, his brother the bishop of Bayeux and Godefroy d'Harcourt that had led to the latter joining the English king.

Edward was thus able, as his clerk Michael Northburgh reported later in the month, 'to disembark the horses, to rest himself and his men and to bake bread until the following Tuesday'.[46] Raids were carried out on nearby towns and villages on the first night after landing, after which Edward issued his proclamation that the inhabitants of his new kingdom were not to be harmed, unless they resisted him. However, this did not prevent further raids across the peninsula, and an attack on the port of Barfleur, which was burnt: this was a legitimate target, as the port contained 'seven curiously fitted-out warships'. Destruction of shipping along the coast, to prevent its being used in naval operations, was a regular feature of operations while the army was within reach of the sea.

When the army set out on 18 July, they marched in the three divisions which had already been organized.[47] Much ink has been spilt over what Edward III had in mind as his army marched into the hills and woods of the Cotentin peninsula. There was certainly a deeper strategy at work, given the scale of the expedition, and a strategy which operated on several levels: the overall English engagement with the French, the immediate objective of the raid into Normandy, the day-to-day effect of the army's destructive actions on the French populace, and the ultimate exit plan for the operation. One objective was to relieve the pressure on the two much smaller English armies already operating in France, and in this he succeeded before he had even landed, drawing the constable and marshals of France away from the siege of Aiguillon to defend the Normandy coast. A second aim was probably to attempt to force Philip VI to face him in battle. Philip had preferred a defensive strategy in Flanders in the late 1330s, and, despite moments when an encounter seemed imminent, had always backed away from engaging with the English army. There is always a danger of reading intentions after the outcome is known, but the argument that a battle was the purpose of Edward's invasion is hard to resist. This in turn dictated his day-to-day conduct: he had to show that the French king was unable to protect the inhabitants of Normandy, so that Philip was forced to prove that he was equal to the task of taking on the invaders. Edward was 'seeking battle' from the outset, and his behaviour was therefore provocative: but he chose his targets carefully, to secure maximum damage with minimum risk to himself. And it is also reasonably clear that his exit plan, whether in victory or defeat, was to join up with the small English force under Hugh Hastings operating in alliance with the Flemish on France's north-eastern border, either to continue the campaign or to re-embark from Flanders.[48]

Edward's hope was that by marching close to Paris, preferably on the north bank of the Seine, he would draw Philip's army to a battlefield of his own choosing. Philip's obvious choice of a rendezvous for his troops would be Rouen, the capital of Normandy, and Edward's route was designed to bring him close to that city, but without any intention of attacking it. He did not intend to besiege any towns, as he would then lose the manoeuvrability which was essential if he was to be able to choose the best site for a battle. The early stages of the march took the army through a series of small towns in the Cotentin: Valognes was taken on the first night, and set on fire as the troops left the following morning. The next day presented a real obstacle: the road eastwards led through Carentan, approached by bridges and causeways across extensive marshes stretching down to the sea on the north and reaching far inland to the south. Fugitives had warned the townsmen of the approaching enemy, and the main bridge was broken to prevent their passage. The army had to encamp at the hilltop village of St Côme-du-Mont while a task force was sent down to repair the damage. The carpenters, guarded by Reginald Cobham, Roger Mortimer, Hugh Despenser, Bartholomew Burghersh the younger, John Stirling and their men, worked through the night, and the army crossed the next morning to Carentan. After a brief resistance, the garrison surrendered and the commanders went over to the English side. It seems that at this stage Edward still envisaged holding the territory which he had invaded, as the commanders were left in charge of the castle in his name. However, it was retaken by the French soon after Edward left, and they were executed for treason.[49] The town itself was sacked by the footsoldiers, who rampaged out of control, wasting wine and food; and local chronicles record that more than a thousand of the inhabitants were killed. Edward had to repeat his edict about the need for discipline, and emphasized 'that no one should waste more food than he needed'.[50] On Friday, 21 July, having crossed the bridges and causeway across the marshes beyond Carentan, scouts found that the next key bridge, in the valley below Pont-Hébert, had again been broken. The prince of Wales's men repaired it the following day, and the army moved on to the town of St Lô. Here Edward signalled his support for Godefroy d'Harcourt and his own status as king of France by burying the heads of three of Harcourt's supporters which had been displayed in the town since their execution for treason in 1343.[51]

Robert Bertrand had retreated in the direction of Caen after his abortive attempt to resist the English landing, and it was reported that he and the constable of France, Raoul count of Eu, had only left St Lô the previous day. Edward was now on the alert for the appearance of the French forces, but they had regrouped within the defences of Caen. Caen lay on the river Orne, and seagoing vessels could come up to the town. It was a rich merchant town, with good defences and a powerful castle, and Edward's tactic was to avoid any fortified place which might delay him or involve the risk of casualties. The presence of the French forces threatened to block his route or at the very least cut off his line of retreat to the ships along the coast. Edward was anxious to keep in touch with his fleet, both as a source of supplies and as a possible means of escape if matters went seriously wrong.

Despite his reluctance to attack a place as strong as Caen, there were therefore good reasons why the army could not simply continue on its way. So Edward encamped in the villages around the town and sent a monk, Geoffrey of Maldon, to offer terms to the citizens, by which their goods would be spared if they surrendered. But Geoffrey did not return. The bishop of Bayeux, Godefroy d'Harcourt's old enemy and now commander of the garrison in the castle, threw him in prison, as a challenge to the English. It was a challenge which was quickly taken up. At dawn the next day, the prince's division and the king's division approached the town, and met with no armed resistance when they entered the landward gates. Half the town was quickly secured, including the twin abbeys for monks and nuns founded by William the Conqueror and his wife: the prince of Wales took up his quarters in the Abbaye aux Dames. The French were hugely outnumbered, as they had only managed to raise 200 armed men and 100 crossbowmen; they had therefore retreated towards the fortified part of the town, the *grand bourg*, around the harbour and the castle, which was separated from the rest of the town by a bridge and a ford. They were backed up by thirty ships in the port, which were positioned to prevent the English from crossing over to the *grand bourg*.

A fierce and undisciplined attack on the bridge, which was guarded by a tower at the entrance, began, and met with equally fierce resistance. Welsh archers fought the Genoese crossbowmen at the ford; it was low tide,[52] and they managed to get at the ships and burn two of them. They then found small boats, and made a landing, while at the same time the English at the bridge overwhelmed the defenders and forced them to retreat and take refuge in nearby buildings. Despite impromptu resistance by the inhabitants, who built barriers using doors and windows from the houses, the English quickly flushed out their enemies, though some found refuge in the castle. Many important captives were taken. Thomas Holland captured the constable, Raoul count of Eu,[53] and a knight in the prince's service, Thomas Daniel, took the count of Tancarville, one of the marshals, prisoner. Nearly a hundred prisoners were taken in all, though in the confusion and lack of discipline, the English footsoldiers killed a number of French noblemen. More than 2,500 men were slain, which implies that a large number of townsmen were among the victims. Edward had his edict against indiscriminate slaughter repeated, but it was clear that the army could not be tightly controlled, and there was in any case a well-established understanding that, under the laws of war, any town taken by storm was open to ravaging by the victors.

The booty taken at Caen quickly became a legend. The *Acts of War* describes how, once the fighting was over, 'the English eagerly returned to the work of despoiling the town, only taking jewels, clothing or precious ornaments because of the abundance. The English sent their booty to their ships . . . [which] followed them along the shore . . . They found such a mass of goods sent to them that they could not transport all the spoils from Caen and elsewhere.'[54] A seventeenth-century French author

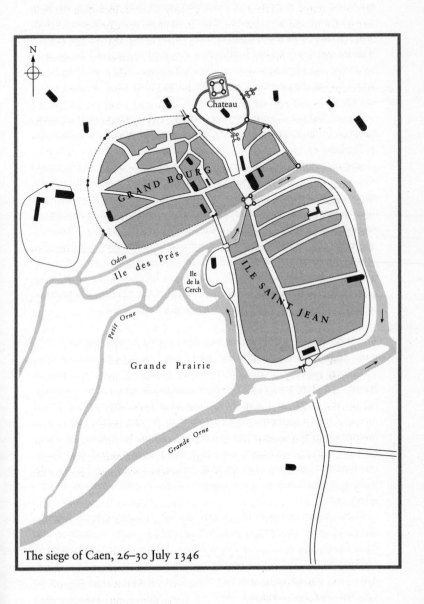

The siege of Caen, 26–30 July 1346

believed that 40,000 pieces of cloth were taken from the town, while in the eighteenth century Thomas Warton dated the rise of certain English families from the sack of Caen and the riches that it brought to them.[55] William Clinton, earl of Huntingdon, returned to England 'because of his grave and perilous sickness, although he was very unwilling to go back', taking the prisoners with him; he was instructed by the king to tell the whole story to the royal council.[56]

Part of William Clinton's report was a splendid propaganda coup for Edward. In the town archives at Caen, a detailed plan for the invasion of England in 1339 by John duke of Normandy was found. This was almost certainly due to information provided by Godefroy d'Harcourt, who would have known about the document. It must have been carefully removed from the archives before they were burnt, and it was sent at once to London, where the archbishop of Canterbury read it out on 14 August at a service of prayers for the king's success in France.[57] Edward was now able to claim that his expedition was not only to secure his title to the throne of France, but was an essential pre-emptive strike to ensure the peace of England. This, together with the reports of the huge prizes taken at Caen, changed the attitude of the nation at large from reluctant acquiescence in the war to positive enthusiasm.

The army remained in Caen for five days, during which time the inhabitants of Bayeux, terrified by the fate of Caen, surrendered to the king. They were probably extremely concerned because it was the bishop of Bayeux who had mistreated Geoffrey of Maldon, and was now holding out in the castle at Caen. According to a local chronicle, Edward arranged for a garrison of 1,500 men to be left in the town, and instructed them to besiege the castle. Once again, this implies an intention to hold the conquered territory on a permanent basis. But a combination of a popular uprising and a sortie by the bishop and Robert Bertrand led to the slaughter of the English garrison shortly afterwards.[58]

On 31 July the English forces moved a few miles outside the town to the great abbey at Troarn, overlooking another natural obstacle, the wide marshlands of the river Dives. A long day's march brought them to Léaupartie, the first village on dry ground on the far side of the valley. They then turned south towards the cathedral city of Lisieux, where Edward met two cardinals sent by the pope from Avignon, who attempted to negotiate a peace between the English and French kings. They had come from an interview with Philip, who was urgently gathering an army at Rouen forty miles away. They offered Edward the duchy of Aquitaine, to be held on the terms that his father had enjoyed, and with the restoration of the same lands, but 'the king thought that their mission was a waste of time',[59] and sent the cardinals back to the papal court after restoring twenty horses which his Welsh soldiers had seized from them.

When the English army set out again on 4 August, the Flemish allies led by Hugh Hastings had invaded French territory south of Calais. France was now under attack in Normandy, Aquitaine and Artois; Philip could only let matters take their course in Aquitaine and summon local militias to deal with the Flemish army, while he concentrated on plans to destroy Edward's forces. On 6 August Godefroy d'Harcourt was sent to reconnoitre Rouen, and was able to report that Philip and his army were now in the castle and city; ditches had been dug in addition to the existing defences, and the main bridges had been broken. Edward was south of the Seine, and urgently needed to cross the river northwards, in order to be able to regain the coast. In a letter of 27 July, he had asked for the ships which had returned to England after Caen with the earl of Huntingdon to be sent back to Le Crotoy, a port on the north bank of the river Somme, with such money and men as the council in England could raise, as well as bows, bowstrings and arrows.[60] If he could not force a battle with Philip, he would at least be able to join up with his Flemish allies.

But Le Crotoy was due north, and for the next nine days he was forced to march down the south bank of the Seine, attempting a crossing wherever he thought it might be feasible, while Philip watched and waited on the other side. There was a marked change in the conditions in which the troops were operating from the first weeks of the campaign. As far as Lisieux, there had been opportunities for replenishing supplies by raiding small undefended towns and villages, and there had been little time for the French to organize the withdrawal of stores into fortified safe places. The terrain was good agricultural land, for the most part. Now, along the Seine valley, the army was repeatedly faced with strongly defended towns, garrisoned and well organized, which they could not take without considerable delay. And delay was not an option: Edward knew that he had to keep one step ahead of Philip, and find a way to cross the Seine before the French army was in position on the other bank. So the troops moved on, testing the defences of the bridges and the towns as they went, from Le Neubourg to Elbeuf, where the Welsh troops managed to cross the Seine by swimming, and brought back a number of small boats after driving off the French who met them on the far bank. Possibly because of the presence of these French soldiers, no attempt was made to mend the broken bridge.

Rather than follow the meandering course of the river, Edward cut across country, 'taking his whole army across country where no one had ever travelled before',[61] and went direct to Vernon to see if he could cross there. However, the town was vigorously defended, and he was unable to gain access to the bridge. The castles at Gaillon, north of Vernon, and at La Roche-Guyon to the east of the town were both attacked, and the first was burnt. The raid on La Roche-Guyon was daring: Robert Ferrers took his men across the Seine in small boats and forced their way into the castle, which surrendered. The *Acts of War* claims that the castle was full of noble ladies, who were released unharmed on promising to raise ransoms for the knights and squires who had been captured. No attempt was made to hold the castle, and the exercise seems to have been a piece of bravado, as there was no question of the army crossing at this point. Edward Attewode[62] was killed here, and either at this castle or at Gaillon Richard Talbot and Thomas Holland were wounded.[63] The following day, 10 August, the army tested the defences at Mantes, and the next day at Meulan, and found them both too strong. At Meulan, the bridge was defended by a tower filled with men at arms and crossbowmen, and there was no quick way of seizing it.

Philip continued to track Edward's movements, and realized that his next target would be Poissy, a major crossing-place ten miles to the west of Paris. The French broke down the bridge because the defensive wall around it had not been reinforced, and evacuated the town, including the convent of which Philip's sister was the prioress. This was Edward's last chance: the march from Lisieux had been arduous, and supplies had been hard to come by, particularly in the deserted country north of Vernon. He could not hope to attack Paris itself, and, if he failed to cross the river, he would be forced to turn back and retrace his steps: he had already requested urgent reinforcements and supplies to be landed on the Normandy coast, and his situation was perilous. The king arrived at Poissy on 13 August, and took up his quarters in the new royal palace, while the prince of Wales installed himself in the old palace, and ordered the carpenters to set about repairing the bridge. That afternoon, the workmen had succeeded in laying a sixty-foot-long beam across the gap when a small French force was seen in the distance. Although the beam was only a foot wide, sufficient English men at arms and archers, led by the earl of Northampton, managed to cross it in time to drive off the French, inflicting heavy casualties. They found twenty-one carts loaded with stone shot and crossbow bolts, evidently intended for an attack on the team repairing the bridge.

This was the most critical moment of the campaign; Edward now needed to gain time for a full repair of the bridge, so he sent out raiding parties to ravage the outskirts of Paris, targeting in particular the royal properties which ringed the city: the castle of Montjoie, Philip's new palace at St Germain-en-Laye and St Cloud were all burnt. Surprisingly, there was no immediate response from the French king, who gathered his army at St Germain-des-Prés on 13 August, and moved the next day to St Denis, to the north of Paris. The 15th of August was one of the great feast days of the Church, the Assumption of the Blessed Virgin Mary, and neither army moved on that day. Despite the reports of English activity on the bridge at Poissy, Philip seems to have believed that the English were heading either for Gascony or for Tournai on the Flemish border, and that, whichever route they chose, they would remain south of Paris. He therefore moved to a position fifteen miles to the south-east of Poissy on 16 August.

The carpenters had had three days in which to work on the bridge unhindered by French attacks. Using timbers from nearby woods and hedgerows, as well as two large pieces fished out of the river,[64] they built a replacement bridge around the sixty-foot beam. As Philip waited for the English to move southwards, the entire force marched north across the newly repaired structure that day. When news of this feat was brought to Philip VI's court, the author of the Grandes chroniques was present, and saw the nobles and knights who advised the king mock the messenger, and call him a liar, because they simply could not believe that it was feasible.[65]

Edward was now on the right course for the intended rendezvous with his ships at Le Crotoy at the mouth of the Somme, and Philip was in the position of having to pursue his enemy, rather than wait at a spot of his own choosing to intercept him. On 14 August, he had issued a challenge to Edward to fight him outside the walls of Paris on the south bank of the Seine, or to the north of Paris. These letters reached Edward three days later, when he was already at Auteuil near Beauvais, forty miles from Paris, and he replied saying that Philip had prevented him from giving battle by breaking down the bridges, and that 'at whatever hour you approach, you will find us ready to meet you in the field', but not on the terms and conditions dictated by his opponent.[66] If Edward moved fast, Philip was even swifter, and by Sunday, 20 August he was in Amiens, where he had given orders for troops to assemble at the beginning of the month: they had been gathering there since 4 August, and for once the French king had his men in exactly the right place. He had brought a contingent under the command of King John of Bohemia with him in the rapid march from Paris.

Edward was only ten miles away, and his men were suffering from shortages of food: on the previous Friday they had had to eat meat instead of fish, and bread was sold in the army for five shillings a loaf. Only the royal household was exempt from eating meat, because the king's fishermen had caught an abundance of fish in the local rivers. Furthermore, there were problems with discipline: Edward gave orders to press on as quickly as possible, but a rebellious detachment, possibly the Welsh archers of the prince of Wales, led by the Flemish knight Wulfart Ghistels, attacked the strongly fortified town of Poix, even though the king twice sent sergeants to order them to halt their activities. The army's progress was hindered by the local militia, and by some Bohemian troops who rode out from Amiens: in both skirmishes, the English were able to beat off the assault, but at the cost of further delays.

Once again, Edward was faced with the problem of escaping from a French army which was closing in on him by finding a way across a major river: Le Crotoy, his objective, was on the north bank of the Somme. According to Jean le Bel, the king waited at Airaines, risking a full-scale attack by the French, because he wished to find an easy passage across the river.[67] He organized a diversionary attack on the town of Oisemont to try to deceive Philip, as it lay in the opposite direction to his intended route; it was taken and set on fire so that the French king's scouts would see it. He sent Thomas Beauchamp and Godefroy d'Harcourt to the nearby town of Pont-Rémy, but found it heavily defended, and they were beaten off before they could capture the bridge. The same thing happened at the bridge at Long-en-Ponthieu, and three

Cassini's map of the mouth of the river Somme, 1790, showing Blanchetaque.

other possible crossings were investigated without challenging the French troops which guarded them. Thomas Beauchamp had ridden thirty miles and fought two skirmishes, but he had nothing to offer the king. However, this was country well known to a number of the English army: Ponthieu had been in English possession until 1338 and Edward himself had been at the castle of Crécy a few miles to the north in 1329. The Somme estuary was shallow and marshy, and there were a number of crossing-places known to the locals, though most of them were quite unsuitable for an army with heavy carts which would require a large ford. The existence of a good ford, known as the 'white spot' or Blanchetaque, was rumoured, but the English had to find it.

The chroniclers give the impression that although the existence of the ford at Blanchetaque was known, its exact nature was a problem. Edward had moved north again, towards Abbeville, the most important town in the area, which his troops had reconnoitred, hoping perhaps to surprise the garrison of this well-defended place. Instead, they had met the French outside the walls, because they had sallied out to meet them. They were victorious in the ensuing skirmish, but the possibility of capturing the bridge was gone.

That evening, encamped at Acheux, Edward sent out scouts to look for the ford. The most probable account of its discovery is given by the Bernier family's chronicle of Valenciennes, a generally reliable source. A squire from the retinue of Wulfart Ghistels came back to the camp and told the king that he had found a good way across: 'and it has a good bottom, because I crossed it several times on horseback when the tide had gone down a little.' Philip was also aware of the crossings in the seven miles of marsh and river between Abbeville and the sea, and had sent Godemar du Fay with three other knights, 500 men at arms and 3,000 of the local militia, to guard these crossings. From the north bank, any movement on the other side of the river would have been clearly visible. By the time the English army was in place at the ford, Godemar had found them, and drew up his men on the north bank. He had Genoese crossbowmen with him. Meanwhile, Philip had set out from Abbeville with his main army in the hope of catching the English before they crossed the ford, and forcing them to engage hemmed in by the river, without being able to choose their field of battle.

The story of the passage of the English army and its dramatic escape from the pursuing French army became the stuff of legend very quickly.

The most reliable accounts, as always, are those brief passages in the English newsletters written within days of the event. They agree that this was not a narrow ford, but a crossing on a broad front: Richard Wynkeley, the king's confessor, wrote on 2 September:

> our lord the king was unable to find a way across except in the tidal reach between Crotoy and Abbeville; here the whole army crossed unharmed at a place which none of the local people knew to be a safe ford except for six or ten people at a time. Our men crossed almost everywhere, as if it were a safe ford, much to the amazement of those who knew the place.[68]

Edward III gives a similar description:

> When we came to the river Somme, we found the bridges broken, so we went towards St Valery to cross at a ford where the sea ebbs and flows ... By God's grace a thousand men crossed abreast where before this barely three or four used to cross, and so we and all our army crossed safely in an hour and a half.[69]

The idea of 1,000 men in line abreast is obviously an exaggeration, as this would need an area nearly half a mile wide, yet it was clearly a broad crossing place. This is confirmed by the account of the Valenciennes chronicle. When the army reached the river bank, the squire

> spurred his horse and went into the water, and he rode down river and up river in the presence of the king and his men. And when he had tested the bottom down river and up river, he came out, and said to the king, 'Did I tell you the truth?' And the king agreed, and at once gave him a hundred *écus*.[70]

The squire does not ride *across* the river, but goes up and down to show that the troops can cross abreast.

The St Omer chronicle describes the ford as being near St Valéry, a place 'where the cattle of the region were accustomed to cross when the tide was out', which would again indicate a broad passage.[71] And Jean le Bel says that Edward was told that a dozen men abreast could cross; 'and carts can cross there safely, too, because there's a bed of good, firm chalk, which is why it's called Blanchetaque.'[72] Henry Knighton records that 'no regular passage there was known to the men of those lands, and so they crossed a wash of the sea about a league wide'.[73] It is quite clear from these descriptions that this is not a river ford, but in the estuary itself. The estuary is sand, but the chalk cliffs at St Valéry indicate that there is a band of chalk on the river bed which reappears at Le Crotoy. Even so, this would be a treacherous crossing without a guide, as the sands would drift over the chalk base. Today there are organized guided walks across the estuary from St Valéry to Le Crotoy,[74] and, although the estuary has silted considerably since the river was turned into a canal in the eighteenth century a couple of miles inland, the basic geology would of course have been the same. The chronicle of Meaux abbey in east Yorkshire says that

> King Edward, instructed by a certain Englishman born at Ruston near Nafferton, who had lived in those parts for sixteen years, went to a ford on the aforesaid river [the Somme] at the towns of St Valéry and Le Crotoy, where the sea flows and ebbs. He crossed there with his men, where previously the local inhabitants had never crossed more than six or four at once.[75]

Nafferton was one of the abbey's larger estates, and this is possibly first-hand information. If the crossing was indeed there, Edward's informant may well have shown the king the way across the difficult sands, which required a knowledgeable guide: the distance was about two miles, and involved the crossing of at least one channel. Similar sand-crossings, for example at Morecambe Bay in England, were crossed by coaches in the eighteenth century, and would easily have borne the weight of carts if the right track could be found.

It was high water during the night, at 3 a.m., and the army left Acheux at dawn, which would have been at 5.30 a.m., and reached St Valéry at low water. The sands would have been passable around 7.30 a.m. It was three days after spring tides, so there would have been little or no tidal water at this point, and only a narrow flow from the river Somme. It was an ideal moment for a mass of men to cross: Edward's luck had held. The English formed up in battle order on the south bank, and moved across ready for action. The archers were in front, as they would normally be on the battlefield, since their range was considerably greater than the crossbowmen they were expecting to encounter. They were followed by the Welsh spearmen, and a contingent led by Thomas Beauchamp and Godefroy d'Harcourt; then came the carts carrying provisions and supplies, and the main divisions of the army led by the king, the prince of Wales and the bishop of Durham. The advance party were detailed to fight off the French defending the north shore. It seems that they did this without any help from the rest of the army. Godemar du Fay, who was a distinguished commander, simply did not have enough men to resist the English onslaught, and was forced to flee after a bitter fight, having lost a large number of his men.

Soon after the crossing was completed, the French army came into sight on the south shore. Philip had hoped to find the English delayed by Godemar du Fay, and at his mercy, but he had already been told by his scouts that they were crossing successfully. He probably arrived at Blanchetaque after 9.30 a.m., when the tide would have turned, and it was dangerous to attempt the crossing when the water was rising if he was to get his whole army safely across.[76] According to Edward's newsletter,

> That same day, soon after we had crossed the river, our adversary appeared on the other bank with a very large force. He arrived so suddenly that we were not in the least ready; so we waited there and took up battle positions, and stayed like this the whole day and the next day, until the afternoon. Finally, when we saw that he did not want to cross but turned back towards Abbeville, we marched towards Crécy to meet him on the other side of the forest.[77]

Edward was now on familiar ground. He had been at Crécy in 1329, and had hunted there; one of his commanders, Bartholomew Burghersh the elder, had been seneschal of Ponthieu at the time, and is likely to have visited the castle of Crécy, while Gawan Corder, a knight in the royal household, had held a manor nearby. The accounts of the clerk of the kitchen record that the army camped that night 'below the forest of Crécy', but this does not imply that the men were in a thickly wooded area. The medieval forest was a place where forest law applied, and, as with the New Forest in England today, it included areas of heathland or open scrub. It appears that the forest area stretched down to the river bank, with the wooded area, which still exists today, to the north.

Edward's move the next day took him out of sight of any French scouts watching from the south bank, and to a site which he quickly identified as an ideal ground on which to meet Philip's army. It has been argued that Edward had considered this as a possible battleground from early in the campaign, and that the request for provisions and men to be sent to Le Crotoy relates to the idea that he could lure the French to

Crécy. This seems unlikely; one of the skills of the medieval general was to choose the right terrain swiftly and under pressure, as the vagaries of any campaign were far too great to allow for much planning. But once Edward was at Crécy, he and his commanders saw the potential of the land to the east of the forest as terrain on which the military techniques they had learnt in Scotland could be deployed to advantage.

The exact site of the battle, generally thought to have been the fields to the east of the village of Crécy, cannot be identified for certain.[78] The greatest problem is that there is absolutely no solid archaeological evidence to indicate that a battle was fought on the area now generally accepted as the battlefield. Added to this is general confusion among the chroniclers as to the description of the site; but it is open rolling country and it is extremely difficult to characterize a given place or even an area. One prominent physical contour on the hillside, a steep bank called the Vallée des Clercs with a drop of sixteen feet, is not mentioned by any of the chroniclers, but would certainly have played a major part in determining the direction of the French attack. All we can say for certain is that the slopes running down from the ridge to the north of the village to the little river Maye, and bounded on the south-west by the bank, are the most likely position for the battlefield. The river may have been wider, and the water table higher, in the fourteenth century, and therefore more of an obstacle to the advance – or retreat – of an army.

The ground is thin soil over chalk, which may account for the lack of archaeological finds. Some of this would have been cultivated land, in the traditional medieval form of strip farming: between the crops there would have been strips of grazing. It was a landscape of small and varied agricultural activities, with no particular features to help or hinder the movement of an army. Edward's defensive positions were evidently towards the top of the hill, as was usual: the uphill slope would slow both the attacking infantry and cavalry. The only prominent object mentioned by a small number of chroniclers is a windmill at the top of the slope, from which Edward is said to have directed his troops.

We can describe the setting of the battle with reasonable confidence. When it comes to the action, the task is much harder.

7

The Battle at Crécy

What happened at Crécy in the following days became an instant sensation: word of this astonishing event spread rapidly through Europe, and its mythical status survives even today. English families will claim with pride that they had an ancestor who fought at Crécy; though these claims are all too often unfounded, deriving from Victorian patriotism rather than any genuine tradition, the battle is an event which still resounds.

The problems of retrieving any real picture of the events leading up to the battle or of the battle itself are extremely difficult. Chroniclers faced with describing such a battle, with little hard information to go on, either tended to rely on the testimony of individuals, or retreated to a summary of the reasons why the English won or the French lost, depending on their viewpoint. Even within a decade of the battle, we can detect these two tendencies at work, and there is a third difficulty: the sheer impossibility of any one single observer being able to know what was actually happening on the ground. What the chroniclers managed to record is the individual impressions of soldiers which were very largely determined by their position within the battle array. The only people who might have been able to give a more coherent account would have been the king himself and his commanders, if the story that the king stationed himself on a windmill to the rear of the battlefield is true, as it very probably is: ten years later, at Poitiers, the prince of Wales established himself on a high point which gave him an overview of the fighting. A handful of men with the king at Crécy might have had some idea of the sequence of events, but would have known little of the details.

The battle of Crécy has been endlessly analysed by military historians with their neat diagrams of oblong blocks of troops, arrows indicating movement, and precise maps of the terrain. Their concern is with military strategy and organization, but none of the chroniclers on whom they have to rely have more than a rudimentary grasp of such matters. They rarely agree as to the number and position of the battalions, their commanders or their manoeuvres. Instead of beginning with the overall picture, it is far more realistic to listen to the witnesses as carefully as we can, and see what conclusions we may draw.

The idea that no one could really know what went on in a medieval battle was admirably summed up by Gilles li Muisit, the abbot of Tournai, writing his account of the battle of Crécy five years later. Anticipating John Keegan's classic account of the difficulty of using eyewitness accounts for the events of Waterloo by six hundred years,[1] Li Muisit roundly declared that, in the heat of the fighting, no one was aware of more than his immediate surroundings:

> Since the events of war are uncertain, and seeing that the conflict is between deadly enemies, each fighting man intent on conquering rather than being conquered, and no one can take account of all those fighting around him, nor can those present form a good judgement of these matters, only the result of their deeds can be judged. Therefore, because many men say and record many things about this conflict, and on the side of the French king and his men some maintain things which cannot be known for certain, and others on the part of the English king also maintain things about which the truth is not known, because of these varying opinions I will not enquire after the event about what cannot be proved, but have tried to satisfy the understanding of those who come after me by setting down only those things which I have heard from certain people worthy of belief, even if I cannot be totally sure that they are what happened.[2]

The only direct eyewitnesses for the events of the battle are from the English side. They are from Edward himself and his administrative staff, in the newsletters sent back to England within days of the battle. What they have to tell us is meagre and disappointing, but the writers were probably well aware that, although they were almost the only people to have any kind of overview of the battle, even they could not describe the action with any precision. The accounts of the capture of Caen had been more detailed, because the stages of the struggle were marked by buildings which could be readily identified and remembered. But here at

Crécy, there had been a mass of men in hand-to-hand combat in the open field. Edward himself is extremely terse as to the action: 'The battle was very fierce and long drawn out, lasting from mid-afternoon until the evening. The enemy bore themselves nobly, and often rallied, but in the end, praise be to God, they were defeated and our adversary fled.'[3] When it comes to the aftermath, he is on surer ground; he has the names of the kings who were killed, and knows that many other nobles died, who have not been identified at the time of writing. And he has seen that in the 'small area' where the first attack took place, 'more than 1,500 knights and squires died'.

Michael Northburgh simply echoes the king's phrases, saying that the battle was 'very stubborn, and endured a long while, because the enemy bore themselves very nobly'. Richard Wynkeley, in contrast, does have some details: 'The adversary himself [i.e. Philip], intending to attack the king personally, stationed himself in the front line; and he was opposed by the prince, who was in our front line. After a fierce and prolonged conflict, the adversary was twice driven off, and a third time, having gathered his men, the fighting was fiercely renewed.'[4] Wynkeley does not say that the battle was won, but lists the kings and nobles who died, and claims that the French king, wounded in the face by an arrow, barely escaped, and that the French standard, the *oriflamme*, was torn to pieces and its bearer killed. He concludes by giving thanks for the escape of Edward and his army 'from great danger'.

These were the immediate messages home. Was there an official account, at greater length, which recorded the battle in more vivid terms? The *Acts of War* is incomplete, and looks very much like an official record of the campaign. It opens with pomp and ceremony: 'These are the acts of war of the most illustrious prince lord Edward, by grace of God king of England and France and of Edward the eldest son of that king, prince of Wales, duke of Cornwall and earl of Chester, which they did at sea and in the kingdom of France, from the last day of June 1346 onwards.'[5] What is striking is that the timespan of the campaign is left in the air: where one would expect a triumphant mention of Crécy and Calais, there is nothing, no ending. There is the question of whether the *Acts* was ever completed. We have no way of knowing, except by looking for traces of it in the contemporary English chronicles. If it was finished in late 1346, Adam Murimuth and Robert of Avesbury, with good access to official records, would almost certainly have used it. Instead, they have only the newsletters. This means that it is unlikely to have been – as has been suggested – the same as the report that Bartholomew Burghersh the elder presented to parliament at Westminster on 13 September 1346, in which he

> declared the graces which God had given our lord the king and others of his company since their arrival at la Hogue in Normandy, such as good towns, castles, and prisons, takings of war, both at Caen and in many other places, and also the victory which God gave them at Crécy, where the enemy was defeated with all his great host . . .

Burghersh went on to outline the king's intention to take Calais, where the siege had just begun, and then to go in pursuit of his enemy and not to return to England before he had brought an end to his war overseas. He then produced the plan for the invasion of Normandy found at Caen, and used this and the king's achievements as a basis for a request for new taxes.[6]

The purpose of the *Acts of War* is therefore not clear. All we can say is that the writer was a clerk deeply involved in the campaign, with access to documents such as Philip's challenge to battle sent to Edward and Edward's reply. What we have is probably written up from notes made at the time, but this could have been done a year or two after the campaign. Judging from his accounts of other military actions, the writer is relying on what he sees himself, and on the immediate talk within the camp. His account of Crécy, if it ever existed, would have been similar: it would have been detailed and immensely valuable, but it would have been gathered from individuals rather than edited as an official history.

There may have been other such documents; indeed, given that we know that a number of letters were sent home, and that some of them were addressed to individuals rather than sent for official circulation, it is virtually certain that the surviving letters are only a portion of those which contained descriptions of the battle. Details that are found in later English chronicles may be from eyewitness accounts. On the other hand, there are no narratives of the battle in the English chronicles which immediately stand out as coming from a single comprehensive version of the events at Crécy. With one exception, Adam Murimuth, whose work ends in 1347, the chroniclers are writing at the distance of a decade or more, most of them after the second great English victory, at Poitiers in 1356; they are inevitably influenced by the stories, true or otherwise, that grew up around the earlier spectacular victory in the interval. But the English historians do not tell those stories; instead, we have a detail here and there which sheds a little light on the events of the battle.

It is less surprising that the French chroniclers have relatively little to tell us about the events of 26 August 1346. Defeat always figures less largely in the history books than victory, and this is no exception. Furthermore, the earliest major chronicle from France that survives today was written more than thirty years after the event. The Flemish chronicles, however, are much more informative, and seem to have drawn on the experiences of knights from Hainault, who fought on both sides. Jean de Hainault, Philippa's uncle, was one of the French leaders, while there was a strong contingent of Hainault knights and squires in the English ranks. Jean le Bel tells us specifically that his information came from Jean de Hainault personally before his death in November 1356; the chronicle of Valenciennes seems to have drawn on English informants. But neither these nor the other Flemish chronicles give us a rounded account of the sequence of manoeuvres. All we have is a series of snapshots, or collections of snapshots, of episodes within the battle, around which the chroniclers attempt to make sense of the stories they have heard.

For the best contemporary overview of the battle, we have to turn, surprisingly, to an Italian source: the chronicle of Giovanni Villani, writing in Florence. Villani specifically tells us that his information came from several sources; in accounting for the casualties, he prefaces his estimates with the words, 'In the said grievous and unfortunate battle most of those who write about it say . . .' Given that he is writing not later than 1348 – he died of the plague that year – his sources cannot have been other chroniclers, but must have been newsletters reaching the great merchant houses of Florence. He seems to have had news from the French side, and possibly from Genoa, since he has details which appear to come from the crossbowmen themselves, and names both their commanders. Equally, he has good information on the English side, and we know that his contacts with England were very close. His account of the battle tells us a great deal about the disposition of the troops, and particularly about the situation to the rear of the army. Whoever provided the original information knew how the English forces had been organized and placed, and it is tempting to think that it might have been a clerk or administrator who witnessed the fighting from the rearguard.

This is Villani's picture of the battle and the events following the crossing of the Somme at Blanchetaque:

> Then they went on their way, hungry and with great discomfort, marching on Friday, 25 August almost twelve Picard leagues by day and night, without rest, with much anxiety and hunger, and arrived six leagues from Amiens at a place and village beside a forest which was called Crécy. And they had to cross a small river, which was deep, and could only go through it one or two abreast as they came out of the ford, which they had not reckoned on. And hearing that the king of France was following them, they encamped in the place outside Crécy on a hill between Crécy and Abbeville in Ponthieu; and to strengthen their position, feeling that they were very few in number compared with the French, and to increase their safety, they enclosed the army with carts, of which they had plenty, both of their own and from the country.[7] They deliberately left an entrance, and, unable to avoid a battle, they made ready to fight and to die in battle rather than die of hunger, because they could not flee. And the king of England arranged his archers, of whom he had a great many, on top of the carts and underneath them, with guns[8] which fired iron shot,[9] to frighten and destroy the French horses. And the next day he organized his knights into three battalions within the carts.[10] The king's son was the captain of the first, the earl of Arundel of the second, and the king of England of the third. All the riders dismounted with their horse to their right to save their energy and to comfort themselves with food and drink.

Villani's focus then moves to the pursuing French army, hard on the heels of their exhausted prey, and full of self-confidence:

> And they felt that they had plenty of good men at arms and knights, because the king of France had a good 12,000 knights, and almost numberless men at arms on foot, while the king of England had hardly 4,000 knights and 30,000 English and Welsh archers, and some men with Welsh axes and short lances. When they came close enough to the English camp to charge them on horseback, on a Saturday after noon, on 26 August 1346, the king of France arranged his men in three groups, called battles. In the first there were a good 6,000 Genoese and Italian crossbowmen led

by Carlo Grimaldi and Anton Doria, and with the crossbowmen was King John of Bohemia and his son Charles, elected king of the Romans, with some other barons and knights, 3,000 horsemen in all. The next battle was led by Charles count of Alençon, brother of the king of France, with several counts and barons, 4,000 horsemen and a good number of men at arms on foot. The third battle was led by the king of France with the other kings we have named and earls and barons, and the rest of his army, a countless number of men on horse and on foot. As soon as the battle began, there appeared above the armies two great ravens, crying and croaking; and then there was a little shower of rain; and when it stopped, the battle began. The first division with the crossbowmen attacked the carts of the king of England and began to fire with their bows; but they were soon rebuffed, because on the carts and under the carts under cover of the canvas and drapes which protected them from the crossbow bolts, and in the battalions of the king of England, which were inside the array of carts drawn up in good order as battalions of knights, were 30,000 archers, as already mentioned, both English and Welsh, who, when the Genoese fired one round of crossbow bolts, fired three arrows with their bows, like a cloud in the air. They did not fall in vain, but wounded men and horses; there were also shots from the bombards, which made such a roaring and tumult that it seems as if God himself was thundering, with great slaughter of men and bringing down of horses. But what was worse for the French army, because the entrance to the array of carts of the English king was such a narrow place,[11] the second battle led by the count of Alençon pressed the crossbowmen so close against the carts that they could not move or fire with their crossbows, so that many were wounded or killed. Because of this the said crossbowmen could not hold their ground, crowded in and pressed against the carts by their own horsemen; so they turned and fled. The French knights and men at arms, seeing them flee, thought they had been betrayed; they themselves killed them, and few of them escaped. Seeing the first division of crossbowmen of the king of France take to flight, Edward the fourth,[12] son of the English king, prince of Wales, who led the first battalion of his knights, 1,000 in number with 6,000 Welsh archers, mounted his horse and they all rode out of the array of carts to attack the French king's cavalry, with the king of Bohemia and his son in the first battle, and the count of Alençon, brother of the king of France, the count of Flanders, the count of Blois, the count of Harcourt, Sir Jean de Hainault and several other counts and great lords. The encounter was bitter and hard, but the second battalion of the king of England followed after him, led by the earl of Arundel, and they put the first and second battles of the French to flight, mainly through the flight of the Genoese. And in this turmoil were killed the king of Bohemia and the count of Alençon, with many counts and barons and knights and men at arms. The king of France, seeing his people flee, charged the array of carts of King Edward with his third battalion, and did such great deeds of arms himself that he forced the English back inside the carts. And they would all have been defeated if King Edward and his third battalion had not left the array of carts by another opening, which they made so that they could attack the enemy from behind and come to the rescue of their comrades, fiercely attacking the enemy from the flank, with his Welsh and English footmen with bows and Welsh lances, whose only purpose was to disembowel the horses. But what most confused the French was that a multitude of their men, who were both on horse and on foot, who intended to charge the English and break their ranks, piled up on top of one another as had happened at Courtrai with the Flemish; and the dead Genoese hindered them particularly, as they lay on the ground from the rout of the first battalion with exhausted and dying horses; and they were attacked by bombards and arrows so that there were no French horses which were not wounded, and innumerable dead. This grievous battle lasted from vespers to two hours after nightfall. In the end the French could not endure it any longer, and fled; and the king of France fled wounded to Amiens that night . . .

Villani then describes the action on the following day, in the course of which some French troops who had remained on the battlefield made a stand, and were put to flight by Thomas Beauchamp and William Bohun. Further levies then arrived from Amiens, and were likewise defeated, leaving the English in control of the battlefield. He concludes with a list of the dead, and with the moral to be drawn from this disaster:

Among the notable lords who died there were King John of Bohemia with five counts of Germany who were in his company, and the king of Majorca, the count of Alençon, brother of the king of France, the count of Flanders, the count of Blois, the duke of 'Renno', the count of Sancerre, the count of Harcourt, the count of 'Albamala' and his son, the count of Salm in Germany who was with the king of Bohemia, Sir Carlo Grimaldi and Anton Doria of Genoa, and many other lords, for we do not know the names of all of them. King Edward remained on the field for two days, and had the mass of the Holy Spirit sung, thanking God for his victory, and for the dead; he had the place consecrated and buried the dead, both enemy and friend, and had the wounded carried from among the dead and cared for by doctors. The common soldiers were given money and dismissed. The lords who were found among the dead he had buried most nobly there at an abbey, and among the rest he held a most grand and honourable funeral for the king of Bohemia, as befitted a king's corpse, and wept for love of him because of his death. He and many of his barons dressed in black, and sent his body with an honourable escort to Charles his son, who was at the abbey of 'Riscampo', and from there his son took it to Luxembourg. And this done, the said King Edward, after his most fortunate victory, in which few of his people died in comparison with the French, left Crécy and went to Montreuil.

O sanctus sanctus dominus deus Sabaoth, runs the Latin, 'holy, holy, holy, Lord God, lord of hosts', great is Your power in heaven and on earth, and especially in battles. Sometimes and often He makes the smaller number and force conquer the greater army to demonstrate His power, and to beat down pride and pomp, and cleanse the sin of the king and lords and people. And in this defeat He showed His power, because the French were three times as many as the English. But it was not without good reason that this disaster befell the king of France, who among his other sins – quite apart from the wrong done to the king of England and his other lords by occupying their heritage and lordships – had ten years before taken the cross and sworn to Pope John, promising to go overseas within two years to reconquer the Holy Land, and had taken the tenths and subsidies from his whole realm, and made war with them unjustly against Christian lords. As a result of this, 100,000 Armenians and other Christians who had begun a war against the Saracens of Syria expecting his help were killed or enslaved: and that is enough to explain it all.[13]

Villani is a good historian, and this is a historian's account of the battle, the first of many attempts to create some kind of order out of the turmoil of the fighting. His final paragraph shows that he is trying to set out his history in the widest context, that of morality and divine judgement, but at the same time he is a master of detail and analysis. There are obvious errors: numbers, as so often in medieval chronicles, are wild overestimates, because very few people ever saw a large gathering of men. And other points can be corrected either from records or from writers with better sources of information. He is writing before the stories had begun to grow up and before writers like Baker and Froissart made the event into a kind of set piece – for Baker, it is an opportunity for a display of Latin rhetoric, for Froissart, a chance to write it up as a series of scenes from a contemporary romance. Both are in their way deeply serious historians; yet Villani's mixture of businesslike analysis and moral judgement is probably the most accurate of the early chronicles.

The story of Crécy was written and rewritten for the next half-century, using the accounts of men who had been there, quickly becoming a legend rather than history. Villani was probably working entirely from written sources, and had a sound grasp of French geography as well as an instinctive distrust of the personal reminiscence. The anonymous author of a chronicle written in Rome a decade after Villani is principally concerned with the dramatic events that led to the declaration of the Roman republic in 1347. It is a very personal document: the author declares that he has told it from the experiences of himself and of men he knows, but he also gives us 'certain information, in brief, about happenings which were concurrent with these' from written sources.[14] All we know about the author is that he had studied medicine at Bologna in his youth, and that he had read classical authors such as Livy and St Isidore's great medieval encyclopedia called the *Etymologies*. He records in the course of his Roman history other 'novelties' which took place at the same time elsewhere in Europe, one of them being the battle of Crécy. His account seems to rely on at least one contemporary newsletter, from which he got some of his figures for the strength of the armies and the number of those killed, and on oral accounts by Genoese and Bohemian soldiers who took part in the battle. These are supplemented by ideas about battle tactics derived from Livy.[15] The result is a strange but very striking document, by turns very detailed and vivid as to events on the battlefield, and hopelessly confused about geography: he seems to believe that Paris lay close to the battlefield. This is what he has to say:

> King Philip had promised to take the field; he knew well that his barons were not loyal to him. He knew well that his barons had bargained with

the English and put them in the midst of France. He grieved greatly to see his enemy wander freely through France unopposed. However, he provided himself with many good men. He had 100,000 knights and 12,000 men on foot. He had the king of Bohemia, named John, with 1,000 Germans. This John liked to fight as a mercenary. He also had the king of Majorca – his name was Jaime – who had been chased out of his kingdom. He too took the king's wages. And there was Louis count of Flanders, who had been chased out of his county. And there were Sir Otto Doria and Sir Carlo Grimaldi with 5,000 Genoese crossbowmen. There were many counts and barons and a good number of soldiers. Now I look at the king of England who encamped for the night in a very broad valley which was eight leagues from Paris. This valley lay below a castle which was called Mount Crécy. On the other side there was a town with more than 5,000 inhabitants called Abbeville. Between these two places, in the open fields at the foot of the slope of Crécy he placed all his men and drew up his host.

The chronicler describes the activity in Paris and the arrival of the news that the English had pitched camp. Armour was in such short supply that a complete suit cost 200 florins:

Day dawned. King Philip's pleasure was that the king of Bohemia was to be his captain-general and should set out in safety; and so it was. John, king of Bohemia, son of the Emperor Henry, Jaime king of Majorca, Louis count of Flanders and all the other barons set out from Paris. As they set out, the English watched the direct road from Paris from a distance, for they had a good view of it. They watched the French setting out and coming towards their camp. They could tell where they were by the flashing of the polished helmets and by the fluttering of the banners lit by the rays of the rising sun.[16] King Edward watched them and knew for certain that he could not escape giving battle. And considering the number of the French it is not surprising that he was a little afraid. He was doubtful and said aloud, 'God help me!' Then quickly, in a small space of time, he surrounded his host with good iron chains with many iron stakes stuck in the ground. This surround was made in the shape of a horseshoe, closed all round, except for a larger space behind like a gateway for the entrance and exit. Then he had deep ditches dug where there were weak places. All the English were set to work. Then this chain was surrounded by carts which they had brought with them. They put one cart beside the next with the shafts up in the air. It looked very like a good walled city and the carts stood in a dense row. Then the king arranged his troops in this fashion. On the left flank, on the side towards Crécy, there was a little hill. On this was a piece of woodland. The corn was also standing, which had not been harvested. It was the month of September, the third day.[17] Because it had been very cold in that country, the corn only ripened in September. In that wood and in the cornfield he arranged 10,000 English archers in hiding. Then he placed in each cart a barrel of arrows. He allocated two archers to each barrel.[18] Then he chose from his army 500 well-equipped horsemen. Their captain was Edward prince of Wales, his son. This was the first battalion. Behind these 500 he placed two wings each of 500 knights, one on the right and one on the left. Behind this 500 he placed 1,000 knights, who were the third battalion. Behind these 1,000 he placed himself with all the other knights, behind the host and behind the chains. When he had done this he comforted his men and commended himself to God and said: 'Ah God, defend and help the righteous cause!'

On the French side, the king of Bohemia was briefed about the English dispositions, and sent a message to Philip that the battle could not be won; but when Philip accused him of being afraid, he denied it, and drew up his army:

Then he ordered the battalions which had been drawn up to advance. For in the meanwhile he had drawn up nine battalions. But three were the famous ones, the principal ones. The first battalion was that of Sir Otto Doria and Sir Carlo Grimaldi, captains of 5,000 Genoese crossbowmen on foot. The second was that of the king of Majorca and the count of Flanders with 3,000 knights. Then there were many individual groups of soldiers. Then there was the battalion of the king of Bohemia with 1,000 Germans and 4,000 Frenchmen and with his son Charles. The first battalion which came into the field in the morning was the Genoese crossbowmen, 5,000 in number. They were ordered to climb the slope at Crécy to take up a position above[19] the English; but this was not done, because the English had occupied the hill and placed obstacles in the corn. So they placed themselves on another hillock further off. Then there was a shower; they could not fire their crossbows, because they could not load them. There had been a little rain. The ground was waterlogged and soft. When they wanted to load their crossbows, each man put his foot on the stirrup. His foot slipped. They could not fix the foot of the crossbow in the earth. Then there was a murmuring among the French and they were afraid that the Genoese had betrayed them because they had not received their pay. They said: 'These men are not firing their crossbows, and if they do fire them they are using wooden shafts without iron tips. Let the Genoese die.' Saying this, the French grew angry with their soldiers. They roughly drew their swords and lances. The Genoese were killed to the last man. Sir Otto complained about the death of his men to the king, who replied, 'We do not need footsoldiers. We have enough men.' This was the first exchange of blows. Five thousand Genoese were killed in an hour. Now the scene of conflict changed to the clash of the battalion of the king of Majorca with Edward duke of Wales. When they came together, the shock was so great, the noise and the clash of spears, that it seemed as if mountains were colliding. One man gave a blow, another took it. They sounded numbers of trumpets and bagpipes . . .

While this was going on, the English archers came down the hill through the corn, and fired continually on the cavalry. They drew their bows and fired arrows – thud, thud, thud. They put everyone in danger. On the left side the horses fell, so that half the army was missing. The wounded knights began to flee. The horses fell dead. The English followed. This battalion was lost.

There are many problems with this account, and it would be easy to dismiss the whole story out of hand. Against this, there are some very striking details, in terms of the general description of the landscape, and the realistic reason given for the failure of the crossbowmen to respond to English fire. What he has to say about the carts corresponds closely with Villani, but is plainly drawn from a different source.

Few of the writers, however, tell us how the English army was drawn up, because most of the French and English chroniclers were concerned to record the battalion in which the great nobles served, and were interested in the honour and deeds of individuals rather than the broader – and much more elusive – question of deployment and tactics. Modern military historians have taken radically different views as to what Edward's battle preparations were, faced with the absence of any real description in the French and English sources. The most striking example of the variation in chroniclers' attitudes is perhaps that of the *Chronicles of*

Flanders, a relatively late compendium which includes early material, and the St Omer chronicle, which is a variant version of it. The writer of the *Chronicles of Flanders* is only interested in the way in which the army was drawn up:

> Edward had the trumpets sounded and the alarm raised throughout the army; he ordered his battalions as we will describe. He made three of them. The first was led by the prince of Wales, son of the English king. This battalion was on a slope leading up to a mill, and behind it there was a wood. The second was led by the king of England but he was not armed in his full arms, and had a surcoat of green velvet with gold letters. And this battalion was behind the other one, and they made a great hedge of their carts, so they could not be surprised. The third battalion was led by the earl of Arundel . . .[20]

The St Omer chronicle, by contrast, wants to tell us about the personnel, omitting all reference to tactics and giving lists of names of those in each battalion instead, though the framework is identical:

> Edward had the trumpets sounded and the alarm raised throughout the army; he ordered his battalions as we will describe. He made three of them, and we will name the banners in the three battalions. The first was led by the prince of Wales, son of the English king, and with him the bannerets who followed him: that is, the earl of Northampton, the earl of Warwick, Sir Roger Mortimer, the Lord Fitzwalter, Sir William Kerdeston, Sir William Carswell, Sir Bartholomew Burghersh and Sir Bartholomew his son, the lord of Man, Lord Say, Sir William Cantilupe, Sir Thomas Dashwood, Sir Aymery de St Amant, Lord Scales, Sir Thomas Ughtred, Sir Robert Bourchier and Sir Robert Verdon. The second was led by the king of England but he was not armed in his full arms, and with him were the earl of Oxford, the son of the earl Warenne, Sir Richard Talbot the king's seneschal, Sir John Darcy and Sir John his son, Sir Reginald Cobham, Sir Maurice Berkeley, Sir John Stirling, Sir John Chevereston, the Lord Poynings, Sir John Lisle, Sir Robert Causton, Sir John Grey, Sir William Fitzwarin, Sir Thomas de Braose, Sir Thomas Bradeston, Sir John Montgomery, Sir Robert Ferrers. And this battalion was behind the other one, and they made a defence out of their carts behind them. The third battalion was led by the earl of Suffolk, the earl of Arundel, the earl of Huntingdon, Sir Hugh Despenser, Sir Robert

Morley, the lord of 'Tringas' and the lord of 'Baruf'. This battalion was the rearguard and guarded the tents and the carts.[21]

The author of the St Omer chronicle, in his enthusiasm to show his knowledge of the lords serving in the English army, has suppressed information which we would find much more valuable. His list is fairly garbled in terms of who served in which division, but shows some knowledge of the leading figures. It probably came direct from one of the clerks with the English army. It was easier to describe the battle in terms of people and personal stories than to give an overview, and we have to build up any picture of the sequence of events from scraps of information.

Returning to the issue of the formation used by Edward, the idea of an array or fence of carts is confirmed by several other chronicles. The Rochester chronicler says: 'The English placed the first battalion, in which were the prince of Wales, the king's son, the earl of Northampton, constable, the earl of Warwick, marshal, to meet the French. They quickly took up their places, and, putting their carts in front of them, fought strenuously and manfully.'[22] The *Norman Chronicle* is particularly valuable as it is not one of the semi-official French histories of the period,[23] which not surprisingly tend to gloss over the whole disaster. The writer makes the carts reinforcements for natural features and other unspecified obstructions:

> and the English were well shielded by their carts and by strong hedges and other obstacles and fired many arrows. And particularly when they saw that the rate of fire of the Genoese diminished, they fired so thickly that the Genoese started to flee and many were killed or wounded. And when the French men at arms saw them turn, many of them charged them and killed more of them. And when the English saw this confusion, they sallied out of their carts and attacked the French and did much harm, more with the arrows than with anything else, for the French horses, when they felt themselves wounded by the arrows, started to break ranks, and many were killed. Then king Edward left the carts . . .[24]

The *Chronicles of Flanders* say that the English made 'a great hedge of their carts',[25] and Mathias von Nuewenburg, who got his information from the Bohemian knights led by King John, makes the most interesting comment of all: he says that 'The English hid all their horses with their attendants near a wood and fought on foot, surrounding themselves with carts so that the French horsemen could not attack them anywhere except the front wing of the army.'[26] This corresponds to the other accounts which describe an opening in the circle of carts, and to the conjectural reconstruction offered in Appendix 1.

This gives us a radically different version of the tactics from that to be found in most military history textbooks, which depend far too much on later accounts. There is a reluctance to admit Edward's use of the carts as a defensive laager, carts drawn up to form a defensive wall, though the evidence for it is consistent in the early documents, particularly those from non-knightly sources.[27] There may be a reason for this, though it can only be conjecture. For Froissart and Le Bel, steeped in the traditions of knightly ideals, the carts reminded them too uncomfortably of one of the great moments of Arthurian romance, when Lancelot, in pursuit of Guinevere's captors, and deprived of his horse, mounts a passing cart, and is known for ever afterwards as 'the knight of the cart', because a knight would only be seen in a cart on his way to a shameful death by execution. Consciously or unconsciously, they suppressed the role of carts in the actual fighting. In 1340, when William Montagu and Robert Ufford were captured, according to Geoffrey le Baker, they 'were callously treated by the arrogant and angry Frenchmen. Although they had given their word not to escape when they surrendered, they were actually shackled in irons and carried, not on horseback, but in a cart like robbers.'[28]

Given that there is good evidence from Italian, English and Norman writers soon after the battle that carts were used, there seems to be a plausible case for a defensive structure of this kind used by the English army at Crécy. Is this then a complete innovation by Edward, or something which was known and used, albeit in different ways, at earlier periods? The idea of using wagons as a means of constructing a defence is found in classical times in Vegetius' famous treatise on warfare; this was the standard textbook in the middle ages: an Anglo-Norman translation was dedicated to Edward I before he came to the throne, and nearly three hundred manuscripts survive of the Latin and French versions. Vegetius notes that 'all the barbarians arrange their carts connected together in a ring like a fort at night, secure against anyone who may approach them'.[29] The Byzantine treatise *Taktika*, written by or for the Emperor Leo VI in the tenth century, also discusses the use of wagons as defensive structures. And in the extraordinary technical treatise *Bellifortis* by Conrad Kyeser, written in 1405, there is an illustration of a square of wagons used as a defence.

The strategy of forming a defensive wagon-fort was the hallmark of the followers of John Hus, the religious reformer, against the imperial armies in the fifteenth century. We have the specifications for the manning of a Silesian battle wagon in 1429, which shows that the idea of fighting from carts was well established by then: it was manned by eighteen men under a captain, six of whom were crossbowmen, two were handgunners and eight were infantry with chain flails and pikes. The supplies for each cart included chains to fasten the wagons when necessary, and each cart was drawn by four strong horses, or six less powerful horses.[30] The wagon-forts were regarded as extremely dangerous to attacking armies: in 1427 an agent of Frederick von Brandenburg advised that such formations should not be attacked until a meeting had been held with two unnamed men, probably Czech anti-Hussite nobles; and another agent wrote that it was better to attack a walled city than a wagon-fort.[31]

The idea of positioning the carts to the rear of the army is a common theme in accounts of medieval battles, often as a kind of wagon park with soldiers detached to guard the valuable contents and vital supplies they contained. Alternatively, they are used in line to prevent an attack from the rear, and simply ranged in a row. However, the further possibilities of such a defensive use of carts had been amply demonstrated some forty years earlier, at the battle of Mons-en-Pévèle, when the French army led by Philip IV was confronted by the Flemish infantry levies led by William of Juliers.[32] The battle was chiefly remembered because William of Juliers was captured and surrendered himself to the count of Dammartin, offering a ransom: the count refused, because his father had been killed at Courtrai two years earlier, and he stabbed William to death. It was therefore an event which was widely recorded in contemporary chronicle accounts. We have four apparently independent accounts written within a decade of the battle which describe the Flemish cart-wall.[33] When the Flemish took up their battle position, they deliberately emptied their carts and deposited the contents elsewhere under guard. The carts were then positioned to the rear of the Flemish army; one wheel of each cart was removed, and they were chained together, so that it was impossible to move the carts quickly and break through the line. One version claims that the carts were in staggered rows, three deep, to make it impossible to break through the line even if horsemen jumped the chains.[34] The French did indeed attack the rear, but were unable to remove any carts and force their way through before the Flemish infantry drove them off.

The length of the battle front at Mons-en-Pévèle is said to have been 1,000 yards; if we assume a space of 6 feet for each cart, a single line would require 500 carts, and a triple line 1,500 carts. Are these numbers feasible? The most recent study of the logistics of supplying a medieval army estimates the ratio of carts to combatants as 1:20,[35] which, given an estimate for Edward's army at Crécy of around 14,000 men, gives 700 carts. Hard data on the military use of carts is minimal. The anonymous Roman chronicler says that Edward embarked with 3,000 carts in 1346,[36] while Jean le Bel claims that Edward III had 'six thousand handsomely fitted wagons, all brought over from England', which stretched for four miles, for his expedition in 1359, the most elaborate of his French campaigns.[37] Given that each cart could carry around a ton, the anonymous Roman chronicler's figure implies 3,000 tons of supplies and equipment for the Crécy campaign, but, as with most such figures in chronicles, it is probably exaggerated. Taking the calculation already quoted that implies that the arrows alone required fifty to sixty carts,[38] a figure of 500 carts would be an absolute minimum (Plate 4).

Edward was fighting a defensive battle, and the terrain at Crécy offered few natural defences. The wood offered some protection to one side, and there were one or two hedges. The Vallée des Clercs, a deep natural bank running down the hillside, was an obstacle, hindering the enemy's approach, but did not offer shelter of the kind he needed. He had to create his defences artificially, and the carts seem to have been central to his strategy. They were an ideal answer on an open site of this kind, and there was no problem in manoeuvring them on the firm ground. The defences were also strengthened with holes a foot square to break any cavalry charge which reached the first line;[39] even though it would be difficult to dig these in the hard chalk, there was more than enough time to do so, since the English army was encamped in the area for two nights before the actual battle.

The position of the archers has been hotly debated, though earlier discussions have largely ignored the evidence about the use of carts. However, not all the archers were stationed on the carts, and there were

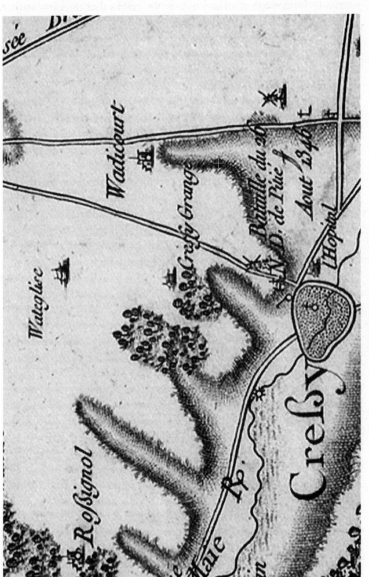

Cassini's map of Crécy, 1790.

certainly formations of archers outside the cart fortress. Robert Hardy, in *The Great Warbow*, makes the good point that if the archers were on the wings, firing across the front of the vanguard, as would be logical, they could not be much more than 500 yards apart from each other to give proper coverage of the ground.[40] Geoffrey le Baker describes the archers as stationed 'almost like wings on the flanks of the king's army',[41] and specifies that they were not among the men at arms. The archers lying in ambush on the edge of the woodland mentioned by the anonymous Roman chronicler are also found in the *Chronicle of the First Four Valois Kings* and in the *Norman Chronicle*, where they lie in wait 'among the hedges'; again, they would be on the wing of the army. There is also the mysterious remark in Froissart about the archers' disposition 'in the manner of a *herse*'.[42] This word is derived, not from the Latin for a harrow or an ecclesiastical frame for candles, but from *ericius*, as the French scholar du Cange recognized in the eighteenth century. The original meaning of the word is 'hedgehog' or 'porcupine'; this could well describe the array of carts with archers on them, shooting arrows like quills.

To echo Gilles li Muisit again, there is no sure evidence as to the disposition of the army, and each modern writer is in effect 'setting down only those things which I have heard from certain people worthy of belief, even if I cannot be totally sure that they are what happened'. Any reconstruction of the English battle formation is bound to be hypothetical; this also applies to the possible solution in Appendix 1, which takes into account what the chroniclers tell us, but ultimately is as much informed imagination as fact. The broad sequence of events is indeed all that we can 'set down' with any confidence. To recapitulate: before the battle, the English army was drawn up in good order, in three divisions, in a position strengthened by improvised defences, which almost certainly included the use of carts, and possibly shallow ditches and wooden or iron stakes. There was little natural cover, but they seem to have set ambushes using the cover of woodland, hedges or standing corn. The personnel in the three divisions of the army prior to the battle is clearly recorded by the author of the *Acts of War*, who very probably had access to official records. He gives us the organization of the English forces at the outset of the campaign on 15–17 July, and this corresponds at several points with the St Omer chronicle, the only other early chronicle to report the names of the leaders of each division. Most of the chroniclers are describing a medieval battle as it was traditionally fought: if the suggestions above are correct, Edward was using highly unusual and innovative tactics, as well as the novel weapons of the longbow and of artillery, which would have made it even more difficult for eyewitnesses to be sure what they were seeing.

The organization of the French army is less clear. There is no doubt that the attack was led by the Genoese crossbowmen; after that, the situation becomes chaotic. According to the Valenciennes chronicler, the second division was the militia from Reims, followed by three battalions of knights and men at arms. The first of these was led by King John of Bohemia, his son Charles and the counts of Alençon, Flanders and Blois. The next was under the command of the duke of Lorraine, with the count of Beaumont, German troops under the count of Salm, and the prior of the Knights Hospitaller of France. The rearguard was led by the king, Jean de Hainault and the members of the king's council and household. Villani claims that the French army was in three divisions, like the English army, and this would be true if he was only counting the knights and excluding the crossbowmen and militia. The anonymous Roman writer makes the first clash of arms after the retreat of the Genoese between a division led by the king of Majorca and the prince of Wales, and seems to imply that the king of Bohemia was to the rear of the army. He is shown as the last to attack, in a futile knightly gesture when the French had fled. This is confirmed by the chronicle of Matthias Nuewenburg which says that 'the Germans remained in the conflict for a long time, and many thousands were killed as a result'.[43]

Since there is general agreement that the French attacked in disorder, it is not surprising that the divisions are harder to disentangle. The usual ordered sequence of attacks, by the vanguard first, followed by the centre, with the rearguard only engaging towards the end of the battle, does not seem to apply to the French manoeuvres. It is fair to say that, once the Genoese onslaught failed, the French forces were more or less out of the king's control. Indeed, if we are to believe Le Bel's persuasive account, King Philip's attempt to check an army which was already raring to attack what they regarded as an easy prey was the moment at which the ranks of the French, already in some disarray because of their hasty arrival on the battlefield, began to disintegrate.

In the circumstances, it is hardly surprising that the survivors' memories of the battle were of isolated moments of drama centred on individual prowess or disaster. The confusion and rage of the contest are reflected by the fact that the sacred *oriflamme*, the French king's standard and the banner of the prince of Wales all went down during the fighting. The *oriflamme* was borne by Mile de Noyers, who wrapped it round his body to prevent its capture; the English claimed that 'it could no longer be venerated as a relic' after this, meaning that it had lost its magical effect, though they failed to capture it. The French king's standard-bearer was killed and the banner torn to pieces. The prince of Wales's banner went down during a fierce attack on the prince himself: Richard Fitzsimon laid it down, and stood over it while he defended the prince, and both he and Thomas Daniel, who raised it again, were richly rewarded once the crisis was over. If banners such as these went down the psychological effect was enormous: it implied that adversaries had penetrated to the core of the army and had either killed the owner of the banner or had managed to destroy the banner itself. The banner acted as the marker for a point where the men fighting in that contingent should regroup; without it, recovery from an attack which had forced them to disperse would be very difficult.

We do know something of the actions of the leaders of the armies, simply because they were the focal points of everyone's attention. On the English side, the fortunes of war of the prince of Wales were recorded in several chronicles, evidently from a number of different witnesses, while, on the French side, dramatic stories about the fate of the king of Bohemia quickly circulated. If we are being rigorous about the evidence, all that we really know is that the prince's battalion bore the brunt of the French assault, as would be expected given that he was leading the vanguard. We also know that the king of Bohemia was killed, probably in the closing stages of the battle.

Only the broadest sketch of the prince of Wales in action survives in the English chronicles: Geoffrey le Baker's rhetorical account of the action gives a glorious but totally imprecise account, describing him as 'showing his mettle to the amazement of the French, running through horses, striking down knights, crushing helms, cutting lances short, skilfully avoiding missiles, commanding his men, defending himself, raising his friends who had been overcome, and setting a good example to all his men'.[44]

At the other extreme, there is a persistent rumour in the Continental chronicles that the prince of Wales was captured at some point by the count of Flanders. This developed into a strange legend, recorded by the anonymous Roman chronicler, that he was only released by the count of Alençon – the implication being that it was not the fighting power of the English but the knightly stupidity of the French which lost the battle. And it underlines the theme of treachery which would later decay into total paranoia on the part of John II himself.

In this battle something unusual happened. The prince of Wales spurred his horse deep into the midst of the enemy. He did great harm by himself. A count called the count of Valentinois[45] saw him and recognized him, and thought that he would win a fortune. He determined to catch this big fish. He rode alongside him and threw his arms around Edward prince of Wales. Then he took him by the fastenings of his breastplate[46] and said, 'You are my prisoner.' Then he stopped and drew him by force out of the conflict and took him into his power. While the count of Valentinois led the son of the king of England thus, the count of Alençon came up, who was the half-brother of King Philip, and saw that young Edward[47] was lost, tied up like a lamb, and said angrily, 'Count of Valentinois, how dare you take my cousin prisoner!' He did not wait for an answer but raised his mace studded with iron which he had in his hand, and struck the count of Valentinois on the head. And he repeated the blows one after another until the count of Valentinois was unconscious. He let go of the bridle and armour of young Edward and fell dead to the ground from his horse. Then young Edward spurred his horse and, not a little joyful, rejoined his company, who had begun to waver.[48]

We are on firm ground with the story that the prince's banner was struck down, and there is no question that the action did centre round the prince. The supporting evidence for the capture of the prince, however, is not very strong, but has perhaps been underestimated. According to the *Norman Chronicle*, which seems generally well informed, 'the prince of Wales, son of King Edward, and Godefroy d'Harcourt rode so far forward to attack the French that it is said that the count of Flanders captured the prince of Wales, but he was soon rescued.'[49] The Valenciennes chronicler confirms that the prince was in the thick of the fighting in his description of this detail of the action:

And the prince of Wales was so hard pressed that he was forced to his knees twice, and Sir Richard Fitzsimon, who bore his standard, took the standard and placed it under his feet and stepped on it to guard it and to rescue his master, taking his sword in both hands and beginning to defend the prince and to shout: 'Edward, St George, to the king's son!' And to his rescue there came the bishop of Durham and many valiant knights who rescued the prince, and Sir Richard raised his standard again.[50]

The prince is shown as fighting on foot, and this would fit the early part of the action. The other detail here is that a contingent from the rear-guard, under the bishop of Durham, was involved in the intense fighting around the prince's position, apparently in answer to Fitzsimon's shouts for help. Geoffrey le Baker confirms this, but depicts the episode on a much smaller scale:

Indeed their non-stop attacks kept the prince and his comrades so busy, that the prince was compelled to fight kneeling down against the masses of the enemy who poured around him. Then someone ran or rode to the king his father, explained the danger threatening his first-born son, and asked for help. The bishop of Durham was sent with twenty knights to the help of the prince, but the bishop found the prince and his men lean-ing on their lances and swords, drawing breath and taking a moment's rest over long mountains of the dead, as they waited for the enemy to return from his retreat.[51]

This rescue is in turn embroidered by Froissart in his usual novelistic style into a refusal of help which enhances the prince's heroic stature – as the king, in Froissart's view, must intend. The sheer vivacity of his story-telling has made this into the 'standard' version of events for gen-erations of readers, and for many historians. A knight named Thomas Norwich was sent to the king to summon help:

On the knight's arrival, he said, 'Sir, the earl of Warwick, the Lord Staf-ford, the Lord Reginald Cobham and the others who are about your son, are vigorously attacked by the French; and they entreat that you would come to their assistance with your battalion, for, if their numbers should increase, they fear he will have too much to do.' The king replied, 'Is my son dead, unhorsed, or so badly wounded that he cannot support him-self?' 'Nothing of the sort, thank God,' rejoined the knight; 'but he is in so hot an engagement that he has great need of your help.' The king answered, 'Now, Sir Thomas, return back to those that sent you, and tell them from me, not to send again for me this day, or expect that I shall come, let what will happen, as long as my son has life; and say, that I command them to let the boy win his spurs; for I am determined, if it please God, that all the glory and honour of this day shall be given to him, and to those into whose care I have intrusted him.'[52]

This episode is probably distinct from the manoeuvre described by Villani; he depicts Edward's army, as we have seen, fighting from within a laager of carts. At the critical moment, the array is opened at the back and the entire rearguard, which included the bishop of Durham and his men, comes to the relief of the hard-pressed vanguard, in a classic encircling manoeuvre which anticipates Poitiers. The battle of Poitiers had not been fought when Villani was writing, so there is no question of accounts of the later encounter influencing what he wrote. A classic tactical manoeuvre has been transformed by other writers, who focus on the characters involved rather than the sweep of the action, into a personal rescue of the prince of Wales.

For the readers of Villani and many of the other chronicles, detached from the Anglo-French courts, it was the mechanics of the great disaster which had overtaken the French that were of the highest interest; personal exploits were far less meaningful. For the French chroniclers nearer to home, on the other hand, the knightly aspects of the battle were paramount; Froissart represents the culmination of this trend. There is, however, one chronicle which, even in this context of heroic deeds, goes against the expected grain. Describing the aftermath of the battle, the Valenciennes chronicler remarks:

> The king of England remained at Crécy for four days with his son the prince of Wales and the other barons who had won the battle on the Saturday. And the king asked the prince of Wales, his son, what he thought of going into battle and being in the midst of it, and whether it was a fine game, and the prince said nothing and hung his head.[53]

The realities and horrors of war fleetingly cast a shadow over the glory of knightly prowess.

The other heroic action in the battle, ending in tragedy rather than glory, was the death of the king of Bohemia. Here the anonymous Roman chronicler has a detailed account, which seems to be based on the first-hand experience of someone in his entourage: the details of the disposal of the bodies after the battle seem to come from someone involved in the operation:

[After the French had fled] the king of Bohemia asked his men how matters stood on the battlefield. The reply was that no one was left alive except him and his men. All the French had been cut to pieces. The English stood strong and firm, with their standard raised. Then the king of Bohemia commanded two of his greatest barons, who were related to him, to make ready to strike. They said to him: 'What do you want to do? All the French have been put out of action. The English are in a strong position. We are not foolish. It would be mad to attack so many men.' The king replied, 'You aren't the sons of my two friends, who were the most valiant in all Germany.' The two barons replied: 'It isn't a question of courage, because we aren't engaged with the enemy.' The king said, 'I wish us to go forward. Let us go forward and die with honour.' The barons said, 'What will you gain from your death and ours?' The king said, 'In good faith, what I say I am saying because I believe we are fighting for the truth.' At this the two barons were convinced. They lowered their voices like lambs and said: 'King, do as you please.'

The king summoned his barons and commanded them to obey his son Charles as they would have obeyed him, and honour him as their king and lord; they were also to rescue him from the battle.

Then he ordered the barons, who were before him, that they should put him directly in front of the English, so that, if there was an encounter, he could not return. Then he chained himself between the two barons and tied the fastenings of their breastplates together, because a common death would be an honour for them. The first squadron was 1,000 Germans from Luxemburg, good troops, Bohemians and gentlemen from Prague. They were followed by 4,000 Frenchmen, Burgundians and Picards. His son Charles served in the rear. Then the trumpets and bagpipes sounded on both sides. Then they lowered their spears and spurred their horses, and fought without mercy. The English had two powerful stratagems: the first was 500 knights reinforced by 1,000 to the rear, the second was two wings of 500 and 500 to the right and left, ranged along the top of the slope. When the Germans engaged with the English in the first line of the centre, the two wings, who had taken up their positions, attacked from the side on each flank. The king of Bohemia was attacked from behind, on his flank and on his side. The king's horse fell. The king was unhorsed and was killed by the horses of the two lords attached to him. The first to fall was a noble French knight who carried the king's banner.[54] He was unhorsed and killed in the first charge. The Germans did not turn their backs but put up a good fight, given that they had neither king nor standard. Many English died. In the end the squadron of the king of Bohemia was broken like salt pounded with a pestle.

Charles wanted to avenge his father's death, but was surrounded by his lords, who seized the reins of his horse and turned him towards Paris:

> [The English gathered the bodies from the battlefield.] ... The 1,000 Germans were taken to Paris on carts. The greater part of the king of Bohemia's body was taken; much of it had been destroyed. These bodies were taken naked from the field to Paris for burial. The other bodies were not collected then but remained for four days on the earth in full view of everyone.[55]

Once again, this is the stuff of popular history, though with more truth in it than the tale of Edward's refusal to help his son. John of Bohemia was closely related to the French royal family by his marriage to King Philip's niece and that of his son to Philip's daughter Blanche, and he was far more at home in the knightly culture of France than in Bohemia itself, where he was regarded as a foreigner: apart from anything else, his efforts to introduce tournaments and knightly ceremonies there had been a failure. The desperate gesture of flinging himself, blind as he was, into the fray, led by two of his lords, gave him the immortal knightly reputation he seems to have craved, and is noticed not only by the likes of Froissart, but even by the Bohemian chroniclers. Beneš z Weitmile, writing about 1374, declares that, when his lords tried to retreat from the battle with him, he declared: 'Be it far from the king of Bohemia to flee! Lead me into the thick of the fray and God be with us. Let us not be afraid, as long as you guard my son carefully.'[56] Weitmile attributes his death to the archers – 'he died pierced by many arrows' – whereas the western chroniclers such as St Omer portray his end in more knightly terms:

> And when the valiant king of Bohemia heard this, he ordered Le Moine de Basle [Heinrich Münch], a very valiant man who held his bridle, to lead him straight to the king of England so that he could fight him. And

Le Moine de Basle led him a long way into the press, striking to right and left at friend and enemy alike, for his sight was poor. His enemies all rushed on him at once, and beat him to the ground, and mortally wounded him; and Le Moine was killed in front of him.[57]

Even Froissart cannot improve on these accounts of John's death, adding only the story that the bodies were found with the horses tied together beside them. And the impact of John's action is probably reflected in the adoption of the black ostrich feather by the prince of Wales. John Arderne, who may have been the prince's doctor, recorded in a medical treatise written about the time of the prince's death that 'Edward the eldest son of Edward the king of England bore a similar feather above his helmet, and he obtained the feather from the king of Bohemia, whom he killed at Cresse in France. And so he assumed the feather which is called "ostrich fether" which that most noble king used to carry above his helmet.'[58]

These were the heroes of Crécy. King Philip, who is the only other figure about whom anecdotes survive, is the subject of a wide variety of stories. There are very divergent opinions about his responsibility for the rash attack on the English while his forces were not yet properly arrayed. Le Bel claims that Le Moine de Basle advised him strongly against any onslaught until the following day; Philip agreed willingly to this, but 'none of the lords wanted to turn back unless those in front of them turned back, because otherwise they would be shamed; so they stood still and did not move, and the others behind them continued to advance, and it was through pride and jealousy that they were destroyed'.[59] We have already quoted the version of the anonymous Roman chronicle, which has a similar but rather more elaborate story attributing the advice to the king of Bohemia instead of one of his knights. The Valenciennes chronicler, who, like Jean le Bel, quotes Jean de Hainault as an authority, contradicts Le Bel's story and, like the Italian chronicler, blames the king himself:

When the king of France had taken up his position and saw the host of the king of England, he realized that the king of England would not challenge him to a battle because he was so close to him; and he told Jean de Hainault and his men that he wanted to give battle because his enemies were in sight. Some praised, others not, because it was Saturday.[60] And all the same Sir John and the other barons said: 'Sir, do as you will: we will follow you.'[61]

The *Norman Chronicle* broadly agrees with this, adding that Philip did not wait for the whole of his army to arrive on the battlefield, but attacked with those forces who were with him. This is confirmed by the aftermath of the conflict, when French troops arrived in quite substantial contingents, which were picked off by the English as they came onto the scene.

We would expect to find stories of the exploits of the two kings. Both were experienced warriors: Philip had been in the fray when he defeated the Flemish at Cassel in 1328, and Edward had likewise fought in several battles in Scotland. Jean de Hainault was at Philip's side from the start of the battle, and talked to Jean le Bel afterwards. His story is that the king took no part in the action, and had to be led away by his companions after the defeat, going first to the nearby village of La Broye and then on to Amiens. Edward certainly took no part in the early stages of the battle, and there is the strong possibility that during most of the action he was directing operations from the windmill which stood at the top of the slope.[62] It is mentioned in the *Chronicle of Flanders* and the St Omer chronicle; eighty years later, a Norman chronicle described how the king had a windmill filled with wood and set on fire to illuminate the battlefield when the fighting had ended.[63] This is not implausible; and, just as carts may have been excluded from the 'knightly' accounts of the battle, the idea of the king in a windmill is not something that would have fitted the scene that Froissart or Le Bel wished to portray.

We therefore know nothing of Edward's personal role in the fighting, and, if Le Bel is right, there is nothing to say on Philip's part either. The Flemish chronicles are ambiguous: they report that Philip reproved his men as they fled, yet it is not clear whether he is simply in the rearguard, 'on the field, facing the enemy', or actually in the thick of the fighting. But the other chroniclers give him an active part in the battle: Richard Wynkeley, reporting to England immediately after the battle, says that he was hit in the face by an arrow, and Villani confirms that he was wounded; later English and Italian writers describe two or three wounds. The French sources, which would have been better informed, say nothing. He was also said to have had two horses killed under him.[64]

Perhaps the entry which is nearest to the truth is that in the *Chronicle of the First Four Valois Kings*: the French lost the battle through haste and disarray, yet 'the French king . . . bore himself that day as a very good knight, but fortune went against him'.[65]

The aftermath of the battle was as dramatic as the fighting itself. The English army remained on the field all night, in battle array, and on the following day isolated groups of French troops, coming up and expecting to join their victorious king, were attacked and defeated. As soon as the main action ended, and in the intervals between these sporadic actions, the horrific task of searching out the wounded and identifying the dead began; the operation lasted four days. The English knew that a large number of French nobles had been killed, because both sides had unfurled their most significant banners to indicate that it was a fight to the death, and that no prisoners were to be taken. The French displayed the *oriflamme*, the sacred banner of the abbey of St Denis, probably red with gold flames, while the English, according to Geoffrey le Baker, flew a standard 'showing a dragon clothed in the king's arms'; the leopards and lilies of Edward III's heraldic device, tempering ferocity with mildness, were changed into the cruelty of the dragon.

According to the St Omer chronicle, the small contingent of German knights on the English side, who were fighting as mercenaries and therefore were keenly interested in the profits of war, remonstrated with Edward, saying that they were astonished that he was allowing so much noble blood to be spilt. If they were taken prisoner, the French command would be weakened and large ransoms could be obtained. The king's answer was that these were his orders, and it was the right course of action.[66] It was a sound military decision: he could not afford to have knights taken out of action as they attended to securing prisoners, when the English were heavily outnumbered and in danger of being overwhelmed. And Baker implies that Edward had the banner unfurled in response to the French declaration that no prisoners were to be taken.

The full picture of the resulting slaughter only emerged gradually. Le Bel says that

> The king then ordered Sir Reginald Cobham, a most worthy knight, to take a herald well versed in arms, and some of the lords and the other heralds, and to go among the dead and record the names of all the knights they could identify, and to have all the princes and magnates carried to

one side with each man's name written down and laid upon him. Sir Reginald did as commanded; and it was found that there were nine great princes lying on the field and around twelve hundred knights, and fully fifteen or sixteen thousand others, squires and Genoese and the rest, while the bodies of only three hundred English knights were found.[67]

Other sources say that the king, Godefroy d'Harcourt and other lords led the search of the bodies; they were stripped of their surcoats or other identifying marks, and only three of the greatest of the French leaders – the king of Bohemia, the count of Alençon and the count of Harcourt – were singled out for special burial. The surcoats, arms and mantlings[68] were taken to the king's tent, where the French heralds later came to help to identify them. In total, 2,200 such items were said to have been collected from the battlefield.[69] The bodies were put in mass graves specially consecrated for the purpose, though the site of these has never been found, while the remaining armour was destroyed.

Godefroy d'Harcourt suffered the most personal loss: both his brother the count of Harcourt and his nephew were among the casualties; it was said that he had tried to protect them, but had been unable to do so in the thick of the fighting. His brother, and the count of Alençon, Edward's cousin, were buried in a chapel near Crécy. Many of the other French nobles would have been known to the English, and there were men in the retinue of Jean de Hainault who would have fought alongside them in Scotland only a decade earlier. As a result of the battle Godefroy seems to have bitterly repented his part in Edward's campaign, and, during the siege of Calais, found an excuse to repudiate his allegiance with Edward and return to the French side, which he did before the year was out.*[70]

The death of the king of Bohemia resounded throughout Europe: it is the one fact which is almost universally picked up by writers who mention Crécy. The death of a king in battle was extremely rare in the period of feudal cavalry warfare, and the circumstances in which it took place, his blindness and the determination – or sheer folly – which led him into the fray, heightened the drama. The uncertainty about the casualties and the problems of identifying them is highlighted by the widely differing versions of his end. Most chronicles confirm that he died in the

---

* He went back to the English side in July 1356, but was ambushed and killed by French troops in November of that year.

fighting, but, according to the St Omer chronicle, which is generally well informed,

> some knights came to the king who said that they had found the king of Bohemia lying on the battlefield and that he was not yet dead. The king ordered that he should be sought out and brought to his tent; and when he saw him he was very sorry for him. He ordered his surgeons to attend to him diligently. And when his wounds were dressed and he was laid in a bed, he gave up his spirit to God.[71]

At the other extreme, the anonymous Roman chronicler claims that 'the greater part of the king of Bohemia's body was taken [to Paris]; much of it had been destroyed'.[72] Edward was deeply moved by his death, and, as Villani says, 'held a most grand and honourable funeral for the king of Bohemia, as befitted a king's corpse, and wept for love of him because of his death. He and many of his barons dressed in black, and sent his body with an honourable escort to Charles his son.'[73] The funeral and requiem mass were conducted by the bishop of Durham, taking up his spiritual role after playing his part in the battle itself. The setting was not a great cathedral, or even the modest church in the village of Crécy or a nearby abbey; it seems to have in the open air, on the battlefield itself.[74]

It is this moment, rather than the heroics of the fighting, which defined the foundation of the Garter. This was the moment of Edward's triumph, when for the first time he had proved himself against the French, and established through trial by battle that he was the rightful king; but it is also a moment of intense tragedy and deep religious feeling. We shall see how the Garter commemorates both the triumph and the tragedy, in that it is a religious confraternity dedicated to remembering the departed and to honouring Edward and his family.

Crécy caused a sensation throughout western Europe. Chroniclers who rarely reported events outside their own country included a brief account of the battle and of the unexpected triumph of the English army. But such victories could be short-lived: a similar disaster had befallen the French at Courtrai in 1302 at the hands of the Flemish militia, when so many noblemen and knights had been killed that it was known as the 'battle of the golden spurs', from the heap of spurs which were gathered from the dead after the conflict. Yet two years later the French were able to overcome the Flemish armies at Mons-en-Pévèle,

him at Calais, having tried and failed to force its way into Boulogne on the day Michael Northburgh wrote. Calais harbour was in the hands of the French, so the English established themselves to the south-east of the town, on the road to Gravelines, which had a small harbour. As at St Vaast-la-Hougue at the beginning of the campaign, ships could also be brought ashore and unloaded on the long sandy beaches closer to the camp. Edward secured the support of parliament for the continuation of the fighting when it met on 13 September; a combination of the heady success at Crécy and a repeat of the reading of the French invasion plan found at Caen was enough to persuade the commons to vote for war taxes for both the present and following year. Letters proclaiming the victory at Crécy, and ordering proclamations to be made that traders should bring their goods and supplies for the proposed siege to Calais, had already been sent to the bailiffs of the major ports and to the sheriffs of the counties on 6 September, almost as soon as the news of the battle reached England. Reinforcements of men and materials were raised, and, in addition, supplies were bought in Flanders and carried in along the coast road. It was another huge logistical effort, coming hard on the heels of the efforts required only a few months earlier to prepare the invasion fleet. Vast quantities of food and building materials were landed over the next few weeks, not without difficulty, since there was a strong French fleet including Genoese galleys now operating in the Channel: twenty-five English ships were attacked and destroyed on 17 September within sight of the coast. After this initial disaster, the English ships were better armed, and the French lost the service of the Genoese galleys when their contract finished at the end of the year. Even before then, houses had been built for the king and the leading commanders, either of timber or of brushwood, and by Michaelmas the encampment, which was christened 'Villeneuve le Hardi', the bold new town, was deemed sufficiently safe and comfortable for Queen Philippa to join her husband. Eventually, the settlement grew to such a size that its market rivalled that of Arras or Amiens, and the Flemish merchants were quick to exploit this opportunity; Villeneuve was after all home to more than 30,000 inhabitants.

Edward had two objectives in besieging Calais, and it is hard to say which was uppermost in his mind. The size of his army suggests strongly that he was hoping to lure Philip into another battle. He could have cut off the town and denied it supplies from the landward side with far fewer men, and he fortified the camp very strongly as if he expected such a challenge. Calais was a great prize, and Philip could ill afford to lose it, since it would give the English a safe port and stronghold on the Continent from which to mount repeated attacks on France. This, too, was undoubtedly part of Edward's calculations. If he did not succeed in making an end of his war, as he had said in his letter of 3 September, he could at least secure a superb base for its continuation.

Even with the huge resources that Edward succeeded in raising for the siege, it was a bold, almost foolhardy, undertaking. Calais was a strongly fortified town, and its defences had been repaired and reinforced throughout the summer, beginning as soon as news of Edward's invasion had been confirmed. It had a double wall, in itself unusual, and in addition to that a double moat. The height of the walls was legendary – they were said to have been built by Julius Caesar – and two of the main methods of attacking a besieged town were impractical. The marshy ground meant that neither undermining the walls nor building huge siege engines was possible, because any mines would be flooded and the siege engines needed firm foundations. The only means of success would be the long, slow process of starving the town out. The citizens were well supplied, and it took some time to secure the harbour so that no ships could enter. It was only with the withdrawal of the Genoese galleys during the winter that the English could be sure of controlling the sea approaches.

Early in October there was a period when it seemed that Philip might rise to the bait, and attempt to relieve the town by attacking the besiegers. Edward sent for reinforcements, though on a modest scale; he and the prince of Wales requested about 400 men at arms and 1,000 archers, the prince ordering the justice of Chester 'not to be so negligent or tardy as he was in the last array'.[78] Neither the French army nor the reinforcements had materialized by the beginning of November, and the request for more men was repeated in mid-November, and again at the end of the month. Edward had concocted an ingenious but somewhat hazardous scheme for getting small boats into the moat surrounding Calais. Scaling ladders would be placed on their decks against the walls, while small wooden siege engines and cannon kept up a bombardment. Fifty boats were requisitioned from Dover as well as hurdles and mattresses to place against the walls, and carpenters were enlisted to make ladders up to forty feet in length. There seem to have been repeated attempts from the end of November onwards to mount a successful assault, until the idea was abandoned the following February.

Sieges were never particularly good for an army's morale, particularly when they threatened to last over the winter, so news of a new victory in England was more than welcome. David II of Scotland had taken the opportunity of Edward's long absence in France to reopen Anglo-Scottish hostilities in support of his French allies. He crossed the border and moved on Durham in mid-October, but William Zouche, the archbishop of York, and the northern nobles were already in the field, and intercepted them at Neville's Cross on 17 October. The fight was fierce, and seems to have been largely an old-fashioned struggle on foot, in which archers played little part. The Scots eventually gave way, and David II himself was captured.[79]

News of the capture of David of Scotland had reached Calais around the beginning of November, and Thomas Bradwardine, chancellor of St Paul's cathedral, who had been with the army since the beginning of the campaign, preached a victory sermon to raise morale and to celebrate the double triumph of English arms. The king had asked for the Church's prayers for divine aid; and Bradwardine took as his text 'Now thanks be unto God, which always causeth us to triumph'.[80] He then explained that those who sought causes other than God's will were in error: some said it was in the stars, or in the workings of fortune or fate, while others said it was their superior numbers (which was patently untrue anyway). Even their military expertise was not responsible, while those who managed to argue that it was all down to the goddess of love, who favoured bold men and lusty lovers, were no better than pagans. Bradwardine, who had written a treatise *On God as Cause* some years earlier, saw only one reason for the English victory: God had willed it.[81] The Church had prayed, and God had answered.

More serious than the lethargic efforts of the French to counter-attack were the conditions in Villeneuve le Hardi: sieges were notorious for the onset of disease, and the marshes were unhealthy places, damp and occasionally flooded by a spring tide. In November there was an epidemic of some sort, which led in turn to desertions from the army. Camp sickness of various kinds continued throughout the winter, as did the desertions. In England, sheriffs and other local officials were warned to look out for deserters, but usually found that they were too weak or too badly wounded to be sent back to the fray. Fire, another hazard in a wooden town of flimsy buildings, also became evident: one chronicle claims that a fire destroyed the king's privy wardrobe, where the jewels, armour and other valuables were kept.[82]

The tedium of the siege did not help, though a series of minor raids helped to occupy the troops: William Bohun, earl of Northampton, led an attack on the nearby town of Thérouanne, and the Flemish attempted an (unsuccessful) assault on St Omer. The chronicler from that town recorded that at Christmas Edward held a great feast, and a solemn crown-wearing, and there were evidently attempts to keep up morale among the knights by holding courtly festivals: at Easter, the king had the rich altar furniture from his private chapel sent over from London for use at Calais.[83] Winter now set in with a vengeance, and the marsh dykes froze over. Thomas Beauchamp seized the opportunity to attack the castle of Hammes, three miles from Calais, by crossing the ice on the moat; it was captured and burnt. Froissart later recorded 'great adventures and fine deeds of arms on one side and the other', but this is his usual highly romantic gloss on affairs. In reality, a series of skirmishes were initiated by the French, written up in detail in the St Omer chronicle, while the English raided the local French fortresses and towns: Marck and Guines were also burnt.[84]

Philip had not been idle during the winter. He had signed a contract with the Castilians to supply galleys to replace the Genoese, but nothing came of this. However, the galleys were to have fought alongside the French naval forces, and the latter were now pressed into service. A major effort was made to assemble supplies and to load them onto convoys sailing out of Boulogne, and twelve galleys from the French naval base at Rouen accompanied the merchant ships. These successfully landed a large quantity of stores and supplies in March and April. But supplies on this scale were needed on a regular basis, and at the end of April the English succeeded in completing the blockade of the town by building a palisade on the sand dune which protected the harbour to the north, and erecting a large wooden fort on the very end of it with a permanent garrison of more than 200 men, archers and men at arms, and with cannon and catapults installed. This was a deadly blow to the hopes of those holding out in Calais. In May, an attempt to run the gauntlet of this fortification failed, and it was not until the end of June that another convoy sailed from the mouth of the Seine. A substantial English fleet was now lying off Calais, under the command of the two

English admirals, John Montgomery and John Howard, the earl of Pembroke and the earl of Northampton. When they approached the convoy on 25 June, the crews of the merchant vessels first threw their cargo overboard in an attempt to lighten their ships and make a quick exit, and then jumped into the shallow water themselves; the escort of galleys turned tail and fled.

Philip matched these naval operations with a plan to raise a new army to challenge Edward. The *oriflamme* was taken from the treasury at St Denis on 18 March, marking the formal start of the campaign. Usually, the administrative skills of the French regime meant that there was little difficulty in raising an army; but the mood of the country after the disaster of the previous year was deeply hostile to the nobility who were the linchpin of any effort to muster troops. Poems circulated accusing them of treachery and of failure to do their duty to protect the realm, and raising taxes had proved extremely difficult during the previous winter. The king was therefore short of money to pay for his army, and the nobles were in even worse case. Many of them had only recently inherited their positions as a result of the death toll at Crécy, and found that their predecessors had incurred heavy debts to equip themselves, quite apart from the problems of a lavish lifestyle. The debts of the Italian bankers had been seized by the crown, so the king was in the position of both asking them for further expenditure and looking for repayment of the existing loans. It was hardly surprising that the response to the summons was lukewarm: and, when the army did assemble at Arras in June, Philip had a further problem. There had been continuous skirmishes and fighting along the border with Flanders during the past year, as the young count of Flanders supported the French, while the towns, mindful of their dependence on the raw wool they imported from England, favoured the English. The French had been unable to deal with the rash of minor assaults and the entrenchment of garrisons in the region, and there was always the danger that, if the army marched against the English, the Flemish would take the opportunity to increase their attacks or even join forces with Edward's troops.

Philip therefore dispatched two divisions, forming the bulk of the assembled army, to deal with this problem. Neither succeeded: one division under Charles de la Cerda, the king's cousin, attacked the Flemish at Cassel, a natural stronghold built on a dramatic hill, and was driven off with considerable losses, while the other, under the lord of St Venant, one of the marshals of France, and Jacques de Bourbon, fought a battle at Béthune which resulted in heavy casualties on both sides and an indecisive result. The Flemish were damaged, but were still free to create problems for the French as they reassembled and marched towards Calais in the second half of June. The royal headquarters were set up at Hesdin, fifty miles south of Calais.

Almost as soon as Philip had established himself at Hesdin, word came of the disaster that had befallen the French attempt to supply Calais on 25 June. On the morning of the 26th, the English saw two small boats trying to leave the harbour as dawn broke. They gave chase, and, as they did so, they saw one of the officers in the French boats tie something to an axe and hurl it into the shallow water as near the shore as he could. The boats were captured, and at low tide the English were able to retrieve the axe. There was a letter attached to it, a dramatic appeal for help written by the commander of Calais, Jean de Vienne, addressed to the French king. Edward read it, and forwarded it to Philip with his personal seal attached, to show that he knew exactly how weak the garrison's position was:

> The town is in desperate need of corn, wine and meat. There is nothing in the place which has not been eaten, no dogs, cats or horses, and nothing to keep us alive unless we eat human flesh. You wrote before this that I should hold the town as long as we had something to eat. Now we are at the point where we have nothing to keep us alive. We have therefore agreed that, if no help comes within a short time, we will make a sortie from the town into the fields, to fight to the death. For it is better to die honourably in battle than to eat one another.[85]

Edward knew that he was now close to his goal of either forcing Philip to give battle, or taking Calais. He had received considerable reinforcements during the spring, including William Clinton, earl of Huntingdon, somewhat recovered from his illness of the previous summer, who brought a contingent with him. More important, Henry of Grosmont, who had until now taken no part in the campaign in northern France because of his military activities in Gascony, arrived in late May with further reinforcements. Almost every important military figure from England was now gathered at Villeneuve le Hardi.

A further sign of the garrison's desperation was the appearance of 500 inhabitants of the town outside the walls, driven out in order to save provisions for the able-bodied survivors who could fight in its defence. Le Bel, who always gives a favourable gloss to Edward's actions, claims that he gave them food and drink and money, and sent them on their way: Henry Knighton, who may have drawn on the memories of the retinue of Henry of Grosmont, says that they perished miserably of cold and hunger in the ground between the town walls and the English army.[86]

On 18 July, Edward sent Henry of Grosmont to ravage the country within thirty miles of Calais, and he returned on 20 July with 2,000 cattle and 5,000 sheep. He also had news of the whereabouts of Philip and his army: they were marching towards Calais, and were now near Wissant. Conflict was close enough for both kings to organize prayers for their success: Edward's letters asking for prayers for his victory went to England on 23 July; the day before, there had been a procession in Paris bearing the relics of St Genevieve for the same purpose. By 27 July Philip had arrived in sight of Calais, and had occupied a position at Sangatte, the hill to the west of the town, which overlooked it and the English camp beyond. He could see the defensive barricade of boats drawn up on the sand, manned by archers and artillery, which formed an immovable rampart barring the passage across the dune to the north of Villeneuve le Hardi. The other flank of the camp, which had been very strongly fortified against a frontal attack, was on the road leading eastwards into Flanders. Here Edward had positioned a formidable force under the command of Henry of Grosmont.

According to Jean le Bel, the two marshals of the French army, the lords of Beaujeu and St Venant, were sent by Philip to survey the English positions and returned to inform him that there was no way of attacking them 'unless he wanted to expose his men to greater losses than those at Crécy'.[87] Philip, to save face, sent letters to Edward asking him to allow him to cross the river defending the English position so that they could fight; Edward, knowing that he had the upper hand, refused. There was nothing that Philip could do except open negotiations, and for three days, under a truce, two delegations explored the possibilities of peace. Henry of Grosmont, William Bohun, the margrave of Juliers, Walter Mauny, Reginald Cobham and Bartholomew Burghersh the elder represented the English; the duke of Bourbon, the duke of Athens, the royal chancellor Guillaume Flote and Geoffroy de Charny spoke for the French. But the negotiations ended in deadlock: Edward was not going to forgo his prize, and was not afraid of a French attack.

By this time, the garrison was desperate, and on the night of 1 August they signalled to the French that they were going to surrender. Geoffrey le Baker says that, when the French army first appeared, they had raised the royal standard of France on the tower of the castle, with those of the king's commanders, and had lit a great fire at dusk to illuminate them: they also sounded trumpets and beat drums for half an hour. The next night they lit a smaller fire and made less noise. When they could no longer hold out, they made a fire that could scarcely be seen from the French camp, and lamented pitifully for almost an hour before cutting down the standards and letting them fall into the ditch.[88] When the French royal army saw this, they burnt any equipment that they could not take with them and destroyed their stores, to make a quick retreat, and left before dawn: the rearguard was harried by Henry of Grosmont and William Bohun as they departed. Philip had done his best, but it was not enough, and his retreat was held to be even more shameful than his departure from the battlefield at Crécy.

The surrender of Calais is one of the famous scenes of English history, immortalized in Rodin's sculpture as well as in numerous popular accounts. Geoffrey le Baker, writing a decade after the event, presents a sober and practical ceremony. Jean de Vienne, riding a little horse[89] so that his feet touched the ground, with a rope round his neck, came into the king's presence, followed by other knights and citizens on foot, bareheaded and barefoot, also with ropes round their necks. Vienne offered the king his sword of war, as befitted a ruler who had won the town from the greatest power in Christendom. Then he handed over the keys of the town. Finally, he offered the king the sword of peace, symbol of the king's righteous justice. Taking this, Edward ordered Vienne, fifteen knights and fifteen burgesses to be sent to England. The other knights and burgesses were allowed to go free and take their money with them, while he ordered the common people to be taken unharmed to the nearby French fortress of Guines.

This orderly scene becomes much more dramatic in the hands of Le Bel (and later of Froissart, who merely retells Le Bel's story). Le Bel tells us that, when Jean de Vienne signalled that he wished to parley, the earl of Northampton, Walter Mauny, Reginald Cobham and Thomas Holland were sent to him. Vienne asked for mercy and to be allowed to leave in peace, as they had only been doing their duty as subjects of Philip, but Mauny, speaking for the king, replied that Edward was so infuriated by their resistance and the harm they had done him that they must all put themselves at his mercy: some would be killed and some ransomed. Vienne asked Mauny to take his request to the king, who at first refused to listen. But, so Le Bel tells us, Mauny himself took Vienne's part, saying that it would be a bad precedent, and that he and other knights in Edward's service could find themselves in the same predicament. At this Edward modified his demand, and asked only that six leading citizens should be brought to him to be at his mercy, for him to do with them 'exactly what I please'. Mauny again pleaded for them, but it was only when Philippa, expecting her eleventh child, fell at her husband's feet, that he relented and granted them to the queen, who spared their lives, and ordered that they should be 'freshly clothed and made comfortable'.[90]

Has Mauny, who was clearly Le Bel's informant, taken this opportunity to write himself into history as he would like to be remembered? It is probably the outstanding example of the way that oral testimony is used by the knights to create their own history – or myth, if you prefer it – with the chronicler's connivance. The story fits Le Bel's knightly agenda perfectly, and the arguments put forward by Mauny and the queen's intervention are all plausible; yet in the end we may be reading a romance.

The campaign of 1346–7 ended in the traditional fashion. Negotiations for a truce were set in hand, and as usual dragged on for a couple of years. Meanwhile Edward landed in England on 12 October, and celebrated his return home with a series of festivals and tournaments. This time, however, the jousts were more in the nature of a Roman triumph than a display of pageantry; and the king's popularity needed no reinforcement among either the great lords or the common people. Edward had ensured that his victories were well publicized; he now made his appearance as the victor of the French campaign, after an absence from England of just over fifteen months, the longest period he was to spend abroad. He celebrated Christmas at Guildford, in the palace there, one of Henry III's most attractive residences, and one of Edward's favourite places for that feast: he was there in 1330, 1337 and 1340. The usual elaborate masks and painted tunics were ordered, in sets of fourteen: six sets of buckram tunics, a set of masks of girls' faces, a set of masks of bearded men, another set of silver angels' heads; there were two sets of crests, one with reversed legs with shoes and the other with hills and rabbits. Peacock costumes, tunics painted with peacocks' eyes, head masks and wings, formed another set, as did white costumes for swans with similar masks and wings and a third set with dragons' heads. It was the most extensive wardrobe for Christmas games of his reign, though the similar list for the following Christmas at Otford runs it close: the centrepiece of this was a complete set of buckram armour for the king and his charger, spangled with silver, and with the king's motto 'Hey hey the white swan, by God I am the king's man'.[91] Fourteen buckram tunics with heads of men, virgins, lions and various other beasts were also provided.[92]

The series of tournaments which followed were at Reading and Bury St Edmunds in February, which seem to have been on a relatively modest scale. At Reading, the king wore blue armour, tunic and doublet. The king's crest was made of pheasant feathers, mounted with copper on stiffened linen, in the manner of the elaborate German crests seen in thirteenth-century manuscripts.[93] The most ostentatious display was reserved for a series of four jousts between 4 May and 14 July, at Lichfield, Eltham, Windsor and Canterbury.[94] The account for the Lichfield event is one of the most detailed that we have, and gives a long list of names; as in earlier years, the jousting circus seems to have moved on en bloc from one site to the next. This would explain why Lichfield has by far the greatest expenditure, while little additional cost was incurred for the other two: 288 masks for ladies and their attendants as against 44 for men and women alike at Canterbury. The king had two sets of armour and horse-trappings. One was of blue velvet decorated with flowers and branches of columbine, bears and lions; the other was white silk stamped with the arms of Thomas Bradeston. Blue was the dominant colour of the event, as blue robes with white hoods were made for the king, his household knights and his squires, and for Henry of Grosmont. The ladies of the court were dressed in blue gowns trimmed with fur, also with white hoods. The king wore blue and white again at the last jousts of the season, at Canterbury on 14 July, whereas the ladies were now dressed in green. The numbers here may have been small, but the costumes for the entry into the city required eight pounds of Cyprus gold thread, five pounds of scarlet silk and 3,000 gold leaves. At Windsor, the king's younger sons made their first appearance in the lists, Lionel, aged nine, in a grey and azure doublet; he, John of Gaunt (aged eight) and Edmund of Langley (aged six) all had armour covered in green velvet. It was an occasion when the scale of Edward's victories was made plain by the appearance of the captives he had taken during the previous two years: David, king of Scotland, the count of Eu, the count of Tancarville and Charles de Blois, 'and many other captives' were present.[95] Suits of armour were provided for the Scottish king and Charles de Blois as the most eminent of the prisoners.

Shortly after the jousts at Canterbury, Prince William, in honour of whose baptism the jousts at Windsor had been held, died, and the court was in mourning for some time after his burial at Westminster on 5 September.[96] In early June the most notorious plague of the middle ages, the Black Death, arrived in England, when an infected ship landed at Weymouth. It spread, largely by sea, first to the west country and then to the ports around the south and east coasts, reaching London around the beginning of October. Its fearsome reputation had preceded it, and men watched its progress with the greatest concern. It was against this background of impending doom that the foundation of a new college of priests at Windsor was announced on 6 August. There were no further tournaments that year.

PART TWO

The Company of the Garter

8

The Royal Chapels and the College of
St George at Windsor

It was almost exactly a year after Calais fell, on 6 August 1348, that
Edward issued letters patent re-establishing the private royal chapels of
St Stephen at the Palace of Westminster and of St Edward at Windsor
Castle, his two chief residences.[1] The two chapels were evidently
intended as twin foundations. The preambles to the letters use the same
phrases, and, thirty years later, Richard II issued letters settling their
affairs on the same day.[2] Both were to become secular colleges, that is,
colleges whose religious members were bound not by monastic rules,
but by a set of ordinances which regulated their life and the organization of the institution. Monks took vows of obedience after a period as
novices; members of a college merely undertook to live according to the
common rules of their establishment. Secular colleges were rare in England before 1348.[3] Most were the early colleges of Oxford and
Cambridge, where the function was entirely different, while others were
almshouses, caring for the poor and sick.[4] Edward's two newly founded
colleges were intended to be his personal contribution to the prayer and
worship which was the essential communal activity of the Church as a
whole.

When Edward's letters were issued, the buildings of both establishments were in disrepair. The chapel of St Stephen was said to have been
founded by King Stephen,[5] and was certainly in existence at the beginning of the thirteenth century. Henry III, who largely rebuilt the Palace
of Westminster, left the building untouched, but spent considerable
amounts of money on furnishings and vestments for it. It may have been
damaged in a major fire in 1263, which would explain why Edward I
set about rebuilding it in 1292. Work progressed erratically, with frequent pauses of several years, until 1331, when one of Edward III's first

acts after he had shaken off the tutelage of his mother and Roger Mortimer was to order the work to be resumed. It took another seventeen years, with a three-year pause during the Scottish wars due to shortage of money, for the building itself to be completed. But in 1348, St Stephen's chapel was still an empty shell, awaiting its furniture, glass and decoration.

At Windsor, the chapel dedicated to St Edward the Confessor had been built by Henry III. It was on a new site in the lower ward of the castle, and was begun in 1240, replacing a smaller chapel about which we know little, and which was part of the buildings around the great hall. The chapel was completed and furnished by the end of the decade. We know from the order to start the work that it was seventy feet long and twenty-eight feet wide, and lay in the middle part of the upper part of the lower ward, with space for a grassed area between it and the royal lodgings. By the end of the century, because Edward I rarely used Windsor, and because of a fire in the royal lodgings nearby in 1295–6, the chapel was in decay, its windows broken by gales, and little was done during Edward II's reign beyond necessary repairs. However, the chapel must have been in a reasonable state in November 1312 when Edward III was born in the upper ward of the castle and baptized in the chapel. Fifteen years later, repairs were again urgently needed: the wind had damaged the windows yet again, and the great joists of the vault were rotten. But there were more urgent claims on the royal income, and nothing seems to have been done. In 1348 St Edward's chapel was in serious disrepair.

Edward's letters patent give no hint of the fact that the chapels in the king's two noblest residences were both in need of work. Rather, the text lays emphasis on the king's personal involvement with them: both had been begun by his ancestors, and he had completed the building at St Stephen's, while he recalled that he had been 'washed in the holy water of baptism' at St Edward's. He then went on to create two new foundations which rededicated the chapels: St Stephen's was to be in honour of the Virgin Mary and St Stephen, while St Edward's received a triple dedication, to the Virgin Mary, St George and St Edward. Edward's personal devotion to the Virgin is recorded by chroniclers on a number of occasions, and is confirmed by the records of his almsgivings and pilgrimages.[6] The famous shrine of the Virgin at Walsingham in Norfolk was at the head of the list, alongside her statue in St Paul's and Our Lady in the Undercroft at Canterbury cathedral. The latter were relatively easy for him to visit, but Walsingham entailed a special journey of more than 200 miles from London. He would offer alms in person at statues of the Virgin which he passed on his travels, but would also instruct members of his household to make such offerings on his behalf to more distant shrines. Most notably, Edward, who was renowned for his bad luck with the weather when attempting to cross the Channel, founded the monastery of St Mary Graces near the Tower in Mary's honour, saying that through her mediation he had escaped from many perils by land and sea.[7] The chroniclers record two occasions when he vowed to found a monastery dedicated to her during a stormy Channel crossing. In March 1343 he returned from Brittany in an Atlantic storm, at the height of which he knelt before a relic of the True Cross 'which had long been with the kings of England' and implored the Virgin not to let him perish in the watery depths of the sea. If he were saved, he would found a monastery in her honour.[8] Similarly, he had prayed to the Virgin during a storm on his return from Calais in early October 1347, saying, 'O my lady Mary, what does it mean that when I set sail for France all goes in my favour, the sea is smooth and my affairs prosper, but when I return to England I always meet with adversity?'[9] While devotion to Mary was commonplace in the fourteenth century, Edward's worship of the Virgin was particularly intense, and this would explain the addition of her name to the royal chapels which he was refounding.

We know a good deal about the decoration, furnishing and layout of St Stephen's chapel, which survived, much altered but with fragments of the original still in place, until the fire of 1834.[10] It was on two storeys, with the lower chapel dedicated to the Virgin and the upper chapel as the private royal family chapel, to which distinguished visitors might also be admitted on state occasions such as baptisms or weddings. There are also references to pilgrims, probably visiting the golden statue of the Virgin in the lower chapel, who were only to be admitted as far as the threshold; but a charter of the canons recorded that they should have access 'without let or hindrance of the King's ministers of the palace'. The upper chapel may possibly have been visible as well.[11] Its decor was certainly such as to imply that it was intended for some degree of public display: it was a carefully planned and elaborate programme laid out in such a way that it portrayed the royal family in parallel with the Holy

Family, interweaving other themes of their personal devotion. The east end had two tiers of paintings, the upper tier showing the Three Kings presenting their offerings to the Christ child to the left. In the centre Mary presented Christ to the High Priest in the Temple, while to the right the shepherds worshipped the new-born child. Linked to these scenes, on the left of the lower tier, were the figures of the king and his sons, with St George drawing their attention to the scenes above them, while the right-hand side showed the queen and her daughters. Between these two sets of portraits stood the high altar.

The emphasis on the Virgin is explained by the dedication of the chapel, but St George seems to be present as Edward's personal patron. The figure of the saint, whose gestures indicate that he is presenting the king to the Virgin and Child in the tier above, is unparalleled in contemporary art: donors often appear in paintings, but their patron saint is usually portrayed as standing over them protectively rather than actively promoting their cause. The Magi or Three Kings, who figure prominently in the upper tier above Edward and his sons, were also the object of the king's personal devotion. He made offerings at their shrine in Cologne in 1338, and continued to give gifts of gold, frankincense and myrrh on the Feast of the Epiphany. Contemporary writers believed that he planned to be buried at their shrine, unlikely as this may seem, and the poet of *Winner and Waster* seems to envisage that, having conquered Paris, Edward would go to Cologne to give thanks for his victory at the Three Kings' Shrine.[12] A mazer made for Edward III with the arms of the Three Kings of Cologne on it was part of the royal treasure at the death of Richard II.[13]

The king's best painters and craftsmen worked at St Stephen's for at least a decade. As many as forty painters were at work there in 1350, and a substantial team of stained-glass makers was also on the site; they were to provide the glass for the Windsor chapel as well. The importance attached to the work is underlined by the problems encountered when the stalls were being designed. The original seating was a two-tiered Purbeck marble bench running round the outer wall,[14] and changing this to the stalls required by a collegiate church proved difficult. In July 1351, after work had been going on for two years, the stalls were removed, and the carpenters were ordered to work on 'raising various panels for the reredos of the said stalls in order to show and exhibit the form and design of the said stalls to the treasurer and other members of the king's council'.[15] In 1355 work was still continuing, and a new carver, Master Edmund of St Andrew, was brought from Newstead abbey, where he was a canon. As well as the thirty-eight stalls, the private 'closets' for the king and queen and their children were built at the eastern end of the nave: the royal family 'would have had an exceptionally good view of the altar murals which, in characteristically medieval illusionistic play, depicted themselves similarly "closeted" in perpetual prayer'.[16]

The murals were hidden behind panelling and forgotten for many centuries. In 1800, the Act for Union with Ireland was passed, which meant that an additional 100 MPs would join the House of Commons. Extra space was urgently needed, and a major refurbishment of St Stephen's chapel was put in hand which led to the destruction of what remained of Edward III's chapel. John Topham, introducing a series of engravings which recorded the paintings in 1795, described the effect of the chapel from the fragments which were still visible:

> It is necessary to observe that the whole of the architecture, and its enrichments, on the inside, are in gilding and colours, appearing extremely fresh; and what is remarkable and singular, the columns are decorated with a sort of patera, and several of the mouldings are filled with ornaments so very minute, that those on the spandrels and grand entablature, could hardly be perceived by the eye from the pavement of the chapel; but the artist designed that the whole of the work should have the same attention paid it, and that one universal blaze of magnificence and splendour should shine around, making this chapel the *ne plus ultra* of the art . . .[17]

To understand the purpose behind Edward's magnificent refurbishment of St Stephen's, we have to look to the Sainte-Chapelle in Paris, the religious focus of St Louis's palace on the Île de la Cité, with a similar relationship to king and government to that of St Stephen's at Westminster.[18] There was a tradition of establishing 'saintes-chapelles' in the French royal family. If we count Edward as part of that family (as he indeed was), his is a relatively early successor to St Louis's foundation: the bulk of such foundations in France are later in the fourteenth century. For England, this was a major innovation on Edward's part; but, as so often with his new ideas, he was looking over his shoulder at his supposed kingdom of France.[19]

The provision for clergy at St Stephen's in the letters patent of

8 December 1355 is identical with that at the Sainte-Chapelle in Paris, the magnificent housing created by St Louis for the relic of the Crown of Thorns which he had acquired from Baldwin II, emperor of Byzantium, in 1239 at exorbitant expense.[20] The architecture of St Stephen's echoed that common to the French royal private chapels, which were similarly buildings on two levels. However, Edward was working with an existing structure, and did not attempt to rival the soaring architecture and dazzling windows of the upper chapel of the Sainte-Chapelle. Nor did he have a relic to match the Crown of Thorns. The result was splendour of a very different kind, and with a different focus.

For the prime purpose of St Stephen's was introspective: it was a dynastic chapel where prayers were to be said for past, present and future members of the royal family, and which was designed to reinforce the idea of kingship as a divine calling, setting kings apart from their subjects. Many of the objects within the chapel were emblazoned with the royal arms, and the arms of the great baronial families were also worked into the decoration. The commemoration of family connections on tombs was becoming a commonplace at this period, with arms and figures of important relatives or colleagues incorporated in the design; but at St Stephen's, Edward is celebrating his living family, looking at themselves as if in a mirror. The paintings were completed during a decade when Edward was consciously creating an elaborate family settlement, involving marriage alliances which could have led to English princes ruling in Flanders and Brittany. And by the end of the decade, all but one of his sons had taken part in the campaigns in France.[21] There is nothing of the past here, no ancestral portraits: it is a bold statement of the power and wealth of the present generation, of their recent military triumph and their hoped-for dynastic success in France.

THE COLLEGE OF ST GEORGE

The letters patent founding the College of St George at Windsor provided for the same number of clergy, fifteen canons, as at St Stephen's. St Stephen's was the larger building, some ninety feet by thirty feet, against seventy feet by twenty-eight feet at Windsor,[22] but the two establishments were clearly intended to rank equally in importance. If Westminster was the pre-eminent royal palace and centre of government, Edward was in the process of making Windsor the pre-eminent castle of his realm. His personal attachment to the place was underlined in the document of 1348; this was his birthplace, from which he got his name, Edward of Windsor, and he had already used the castle for the greatest festival of his reign, in 1344. Windsor had always been the castle which he used most frequently; he was at Westminster more often, but this was due to the requirements of government. Woodstock, his other favoured residence, was a hunting lodge on a palatial scale with a park and pleasure gardens, a private place with no military or political significance; Edward's first three children had been born there, and its atmosphere is best summed up in the payment in 1354 for building a balcony for Princess Isabella so that she should have a view of the park.[23] He took up residence there for months at a time in the 1330s, but visited it only briefly and occasionally after 1340.

On the face of it, a more likely candidate as the home of a new institution might have been Winchester Castle. Winchester had been much patronized by his grandfather, and had strong Arthurian connotations, but the castle had been partially destroyed in a fire in 1302 in which the king and queen narrowly escaped with their lives. The damage does not seem to have been repaired until the 1330s.[24] Edward stayed there very rarely, though the great hall was repaired in 1348–9. It has been suggested that the Round Table was first mounted on the wall of the great hall during these repairs, and that there is a link with the supposedly Arthurian Company of the Garter at Windsor. However, we shall see that the Company of the Garter is in no way Arthurian, and there would be no point in these elaborate exercises in Arthurian propaganda at precisely the moment when Edward was moving away from the Arthurian imagery of the years prior to the Crécy campaign.[25]

The underlying question remains, however: why did Edward choose to found two new colleges rather than just one at Westminster? St Stephen's celebrated his dynasty and his military prowess in terms of princely magnificence. What else did he want to celebrate or commemorate? Much of the answer lies in the nature of the foundation, which we can only understand if we read it in conjunction with the religious provisions of his new institution. St Stephen's was at the heart of the seat of government, while St George's was established in the castle which best typified the king's military power.

Dedications to St George were relatively rare in England; most church dedications date from the twelfth century or earlier, and only 120 instances of St George as patron are recorded.[26] Despite the fact that the first dedication of the chapel at Windsor is to the Virgin Mary, it is as St George's chapel that it is remembered. It crystallizes the long process by which St George is identified with the triumph of the English armies. The red cross of St George, the great patron of military endeavour and of the crusades, had been adopted by Edward I in 1277 on his Welsh campaign, and was used again in 1290.[27] In the Scottish wars, his banner, alongside those of Edward the Confessor and St Edmund, was displayed by Edward I at the siege of Caerlaverock in 1300. The king's personal devotion to St George led him to present a gold statue of him, together with one of St Edward, to the shrine of Thomas Becket at Canterbury in 1285, at the very substantial cost of £374.[28] Edward III was very conscious of his grandfather's military reputation, and consciously took up many of the themes of his reign.

St George seems to have been established as a royal symbol of power and good government by the end of Edward I's reign, and this may be the message behind two magnificent manuscripts produced in the 1320s. In the margin of a devotional book, the Douce Book of Hours, two knights face each other: one is St George, while scholars believe that the other represents Thomas of Lancaster, cousin of Edward II and his bitter opponent, leader of the baronial opposition which had seized power in 1312 after Edward's favourite Piers Gaveston had been executed.[29] By the end of Edward II's reign, when this image was painted, Thomas of Lancaster had become a symbol of good government, and a popular cult had grown up around his tomb, even though he had died as a rebel fighting against the king. The image may therefore show St George as the representative of rightful royal government which Thomas of Lancaster had attempted to uphold.

The other manuscript was very probably presented to the young Edward III around the time of his accession to the throne. St George stands facing a young man whose surcoat bears the three leopards of England. He is about to hand him a shield bearing the same device, to complete his arming. This image is from a lavish manuscript apparently intended for Edward II, but hastily adapted for presentation to Edward III just as he became king. The book had been started in the dark years of his father's reign, when Edward was in his early teens. The text is a treatise on 'the nobility, wisdom and prudence of kings', and it is

1. Edward III, on the lion of England, is given a sword by
Philip V of France, as a symbol of his inheritance of the
French throne, while Philip VI cowers beneath. From a
manuscript of c. 1360–70.

2. (*above*) Edward III gives the charter for the principality of Aquitaine to Edward prince of Wales. From the original charter of 1362.

3. (*left*) Philippa of Hainault, from the manuscript she gave to Edward at the time of their wedding.

4. Four-wheeled cart of type used by Edward's army in 1346. From a manuscript of *c*. 1344.

5. Archery practice, from the Luttrell Psalter, *c*. 1330.

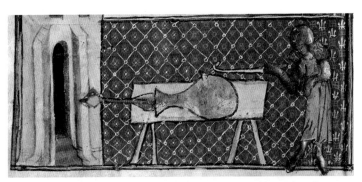

6. An early bombard, from the treatise presented by Walter de Milemete to Edward III in 1327–8.

7. Tents, from the *Roman d'Alexandre*, *c.* 1344.

8 (*above right*) A reconstruction of the Garter pavise of *c.* 1350.

9 (*below*) An army on the march, with prisoners and oxen, from a manuscript of *c.* 1350–75.

10. (*above*) St George in Garter robes, with the duke of Bedford kneeling before him. From the Bedford Hours, 1423.

11. (*below*) St George's chapel in the 1430s. It is the building with three windows to the right of centre, near the outer wall.

12. William Bruges, Garter King of Arms, with St George, from his Garter Book of *c.* 1430.

13. The earliest known representation of garters: a figure from the Luttrell Psalter, *c.* 1330.

14. A knight wearing the Garter, possibly Sir Edward Despenser, from an Italian fresco of *c.* 1370.

15. Dancers and musicians with 'vizors' or masks covering head and shoulders. From a French manuscript of 1275–1300.

intended as a book of advice to a king, a king whom the author addresses in the most flattering terms. If it was addressed to his father, it would have been a reproof, for much of the counsel that it offers runs exactly contrary to Edward II's behaviour in real life. For Edward III, on the other hand, the text as much as the image of St George foreshadows his future achievements.

The treatise was composed by a clerk in royal employment, Walter Milemete, as a companion volume to another work of the period which was celebrated for its section on kingship; it also contained a great deal of medical advice, and this curious miscellany, known as *The Secret of Secrets*, supposedly written for Alexander the Great by his tutor, was very popular in the thirteenth and fourteenth centuries. When the great expert on manuscripts, M. R. James, produced a lavish facsimile of Milemete's treatise, he dismissed the text as 'second-hand book-learning'.[30] But in recent years scholars have looked at Milemete's work more closely, and found a text which is rather more interesting than James suggested. The advice that Milemete offers is designed to encourage a partnership between the king and his great lords; and it was exactly this collaboration that had been so singularly lacking in Edward II's reign.[31]

So far St George had been a saint to whom the king had a special relationship. In the late 1330s, with the advent of the war against France, his red cross on a white ground becomes a nationalist symbol, emblem of the English nation as well as the English king. When the constable of Bordeaux in 1338–9 was fighting to recover territories lost to the French in the previous decades, he ordered standards to be flown in the fortresses and towns he reconquered. Nine of these bore the arms of St George, and six bore the king's arms. The French enemy were evidently expected to recognize that St George was the emblem of English power, in opposition to St Denis. And in the satirical poem about the French wars, *The Vows of the Heron*, Edward's vow to fight for the French throne is sworn by 'St George and St Denis', seen as the patron saints of England and France.

The triple dedication to Mary, St George and St Edward may also have further resonances. In late fourteenth-century English popular poetry, St George appears as 'Our Lady's knight', a title that draws on stories about St George being raised from the dead and armed by the Virgin. This story seems to arise from the legend of St Mercurius (sometimes said to be St George's cousin) being confused with that of

St George. In the great repertory of saints' lives, *The Golden Legend*, St Mercurius is raised from the dead by the Virgin to kill the apostate Emperor Julian, and this episode is illustrated in the Lambeth Apocalypse in the mid-thirteenth century, where St Mercurius bears arms similar to those of St George. The version of the same episode in Queen Mary's Psalter is unambiguous: the arms are those of St George. Two manuscripts close in date to Milemete's treatise also have this miracle as a marginal illustration: the Smithfield Decretals (*c.* 1330–40) and the Taymouth Hours (*c.* 1325–35).[32] It would seem that the link between St George and the Virgin was established by the beginning of Edward's reign, though it is only in the chorus to the famous Agincourt carol, nearly a century later, that the phrase appears in literature: 'Enforce we us with all our might / To love Saint George, Our Lady's knight'.[33] It is tempting to speculate that Edward, a devotee of the Virgin with a victorious campaign behind him, might identify himself as 'Our Lady's knight', and thus also with St George. Furthermore, the Virgin had a special meaning in connection with his claim to the French throne. The French kings claimed the favour and protection of Our Lady, and the lilies which Edward now quartered with the English arms were her flower.

THE GARTER BADGE AND THE PLANNING OF THE COMPANY OF THE GARTER

The early history of the Company of the Garter has long baffled historians, because we no longer have the records of its foundation and of its early years. There are a handful of chronicle entries, mostly from the end of the fourteenth century, that mention the founding, and we have to fall back on the highly problematic evidence in the royal accounts. The garter first appears as a badge, with an associated blue-and-white colour scheme, on garments ordered for the king and his companions: yet even here there is a mystery.

Garters are an uncommon item of clothing, and in the fourteenth century the word is very rare except in connection with the Company of the Garter: there are perhaps half a dozen instances of it simply as an item of clothing. It derives from the Latin *garetta* and French *garet*, the crook of the knee, and was a piece of material tied round a man's leg to keep up stockings, usually called hose. Garters were so simple that purchases would not have warranted an entry in the royal accounts. However, garters as expensive decorative items do appear: they are recorded as early as 1307, in the accounts of Edward II as prince of Wales, who was provided with 'four garters for the prince's person decorated with silver silk' by his armourer Hugh of Bungay, who also provided eight pairs of gilded shoes.[34] In 1322 there is a entry for garters decorated with silver and red enamel.[35] Both these records imply that the garters were visible, and this may mean that the general assumption that male hemlines were below the knee until the 1330s is incorrect.[36] The first record of garters belonging to Edward III is in 1332, when the king's armourer and supplier of costumes John of Cologne makes a pair of pearl garters for the king for the tournament at Woodstock on 16 June. These may be the same as the 'pearl garters encrusted with gold' listed in the treasurer's accounts in 1334.[37] About five years later, 'a pair of garters the band of which is of red velvet' were bought for the eight-year-old Edward prince of Wales.[38] There is another account entry for two pairs of silver garters in 1341.[39] We know that the king's close friend Henry of Grosmont was fond of garters: in his treatise *The Book of Holy Medicines*, he confesses to his pride in his appearance as a young man. In the convoluted imagery used by writers of such texts, he describes how pride attacked him through various points of his body; it entered him through his feet, which, it seemed to him, 'look good in the stirrup, or in hose or in armour, or as I dance with a light foot; and garters suit me well, in my opinion'.[40] The use of garters was a relatively new and unusual fashion; Walter of Bibbesworth's Anglo-French glossary in about 1250 describes the garter as an item of apparel used by fashionable squires, but it is another fifty years before we have a definite record of them. When a new fashion for 'paltoks', a very short padded garment which came down to just below the hips, appeared in the 1360s, the chroniclers noted that hose were now laced to the paltoks,[41] which must have made garters superfluous.

The Luttrell Psalter, famous for its illuminations of everyday life and the grotesques which inhabit its borders, has a little scene in which one of the figures is clearly wearing garters, tied with a decorative end hanging down (Plate 13). It seems to display a curious game, or perhaps a symbolic group, in which one man is trying to lift a pole over a molehill, and is prevented by his companions who are standing on the ends. The verses above from Psalm 88 lament the loss of friends; the dress of the gartered figure is in the latest fashion, and, together with the apparent game, seems to imply that the scene represents lost youth, a distant echo of Henry of Grosmont's self-portrait as a young man.[42]

Garters do not appear as part of women's dress until the fifteenth century: about 1400, a writer claimed that 'from the men [i.e. knights] of the garter came the use of the garter', and the first reference to women wearing garters is about the same date.[43] Men's garters were of course visible, and women would have worn a gown over their hose, so it may be that they were simply not mentioned, though, if women did indeed use them, one would expect to find silk garters in the detailed accounts for Queen Philippa's often extravagant apparel. Garter robes were issued for the ladies of the royal family from the beginning of Richard II's reign onwards,[44] but there is no specific mention of garters being issued to them. Until the end of the fourteenth century, the badge is therefore a strictly male emblem.

After 1341 there are no further references to garters in a context which implies that they are simply items of clothing. They emerge gradually as a badge around 1348, again in the accounts of the king's armourer, John of Cologne. These records show the extent to which he was responsible for supplying not only armour, but also many items of clothing and furniture, often with heraldic insignia. The details are found in three main documents, two of which are copies.[45] The first is an indenture between John of Cologne, the king's armourer, and Thomas Rolleston, clerk of the privy wardrobe, 'attesting to the delivery between 25 March, 19 Edward III [1345] and 22 June, 23 Edward III [1349] of divers garments and equipment made by John for the king within this period'. The second is a copy of this indenture on Thomas Rolleston's account roll for the period, and the third is a copy on the general account roll, or pipe roll, for 1349. The list seems to have been made up from notes of the king's purchases kept in John of Cologne's shop, and the dating and sequence of the material is a real problem, given that it covers four years. Sometimes a year is given; very rarely, there is an actual date. We can place some items by what we glean from other documents. A further complication is that the original is fragmentary, and the copy on the account roll is a version written up by Rolleston's clerks. The masks for an entertainment at Guildford which

John of Cologne describes as 'fourteen girls' faces with *bosettis*' evidently baffled the copyist, and remains a mystery today. 'Fourteen angels' heads' a line or two later become 'fourteen Englishmen's heads', the old confusion between *angeli* and *angli*.[46] John of Cologne's accounts were next made up in 1351, for the period 1349–51; the long period of the previous account is probably due to the king's absence abroad. John of Cologne first appears in the royal accounts in 1328–9; he seems to have died about 1367, when he is described as a merchant and citizen of London, and his executor, William of Cologne, is trying to collect long overdue debts.[47] John would have commissioned the making of a wide variety of armour and clothing, rather than manufacturing it himself, though he may have had a workshop for finishing such items. The supplies were probably authorized by a letter under the privy seal and individual items would then be ordered by the clerk of the wardrobe as and when needed.

Our next piece of evidence is even more confused than John of Cologne's records. It is in the register of Edward prince of Wales, the official copy of documents issued by his council, and is an account submitted in 1352 by William Northwell, who had been keeper of the prince's wardrobe between June 1345 and January 1349.[48] This is therefore a copy of Northwell's account, which in turn had been made up from notes relating to transactions going back to at least 1345.[49] Here there is a different problem. There are a number of dates, but many of the entries simply say 'bought the same day' when it seems highly improbable that these were the actual dates of purchase: if we are to believe the records, the prince of Wales bought all his new year's gifts – the traditional day for gift-giving at court – on 24 June the previous year; and furs, also a traditional winter gift, were bought on 28 June. The dates do not seem to relate to the actual transactions.

This may seem a rather long-winded disquistion on medieval accounting: but these entries are the most tangible evidence of the Company of the Garter in the course of formation. Another way of looking at the entries is to see how they are grouped. In the case of John of Cologne's accounts, there is some kind of pattern: he puts together all the entries relating to William of Windsor, the king's son, born in May 1348, who died in September 1348. The entries for his funeral precede those for the celebration of the churching of the queen after his birth, in June 1348. Similarly, there is a series of entries for the items made for the king's entertainments, and another series for the purchases for the king's jousts. It is therefore no surprise that there is a group of entries which relate to the use of the symbol of the Garter on royal and other clothing, armour and furnishings. The groupings are not absolute: there are stray entries elsewhere, but, as far as there is any principle in the drawing up of the account, it appears to be by topic.

The first items in the sequence as we have it are two worsted streamers, one with the image of St Lawrence with a white *pale* or stripe powdered* with blue garters. This is for a ship and there are a number of ships in the records called the *Lawrence*. Streamers could be prepared for diplomatic journeys abroad by the king as well as for military expeditions: in 1338 the accounts show streamers being prepared for his crossing on his way to Cologne to meet the emperor, in a very similar style.[50] The most likely dating is that the streamers were prepared for Edward III's journey to Calais to meet the count of Flanders in 1348.[51]

The streamers are followed by a blue silk bed, on which the garters carry the motto 'Hony soit qui mal y pense'. (The motto is frequently cited in the accounts without the word 'y': this changes the meaning from 'Shame on him who thinks evil of it' to 'Shame on him who thinks evil', but is probably just a scribal error.) Then there are items of clothing, beginning with a blue cloth *chlamys* or short military cloak: this classical word is very rare in English sources before its use for the Garter costume, and is a deliberate echo of the costume of Roman knights. It is only in the fifteenth century that it is found in more general use.[52] Two silk jupons or close-fitting tunics of different kinds complete the list: on both the *chlamys* and the jupons, the garters have buckles and pendants of silver-gilt. These items, apart from the streamer of St Lawrence, may have been made for the Eltham tournament of 1348, at which the king appeared in a robe powdered with twelve blue garters with the motto 'Hony soit qui mal pense'. Three sets of armour were made for the king for the Windsor jousts at midsummer that year, worked with blue garters and wild men or wodewoses, also in blue.[53] At Canterbury a month or so later, blue velvet was used for a *lappekyn* or cloth covering the helmet and leg-armour all decorated with garters, as well as for eight tunics and hoods for the king, and twelve gowns for

---

* Decorated with an irregular pattern.

their ladies. There is also a cloak and hood with no less than 100 silver garters with buckles and pendants.

Blue is suddenly the colour of the month, and the significance of the costumes for the tournaments of 1348 which we noted earlier becomes clear.[54] The heavy emphasis on it this year is evidently related to the imagery of the Garter. Apart from blue cloth, there are blue hands on white velvet armour, and dancing blue men embroidered on white hoods. Probably at the end of the year, Henry of Grosmont was given a set of armour and horse-trappings in blue and white silk.

So far, the symbol of the Garter and its colour might simply be one of the many decorative schemes adopted by Edward at various times during his reign. It has been suggested that it might have originated as a tournament badge; against this, there is no sign of the use of such badges in tournaments, and there must be some kind of reason behind the adoption of the symbol.

There is no reference in the royal accounts for 1348 to any form of company or order called 'of the Garter'. However, when we turn to the prince of Wales's account as recorded by Northwell, we find the phrase 'de societate Garteri',[55] of the Company of the Garter, used twice, and two other references which must be to decorative garters:

A plate, gilt and enamelled, of the company of the Garter, with a hatchment, made for a herald of arms, bought the same day, to William de Stafford, herald of arms of Alvan'.

Twenty-four garters made for the prince and bought the same day; to the knights of the company of the Garter.

Thirty buckles, sixty girdle-tips and sixty bars, bought the same day; to sir John Chaundos for his robes, of the prince's livery.

Sixty buckles, sixty girdle-tips and a hundred and twenty bars, bought the same day; to the knights of the prince's company for the tournament of Windsor.[56]

The only certainty about Northwell's account is that it ends in January 1349; the problems over the phrase 'bought the same day' make it impossible to be more precise about the date of the Windsor tournament. However, the preceding entries do give some clue. Two entries above the gift of a plate to William Stafford is an item which seems to conclude a list of gifts to ambassadors who came to England in the autumn of 1347 in an unsuccessful attempt to persuade Edward III to stand for election as Holy Roman Emperor: it is a gift to the notary who accompanied the ambassadors. The next entry consists of presents to the nurse and attendants of William of Windsor, in honour of whose baptism the midsummer 1348 tournament appears to have been held. It therefore looks as if these entries are copied from a new list, which should have been given a new date.

The gifts to Chandos and the prince's knights are for making up garters to attach to their clothing or armour, and we know that armour decorated with garters was worn by the king. The key item, however, is the reference to the twenty-four garters given to the 'knights of the company of the Garter', as this is the first time that we meet the Garter as a formal institution. This does not mean that the Company of the Garter was fully functioning at midsummer 1348. It seems most likely that the members had been chosen, and that the statutes at least drafted, and that the decision to make it an adjunct of the new College of St George at Windsor had been taken.

This tangled web of evidence therefore shows us little more than that the idea of the company was in the air in 1348 and possibly earlier; but this is hardly surprising, since Edward created the College of St George on 6 August 1348. This may have been the occasion when both the college and the company were set in motion. Neither were questions of great moment; indeed, the huge half-finished shell of the Round Table building in the upper ward of the castle was a reminder to the king not to overreach himself with ambitious plans. The membership of the company may well have been settled between April 1348 and New Year 1349, and the wording of the entry in the prince's account, made in 1352, reflects the situation at the time of writing. The items in question were perhaps given to the *future* companions at the end of 1348, who became knights of the companionship of the Garter at the first annual assembly on St George's Day, 23 April 1349. This is borne out by two payments to John of Cologne, which were modest advances against the costs of the first Garter robes; he received £30 on 11 January 1349, and a further £30 on 2 March, 'for various works for the king's person and for his companionship of the Garter', and for 'robes and garters for the king'.[57] A date of 23 April 1349 is therefore the most likely moment for the initial meeting, which implies the selection of the members well before then.

Another way in which we may be able to find clues as to how the Garter companions were chosen is to look at what we know of the actual creation of the company. The statutes place its institution firmly in 'the twenty-third year' of Edward's reign, that is, between 25 January 1349 and 24 January 1350, which would point to 23 April 1349 as the most likely date for its inception. The only historian writing within a decade of the foundation who gives a detailed account of it is Geoffrey le Baker, and he dates it firmly to 1350. Chronology is not his strong point: he places the Windsor tournament of 1348 a year later, and in the earlier part of his work uses a system of starting the new year at Michaelmas, taken over from Adam Murimuth, on whose chronicle he bases this part of the narrative. He also merges the institution of the college with that of the company, and it is clear that he has good information about both, except for the question of the timing. If he is right about the two institutions being founded at the same time, which would be logical, that evidence would support a date of 23 April 1349 as the moment when both schemes were set in motion. The college was the first to be officially confirmed, while the company's statutes had to wait for the approval of the first gathering of the knights a year later. On balance, this is the best reconstruction of the sequence of events that can be offered.

What then is the significance of the adoption of the garter as an emblem, and of the motto 'Hony soit qui mal y pense'? The first appearances of the garter in the royal accounts are within a few months of the probable foundation date, so it is likely that it was always intended as a knightly symbol for the planned company: garters embroidered with the motto appear very early on, and the two are virtually inseparable. William Camden, the great antiquary of the early seventeenth century, whose *Britannia* is one of the classics of the period, makes a remark which seems to have been overlooked by modern writers. He tells us in suitably rhetorical prose in his entry for Windsor: 'In this place, king *Edward* the third, for to adorne martiall prowesse, with honors, the guerdon of vertue, ordained that most noble order and society of knights, whom (as some report) for his owne garter given forth as signall of a battaile that sped fortunately, hee called knights of the Garter . . .'[58] This would be a strong possibility if we knew that garters were used in this way, as a kind of coded badge in a battle. Juliet Vale has suggested that the garter could have been adopted as a general emblem for the invasion of France in 1346; it is an attractive suggestion, but again, there is no evidence of such usage and the mystery remains.[59] The motto is now generally accepted as a reference to Edward III's claim to the French throne, a defiant challenge to those who denied or opposed his right. However, if it were a propaganda statement as part of the general campaign to present Edward III as the true king of France after his assumption of the title in 1340, it should really appear at a much earlier date. I would suggest that the motto also has a particular resonance *after* the battle of Crécy. The French were not only defeated, but their nobility were shamed, a shame and loss of honour which went like a shock wave through France, and is expressed in surviving poems. *Honi* is literally 'shamed' rather than 'shame', *honte*, and the usual English translation is misleading: it should be 'Shamed be he who thinks evil of it'. It is a motto which fits perfectly the situation after Crécy, when Edward had shamed his opponents.

There is a third aspect to it: like all good mottoes of this kind, it has multiple meanings. One of these was directed at the critics of the war in England, who, though largely silenced in the aftermath of the events of 1346–7, were still a force to be reckoned with. In particular, the parliaments of January and March–April 1348 were dominated by the commons' attempt to restrain the king's efforts to raise new war taxation, and to bring such exactions under their control. From this point of view, the war was highly unpopular. The commons carefully avoided any formal opposition to the war in principle – 'as regards your war and the array of the same, we are so ignorant and simple that we neither know nor are able to give counsel thereon' – but had a great deal to say on the question of the resulting taxes, which they called 'a very great charge from his poor commonalty'. The king got his money, but the commons did their best to hedge the grant, 'made to their great misfortune', with as many conditions as possible.[60] The complaints and unspoken hostility to the war were, in Edward's view, shameful, when he had just won such a glorious victory.

The blue and gold of the garter are the French colours, and the form of the garter – not a simple tie, but a minute version of the knight's belt, the *cingulum militare*, which was a central part of the knighting ceremony, and which was used to gird on the new knight's sword – proclaims its military intent. The choice of the garter as emblem is also practical, since it could be displayed over armour without difficulty, like the Spanish Order of the Sash, founded in 1330, and which William Montagu and Henry of Grosmont would have known from their mission to Spain in 1343.[61] The statutes of the institution focus on commemoration and religious ceremony; the badge reminds us that the company is, in its original form, a memorial to a great victory, which also looks forward to the continuation of the spirit which had made that triumph possible, and the pursuit of the ultimate goal, Edward's coronation as king of France.

The closest that we can get to Edward's own concept of the new institution is by looking once again at the royal accounts. From the earliest mention of the knights of the Garter until the end of his reign, the clerks of the great wardrobe and of the prince of Wales consistently call it a *societas* or company.[62] Only at the end of Richard II's reign is it called a *fraternitas* or brotherhood by the clerks, although Geoffrey le Baker describes it as such around 1360.[63] It is not called an order in the exchequer records until the end of Henry V's reign, though in 1403 the parliamentary clerks refer to it as 'an order of knighthood'. There is one exception to this, when in 1353 John Buckingham records the alms given by the king for masses for 'the deceased brothers of the said order [i.e. of St George]'. Here the Company of the Garter is seen in religious terms as an organization within the Church; it is not being portrayed as a secular order of knighthood. If it were, the text would read 'the deceased *knights*' instead of 'the deceased brothers'.[64]

The surviving copies of the early statutes are all later than 1415, and some of them refer to the 'company or order of knighthood' of the Garter; these probably reflect usage at the time the copies were made rather than the original lost text. The absence of any straightforward copy of the original statutes means that the texts have to be used with caution. It seems that modifications were made in Richard II's reign and again in Henry IV's reign, and the extent of those changes is not clear.

The twin victories of Crécy and Calais lie at the heart of the function of St George's chapel. The statutes of the Company of the Garter lay a stronger emphasis on the religious duties of the knights than on anything military or knightly.[65] Only two clauses deal with secular matters: the requirement that the knights are of good behaviour and noble birth, and the stipulation that knights shall be given preference when summoning forces for a campaign: and it is not impossible that the second is a later addition. As portrayed in the statutes, the Company of the Garter was a religious confraternity, and the chief duty of its members was to attend the annual service at Windsor on St George's Day.[66] Penalties for non-attendance at the services, without permission of the king, were severe. A knight who failed to appear was to be publicly shamed the following year, and, if he missed two such occasions without excuse, he had to offer a jewel worth twenty marks on the altar, a fine which was doubled for each consecutive repeated absence. The day after the St George's festival all knights had to attend a requiem mass before departing. Even if a knight had permission to be absent, he had to observe the feast wherever he might be.

On the death of a knight the king was to have 1,000 masses said for the knight's soul, and other members were required to provide masses according to their rank, ranging from 700 from the prince of Wales down to 100 from a simple knight. In effect, at least 5,000 masses would be said within three months of a knight's death. Even by medieval standards, this is a very large number. Furthermore, in common with other religious confraternities of this type, it meant that, if a knight died on campaign without leaving a will which made provision for such masses, his soul would not be left to languish in purgatory. Since the majority of knights do not appear to have made wills before they departed on campaign, this was 'a type of insurance policy for the soul'. In the case of John Chandos, who died intestate in 1370, 'his fellow companions in the order paid for at least 5,300 masses to be said to speed his soul through purgatory'.[67] In 1372 John of Gaunt paid for 500 masses to be said for the soul of Walter Mauny, 'our most dear companion, one of the knights of the Garter', at a cost of 41s. 8d., so the total expenditure by members of the company on the death of one of the knights would have been around £23, the equivalent of the annual fee of a banneret in the king's household.[68]

Given this emphasis in the company's statutes on the observance of St George's Day and on the remembrance of the dead, it is clear that the prime object of both company and college is commemoration. Founded a year after the end of the Crécy–Calais campaign, possibly on the anniversary itself of Edward's entry into the conquered town, it is a memorial to the triumph of England. Anniversaries were hugely important in the medieval Church: on the anniversary of the death of anyone of rank, lay or clerical, masses would be said for their soul. And those masses, in the case of the company, would include not only the handful of dead on the English side, but the vastly more numerous souls of the enemy casualties, included as part of the Christian world at large in the annual requiem mass 'for the souls of all those companions who have died and all Christians'[69] held on the morrow of St George's Day. Crécy had been a great victory; but it had also been a massacre on an almost unprecedented scale, not simply of a faceless enemy, but of men who were close friends and relatives of the members of the company.

The statutes of St George's College are carefully designed to prevent that scourge of many religious institutions of the time, the absentee holder of a sinecure. Edward III therefore provided that a canon who failed to reside at Windsor received only 40s. a year, while a resident could receive as much as £20 5s., since a payment of 1s. was made each day to those canons present at services in chapel.[70] The king's concern for continuous celebration of masses is further evidence of the commemorative aims of the foundation: he 'wanted the flow of intercession to be unceasing'.[71] And it was to continue, of course, beyond his death, particularly for himself: in 1416, apart from the general requirements for masses contained in the company's statutes, specific obits were observed for Edward III, Philippa and Edward prince of Wales, Henry of Grosmont, Thomas Beauchamp and William Bohun.[72]

The only official of the company recorded before the fifteenth century was William Whitehorse, the usher or verger of the company, who seems to have been appointed before 1352. In 1352–3, the building accounts have entries for his lodging, a half-timbered building which was not part of the college, but probably stood in the middle ward.[73] Whitehorse was one of the king's yeomen, and in 1353 he was granted permission to have a substitute for an office he held in York because he 'stays continually in the king's service at his side'.[74] He had been in the king's service since 1343, and in 1347 was made constable of Conisbrough Castle; he had evidently been with the king at Calais and possibly also at Crécy, and was described as 'the king's beloved squire'. In 1360 he was again rewarded for 'his sedulous service at the king's side', and the next year he retired to Wenlock abbey to be maintained by the abbey. In 1366 he went abroad, possibly on pilgrimage.[75] He was evidently one of the king's personal attendants, and seems to have had charge of the king's jewels, perhaps as receiver of the chamber.[76] As such, he would have been familiar with the knights of the Garter even before the company was established. They in turn gave him gifts and lands: he received £5 from Prince Edward in 1355 and later a grant of lands, and Thomas Holland also granted him lands.[77] His role as usher was largely ceremonial, and fitted in with his duties about the king's person: he was 'to bear the rod in [the king's] presence before the college of the chapel in processions on feast days'.[78] The post of usher was merged with that of the verger of the College of St George when Thomas Sy was appointed by Henry IV in 1399; Sy was also keeper of the knights' robes and black rod of the Company of the Garter.[79] This seems to have been the first move in Henry's reappraisal of the Company of the Garter.

The biggest question about the nature of the Company of the Garter under Edward III is that of the supposed tournaments which, according to many historians, were a central part of its ceremonies. If we look carefully at the records, we have only two positive records of jousts at Windsor after the St George's Day ceremonies, those of 1349 and 1358. The 1358 occasion was certainly impressive, but it was not a customary occasion, despite the claim of Thomas Gray in his *Scalacronica*, apropos of these jousts, that 'At that place of Windsor, the said King Edward held his great feast with jousts and revelry on St George's Day, as was customary'.[80] It seems to have been on a similar scale to the Round Table of 1344, a tournament 'open to all wishing to compete within their degree'. At the beginning of March, heralds were sent to France, Germany, Brabant and Flanders to proclaim the jousts; personal letters were sent to English lords, and countesses and other ladies were similarly summoned.[81] The jousts were proclaimed by Roger Mortimer, earl of March, who borrowed £1,000 from the prince of Wales on 17 February, probably to finance his part in the tournament. The prince himself gave no less than £100 to the attendant heralds and minstrels.[82] Edward and his prisoner King John were present, as were Isabella, Philippa and Joan queen of Scotland, and as usual the chroniclers declared that it was 'a solemn banquet and round table such as had never been held in England since the time of King Arthur'.[83] It was also a diplomatic occasion, since John himself wrote to the citizens of Nîmes a week or two later saying that at this splendid festival he had been given assurances that full peace negotiations would soon be under way.[84] Matteo Villani describes it as a 'solemn and vain festival of knights errant in the city of London', where, 'renewing the ancient fables of the Round Table, twenty-four knights errant were created, who, in imitation of the fallacious romances which were spoken of in olden times, challenged and were challenged to joust for the love of ladies'. The knights do not seem to have assumed Arthurian identities, but merely to have echoed the proceedings in the romances: 'the ladies and knights came before the king with pretended claims of grave misdeeds' which were settled by jousts between the lady's champion and the supposed offender. Villani's repeated description of the event as 'vain and pompous and full of stupidities', with few specific details, shows that he is more concerned to make a moral point than to record the event accurately; he ends with the notion that it all ended in tears, because soon afterwards the king's sons fell ill of the plague, though he fails to note that Henry of Grosmont was wounded in the crotch in the tournament itself.[85] King John is said to have remarked that he had never seen 'so royal and costly a feast made with wooden tallies, without paying in gold and silver', a reference to the English exchequer's system of issuing promissory notes in the form of a stick split in half; the creditor's half had to be matched to the exchequer half before payment could be made.*[86]

Much has been made in recent years of the idea that the company might have been based on two tournament teams. Juliet Vale wrote in 1982: 'It is immediately apparent that the seating arrangement [i.e. in the chapel] also provided two potential tournament teams.'[87] She sees the selection of the king's and prince's companions in the company as being driven by this idea: 'Age and experience seem very carefully matched in the two sides, who would evidently provide an evenly balanced encounter. In itself this parity strongly suggests that Edward's distribution of the knights was influenced by the need to compose two fairly matched tournament teams.'[88] Ian Mortimer claims that 'Geoffrey le Baker ... states that Edward founded it *at* (not before) this tournament on St George's Day 1349 ... The implication of le Baker's description

---

* It was a highly unpopular system: in the late 1330s the poem 'Against the King's Taxes' complains that it would be better for the king 'to eat from wooden platters and pay in coin for food, than to serve the body with silver and give pledges of wood'.

is that the founder members were defined by their being there that day: *they took part.*[89] Baker actually dates the event to 1350, but this is a different question. Whether he is talking about 1349 or 1350, the event he describes is a *convivium*, which has the specific meaning of feast, particularly a feast in terms of an ecclesiastical festival or celebration: mass is sometimes referred to as *sacrum convivium*. If Baker says nothing at all about a tournament, the accounts of Thomas Rolleston do indicate that there was a tournament at the same time as the first Garter feast, because, after a list of items for the chapel of St George for the 1349 Garter feast, he accounts for 'cloth of Dest, canvas and satin bought and used to make four suits of armour of cloth of Dest at the same time'.[90] This is the only moment at which there is evidence of a possible tournament in connection with the Garter feast. The issue of robes for subsequent feasts is never connected to the gifts of arms which are typically found for major tournaments, and the 1358 event is the exception, rather than the rule.

Furthermore, if we look at other contemporary knightly companies or orders, discussed in Chapter 12, we find that tournaments are specifically mentioned in their statutes. The oldest known order is the Hungarian Fraternal Society of St George, founded in 1326.[91] Here the statutes specifically required participation in tournaments if the king was one of the jousters: the fifty knights of the order were required to 'follow the king in every recreation and especially in the military games'.[92] The members of this Hungarian order hold a position nearer to that of the English household knights, but are organized, like the Garter, as a fraternity.

The Castilian Order of the Sash was unique among the early knightly orders in making the tournament a central element in the order's proceedings. The knights were to gather at Whitsun each year for the specific purpose of tourneying, 'if the king should have time for this'.[93] If at any time there was a tournament within thirty miles of wherever they happened to be, they were bound by their oath as members of the order to take part in it, 'so that it shall seem that wherever knightly deeds are performed, some knights of the Sash will always be there'.[94] There were complex rules for gaining admission to the order by challenging current knights of the order to joust, and this was a dominant feature of membership. The contrast between the statutes of this Castilian order and those of the Garter is therefore very striking, and reinforces the idea that the Garter is essentially distanced from purely knightly displays.

The Company of the Garter is much closer to the proposed Company of the Virgin and St George in France, a project which antedated it by five years. The letters patent of Clement VI, giving John II, who was at the time duke of Normandy, licence to found a church and college of 200 knights in 1344, specify that the knights shall, on the feast days of St George and of the Assumption of the Blessed Virgin, meet 'not for jousts or tournaments or any other deed of arms, but only for the purpose of devotion to the said church ... assembl[ing] there annually in person'.[95] The Company of the Garter and the proposed French Company of the Virgin and St George are both centred on an actual ecclesiastical establishment, with a royal chapel as their focal point. And in the French case it is specifically stated that tournaments are not to have any place in the company's proceedings.

It is not therefore surprising to find that the tournament element of the Garter is probably a mirage: the surviving evidence consists of Thomas Gray's throwaway remark that the king did this every year. He may well have meant to say that the king held a great annual festival on St George's Day, and assumed that 'jousts and revelry' were automatically part of such an occasion: given his remoteness from court life at this time, his information is by no means conclusive. It is much more likely that tournaments, however largely they figured in knightly ideals and in the mindset of Edward and his companions, were not part of the religious festival at the heart of the Company of the Garter.

St George's Day was undoubtedly transformed into one of the major court festivals, on a par with the four great Church festivals on which the king and his household traditionally gathered.[96] It is not unreasonable to see the ceremonies at Windsor on the feast of St George as the medieval equivalent of Remembrance Day. In 1353 the expenditure on food during this period was the highest of any of the year's festivals, and the reunion may have extended beyond the royal family to a larger group, whom we can only occasionally discern.[97] In 1357, during a session of parliament at Westminster from 17 to 30 April, the king appears to have declared a recess in order to go to Windsor.[98]

The bishop of Winchester was also present as the prelate of the company. It has been claimed that Winchester was chosen as prelate, despite the fact that Windsor is in the diocese of Salisbury, because of its Arthurian associations, being traditionally identified as Camelot. In fact, there were just three prelates for the first century of the Garter's existence: William Edington, Edward's right-hand man during the period of the Crécy campaign, William of Wykeham, the rebuilder of Windsor, and Henry Beaufort, son of John of Gaunt and a major figure in early fifteenth-century politics. These men were all part of the inner royal circle, and what may have been intended as an appointment at the king's will became a tradition (that the prelate was from Winchester) because of their longevity: Beaufort died two years before the centenary of the foundation of the Company of the Garter. Again, the evidence tends to point to this being a reunion each year of a small group, the king's family and intimates, rather than a gathering with wider resonances.

The requirements for the celebration of large numbers of masses may have encouraged the striking development of St George's into one of the major centres of the new polyphonic music from 1360 onwards. The records of the chapel are much fuller than for most other centres, so it is not easy to compare with other cathedrals, while we know very little about St Stephen's. What we can say is that St George's was home to John Aleyn, composer of the motet in praise of Edward entitled *Sub Arcturo plebs vallata*,[99] 'one of the most complex and remarkable ... motets ... to have survived from anywhere in Europe' from this period. Aleyn was a canon from 1362 to 1373, and the implication is that from the start St George's was one of the major musical centres of England,[100] and that the Garter services were performances of a rare quality.

If we know a great deal about the St George's music and almost nothing about that at St Stephen's, the reverse is true about the architecture and decoration of the chapels. Henry III's chapel at Windsor was superseded by Edward IV's new chapel in the 1470s, though the former was left standing.[101] Most of the original chapel was demolished when Henry VII's Lady Chapel was added to Edward IV's chapel in 1494–8, and we have no images of the interior. A small fifteenth-century sketch of the outside does survive in a drawing of the whole of Windsor Castle, and we know the dimensions of the chapel and its general architecture from the original writs of Henry III commissioning the building. It was twenty-eight feet wide and seventy feet long, and it was to have 'a high wooden roof ... in the manner of the new work at Lichfield, so that it resembles stonework'; there was to be a turret in front of it with three or four bells (Plate 11).

Something of this original chapel remains. The masonry of the north wall of the original chapel is the south wall of the dean's cloister, with its blind arcades; it survived because in order to replace it the cloister would have had to be rebuilt. It is the narthex or west porch of Henry III's chapel which is the most important survival, forming an ambulatory between the east end of Edward IV's chapel and the chapel beyond. Henry VII made this into a Lady Chapel, and it was remodelled in Victoria's reign as the Albert Memorial chapel. Again, there are blind arcades with fine Purbeck marble columns: in the centre of the wall is a magnificent pair of wooden doors decorated with iron patterns, the original entrance to both Henry III's chapel and Edward III's remodelled

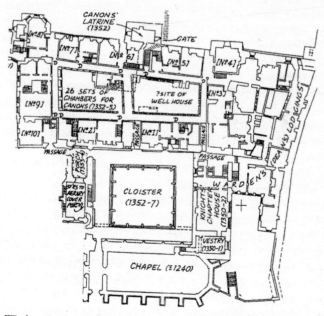

Windsor Castle, showing the original site of St George's chapel.

Garter chapel. These seem to have been the work of a goldsmith named Gilbert Bonington, one of the moneyers responsible for minting the new silver pennies issued in 1247; his mark, '+ Gilebertus', is stamped on the metal, the only example of marked English medieval ironwork.[102]

The interior of the chapel was filled with elaborate furnishings, relics and statuary, and the glass was made by the glaziers working at Westminster. Work started in 1352, and seems to have been complete by November; the glass was put aside and stored for the winter, before being sent to Windsor the following spring, in boxes packed with hay and straw, and installed in time for the Garter festival of 1353. The glass was therefore similar in style to St Stephen's, but nothing survives from either set of windows.[103]

The nearest approach to what the glass of the original Garter chapel might have been like is the great east window at Gloucester cathedral, a work on a monumental scale which is the largest surviving example from the fourteenth century. At the foot of the serried ranks of the hierarchy of heaven, there is a row of shields. Some have come here by chance, but there is a core of the original heraldry, and the owners of these shields can be placed at Crécy and Calais: Richard Fitzalan, Thomas Berkeley, Thomas Beauchamp, William Bohun, Laurence Hastings, Richard Talbot, Maurice Berkeley, Thomas Bradeston. Higher up there are the shields of Prince Edward and Henry of Grosmont. The window is dated in the most recent study to 1350–60, and seems beyond reasonable doubt to celebrate the campaign of 1346–7. The windows at St George's chapel would almost certainly have contained this mixture of religious themes and topical heraldry, and would have commemorated the same events.[104]

Although there had been extensive painting by Brother William of Westminster in 1248–56 in the original chapel, there is no record of painting being carried out at St George's during Edward III's remodelling of the interior. However, it is possible that there was no space for an ambitious iconographic programme like that at Westminster. If a fifteenth-century sketch of Windsor Castle, done before Edward IV's chapel was built, is reasonably in proportion, the walls must have been about thirty feet high, with a series of substantial windows whose sills were fifteen feet above the floor; and we know that below these windows were the elaborate stalls of the knights and canons.[105] There are no real parallels for a chapel with seating for both laymen and clergy, and any reconstruction must be conjectural. We do have surviving choirstalls from a set made in the 1360s for the chapel of the hospital of St Katharine's by the Tower, under the patronage of Queen Philippa.[106] These are probably in the same style as those for St Stephen's and for Windsor, and measure approximately twenty-seven inches across. The knights' stalls must have occupied a space of about twenty-seven feet on each side, and, assuming that the canons also had stalls against the walls, the total run of stalls would have been fifty-four feet. However, the placing of these presents some problems. The king and the prince of Wales had separate seats, which were likely to have been in a place of honour close to and facing the altar, and it would be logical for the knights' stalls to be adjacent to these. A second but less likely possibility is that the canons may have been close to the altar, with the king, prince and knights further down the choir. If we look at the arrangements when Edward IV's new chapel came into use in the late fifteenth century, it seems that the knights and canons sat either in the two higher rows or in alternate seats.[107] In front of the stalls were cloth-covered benches.[108] Here the choristers sat: if a knight was late for the service on the eve of St George's Day, he was not allowed to enter his stall, but had to sit 'lower down, in front of their stall, in the choristers' place'.[109] At the end of the stalls, presumably forming a return running across the end of the choir against the pulpitum, was a pew for the queen.[110] As there was a doorway to the vestry on the north side, this pew would have been to the south.[111] In addition to the high altar, there were two other altars at the east end. One was behind the high altar, for the use of the priest celebrating mass. The other, against the north wall, was probably dedicated to St George, as it had on it a wooden board with brass plaques illustrating the saint's life.[112]

The main visual feature of the choir must have been the tracery and carving of the stalls, on which a great deal of time and money was expended in 1351–3. Between twelve and fifteen carpenters worked on the stalls for sixty-four weeks, and the turning of the capitals for the stalls took the king's master carpenter, William Hurley, and his assistant about forty weeks, quite apart from the carving of figures on the misericords, carried out by Robert Burwell and Robert Kynebell, and the production of pinnacles and other ornaments for the upper part.[113]

Above each stall was a fitting on which the knights' swords were hung. Twenty-four such 'crooks' were bought 'for the stalls in the choir of the chapel'.[114] This tells us that the knights were within the choir, a highly unusual arrangement. Normally the choir was reserved for the clergy, and this placing may underline the religious connotations of the new company. It also suggests that the number of knights had not yet been increased to twenty-six. The problem of the difference in numbers, here as elsewhere, may be that the king and prince of Wales are not treated as knights in the strictest sense, but have a different status.[115]

On the pulpitum or stone choir screen were the organs, an altar and a desk from which the Gospel and Epistle were sung. Beyond it lay the antechapel, with two altars on either side of the doorway to the choir: one of these was dedicated to the Virgin. The font was probably in the antechapel: it was described in the seventeenth century, in a list of items taken by the Puritan army in 1642, as a 'Great Brasse Bason or Font for Christenings given by the founder Edward III', and would have resembled the brass fonts which survive at Rostock, Schwerin and Wismar in eastern Europe. It may have come from Flanders, where there was a long tradition of highly skilled metalwork of this kind.[116] William of Windsor was probably baptized here in 1348.

Statues of St George and the Virgin stood on either side of the altar; St George was in wood, and was carved in 1352, possibly by William Herland.[117] The reredos was not installed until 1367, but it had probably been in the making for some time. It was of alabaster, and cost the huge sum of £166 13s. 4d. Even more surprising is the fact that it needed ten carts, each pulled by eight horses managed by two men, to transport it from Nottingham to Windsor. English alabasters of this kind were just coming into their own at this date. Although the stone had been used locally for effigies for some decades, the first document referring to alabaster from Tutbury, the main quarry in the medieval period, is dated 1362, and the first reference to an alabasterman in Nottingham is in fact that for the making of the St George's reredos.[118] As in the case of the music to be heard in the chapel, St George's was at the cutting edge of the art of the period. The largest surviving alabaster reredos recorded seems to be that at St Seurin in Bordeaux, consisting of fourteen panels in three rows, and that at St George's would have been on a similar scale.[119] Like most medieval sculpture, alabaster was painted; it was a good surface for the purpose, and the effect was as powerful as frescoes, but with the added depth given by the three-dimensional carving. It was this reredos that provided the main pictorial element in the chapel, but it did not survive the demolition of the original building.

The reredos had both carved and painted panels and blank niches, where jewels and relics could be displayed, and it had two wings which could be closed to form a cupboard.[120] An inventory of 1384 lists twenty-one items on the reredos shelves, most of which are jewels. On the altar stood a reliquary in the shape of an arm, containing part of the arm of St George, while the total number of relics possessed by the chapel was around two dozen. The most important was the Neith Cross, containing a fragment of the True Cross. This was presented to Edward I by the Welsh in 1283 at Conway following his defeat of Dafydd of Gwynedd and the final subjugation of Wales. It was paraded through the streets of London in 1285 at the head of a procession which included the king and his family and many of his magnates, as a visible symbol of his victory. It was therefore an important talisman, and was presented to St George's by Edward III as the principal relic of the chapel, a reminder of his ancestor's military triumph.

From the beginning, St George's seems to have possessed an outstanding collection of vestments. Earlier in the century, Canterbury cathedral owned sixty-nine sets of vestments and forty-nine copes; St George's, a much smaller establishment, owned twenty-five sets of vestments and no fewer than forty-three copes,[121] including such items as a vestment of cloth of gold 'powdered with various birds', in which Joan countess of Kent was married to Edward prince of Wales and Aquitaine, and two vestments with stars and eagles and a golden cope given by her husband.[122] Many of the items were evidently either made of cloth intended for secular purposes or are reused from secular garments: the cope given by Edward prince of Wales is an exception, showing 'various martyrdoms of various saints'.

A number of the furnishings listed in the inventory of 1384 proclaimed that the chapel was home to the Company of the Garter. There are two cushions embroidered with garters and the arms of St George; and the veil used to cover the altar during Lent is 'powdered with Garters and golden eagles'. Carpets with heraldic designs covered the floor of the choir: six of these had the king's and prince's arms, or those of Garter companions (Thomas Beauchamp and Pembroke).[123] Six other carpets had garters on them, on blue or red backgrounds. Only four plain carpets are listed.

Finally, there are the swords and helms above the stalls. We have seen how 'crooks' were provided for the swords, and the inventory of 1384 lists eight helms and three of the swords, so the helms were part of the original scheme. We shall see that the stall plates are likely to have been an innovation on the part of Henry V, as part of the attempt to recover the lost early history of the company. The practice of hanging helms and swords over a knight's tomb is particularly English, and there is little evidence of it before the mid-fourteenth century. There are wills in which the horse and armour used at a knightly funeral are left to the church in which the knight is buried, but these are probably donations in kind rather than items for display in the church.[124] There was certainly a tradition of knightly splendour at such funerals, to the extent that other wills specifically prohibit such demonstrations of worldly status. An alternative reading of the presence of the swords in St George's would be as a kind of ex-voto for victory.[125] It is possible that the helms and swords in St George's chapel may represent the beginning of this fashion for heraldic display in churches, particularly since the most spectacular of all funerary monuments of this kind is the tomb of Edward prince of Wales in Canterbury cathedral, dating from the late 1370s. Here, not only the helm and sword are preserved, but also his shield, gauntlets and heraldic surcoat.

The external appearance of the college was relatively modest, in line with its status as the king's personal foundation within the castle. A visitor to Windsor in 1360 would have found a broad open space inside the great gatehouse, with buildings on the far side. Crossing this area to the great hall, the major state room of the castle, he would have seen to his right, at the top of the slope of the lower bailey, an elegant two-storey porch. The walls on either side ran from the chapel to the buildings against the outer wall of the castle, forming a self-contained space within the castle, which proclaimed that this was a separate entity. The porch itself was in the latest architectural style, related to the great porch of the twin establishment at St Stephen's.[126] Its elaborate and ingenious vaulting and decoration formed the entrance to the cloisters within. The buildings (particularly the cloister) have largely survived, buried in later constructions, but the enclosed nature of the college has been lost.

Within the college, the accommodation was mainly for the canons and vicars. The twenty-six poor knights, elderly or disabled men supported out of charity as specified in the college's foundation charter, were a negligible element in the establishment until long after the Reformation; owing to Edward III's failure to provide adequate endowments after his initial grants to the college, there were never more than three of them in the medieval period, instead of the twenty-six envisaged in the charter. The knights themselves were only occasional visitors to Windsor, and did not require permanent quarters, and the one building associated with their gatherings was the chapter house of the company.[127] The annual chapters of the knights and the elections were not attended by the canons, though one of the latter would probably have acted as registrar. How formal this appointment was in the early years we cannot tell, but, before the creation of the post of Garter king at arms under Henry V, such records as the company had were certainly kept in the college.[128] Architecturally, the chapter house is modest. Although it is quite large, it has a ceiling rather than a vault; built of stone, it was originally thirty-eight feet by twenty-three feet. The dominant feature is the elaborately traceried windows, one of which still survives, though without the stained glass.[129] The chapter house glass must have been magnificent: it was made at the same time as the glass for the chapel itself, at Westminster, and was shipped up the Thames in the same fashion. There is a reference to the drawing of 'images' in the windows, and to a wide range of colours of glass: there is no record as to whether the images were of knights or saints, or both. The knights would have used the room for elections as well as their annual chapter; but it was an occasional meeting-place rather than a central element in the company's life.

The worshipper in St Stephen's was surrounded by a dazzling display of the power and wealth of Edward's dynasty, lavishly executed in the latest style of painting. St George's, by contrast, uses a rich interior and rich apparel to focus on the religious purpose of the chapel, while the helms, swords and carpets proclaim the high reputation in arms of the knights, who are accorded higher status than the clergy in the choirstalls. Here the king and his sons appear in a different context, that of their military prowess, seated as the leaders of the victorious English

9

'The company of the knights of Saint George *de la gartiere*'

The earliest surviving version of the statutes of the Company of the Garter dates from the reign of Henry V, and was probably issued in a chapter of the company on 22 April 1415, about sixty-five years after the company's first gathering.[1] The opening of the statutes declares:

> 1. In honour of Almighty God, of St Mary the glorious Virgin, and of St George the martyr, our supreme lord, Edward III, king of England, in the twenty-third year of his reign ordained, established and founded a certain company or knightly order within his castle of Windsor, in this manner: Firstly, he decreed himself to be the sovereign of the said company or order, his eldest son the prince of Wales, the duke of Lancaster, the earl of Warwick, the captal de Buch, the earl of Stafford, the earl of Salisbury, Lord Mortimer, Sir John Lisle, Sir Bartholomew Burghersh the younger, Sir John Beauchamp, Lord Mohun, Sir Hugh Courtenay, Sir Thomas Holland, Sir John Grey, Sir Richard Fitzsimon, Sir Miles Stapleton, Sir Thomas Wale, Sir Hugh Wrottesley, Sir Nigel Loring, Sir John Chandos, Sir James Audley, Sir Otho Holland, Sir Henry Eam, Sir 'Sanchet d'Abridgecourt', Sir Walter Pavely.
>
> 2. It was agreed that the king of England, whoever it shall be at the time, shall in perpetuity be the sovereign of this Order of St George or Society of the Garter.[2]

In other early copies of the statutes, variations occur in the spelling of names, which is common in medieval manuscripts, but apart from this the list is consistent. The wording implies that these are the first founders. However, the opening sentence itself and the first clause listing the founders do not really connect. Edward establishes a company 'in the following manner' in the preamble, and the text which follows should describe the regulation of the company, as indeed it does from the second clause onwards. The fourth clause simply says that 'the aforesaid twenty-six ... shall wear the mantles and garter as ordained at the said castle as often as they shall be present there' for the ceremonies of the company. It is only in the next clause that there is a reference to 'the aforenamed founders'. Later in the statutes, there are references to the 'first founders'; when any member of the company dies, his successor shall have the same stall in the chapel, even if he is not of the same rank. An earl's stall may be taken by a simple knight, and vice versa: there is to be no precedence by status within the company, with the exception of the king and the prince. 'And this is ordained so that it shall be known who were the first founders.' Again, clause 24 reads as if it were drafted after some of the 'first founders' had died; it provides for the famous stall plates to be mounted on the back of the deceased knight's stall, but also says that any subsequent plates are to be placed below those of the 'first founders'.

A further possible problem is clause 10, which provides that, if St George's Day falls within the fourteen days after Easter, the actual ceremonies shall be deferred to the second Sunday after Easter, so that the knights are not obliged to travel during the Easter period. This would mean that the ceremonies should have been deferred in 1351, 1356, 1359, 1362 and 1367. In 1356 and 1359, the new dates would have been on 6 and 3 May respectively, and the king was definitely at Windsor. In 1351 and 1362, he could have been at Windsor, but there is no evidence either way.[3] And in 1367, when the date was 1 May, he was at Sheen. Against this, he was consistently at Windsor on 23 April each year, unless he was abroad. It is difficult to judge from the slim evidence, but his presence elsewhere in 1367 might imply that this clause was not introduced until after the end of Edward's reign.

Taken together, these minor discrepancies might simply be the result of hurried copying, the omission of a sentence at the beginning of the first clause saying that these are the names of the first founders. But they are consistent across a large number of copies, and therefore may indicate something more serious: that the statutes are a reconstruction, from a somewhat damaged or fragmentary text, of the company's rules. The text itself does not have the clarity one would expect from Edward III's highly experienced clerks, and there is no question that this earliest version of the statutes dates from the reign of Henry V; they must have been written from copies of documents which no longer survive and which certainly went back to the early days of the company.

It has long been known that the records of the succession of the knights in the early years is a major problem, and that the tidy lists of knights produced by heralds in the sixteenth century are difficult to support from any other evidence. Henry V's motives in producing this set of statutes have been described as follows: 'it might have been brought to his notice that there were no actual formal statutes for his Order to be found. More likely there existed a series of documents containing Edward III's original regulations for the Order and numbers of subsequent chapter ordinances.'[4] This idea is supported by a document from 1378, when a visitation of the College of St George was made. As an ecclesiastical establishment, it was liable to regular inspections by its superior, the bishop of Winchester, and one of the defects found during the visitation was that the deeds and records of the college, which are likely to have included those of the companions of the Garter, were 'remissly and negligently kept'. The prior of the college was ordered to obtain a proper chest in which to keep the papers, and to maintain his records in a more regular fashion.[5] There was no proper provision for a registrar for the company itself until the early fifteenth century, and the lack of such regulations combined with the general disorder of the college records would adequately account for the disappearance of the original statutes.

In 1400, when Henry IV had come to the throne and there was renewed interest in the Garter – his grandfather Henry of Grosmont had of course been a founding member – two tables listing the knights were made for display in the chapter house of the company. Such tables were used elsewhere as a way of informing visitors of the history of a church, the best surviving example being the 'great table' at Glastonbury, now in the Bodleian Library.[6] This consists of three boards, just over three feet high, which, when unfolded, form a hinged screen three feet wide. They are mounted in a wooden box, which was positioned in a prominent place inside the abbey church, where visitors could consult them. There are two similar examples at York, with general historical information; another, specifically relating to the life and miracles of St William of York, was kept near his shrine. There are records of similar tables in five other English cathedrals, and in five monasteries. The earliest known examples are a table at Seaford in Sussex, recorded in the late eleventh century, and the late twelfth-century tables which were at Bury St Edmunds. There seems to have been a vogue for such tables from the late fourteenth century onwards, as the vast majority date from this period, the Windsor tables among them.

There is a considerable amount of material in the Glastonbury tables, and they are not intended as a kind of placard of the sort that is found at historic sites today, with perhaps two or three hundred words in all, to be read easily and quickly. The modern edition of the contents runs to fifty pages, and the impression is of a collection of texts for reference, where the curious visitor can look up the answer to a question. They may well have been used by the monks themselves, to save them looking up a passage in one of the monastery's manuscripts. The Windsor tables were simply a list of the knights, rather like the last page of the Glastonbury tables, which gives 'a brief listing' of all the saints buried at Glastonbury.[7]

We first learn of the existence of the Windsor tables listing the Garter knights in the entries in the precentor's rolls at St George's in 1400–1401, when John Page was paid fourpence for 'writing the names, that is, of the king, prince and other companions of the Garter in the tables'.[8] A new table was probably written in 1416–17, because parchment costing sixpence was bought for Henry Bourne to 'make the tables' in 1416, and he was paid twenty pence for writing the responses for the feast of the exaltation of the Holy Cross and entering the names of the Garter companions on the tables in September 1417.[9] The feast of the Holy Cross was an important date in the calendar of St George's, because the chapel's chief relic was the Neith Cross, containing a fragment of the True Cross, and the table may have been prepared for that occasion.

After the Restoration, Elias Ashmole, one of the great antiquaries of the period – founder of the Ashmolean Museum as well as Garter king at arms – produced a full account of the Company of the Garter, and printed as an appendix the text he found on the two tables 'remaining in the Chapter-house at Windesor'. The list gives the division of the knights into the 'king's side' and the 'prince's side', information which is not in the fifteenth-century statutes, and it probably derives from John Page's original table of 1400. However, in the form in which Ashmole saw them, the tables date from Edward IV's building of the new chapel in the 1470s, as the names down to that date are all written in the same hand, with additions up to 1495. The information on the tables does not always correspond with the contemporary records of knights' names, which are reasonably full and consistent, and a number of names are simply omitted. It appears from this that the tables, which should be a prime witness, were obviously not prepared with a great deal of care, and so cannot be relied upon in our exploration of the founder knights.[10] The tables were last seen in the eighteenth century, and were probably destroyed.

A further source of information should be the stall plates, which were taken from the original Garter chapel when it was demolished, and placed in the new chapel when it was furnished. Again, these are a highly fallible guide. William St John Hope, who studied the architecture of Windsor Castle in the late nineteenth century, examined the stall plates carefully, and found that the majority of them had not been made until the time of Henry V, in Ashmole's words 'that happy restorer of the honor of the Order, having (at his entrance to the Royal Throne) found its glory upon abatement, not only raised it to its former lustre, but very much increased the honor thereof'.[11] The same error occurs both in the Windsor tables and on the stall plates, where the captal de Buch, Jean de Grailly, is called 'mons. Piers', and the style and size of the plates show that the majority of them were made in one batch. Only one plate, that of Ralph Bassett, actually dates from before 1400, and even this appears to have been adapted from a memorial brass.[12]

There is therefore nothing in the Windsor records which we can securely date to before the end of the fourteenth century – statutes, tables or stall plates – but there is an earlier list, dating from around 1360, and this may well be the most reliable witness to the identity of the founder members, though it gives us only thirteen names. It is in Geoffrey le Baker's chronicle, and the date of the list that he had in front of him can be fixed, because Roger Mortimer is described as a simple knight, with the added comment that he is now earl of March. He was restored to his father's earldom in 1354, so the original list predates that year. Geoffrey le Baker's account reads in full:

> In that year on St George's Day the king held a great feast in his castle at Windsor. During it he instituted a chapel of twelve priests and founded an almshouse in which impoverished knights whose own resources were

inadequate could obtain sufficient assistance from the perpetual alms of the founders of that college. The other people who contributed to the founding of that almshouse besides the king were of course the firstborn of the king, the earls of Northampton, Warwick, Suffolk and Salisbury, other barons and also some who were merely knights, namely Roger Mortimer who is now earl of March, Sir Walter Mauny, Sir William Fitzwarin, Sir John Lisle, Sir John Mohun, Sir John Beauchamp, Sir Walter Pavely, Sir Thomas Wale and Sir Hugh Wrottesley. These men who were merely knights were linked with the richest earls because their worth had been tested and tried.

All these together with the king were clothed in russet gowns, spangled with gold, and with armbands of Indian blue. They also had similar garters on their right legs, and they wore a mantle of blue with the escutcheons of St George. Dressed like this and with bare heads they solemnly heard a ceremonial mass sung by the prelates of Canterbury, Winchester and Exeter, and then in due order seated themselves at a common table in honour of the holy martyr to whom they specially dedicated this noble fraternity, calling it the companionship of the knights of Saint George *de la gartiere*.[13]

The names of the founding knights given by Baker correspond with the record of the statutes and the Windsor table, with three exceptions: Robert Ufford, earl of Suffolk, William Bohun, earl of Northampton, and Walter Mauny. All of these are given in the Windsor records as subsequent appointments to the company: Ufford and Bohun succeeded to the stalls of Richard Fitzsimon and Hugh Courtenay, both of whom are said to have died in 1348–9, while Mauny took the place of John, Lord Grey, as late as 1359. If the list which Baker was using predates 1354, then there is a serious conflict of evidence with the Windsor records. But it is also possible that Baker was simply confused about which of those knights who were members of the company at the time when he was writing had been among the founders. On the other hand, the three knights he names who are not in the Windsor list are obvious candidates as 'first founders'.

Baker's summary follows the sequence of the statutes of 1415, which mention the priests in clause 5, followed by the poor knights in clause 7. The qualification for the poor knights is given in similar terms: the statutes say that 'it is ordained that twenty-six veteran knights, who have no means of sustenance, shall have there in the honour of God and of the blessed George a sufficient maintenance', in the new foundation. There is reason to believe that he was working from a document rather than an oral report. He also describes the robes correctly,[14] which are not given in the 1415 version of the statutes; clause 4 simply speaks of the 'mantle and garter as ordained', but does not specify them, although clause 8 is precise about the mantles for the poor knights.

It is impossible to determine whether Baker is right and the surviving Windsor records are wrong. But it is very important to realize that the names of the original twenty-six knights are by no means certain, and the succession is even more open to challenge; we shall look at instances where there is new evidence that may disturb the accepted lists in a moment.

Historians have commented on the uncertainty of the lists; Nicolas Harris Nicolas wrote in 1842 that

> the deficiency of materials for the ancient History of the Order renders it more than probable that many knights may have been elected whose names are not recorded; and it is not impossible that a few are erroneously supposed to have received its honours ... The precise date of the elections of many of the companions is very doubtful ... [the effect] of numbering the knights, and calling any one of them the 'twentieth' or 'the hundred and second knight of the Garter', is to mislead.[15]

Yet numbered lists continue to appear, as though we were as sure of the succession of knights as of the kings of England. In fact, the evidence as to the identity of the original knights and as to the succession before 1400 is very much open to question, even if it is difficult to propose an alternative list of members of the company.

We can get a little further by looking more closely at the Windsor list in terms of who the knights were, when they died, and their successors in the stalls. The sequence of admission to the company derives from the Windsor tables, and, for most of the knights, the dating is not a problem. However, the early admissions do present serious issues. Three of the original twenty-six knights are said to have died before the end of 1349, and to have been replaced. These are 'Sauchet' d'Auberchicourt, Richard Fitzsimon and Hugh Courtenay. It is very probable that 'Sauchet' d'Auberchicourt is actually Eustace d'Auberchicourt, who died in 1372.[16] We have no definite date for Richard Fitzsimon's death, as, apart from his appearance in Henry of Grosmont's retinue in Aquitaine in 1345 and as the prince of Wales's standard-bearer at Crécy, there is nothing further in the military records about him. We can be certain about Hugh Courtenay's death, as the queen paid for a cloth to be laid on his tomb on 2 September 1349.

If Eustace d'Auberchicourt is one of the founding knights, the succession to his stall presents serious problems. William Fitzwarin, who is said to have succeeded him, died in 1361, eleven years before the stall became vacant. We know that Fitzwarin was definitely a companion of the Garter, as his tomb effigy shows him wearing a garter over his armour on his right leg. There is a similar problem with Henry Eam, or Oem, whose death can certainly be ascribed to 1353;[17] his successor is supposed to have been Thomas Ughtred, on the basis that Oem died in 1358. The succession list is based solely on the sequence of supposed dates of death of the knights, and assumes that the rule providing for prompt election of successors was often disregarded.[18] It would make logical sense for Eam's successor to be John Sully, who took over Eam's position as the prince of Wales's household knight shortly after his death.

Confusion over the succession of knights may well be due to the high rate of mortality among the knights in 1359–61, when no less than nine companions of the Garter died. This was partly due to the second great plague of Edward's reign, in 1361, which, as the chroniclers noted, caused a great mortality among the nobility, who had largely escaped the Black Death. Henry of Grosmont was the most notable victim, but Thomas Holland, earl of Kent, William Bohun, earl of Northampton, Reginald, Lord Cobham and William Fitzwarin also died between September 1360 and October 1361.[19] It was probably the death of Henry of Grosmont in March 1361 that was the reason for the issue of black cloth for Garter robes in this year.[20] A further spate of deaths occurred in 1368–9, when seven knights died in fourteen months. If – and this can only be a hypothesis – in such periods of rapid turnover, the sketchy record-keeping of the company broke down, this would account for the difficulties in reconciling the succession recorded in the Windsor tables with what we know of the knights from other sources. The very strict provisions in the statutes that elections are to take place within six weeks of the certification of the death of a knight by the sovereign, and that a knight must be installed within a year of his election or the election is void, may well be a later addition, as a result of problems in earlier years.[21]

THE FIRST GARTER KNIGHTS:
A CLOSE-KNIT GROUP

For present purposes, we shall look at the first thirty-seven names in the list of Garter companions as generally accepted, which takes us down to 1360, a group we shall call the 'companions to 1360'. In that year three of the king's sons were elected, and over a quarter of the knights were from the king's immediate family, changing the nature of the company away from knights of lesser rank but greater military accomplishment.[22]

If we look first at the 'traditional' list of twenty-six founders from the statutes, including the king and the prince, they fall into four groups by age. Four of them are under twenty, contemporaries of the eighteen-year-old prince of Wales, and a further ten are between twenty and thirty, knights with up to fifteen years' experience of warfare. Nine are between thirty and forty; some are experienced commanders, the king's contemporaries, while others are not yet bannerets. Finally, there are three men senior in age to the king, but interestingly not in the first rank of the leaders of the army. The eleven knights appointed after the foundation and before the king's three sons in 1360 have a rather different profile. Five of them are found either as in command of a division in a major battle or as acting as independent commanders, four are older knights, and only two are under thirty. The average age for this additional group is forty-three, compared with thirty for the first group.

Overall, the average age of the companions to 1360 is thirty-three. The companions of the Garter are the new men of Edward III's reign, with little involvement in the convoluted politics of his father's time. Three of them had served as young knights in 1324–5, mostly abroad, and only Thomas Ughtred, the oldest member of the group, had had any serious political engagement in the 1320s. He had sided with the king against Thomas of Lancaster in the civil war that led to the latter's execution; Thomas of Lancaster came to symbolize the baronial and popular resistance to Edward II's rule, and his tomb became a place of pilgrimage. Ughtred was only elected to the company around 1358, when he was sixty-seven and his solid record of military and political achievement under Edward III outweighed any memories of his youthful activities; he was one of the oldest men serving in the army on the Reims campaign of 1359–60.

The overriding common factor among the companions to 1360 is that all save two were present at the siege of Calais, the exceptions being the Gascon lord Jean de Grailly, captal de Buch, and Thomas, son of Robert Ufford, earl of Suffolk, who was only twelve at the time. The majority of them had also served on the Crécy campaign; the exceptions were those who had been fighting in Gascony at the time: Henry of Grosmont, Walter Mauny and Frank van Hale. We do not have direct proof for Henry Eam, but he had been knighted by the prince of Wales before January 1348, and thus was almost certainly with him at Calais, if not earlier in the campaign.

If the list of founder knights in the statutes is correct, only one of the commanders at Crécy was included when the company began: this was Thomas Beauchamp, marshal of the army and commander of the prince's division, which bore the brunt of the fighting. Two other commanders may have been founders, or were appointed shortly afterwards: these were William Bohun, earl of Northampton, also a commander in the prince's division, and Robert Ufford, earl of Suffolk, commander of the rearguard. Six of the list in the statutes – John Beauchamp, Lisle, Burghersh the younger, Mohun, Grey and Audley – fought as bannerets at Crécy, with their own retinues; two more bannerets were among the companions to 1360, William Fitzwarin, who may have been a founder, and Reginald, Lord Cobham. Eleven of the group were mere knights at the time of the battle. Of the total of twenty-five men who fought in the battle as ordinary knights, twelve had fought in the king's division, ten in the prince's division and three in the rearguard.

For the most part, we can only conjecture about the reasons for selecting these particular men. In one case, that of Richard Fitzsimon, there is an individual act of heroism, the defence of the prince's banner, which would account for his choice. William Montagu the younger had been knighted with the prince at La Hogue, and several of the knights later closely associated with the prince – John Chandos, James Audley, Nigel Loring and Bartholomew Burghersh, son of the master of his household – were chosen. Henry Eam and Auberchicourt, like Walter Mauny, were part of the 'Hainault connection'. Another group of knights are part of the king's entourage, and there are members of a key group of men who had been involved in the overthrow of Mortimer in 1330. Where members of the conspiracy had died, their heirs or relatives were elected to the company. William Montagu, first earl of

Salisbury, Edward's closest friend, had died in 1344, but his son was among the prince's companions at Crécy, and there was hence a double reason for his inclusion among the founders. There was a similar double reason for the inclusion of William Bohun, earl of Hereford and Northampton; he and his twin brother Edward Bohun had both been among the plotters, but Edward had drowned while trying to rescue his squire from a wild beast in Scotland in 1334. Robert Ufford, earl of Suffolk, also comes within this group; like Bohun, he was elected in the first years of the company, by 1350. The namesake and heir of one of the plotters, William, Lord Latimer, was, like the young William Montagu, with the prince at Crécy, but was not elected until much later, in 1361.

Another way of trying to define the qualities of the Garter companions or the reasons for their election is to look at those prominent figures who might have been expected to appear among them, but who were left out. Of the six earls created by Edward in 1337, three were members of the company. William Montagu the elder's son, the second earl of Salisbury, was included. Hugh Audley, earl of Gloucester, died in 1347; he left no sons, but Ralph Stafford, his son-in-law, was one of the first knights. This leaves one surprising omission: William Clinton, earl of Huntingdon. Clinton had set out on the Crécy campaign, but was forced to return home because of a 'most serious and grievous illness',[23] and did not take part in the battle. He did return to the siege of Calais in the spring of 1347. In 1350, he petitioned the pope for a private chapel at his castle at Maxstoke, on the grounds that he and his wife spent much time there and had difficulty in getting to the parish church in bad weather; this, together with his virtual disappearance from the public records after 1347, suggests that the illness he had contracted was the cause of his retirement. If this is correct, it implies that the company was intended not simply as a gathering of participants in the Crécy–Calais war to commemorate the momentous events of those months, but as a group united by their common recollections and by their service to the king, who were going to build on those achievements. In other words, these were the men who were going to take forward Edward's plans for the conquest of France.

We can account, therefore, for the new earls of 1337; there were six other earls who might also have qualified,[24] but of these the earls of Hereford and Lancaster were permanently incapacitated by sickness and blindness, and John de Vere, who had fought in the king's division at Crécy, was, like Clinton, the victim of long-term illness, though he resumed his career in 1355.[25] The earl of Devon, Hugh Courtenay, never seems to have been active outside his own lands, but his son was briefly elected to the company, dying in 1349.[26] Of the two remaining earls, Thomas Beauchamp was a prominent member of the company, but the absence of the earl of Arundel from the list is a real puzzle. Richard Fitzalan was an ambitious and energetic man, who rebuilt the family fortunes from a very low ebb at Edward III's accession.[27] His father was a supporter of Edward II when Isabella and Mortimer invaded England in 1326, and was summarily executed as a traitor in November 1326. His lands were forfeited, and Richard, aged thirteen, fled abroad, having been involved in a plot against Mortimer. He returned in 1330, and petitioned for the restoration of his inheritance, which was granted in parliament in 1331. He and Edward had been brought up at the royal court together, and Edward regarded him as a trusted servant of the crown. His career was wide-ranging: from 1343 onwards, he was one of the leading diplomats in English embassies abroad. He was something of a financial wizard: as one of the most active administrators in Edward's government, he was well rewarded for his work, but he chose to use his money shrewdly rather than indulging in spectactular displays of wealth. If he bought jewels, they were as a form of ready cash;[28] he lent huge sums to both the king and the prince of Wales, and the record of his transactions in royal writs makes it seem that he was banker to most of the leading captains of the time. He was also prepared to speculate: we find him lending money to London merchants 'to trade therewith to the earl's profit'. Moreover, he himself was a highly experienced captain, and was on five campaigns in Scotland between 1333 and 1342; he fought at Sluys and Winchelsea, and on the Reims campaign. Most important for our purpose, he was on the Crécy campaign, and commanded the rearguard with Robert Ufford. Why then might he have been excluded? There are three possible explanations: one is that, in the financial and political crisis of 1341, Arundel had spoken his mind against the king (as had Huntingdon), and that Edward had never forgiven him for this. Yet his continued active employment in the royal service argues against this, and the king and queen were present at his scandalous marriage to Eleanor, sister of Henry of Grosmont, in February 1345: Arundel was already married to Isabella, daughter of Edward II's favourite, Hugh Despenser the younger, but his wife was now a political liability. A month later, the first marriage was annulled by the pope, on dubious grounds.[29] And in 1351 Edward specifically confirmed Arundel's title to his lands, in case there was any doubt because his father had forfeited them. There is no reason to believe that Edward was harbouring a grudge against him.

The second explanation is that Arundel's banking activities were seen as unchivalrous, and not suitable for a member of a company designed to celebrate knightly and religious ideals. The curious nickname 'Copped Hat' which has been attached to him[30] has an obscure origin. 'Copped' means peaked or pointed, and these pointed hats were a new fashion. When John II entered Paris after his coronation at Reims in 1351, the Parisian trade guilds each wore their own livery. Among them were the Lombard bankers, dressed in cloth of gold and 'tall pointed hats'.[31] These are the only costumes described, which suggests that they were novel and unfamiliar. Arundel was famous for his banking activities in Europe as well as England: in 1364 the abbot of Cluny commented on his extraordinary wealth. He was also descended from a Lombard family, his grandmother being the daughter of the marquess of Saluzzo in Piedmont; a chronicler noted this, saying that his father was descended from 'the impious Lombards'. The tension between the old knightly nobility and the rising merchant class is reflected in 1381 in the statutes for the Order of the Ship in Naples, which forbid the membership of bankers,[32] and in the next century in Germany by regulations banning anyone who partook in trade from entering tournaments. Could a similar prejudice be at work here?

The third alternative raises the question of how seriously the third of the statutes of the company was taken: it provides that no one shall be elected to the company unless he qualifies both by descent and by reputation. Candidates must be 'of noble birth and a knight without reproach'. Arundel's bloodline amply qualified him for election, and it therefore comes down to whether he would not have been seen as 'a knight without reproach'. His remarriage, and the attendant lawsuits, were in process at exactly the time when the first knights were being chosen, and it would seem that it was this that was the stumbling block. His honour and fame were in dispute, and, given the consistent importance attached to these in the evidence in the Court of Chivalry, the idea that a newly proclaimed company which specifically required good repute could admit him seems unlikely. There is nothing in the record of any of the Garter companions prior to the foundation of the company which is as notorious as Arundel's behaviour; it is only in subsequent years that renegades like Auberchicourt and Wrottesley indulge in profitable lawlessness. This, then, is the most likely reason for his exclusion, though his behaviour generally with regard to trade speaks of a character with an eye to the main chance, ambitious in the extreme and not given to consideration of the finer points of honour.[33]

The other aspect of warfare reflected in the Company of the Garter was the close companionship of men who had fought side by side for as many as fourteen months, from the beginning of the campaign on 11 July 1346 to the return from Calais in September 1347. This service formed a strong bond, as the great majority of the founding knights had taken part in the campaign, the exceptions being the leading commanders in Gascony at this period. The hardships and difficulties of the months in camp and the dramatic moment of victory meant that this was a group with a very large degree of common experience.

The victory at Crécy and the taking of Calais had transformed Edward's situation with regard to recruitment, because the lure of profits of war was now a real one. Accounts of the taking of Caen in 1346 emphasize the riches that could be won if a town was taken:

> And those who could carry away booty came back with a vast amount of treasure from the houses ... The English eagerly returned to the work of despoiling the town, only taking jewels, clothing or precious ornaments because of the abundance. The English sent their booty to their ships ... [which] found such a mass of goods sent to them that they could not transport all the spoils from Caen and elsewhere.[34]

If the Round Table festivities had been aimed at attracting a wide range of knights who were likely to bring retinues to an army, the Company of the Garter included those likely to provide the largest retinues as well as potential captains who might build up a following. One of the Garter statutes provides that 'if some knightly expedition arise, or anything else which may be perceived to result in knightly honour, the sovereign of the order shall be obliged to prefer by his grace the companions of the order to all others in such knightly actions'. The original companions of the Garter had been chosen because of their military prowess, and their successors were expected to be the elite commanders of the future.

FAMILY NETWORKS:
THE ROYAL FAMILY

Companionship in war was one bond. There was another, almost as important. The families of the companions of the Garter were a very closely linked group, even by comparison with the royal houses of Europe and the aristocracy of England, who continually intermarried in pursuit of political or economic goals. Marriage between members of such groups, who were very often already related, was not a secular matter. It was controlled not in the king's courts, but in the ecclesiastical courts, and the result was a complicated interplay between politics and religion. Canon law forbade marriages within the prohibited degrees, and the degree of consanguinity specified – the so-called third degree of kinship – meant that any couple who had one great-great grandparent in common required papal dispensation in order to marry. Usually this dispensation was forthcoming for second or third cousins, but grew more difficult as the relationship became closer. In terms of aristocratic and royal matches, it was all too often less about the pair in question than about the political and dynastic implications: during the papacy of Clement VI, whose earlier career had been in the French administration, the political matches made by Edward III in pursuit of Continental alliances were usually disallowed if they did not suit the interests of the French kings. It gave the pope a considerable degree of control over this aspect of European politics.

There were other complications to marriage as well, because, although it was a sacrament of the Church, there was no requirement that a priest should be present if a marriage was to be valid. Spousals, as opposed to marriage, were valid in the eyes of the Church, and a couple could wed by declaring that they would take each other as man and wife, either at the present time or at some future date, in the presence of witnesses, provided there were no impediments of relationship or previous marriage. If a promise of future spousal was followed by consummation, then it automatically became a de facto marriage. The priest's function was to bless the spousal, and thus to turn it into a sacrament. Even in a church wedding, these aspects were kept firmly separate: in the *Canterbury Tales*, the Wife of Bath declares that she has had five husbands 'at the church door', because the contractual part of the wedding, the spousals, were a public ceremony before the couple actually entered the church for the liturgical blessing.

Of all the women who married Garter companions, the most famous case is that of Joan of Kent. She was married to three Garter companions in turn and her connections among the knights include five brothers-in-law[35] and three sons. Joan was the eldest child of Edmund earl of Kent, half-brother to Edward II, and Margaret Wake, sister of Thomas, Lord Wake. Thomas Wake, although married to the sister of Henry of Grosmont, had no children, and Joan was (through her mother) heiress in her own right to his lands.

Her father was executed for treason when she was two, and Joan was subsequently adopted by Queen Philippa, spending much of her childhood in the royal household. In 1337 Joan may have gone with the rest of the royal family to Flanders. By the time they returned to England Joan was twelve and already seems to have had a reputation for beauty and gaiety: later generations were to remember her as 'the Fair Maid of Kent', though contemporaries ironically called her 'the virgin of Kent' because of her marital record. At this early age, she had attracted the attention of Thomas Holland, a dozen years older than herself and at that time a knight of the royal household. They married in the spring of 1340 in conditions of utmost secrecy: Joan, although her prospects of inheritance were far from certain, was a member of the royal family. The marriage was a spousal – the recognized term was *per verba de praesentis*, in front of witnesses – and the match was duly consummated. Holland was with the English army all that summer, and set out for Prussia in late 1340, remaining there until the middle of the following year. In the meanwhile, Joan's marriage seems to have remained a secret, because her mother arranged for her to wed William Montagu, the son of the first earl of Salisbury. She was married to Montagu, this time with due ecclesiastical ceremony, in the winter of 1340–41, and remained with her new husband even after Thomas Holland's return in 1341. The latter became steward to the young couple shortly after the younger Montagu succeeded to the earldom in 1344, an appointment which implies that Montagu knew nothing of the past history of Thomas and Joan.

It was almost certainly lack of funds, and perhaps also his financial dependence on Montagu as his steward, that had prevented Holland from reclaiming his wife before 1346. Following the sale of the rights in the ransom of the count of Eu to Edward for 12,000 florins, he was now in a position to proceed; furthermore, as steward to the Montagu household, he knew that they were short of money, the revenues from the young earl's inheritance being in the king's hands because he was still under age.[36] Within a few months of the king's grant of the purchase money in June 1347, he began proceedings at Avignon for the return of Joan, declaring that he and Joan had been lawfully wedded and that the marriage had been consummated. Later, 'not daring to contradict the wishes of her relatives and friends', she had been married to the earl 'by their arrangement' in Holland's absence.[37] The earl, aided and abetted by Joan's mother, refused to acknowledge Thomas's claim, who had therefore brought the present case.

It was a case which would not normally have been heard in a papal court, but the pope, either feeling that Holland would not get a fair hearing in England, or seeing it as an opportunity to cause trouble for Edward, authorized its hearing and summoned William Montagu to put in an appearance, as well as Joan. However, the papal envoys were unable to get the earl to plead before the court, and Holland, in a subsequent petition, alleged that the earl and his accomplices were holding Joan against her will and in seclusion. The pope intervened on Joan's behalf in May 1348, but a further eighteen months elapsed, largely through the delaying tactics of the earl and his attorney, before a papal bull, dated 13 November 1349, declared Joan's marriage to Montagu void, and ordered that her marriage to Holland be properly celebrated in a church ceremony, which took place shortly afterwards. At about the same time Joan became heiress to the Wake estates when her uncle died without children.

Joan and Holland had five children in the next few years; both the eldest, named Thomas after his father, and the second son, John, were later companions of the Garter. Otho, Holland's younger brother, was one of the original members of the company. In 1352 Joan's younger brother, John, died unexpectedly, and she became countess of Kent in her own right. Thomas, her husband, also died unexpectedly, in Normandy on 28 December 1360. Joan's widowhood was, however, brief. At some time in the spring or early summer of 1361, Edward prince of Wales asked for her hand in marriage. She accepted him and they contracted a clandestine marriage, just as she had done with Thomas Holland twenty-one years earlier. The betrothal seems to have been an entirely private affair, and in view of Joan's previous marital history and her status, this was a surprising turn of events. In addition, the pair were related within the prohibited degrees – they were cousins, and the prince was godfather to Joan's eldest son. The match has given rise to much speculation. At the time of his betrothal to Joan there were plans for the prince to marry Margaret of Flanders. Matteo Villani says that everyone who knew the prince was surprised by the marriage.[38] One French chronicler produced a fanciful romance telling of the unspoken love of Joan for the prince of Wales, and of the prince for Joan, and of the king's subsequent fury.[39] According to the *Chronicle of the First Four Valois Kings*, one of his knights, the sieur de Brocas,[40] asked the prince of Wales to approach the newly widowed Joan on his behalf. The prince went gladly to see Joan, whose beauty and poise 'pleased him marvellously', but his representations were in vain; and, after repeated visits, the prince declared that, if they were not related, 'there is no lady under heaven whom I would hold so dear'. The countess, portrayed as mistress of every feminine wile, declared that she would never marry because she was in love with 'the man of most prowess under the sky'. The prince insisted on being told who it was, and, after a suitable show of reluctance, Joan told him that he was the object of her affections. They were married, and Joan insisted that she must leave England 'because the king of England would put her to death' if she stayed; and so the prince of Wales and his wife went to Aquitaine. It is a wonderful little set piece – the editor goes as far as to call it 'a masterpiece' – but it is a masterpiece of fiction. In fact it seems unlikely that the king was outraged, since Edward III, as well as his son, petitioned for a papal dispensation, which was granted on 7 September 1361. It is from this document that we learn that there had been a clandestine marriage, and that the couple were to endow two chapels as penance for it.[41]

On 6 October Joan publicly plighted her troth to the prince of Wales in the presence of the archbishop of Canterbury, and four days later, in the presence of most, if not all, of the royal family, including the king, and a large congregation, the wedding was celebrated at Windsor. The prince was thirty-one, and Joan probably two years older. They spent Christmas at Berkhamsted, one of the prince's favourite residences, where the king and queen visited them. Joan's style of living, which had once been restricted by her lack of income, had improved when she became countess of Kent and also inherited the lands of her uncle, Lord

Wake; now it seems to have become positively extravagant. The prince, already renowned for his lavish gifts, spent large sums of money on clothes and jewellery for her early in 1362.[42] She brought to his household her two sons and two daughters, one child having died in infancy. When the prince of Wales set sail for Aquitaine from Plymouth on 9 June 1362, the whole family accompanied him.

During the nine years that they spent in Aquitaine the couple had two sons. The elder, Edward, was born in 1365, but died five years later. His younger brother, the future Richard II, was born in January 1367. Relatively little is known about Joan's life in Aquitaine; she seems to have spent most of the time at Angoulême or Bordeaux. It was at Angoulême in April 1365 that the prince of Wales held the most magnificent tournament of his time in France, to celebrate Joan's churching after the birth of their first son, and the scale of the festivities gave rise to stories about the princess's love of luxury and the latest fashions. As early as 1363 French visitors to the prince's court had reported that the princess and her ladies wore furred gowns with slit coats and great fringes; in the French view, these were copied from the mistresses of English freebooters, and were unsuitable for courtly society. The prince's affection for Joan is evident in his letter to her after the battle of Nájera; and on his return from Spain she met him at the cathedral at Bordeaux with his eldest son: he dismounted, and 'they walked together holding hands' to the bishop's palace, where they were staying.[43]

On the prince's death in 1376 Joan became guardian of the person of the young Richard, and received his allowance, while one-third of the revenues of Wales were reserved to her once he became prince of Wales. For the second Garter feast of his reign, in 1379, she and eleven other ladies were issued with the Garter robes, an innovation which was to become a regular occurrence under the new king.[44] Apart from administering the estates that had once belonged to her husband, Joan seems to have had considerable influence with the king: a large number of pardons and grants in the years 1377–85 are recorded as being 'at the request of the king's mother', and it is probable that the idea of the issue of robes to the so-called 'ladies of the Garter' was hers. The ladies so honoured, however, had no part in the fraternity itself; the robes were an ad hoc recognition of their standing, and conferred no formal title or association with the Garter knights themselves.[45]

Joan became ill and very overweight in her last years, and died, probably at Wallingford Castle, in 1385. The St Albans chronicler believed that it was out of grief because her second son, John Holland, earl of Huntingdon and companion of the Garter, had murdered Ralph Stafford, whose grandfather had been one of the original companions, in cold blood in the course of a feud, and Richard, swearing to see that justice was done, had refused to listen to his mother's pleas for mercy for his half-brother, and had him executed. She asked to be buried, not with the prince of Wales at Canterbury, but near the monument of Thomas Holland in the Minorite church at Stamford. She left to the king her new bed, decorated with golden leopards and with the silver ostrich feather badge of his father.

By 1376 no fewer than eight members of the company were also members of the royal family. Apart from Edward and three of his surviving sons,[46] the king's first cousin once removed, Humphrey Bohun, and the three royal sons-in-law, the earls of Pembroke, Richmond and Bedford, were all Garter companions. Other knights of royal blood already deceased included the king's second son, Lionel, his cousins Hugh Courtenay and William Bohun, and his second cousin Henry of Grosmont. Two of the knights from Hainault were linked to the royal family by marriage: Walter Mauny's bride was Margaret of Brotherton, the king's cousin, and Eustace d'Auberchicourt had married Philippa's niece, Elizabeth of Juliers. Approximately a quarter of the sixty-three knights belonging to the company before Edward's death were thus family members.[47] The company founded to celebrate Edward and his dynasty became a way of binding that dynasty together.

FAMILY NETWORKS: THE GREAT LORDS

But there were other networks present within the company as well as that of the royal family itself. The most extensive of these linked John Mohun with the Burghersh, Montagu and Mortimer families. John had been the ward of Bartholomew Burghersh the elder, and was married to Burghersh's daughter Joan. Their daughter Elizabeth married William Montagu, after his supposed marriage to Joan of Kent had been dissolved, and William Montagu's sister Philippa married Roger Mortimer. Another set of marriages linked Thomas Beauchamp, Ralph Stafford and Henry of Grosmont, through Ralph Stafford's sons: the eldest, also called Ralph, who predeceased his father, married Grosmont's daughter Maud, while the second, Hugh, who inherited the title, married Beauchamp's daughter Philippa.

In both cases, this was largely a question of social advancement: the Burghershes and Staffords were from a relatively modest background. Ralph Stafford himself was highly ambitious, as his own marriage to Margaret Audley, daughter and heiress of the earl of Gloucester, shows. Bartholomew Burghersh the elder and his brother, Henry Burghersh, bishop of Lincoln, were key figures in Edward's administration: Bartholomew Burghersh the younger, John Mohun's brother-in-law, married money rather than rank: both his wives were from the city of London, and the second was the heiress of one great merchant and the widow of another. These were unusual matches for a companion of the Garter, but perhaps less unexpected given the family's background. His sister's match balanced this with an alliance to a family very close to the king.

At the other extreme, there were five knights who appear to have remained bachelors. John Chandos and James Audley were the most prominent of these; both definitely died unmarried, whether by inclination or simply because they were so continuously engaged in warfare. Other knights married locally: this was true of men such as Nigel Loring, Hugh Wrottesley and even Robert Ufford, earl of Suffolk. And for a handful of knights, we have simply the name of their wife or the fact that they were married, and nothing more.

THE WOMEN OF THE GARTER FAMILIES

Not all marriages were for dynastic reasons: and the most important exceptions come from members of the royal family themselves. The majority of Edward's children were swept up as pawns in the endless game of diplomatic alliances sealed by betrothals. The recital of Edward's failed attempts to use marriage as a tool in such negotiations would cover at least twenty years of his reign. John of Gaunt did in fact marry the heiress of Castile, with dire consequences for both English and Spanish politics, and Mary married the son of Jean de Montfort, who succeeded to the duchy of Brittany. Edward's sister Joan had married David II of Scotland, an unhappy match both politically and personally. Lionel duke of Clarence died in Italy just after his marriage to Violante Visconti, daughter of the duke of Milan, while Joan, Edward's second daughter, died of the plague in Bordeaux on her way to marry the son of the king of Castile.

However, Edward's two eldest children, the prince of Wales and Isabella, both chose their own partners. We have already looked at the prince of Wales's sudden marriage to the newly widowed Joan of Kent. Four years later, Isabella married, at the relatively late age of thirty-three, a French nobleman, Enguerrand de Coucy; again, this seems to have been a love match. Coucy was one of the hostages for John II, and had been at the English court for four and a half years; Froissart said that he was 'much in favour with both French and English', and he was partly of English descent. Furthermore, as we have seen, the king's cousin Eleanor also made a love match, in more scandalous circumstances. After her first husband died, she had become the mistress of Richard Fitzalan, earl of Arundel, the wealthiest man in England. He was married to the daughter of Hugh Despenser the younger, executed as a traitor at the overthrow of Edward II; it had been a good match politically at the time, but in 1344 it was of no consequence, following her father's disgrace. If the king's cousin as mistress of a great magnate was a scandal, the divorce proceedings were even worse. The petition sent to the pope stated that 'Richard earl of Arundel and Isabel, daughter of Hugh Despenser ... at the respective ages of 7 and 8, not by mutual consent, but by fear of their relations contracted espousals, and on coming to years of puberty expressly renounced them, but were forced by blows to cohabit, so that a son was born',[48] and asked for the dissolution of the marriage. The fact that two daughters were also born of the marriage was not mentioned. The son, Edmund, was formally declared a bastard and disinherited, though he retained a place at court and married the sister of William Montagu, second earl of Salisbury, in 1349.

Independence of choice of husband among royal women was unusual; and Eleanor was fortunate to get off so lightly for her affair with the earl of Arundel. Edward's mother Isabella, who might have continued as regent and as a power in the land during Edward's younger years, was fatally weakened by her association with Mortimer, and after the coup of 1330 her life was passed in enforced retirement – a genteel captivity similar to that of a royal prisoner being held for ransom, with some freedom of movement and a suitable but not luxurious lifestyle. Far worse was the penalty for clandestine adultery if detected: the affair of the tour de Nesle in France in 1314 showed what could happen to errant royal spouses. Isabella had three sisters-in-law, all daughters of the dukes of Burgundy. In April 1314, while Isabella was visiting her father in Paris, a scandal erupted at the French court. Margaret and Blanche, the wives of Philip the Fair's sons Charles and Louis, were accused of adultery with two household knights from Normandy, and arrested. Their sister Jeanne was accused of knowing of the affair, and aiding and abetting them. They had apparently been in the habit of meeting in a guard tower called the tour de Nesle, overlooking the Seine. The knights were executed by breaking on the wheel, and Margaret and Blanche were found guilty of adultery, and sentenced to life imprisonment. Jeanne was confined to the castle of Dourdan, and released in 1315 after a trial in which she was found innocent.[49]

Thomas Gray, writing fifty years later, claims that 'common gossip had it that this scandal was revealed to the king of France by his daughter Isabella, queen of England, though many considered this was not true'.[50] His account of the affair is highly coloured, as with his other stories from Continental Europe, but the tradition survived in later chronicles, with elaborate details explaining that Isabella suspected the knights when she saw them wearing purses which she had given to her sisters the previous year. There may be a reference to the affair in a verse chronicle written close to the time of the events. The author praises Isabella's beauty and wisdom, and says that 'through her many things were later disclosed and revealed in France' which later proved to be true, 'which we will speak of when we come to the next year'; the promised entry does not materialize. There is no way of telling whether the accusation against Isabella is true; the scandal itself was real enough, and extremely serious for the French royal house. Later writers attributed the affair to a curse placed on Philip the Fair and his family by the master of the Order of the Knights Templar, burnt at the stake on the king's orders in March 1314, a month before the affair came to light.

Adultery by a queen consort had the most serious of implications, in that it might cast doubt over the legitimacy of her children and lead to disputes as to the succession to the throne. For the other aspect of the role of women in marriage was that of landed wealth and inheritance of estates. It was this that lay behind the child marriage of Richard Fitzalan and the daring coup by Ralph Stafford in carrying off Margaret Audley: in the first instance, the Despensers, as newcomers to the nobility, were anxious to make an alliance with a wealthy and old-established family; in the second, Stafford, as an ambitious newcomer with little property of his own, was securing a marriage to an heiress who would bring valuable lands with her.

Interestingly, there is only one other example of marriage to a great heiress among the Garter companions, that of Walter Mauny to Margaret of Brotherton, the king's cousin and heiress to half the lands of the earldom of Norfolk, and widow of John Seagrave, who died in 1353. Again, the marriage was made without permission, in this case in defiance of the king himself. There was obviously more to this than a merely political match. At some time in 1350, Margaret seems to have set off for Avignon to seek a divorce while her first husband was still alive, despite a royal prohibition against direct appeals to the pope.[51] She crossed the Channel, where a servant of Mauny's met her at night to help her on her journey. Unfortunately he broke his lantern, apparently by treading on it; the pair were caught and arrested as they tried to escape in the dark. In 1354, soon after her second marriage, both she and Mauny were summoned to explain the breach of the prohibition four years earlier, which implies that this was a love match. Mauny had some links with her father's household; Thomas of Brotherton had appointed him marshal of the king's Marshalsea prison in 1331, and he had therefore probably known Margaret for some twenty years.[52] She was briefly restricted to Somerton Castle in Lincolnshire (imprisonment is perhaps too severe a term), but was soon at liberty again. Margaret was a strong-minded and determined character, and this must have been very much a marriage of equals; she was indefatigable in pursuit of her rights and inheritance, in which Mauny aided and abetted her. That she was the prime mover is shown by her claim in 1382, after Mauny's death, to the title of earl marshal, which had belonged to her father, and to a debt of £2,000, outstanding since the time of Edward II. She was treated, as she expected to be, as a magnate in her own right, exchanging new year's gifts on equal terms with John of Gaunt. When she died, she left money for new choirstalls to the church of the Greyfriars in London, and asked to be buried there.

At the other end of the scale, those Garter companions who never rose to the peerage tended to make marriages which reinforced their local standing. We have looked at the marriage links within the company, which show that some of the knights saw their natural allegiance as being with other families represented among the order's members. Of those who married outside, and setting aside the possible love matches discussed above, there was occasionally a match with the daughter of a powerful lord: Reginald Cobham's wife was daughter of Thomas Berkeley of Berkeley Castle, of whose household he had been a member. Berkeley's retinue included other distinguished knights: his cousin Maurice Berkeley and Thomas Bradeston would both have been candidates for the Company of the Garter. Maurice died in February 1347, however, and Bradeston was relatively old, having served in Edward's Scottish wars.[53] Age may have been the reason why he was not chosen, as he would otherwise seem to be a prime candidate, having been involved in the capture of Mortimer in 1330, and a close companion of Edward in the tournament field.

Miles Stapleton's marriage to Joan Ingham was a similar alliance to that of Reginald Cobham. Though Joan's father, Oliver Ingham, had served much of his life in Bordeaux and did not have a following in England, he was a powerful and respected figure, and it is interesting that Stapleton moved the centre of his estates from Yorkshire to Joan Ingham's home territory on the Norfolk coast, and that he founded a priory and chantry at Ingham rather than at Bedale, where his father's estates had been.

Marriages such as Hugh Wrottesley's to Isabel Arderne, daughter of a neighbouring landowner, and those of John Grey to Katharine Fitzalan of Bedale, and to Avice Marmion, were probably part of a network of local friendships and alliances, perhaps involving modest inheritances. That of Robert Ufford to the daughter of William Norwich may reflect an attempt to extend the Ufford estates in East Anglia. In one case, we know the specific reason for a marriage: when William Bohun married Elizabeth Badlesmere, the widowed daughter-in-law of Roger Mortimer, in 1335, it was made known that the match was taking place to help the reconciliation between the Mortimer and Bohun families, who were neighbours on the Welsh borders.

CASTLES

Five of the Garter companions came from well-established families, whose estates centred on a castle built by their ancestors. Of these, only Thomas Beauchamp undertook extensive building works, at Warwick Castle, part of a programme of reconstruction which lasted into the 1390s. He used the wealth he had garnered in the wars in France to remodel the eastern defences, beginning with the gatehouse and what is now called 'Caesar's Tower', and including the watergate. Caesar's Tower and the watergate are both unusual in plan; the inspiration seems to have been from local architecture rather than from abroad, particularly in the layout of the interior spaces – a trefoil plan in the tower, and a polygonal entrance in the watergate, which also has striking octagonal towers. Thomas Beauchamp spent much of his life abroad, as the most energetic and most feared of Edward's commanders, and he may have left the construction in the hands of his household officers, which might explain why the work drew on local styles rather than the international fashions which might have been expected.[54]

Other Garter companions had been granted estates which included castles, but, in at least one instance, a knight, Ralph Stafford, had risen to new eminence, but had no castle. However wealthy he had become, he could not simply build one: he needed a 'licence to crenellate', broadly speaking royal planning permission to build a castle or convert an existing manor into a fortress. Originally devised to give the king control over potentially dissident barons who might raise castles which could be used against him, by the second half of the fourteenth century this was largely a mark of status.

When Ralph Stafford started his new castle at Stafford in 1348, he, like Thomas Beauchamp, drew on local styles; the contract with his mason, John of Burchester, specifies that John is to work to plans provided by the earl. It was a stylish building, again with polygonal towers, and reflects his sudden rise to fortune in 1347. He had married in 1336 Margaret, daughter of Hugh Audley, earl of Gloucester, against her father's wishes; he seems to have been reconciled with his father-in-law, and certainly enjoyed the king's favour. In 1341, during the king's dispute with Archbishop Stratford, he had played a key role, and as steward of the royal household had tried to prevent the archbishop from attending parliament in April. This angered the fiercely independent peers, and one of the most senior of them, John, Earl Warenne, had turned to the king and said, 'Everything is turned upside down: those who should be the principals are shut out, and hired servants sit here in parliament who should not belong to your counsel.'[55] It was, however, Stafford who had the last laugh. When his wife came into her inheritance in 1347, he actually commissioned the castle a few weeks before having the necessary licence to do so: he was confident that he was now recognized as one of the leading men of the realm, in the light of a decade of military success combined with loyal service to the king. The new building also anticipated his creation as an earl in 1351, and is very much a visual statement of his social rank. A description of it in 1521 speaks admiringly of its excellent design and position, so it would evidently have succeeded in making a suitable impression on his contemporaries.[56]

Men with less substantial estates, often scattered across the country, might have to make do with older castles, such as the timber castle at Rougemont by which John Lisle 'of Rougemont' was distinguished from other men of the same name. This was an enlarged twelfth-century castle, with the necessary buildings from which to administer his manor of Harewood. Bartholomew Burghersh the younger, who spent most of his life in the service of Edward prince of Wales, held the castle of Ewyas Harold in Herefordshire, which appears to have been the most important building on his estates. However, it remained ruinous at the time; his absence on the prince's business and his close links with the City of London meant that he lived elsewhere.

And about half of the members of the company were household knights, who were not in a position to aspire to more than the grant of a comfortable income paid by the king or the prince. Men like John Chandos, one of the prince's closest councillors, might find themselves granted a castle in Normandy, in his case that of St Sauveur-le-Vicomte, formerly the property of Godefroy d'Harcourt and retained by the English after he returned to the French side. Chandos was put in charge of the garrison there in 1360,[57] and the grant was made by Edward III in 1361 after the treaty of Brétigny. It was ratified by the French king, and Chandos held it until his death.

We know little about how any of the Garter companions ran their estates, with one striking exception: that of Hugh Wrottesley.[58] This takes us away from the court and the world of great military victories to the murky local politics and feuds of ordinary life and the darker side of the Anglo-French wars. Wrottesley came from Shropshire, from a family without obvious connections to the court. His first appearance in the records is in the patent rolls in 1334, when he was twenty, and was proposing to join the crusade planned by Philip of Valois; he was granted letters of attorney to cover the management of his affairs in his absence. The crusade came to nothing; in the same year, deeds relating to the feuds over property which were to occupy him for the rest of his life appear. Since the original archive survives, there is a welter of detail, and we can trace the interminable progress of his main quarrel, beginning, in 1337, with the Perton family. He accused them of an armed raid in August 1336, when twenty-nine men carried off his harvest, to the value of £20. This was followed by counter-accusations and counter-attacks, and the king was forced to issue a special commission to inquire into the disturbances, which had resulted in the death of John Perton, to be headed by William Shareshull. Shareshull was a neighbour of Wrottesley's; it is suspicious that Wrottesley, about the time the commission was set up, departed for Scotland with William Montagu, taking with him all his supporters who were named in the inquiry; they duly got letters protecting them from prosecution during their absence on military service, and it may be that Shareshull warned him of what was afoot.

Almost as soon as he returned from Scotland in June 1338, he departed, again with letters of protection, to serve under Montagu in Flanders. By the end of the year, he had distinguished himself sufficiently to get a full pardon for the death of John Perton because of his good service. But he lost another lawsuit brought by his father-in-law, to whom he had mortgaged the rents from his estate, which Wrottesley had then attempted to collect himself. This left him very short of ready money, and he solved the problem by confiscating twenty-seven and a half sacks of wool which the tenants at Wrottesley had hidden from the official collectors; the wool had been granted to the king by parliament, because he too was short of ready cash to pay for his expedition. Wrottesley's export of the wool without paying dues was noticed, and entered as a debt in the exchequer records, but in 1348 the money was written off. His next move was to eject his mother and stepfather from lands to which they seem to have been entitled under his father's will, with the help of a dubious judgement from William Shareshull.

In 1342 he was in the retinue of Ralph Stafford in Brittany, where he remained until 1343. During the summer of that year, there was an uneasy truce, complicated by the fact that, although Philip of Valois had promised to release Jean de Montfort, the claimant to the duchy supported by the English, he had failed to do so. In October 1343 the pope wrote to Edward to complain that a man named Hugh Wrottesley with others from the English army had seized Ralph de Montfort and his companions from their beds and abducted them from the French camp, robbing them as they did so. Ralph and the others were still captive, and the pope demanded their release. It seems that this was a case of mistaken identity, or perhaps an attempt to obtain a bargaining counter, the object being to release Jean de Montfort from captivity rather than seizing his namesake Ralph. Somewhere along the line, Hugh Wrottesley appears to have collected a considerable ransom, since on his return to England he repaid his very substantial borrowings in the course of the next year.

He served in the prince's division at Crécy and Calais, and evidently distinguished himself, because in 1350 he became a knight of the king's chamber. At the same time, his debts at the exchequer dating back to 1337 were written off over a period of time by order of the king: they may have totalled as much as £2,000. Hugh was now a reasonably wealthy man, and held an important post at court; but disaster was at hand. A new sheriff was appointed in 1352, who evidently intended to collect the debts which had not yet been notified to him as forgiven; moreover, he was the brother-in-law of John Perton, killed by Hugh in 1337. The posse raised by the sheriff was met by Wrottesley and his men at dawn on 29 November, and in the ensuing affray the sheriff and his clerk were killed, and a third man died soon afterwards. Two of the widows charged Wrottesley with the murders in the court of king's bench in spring 1353, and Wrottesley was imprisoned in the Marshalsea. He and his companions proceeded to escape at some point later that year, and in 1354 a sentence of outlawry was pronounced. Wrottesley had made his way to Brittany and had joined the English army there. Here his luck ran out: he was captured, and had no means of raising a ransom or even of getting funds for his maintenance while in enemy hands. How he obtained his release is unclear, but, when proceedings against him were renewed in October 1355, he was able to get the outlawry lifted because he was not in England at the time sentence was pronounced. Furthermore, he was able to produce the king's pardon for his part in the murders and for breaking out of prison, granted on 5 March 1355. His lands were restored to him in November, and in the following April he arranged to rent his lands for a fixed sum, implying that he was planning to leave England again. He probably served with the prince of Wales at Poitiers, since he does not reappear in the English legal records until November 1357. He was with the king as a house-hold knight on the Reims campaign in 1359–60, evidently fully restored to favour. He appeared at the Garter feasts with some regularity: robes were issued to him in 1363 and 1364, and again in 1372. In 1366 he made a settlement of his property which may imply that he was about to go abroad again: since the next entry in the legal records is in April 1368, it seems likely that he went with the prince on his Spanish ven-ture, and may have fought at Najéra. Evidence of the same sort would place him on the abortive expedition of 1372 to Aquitaine, when the king's fleet was driven back by storms in September. He attended all the Garter feasts from 1374 to 1379.

The absence of military activity in the late 1370s meant that Wrottes-ley was back in England, terrorizing his neighbours once again. A dispute with Adam Peshall led to a petition to Richard II, in which Adam described how, when he was returning from the king's coron-ation, 'Hugh de Wrottesley, designing his death, had made various ambushes of men . . . on the high roads between London and the coun-try, and he had himself laid in wait with many armed men at a place called Foxhunte Ledegate . . . with a view of killing and murdering the said Adam.'[59] Hugh's answer to this was a series of counter-charges, though at first he hoped to get away with mere bluster, only to find that the council were no longer in a mood to favour lawless knights, how-ever well connected. There is no further word of the suit; Wrottesley died in January 1381, aged sixty-seven.

His career is typical of many of the knights of the period: valuable as warriors, they were almost as lawless as their freebooting counterparts in France: to take just one example, James Audley of Heighley, name-sake and distant relative of the James Audley who was a knight of the Garter, was also one of the prince's military commanders. The prince's domain of Cheshire was a palatine county, not subject to royal author-ity, and was renowned for its lawlessness. James Audley of Heighley was accused of corrupting the prince's officials in the course of his crimes and was outlawed, with an additional fine of 700 marks for his extortionate behaviour while serjeant of the peace. Three years later, he fought at the prince's side at Poitiers.[60] Ironically it is only through the sporadic efforts of their victims and of the law courts to bring them to book that we know about this other side of the coin. Even more notorious were the activities of the Coterel and Folville gangs, in the Peak District and in Leicester, at the beginning of Edward's reign, whose activities in the years between 1327 and 1332 went as far as issuing forged royal writs for fines, which they collected with menaces and the often complete suborning of the local and even national justices and judges. In both cases, some semblance of order was restored when the ringleaders took up service in Edward's Scottish wars: the king's armies may have included criminals and evildoers, but, by recruiting them, the royal officials and local lords solved the problems of local society, for a time at least. The lawbreaker, often with a grievance over their treatment by the law, and the respected knight on campaign, were often one and the same.[61]

BACHELORS

A smaller group of Garter companions were younger sons and knights who remained bachelors. Such men had modest estates of their own and were career soldiers: three of the prince's retainers, Loring, Audley and Chandos, who appear together in a writ of 1351, had highly distinguished careers. Perhaps partly because they were not in the king's service but in the prince's household, they were less richly rewarded than other comparable commanders. Nigel Loring's estates, apart from his own lands in Bedford, were mostly in the earldom of Cornwall, given for his service by the prince. James Audley had an income of £400 a year from the Cornish tin mines and estates in France and was lord of the Île d'Oléron near La Rochelle; apart from these grants, he had only his father's manor at Stratton Audley in Oxfordshire. John Chandos likewise had both gifts and grants of estates from the prince; his career was almost entirely in France, and he spent the last ten years of his life in Aquitaine, Spain and Normandy.

Two of the original knights came from Hainault, in the wake of the death of William II at the battle of Staveren in 1345, and depended entirely on what they could earn as household knights, in effect trans-ferring from William's household to that of the prince of Wales. Both Eustace d'Auberchicourt and Henry Eam have mystified historians of the early years of the Company of the Garter.[62]

Curiously, the key evidence about Henry Eam has been in print since 1931 but has not previously been noticed. It was known that he was a foreigner, because when he became one of the prince's household knights in 1348 he pledged obedience to the prince of Wales, saving only his duty to his liege lord, the duke of Brabant. In 1351 he was given letters of protection by the prince when he went to Flanders, since anyone from Brabant was liable to be arrested there. There is a further docu-ment in the prince's register addressed to his aunt, Margaret countess of Hainault, which gives his Dutch name, Oem. Although there is no abso-lute proof of this, he is almost certainly the squire called Heinken (Heynric) Oem who accompanied William II, the prince's uncle, to Prussia in 1343-4.

For his career at the court of Hainault, we have the detailed accounts of the count's household for 1343-5, and Heinken Oem first appears in July 1343, when the count paid his farrier for tournament armour which the latter had supplied for Heinken's use.[63] As a serving squire, who had completed his basic training in arms, he is likely to have been between fourteen and sixteen, which gives a probable birth date of around 1330. This would make him a similar age to the prince of Wales. Later in the same year, he accompanied William II on a pilgrimage to the Holy Sepulchre. William had originally intended to go to Granada, but instead, on 8 August, he set out for Palestine.[64] On 11 August Heinken offered five 'angels of Luxemburg' on behalf of the count at a church at Kaisersberg, south-west of Strasbourg. The same day, a bay tournament horse was bought for Heinken by the count at Colmar.[65]

Four weeks later, the count and his entourage had evidently travelled to Venice, and taken a ship to Ragusa, now Dubrovnik, on the Dalma-tian coast, where the count instructed Heinken to give alms to two monks who had come from Mount Sinai.[66] By December, the accounts show that they had returned from Palestine and had reached Vienna: the duchess of Austria gave the count a fur cap, a girdle and a purse, and the bearer was rewarded by Heinken with six gulden; the minstrels of the town of Vienna performed for the count while he was there, and received seven gulden from Heinken. The duke presented the count with a black horse, and the man who brought it was given six gulden by Heinken; the count rode the horse at Vienna, but with suitable lordly generosity then gave it to one of the local knights.[67] The party went on to Prussia, but the success or otherwise of their crusading is not recorded; by 8 April 1344 they were back in The Hague. Apart from acting as the count's go-between when it came to rewarding messengers and minstrels, Heinken seems to have occasionally bought horses for the count, in particular during their return to Prussia from December 1344 to the end of March 1345. While they waited for the winter campaign to begin, William II won 600 gulden at dice from Louis of Hungary, who was very angry that he had lost so much. William made matters worse by saying, 'Money that I win at gambling, I don't hold on to', and threw his winnings to his followers.[68] William did not have the same luck with the campaign, which proved to be fruitless. Heinken is the most frequently mentioned of the squires who accompanied the count during this period, and it may be that he was something of a favourite.

We do not know whether he was on the fateful expedition to Friesland in September 1345. All that we can say is that his career in Hainault ended some time between 1345 and 1348, when we learn that he had been knighted by the prince of Wales and was a member of his household. The best explanation would be that he had sought another master on William II's death, and had not unnaturally turned to the latter's nephew, who had an equally knightly reputation. It is tempting, and probably plausible, to fill the gap by making him one of the 264 esquires who accompanied the prince on the Crécy campaign; we might also assume that he was knighted in the course of the English march from La Hogue to Calais. In January 1348 letters patent from the king confirmed a grant to Henry Eam, as he was now known, of an annuity of 100 marks to support the estate of knighthood. He became 'the prince's bachelor', one of the household knights, while retaining his connections in Brabant.

The final notice of him in the prince's records was also missed in earlier accounts of his life. On 12 March 1353, 'the prince, on the death of Henry Eam, who . . . had 100 marks yearly as his fee by the prince's grant out of the issues of the manor of Bradenynche, has retained Sir John [Sully] at a yearly fee of £40 out of the same issues'.

The most plausible reason for Henry Eam's presence among the Garter knights is a personal friendship between himself and the prince of

Wales, based both on his connection with the prince's uncle, and on a shared love of jousting and the knightly world; there may well have been military accomplishments to his credit as well, but of those we know nothing.

RELIGION AND RELIGIOUS FOUNDATIONS

The Company of the Garter was a religious confraternity, in an age when religion loomed very large in personal lives. We know something of the attitudes of individual knights to religion, though the private devotions of the middle ages come down to us largely by chance: an inscription in a book of hours, a gift recorded in the royal accounts, an anecdote recorded in a chronicle. Very rarely we have a book written by a layman of high rank, and there is sometimes a personal element that can be disentangled from the formal piety of the foundation of chantries and monasteries or the commissioning of tombs. There is no narrative of knightly piety, only a fragmentary mosaic.

The most valuable evidence that we have for the religious attitudes of the Garter companions is *The Book of Holy Medicines* by Henry of Grosmont.[69] He wrote this in 1354, not long after the foundation of the Company of the Garter, but, more importantly, while the memory of the Black Death was fresh in men's minds. It may have been undertaken on his confessor's instructions as a penitential task. The text as a whole is hard to read with any great enthusiasm today, unless one is steeped in the devotional literature and imagery of the fourteenth century. It is allegorical and confessional in tone, and tells how the author – perhaps one should say simply the sinner – has been invaded by the seven deadly sins through each of his five senses, which have even penetrated to his heart, the keep of the castle, so that the fortress of his body is infected by evil. He prays to Christ as physician of the soul, through the 'sweet lady' his Mother, to provide remedies for the infection in all its manifestations, remedies which he himself suggests.

If this was all the book contained, it would have been just another devotional treatise of the kind that were produced for pious laymen by the clergy. What gives it its colour and interest, particularly for a modern reader, is the way in which the religious allegory is continually reinforced by reference to Henry's own life and experiences. From the image of his body as a castle, the similes extend outwards, from military operations to hunting, travel and everyday life. His similes are like the illuminations at the foot of the page of the psalter or book of hours: the scenes of foxes and hounds, of carriages full of ladies, of marketplaces and cookery which we look at today for our amusement are really there as yet another piece in the great jigsaw of God's design of the world for our spiritual instruction. Here in literary form is a version of the rich vein of medieval preaching which used examples from everyday life as a basis for sermons that spoke more directly to a congregation; but the difference is that these pieces are written from experience.

The castle, Henry observes, is as often taken over the walls as through the gates, because men guard the former less carefully; the seven deadly sins undermine the walls, and can then enter as easily as through a gate. He links this to his underlying image of the body by comparing the walls of the castle to his feet:

> pride has entered me through my feet when I have advised myself badly, for it seems to me – and to no one else – that my feet look good in the stirrup, or in hose or in armour, or as I dance with a light foot; and garters suit me well, in my opinion: all of which is worthless, and if I dare to say so, my mad joy in this was greater than all else, and quite without restraint.[70]

The vividness of the scenes from everyday life which Henry cites contrasts with the repetitive and conventional piety of his self-reproaches for his sins, which to a modern reader are unrealistic and difficult to take seriously. Yet these are just as much Henry's own words as those of the descriptive passages; this is how devout laymen would have expressed themselves, echoing the words of their confessors and the sermons of the preachers they listened to, using a vocabulary which no longer speaks directly to us. The penitential attitudes which underlie this deliberate rejection of worldly pleasures by a man who nonetheless indulged in them point us towards the confessional wills of the later fourteenth century, where the writer emphasizes his spiritual unworthiness, and demands an ascetic funeral without the least trace of worldly glory.

There are occasional glimpses of aspects of personal devotion in other Garter companions, but they are few and far between. Miles Stapleton's reputation for being 'wonderfully devoted to the blessed Virgin' is a throwaway remark by the chronicler Geoffrey le Baker, sandwiched between his trustworthiness and his unusual experience in the business of war. But his religious faith is confirmed by the evidence of a witness in the case of Lovell versus Morley in the Court of Chivalry, who records that, when Robert Morley died on Edward III's ill-fated expedition in 1359–60, 'Miles Stapleton preached to him of the faith of Holy Church and the mercy of God shortly before his death.'[71]

One of the permanent concerns of medieval knights was the possibility that they would die unconfessed in battle; there were few clergy with the army, though Geoffrey le Baker notes at Bannockburn in 1314 that the king had 'his bishops and other men of religion' with him in his division in the battle. The solution for those who could afford it was to have a private confessor and a portable altar at which mass could be said regularly, or, in rare cases usually affecting those of the highest rank, to petition for plenary remission for their sins at the hour of their death. Successful petitions for this privilege in 1343 before the renewal of war in Brittany included Henry of Grosmont, William Bohun and Thomas Beauchamp; during the preparations for the Calais campaign, Ralph Stafford and John Beauchamp also obtained it. Portable altars and private confessors were often combined with the right to celebrate mass before daybreak, otherwise contrary to canon law, but often essential on a fast-moving expedition, or on the morning of a battle. William Montagu was granted a portable altar and a confessor in October 1333, a licence renewed for him and Henry of Grosmont when they went to Algeciras in 1343. And during the troubles in Aquitaine from 1365 onwards, Nigel Loring, Walter Pavely and John Chandos from the prince's household were granted the same privilege; furthermore John Lyons, Chandos's chaplain, was granted the faculty to hear the confessions of English soldiers, because, in the past, 'being ignorant of the language, [they] have died imperfectly confessed'.[72]

As to the personal worship of the members of the confraternity, the prince of Wales's devotion to the cult of the Trinity is the best documented. He and Joan of Kent founded a chantry chapel at Canterbury on their marriage, and in the foundation charter the prince mentions his especial worship of the Trinity. This is reiterated by several chroniclers, and confirmed by three works of art: a lead badge showing the prince kneeling before the Trinity, of which two examples survive,[73] the frontispiece of a manuscript of Chandos Herald's life of the prince with a similar composition, and the magnificent painting on the tester or head-board of his tomb at Canterbury. The same particular form of the Trinity, the so-called 'Throne of Grace', is used in all three, so that the kneeling prince is praying for God's mercy in these images. The cult of the Trinity had been established at Canterbury in 1162 by Thomas Becket, and the cathedral was rededicated to the Holy Trinity. It was only in 1333 that the festival of the Holy Trinity was generally adopted by the Church as a whole on the instructions of John XXII. The earliest evidence of the prince's devotion to the Trinity is in a letter of Bishop Grandisson of Exeter to his clergy in the autumn of 1356, announcing the news of the victory at Poitiers, as the king had requested; Grandisson adds instructions that particular thanks should be offered to the Trinity and that the mass for Trinity Sunday should be celebrated. The following Trinity Sunday, the prince ordered sixteen swans for a feast on that day. The prince had undoubtedly made frequent visits to Canterbury, though the only pilgrimages that are recorded are those in 1343 and 1346 when he accompanied his father. He also went to the chief shrine of the Virgin Mary in England, Walsingham, before his two major expeditions to France, in 1346 and 1355; in 1346 he was with his father, and, on the second occasion, he may have been accompanied by Bartholomew Burghersh the younger.[74]

The prince's choice of devotions overlapped to some extent with that of his father, but Edward himself was a staunch and traditional worshipper of Our Lady, the first-named of the three patrons of the Company of the Garter, and he does not seem to have had any interest in the cult of the Trinity. His preferred shrines were those of the Virgin, not only at major centres of pilgrimage such as Walsingham, but also any local sites where she was worshipped which he passed on his travels. For instance, he may have visited the shrine of Our Lady of Grace at Ipswich in 1340 before he embarked to engage the French fleet at Sluys, as he sent an offering there 'out of special devotion' in 1342, and this may explain the choice of St Mary Graces as the dedication of his London foundation in her honour.[75]

The king was also a very frequent visitor to Canterbury. He was of course a worshipper at the Lady Chapel, and he also made offerings at the tomb of Becket, as the English kings had done since Henry II, in expiation of his murder at Henry's behest: he was now considered one of the patron saints of England. Edward also honoured St Edmund, the royal martyr, and St Edward the Confessor, his name-saint, his predecessors as king before the Norman Conquest and also revered as national patrons. He had been baptized in the castle chapel at Windsor dedicated to St Edward, on St Edward's feast day, in the great bronze font which later stood in St George's chapel. These were the traditional royal saints, who had been invoked in support of royal ambitions since the mid-thirteenth century.

We have already mentioned his other enthusiasm, which was rather more unexpected: the shrine of the Three Kings at Cologne Cathedral.[76] This was linked to his appointment as vicar-general of the Holy Roman Empire in 1338 as part of his alliance with the Emperor Louis, and his relations with the cathedral were a reflection of his imperial connections and ambitions. However, this did not last; it was reported that in 1359, before the Reims expedition, Edward had said that, although people thought that he was to be buried between the Three Kings there, this was not true, because Westminster was far more beautiful. The three kings among whom he wished to lie were all buried there: Edward the Confessor, Henry III and Edward I, 'a most noble king and my ancestor, who in all his life was the most illustrious and daring in deeds of arms, and in the commanding of armies'.[77]

Pilgrimage figures in the biographies of other Garter companions, for all of whom it was probably a common experience, with varying degrees of enthusiasm. Bartholomew Burghersh the younger was actually buried before the high altar in the pilgrimage church of Our Lady at Walsingham, in 1369; he had projected a pilgrimage to Jerusalem with his father and Walter Pavely in 1354. Henry Eam probably went to Jerusalem with William II of Hainault as a squire. In 1350 William Fitzwarin was the leader of a group of no less than 168 named pilgrims[78] who were given permission to leave England on pilgrimage to Rome, embarking from Dover. William took with him six yeomen and seven horses, and there are a number of other illustrious names in the company, so it must have be a troop of at least 350 people, all on horseback. If there were any pilgrims on foot they would have made their way separately once they landed.

The list of pilgrims who went with Fitzwarin shows that they were mostly nobles, knights and clerics. Two widows of great magnates were in the party, and had the most substantial retinues. Blanche, widow of

Thomas, Lord Wake of Liddell, was the sister of Henry of Grosmont, and brought thirty attendants and three damsels with her. Ida, Lady Neville, daughter of Robert, Lord Fitzwalter and widow of John, Lord Neville, two of the great families of Essex, travelled with an escort of twenty attendants, male and female. There was one other widow, six married couples and three apparently single women. Beatrice Luttrell, daughter-in-law of the Geoffrey Luttrell who commissioned the Luttrell Psalter, came without her husband Andrew. Seventeen of the men are identified as knights or men at arms, but others were certainly of knightly standing. The largest group were, not unexpectedly, the thirty-seven clergy; the foremost of these was the prior of Worcester, travelling with two of his fellow-monks.

How this group was assembled is hard to say. It may be that Fitz-warin had been named as leader, and that anyone who wished to go on pilgrimage had been told to assemble in London at the beginning of September. Despite Fitzwarin's service with the queen, there is no obvious link to the queen's household, but there are a number of men from the Welsh marches, and another group from Lincolnshire. This would imply that Fitzwarin's group was simply one of several such companies for whom a record has survived; but it was almost as diverse a collection of people as Chaucer's famous pilgrims to Canterbury.

The reason for this particular expedition was that 1350 had been declared a jubilee or holy year by Pope Clement, when exceptional privileges would be granted for those who came to Rome. The jubilee year, which is still one of the major celebrations of the Roman Catholic Church, had never before been officially declared in advance. Its origin was curious, although the idea of the jubilee, originally a time when salvation was especially near for the faithful, had entered the language of preachers from Jewish tradition in the twelfth century and the first jubilee seems to have happened spontaneously.[79] The end of the century was always a moment when apocalyptic predictions of the return of Christ were rife, and in 1299 this led to rumours that exceptional indulgences[80] would be granted for those in Rome on 1 January 1300. Pope Boniface VIII validated this belief retrospectively on 22 February, and extended it for the whole year, declaring that such a jubilee would be held every hundred years. However, in 1343, Clement VI, partly for financial reasons, and partly appealing again to the Jewish tradition which specified a fifty-year interval, changed the interval to fifty years, and thus gave notice that 1350 would be a jubilee. Despite the ravages of the Black Death, which had not quite died out in the northern parts of Europe, the event was a huge success, and, although the records imply that William Fitzwarin's party was the largest by far to leave England, many other Englishmen at a humbler level took part in the pilgrimage that year, alongside a throng of travellers from the rest of Europe.

We know that the party crossed from Dover. Given that Englishmen were not welcome in France during the uneasy truce that existed between the two countries, and the political turmoil there, it is unlikely that they followed the old pilgrim road through eastern France. Instead, they probably took a route to Rome through the Low Countries, Germany and Switzerland to Milan, via the St Gotthard pass, which had been opened up in the thirteenth century.[81] It took them through a series of substantial towns and cities, where accommodation for such a large party would have been possible, such as Bruges, Ghent, Cologne, Koblenz, Speyer, Strasbourg and Basle. The difficult part was the journey over the St Gotthard itself on the steep and narrow Alpine roads. Since William Fitzwarin and his companions were on horseback, they should have averaged around twenty miles a day,[82] which would have brought them to Basle around 10 October, and to the pass before the first snowfall. The route through Italy would again take the group through large cities, accustomed to dealing with sizeable groups of travellers. Once in Rome, they spent only a few days in the city, because of the huge crowds; the Romans, in order to extract the maximum profit from their visitors, had initially put word about that to obtain the sought-after indulgences, the main churches had to be visited repeatedly. But this abuse was ended when the papal legate issued an edict that pilgrims should only spend six days in the city.

The return journey is much more difficult to assess, as we do not know when they landed in England again; the group would not have reached the Alps until late November at the earliest. This meant that they would have to struggle through snow and ice: pilgrims did cross the passes in winter, but only at great personal hazard. The cost of staying in Italy until the spring would have been considerable. For such a journey, it was clearly vital to have a trusted leader, and someone like William Fitzwarin, with military experience, was almost essential if a pilgrimage on this scale was to be successfully completed.

Elsewhere, we have to rely on records of royal, princely and knightly charity for an idea of the religious enthusiasm of the Garter companions. The foundation of religious establishments, particularly in the later years of life, was a common theme among the magnates of the time, and the Garter companions were no exception. In addition to the chapels of St Stephen and St George and the abbey of St Mary Graces, Edward founded a nunnery at Dartford. The prince of Wales re-founded the house of canons at Ashridge in Hertfordshire which his predecessor as earl of Cornwall had established as a house of the *Boni Homines*, or Brothers of Penitence; and he also gave them Edington college in Wiltshire, and a rector was appointed there from the brethren at Ashridge.[83]

Other collegiate and monastic institutions founded by Garter companions included the college of canons at Newark of which Henry of Grosmont was the patron, and the London Charterhouse, which Walter Mauny sponsored. The Newark college, established in 1356, was on much the same scale as St George's itself, as one might expect from someone of the rank and devoutness of the duke of Lancaster. There was a dean and twelve canons, with thirteen vicars, and it was actually more substantially endowed than St George's, which Edward neglected somewhat after the first flush of enthusiasm. It was a re-foundation of the hospital at Newark which Henry's father had begun twenty-five years earlier, and the fifty poor folk it housed were the equivalent of the twenty-six poor knights at Windsor. Many of the statutes of the college concerned the commemoration of Henry's family, just as St George's focused on Edward and his dynasty; while neither were chantries, whose prime purpose was the celebration of masses for the departed, they were novelties in their time, colleges which were neither monastic nor a group of secular clergy based on a cathedral.

Walter Mauny's Charterhouse (as Carthusian abbeys were called) in London stemmed from his lease of a plot of thirteen acres from St Bartholomew's Hospital in Smithfield, outside the city's walls, for the burial of victims of the Black Death in 1349.[84] This was next to a plot purchased by the bishop of London, Ralph Stratford, which had already been filled by the end of 1348. At the dedication, on the feast of the Annunciation, the bishop of London preached on the first word spoken by the angel Gabriel to the Virgin, 'Hail'. The Charterhouse, when it came into being, was known as the House of the Salutation of the Mother of God. Mauny's first intention was to set up a college similar to that of Henry of Grosmont at Newark, but in the end a modest hermitage was built instead, with two occupants whose duty was to pray continually for the dead.[85]

The idea of offering the unused part of the plague burial site to the Carthusians appears to have been the work of Michael Northburgh, bishop of London from 1355; on his travels as a diplomat he had seen the new Charterhouse at Paris. The Carthusians had originally sought out remote and desolate places for their monasteries, but had recently adopted a policy of creating secluded communities within the bounds of great cities, as an example of holy living in the midst of the temptations of the metropolis. Mauny may have seen those at Liège and Bruges; when Northburgh approached him, he readily agreed to the new plan, and it was supported by the priors of the two leading Carthusian foundations in England. Unfortunately both died shortly afterwards, and the plan was not revived until the late 1360s. Mauny agreed once more to proceed, and the terms were agreed with the order in 1370. The foundation charter was issued in 1371, and Mauny gave the house rich endowments. When he died the following year he was buried at the altar of the old graveyard chapel, which was to become the church of the new Charterhouse. But his gifts were rendered ineffective by his death: one of the estates was seized by other claimants, and the £4,000 which the king owed him – perhaps from the loan in the Netherlands thirty years earlier – was never repaid. If he had been alive to claim the debt, he would probably have obtained at least some of the money as a personal favour from the king. The Charterhouse was built and the community came into being, but at times it led a hand-to-mouth existence rather than the secure living that its founder had intended.

Walter Mauny also played a small part in the foundation, or at least the early years, of two Cambridge colleges. In 1347–8, shortly after his return from Calais, he helped Edmund Gonville, a member of an old Norfolk family who had some connection with Henry of Grosmont, to found the college that bears his name, dedicated to the Annunciation of the Blessed Virgin (like his cemetery and proposed college of canons in London). The charter, dated 28 January 1348, states that Gonville's petition had been supported by Mauny. A few years later, he and his family were enrolled in the Guild of Corpus Christi around the time that the College of Corpus Christi and the Blessed Virgin Mary obtained its charter in 1352. The college was unusual in that it was a creation of the united guilds of St Mary, whose history goes back to the late thirteenth century, and that of Corpus Christi, instituted in 1350. Like Gonville College (now Gonville and Caius), the new college was a response to the urgent need for more clergy, in the light of the huge death toll of the Black Death. Henry of Grosmont, as alderman of the Guild of Corpus Christi, petitioned for the grant of the charter. A further link is the figure of William Bateman, bishop of Norwich, and fellow-diplomat of both Henry of Grosmont and Walter Mauny on an embassy to the papal court at Avignon in September 1348: he founded Trinity Hall in 1350, and took up the affairs of Gonville College after Gonville's death in 1351 with the work only partly completed. Mauny and Grosmont had been companions in arms in 1345–6 in Gascony, and again at Calais, so knew each other well, but how their common interest in the new foundations in Cambridge came about is a mystery. Equally, Mauny's relations with Gonville are a mystery, though Gonville seems to have been a manager of landed estates, and Mauny was an equally business-minded character.[86]

It is possible that we can trace the way in which Henry of Grosmont himself was drawn into the foundation of Corpus Christi. The records of the Guild of Corpus Christi note that John Clement of Tamworth 'was and is the best councillor and helper in London in all the business of the Guild and college'.[87] Tamworth lies to the west of Leicester, the centre of Grosmont's lands; at Leicester, Grosmont was well acquainted with the townspeople, and a popular figure with their leaders; there are records of friendly exchanges between the duke and the corporation, and he sent them news of his progress in Aquitaine in 1346. On his return they gave a dinner in his honour, which indicates a degree of warmth unusual in the relations between a town and a neighbouring lord. John Clement may well have had some connection with Grosmont, perhaps through John Gynewell, who was Grosmont's steward from 1343 to 1345 and held a prebend in Tamworth as well as at St Mary's in Leicester Castle. And, given Grosmont's known openness towards townsfolk, Clement may have regarded him as both approachable and extremely prestigious. It is no more than a speculation, but no other figure in courtly circles had the same kind of civic reputation.

These were major foundations: other companions of the Garter worked on a humbler scale. The commonest examples are extensions or rebuildings of churches already associated with their families, whether to create a new chantry chapel or even a modest religious house associated with the church. At Ingham in Norfolk, Miles Stapleton rebuilt the parish church with an impressive tower and spacious nave, out of scale with the small village which it still dominates. In 1360, after the work was completed, it was attached to the Trinitarian priory which he founded, part of whose purpose was to ensure that the necessary masses were said for himself and his wife, and her father, Oliver Ingham. The Trinitarians as an order were particularly concerned with the redemption of captives, especially captives who had fallen into the hands of infidels, and one-third of its income was set aside for this purpose. At this period, there was relatively little warfare which involved this kind of transaction; in Prussia, where Stapleton had fought, ransoms appear to have been unknown, and it is possible that Stapleton's choice could have been influenced by the prince's enthusiasm for the Trinity.

Only one other Garter companion is recorded as founding a priory or monastery; Ralph Stafford created an Augustinian priory at Stafford in 1344, in memory of his first wife. She and her family were to be remembered with prayers, as was the king. Although this preceded the building of his castle and his earldom, it was undoubtedly intended as part of a building plan appropriate to his new status. He later founded a chantry at Cold Norton priory for himself and his second wife. William Fitzwarin, soon after he returned from his pilgrimage to Rome, obtained a licence in 1351 to give lands and rent to support three chaplains at the parish of Wantage. He also included the king as a beneficiary: the chaplains were to celebrate masses 'for the good estate of the king, Queen Philippa and him, and for their souls when they are dead'. Nigel Loring, though he did not found a new establishment, was a benefactor of Dunstable priory, added a chantry chapel to his parish church at Chalgrave where he is buried, and is commemorated in the book of benefactors of St Albans abbey for his gift towards the building of the cloister there. The miniature of him in the abbey's book of benefactors, painted about 1380, is the earliest representation of a Garter companion, and shows him in a white robe powdered with blue garters.[88]

At Warwick, Thomas Beauchamp began the rebuilding of St Mary's, the largest parish church of the town, which was still incomplete when he was buried there in 1369. Reginald Cobham was buried in the parish church at Lingfield in 1361, but after his death the church was rebuilt and enlarged, and the college there was only founded in the fifteenth century. Other Garter companions were simply buried in churches which were already family mausoleums, and which did not undergo any rebuilding in honour of their distinguished occupants: this is true of William Montagu, second earl of Salisbury, at Montacute priory at Bisham, of William Bohun, earl of Northampton, at Walden priory in Essex, and of Roger Mortimer, earl of March, at Wigmore priory.

FUNERALS

Funerals were great ceremonial occasions and in most cases remained so for the nobility, despite the preaching of the reformist Lollards against such worldly pomp and show in the setting of a church service. The prince of Wales specified very precisely in his will in 1376 what the procession and its heraldry should be:

> And we wish that at the hour when our corpse is taken through the town of Canterbury to the priory that two warhorses covered in our arms, and two men armed in our arms and helms go in front of our corpse, that is to say, one equipped for war with our whole arms quartered, and the other equipped for peace with our badges of ostrich feathers with four banners of the same, and that each of those who carry the said banners shall have on his head a hat with our arms. And the man who is armed for war shall have an armed man carrying near him a black pennon with ostrich feathers. And the hearse shall be built between the high altar and the choir, on which we wish our corpse to be placed while the vigils, masses and divine services are performed; and when those services are performed, our corpse shall be carried to the chapel of Our Lady and buried there.[89]

He also gave very precise instructions for the design and imagery of his tomb, and the epitaph to be used on it, which was a traditional text contrasting the glory of this world and the state to which his body was reduced.

The prince's instructions were largely carried out, though his tomb is in fact near the chapel of the Trinity rather than in the Lady Chapel. Walter Mauny told his executors to bury him in a style befitting his rank, without 'worldly show, and without too much expense, but in a reasonable style, according to current fashion'. The tomb was to be in the middle of the choir of the Charterhouse he had founded at Smithfield, and was to be of alabaster, with 'a knightly effigy with my arms, like that made for John Beauchamp at St Paul's in London, in remembrance of me and so that men may pray for me'.[90] Froissart claims that the burial was attended by the king, prelates and nobles, but there is no supporting evidence: he is (not for the first time) describing what he thinks should have happened.[91]

The only other funeral of an early Garter companion of which we have any record is that of James Audley at Poitiers in 1369: Froissart, who was in Brabant at the time, can tell us only that the prince of Wales attended in person.[92]

MONUMENTS

Most of the tomb effigies of the first Garter companions did not survive the ravages of the Reformation. The earliest surviving effigy, that of William Fitzwarin at Wantage, is much damaged; the Garter can be seen as a raised band on his leg, but no details or painting remain. In many cases, there may not have been an effigy, particularly where there were no surviving family members; in other cases, the memorial may have been a brass. None of the brasses survive, but we do have a drawing of that of Miles Stapleton. Surprisingly, there is no sign of the Garter, perhaps because it had worn away; but the drawing appears to have been done from a brass in good condition. Alternatively, the absence of the Garter may be because the brass was a relatively standard one, bought from a workshop in London.

The three great monuments relating to the Garter which do survive largely intact are the tomb of Reginald Cobham at Lingfield, a chest tomb with a series of shields around the base, the effigy of Thomas Beauchamp at Warwick, and the brass of Hugh Hastings at Elsing in Norfolk: although Hastings was not a companion of the Garter, it includes images of several members of the company.

And it is from tombs that we get our shadowy glimpse of the physical appearance of the members of the company. On two occasions, the tombs of Garter companions have been excavated. Walter Mauny's resting place was found before the high altar during an exploration of the remains of his Charterhouse in 1947, following its destruction in an air raid in 1941. His coffin was opened, and revealed the remains of a man a little over 5 feet 7 inches tall, with most of his hair and a full beard but lacking most of his teeth. He was strongly built with a large round head and broad face, and appears to have been fit, with little signs of disease or arthritis. It seems that a papal bull had been hung round his neck; the ribbon and lead seal survived, and it may have been the licence granted to him by Clement VI in 1351 to choose a confessor who would give him full remission of sins at the hour of death.[93]

Bartholomew Burghersh the younger's tomb at Walsingham was found in 1961, during an excavation of the chapel of the Holy House.[94] This had held the replica of the house in which the Annunciation had taken place, built in the eleventh century by Richeldis, after a vision of the Virgin Mary had appeared to her. Burghersh was buried in front of the high altar, with the image of the Virgin, as he had specified. He was around fifty when he died, and his skeleton showed him to have been a little under six feet tall, with a strong physique, and only slight evidence of wounds given his long career in the field: a damaged ankle and broken ribs. His face was narrow, with the eyes set high; he had a full set of teeth, though much worn by the coarse medieval diet.

PART THREE

The World of the Garter Companions

IO

Knightly Associations: Orders, Companies, Fraternities

The idea of an 'order' of knighthood springs from two sources. The first is in a religious context, of knighthood as one of the three 'orders' of society: those who pray, those who labour and those who fight to defend the other two. This was the rationalization of society made and preached by the Church, a background to the way knighthood was seen rather than a direct inspiration for the actual orders. The Church had a second and more precise meaning for 'order', a group of men living under a common rule, as in the orders of monks which evolved within Christian society from the third century onwards, and of which the most influential model was that of the Benedictines, whose rule dates from the first half of the sixth century. From this monastic ideal evolved the idea of an order as that of a select group of knights living according to a common rule which became the 'military orders' of the Church, the monastic knightly orders of the twelfth century designed as a bulwark against the heathen, both defending Christendom and its holy places and aggressively expanding its boundaries by conquest.

The idea of such orders was a direct result of the crusades: the original orders were groups of knights who vowed to protect and care for pilgrims to Jerusalem, and who lived according to a religious rule; they were in effect the 'monks of war'. From their humble beginnings, these military and religious orders grew immensely wealthy, as the kings and nobility of western Europe gave them lands to provide them with the income they needed for their work. This gradually extended from the protection of pilgrims to cover the defence of the kingdom of Jerusalem and the other western principalities in the near east. By the end of the thirteenth century the orders were huge and complex international organizations. The Knights Templar and the Knights Hospitaller remained in Palestine, while the Teutonic Knights had transferred their attentions to the pagans on the eastern borders of the Holy Roman Empire. But the Templars and Hospitallers had failed in their objective of maintaining a Christian presence in the east, when the last crusader stronghold fell to the Arabs in 1291.

If the war in the Holy Land had ended in defeat for the two great orders, the struggle against the infidel continued elsewhere. In Prussia, the Teutonic Knights were lords of a secular state of their own, a situation which had never arisen in the Holy Land. However, by the mid-fourteenth century the Hospitallers were in a similar position as rulers of the island of Rhodes. The Templars had been the scapegoats for the loss of Palestine, and had been disbanded on trumped-up charges in 1311; those of their leaders who protested their innocence were burnt at the stake. The two surviving orders were therefore both political and territorial powers, and the monastic and religious element had sharply diminished.

Both Templars and Hospitallers had played a major part in the *reconquista*, the wars which attempted to destroy the power of the Muslim kingdoms which had been established in the south of Spain since the eighth century. From this base, the Muslims had nearly succeeded in overrunning the peninsula by the mid-tenth century. There had been no international crusades in Spain after the eleventh century, and the religious zeal to be found in Palestine was muddied in Spain by the shifting allegiances of local lords, as well as a considerable degree of religious tolerance on both sides. But there was a proliferation of knightly orders in the Spanish peninsula. The Order of Santiago, founded about 1170, is particularly interesting, as it arose out of a peculiarly Spanish phenomenon, the *hermandad* or confraternity of knights. These were at first informal associations in which knights would come together to choose a leader and fight against the Muslims. The knights of Santiago were not technically a religious order; their members could marry, and their role was that of a secular religious fraternity whose purpose was the defence of the kingdom as well as the crusade against the Muslim princes of southern Spain. By the early thirteenth century the Order of Santiago had an established constitution and an elected master, and it was envisaged as a permanent foundation. The members of the order fought alongside the king's troops, and it quickly became a vital element in the royal armies. By 1254 the king expected to have a say in elections;

five years later the order's statutes were amended to insist on noble birth for anyone wishing to become a knight, and its secular aspect became more prominent. When the order was in crisis after most of its knights had been killed in a disastrous battle near Granada in 1280, Alfonso X of Castile merged Santiago with another order which he had recently helped to establish, but retained the name of the senior order.

The disappearance of the Templars left a gap in the defences of Spain. In 1307, Philip the Fair of France seized the goods of the Order of Knights Templar in his kingdom, and persuaded the pope to suppress the order on charges of heresy. Their real fault was the acquisition of a political and financial power in the west which went hand in hand with the decline of the crusading presence in the east. They had become bankers on a large scale, originally in order to transfer money from western Europe to the Holy Land, as well as diplomats and administrators, often carrying out royal commissions. The complex story of the trial of the Templars is outside our present subject; but much of the property belonging to the Templars passed, at least temporarily, into the control of the kings and princes of Europe. Some of it ended up in royal treasuries; much of it went to the Hospitallers.

However, in Portugal and Aragon, the kings were anxious to maintain the armed support which the Templars had supplied. So, instead of simply letting the Hospitallers take over, as happened elsewhere in Europe, they set about establishing replacement orders on the lines of the Order of Santiago. The first of these was the Order of Christ in Portugal, set up in 1317 by King Dinis, and approved by the pope; similarly, in Aragon, King Robert set up the Order of Montesa two years later, and papal bulls were issued in March 1320. The exact power wielded by the kings over the two orders is not defined in their statutes, but there is clear evidence in their subsequent history that, like the Castilian orders, they were a hybrid of religious and secular orders of knighthood, with a large element of royal influence that had been totally lacking in the days of the Templars. Furthermore, these were no longer international orders, but had a specifically national base. However, Alfonso XI of Castile was slower off the mark, and, after long negotiations over the fate of the Templar lands and castles, he asked for the establishment of a new order in 1331 to take over these estates, only to be told that it was too late to do this, as the pope had given the lands to the Hospitallers.[1]

*

Five years earlier, in 1326, the Hungarian king, Károly I, founded an entirely new type of institution to which he gave the title of 'fraternal society': its full title was 'The Fraternal Society of St George',[2] echoing the Latin title used for the Knights Templar, 'brothers of the knighthood of the Temple'. St George was widely regarded as patron of knighthood by this time, and, although there was to be a strong knightly element in the statutes, the preamble to the charter of 1326[3] establishing the society defines its purpose in terms which imply that it is a direct descendant of the military religious orders:

> since the kingdom touches everywhere on the borders of the infidels and
> pagans, and therefore the government of the kingdom is entirely given
> over lest the pagans have the upper hand; and the lord of the same king-
> dom shall benefit from such a friendly society by which his life and body
> shall be made safe and the kingdom shall be defended from the infidel.[4]

The one problem with this statement is that the reality of Hungarian politics was rather different. Károly's energies were directed not against Hungary's external enemies, but against the independent-minded oligarchs within his kingdom. Károly came from the Angevin royal house of Naples, who had wide estates in both southern Italy and Provence, and therefore had a Franco-Italian background. His claim to the throne, through his grandmother, was only recognized by a small minority of the nobles, and, when he appeared with a handful of knights at Esztergom early in 1301, it was only the support of the pope and of the archbishop-elect of Esztergom that led to his coronation. Almost immediately he was forced to surrender the throne to a rival claimant, the king of Bohemia, and it was not until 1309 that Károly was able to win back the throne, if not the kingdom. He was now in a position to start to enforce royal authority, demanding the return of lands usurped from the crown, and forbidding the oligarchs to conscript the local nobles into their service. This met with fierce resistance, and only after a series of victories over the various rebellious oligarchs, particularly in the long-drawn-out war against Matthew Csák, which ended in 1321, was he in effective control of his lands. His ultimate victory was as much due to the failure of the oligarchs to unite in resistance to the king as to outside support. It is at this point, when the court was moved from Timişoara on the western border of the kingdom to Visegrád near Buda, in the centre of his lands, and the internal battles seemed to be at an end, that the Fraternal Society of St George was established to emphasize his sovereignty, a point also made by the new gold coinage issued in 1325.

Károly's strategy was to ensure that the representatives of the old families were given posts which removed them from the centre of power, and to bring forward a new aristocracy drawn from the next tier down in the feudal hierarchy, the lords who had been subject to the princes. By 1333 only one of the numerous counts, who had previously been barons and members of the royal council, was still entitled to a place on the council. Károly also created a royal household on the model of the French court, and we find knights of the household from 1324 onwards.[5] Károly also reorganized the royal domain, using the castles which had been usurped from.the crown by the princes and were now once more under royal control. They became administrative centres, controlling the lands of the royal domain, collecting taxes and meting out royal justice. The counts were deprived of their automatic right to carry a banner, in other words to command a retinue similar to that of a banneret in the English army; instead, the bannerets were appointed by the king. Under the previous regime, the oligarchs had maintained troops in each of their castles as part of their power base, and these also disappeared, to be replaced by a more general royal levy.[6] These made up the royal army in a way very similar to that of the armies of Edward III. By the end of his reign, royal power in Hungary was firmly established thanks to measures of this sort, and the princes or 'true barons of the kingdom' no longer challenged the king's authority.

It was to these new bannerets that the Fraternal Society of St George was addressed. Károly's institution was designed to strengthen the ties of these new men to the king's person. Although on a strict interpretation the king had no direct authority over the society, it is clear that he was the driving force behind it. He harnessed the ideals of knighthood to a political end, just as the military orders had harnessed religious ideals for the same purpose, but it is interesting that he felt the need to appeal to the old crusading concepts to justify his creation of the society. This is particularly striking because the content of the rest of the statutes labels the society as a firmly knightly institution but with distinctive features which are not found in any similar organization. These look like the work of Károly I himself, a practical and far-sighted ruler, in touch – like his contemporary John of Bohemia – with the ideas current among the nobility of western Europe. In the early 1320s, John was attempting to arouse enthusiasm for tournaments among the knights of Prague; when he met with little success, he went off to France to fight in tournaments there. John's exploits were highly personal, but they are evidence of the strong cultural influence of French knighthood in central Europe at this period. Coats of arms and crests were granted by the king for the first time in 1324. Károly's upbringing would have been that of a French prince, and he was hoping that the new lords whom he was installing in positions of power would take their cue from him.

This is the context in which the Fraternal Society of St George was founded. We know nothing of it apart from the charter of 1326, which repeats the text of the foundation charter and adds an amendment. From this we can get a clear idea of what was proposed, but we have little idea how it worked in practice. The constitution is striking: the members were limited to fifty, and the society was under the control of two judges, one lay and one clerical, elected by the members themselves. The original members must have been nominated, presumably by the king; anyone could offer himself for membership, subject to election, again by the existing members. If this is a hint of the egalitarian streak found elsewhere in knightly culture – the round table at which all are seated equally or the custom of kings and heroes fighting incognito – this is counterbalanced by the stated purpose of the society, to protect the king's person.

The political purpose of the society is reflected in the extraordinary status which the members enjoyed. They could be tried only by the two judges of the society, and were exempt from normal jurisdiction; and they could request the judges to intervene in cases in the ordinary courts in which they were involved. No subsequent order of knighthood contained such sweeping privileges for its members; but in return there were sweeping, though often vague, obligations. There is a wide duty to protect the king and his interests, including the requirement that knights should report any rumours hostile to the king. When the knights are at court, they are to meet monthly, and to dine together each Monday, so that they form a distinct and close-knit group; they are also to take part in the three general assemblies each year. There are detailed provisions about relations between the members, but these are not very different from those found in other lay confraternities of this period. Once a month at their weekly assembly, if the judge requires it, the knights are to discuss the welfare of the king and the kingdom and practical matters concerning them. This makes them a kind of royal council, rather larger than a privy council, and similar to the 'continual council' of the kings of England in the fourteenth century.[7] If all the prescribed meetings were held, they amounted to fifty-five days a year, a demanding schedule.[8]

The knights were required to follow the king in all his knightly pursuits and tournaments, and there was a strong social element to the fraternity. Károly himself was evidently an enthusiastic tourneyer, since in his funeral procession three knights carried his armour, one his decorated tournament armour, the second his armour for jousting and the third his armour for war.[9] The first known tournament in Hungary had been held in 1319: the king knocked out three of a knight's teeth, and granted him three villages by way of compensation. Furthermore, he decreed that knights in royal service should have heraldic arms, because in the royal service, 'namely in the army, in tournaments and other military processes and expeditions', they needed to be distinguished from one another; the first grant dates from 1324.[10] When the friar Walter atte More was sent on an embassy to Hungary by Edward III in 1346, his account for expenses submitted on his return included a payment of 3s. 9d. for 'painting the shields of the Hungarians', presumably as a manuscript roll recording their arms, information which was not known to those expert in heraldry in the west.[11] The knights of the fraternity themselves had a uniform, a black hooded mantle embroidered on the back with the words 'In truth I am a rightful member of this society'. No later secular order had a habit of this kind; we shall see that they all relied on a device or badge instead, and this too marks a transitional stage between the military religious orders and their new secular successors.

We know nothing of the Fraternal Society of St George after the issue of the charter and amendments in April 1326. It may well have been no more than a project which failed to prosper, and there is no evidence, therefore, that it was active in 1346 when Walter atte More went to Hungary, but there would certainly have been members of the court who remembered the attempt to create it. Given More's apparent interest in Hungarian heraldry, it is tempting to conjecture that he carried some information about the society back to Edward III. But apart from the dedication to St George, the restricted number of knights and the obligations of confraternity in both orders, the Fraternal Society of St George has very little in common with the 'Company' or Order of St George founded by Edward III shortly after More's return.

THE ORDER OF ST CATHERINE

At some time in the 1330s, statutes for an Order of St Catherine were drawn up in the principality of Viennois (today called the Dauphiné) in south-east France, whose ruler was Humbert II.[12] The statutes are a very curious document. The preamble states that in the present troubled times, 'new counsel' is needed, particularly in view of the wars, dissensions and other similar pestilences which might disrupt the good faith and affection between the dauphin and 'the good people of his country'. The purpose is to create an order, which is to be named 'of St Catherine', to guard the honour and estate of the dauphin, his people and his country. The lords responsible for the document – whose names are evidently missing – protest that if anything is written in the ordinances which displeases the dauphin, they will amend them as he desires.

This is therefore – at least in theory – a voluntary association of nobles in support of their ruler, though this may simply be a fiction. The preamble is followed by a fairly simple set of rules. The badge of the order is to be an image of St Catherine in red, holding a white sword in her right hand and in the left hand a motto 'To be more worthy', on an azure ground: each knight is to have such a shield made as soon as possible. The knights are to meet once a year (unless sick or more than three days' journey away) on the eve of the feast of St Catherine (25 November) at La Côte St André between Vienne and Grenoble, the meeting-place of the estates of Vienne, where a chapel in honour of St Catherine is to be founded. The lord of Anjou and Guillaume Alamans are to be captains of the order, with two captains from each of the three 'marches' of the principality. These captains are to deal with any 'riots, dissensions or disagreements' between companions of the order and are empowered to expel them if they are disobedient; they can also summon them to assemble for the good of the dauphin, the order and the country. Companions are always to have their arms and armour in readiness for the dauphin's service. They are to do their best to dispel or counter any rumours to the detriment of the dauphin or the order, and are to help the clergy, widows and orphans if so requested. Only one provision relates to tournaments: if at a joust one of the companions is without a horse, the others must lend him one, and are not entitled to refuse the request.

On the evidence of this document, the Order of St Catherine was similar to the confraternities of knights which came together to fight on the Spanish frontier, in that it appears to have been a spontaneous creation among the nobles, troubled by the prospect of civil strife. Humbert was an unsatisfactory ruler, more interested in the idea of a renewed crusade in the east than in the good government of his domains, and after 1335 he was actively trying to sell his principality, first to the pope, and then successfully in 1349 to Philip VI of France. The only hint that the order might have had something to do with him is the dedication to St Catherine, who was associated with the monastery of Sinai, and hence appropriate for a would-be crusader. On the other hand, given that Humbert was related to Károly I of Hungary, the parallels with the Fraternal Society of St George, also charged with supporting the sovereign and with a network of members across the country, may be more relevant. Whether the order ever came into existence is not known, but it is valuable evidence of the way in which princes and nobles regarded such institutions. Here we have a knightly brotherhood, with some religious commitments, but also with obvious political reasons for its existence.

What these shadowy 'orders', 'societies' and 'fraternities' tell us is that the idea of a group of knights coming together for secular or religious purposes was something that was very much in the air in the decades after the sudden decline in prestige of the great military orders after the loss of Palestine. Groups like this do not appear to have existed in the thirteenth century, and this is a real change in knightly attitudes. In France and England, the greatest centres of knightly culture of the mid-fourteenth century, no fewer than five proposed or actual groups emerged between 1344 and 1352, in a more fully developed form than any of those which we have already described. These were Edward's proposed Order of the Round Table of January 1344, the Congregation of the Virgin and St George of John duke of Normandy (later John II) later the same year, Edward's Company of the Garter in 1348–9, John

II's Company of Knights of Our Lady or of the Noble House, or Company of the Star, in 1351, and Louis of Taranto's Company of the Holy Spirit in Naples also in 1352.

Edward's proposed Round Table, the nebulous nature of which we have already explored, survives as little more than a curiosity, with the remains of a building destroyed soon after it was created as the only tangible evidence of its existence, and with only the vaguest indications of what was in Edward's mind in the accounts of very well-informed chroniclers. For the second of these orders, we have a full-scale written proposal.

THE CONGREGATION OF THE VIRGIN AND ST GEORGE

At some time in 1344, John duke of Normandy, heir to the French throne, applied to Pope Clement VI for letters granting religious privileges to the order which he was proposing to found. Károly I's fraternal society had had the approval of the Hungarian bishops, but this was the first occasion that full ecclesiastical authority for the creation of an order to be headed by a prince or monarch had been sought. The scheme for which John sought and obtained approval was centred on the foundation of a new church in honour of the Trinity and the Virgin Mary, in the names of the Virgin and of St George. The pope's letters tell us that it was to be a collegiate church of twelve secular canons and twelve resident priests, and it fitted broadly into the pattern of 'saintes-chapelles' founded by members of the French royal family. John's father, Philip VI, had founded a chapel of this kind near Le Mans in 1329,[13] and the clergy of John's chapel were to celebrate their offices 'according to the manner that has been and is used in the royal palace chapel',[14] the Sainte-Chapelle in Paris, making the link between the two quite explicit: the act of foundation of the 'sainte-chapelle' at Bourges in 1405 specifies that the offices shall be celebrated 'in the manner and style that one does so in the chapel of the lord king in his royal palace in Paris'.[15] The distinctive feature of the scheme for the new company, however, is the presence of a

> communion or congregation of two hundred knights, and these knights shall gather in person each year on the feast of the Assumption of the Blessed Virgin Mary [in August] and the feast of the Blessed George the

Martyr in the month of April, not for jousts or tournaments or any deeds of arms, but solely out of devotion to the said church, including both those usually absent as well as those of them who through pious and charitable arrangements and right intent shall reside there through the goodwill and desire of the said duke of Normandy.[16]

The knights of this 'Congregation of the Virgin and St George' were granted ecclesiastical privileges in the papal letters relating to confession and absolution. John's intention seems to have been to found a specifically religious confraternity of knights attached to his new college, but beyond that we cannot say what particular circumstances may have given rise to the project. The other qualifications for a 'sainte-chapelle' were physical: it had to be a palace or castle chapel, its architecture had to be modelled on that of the Paris building and it had to contain relics of the Passion. The scheme never went beyond the stage of papal approval to actual planning and construction, and there is therefore no evidence on these points. Indeed, John's proposals could simply have been intended to provide similar lay support for a 'sainte-chapelle'.

The reasons for the suspension of activity after the papal letters of 1344 are not far to seek: from mid-1344 onwards, the renewal of warfare between England and France was imminent, even though the truce negotiated at Malestroit between the two kingdoms was due to run until 1346. By the autumn of 1344 it was increasingly evident that Edward intended to repudiate the truce, and he did so in February 1345. The Crécy campaign and its disastrous consequences for Normandy and France as a whole were followed by the Black Death, and the projected foundation faded into oblivion. There are no traces of it in French chronicles or records.

THE COMPANY OR SOCIETY OF KNIGHTS OF OUR LADY OF THE NOBLE HOUSE OF ST OUEN

Historians have tended to treat the 'Congregation of the Virgin and St George' of 1344 as the same institution as the knightly company which John II founded soon after he came to the throne in 1350. The distinction is that the congregation was designed by its founder as a religious institution, whereas the new company was definitely secular.

It seems that John II never abandoned the idea of some kind of knightly fraternity. He succeeded his father in 1350, and in 1351–2 he put new plans into effect. The document which tells us most about his thinking is a charter of 1352 in favour of the newly founded 'Noble House' and collegiate chapel at the royal manor of St Ouen, outside Paris. It is a splendid piece of rhetoric, but beneath the flowery prose is an acute perception of the realities of power: a well-motivated knightly class is essential to the peace and power of the kingdom. In the background looms the French defeat at Crécy, a defeat which John saw as humiliating, partly because his father had fled from the battlefield. He also concurred in the wave of criticism launched against the French nobles for their pride, ineffectiveness in battle and quarrelling between themselves. The prologue to the charter was probably written by a royal clerk, but we can probably detect in it the king's own concept of the place of knighthood in the state. It starts from the premise that the ancient high ideals of knighthood in France, which had assured the kingdom's peace and security, are in sharp decline, and by appealing to those 'faithful knights' who remain and bringing them into a 'perfect union', the desperate state of the kingdom may be redeemed.[17]

The company is to be in honour of the Virgin alone, instead of the Virgin and St George in the scheme of 1344. The change may be an indication that St George was now becoming the accepted patron saint of England. It is to be called 'the Company or Society of Knights of Our Lady of the Noble House of St Ouen' and there is to be an associated college of canons to celebrate the divine offices. The king hopes that, through the intercession of the Virgin, Christ will so inspire the knights that they, 'starved of honour and glory, will henceforth bear themselves with such concord and valour that the flower of knighthood, which for the reasons we have already described has, so to speak, wilted in the shade, will flourish under our sceptre and shine again in perfect harmony to the honour and glory of our kingdom and our faithful subjects'. This is a clear reference to John's continuing dismay over the behaviour of the French nobles at Crécy and in its aftermath. The charter itself is concerned with the financing of the new college of canons, and tells us nothing more about the company as a whole.

In November of the previous year, he had sent out letters to the knights whom he had chosen as the founder members. The only surviving copy of these letters is addressed to his 'beau cousin', a term which could apply to a large number of kinsmen of the royal house, and gives an outline of the rules of the new institution. The king explains that 'in honour of God and Our Lady, and to encourage chivalry and increase honour, we have ordained that a company of knights shall be made who will be called the Knights of Our Lady or of the Noble House.'[18] This letter is to inform the addressee of his election to the company, and to summon him to its first gathering. The badge of the company is to be a white star with a blue circle in the middle, in which was a golden sun: Jean le Bel called it 'the Company of the Star', and this is its usual but incorrect title. The knights are to swear to give 'loyal counsel' to the king in matters of arms and other affairs, and are obliged to resign from any other company. If they cannot honourably do this, the present company is to take precedence. If any knight leaves the battlefield or otherwise disobeys orders, he is to be suspended from the company. They are to attend the annual festival on 15 August, the Assumption of the Blessed Virgin, if they reasonably can, and are to celebrate it wherever they might be.

John II's view of the company as founded on knighthood rather than religious devotion or fraternity emerges in the subsequent paragraphs:

> It is ordained that in the Noble House there shall be a table named the table of honour, at which there shall be seated on the eve and on the day of the first feast the three most excellent princes, the three most excellent bannerets and the three most excellent knights bachelor present at the feast who are to be received into the said company; and on each eve and festival of mid-August each year following there shall be seated at the said table of honour the three princes, three bannerets and the three knights bachelor who during the year shall have done the most in deeds of war, because deeds of peace shall not be counted for this.
>
> And it is also ordained that everyone shall bring his arms and his badge painted on a sheet of paper or parchment so that the painters may put them promptly and correctly in the place where they belong in the Noble House.

The knights are to be 500 in number, and the king, as 'inventor and founder' of the company, is to be its prince, as are his successors. We learn a little more of the details of the statutes from Jean le Bel, who has his own ideas about the name and origins of the order:

In the year of grace 1352* King John of France founded a splendid company, great and noble, modelled upon the Round Table that existed of old in the days of King Arthur. It was to be a company of three hundred of the outstanding knights in the kingdom of France and was to be called the Company of the Star; each knight was to wear at all times a star of gold or gilded silver or pearls as a badge of membership. And the king promised to build a great and handsome house near Saint Denis, where all the companions and brothers who were in the land and had no reasonable impediment would meet at all the most solemn festivals of the year; it was to be called the Noble House of the Star. At least once a year the king would hold a plenary court which all the companions would attend, and where each would recount all the adventures – the shameful as well as the glorious – that had befallen him since he'd last been at the noble court; and the king would appoint two or three clerks who would listen to these adventures and record them all in a book, so that they could annually be brought before the companions to decide which had been most worthy, that the most deserving might be honoured. None could enter this company without the consent of the king and the majority of the companions present, and unless he was worthy and free of reproach.

Moreover, they had to vow never knowingly to retreat more than three hundred yards[20] from a battle: they would either fight to the death or yield as prisoners. They vowed also to help and support each other in all combats, and there were a number of other statutes and ordinances to which they all swore, too. The Noble House was almost built; the idea was that when a knight became too old to travel the land, he would make his home there at the house, with two servants, for the rest of his days if he wished, so that the company would be better maintained.[19]

The Round Table may be the inspiration for the Noble House, but the parallel is not that close; any description of a knightly event in the fourteenth century tends to invoke Arthur's name as a kind of benchmark. The idea of a book in which the knights' deeds should be recorded is an obvious echo of Arthur's command at the end of the romance of the Holy Grail:

the king made great clerks to come before him, for cause that they should chronicle of the high adventures of the good knights. So when Sir Bors had told him of the high adventures of the Holy Grail such as had befallen

* In fact, November 1351.

him and his three fellows, which were Sir Lancelot, Perceval and Sir Gala-
had and himself, then Sir Lancelot told the adventures of the Holy Grail
that he had seen. And all this was made in great books which were stored
in cupboards at Salisbury.[21]

Likewise, Alfonso the Wise had recommended in his laws that 'the
ancients' had established the custom that 'narratives of great deeds of
arms performed by others should be read to knights while they ate, as
well as accounts of their wisdom and power by means of which they
were able to conquer, and accomplish what they wished . . .'[22] Knightly
ideals were something to be recorded in books and debated among
knights, a sentiment which Froissart and López de Ayala would reiter-
ate when they came to write their chronicles later in the century.

Like the Company of the Garter, the Company of the Star had nothing to do with secular activities such as tournaments. The royal letters
notifying knights of their election have no mention of jousting; the
badge of the company is to be worn on secular clothing or on war
armour only.[23]

The first assembly and feast of the Company of the Noble House was
held on 6 January 1352, and we can glimpse some of its splendours
from the royal accounts.[24] Edward might put up a good display of
wealth in his great festivals, but the wealth of the French court made it
hard to compete with them. Thousands of ermine furs were used for the
knights' clothing; three great embroidered stars for the king's chamber
had to be made 'in great haste, working night and day', by his armourer
Nicolas Vaquier; red sendal and velvet and silver damask were provided
for the king's use. Haste and confusion appear elsewhere in the records:
cloths of azure sendal scattered with gold stars were put aside unused,
in favour of cloth of gold and silver. The king's throne was set up on a
dais surrounded by clouds made of cloth of silver, each containing a
star. There was an exceptional display of jewellery, much of it sewn onto
clothing or worked into the stars. The dauphin's armourer produced a
tapestry of the oceans, in which there were people like angels, 'made of
Cyprus gold'.[25]

The Company of the Star evidently included the majority of the great
nobles of the realm. We have no official lists of the members, but the
accounts name twenty of them. The largest single group is that of the
younger members of the royal family. All four of John II's sons were

included, from the future Charles V, aged fifteen, to the youngest, aged nine, who was to become known as Philip the Bold, duke of Burgundy; and the king's younger brother and four of the king's cousins were also named. Knighthood was conferred on five of them on this occasion, the other four presumably already being knights. The core of the company was therefore the royal family itself, and it was seen as the forum for their knightly upbringing. This is in line with the tone of John's preface to the charter, in which he looks forward to the future of knighthood in France: how many of the knights and lords who had so signally failed to defend the kingdom at Sluys and Crécy were given the badge of the star, we cannot tell, but among the remaining names the great majority are the household officers of the king and of the dauphin Charles, reinforcing the idea that this is a tightly knit group centred on the royal family. There are three outsiders, all notable in their own way. Humbert II of Vienne, who had sold the Dauphiné to the French crown in 1349, was obsessed by the idea of reviving the crusades, and, after an abortive attempt in the 1330s, had been appointed leader of a papal fleet directed against a Turkish prince in 1345. He had left the expedition before it achieved anything, and, when he had sold his principality, he took holy orders and became patriarch of Alexandria.[26] Despite this he returned to France and appeared at the knightly gathering at St Ouen as a knight and seems to have been admitted to the company. One foreigner was present, a knight from Naples named Giacomo Bozzuto, whose grave in the cathedral at Naples records that he 'was of the Company of the Star of the illustrious lord John king of France' and was also a councillor of the king of Naples. And finally, although he is not noted as being given the insignia of the company, the name of Geoffroy de Charny, famous for his prowess and his expertise in knighthood, appears in the records. As he was certainly a member of the company very soon afterwards, he is likely to have been one of the founders.

The splendid inauguration of the Company of the Noble House might have led to great things, if it had not been for the continuing misfortune of the French armies and of the French royal family. Jean le Bel records the disaster which almost immediately befell a large number of the lesser, anonymous members of the company at the battle of Mauron:

But in the year 1353* a large English force of men-at-arms came to Brittany to aid and support the valiant Countess of Montfort and to lay waste the region that had sided with lord Charles of Blois. As soon as the King of France heard the news he sent a great body of men-at-arms to oppose them, including knights from the Company of the Star. But the English, on learning of their approach, sprang such a brilliant trap[27] that all those French who rushed to engage too soon and too recklessly were routed and slaughtered. No fewer than eighty-nine knights of the Star were killed there, and all because of their vow about not retreating: had it not been for that vow, they would have been perfectly able to withdraw. Many others died, too, on their account: men they might well have saved had it not been for this vow of theirs and their fear of reproach by the company.

This noble order was never spoken of again, and I think it has come to nothing and their house has been left empty. So I'll leave this now and tell of another matter.[28]

Le Bel was writing in 1358, and he was correct in saying that the Company of the Noble House was effectively extinct by then. There is no trace of any meeting after the initial festivities, although John kept the project alive, and continued to give grants to the college until his capture at Poitiers in 1356. Thereafter the problem of raising the huge ransom demanded by the English precluded any further expenditure on the company. The star briefly became a royal badge in the reign of Charles V, but then disappeared altogether.

However, the legacy of the company, shortlived as it was, was not insignificant. It served as the model for the Company of the Holy Spirit in the kingdom of Naples, founded by Louis of Taranto and which first met in May 1352.[29] The statutes are more elaborate and less practical, and read like excerpts from a romance. Here the table of honour is reserved for those who have fought in a full-scale battle, and were therefore entitled to wear their knots untied. There was also a table of disgrace, for knights who had left a battle or were otherwise in dereliction of their military duty. Like the Company of the Noble House, the Company of the Holy Spirit did not survive for long: it was too

* In fact, August 1352.

elaborate and overlaid with romantic ideas to be taken very seriously, and Louis of Taranto himself was characterized by his contemporaries as a 'lord of little weight and even less authority ... He took little trouble about feats of arms ... He was eager to make money, administered justice softly, and made himself little feared by his barons.'[30] The order was almost certainly devised by his chief councillor and *éminence grise*, the Florentine Niccolò Acciaioli, as a somewhat desperate attempt to create a body of knights loyal to his rather dubious master and to bring an end to the civil war within the kingdom. He overlaid a fairly severe list of commitments to the king's service with a scenario drawn from the Arthurian romances in an attempt to restore 'the tarnished glory of his master's kingdom, house and person ... by performing great deeds of honour and knighthood'. Such deeds were supposed to be written in a book to be kept by the company, and this does seem to have existed, because Giovanni Boccaccio, who could have seen it when he stayed with Acciaioli in Naples in 1362, mocked it in a letter to a friend, saying that Acciaioli had written it 'in the style in which certain others in the past wrote of the Round Table. What laughable and entirely false matters were set down, he himself knows.'[31]

The idea of a secular order of knighthood which emerged in the first half of the fourteenth century starts from the model of the military religious orders. The binding force in the great crusading orders was religion, and a belief in the spiritual righteousness of warfare against the heathen. Philip the Fair's opportunistic attack on the Templars in their moment of weakness did not destroy this ideal, but opened up the idea that such orders should be under royal rather than ecclesiastical control. The creation by the kings of Portugal and Aragon of new, smaller orders to continue the work of the Templars and take over their possessions was possible only because of the continuing wars against the Moorish kingdoms of southern Spain. Castile might well have followed suit, but Alfonso XI was too late to secure the lands of the Templars for the use of such an order. Instead, we have the first purely secular and monarchical order, the Order of the Sash, which has no religious element whatsoever. The Fraternal Society of St George in Hungary represents another approach, in a different context. Károly I paid lip-service to the idea that such an order has a function in the wars against the heathen, but seems, from the sparse documentation that survives, to have provided himself with a group of selected retainers bound by special ties to the crown. This body was entirely devoted to the service of the king, despite the invocation of the religious aspect of warfare in the prologue to the foundation charter, and the inclusion of religious duties as part of the order's statutes, together with a dedication to a patron saint.

THE ORDER OF THE SASH

We have already seen how Alfonso XI had applied to the pope to create a new religious order to replace the Templars and take over their lands. In the same year that he wrote to the pope, and, very probably knowing that the request would be declined, he established his own secular order. Compared with the Fraternal Society of St George, we know far more about the Order of the Sash,[32] which is the first secular order on record to be headed by a monarch. In the *Chronicle of Alfonso XI*, we are told that in 1330 the king established a uniform of white clothing with a dark sash that was 'as broad as a man's hand, and was worn over cloaks and other garments from the left shoulder to the waist' which he gave to selected knights and squires of his household. This was to encourage knightly deeds, and other knights could join the order by challenging those who wore the sash or performing suitable knightly exploits.[33]

Although the qualification for membership was thus relatively loosely defined, the group quickly developed into a formal order, whose statutes survive in a copy whose elaborate decoration implies that it was prepared for use by the order itself.[34] The preamble lays heavy stress on knighthood: '[the king] ordered this book to be made of the Order of the Sash, which is founded on two principles: chivalry and loyalty . . .' The most obvious difference between the Order of the Sash and the other fourteenth-century orders is that it has no spiritual element, and the only religious stipulation is that knights shall attend mass each day. Given Alfonso's rebuff from the pope over the foundation of a new order using the assets of the Templars – a new order which would have been largely religious – his purely secular society could be seen as a riposte. This secular approach also distinguished it from the Order of Santiago, which, as we have seen, was partially under royal control.

The statutes seem to aim at a distinctive *corps d'élite*, set apart both by their way of life as the most polished of courtiers and by their special oaths of loyalty, as well as their function as the royal bodyguard in war. Two things stand out: the knight of the Sash is obliged to be a vassal of the king or one of the king's sons for the rest of his life: if he should leave their service, he is to surrender the insignia. This implies that many of the knights would be retained for a fee rather than holding lands from the king, since the landholders could only switch allegiance if there were two claimants to the throne. The knight is also obliged to treat the other knights as brothers. In most fraternal orders, there is a clause of this kind, but here it is strongly worded.

The ritual for admission then follows: both knights and squires are eligible for admission, and that the procedures of admission to the order are unusual. All other orders require the candidates to be knights, whereas Alfonso envisages the possibility that squires might become members. There was a good reason for this, because, when the order was founded, Alfonso himself had not yet been knighted: his knighting and coronation took place later in 1332. As was the custom when one of the royal family was knighted, other squires were knighted with him. Of the 110 participants in this mass ceremony, a handful were already members of the order, so the provision about squires was not a special exception made for the king.

As to admission to the order, when we look at the names of those known to have been knights, it is clear that Alfonso controlled the appointments fairly closely. Lists of the early members of the order survive attached to the two versions of the statutes, and over half of these can be identified.[35] Of the thirty-six knights whose names are recorded, six were of the highest rank: two cousins of the king, two magnates and two of the foremost royal officers. Next came four of the men in charge of the households of the king's sons. About the remainder, we have no information; the Castilian records for this period are relatively sparse. But, on the basis of their surnames, only ten families are represented, so it is a tightly knit group which probably represents the major aristocratic dynasties of the period.

The clauses which follow are surprisingly detailed, obliging them to hear mass each morning, prescribing the arms and armour they should possess, forbidding them to boast, complain or gamble, and regulating their clothing and table manners. Some of these passages reflect a traditional view of knighthood set out by Alfonso's grandfather, Alfonso X,

16. The Butler-Bowdon cope, a magnificent example of *opus anglicanum* embroidery. The colours of the silks have faded.
Made in England *c.* 1330–50.

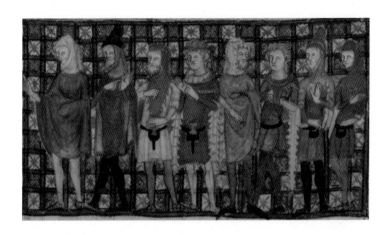

17–18. Gilles li Muisit, poet, historian and monk of Tournai, complains in his poems of the lavish dress of the gentry and of the women of Tournai. The miniatures date from the end of his life, 1352–3, and represent accurately the high fashion of the period.

19. (*above*) A group of fashionable courtiers dancing.

(*below*) men wearing vizors and dancing
From the *Roman d'Alexandre c.* 1344.

20. (*above*) Feast given at St Denis in 1378 by Charles V: the siege of Jerusalem and the ship at sea were both dramatic interludes staged in the hall. The miniature dates from the following year.

21. (*left*) Embroidered purse, French, second half of the fourteenth century.

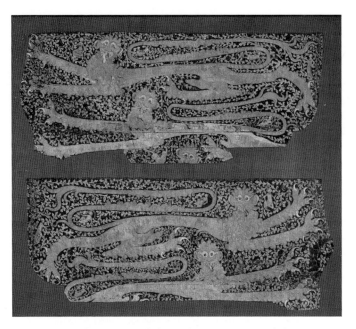

22. (*above*) Leopards from a horse trapper, English,
fourteenth century.

23. (*below*) Tapestry of Scrope arms (*azure a bend or*), differenced here
for an eldest son, fifteenth century.

24. Carriage from the Luttrell Psalter, showing the elaborate decoration. The figure at the front with a squirrel may well represent Philippa.

25. A tournament *mêlée*, from a North Italian manuscript of 1352. Edward's son Lionel married the daughter of the duke of Milan, and the costumes and armour are not very different from those in England.

26. (*above*) The chest made to contain the documents regarding the truce at Crécy in 1347, with the arms of some of the signatories.

27. (*below*) Replicas of the heraldic achievements of Edward prince of Wales at Canterbury Cathedral.

known as 'the Wise'. Alfonso X's *Las siete partidas* is one of the great law codes of western civilization, not merely a list of legal enactments but a veritable encyclopedia of the medieval way of life.[36] The behaviour of the knights is regulated by the statutes, and these sections are a much abbreviated version of the laws on knighthood in *Las siete partidas*. Alfonso the Wise writes at length, giving the history of the practices he prescribes; in the statutes, there is none of this elaborate background.

The real purpose of the Order of the Sash emerges in the statutes following those on weddings and funerals. The knights are to form a single squadron when the royal army is on campaign, and it is clear that the order was intended to be the elite corps. Throughout the statutes, there is an emphasis on excellence, whether of arms and armour or of skill in arms. The knights are to meet once a year at Whitsun,[37] for a tournament, and to hear *The Book of the Sash* read to them. The implication is that this book may contain the deeds of the knights as well as the statutes of the order, for rewards and punishments are to be meted out by the king accordingly. A mass is to be said in honour of St James, the patron of the Spanish armies in the war against the Muslims, and also patron saint of the release of the captives taken in warfare and in raids on Christian territory: each knight was to give enough alms to release seven captives.[38]

Tournaments are as much of a driving force behind the workings of the order as the role of the knights in the royal squadron in warfare. Knights of the Sash are required to attend any tournament within thirty miles of the place where they are staying, 'so that it shall seem that, wherever knightly deeds are performed, some knights of the Sash will always be there'. Refusal to go is a punishable offence: the offender is banned from wearing the sash for a month, and is required, dangerously, to run three courses with another knight of the order without having a lance himself.

Alfonso had particular reason to value loyalty to his person and peace among his knights. He had come to the throne before he was two, and a troubled regency of thirteen years had followed. Continual revolts and intrigues had seriously weakened the kingdom, and much territory was lost to the Moors. Though Alfonso's first campaigns in 1327 and 1330 regained some of this, his domestic troubles continued. He had one of the former regents assassinated in 1326, but another former regent was still rebellious in 1332, and became a vassal of the king of Aragon at about this time. So the Order of the Sash may have been an attempt to bind the nobles in personal loyalty to himself, improve the royal army for campaigns against the Moors and provide an alternative to the existing military orders.

The Order of the Sash, unlike the Fraternal Society of St George, survived and flourished for nearly forty years. At the battle of Nájera in 1367, Pero López de Ayala carried the 'banner of the Sash' in the vanguard of Henry's forces; 'and those on the side of King Pedro and the prince of Wales wore as their badge white shields and surcoats with red crosses, for St George; and all those on King Henry's side wore that day sashes on their surcoats'.[39] Here, however, it is not a question of the Order of the Sash, but of using the sash as one of the royal emblems. There are other examples where the badge of an order is displayed on battle standards and pennants, as the king's symbol, rather as the badge of the Garter was displayed on English pavises. Henry and his son are shown in a contemporary painting wearing the Sash in the approved fashion. Henry's son Juan II minted gold coins from 1406 onwards showing a plain shield with the sash, held at each end by lions' heads. It seems as if the order itself ceased to exist after the death of Pedro in 1369, and it was thereafter simply a royal badge or device.

The Order of the Sash was purely knightly and military. Its purpose was to provide a body of knights closely associated with the king, skilled in arms, who would fight with him in the continuing battles of the *reconquista*, and who would also play a political role as a group of vassals with a particular sworn loyalty to the king's person. If Alfonso knew of the existence of the Fraternal Society of St George, he may have taken these ideas from Károly I's creation. It is more likely that these concepts were more broadly current in European courts at the time, particularly in the context of the decline of the religious military orders, but Alfonso's solution is more extreme, in that it ignores all religious elements and the Order of the Sash is entirely secular.

With the exception of the Order of the Sash, the groups of knights formed or proposed up to 1350 are therefore not knightly orders in the later sense of the word. However, they have one central element, which is that they focus on the monarch as their leader, even when they are specifically religious in purpose, as with the Company of the Garter and the Company of the Noble House. The way forward was to be that foreshadowed by the Company of the Knot, where the honour of the individual knight was paramount; the fully fledged knightly orders of the fifteenth century were essentially honorific, and the only one of the early companies to survive into the next century did so by moving with the times. Membership of the Company of the Garter, originally based on fellowship and a common religious celebration, became an election in which the final choice lay with the monarch. Reputation was everything; one such victory as Crécy, however tremendous, could easily have been eclipsed by subsequent defeat. Instead, the companions of the Garter were to become famous for their remarkable series of successes on the battlefield.

II

Knights in their Own Words

The first manual on knighthood to be written by a knight – in this case, a former knight turned philosopher and missionary – is *The Book of the Order of Knighthood*, by Ramon Llull. Llull was one of the greatest intellectual figures of his age, born in Catalonia in the 1230s into a knightly family. His career was as a knight and courtier, until, in 1265, so he tells us himself, he was composing a song to a lady he loved when he had five visions of the crucified Christ. He went on pilgrimage to Santiago de Compostela, and then devoted himself to planning a great crusade to north Africa in imitation of that of St Louis, and to writing religious and philosophical treatises. He was deeply concerned about the conversion of the Arabs, whether by force or persuasion, and proposed that schools should be established where missionaries could learn Arabic so that they could preach more effectively. He taught at Paris and Montpellier universities, and led an extraordinarily active life. He wrote more than 250 works, and managed also to make a series of visits to north Africa to debate with Jewish and Muslim philosophers, and then to preach to the Muslims when he was in his late fifties. In the course of one of these journeys he was nearly stoned to death by his infuriated listeners.

Despite his formidable reputation as a philosopher, Llull was well aware of the requirements of his audience in *The Book of the Order of Knighthood*. He did not expect knights to settle down to read a dry treatise, and dressed his text up in the trappings of a romance, so that it is told by a knight who has retreated to a hermitage after a lifetime of activity: he 'had long sustained the order of knighthood and ... by his nobility and strength and high courage and wisdom, and by risking his life, had been through wars, jousts and tournaments, and had had many noble and glorious victories in battle'.[1] His teaching is addressed to a young squire who fell asleep while on his way to the king's court, and whose horse carried him to the hermit's door. On learning that he seeks to be knighted by the king, the hermit offers him a little book, which will tell him all he needs to know about knighthood – which is of course the book that Llull has written.

Llull is not concerned with the practice of knighthood, but with its place in a philosophical world-view. What follows is cast in the form of a reminder to knights that their true calling is the defence of society: he calls for them to 'return to the devotion, loyalty and obedience which they owe to their order'. This is typical of medieval thinking: the appeal is always to the authority of the past, and not to a new ideal. 'Order' in this case refers to knighthood in general as one of the three orders of society, and it is from this general concept that the idea of specific named 'orders of knighthood', whether religious or secular, comes. Llull sets his treatise firmly in this context: knights have a specific place in the hierarchy of society, below the authority of the prince and with authority over the people, and a specific task, to defend both society and the Church. Llull particularly emphasizes the defence of the people and the maintenance of justice; for this purpose, the knight must appear terrifying, his mere appearance a deterrent to evildoers. Bodily strength, boldness and armour are the outward signs of this, but these are no help unless the knight is inspired by the right motives, and has 'true courage':

> Seek not noble courage in speech, for speech is not always truth; seek it not in rich clothes, for many a fine habit conceals cowardice, treachery and evil; seek it not in your horse, for he cannot speak to you; seek it not in fine harness and equipment, for they too often conceal an evil and cowardly heart. Seek noble courage in faith, hope, charity, justice, strength, moderation and loyalty . . .[2]

This is the stuff of sermons, and knights were doubtless used to such exhortations; but Llull, a knight himself, has a sharp sense of the knight's psychology, his enthusiasms and weaknesses. He is happy for knights to 'ride great horses, joust, go to tournaments, hold round tables, hunt stags and rabbits, boars, lions and similar creatures'[3] because such exercises make him a better horseman and more adept at handling his weapons. He is also aware that knights have a role to play within the hierarchy of the state: they not only support and enforce justice by their power, they are also a key part of the administration of society, and should 'love the common good' by serving as royal officials, as he himself had done when he was a knight.

Underlying Llull's portrait of the ideal knight is a call for reform, a sense that in real life the conduct of knights is all too often the reverse of the picture he paints.[4] For each knightly virtue that he describes, he is all too aware that the opposite may well prevail, as in the passage above, where the splendid appearance of the knight only acts to conceal the vices within. Ultimately, *The Book of the Order of Knighthood* may more often have been found in the hands of preachers and confessors who needed to address a knightly audience than actually read by the knights themselves.

When Ramon Llull wrote his little treatise, his days as a knight were past, and he speaks from the point of view of a philosopher rather than that of a practical man at arms. Geoffroy de Charny, writing seventy years later, was in the thick of the fighting in the Anglo-French wars, and never claimed to be other than a warrior. That is not to say that he was not a devout man, and he is today most famous as the first recorded owner of what is now called the Shroud of Turin. His books were written in the context of the years after Crécy, and particularly in relation to the founding of the Company of the Star. And they were written while he was in his prime; they are not the admonitions of the retired expert, looking backwards, but are very much concerned with the here and now.

Geoffroy de Charny was the younger son of a younger son, and from a minor knightly family in Burgundy; his grandfather was Jean de Join-ville, companion and biographer of St Louis, but none of the wealth or prestige of his ancestor had come down to him.[5] The connection may have been useful in obtaining service under the count of Eu, constable of France, with whom he had a distant link by marriage. His first appearance in the records was in Raoul count of Eu's retinue in Gascony in 1337, accompanied by five squires; he had some small means of his own, probably through his marriage. He was still with Raoul count of Eu when Tournai was besieged in 1340, and was among the successful defenders. His next venture, in the wars which began in Brittany in 1341, was in the service of John II, then duke of Normandy, who was attempting to enforce Charles de Blois's claim to the duchy. He had evidently distinguished himself in action by 1342, when he was put in command of the vanguard at the attempt to relieve Morlaix. After the French army were repulsed, a number of prisoners were taken: Adam Murimuth tells us that 'among them was Geoffroy de Charny, who was reputed to be one of the best and wisest knights in the French king's army; he was captured by Richard Talbot, and sent to Castle Goodrich on the borders of Wales'.[6] It seems that he was purchased from Talbot by the earl of Northampton as commander of the expedition, the usual practice with important prisoners, for in 1343 it was the earl who appointed attorneys to receive Charny back into captivity when he returned from a journey to France to raise his ransom.

Despite being still on parole, Charny seems to have been back in action against the English in Brittany in late 1342,[7] just before a truce was arranged. We next hear of him on crusade, with Humbert dauphin of Viennois, in 1345, sailing to support the fleet of galleys raised by Pope Clement which had just seized Izmir (Smyrna) on the Anatolian coast. Humbert was more of a scholar and idealist than a military leader, and nothing was achieved; Charny returned in 1346, while Humbert resigned his position in 1347 prior to abdicating and becoming a monk. Charny rejoined the duke of Normandy's army, and fought in Gascony in 1346 until the army returned to Paris in haste on hearing the news of the defeat at Crécy. Charny was named standard-bearer of the *oriflamme* when Philip took his army to the relief of Calais in July 1347, only to retreat in humiliating circumstances. Charny was one of the French negotiators of the truce of September 1347.

Criticism of the king and of the French knights was rife at this time: there are a number of surviving poems attacking them for their disastrous failure at Crécy. Philip responded by appointing new advisers, and Charny became a member of the royal council in January 1348, with a house in Paris in acknowledgement of his services. Valued though he was as diplomat and councillor, Charny preferred action, and it was he who dreamt up the scheme to recover Calais by bribing the mercenary whom Edward had appointed as master of the king's galleys, Aimeric di Pavia, to open the gates to a small French force which he was to lead.[8] The plot led to his defeat by Edward's household knights under the king and the prince of Wales in person, and his capture by John Potenhale after he was wounded. He began his second English captivity as the king's prisoner, Potenhale having been given 100 marks for his good service in taking Charny. This time the ransom was substantial, and, soon after the duke of Normandy came to the throne in 1350 as John II, he is said to have paid 12,000 *écus* towards Charny's ransom. He was back in France by June 1351, and defended Ardres near Calais against an English attack: he was now the commander for Picardy and the Norman frontier, and he used this post to settle scores with Aimeric di Pavia, whom he regarded as having broken his word, and with the captain of Guines, who had sold his fortress to the English. Both were seized and summarily executed: Charny regarded treachery as one of the cardinal sins of knighthood.

Charny was one of the founder members of the Company of the Star in 1352, and it is possible that he had been connected with the plans for this order since John II originally proposed it in 1344, as he had been in John's service in Brittany prior to that. He certainly wrote one of his works specifically for the order, the *Questions on Jousts, Tournaments and War*, and it is possible that his *Book of Chivalry* was also intended for the knights. He also wrote a *Book of Charny*, a personal account of his life; it is tempting to suggest that this was the product of his enforced leisure in England in 1349–50, since we can point to a number of knights who wrote while in captivity: Thomas Gray, author of the *Scalacronica*, the poems of Charles of Orléans, and, most famously, Thomas Malory's *Le Morte Darthur*.

In June 1355, as preparations for the renewal of the war began, John II again appointed Charny bearer of the *oriflamme*, and he carried the sacred banner at the battle of Poitiers the following year. Here Charny was killed in the final moments of the battle, in the small knot of knights who made a last stand in defence of the king and of the standard. Geoffrey le Baker wrote of him that he was 'more practised in military matters than any other French knight, and that, besides his long experience of war, he had been given the excellent gift of the quick wits of a lively nature',[9] while Froissart simply called him 'the most worthy and valiant of all'.

The *Book of Chivalry* is therefore the work of a central figure in the knightly world of the mid-fourteenth century, well known in both France and England, and with experience of both countries. It is as close as we shall come to understanding the mindset of the companions of the Garter, belonging as it does to the common culture of knighthood which transcended the political divisions between England and France.

Charny begins by defining a scale of prowess, and here we immediately encounter a vital element in knightly ideas of the mid-fourteenth century. It is that much of knightly life is competitive: the focus is on the individual, not on the team aspects of warfare. The objective towards which knights strive is personal fame and reputation, their model the heroes of romance rather than the great commanders of history. This cult of the individual is underlined in heraldry, where the coat of arms is unique and personal, and cannot be borne by anyone other than the rightful holder. The first cases concerning unauthorized use of arms in the Court of Chivalry date from this period, notably from the siege of Calais in 1346–7, when Robert Morley and Nicholas Burnell both laid claim to the same arms, and a similar case was heard between John Warbleton and Theobald Russell.[10] Charny is in search of the superlative individual, as his introduction makes clear: 'And always the noblest way rises above all others, and those who have the greatest heart for it go constantly forward to reach and achieve the highest honor.'[11] He discusses knightly activities in terms of this 'scale of prowess', with deeds of arms in tournaments at the bottom, then deeds of arms in local wars, and finally deeds of arms in full warfare: 'it is from good battles that great honors arise and are increased'. The reputation of the individual Garter companions arose from their 'good battles', and together their fame became that of the company as a whole.

He then looks at other activities which can enhance a knight's reputation, in a series of short discussions on travels to distant places, serving for pay and performing feats of arms for the love of a lady; each ends with a variation on the refrain, 'I therefore say: whoever does best, is most worthy.' He gives us a series of character sketches: the knight who spends extravagantly on 'great state and outward show', but cannot afford to keep up his expenditure for long enough to wait for the action in which he might distinguish himself; the men whose deeds are undertaken in remote places, and which nobody knows about; the men who are too eager for plunder and then lose both their booty and their reputation. He sketches his ideal knight, an enthusiast who listens carefully in his youth to men of experience talking about deeds of arms or weapons, armour and horses, learning all he can about the skills of a knight, and about how a knight should conduct himself. He learns how to handle arms, first through jousting, 'the first exercise in the use of arms which he can encounter', and then through tournaments, from which he progresses to real warfare 'in order to achieve the highest honor in prowess'. In order to take part in warfare, he observes the techniques of managing an expedition and deploying troops, whether attacking or withdrawing, as well as siegecraft against castles and walled towns. He seeks out places where sieges are in progress and, stationing himself there as observer, watches all the different siege machines and techniques of mining, bombardment and scaling walls. He then travels to find countries that are at war, so that he can take part in a battle, and so his career begins. Charny recognizes that the best way to advancement is through service with a great lord, because his retinue will be larger, and will be a better milieu for learning knightly skills; the lord will be able to choose the best men at arms and is more likely to be a good leader.

Having won high renown in the field, the knight must look to his reputation, 'for there will be much greater talk and notoriety about their shortcomings than there would be concerning someone without such a great reputation'. And, in order to ensure that scandal does not touch the ambitious knight, he must adopt the right kind of lifestyle from the outset. So Charny becomes a kind of medieval life coach, and launches into a detailed discussion of the vices and virtues involved, with vivid glimpses of contemporary manners. He condemns drunkenness and gluttony, and even being a gourmet is forbidden: 'do not concern yourself with being knowledgeable about good dishes and fine sauces nor spend too much time deciding which wines are the best . . .'[12] Gambling is another besetting sin, and the evidence from the royal accounts shows that this was a very frequent failing. More curiously, he condemns real tennis, a specialist game with a small but avid following; but this is because of the wagers which were placed on the outcome. Jousting and dancing naturally meet with approval, as do conversation and singing; these are social pastimes and always to be recommended in good company. 'Yet fine games are good where there is no anger, but when tempers rise, it is no longer play';[13] so the choice of companions is important, and lords whose entourage includes men who are a bad influence are to be avoided.

Above all, the ambitious knight needs to be single-minded in his pursuit of honour. Charny would have been horrified by Falstaff's view of honour: 'What is honour? A word. What is in that word honour? What is that honour? Air – a trim reckoning!' Honour is a word Charny cannot use often enough, and his sermon on honour is the central part of his teaching, in the course of which he moves on from the almost fanatical pursuit of honour earned to the inspiration for such deeds. Here his book takes up the traditional theme of love as the fount of honourable deeds: it is perhaps the least original part of his text, rather as if he himself is repeating a lesson learnt, a convention that is beginning to outwear its time.

Having paid his respects to courtly love, Charny quickly returns to instructing his knight in less ethereal matters. In the section on physical strength and courage, he gives a splendid list of the terrors that await a knight who loves comfort too much once he is in the field. He lives in fear of walls that might fall on him, rivers that can drown him, bridges that might collapse; he will go miles out of his way not to cross a boggy patch, is frightened by the least illness and cannot stand the sight of blood. He cannot sleep at night in case the wind brings down the house he is sheltering in.

The closing sections of Charny's book return to the conventional religious view of society and knighthood; there is less about the practicalities of knighthood in this theoretical section, and his ideas are largely derived from Ramon Llull and the concept of the three orders, though he turns aside to discuss the virtues relevant to a good man at arms, condemning those who are outwardly devout but harbour secret vices, those who are too clever to take practical decisions because they are always seeing subtle complications, the rash, those who avoid responsibility and will not lead. And in his final pages, he gives a sermon against richness of dress in men which runs counter to the personal extravagances of both the English and French kings. But it is the presence of this section, however stereotyped, which is important: Charny is trying to mould his knight to be both practical and effective, and with a strong spiritual background, understanding where his power comes from and how it should best be used.

Charny's other works illustrate knightly life in different ways. The *Book of Charny*, written in simple verse, covers some of the same ground as the *Book of Chivalry*, but the images that Charny provides of the knight's actual experience in the field are intriguing. Here he is on the subject of what might happen in the course of a siege:

If they are attacking a castle or tower, be there to take part in the assault.
You will have to suffer great blows, and often fall to the ground; rocks

will be thrown at you from mangonels,* arrows and crossbow bolts will fly around you and some will strike you and wound you, of course. Now you are up to the walls, and the blows are so hard that I am not sure you will come back. Everyone is looking out for a chance to wound you, and nothing can protect you any more, I know this for a fact, unless God shields his own, finding some good in them; then he will be gracious to them and let them escape, and hide them under his mantle; at least so it seems to me when men often escape from such great danger.

Now the scaling ladder is against the wall, be the first man up; but you will come down badly, head first. Lances and swords will attack you, and very heavy stones will fall on you. Then you will have to be picked up and carried to your lodgings on a shield. They will shout in your ear, and you will not say a word. It will be a great miracle if you are alive. Your eyes are closed, your face is pale and your blood is everywhere. If you are alive, thank the Son of the Virgin Mary with all your heart. If He wishes, He can rescue you but you cannot do anything without Him. So you see that an ass that munches thistles or a beast harnessed to a cart are not as unfortunate as he who learns to be a knight.[14]

Charny paints similarly gloomy vignettes of the battlefield and of sea voyages in search of adventures in the east. But doing nothing is not an option: if the knight gives up, he will become like a horse crowded into a stable for a long time and badly looked after, that loses all its qualities. Faced with danger, he should trust in God, and continue to strive to do his best: he will win honour and praise when he returns home. The last section of the poem deals with the education of the aspiring knight, with a strong emphasis on religious observance, and a discussion of the seven deadly sins, before Charny concludes very much in the same vein as in the *Book of Chivalry*.

The last of Charny's works, *Questions on Jousts, Tournaments and War*, is the only one definitely associated with the Company of the Star. It consists of a series of problems to be put to the knights for their decision, acting as a kind of court of knightly behaviour. We have only the questions: Charny probably never wrote the answers, and genuinely intended them as matters for the knights of the Star to discuss, after which decisions might have been recorded. There are three sections, on

* A type of siege engine.

jousts, tournaments and warfare. In the sections on jousts and warfare, the main topic is the booty to be acquired, how title to a defeated knight's horse in a joust or to a prisoner for ransom can be established. The questions on ransom and the conditions connected with the terms of captivity are his main concern, forming a third of the text. The section on warfare is detailed, and includes two items on the status of the standard-bearer, the position that Charny himself held. There are occasional mentions of honour and prowess, but by and large these are matters which reflect the business of war, and much of it seems more appropriate to matters of trade than matters of knighthood. Occasionally the purely romantic ideals intervene, as in question 88, which pits two companies of fifty knights against each other: one company has just come from seeing their ladies, while the others are on their way to their paramours: which, asks Charny, will fight the better? Sadly, we shall never know the answers.

The importance of these books is that, unlike earlier treatises, which belong on the bookshelves of preachers or clergy in a great household, these do seem to be books whose readership is genuinely envisaged as the knights themselves. However, Charny's desire to reach an audience of his peers was to be disappointed: perhaps because of his death at Poitiers, the books never reached a wide circulation, and survive only in two manuscripts, with little evidence that they were known to other readers.

Knights and books did not mix, on the whole. If reading was widespread among knights, we would expect to find a larger number of manuscripts on knightly matters surviving, even allowing for the massive destruction of medieval books in succeeding centuries. Major works often survive in unique manuscript copies, whether historical texts such as Jean le Bel's chronicle, Thomas Gray's *Scalacronica*, or romances such as *Sir Gawain and the Green Knight* or Thomas Malory's *Le Morte Darthur*. We may know something about lost works through references to them by other writers or from medieval library catalogues and inventories, but there is little to suggest that what we have seriously under-represents the ownership of such books by knights. Literacy was largely a matter of rank. The great magnates were the most likely to own, and probably therefore to read, chronicles and romances and works on knighthood. It is not until the fifteenth century that we find aspiring knights like John Paston collecting texts about knighthood as part of their efforts to improve their social standing.[15] In France, where warfare affected almost every part of the kingdom in the second half of the fourteenth century, there was a lively debate on knights and the conduct of military affairs, which only appears in England once the English war effort faltered at the beginning of the fifteenth century.[16]

How then did the majority of knights know about the content of these books, and about romances? Ideas about knightly ideals, and about the knights' place in society, were mediated through preachers; sermons are full of exemplary stories about how knights should behave, and the dire fate that awaits knights who succumb to the sins of pride and luxury, to which they are supposedly exceptionally prone. The same ideas would be mediated through tutors in the households of great lords, which acted in a sense as schools of knighthood; it was common practice for knights to send their sons to such a household to serve as squires, and they would be taught, it seems, alongside the lord's own sons. And at court the idea of discussions on knighthood was encouraged; Alfonso IX of Castile decreed that texts concerned with knighthood should be read during mealtimes, just as monks might have the Scriptures read to them at dinner. The household ordinances of Edward IV provide for discussion of knightly matters after supper. And finally, there were always a small number of knights who were interested in books and learning, such as Charny and Henry of Grosmont, as well as the 'knight-prisoners' like Thomas Malory, Thomas Gray or Charles duke of Orléans who turned to writing to relieve the tedium of captivity.

In short, the world of the romances and treatises may reflect the ideals of knighthood and the theory of the place of the knight in society. But we cannot assume any very direct link or any very great influence of books on the everyday attitudes and thinking of the majority of knights. To learn something of their mindset, we have to turn to legal records.

THE COURT OF CHIVALRY

Chivalry, we have to remind ourselves, is one of those English words which makes a distinction which is not present in other languages. Chivalry and knighthood are united in the French word *chevalerie*, which Charny uses, and he does not recognize the division of the ideals and practice of knighthood found in the English vocabulary. This is well illustrated by the so-called 'Court of Chivalry', as it is now generally called in legal textbooks. It was originally the military court, *curia militaris*, which dealt with army discipline in the field. Its French name was *court de chivalrie*, and it was this name that persisted, rather than the 'Court of the Knighthode of Engeland' which appears in the late fourteenth-century documents.[17] The Court of Chivalry appears for the first time in the records during the siege of Calais, though it had existed before then in a less formal way. It was effectively a system of military justice, administered by the constable and marshal of England, the two officers responsible for the discipline of the army. By 1390 the court was important enough for parliament to be alarmed by its activities, and to petition the king that it should not interfere in 'any kind of contract made within the kingdom of England which may be tried by the common law, unless solely concerning [heraldic] arms, which cannot be tried by the common law'.[18] This was granted; the implication is that the constable and marshal and their court still have jurisdiction over matters outside England, such as the questions of ransoms for prisoners taken in France. We shall return to the ransoms, but for the moment it is their authority over disputes about arms that interests us.

The organization of the army depended on small units grouped around a knight or banneret, who in turn answered to a commander; that commander might be in the pay of a great lord. The visual signs which identified the groups and sub-groups were the banners and coats of arms of the various levels of leaders. It was therefore important in any large army that there was no duplication of the arms borne by leading knights, and from the beginning of the fourteenth century we have pictorial records of the coats of arms displayed in some of the campaigns, either as a commemoration of the event, or as a fair copy of working notes used in the field.

It is significant that the first recorded disputes about the right to bear particular arms arise out of the Crécy campaign, the largest English army to have fought abroad up to that date. An engraving of a lost document settling a dispute at Calais describes the group of lords who issued the decision as appointed to 'try and judge all manner of debates over arms and helms in the army and in the siege before Calais'.[19] The implication is that the two cases at Calais which have come down to us are only a small remnant of a good number of such claims, and that this was a serious issue. The judges are of the highest rank: Henry of Grosmont, duke of Lancaster, as steward of England, William Clinton, earl of Huntingdon, Reginald Cobham, Walter Mauny, William Lovel and Stephen Cosington.

Confusion over arms could have practical repercussions in the field, and the only authorities who could settle the matter were those responsible for army discipline. It was not the heralds who were called in, because their jurisdiction in such matters was not recognized until the early fifteenth century. Nor were they called as witnesses in such cases; all the testimony in the records that have come down to us is from fellow-knights, with the single exception of John Suffolk, herald to Robert Ufford, earl of Suffolk, in the case between John, Lord Lovell and Thomas, Lord Morley, in 1386–7.[20] Knowledge of arms was something which every knight was expected to acquire, as we shall see from other evidence in this case.[21] Arms, and the reputation attached to those arms by virtue of the deeds of the men who had used them in the past, were an essential part of knightly morale. This is best illustrated by cases where shaming a knight by displaying his arms upside down was used as a means of trying to get him to pay up on a ransom on which he had defaulted. Henry Pomfret did this to the count of Tancarville in the 1360s, though the count denied that Pomfret had taken him prisoner according to the laws of war; and Lord Scales suffered the same treatment at the hands of a French captain in the 1430s.[22] And for a knight convicted of treachery, the surcoat of his arms would be torn from his body and replaced by one of his arms reversed.

A claim by a rival knight to a coat of arms which another family believed was theirs by right challenged the very roots of their existence. But part of the reason why these disputes arose at Calais was that coats of arms would only be seen together in a large army. The arms disputed by Richard, Lord Scrope, and Robert Grosvenor were also borne by an obscure Cornish family, who, despite the duplication with Scrope, had already been permitted to use them.

The cases in the Court of Chivalry are the most immediate witnesses we possess to the real world of medieval knighthood. Detailed records survive for just two cases, that of Scrope versus Grosvenor and the case of Lovell versus Morley; actions at law of this kind were highly unusual. The cases were heard by commissioners, who recorded the actual words of the witnesses – or something very close to them – in their reports. These report rolls were then written up in more formal style as a statement of the case. From the reports, we learn at the outset the bare outlines of the witness's career, his name, status and age. There are three types of evidence: occasions on which the plaintiff or defendant was seen wearing the disputed arms, descriptions of items on which the arms appeared, and a more general assessment of whether the party for whom the witness was speaking was believed to be entitled to these arms.

What do these witnesses have to tell us about the world of the knight at the time of the founding of the Company of the Garter? The picture that emerges is of an England where regional loyalties are gradually giving way to a national view, and where there is an increasing emphasis on the fame and honour of individuals and families. There is little evidence that arms were regarded as exclusive to one lineage before the beginning of Edward III's reign, simply because the lives of knights in Cornwall and Yorkshire were unlikely to overlap. The armies of Edward I in Scotland were still substantially regional, drawn – for good practical reasons – from the north of England and reinforced by the king's household troops and those of the great magnates. This remained true in Edward III's reign, and it is very striking that the first northern knight to become a member of the Company of the Garter is Henry Percy in 1365, sixteen years after the company's foundation. In turn, this meant that reputations were local, and confined to a fairly small circle, that of the magnates of the area. The Grosvenors were long established in Cheshire, and, for a Cheshire man at arms, his arms would be part of the knightly tradition of that county. The Scropes were known and honoured for the same arms in Yorkshire, but had entered royal service and were therefore recognized in London and at court as the rightful bearers of those arms.[23]

The personal reminiscences recorded in the Court of Chivalry cases are very striking, and the memories of the witnesses stretch back for a surprisingly long timespan. John Sully, a companion of the Garter, claimed to be 102 when he was interviewed, and his squire was 84. In the 1380s there were men like Richard Fyfield who could remember the battle of Bannockburn in 1314, in which he had taken part. The length of military service is surprising: Nicholas Sabraham had been with William Bohun at Lochmaben in 1335 and went to Spain with the prince of

Wales in 1367; he had been 'armed thirty-nine years'.[24] The witnesses in support of Lovell's claim are even more remarkable: forty-eight of them claimed over forty years in arms.[25] Because men who could remember what might be the earliest evidence for use of the arms were particularly sought out, this length of service must be treated as exceptional; but it overturns the popular image of medieval life as 'nasty, brutish and short'. It also underlines the sheer experience of Edward's armies: many of the men who had fought in Scotland in the 1330s were still active on his Reims campaign of 1359–60. Most of the witnesses recollect their 'first arming', a crucial moment in the military career of knights and squires, in a similar way; sometimes it refers to the actual knighting ceremony, as at La Hogue in 1346, at other times it simply means 'the first battle in which I fought'. And there is much detail in many of the depositions which allows us to get a general idea of the pattern of military careers in Edward III's reign, though it has to be treated with caution because the evidence concerns a limited number of engagements. Furthermore, the range of witnesses indicates the increasing role played by the esquires – the gentlemen of later centuries – who were not knights. More than two-thirds of those in the Lovell–Morley case belonged to this rank, and were treated with the same respect as their knightly superiors.[26]

Much of the evidence is concerned with the use of the disputed arms on a campaign, and all the great battles of Edward's reign are frequently recalled, as well as many lesser encounters. A number of witnesses also recall seeing the knights in their arms at tournaments of which we have no other record. Ralph Ferrers told the court that 'tournaments are where arms are taught and studied'; heraldic arms had in large part originated at twelfth-century tournaments, and they were still essential to the spectator at such an event two centuries later.[27] These glimpses can be a real window into the past, as in the case of Nicholas Sabraham's account of Stephen Scrope, dressed in the gold and blue of the disputed arms, receiving knighthood from King Peter of Cyprus on the crusade of 1365, at the siege of Alexandria.[28] Geoffrey Chaucer remembered walking down a London street, and seeing what he believed to be Scrope's arms above the door of lodgings; on enquiry, he was told that these were the arms, not of Scrope, but of a member of the Grosvenor family. This, he said, was the first time he had ever heard of the Grosvenors' claim to the arms.[29]

The visual evidence reveals a world where arms were displayed, not merely in the grey remnants of heraldry we see on tombs today, but seemingly everywhere – on silver, on the walls of great chambers, on embroidered vestments presented to churches, in church windows, on church walls, and in vivid colours on monuments. The expensive accoutrements of the knight, surcoat, shield and horse-trappings, were only a small part of this (Plates 22–3, 26–7). On the other hand, this impressive catalogue of images rarely includes armorial displays in churches similar to those on the Garter stalls or on the prince's tomb at Canterbury, where helms, swords and surcoats were preserved as heraldic memorials. The only such memorials recalled by witnesses are the banners set up to commemorate Robert Morley's death on the Reims campaign, and the heraldic armour of William Morley at Somerton.[30]

Another test was 'public fame': was it generally acknowledged that the family in question had the right to the arms? This brings us into the elusive problems of reputation and honour, the remembrance of the great deeds of arms done by knights wearing the disputed coat of arms. Occasionally, old chronicles and documents are quoted, usually by clerics, as supporting evidence, but this was principally a matter of word of mouth, the stories attached to the family and sometimes evidence of their activities abroad. The more battles at which a knight had displayed his banner, the greater was the honour attaching to that coat of arms; and battles against the heathen had a particular value. Hugh Hastings II, unfurling his banner for the first time in a battle against the Saracens, had done 'special honour' to those arms; and the same idea was echoed by Anne Mauny, daughter of Walter Mauny and married to John Hastings, earl of Pembroke, when she thanked Hugh Hastings III 'for the honour you have done to the arms of Hastings in the past', and hoped that he would continue to do so in his own forthcoming journey to the east. And to ensure his reputation, Hastings duly left little shields with his arms at the places to which his travels took him.[31]

CRUSADING

Most of the evidence for the participation of English knights in the Prussian crusades in the mid-fourteenth century comes from the Court of Chivalry proceedings. In this international setting, knights were eager that their arms should be recorded as participants in the wars against the heathen, and the expeditions to the lands of the Teutonic Order combined both the quest for honour and the spiritual rewards of going on crusade. What may seem false and unreal to us, the attempted conversion by force to Christianity of the pagan tribes living on the eastern borders of the Holy Roman Empire, and the elaborate conventions of the 'table of honour', were eagerly sought after by knights from all over Christian Europe in times of truce or peace. They could gain spiritual merit, earthly glory and practice in arms and warfare through the 'Prussian journey'.

With the fall of Acre in 1291, the first series of crusades, grandiose expeditions aiming to recover Jerusalem from the infidel, had come to an end; there was no longer a base on the mainland from which to mount a campaign in Palestine. The idea of a great crusading expedition persisted, however, and one of the objectives of the popes at Avignon for much of the period of the Anglo-French wars was to persuade the two sides to make peace so that a new crusade could begin. However, it was not until 1395 that these efforts were successful and a new crusade was launched; but the disaster that befell the Christian army at Nicopolis in that year effectively marks the end of the eastern crusades.

Crusading in the mid-fourteenth century meant a rather different kind of activity. Since the mid-twelfth century, there had been an ongoing war on the eastern frontier of the Holy Roman Empire against the heathens in Poland, Lithuania and Latvia, led by an order of knights which had begun life in Palestine as guardians of a hostel for German pilgrims. Like the other crusading orders, the Teutonic Knights, as they are usually called in English, had developed a belligerent life of their own, carrying the attack to the invading Muslim armies. But towards the end of the twelfth century the order acquired lands in eastern Germany, particularly in what became Prussia, and began to campaign there with the object of converting the pagan tribes by force to Christianity, and settling their land with German inhabitants.

The Teutonic Knights were fighting a different kind of warfare to that in Palestine. The latter was a war of conquest and counter-conquest, as huge Muslim forces swept in and were confronted with varying degrees of success. The war in Prussia was a war of attrition, punctuated by occasional moments when the heathen tribes united under a single leader. It was fought in a landscape even more hostile than the Palestinian desert, a trackless wilderness of swamps and waterways with islands of habitable land, which was impenetrable for much of the year: it was sometimes passable in a dry summer, but the majority of campaigns (called *reysen,* 'journeys') were fought in the winter, when the swamps would freeze hard and horses and baggage trains could cross. One of the most famous encounters – in which the Teutonic Knights were defeated by an army from Novgorod led by Alexander Nevsky – was the 'battle on the ice' on lake Peipus in 1242.

The Teutonic Knights were a small order, though relatively wealthy. They were a sovereign power, and, under the leadership of their best masters, they encouraged trade and settlement, and were able to supplement their revenues from their extensive landholdings in Germany, given to them by pious supporters. But their resources of manpower were relatively slender, and like their fellow-knights in the great crusading orders in the east, they needed reinforcements from the west. Large armies were a liability in the terrain in which they had to fight, and they developed a system by which small groups of knights, or even individual knights, were encouraged to come to their headquarters at Marienburg, for a *reyse*, a summer or winter expedition.

The Teutonic Knights were not slow to see the possibility of using the pent-up desire to go on crusade as a means of furthering their own conquests, and they were able to offer all the spiritual benefits that would have derived from participation in a crusade to the Holy Land. Despite a dubious reputation for ferocity and high-handed behaviour in the lands they ruled, they were still regarded in most western European courts with the same respect that had been accorded to the Templars and Hospitallers in the previous century.

Small numbers of knights had been recruited by the Teutonic Order in Germany for specific campaigns in the thirteenth century, but it was from 1328 onwards that the Prussian crusades became part of the international knightly scene. King John of Bohemia, an impractical ruler but an inspirational figure in terms of knightly enterprises, led a group of Bohemians to Prussia in that year, and returned twice in 1344–5. A Prussian chronicler notes that 'many nobles from England and Germany' also came in 1328, and this expedition seems to have set a fashion that was to last for almost a century, until the order's disastrous defeat by Vladislav II of Poland at Tannenberg in 1410.

Knights from France and Hainault joined the crusades in the mid-

1330s, but the peak of enthusiasm for crusading was during the truce of Esplechin, which suspended fighting in France more effectively than during the truces after 1346. The crusading seasons of 1343–5 saw, in addition to the king of Bohemia's two journeys, two similar expeditions from Hainault and numerous knights from France.[32] A year of victories in 1348, similar to the English *annus mirabilis* of 1346, saw three successful expeditions against the Russians, Lithuanians and Samogitians. The grand master elected in 1352, Winrich von Kniprode, presided over the most glorious period of the order's history. In the next century the chronicle of the order would look back to this period nostalgically as a time when 'many lords, knights and squires from Christendom desired to see the order, and came with their forces to Prussia, and stayed at Königsberg with great provisions, many waiting for a whole year for a *reyse* against the enemy'.[33]

Surviving records name more than sixty English knights, about a hundred from Holland and Hainault, and more than a hundred from France who went to Prussia during Edward III's reign. Because of the order's close connection with Germany, the numbers from the Holy Roman Empire probably exceeded all the rest put together. Most of these names come from the accounts of great lords, and are of knights and squires serving with them. For the smaller retinues, there is no documentation, and only a few individual names of leaders of such retinues have come down to us; any records of the order which might have named the guests of the grand master have disappeared, so we are only able to identify a small proportion of those who reached Prussia.

Typically, the number of men in a group was very similar to that of a lord's or banneret's retinue in one of Edward III's armies. They would rarely stay for more than a year, and there was a constant traffic to and fro from Prussia; the journey was not a lengthy one, like the overland route or the sea voyage to Palestine, and it was possible to travel from England or France in a little more than a month. In 1344, William II of Hainault, Edward III's brother-in-law, took thirty-six days to reach Marienburg starting from Haarlem in Holland, leaving on 14 December. The count and his retinue arrived back at Valenciennes on 30 May 1345, having taken part in the *winterreyse*.[34] Henry Bolingbroke (later Henry IV), who led the largest English expedition to Prussia in 1390–91, left Boston in Lincolnshire on 22 July 1390; the journey was quicker by sea, and took twenty-six days outwards and thirty days on the return voyage, reaching Hull on 30 April the following year.

Knights arriving at Königsberg found themselves in an atmosphere which was very like that of a great lord's castle in their homeland. There were, of course, the monastic observances of the order; but alongside these, there was a knightly existence on a grand scale. Because the *reyse* depended so much on the right weather, there were long periods when Königsberg was crowded with would-be crusaders: such waiting time was a regular occurrence, and a tradition of feasting, courtly gatherings and display evolved. This knightly culture was not deliberately encouraged by the order, but seems to have arisen spontaneously from the numbers of knights present at Königsberg.

However, the order saw the possibilities of using knightly pride to assist it in recruiting those who were interested in joining its crusades. It was probably the grand master Winrich von Kniprode who created the focal point of social life during this enforced idleness, the table of honour, an idea which he almost certainly took from the short-lived Company of the Star, announced by John II in 1351.[35] The *Ehrentisch*, to give it its German name, is famous from Chaucer's portrait of the Knight in the *Canterbury Tales* who 'had often sat at the head of the table above all the other nations in Prussia'; in other words, had been chosen as the most distinguished of the guests.[36] This was not a metaphorical honour, but literally a table at which the chosen knights sat. In 1413, Gilbert de Lannoy saw 'the arms, the place and the table of honour' in Königsberg, implying that it was set apart, possibly in the main refectory of the order's castle there, and that the walls were hung with the shields of those who had sat at it. Other accounts indicate that twelve or fourteen knights sat at the table, and that only those who had come at their own expense were eligible: in 1400, knights paid by the duke of Lorraine as part of his retinue were disqualified, even though they were regarded as worthy of the honour in all other respects. The ceremonial dinner took place in winter, often before the *winterreyse* began, in late January or early February, and the choice of knights was therefore based on their reputation and not on their performance on the *reyse*. Furthermore, the choice of knights seems to have been made by the heralds who had accompanied the crusaders to Prussia. Occasionally there is a hint in the texts of why a knight was chosen: he might simply be 'a good knight', or have shed his blood 'in many countries'. Another was honoured as standard-bearer of the order's banner of St George on a previous *reyse*.

As to the dinner itself, we have a description of that held in 1375 according to an eyewitness:

> The grand master ... wished twelve knights from different kingdoms to be seated at the table of honour. And from France Sir Hutin de Vermelles and Sir Tristan de Maignelay sat at the high table, whom all men called good knights, and from other countries two from each up to a total of twelve, in the places specified by the master; and they were served in accordance with the glory of the day. And after grace was said, these twelve were told about the institution of the table and how it had been established. And then one of the brethren of the order pinned a word written in golden letters onto their shoulders, 'Honour conquers all'.[37]

The idea of the table of honour is found in two contemporary orders of knighthood in western Europe, those of the Star and the Knot, which predate the first recorded appearance of the table of honour in Prussia by twenty-five years. Both were orders relating to kingdoms, or monarchical orders. The statutes of the Company of the Star of 1351 include a provision that at the annual feast of the order,

> there shall be a table called the table of honour, at which shall be seated on the eve and the day of the first festival the three most distinguished princes, three most distinguished bannerets and three most distinguished knights among those who shall be members of the said company and who are present at the said feast; and at each eve and festival in mid-August, every subsequent year, the three princes, three bannerets and three knights who have performed the greatest deeds in war shall be seated there, for no deeds in arms of a peaceful nature shall count towards it.[38]

The idea of a table of honour was less impressive within the context of an order whose knights had already been chosen because they were supposedly outstanding in knighthood. In Prussia, where a different group of knights assembled each year, there was more purpose in such a table; it formed a focal point for the knightly ambitions of the crusaders, while the ordering by nations made it an international body which also served to unify the temporary army which arrived for a single campaigning season. It does not seem to have survived beyond the end of the century.

Any knight who came to Königsberg towards the end of Edward III's reign would be instantly reminded of the enthusiasm with which his predecessors had made the journey to Prussia. The cathedral was filled with knightly paraphernalia, massive quantities of painted shields recording the arms of the crusaders; the inns where they had lodged had similar displays, as did other castles in the territory. The accounts of Jean count of Blois in 1369 show huge expenditure on painting his arms and those of his companions, and the concern for accurate recording of exactly who was with him. He set out on the *reyse* with forty-three knights, but seven others joined him in the field, and their arms had to be added when the campaign ended. More ominously, the arms he had put up on his first visit in 1363 had to be replaced 'because the English had torn them down'.[39] Arms of this kind were to be found as mementoes of pilgrimage, at Santiago de Compostela and on the road to Jerusalem and in the Holy City itself, but there was no display elsewhere remotely on this scale.

THE *REYSE*

The hardship of the *reyse* must have seemed a direct contrast to the glories and festivities of Königsberg. But only a small number of knights actually experienced warfare in Prussia. There were on average three *reysen* a year from 1305 to 1409, but less than a third of these had a contingent of foreign knights. And on many occasions, the weather prevented any expedition taking place while a crusader was in Prussia. The duke of Geldern went on crusade seven times, but only once was he able to take part in a *reyse*.[40] Often the winter was too mild for the ice to form, so that the swamps remained impassable, or there was a sudden thaw, as in 1344, when floods from melting snow and ice forced a hasty retreat. In 1352 heavy rain nearly destroyed the army: knights had to make their way back on foot because their horses starved to death, or both knights and horses drowned in swollen streams. On the other hand, in 1364, there was such a hard winter, lasting three months, that numerous forays were possible.

Prussia was not therefore a place where encounters with the enemy were frequent. Even if the army entered pagan territory, there was often no resistance and little fighting. However, if a knight was fortunate (or perhaps unfortunate) enough to go on a *reyse*, the experience of campaigning in harsh and unfamiliar territory was a swift initiation into the hardships of life in the field, given the extremes of weather and the lack of obvious routes into the wilderness which sheltered the enemy. When Edward III unexpectedly launched a winter campaign in France in late October 1359, many of the leaders of retinues in the army had had experience of winter warfare in Prussia.

Almost half of the founding Garter companions made the journey to Prussia. The earliest who can be traced precisely is Thomas Holland, who travelled there for the *winterreyse* in 1340–41, and probably took part in an attack on Livonia, which was abandoned because of humidity: the warm air produced fogs and thawed the ground. Reginald Cobham and William Fitzwarin seem to have gone on one of the expeditions led by nobles from the Low Countries in 1340–45.[41] Their arms are included in the records of the herald Claes Heynenzoon, which seem to be based on a list of crusaders from that period, and the link between them, perhaps begun on this journey, continued as late as the 1360s.

In the absence of fighting in France in 1351, Henry of Grosmont led a major expedition to Prussia. His company included four members of the order: the young earl of Salisbury, William Montagu, and three knights, Nigel Loring, Walter Pavely and Miles Stapleton.[42] The advance party of his army were guarding the duke's treasure as it was taken across northern Germany, when it was attacked by men led by two local magnates, and the treasure seized. Henry and his men were captured, and forced to pay a ransom of 3,000 gold crowns. Despite this setback, Henry and his men reached Prussia, only to find that they were too late for the *reyse* and that a truce was now in force. It seems that he continued to Poland, in the hope that the king of Poland might need his help against the Tartars, but found that they had just retreated.[43] Henry later accused Otto duke of Brunswick of having arranged the ambush in order to take him prisoner and hand him over to King John of France, and the affair ended in a judicial duel between Henry and Otto at the French court. As so often, the participants were prevented from fighting and were reconciled by the king.

With the exception of a Prussian journey by Jean de Grailly (and probably James Audley and Miles Stapleton as well) in 1357–8,[44] English knights did not return to Prussia until after the treaty of Brétigny. Of the Garter companions, Humphrey Bohun, who had just succeeded his uncle as earl of Hereford and Northampton, was there in the winter of 1362–3, a year before his election to the order, with four squires and several other knights. Thomas Beauchamp, earl of Warwick, spent both the summer of 1365 and the winter of 1365–6 on crusade. Both earls returned for a further crusade in 1367–8. They very probably took part in one or more campaigns, as numerous expeditions are recorded by the historians of the Teutonic Order in this period, and none of them seemed to have encountered adverse weather.[45]

The majority of those who went to Prussia were in their twenties; some of them were already experienced soldiers, while for others it was their first experience of war. But the journey to the headquarters of the Teutonic Knights at Königsberg was for many an introduction to the international world of knightly display and festivities, particularly for squires in a lord's retinue. It was in this role that Henry Eam and Eustace d'Auberchicourt saw Prussia, in the retinue of William II of Hainault in 1344–5. This was the place where the rivalry for knightly fame and honour was probably most evident; in the 1350s and 1360s tournaments, the usual outlet for this competitive spirit, were rare in England and the Low Countries, and almost unknown in France, during the most destructive phase of the Anglo-French wars. Equally, it was the one place where the English and French knights met on largely friendly terms and made common cause against a very different enemy. Many of the leaders of the French armies were veterans of the Prussian crusades: the count of Eu surrendered at Caen in 1346 to a fellow-crusader, Thomas Holland. A very large contingent of about a hundred French nobles, knights and squires came to Prussia at the time of Humphrey Bohun's visit in 1362–3. After 1370, however, the French continued to appear in Prussia regularly, while there is only one recorded English crusader between 1369 and 1383.

Just as the secular orders of knighthood sprang up in the vacuum created by the decline of the military religious orders, so the crusade itself in Prussia had acquired a heavily secular veneer. It was less demanding in terms both of time and of actual warfare than the eastern crusades, and the customs of secular war in the west had extended to such matters as ransoming. In the thirteenth century, the knights of the Teutonic Order rarely took prisoners, and were usually killed by the pagans if they were captured. With the appearance of the first western crusaders, customs began to change, and by the mid-fourteenth century ransoms were commonplace, to the extent that, under Winrich von

Kniprode, the order guaranteed to ransom any captured crusader, though the ransom had to be repaid once he was freed.

The predominantly winter campaigns meant that a knight could fight in France during the larger part of the spring and summer, go to Prussia and be back in time for the next season's warfare in the west. Like Jean Boucicaut at the end of the fourteenth century, he probably went 'because it seemed to him that there was a great lack of warfare in France at that time . . . he returned to Prussia for the second time because he had been told that there was bound to be fine fighting there that season'.[46] In peacetime, such a crusader might occupy the summer in tournaments. The best example of this is William II of Hainault, whose brief reign ended in a burst of knightly activity, with two expeditions to Prussia in 1343–5, punctuated by a series of festivals and tournaments (as well as a pilgrimage to Jerusalem) before his death in the disaster at Staveren, where knightly overconfidence was no match for the determination and numbers of the enemy. His crusades had involved little action – two abortive raids and a brief siege had scarcely added to his military experience.[47] Prussia was not the place to learn about the larger issues of strategy and tactics, and the handling of an army in battle.

12

Laws of War and the Reality of Warfare

What was medieval warfare really like? Most descriptions of medieval warfare that have come down to us are by poets or chroniclers who (like modern historians) have never been in a battle. The images which Geoffroy de Charny conjures up are at the opposite pole from the rhetoric of Froissart or Baker: blunt, direct and pulling no punches about the possible outcome.

Jean le Bel also wrote from direct experience about the hardships of a campaign in enemy territory. He vividly remembered Edward's first expedition into Scotland in 1327, with both sides in equally dire straits:

As soon as they [the enemy] had been found we were told to strike camp and take ourselves and all our gear to another mountain directly facing them. Then we formed our battle line and made as if to advance, but as soon as they saw us coming they left their shelters and smartly planted themselves close to the opposite bank of the river; but they wouldn't cross to meet us, and attacking them was impossible: we would all have been miserably slaughtered or captured.

So there we encamped, confronting them on that second mountain, for eighteen days in all. Every day we'd draw up our lines to face them, and they to face us; but they wouldn't cross the river to meet us, or give ground on their side to allow us to deploy, or accept our offer of ground on our side where they could do the same. And all the while they had no bread, no wine, no salt, and no leather or material to make hose or shoes: instead they made shoes out of raw cowhide, the hair still attached. Not that we were much better off: we had nowhere to lodge or shelter, and nowhere to forage but moor and heath. I can't tell you how frustrated we were about our tents and tools and baggage-carts: we'd brought them to make our lives easier and then had left them in a wood, unguarded, with no way of recovering them – we didn't even know where the wood was!

We spent a month in this abject, miserable state, with all our supplies missing when we needed them most. It's true that provisions were daily brought for sale from all directions throughout the time we were besieging the Scots and were stuck there facing them – but at what a price! A badly baked loaf (of low-grade grain) cost three pence when it would have been worth just a *parisis* in the town, and a gallon of warm, poor-quality wine cost twelve when a barrelful would have been worth but three. We had to feed ourselves and our pages very sparingly, constantly fearing greater hunger still and that our money would run out if we had to stay much longer.[1]

Edward's armies rarely found themselves in such dire straits again, but any long campaign would mean problems of supply, serious wear and tear on armour, clothing and shoes, and horses with patched-up harness who were often unshod. The English army at Crécy was the worse for wear after six weeks in the field, even though their baggage train was intact, and they were reasonably well provisioned. But there were also benefits from time spent on campaign in a well-disciplined army, notably the growth of *esprit de corps* and a mutual trust between the commanders and their men.

As to the battles themselves, the terror and chaos of the action itself is never evoked in the chronicles, which generally resort to clichés and to vague overall descriptions. We have no descriptions of what it was like to be met by a hail of arrows from the English archers, or to withstand a French cavalry charge on foot. Only at one moment do we get some feeling of what participation in a battle might have been like, in the descriptions of Prince Edward and his men at Crécy. Prince Edward was 'compelled to fight kneeling down against the masses of the enemy who poured around him', and when the bishop of Durham arrived with reinforcements, he 'found the prince and his men leaning on their lances and swords, drawing breath and taking a moment's rest over long mountains of the dead, as they waited for the enemy to return from his retreat'. The dead, of course, had not been slain by Edward and his companions alone; most would have died at the hands of the archers or simply been crushed against the bodies of men and horses which blocked their way.[2] And in the aftermath, the king asked his son 'what he thought of going into battle and being in the midst of it, and why it was a fine game and the prince said nothing and hung his head.'[3]

The most controversial and sometimes the most gratuitously violent moments of Edward's campaigns came during the raids into France, which were intended to demonstrate to the populace at large that the French kings could not defend them, and were therefore not the true rulers of the country. At the same time, they were intended to provoke the French to put an army in the field and fight a pitched battle. Despite Edward's claim at the outset of the Crécy campaign that he intended to protect the civilian population, there were excesses from the start, largely because it was extremely difficult to control an army in which there were undoubtedly men out for pillaging and rape. As early as the siege of Caen, in the second week of the Crécy raid, there were severe problems of this kind. And there was official brutality, the burning of towns and destruction of crops and property, in the name of economic warfare.

None of this was as bad, however, as the lawlessness which followed the French defeat at Poitiers, banditry over which neither the French nor English king had control, though Edward undoubtedly exploited it when he could, as did Charles of Navarre. Only one of the Garter knights, Eustace d'Auberchicourt, seems to have been involved, and that fairly briefly. This brigandage, however, stemmed from the troops made unemployed by the truce between England and France, and led to the formation of the 'great companies', whose organized depredations were the most terrifying of all. The narrow border between these ex-brigands and the royal armies was underlined when they were incorporated into both the French and English expeditions to Spain in 1366–7.

THE FINANCES OF WARFARE

For the English knights, and for some fortunate footsoldiers, there were fortunes to be won (and sometimes lost) on the battlefield and on campaign. The Garter companions occupy a very wide spectrum in this respect, from men who had only just been knighted to the greatest magnates of the realm. A man like Henry Eam would have had at most half a dozen men in his retinue, and possibly just a squire. His main expense would have been his horses and armour; an adequate warhorse cost between £15 and £30, and he would need one or two lesser horses besides as reserves, or for riding if he wished to rest his best horse.[4] His armour would cost somewhere around the same amount: a helmet could cost £5, and a pair of plates (the coverings for chest and back) as much again. The knight's basic equipment represented a substantial investment, and the ongoing expense of maintaining even a modest retinue required the income from a small manor at least: the grant to Sir Henry Eam when he took service with the prince of Wales was for £66 13s. 4d. to be paid out of the revenues of the manor of Bradninch. This was in fact an honour, or group of manors, and therefore an important source of income for the prince, and only from such a source could fees on this scale be paid. Sometimes the grants were in the form of annuities to be paid until a suitable holding was free, which would provide the equivalent in income.

The system under which the companions of the Garter and other knights of similar rank served was relatively new; it had been introduced in the 1340s after Edward's bitter experience with hiring foreign troops in Flanders. Because the feudal obligation to serve the king could be directly invoked only if there was a threat of invasion, a new system was needed, and rates of pay were critical. Men had to be paid to fight abroad; Edward paid a *regard* or retainer to the leaders of retinues, whether knights or bannerets, and then wages, again payable to the leader, which were quickly doubled for the overseas campaigns. The problem was that the king was always short of ready cash, and at the end of the campaign the knight might be owed a substantial sum because he had had to pay his men out of his own pocket. Typically, the wages owed by the king to the leaders of retinues were paid in part during the campaign, and the settlement of the balance might take as much as twenty years. Some knights evidently could not afford to finance their men: in the record of payments for the 1355 Gascon campaign kept by John Henxteworth, John Mohun is paid a series of small sums at regular intervals, while his fellow-knights are paid large lump sums occasionally.[5] The explanation for this seems to be that Mohun lacked the cash resources to which the others had access, and his financial problems are indeed documented in the law cases in which he was involved at the time.

Many knights would resort to borrowing for a major campaign.

Quite apart from the direct and unavoidable costs they had to meet, there was the temptation to spend money on display; Charny observes that there are men who commit themselves to 'great state and outward show', the cost of which exhausts their resources. Visual display was part of military life, and it was always tempting for an ambitious knight to make a brilliant appearance in terms of fine warhorses, elaborate trappings and the best armour. A case in point is Walter Mauny: in 1342–3 he led a small force to Brittany, and the accounts for payments for horses lost show that his retinue had horses of much higher than average value, while he himself rode a *destrier* worth £100, the highest valuation in the record. Mauny was a great polisher of his knightly image, and turning up on campaign on the equivalent of a Rolls-Royce may have all been part of this, along with the splendid stories he told to Jean le Bel and later to Froissart. His squadron, also on fine horses, would have made a strong impression and enhanced his reputation.[6] Mauny had already made money from ransoms and was in a position to lend the king £4,000 in 1340, so could clearly afford such a display.

For those who could not, raising money was not difficult. A lease could be sold on an estate or the revenues pledged for a loan; Hugh Wrottesley's tangled finances included several transactions of this kind. Many knights resorted to straight borrowing from magnates or merchants. A number of these transactions were recorded at the exchequer, and we can trace the fortunes of individual knights. The greatest lender in the country was Richard Fitzalan, earl of Arundel. We have already noted his absence from the Company of the Garter, despite his military record, with the suggestion that it might be this financial record that was the reason. In the decade between 1350 and 1359, he lent sums varying between 200 marks and £2,000 to five different Garter companions. The last transaction is one of a class of somewhat mysterious dealings on the eve of military campaigns. In this case William Bohun, earl of Northampton, lends Richard Fitzalan, earl of Arundel, £2,000; and Arundel lends Northampton £2,000. Such back-to-back loans are often found in connection with performance of a contract, such as an engagement between the heirs of two families; if there is a default, then the defaulting party loses his money. But in the context of imminent departure on an expedition, this must have a different function. Until we find an example of one of these loans which was actually called in, the most likely explanation is that it is some kind of mutual insurance, against a ransom perhaps, or simply shortage of cash: if for example Northampton could not pay his men, he could go to Arundel and draw on the pre-arranged loan for ready money.

For lesser men, the entries at the exchequer are of a series of more modest debts – modest in comparison, but a heavy burden for knights with small resources. John Mohun appears with five debts between 1350 and 1355 totalling £468, of which only £9 13s. 4d. is shown as repaid: the lenders include John Beauchamp, the bishop of Worcester and the king. William Fitzwarin borrows £100 from his patron Queen Philippa in 1345. Knights whose careers are largely abroad appear less frequently in these lists: there are only a handful of entries for Audley, Chandos, the younger Burghersh and Loring.

Against this, we have to set the income from warfare. Firstly, there are the king's wages and the *regards* paid to the leaders of retinues. For the ordinary knight, it was only the wages that counted, and these were paid at the standard rate of two shillings per day.[7] This was twice that for an ordinary man at arms, and half that for a banneret. The responsibility for feeding the troops lay with the commander of the retinue to which they belonged; the Garter companions, unless they were magnates, were attached either to the prince's or to the king's household. We know a great deal about the king's household and its provisioning on campaign, for the detailed accounts of the Crécy campaign survive. The quantities involved indicate that the supplies were for the king's personal entourage only, rather than feeding his whole retinue. There are episodes in the chronicles where, describing acute food shortages during a campaign, the writer says that bread or other food was sold very expensively, which implies that there was some purchasing of supplies within the army. In the circumstances two shillings a day, which was the equivalent of £36 p.a., was in itself enough to make a cautious man reasonably wealthy simply by his presence in the army.

The real money was to be made where there was booty to be had, and particularly where there were ransoms to be secured. After the sack of Caen, writers say that an astonishing amount of loot was sent back to England. Once it was unloaded from the ships which had been sent back to fetch more supplies, we hear nothing more of it; it may have been quickly sold on to London merchants, or it may have gone to adorn manors up and down the country. But booty is cited only in general terms as a profit of war; it is difficult to quantify from the records we have. The principles, however, were established by the laws of war, by contract and by custom.[8] For the most part, the knights with whom we are concerned were fighting either in the king's name or under his command. This meant that they were fighting in a 'just war', a war declared by a sovereign or a great prince. Under these conditions, there was no doubt as to the legality of their spoils; the activities of English captains in France after 1356, when the official truce after Poitiers degenerated into a free-for-all, were much more questionable in terms of the law of arms. In the case of a siege, the loot was entirely the king's property, and this would have been the case at Caen. But the king had already agreed terms with his commanders, and they in turn had contracted with the knights in their service as to the division of spoils. The English custom was generous: for most of the campaigns of Edward III's reign, the spoils were divided evenly between the captain and the soldier who had taken the booty.[9] In France, the captains had only a tenth; the incentive to loot was therefore much greater for the English, even though it was directly at odds with Edward's sporadic efforts to win over, rather than terrify, the French people he claimed to rule.

Even if we cannot put figures on the total of booty taken – the king's share was treated as his private income, and did not pass through the exchequer records – the real concern of soldiers about its acquisition and distribution is reflected in Charny's *Questions on Jousts, Tournaments and War*. There are fifteen headings for discussion, which deal with the problems that might arise, such as the case where part of a troop of soldiers have fled from the action and the remainder have fought on and won substantial booty: are they all entitled to a share, or do those who have left the battle forfeit all right to booty?[10] Charny's basic premise in all the discussion points is that booty is taken for the common good of the whole force engaged in the combat, and is only divided afterwards: there is no question of individual profit. Furthermore, the division of spoils is after an individual engagement, rather than at the end of a campaign. Beyond this, we know little of how the actual goods were handled, transported or sold to merchants. Records of the sharing out of ordinary spoils are extremely rare: I have found only one specific payment for booty, when Chandos and his men were paid £118 16s. for 215 cattle on 22 June 1356 near Périgueux.[11] At the other extreme, where individual objects of great value are concerned, we know that the prince of Wales acquired the crown, badge of the

Company of the Star and a silver table centrepiece in the form of a boat found in John II's tent at Poitiers; he promptly pawned the last two items to the earl of Arundel in return for a loan.

Ransoms were quite another matter.[12] If the right captive fell into a knight's hands, it was like winning the lottery; and precisely because large sums and important political figures could be involved, there was a considerable body of law about the capture of prisoners, the way in which they should surrender and how the rights of the captor could be enforced. In the tumult of a medieval battle, it is extraordinary that a transaction of this kind could be carried out in a way which ensured that both captor and captive recognized its legitimacy, and which in turn was acknowledged by the rest of the army. For the lawyers in the calm of their chambers, the capture of a prisoner established a contract in law, sealed by an oath: the prisoner literally became his captor's property, and could be inherited, subject to the terms of his ransom, like any other asset. In return for surrendering his liberty, the captive gained the protection of his captor. In the heat of battle, there had to be a good deal of trust: the ransom could not be settled on the spot, and the initial duty of the captor was to ensure his prisoner's safety. In practice, the prisoner would have been taken out of the battle by a squire to the rear of the army, where he would be guarded until the action had ended. If the captor's side was defeated, that did not mean that prisoners necessarily gained their liberty, as they would usually remain with the retreating losers.

The most famous case is that of the count of Dammartin, whose case was entered as a matter of public record in the prince of Wales's register, three years after his capture at the battle of Poitiers. Thomas Beauchamp, earl of Warwick, and Reginald Cobham, as constable and marshal at the time, and therefore the highest authorities of the army in terms of military law, testified that the prince had made an ordinance, publicly proclaimed before the battle, that 'no man should linger over his prisoner on pain of forfeiting him, but that each man without hindrance or dispute should have the prisoner to whom he should first be pledged'. The count himself then declared before the prince's council and his notary the events of his capture. The first to approach him to surrender – by implication he was clearly in no fit state to resist – was a squire who identified himself as John Trailly, of the prince's household. 'He called on me to surrender,' recalled Dammartin, 'and I gave him my fealty in such wise that he should save me.' Trailly took off his prisoner's helmet, and, when he protested, said that he would be quite safe. He also took off his gauntlets, and someone else cut off his sword, which Trailly collected. Trailly put him on his own horse, and gave him to one of his retainers to guard. But the retainer went off, and left him. A Gascon appeared, and demanded that Dammartin should surrender to him. 'I answered that I was already a prisoner, but all the same I gave him my fealty, simply so that he should save me.' He took a badge from his armour, and left: as the Gascon went, Dammartin said that if anyone else came up and asked him to surrender to him, he would do so. 'Save yourself, if you can,' was the answer. The next to appear was one of John de Blankmouster's retainers. Dammartin explained that he had already been taken prisoner twice, but surrendered yet again. 'This man stayed with me, guarded me and brought me to the earl of Salisbury, and I gave my fealty to the earl at the wish and consent of my last captor.'[13]

This must have been typical of the chaos surrounding the taking of prisoners; it usually happened in the last and most confused stages of the battle. Presumably Trailly, his retainer and the Gascon either felt themselves to be in danger or went off in search of more profitable booty; even if they understood who their captive was, they might well have little idea of his importance unless his armour and arms made it clear that he was someone of the highest rank. This takes us back to ransoms as a contract: in return for the prisoner's surrender, the captor was guaranteeing his safety. If he wandered off and left him, and failed to guard him, the contract was valueless, and the process could begin again. The prince of Wales claimed Dammartin as his prisoner, because his squire was the first to take him, but the court adjudged that this contract was broken, as was that with the anonymous Gascon, and that Dammartin was the prisoner of William Montagu, earl of Salisbury. A charter was duly drawn up, putting in writing the conditions of the ransom. The prisoner had to promise to obey and be loyal to his captor, and to renounce any attempt to dispute his captor's right to ransom once he had signed the document. If he failed to carry out these obligations, he was to suffer the penalties, both spiritual and secular, for perjury, and his captor could disgrace him by displaying his arms reversed[14] as a traitor.

Further documents would set out the terms of captivity, and the arrangements for paying the ransom. Even if the prisoner was rescued by his own side, he was still bound by the agreements, and, while he was subject to ransom, he could not fight against his captor or his allies. The conditions of his captivity were specified, which varied from actual imprisonment to the requirement that he should return to the place of captivity each evening. As to raising the ransom, this was the most difficult point of all. The price had to be set, and was in principle a sum which the prisoner would be able to raise, though this was not always the case. There are many instances of ransoms not being paid in full, as with John II after Poitiers, either by agreement or because the knight in question absconded after a substantial payment had been made. In the end, of the huge sum of thirty million gold crowns demanded as John II's ransom, between 45 and 55 per cent of it was paid; as much of it went directly to the king's private treasury, we do not have exact accounts.[15] Other prisoners spent much of their life in prison awaiting ransom; and exceptionally a prisoner might be so important that his release was forbidden. Henry V forbade the release of Charles duke of Orléans after Agincourt, because he was head of the Armagnac family, rival claimants to the throne of France; and Charles's son, born after his release in 1440, did indeed become Louis XII of France.

More typically, a reasonable ransom would be set, and the prisoner would be allowed to travel on licence to his home to set about raising it: his status was in effect that of a non-combatant. He would have to find men, usually from his own retinue, to act as sureties for him and remain with his captor while he was away. Charny does outline a case where a prisoner, on the advice of his surety, passes all his estates to his heirs, and fails to return or pay up; the surety then excuses himself on the grounds that the prisoner has no assets. In real life, legal manoeuvres of this sort seem to have been very rare, and Charny is probably asking a rhetorical question.[16] If the prisoner failed to reappear, the sureties would be liable for the ransom themselves; there was little effective recourse against escaped prisoners in these circumstances, since their assets were in enemy territory and a lawsuit would be almost impossible. The only real recourse was that of dishonour, which was said to be taken extremely seriously: the aggrieved captor could display the escaped prisoner's arms in a public place, but just as important was to spread the word that the captive had broken his word.

In 1360, the treaty of Brétigny had stipulated that, if John II travelled to France to organize his ransom, his younger son, Louis duke of Anjou, should go to England as one of his sureties. Anjou went in 1361, very reluctantly: on his arrival, he was fêted by the English court, particularly by Queen Philippa, along with the other dukes who were John's sureties. The usual state occasions and feasts were laid on, and also many informal social gatherings.[17] It must have been about this time that Louis was presented with the only Garter badge from Edward III's reign of which a record survives:

> Another brooch, made in the manner of a garter, and it is enamelled in blue. And on it is written: *honny soit qui mal y pense*. And in the middle a little boar which is on a green ground. And to one side there is a balas ruby. And above its back there are six little diamonds. And around the said boar there is also a white rose, on the leaves of which are six little escutcheons in the midst of which is a diamond. And the whole of the brooch is surrounded with pearls, and there is a little escutcheon of St George.[18]

The symbolism of this is difficult to disentangle. Both Edward and the prince of Wales were referred to as 'boars' in the symbolism of political poems and in chronicles. As the boar is a 'pourcel', literally piglet, it may refer to the prince of Wales rather than his father, and Geoffrey le Baker calls him the 'boar of Cornwall' in the context of the victory at Poitiers.[19] But why was such a symbol of English victory and French humiliation handed to Louis of Anjou?

Despite the lavish festivals, Louis chafed at his captivity, and contrived to escape in September 1363; he was being held by the English in Calais, and was allowed to leave on parole for three days at a time to visit his wife, whom he had married in 1360, at the nearby castle of Guise. After one such visit, he simply failed to come back, and, when his father tried to persuade him to return, he flatly refused. It was an act with huge consequences: a private treaty between John II's sureties in England and Edward III which would have settled the problem of the ransom payments became valueless, and Anjou's escape was one – but not the only – reason for John II's return to England and death there in 1364. This was the most dramatic breach of faith over a ransom; but there were other, more marginal cases, particularly those of Arnoul d'Audrehem and Bertrand du Guesclin after the battle of Nájera in 1367. Both had been captured by the English and ransomed, Audrehem at Poitiers and du Guesclin at Auray in 1364. Both had only paid part of their ransoms, Audrehem to the prince of Wales and du Guesclin to John Chandos. Both therefore faced the same accusation: that they had fought against their captors in breach of their oaths. According to the Spanish chronicler Pero López de Ayala, who may have been present, the prince called Audrehem 'a false traitor'. Audrehem replied, 'Sire, you are a king's son and I do not answer you as respectfully as I should: but I am neither a traitor, nor false.' The prince agreed to a trial by twelve knights from his army, four from England, four from Aquitaine and four from Brittany. He made a speech outlining the charges. Audrehem asked if he might defend himself without incurring the prince's wrath, and the prince told him to speak freely since it was a matter 'of knights and of war'. Audrehem then came up with a convincing argument: in response to the prince's charge, he pointed out that he was not fighting the prince, but Pedro of Castile; they were both hired swords, serving other masters, and he had not therefore attacked the prince's interests. Ayala, preferring the chivalrous rather than the practical view of such matters, claims that 'the prince and the other knights were very pleased that the marshal had found such a good reason to excuse himself, because he was a good knight'.[20] Even allowing for Ayala's knightly attitude to the matter, this shows how the 'laws of war' operated in reality. There was nothing to prevent the prince of Wales from taking justice into his own hands, as Philip VI might have done, and simply executing Audrehem; the court of law which tried the case was one which he had himself created, and the authority was that of the common interests and ideals of knighthood. Ayala's account is confirmed by a judgement in a similar case involving du Guesclin in 1390 before the highest court in France, the parlement of Paris; the defendant cited Audrehem's argument that the prince was merely a 'soudoier' or mercenary in Pedro's service.[21]

After Nájera, du Guesclin was apparently challenged to set his own ransom by the prince: as a man of relatively humble estate, he was in no position to pay a high price himself, and the prince of Wales knew that he was the most skilful of the French commanders. Indeed, his advisers were aghast when the prince made the offer, as they would have preferred to see him safely out of the way for as long as possible. Du Guesclin named a high sum, of around £20,000, which placed him on the same level as most great magnates,[22] and, as soon as it was agreed, obtained financial help from Charles V and was released a few months later.

Getting ransom money, for the ordinary knight, was a matter of luck. The commanders, however, were entitled to a share of any payments arranged with men in their retinue; just as with the knights, this was income used to defray their expenses, and to make a profit, though it would be difficult to judge what contribution it made to the huge outgoings involved. With individual knights, we can see the effects of ransoms on their fortunes much more clearly.

Many minor ransoms have left no trace in the records, so, when we look at the prisoners taken by the Garter companions personally, it is not surprising that we can find only eight of the thirty-six knights who are known to have profited from such transactions. Of the seven named captives, the majority are of the highest rank, as the list below shows. There were also eight other unnamed knights or groups of knights for whom Garter companions received ransoms on recorded occasions, but there must have been a far larger number of transactions of this kind which were on a small scale. For instance, Hugh Wrottesley's improvement in fortunes in 1343, after his rather dubious seizure of prisoners in Brittany, is almost certainly due to ransom money. At the bottom end of the scale is the income that Eustace d'Auberchicourt made from freebooting in 1358–9 in Champagne, less a question of ransoms than of extortion from the local populace in best Mafia style.

Prisoner:	Captor:	Battle:
Jacques de Bourbon	Captal de Buch	Poitiers 1356
Archbishop of Sens	Thomas Beauchamp	Poitiers 1356
Count of Longueville	Reginald Cobham	Poitiers 1356
Bertrand du Guesclin	John Chandos	Auray 1364
Raoul count of Eu	Thomas Holland	Caen 1346
Guy of Flanders	Walter Mauny	Cadzand 1337
John Crabbe	Walter Mauny	Roxburgh Bridge 1332

Poitiers was unusual for the high number of captives taken: the prince's edict before the battle seems to have worked well, in that the large-scale ransom operations did not interfere with the course of the battle. At Crécy, where both sides had signalled that no quarter was to be given, we know of very few prisoners, and none of any rank. At Poitiers, the captives were about 40 per cent of the total of enemy losses, while at Agincourt the ratio was 25 per cent; far more were killed in proportion to those captured.

Ransoms worked both ways, of course. Six Garter companions had to be ransomed during their career, from Robert Ufford, captured with William Montagu in 1340 due to a rash escapade in enemy territory, to Jean de Grailly, taken prisoner at Cocherel in 1364, and again at Soubise in 1372, dying in prison in Paris in 1377 because he refused to abandon his allegiance to the English. Eustace d'Auberchicourt was also captured twice in the course of his career as a freebooter, and on one occasion narrowly escaped being put to death on the spot. Wrottesley was captured in Brittany in 1354; his finances were always poor, and this was a serious matter, since he was outlawed in England and had no means of raising money. How he escaped and regained the king's favour is something of an enigma. John Beauchamp was taken in similar circumstances to those of Robert Ufford and William Montagu, leading a raid out of Calais, where he was captain of the town, in 1351. Thomas Ughtred was ransomed with help from Edward II early in his career, after the battle of Byland in 1322, when the Scots raided as far as north Yorkshire; ransoms in Scotland were usually modest compared with those demanded in France, because of the poverty of the country. For the English knights in general, the debit side of the ransoms, however, was very much smaller than the credit side.

Ransoms proved an excellent safeguard against death in battle, as long as you were on the winning side. It is astonishing how light were the English casualties in the early decades of the Hundred Years War. The French lost many more knights at Crécy alone than the English did in the whole period up to the end of Edward III's reign. Only two Garter companions fell in battle. John Lisle died, in what may have been an accident, early on the prince's raid towards Toulouse in 1355: in John Wingfield's words, he was killed 'very strangely, by a crossbow bolt'. Fifteen years later, John Chandos was killed on the bridge at Lussac. Froissart tells us that he slipped on the ice, because he was wearing a long surcoat embroidered with his arms, and that his attacker was on his blind side, as he had lost an eye many years earlier, so that he did not see the fatal blow. His great comrade, James Audley, narrowly escaped death at Poitiers, while Miles Stapleton probably died of wounds received at Auray. Most of the deaths recorded on campaign were due to other causes: Roger Mortimer died, much to Edward's grief, on the ill-fated Reims campaign, and it is surprising that no other Garter companions appear to have died in the field or at sieges, as the mortality rate at the siege of Calais far exceeded that for the battle of Crécy. Of the illnesses brought on by years of the harsh life of the camp and battlefield we know little. Three other knights who had been on the 1359–60 campaign died in the following two years: Henry of Grosmont, William Bohun and John Beauchamp, but this was due to the outbreak of plague in 1361 which, in comparison with that of 1349–50, took a far greater toll of the nobility. By the end of 1361, half the original founders were dead.

LAWS OF WAR

The existence of a system of ransoms depended on the laws of war. Behind the confusion of battle, the *chevauchées*, sieges and skirmishes of the official campaigns, and even behind the activities of the brigands of the companies there was a concept of a set of laws which applied to all warfare. The moral justification for any kind of warfare was a huge problem for theologians: Christianity – strange though this would have seemed to the Garter companions – is in theory an essentially pacific religion, and warfare posed all kinds of difficulties when it had to be reconciled to the teaching of the Gospels. In practice, theology was supplemented by a system which was more in tune with the harsh realities of life, the so-called law of arms, which tried to regulate the conditions of combat, appealing to the idea of the 'law of the nations' found in Roman legal writing. This rather vague concept was based on the idea that there was a 'natural' law, to which all men, whether Christian or heathen, were subject, and it therefore enabled the lawyers to deal with cases in which both believers and infidels were involved, even if the latter did not recognize the 'law of nations'; it was a legal fiction which attempted to solve an intractable problem, but at the same time it provided some kind of framework which meant that there were generally understood principles behind the waging of war.

Few, if any, of the knights fighting with Edward's armies would have troubled themselves with these high-minded ideas. What would have been familiar to them were the rules of engagement, the limits which both sides generally observed, either from a sense of honour or out of an instinct for self-preservation. The treatment meted out to their victims or captives might be what they themselves would face if the fortunes of war went against them. Their concept of these rules would have derived, not from the legal texts, but from the ideals promoted in the romances or sermons which we have already looked at. One stumbling block was that these ideals present the knight as a *defender*, and have little to say about his role as aggressor. This was where the 'laws of war' came into play: they restrained the aggressor from overstepping certain limits, and provided some relief to those who were on the losing side.

The 'laws of war' do not seem to have existed as a formal written legal code, but as a set of customs; when it came to a lawsuit, these customs would be taken into account, but the higher principles of the 'law of nations' might override such customary law. There is a tantalizing mention in an early fifteenth-century French chronicle whose author may have met Henry of Grosmont's grandson, the future Henry IV, during his exile in France in 1399.[23] Speaking of Henry of Grosmont, he tells us: 'Henry the duke of Lancaster, earl of Derby, who was so skilled in the law of arms and other matters, and who for the instruction of nobles made the book of the laws of war . . .'[24] Henry of Grosmont was certainly capable of writing such a book on the evidence of his authorship of *The Book of Holy Medicines*; but there is no trace of this book.

In legal terms, a case brought under the 'laws of war' was likely to be inconclusive, and difficult to enforce; as a result, such matters as ransoms were dealt with by contract. So the 'laws of war' are really an extension of mutually accepted conventions in warfare. For example, to display a banner implied that a state of war existed, whether it was a royal banner or that of a banneret. The unfurling of such a banner was a declaration that the rules of war now applied, and that a formal challenge to fight had been issued. In skirmishes, the only display might be of knights' pennons, even though a man of high enough rank to display a banner was present; in this case there was no formal engagement between the combatants. At the other extreme was the display of a specific banner which indicated that it was war to the death, *guerre mortelle*, and that no prisoners were to be taken: the banner for such occasions usually had a red background, and would be displayed by the king: the *oriflamme* unfurled at Crécy and Poitiers by the French, and the dragon banner attributed to Edward III at Crécy, are examples of this.

Outside the major campaigns, and particularly in periods when a truce was in force, much of the fighting was in fact outside the scope of the 'laws of war'. A knight was entitled to wage private war against an individual, provided he had good and lawful reason to do so, and had sent a defiance to his opponent. The cat-and-mouse fighting on the Gascon border might occasionally have qualified as private war, but was usually a simple breach of the truce when one side saw an opportunity to seize a fortress or capture an important opponent. Technically, the operations of men like John Chandos and James Audley were sometimes on the wrong side of the 'law of arms', but both sides were equally guilty in this respect. More serious were the activities of Eustace d'Auberchicourt as a leader of a private company in Champagne; not only was he in breach of the truce, but he actually defied a specific order from Edward III to desist from his activities.

A display of banners clearly identified the leader in whose name the action was being fought. The war cry could also be used as a means of proclaiming the army's nationality or allegiance. This took various forms: the early war cries were national ones, 'Montjoie St Denis' for France and 'St George' for England. These could be coupled with other words indicating allegiance, as in the cry 'Guyenne, St George', used at Poitiers ten years later, Guyenne being another name for the English domains in Aquitaine. Individual war cries were later attributed to families: if an army attacked using the cry of a great lord, it was assumed that they were acting either under his personal leadership or on his instructions. At Cocherel in 1364, according to Froissart, the count of Auxerre, technically the senior officer in the French force, declined to have his cry used, and ordered that du Guesclin's name should be the signal, as the latter already had a great reputation: so the cry became 'Notre Dame, Guesclin'.[25]

SAFE CONDUCTS

In wartime, certain of the enemy were automatically granted safe conduct: messengers, heralds and ambassadors. For the ordinary knight, safe conduct usually only applied under strict conditions; if he was taken prisoner, he might travel home under safe conduct in order to raise his ransom. He would also need safe conduct if he was not involved in the war, and needed to travel through hostile territory. This was all well and good if that territory was under the control of a recognized authority; the king's safe conduct was generally effective, but in the periods when the free companies were operating, safe conducts might be needed from a number of captains active along the route the traveller was taking. And such freebooters would not necessarily respect the safe conducts given by their allies.[26] One of the most famous cases involved Walter Mauny. In 1346 he was one of the captains at Aiguillon in Gascony when it was besieged by John duke of Normandy. In the course of the siege, he captured one of John's knights, and ransomed him in return for a safe conduct from the duke to travel through French territory to Hainault. When he tried to use it, however, he was captured and imprisoned; he escaped, but was caught again and sent to Paris. Here, John's first attempt to persuade his father the king to release him was refused, and, according to Jean le Bel, John was 'so upset by this that for as long as [Mauny] remained imprisoned he refused to be part of his father's household', and in the end he secured Mauny's release.[27] To disregard the duke of Normandy's safe conducts was to dishonour him, and Henry V decreed towards the end of his reign that anyone who defied a royal safe conduct should meet the same fate as a traitor: he would be hanged and drawn. But as with so many other legal aspects of war, what happened in the field had little relation to what custom and royal decrees might dictate.

SIEGES

The most striking application of the laws of war was at the end of a siege. Sieges could end in three ways: the castle, town or city could be taken by storm, the besieged could surrender unconditionally, or the two sides could reach an agreement as to the terms on which the siege would end. In addition, there was of course the not uncommon possibility of treason.

For a fortified place to be taken by storm was a disaster of the first magnitude. The laws and customs of war were stark: the goods and chattels of the citizens were at the disposal of the conquerors, and they themselves, with the exception of women, children and priests, were fair game, particularly if they offered resistance to the seizure of their worldly wealth. In the heat of the fighting, however, murder, rape and assault were regarded by the chroniclers as to be expected. Caen in 1346 is a prime example of the scenes which followed a victorious assault by the besiegers; even the high-ranking leaders of the French garrison narrowly escaped with their lives. The garrison, as frequently happened, was able to retreat to the castle keep, and to hold it until the English army had moved on. It was therefore almost always the civilian population that bore the brunt of the siege. Behind the scenes of devastation lay Edward's decision to make an example of Caen, and to show that resistance to his authority on the part of his French subjects would not be tolerated. From the point of view of his men, the booty and ransom from Caen became a legendary moment in the war, when the possibility of profits of war was realized for the first time. As we have seen, it also influenced popular opinion in England in favour of Edward's campaigns.

At Calais, the surrender was negotiated, but was unconditional. The town was therefore at Edward's mercy just as if it had been taken by storm. It was, however, unusual for a brutal pillaging of a town to follow such a capitulation. Instead, the goods would be taken on the king's behalf in a systematic and orderly fashion, and would be divided out as spoils according to the terms of the agreements he had made with his captains. The famous scene of the surrender of Calais, as described by Jean le Bel, makes absolutely clear that Edward was within his rights to put everyone in the town to death; the alternative was to punish the leaders of the resistance to his authority, and in practice this was the norm. Cold-blooded massacres of an entire population are unknown, though on occasion all the occupants of a castle that surrendered might be killed. The likelihood that Edward would order the execution of the six burghers who came to surrender to him is what makes the tension of Le Bel's narrative so acute, and the drama of the intervention, first by

Walter Mauny and then by the queen herself, so vivid. Le Bel makes Edward's action one of simple mercy.[28] When Froissart came to rewrite Le Bel for the first time, he made it a more pragmatic deed: Mauny, he says, argued that, if the leaders of Calais were executed, the same might happen to English commanders under such circumstances.[29]

The most notorious siege of the period was that of Limoges in 1370. It was surrendered to the French without resistance by its lord, the bishop of Limoges, who was godfather to the prince of Wales's eldest son. According to Froissart the prince retook the city by storm, and, furious at the bishop's betrayal of him, threatened to execute him. The city was then pillaged and the inhabitants slaughtered to a man. The English chronicler Thomas Walsingham seems to confirm this, claiming that 'the prince almost totally destroyed it and killed all those he found there, a few only being spared their lives'. However, the city's own chronicle merely says that the inhabitants were taken prisoner, including the bishop, while a note in the chronicles of the monastery of St Martial of Limoges written very soon after the event put the death toll at 300. A careful study of the tax records before and after the siege by a local historian arrived at a similar figure, perhaps 10 per cent of the population. These were probably casualties of the fighting, and the 'massacre' is very unlikely to have taken place. What the episode reveals is not the prince's cruelty – it is sometimes cited as having given rise to his nickname 'the Black Prince' – but what chroniclers expected to happen at a siege where the ruler's honour had been seriously slighted by treachery.[30]

For a complex arrangement for the ending of a siege, Edward III's capture of Berwick just before the battle of Halidon Hill in 1333 is an excellent example. It specifies the time by which the relief force must reach the city if the surrender is not to take place, and even the direction from which it must approach. The relief force did not have to enter the town, but merely to encamp near it. In this case, a small army appeared, but from the wrong direction: they entered English territory, and attempted to attack from the south, so the agreement was null and void. Calais is another case where a relief agreement was made and failed, even though Philip VI had raised a huge army and brought it to within a few miles of the town. His retreat was held to have dishonoured him, and the question of honour recurs again and again in relation to sieges. Even the precise specifications for relief are part of this: the two armies were not regarded as fighting a campaign when these details were drawn up, but rather participating in a formal judicial combat. If the garrison refused to surrender a fortress when they should have done so under an agreement, any hostages given by the besieged were liable to be executed; and they often were, the death of Alexander Seton's son at Berwick being an example. It was a symbolic penalty for the treason of the besieged, and treason was above all a crime against honour.[31]

PART FOUR

A Question of Honour

13

The Garter Companions at War

Sixteen months after Calais had been taken, in December 1349, Geoffroy de Charny approached a Genoese mercenary, Aimeric di Pavia, who was stationed there as master of the king's galleys, to see if he would betray the town to the French for a suitable fee. Charny may well have known Aimeric from the days when he was in French service, because he had been in the French garrison during the siege, and had changed to the English side when the town was captured. The price agreed was 20,000 gold pieces,[1] and the date of the operation was set for the very end of the year. Aimeric was to obtain the keys to one of the towers, and would admit Charny and his comrades by night. Aimeric, however, decided to play a double game, and wrote to Edward revealing the entire plot: Baker claims that he had pangs of conscience, but as a mercenary Aimeric had probably simply weighed up the situation and decided that Edward was likely to reward him better for the information.

The news reached the king at Havering on Christmas Eve, and he hastily assembled a small group of knights from his household, including the prince of Wales and Roger Mortimer, with a number of men at arms and archers. They reached Calais just before the town was due to be betrayed, and set up an ambush for the French. Baker describes in great detail how the knights were hidden by a specially constructed dry wall, which could be pushed down at the right moment, and how the drawbridge was partly sawn through so that it could be broken by a stone toppled from the parapet above. This is probably an elaboration: he claims that the knights were concealed there for three days, 'like hermits'. It is more likely that the trap involved the double walls and moats surrounding the town, and that a special arrangement for bringing up the outer drawbridge, supplementing the usual mechanism and invisible to the scouts, was put in place.[2] When Charny arrived before dawn on 4 January, unaware of the double-dealing that had taken place, he was certainly cautious. The French standard was flying over the gate by which he was to be admitted, but he sent in scouts to ensure that the entrance was safe and that there were no suspicious signs. He demanded Aimeric's brother as hostage, and sent him as a prisoner to the nearby castle of Guines. Only when he was reassured that all was well did he hand over the first payment to Aimeric. Charny ordered the advance guard to move into the town, and as soon as the first body of men had crossed the bridge, it was raised. Since the inner drawbridge was not yet lowered, they were trapped between the inner and outer walls; the English knights emerged from their hiding places and captured them. The French standard was replaced by that of England, and Charny and his men realized that they had been betrayed. They started to withdraw across the narrow causeway through the marshes, but the king led a handful of men out of the gate and pursued them.

When the French realized how few the king's companions were, they turned to fight, and for a moment it seemed that Edward had put himself in serious danger; he later rewarded his standard-bearer, Guy Brian, for his bravery in carrying the standard and defending it in the fighting. However, the king had sent archers to find dry places in the marsh where they could station themselves, and the prince of Wales brought reinforcements out of another gate. A brief but fierce fight ensued, ending with the capture of Charny and Eustace de Ribemont, the other French commander. The archers probably accounted for the majority of the 200 French killed in the encounter. Le Bel has a typical romantic story of the aftermath. According to him, when the French commanders were brought before Edward, he reproached Charny, the supposed model of knighthood, for his treachery in trying to take Calais by deceit and sent him to England as a prisoner; but set Ribemont free: the king crowned him with a chaplet of pearls in honour of his bravery, and released him on condition that he wore it for a year whenever he was in the company of ladies. In fact, Ribemont was sent by Edward on parole to Philip of Valois to tell him what had happened, after which he went to England as a prisoner. Two years later Charny, having paid a substantial ransom for his freedom, had his revenge on Aimeric di Pavia, whom he captured in the course of an attack on Guines, now in English hands, and the outposts of Calais. He took his prisoner to St Omer, where he was tortured and executed.[3]

The truce was supposed to include the Castilians who had supplied ships to fight with the French navy, but the Castilian seamen had continued to harass English shipping in the Channel on their own account, combining this with trading with the Flemish ports. Their activities became so alarming in the summer of 1350 that Edward decided to take action against them. The Castilian ships were armed merchantmen, considerably larger than cogs or galleys; these were busses, with high 'castles' forward and aft. A buss was less manoeuvrable than the smaller ships, but had the advantage in a sea-battle, because missiles could be dropped on a cog or galley which came alongside to grapple it. Edward requisitioned ships to assemble at Sandwich, ordering them to have similar wooden castles fitted, and raised a small army with which to man them. A major attack on the Castilians was intended, as the whole fleet was under his command, and the prince of Wales, Henry of Grosmont, William Bohun, William Montagu, Richard Fitzalan, William Clinton, Hugh Audley and Thomas Beauchamp were given squadrons.[4] Reginald Cobham, Walter Mauny, Robert of Namur and John Chandos were also present, as well as John Lisle, Lord Basset, Thomas Holland and Guy Brian.[5]

The Castilians had previously attacked a wine convoy from Gascony, and appear to have been cruising close to the English coast looking for places where they could land and loot the ports. This would explain why Edward was able to intercept them without difficulty off Winchelsea. It would have been hard to find such a fleet if it was even as close as mid-Channel; by the time a small vessel, however fast, had found the fleet and reported its whereabouts, pursuing ships would have been unable to catch up. It seems more likely that coastal watchers were able to sight it and send word by land to Sandwich so that the English ships would be well out to sea before the Castilian fleet passed. The Spaniards had twenty-four great ships, loaded with valuable Flemish cloth, which towered over the English ships, in Geoffrey le Baker's vivid phrase, 'like castles over cottages', as well as other smaller ships. When the fleets engaged, the English archers were able to open fire out of range of the Spanish crossbows. However, they were unable to clear the decks and when the English engaged at close range and tried to board the ships, they suffered heavy casualties alongside because of the shower of missiles which rained down on them. Once the English boarded, they were able to overcome the lightly armed Castilian crews; in several cases they had to take refuge in the captured ships because their own vessels had been sunk while grappled to the Spanish. The battle ended at dusk, and, when the English prepared to renew the conflict the next day, twenty-seven ships had escaped, leaving seventeen in their hands. To celebrate the victory, the king knighted eighty squires.

Shortly afterwards 1,000 pavises, shields used to protect archers on ships and to shelter men involved in siege works, were delivered to Robert Mildenhale, keeper of the armoury at the Tower: they were painted white, with the royal arms encircled by a blue garter; a further 100 were of burnished silver-gilt, with a garter above the king's arms. Pavises such as these were a novelty in England at the time and these would have made a dramatic display, very probably in a naval battle. Although we cannot associate them with a particular event, they were a powerful statement of the place of the Company of the Garter at the heart of the English military effort.[6]

The pavises also remind us how little we know about display of arms on the battlefield. The debate in the contemporary poem *Winner and Waster* takes place before a king who is clearly identifiable as Edward: Winner argues for austerity and saving, while Waster advocates expenditure – 'with our feasts and prosperity we feed the poor' – and argues that money 'huddled and hidden and hoarded in coffers' does no good to the people at large.[7] The poem is often said to be a satire on Edward's expenditure, but the debate is balanced, and, at the end of the argument, the king pronounces an even-handed judgement; the views of the protagonists have a strong echo today. The poet sets the scene on a battlefield where the opposing armies of Winner and Waster are drawn up, and depicts the king's camp on the cliff above, a scarlet tent decorated with gold ornaments encircled by blue garters: between them were woven the words 'Hething have the hathel that any harm thinketh!', a paraphrase in English of the Garter motto. Its guardian has a magnificent helm with a golden leopard crest, and a cloth with the arms of England and France quartered. The king sits nearby on a silken bench, in a brown mantle embroidered with ducks so realistic that they seemed to tremble in fear of the falcons who threatened them. This is an allusion to Edward's love of falconry, but the interest for us lies in the image of the tent resplendent with garters. We have no details of the decorations of Edward's war pavilions; perhaps the poet had indeed seen one of them, and, as with the pavises, the Garter was the dominant theme in the 1350s, the decade to which the poem is usually attributed. If the French associated the Garter with the English victory at Crécy, it would have been a potent and threatening visual symbol.

But was the sea-fight off Winchelsea a victory? Geoffrey le Baker, whose account we have quoted, certainly thought it was, and many other writers agreed with him. Gilles li Muisit, writing from Tournai, and relying on news brought back to Flanders, was more doubtful; although he could not really decide what could be said about the occasion, he thought the king of England had suffered greater losses than the Spaniards, because his forces were the flower of his army, and the Castilians were a ragbag collection of merchants and mercenaries from Flanders.[8] The majority of the Castilian fleet had escaped, and he had simply ended up with less than half their cargo – and it was this which the English were really interested in. This cynical account is somewhat contradicted by the fact that a formal truce for twenty years was signed with Castile very shortly afterwards, because the Spaniards realized that they could not overcome the English; and since, quite apart from the raid on the wine fleet, Edward had made considerable arrangements for the militia to defend the English coast that summer, the Spaniards were clearly the aggressors.

Le Bel, for once, is silent about this occasion; Froissart has a very full account, probably from his patron Robert of Namur, who was one of the commanders. If we reduce it to the basic information, what he has to say is credible: the fight was very severe, because of the Spanish advantage of the height of their castles. The king's ship rammed and dismasted one Spanish ship, the mast destroying the Spanish after-castle as it fell, but the force of the collision made the English ship spring a leak. Despite this, the king grappled another Spaniard, and eventually abandoned his own ship and boarded and took the Spaniard. The prince of Wales had a similar adventure, but was in danger of losing his victim and sinking with his ship when Henry of Grosmont grappled the Spaniard on the other side. As soon as the prince's men were able to storm the Spaniard, their own ship sank. Robert of Namur, in a ship called *Salle du Roi*, was grappled by a Spanish vessel which towed him away from the battle; one of his sailors got aboard and cut the main-mast stays, bringing it to a halt, and Robert and his men were able to conquer it.

The general pattern of the fight, the sinking of the English ships and the capture of the Spanish vessels is plausible enough. Froissart turns it into a much more knightly occasion than it is likely to have been in real-ity. Before the battle begins he presents us with this scene:

> The king posted himself in the fore part of his own ship: he was dressed in a black velvet jacket, and wore a small black beaver hat which suited him well, and he was, as I was told by those who were there, as joyful that day as they had ever seen him. He made his minstrels play for him a German dance which Sir John Chandos, who was present, had recently brought back. For his amusement, he made the said knight sing with his minstrels, and took great pleasure in it. And from time to time he looked up at the forecastle, where he had placed a lookout to tell him when the Spanish hove into view. And as the king took his pleasure and all the knights were happy to see him, so full of joy, the lookout, who had seen the Spanish fleet coming, running before the wind, cried: 'Ahoy! I see a ship coming, and I think it is from Spain!' Then the minstrels ceased . . .[9]

The king knew that it was at best a partial victory, because on 8 Septem-ber he wrote to the citizens of Bayonne, his southernmost city in Gascony, whose sailors were deadly rivals of the Castilian seamen and more or less permanently at loggerheads with them, that the Castilian fleet was on its way home and that they should arm themselves against a possible attack: in October, the Bordeaux wine fleet was given a pro-tective escort. On the other hand, the discipline and co-ordination of the English had been impressive, against considerable odds; for once, they were fighting at a disadvantage, and their commanders had been able to keep up the morale of their men amid the unfamiliar and difficult situ-ation of a battle at sea.

For a decade or more, the main theatre of the war between England and France had been northern France, from Brittany to Flanders. Gascony, where the French had taken substantial territory from the English, had been the scene of continuous skirmishes, but only one major campaign, that of Henry of Grosmont in 1345–6. When it became clear in early 1355 that the series of truces and peace negotiations which had maintained an uneasy calm for eight years was finally exhausted, Gascony became the focus of attention. The French lieutenant-general, Jean d'Armagnac, appointed in 1352, had successfully extended the area under French control, particularly along the valley of the river Lot, and was now continuing his successes closer to Bordeaux. Ralph Stafford, the commander in Gascony, had failed to prevent this creeping erosion of English authority, and Jean de Grailly, captal de Buch, and the lords of Lesparre and Mussidan came to England to meet the king and his council. At first the plan was to send Thomas Beauchamp to Gascony, and orders to requisition ships for him were made on 10 March. At the end of March, Henry of Grosmont returned from the failed peace nego-tiations at Avignon, and, at a great council in April, it was decided that the prince of Wales should lead the expedition. According to Chandos Herald, whose biography of the prince in verse was probably written around 1380, the prince told his father that 'one of his sons' should be sent to Gascony because the nobles there needed encouragement. As Lionel, the second son, was only sixteen and had no experience of war-fare, it was obvious that he was asking to be given the command himself. The prince himself, in a writ to his steward in Cornwall on 24 April, says that he 'has prayed the king to grant him leave to be the first to pass beyond [the] sea', ahead of the troops being sent to Normandy at much the same time.[10]

The formal indenture between Edward and the prince of Wales setting out the terms of his appointment as royal lieutenant in Gascony was drawn up on 10 July, and names Thomas Beauchamp, Robert Ufford, John de Vere, William Montagu the younger, John Lisle and Reginald Cobham as his companions. The prince was given full powers to act 'as if the king were there in person' in all matters concerning the government of the province, and in making truces and armistices. There was a safety clause as well: 'the king has ... promised that, if it shall happen that the prince is besieged or beset by so great a force that he cannot help himself unless he be rescued by the king's power, then the king will rescue him in one way or another.'[11] The principal means of such a rescue would have been the expeditionary force which was sent at the same time to Normandy under the command of Henry of Gros-mont, and the leaders of this army swore to undertake such a mission if required.

The prince of Wales was by now an experienced soldier, but, despite his nominal command of the vanguard at Crécy, he had never undertaken a campaign alone before this. The men who accompanied him were also highly experienced, and among them were the leaders of the 1346 campaign, who, like the prince, had been part of Edward's council of war. If the ultimate authority rested with the king, the evidence – though we have no formal record of how decisions were made – suggests that Edward listened to the opinions and advice of his commanders, and that the great strength of the English high command was the closeness and trust between the group who led the army from the landing at La Hogue in July 1346 to the departure from Calais in October 1347, a very long time for an army to be in the field in the middle ages. As we have seen, the majority of this group became companions of the Garter, and, of the twenty-six members of the company, fourteen were definitely with the prince in 1355–6. Five were engaged in military activity elsewhere, and for the remaining seven we have no definite information. The commanders of the divisions during the raid and at the battle of Poitiers were all Garter knights, with the single exception of the earl of Oxford, who never became a member of the order. The prince's companions were therefore old comrades in arms and accustomed to working together. Robert Ufford, titular head of the prince's council since the latter's coming of age in 1337, was the oldest of the group, aged fifty-seven, while there were two contemporaries of the king, in their forties: Thomas Beauchamp, marshal of the army on that expedition and commander of the prince's division, and John de Vere, both veterans of Edward's Scottish and Flemish wars. Of the other lords who brought retinues, Reginald Cobham had fought in Flanders, and was the same age as Robert Ufford, while William Montagu the younger was the prince's contemporary, and had been knighted with him at La Hogue. John Lisle had fought in Gascony in the 1340s.

Among the Garter companions with the prince of Wales, several had been in Gascony before, with Henry of Grosmont in 1345–6; these were the prince's chamberlain, Nigel Loring and James Audley. John Chandos had been a companion of the prince's since 1339, and he and Audley seem to have been the prince's personal advisers. Other knights, such as Bartholomew Burghersh the younger and Eustace d'Auberchicourt, had probably been in the prince's household since Crécy. Edward Despenser, who became a Garter companion in 1361, was on his first military expedition.[12] There was a mixture of great military experience and youthful enthusiasm, and a strong sense of loyalty to the prince – already a heroic figure after Crécy – which, taken together, contributed greatly to the success of the subsequent campaigns.

As usual with an expedition on this scale, the departure for Gascony, planned for early July, was delayed by weather and logistics. Everything was ready on land by the end of July, but a steady south-westerly throughout August prevented ships from coming down the Channel, and as the bulk of those requisitioned came from the east and south coast, with relatively few from Devon and Cornwall, this meant that the whole expedition was delayed. Plymouth was always the most difficult port from which to move an army to the Continent, but it was also the only practical option if a fleet was destined for the south-west of France.

The fleet finally disembarked at Bordeaux on 20 September, and the prince's council, having consulted the chief supporters of the English cause in Gascony, decided on immediate action. In the remarkably short time of a fortnight, the army was on the move. The aim was to take the war into the lands of the man who had done the most damage to the English in the past decade, Jean d'Armagnac, the king's lieutenant in Gascony; these territories lay south-east of Bordeaux. This was to be a raid or *chevauchée* like that in Normandy ten years before, through much more difficult terrain, and with the objective of causing as much damage as possible. This was partly in order to draw d'Armagnac into battle if he would rise to the bait, but also to weaken the economic base of his power. On 7 October the army entered d'Armagnac's territory, twenty miles from Bordeaux. The vanguard was under the command of Thomas Beauchamp, as it had been at Crécy, with Reginald Cobham. The prince of Wales took the king's role, in charge of the second column, with John de Vere, Bartholomew Burghersh the younger, John Lisle and the Gascon Jean de Grailly, the chief supporter of the English in the region. The rearguard was under the relatively inexperienced William Montagu the younger. Very early in the campaign, at the town of Monclar, fire broke out while the prince was lodging in the town; as a result, for the rest of the campaign he insisted on sleeping in tents pitched in the open countryside, because of the risk of fire and surprise attacks. John Lisle was the first serious casualty of the raid, wounded by a crossbow bolt at a village near Monclar; he died the next day. The only major town to be sacked in the first fortnight was Plaisance, on the river Adour, whose inhabitants had deserted; on two occasions, possible targets were spared because they were Church property. The general impression is of much greater discipline than on the Crécy raid, though one village, Seissan, was later burnt in direct contradiction of the prince's instructions. This was unknown territory, and John Henxteworth's day-book of expenses includes payments to guides on several occasions: the substantial sum of 22s. 6d. was paid to two men who showed the prince the way on 6 October from Castets-en-Dorthe to Bazas, 'a hard day of marching through the woods'. Arnaud Bernard was the prince's chief guide, and was even more highly paid, receiving £9 for his services on 28 November. Even at the very end of the expedition, guides were needed near the border of the English lands in Gascony. [13]

By 26 October the English army was approaching Toulouse, head-quarters of Jean d'Armagnac. Preparations had been made for a possible invasion even before there was definite news of any attack: the local nobles and militia had been summoned, and their followers were instructed to wear a white cross badge for identification. Stocks of pro-visions were to be laid in, and those living in the countryside were told to be ready to take refuge in the nearest fortified castle. These tactics point to a decision to fight a defensive war; in addition, Jean d'Armagnac had a fairly mixed force at his disposal. There were a small number of royal soldiers under the constable of France, Jacques de Bourbon, and the marshal of France Jean de Clermont, the local nobles and their reti-nues, and a number of hired crossbowmen. He could not be sure of the quality of his men, and knew that, if he was besieged, he was unlikely to receive any help from distant Paris.

The prince of Wales did not know that Jean d'Armagnac was actually in Toulouse until he had passed the city. To besiege Toulouse was impos-sible, since the army had no siege train. If he continued, he could find his way back blocked. If he went north, he knew that the countryside had been stripped in preparation for a possible invasion. It was late in the year, and the weather was worsening, but he decided on a bold stroke: to continue to the east, where the towns and cities felt they were safe from marauders, because any raiding army would not risk penetrating so deep into enemy territory. Furthermore, the terrain was difficult, and the Garonne and the Ariège had to be crossed, swollen with rain, and an unknown ford had to be found – 'yet by God's grace we found it', wrote John Wingfield, the prince's steward. [14] The expedition was now, in le Baker's phrase, 'in lands where the fury of war had never been seen

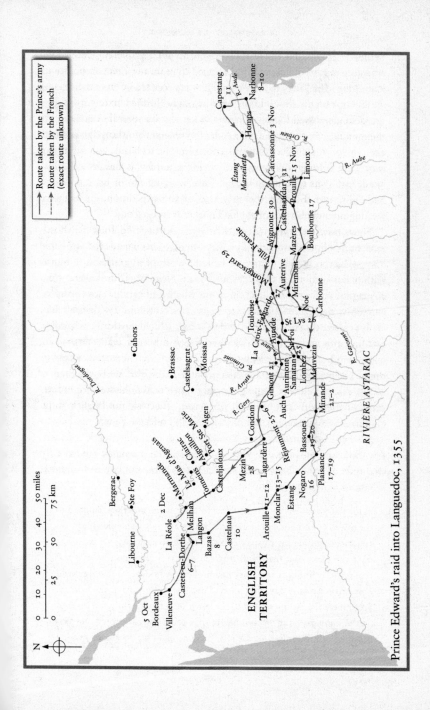

Prince Edward's raid into Languedoc, 1355

before'.[15] Towns and windmills were burnt; at Carcassonne, the citizens offered 25,000 gold crowns but refused to renounce their allegiance to King John. The lower town, or *bourg*, was occupied by the English, and an attempt was made to besiege the strongly fortified citadel itself, but the defenders used flaming arrows to set the wooden houses beneath them on fire, and the prince's men had to withdraw. Much damage had been done, but the French were a force to be reckoned with now that they were fighting a defensive war. Pressing on to Narbonne, the army again met with serious resistance, since word of the prince's activities had led to rapid defensive preparations. The town was burnt by using flaming arrows, but the castle held out.

News now came that Jean d'Armagnac had left Toulouse, with the intention of finding the prince of Wales to do battle with him. Soon after leaving Narbonne, the prince, as he later wrote, was expecting 'a battle within the next three days',[16] but by 15 November he realized that Armagnac had retreated, and the army, which had been in close order in case of battle, resumed its formation as three divisions. The prince's division crossed three rivers in one day, a feat which earned them a day's rest 'in calm and delightful weather',[17] but this enabled Armagnac to come within six miles of the rearguard, evidently hoping to surprise them. The prince drew up his men in battle order, and, when the French scouts discovered this, Armagnac once more withdrew, but not before most of the forty knights who had been observing the English were captured by Burghersh, Chandos and Audley and their men.

We have no contemporary French version of the events of the next few days, and the prince of Wales's report on the campaign puts a positive spin on what happened. According to him, the capture of their scouts

> made the enemy retreat in great fear to their camp, and they marched to the towns of Lombez and Sauveterre, which are only two miles apart. We encamped outside the towns that same night, so close that we could see their campfires. But there was between us a very large deep river,[18] and that night, before we came, they had broken the bridges, so that we could only cross the next day after we had got our men to repair the bridges. From there the enemy moved to the town of Gimont, which we reached on the same day as them, and before they could enter the town our men captured or killed many of them. That same night we encamped outside

the town, and waited there the whole of the next day, hoping that a battle might take place. And the following day we and the whole army were in battle order before sunrise, when news came that before daybreak most of the enemy had left.[19]

The prince held a council of war, and decided that, since the enemy did not want a battle, they should turn for home. What he does not say is that the French had successfully obstructed his progress, and had gained their objective, which was to see him safely back in English territory as soon as possible. Without their manoeuvres, he would have continued to ravage the countryside and destroy the smaller towns, even if he now knew that the large towns and cities were too heavily defended. Nor could he afford to continue such a game of cat and mouse well away from his supply bases, against an enemy who only had to retreat to nearby Toulouse for new supplies and reinforcements. It was a foretaste of the defensive tactics which were eventually to nullify the glories of the English triumphs on the battlefield: but Jean d'Armagnac's caution was not to the liking of the constable of France, Jacques de Bourbon, his fellow-commander. In the spirit of the overconfident knighthood that had helped to destroy the French at Crécy, he roundly condemned Armagnac's tactics, and returned to Paris to resign his post.[20]

Nonetheless, the prince could claim a notable military achievement, chiefly in terms of damage to the economic base on which the French relied for the continuation of the war. John Wingfield, the prince's steward, wrote home to England to report the destruction that had been wrought with the eye of a man used to assessing revenues and estates:

It seems certain that since the war against the French king began, there has never been such destruction in a region as in this raid. For the countryside and towns which have been destroyed in this raid produced more revenue for the king of France in aid of his wars than half his kingdom; and that is without the profits of recoinage and the profits and customs which he takes from those of Poitou, as I could prove from authentic documents found in various towns in the tax-collectors' houses. For Carcassonne and Limoux, which is as large as Carcassonne, and two other towns near there, produce for the king of France each year the wages of a thousand men at arms and 100,000 old crowns towards the costs of the war. According to the records which we found, the towns around

Toulouse, Carcassonne and Narbonne which we destroyed, together with Narbonne itself, produced each year, over and above this, 400,000 old crowns as war subsidies.[21]

Matteo Villani estimated the booty at 1,000 carts loaded with the possessions of the inhabitants, and 5,000 prisoners; but given that there is little mention of either booty or prisoners in the English letters home, and looking at the march which the army undertook, it seems unlikely that anything on this scale had been taken.[22] If the result in military terms had been a stalemate, in that the two armies both returned to base with minimal casualties, the propaganda advantage was definitely on the prince's side: in the view of the French public at large, Jean d'Armagnac had failed to protect the population of the territory for which he was responsible, and had shown himself a coward by not attacking the English army. The prince, on the other hand, had shown that the military skills of the English enabled them to raid at will deep into lands which had been regarded as impregnable, demonstrating that no Frenchman could safely rely on being protected by John II. Yet when forced to choose between the two sides, John was still regarded as the better bet, as the refusal of the inhabitants of Carcassonne to renounce their allegiance showed.

The winter of 1355–6 was passed in skirmishes and raids of the kind that had been endemic in Gascony ever since the official seizure of the English territories there by the French king in 1324. The English had not deployed so many troops or such skilled commanders since Henry of Grosmont's activities in 1345–6, and a satisfying amount of territory was recovered. In the spring of 1356, an ambitious war plan was developed: reinforcements were to be sent to Gascony so that the prince of Wales could continue his activities, and in Brittany Henry of Grosmont was also to be reinforced. Edward himself was planning, it seems, a third army which was to join up with Henry of Grosmont and then draw the French into battle west of Paris, while the prince moved up from Gascony to cut them off from the city and attack them from the rear. By July, troops had been sent to Gascony and Brittany, but Edward's own role had not yet been decided.

The French knew that such plans were afoot, but had no idea of their nature. As far as the prince of Wales was concerned, they assumed he

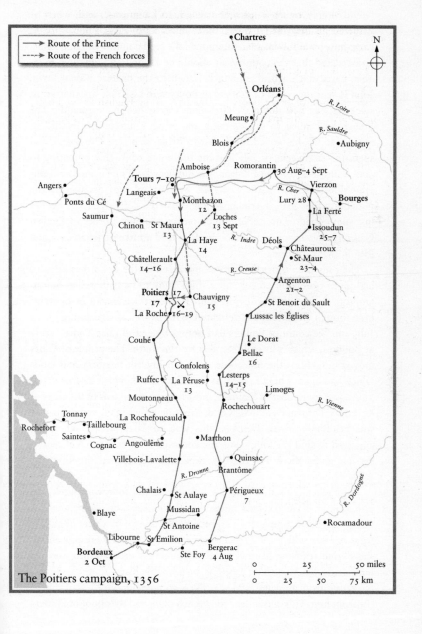

Route of the Prince
Route of the French forces

Chartres

Orléans

Meung

R. Loire

R. Sauldre

•Aubigny

Blois

Amboise   Romorantin   30 Aug–4 Sept

Tours 7–10   Vierzon

Angers•   Langeais•   *R. Cher*   **Bourges**

Ponts du Cé   Montbazon   Lury 28

12   La Ferté

Saumur•   Loches

Chinon•   St Maure   13 Sept   Issoudun

13   Déols   25–7

La Haye   *R. Indre*   Châteauroux

14   St Maur

Châtellerault   *R. Creuse*   23–4

14–16   Argenton

21–2

Poitiers 17   Chauvigny

17   15   St Benoît du Sault

La Roche• 16–19   Lussac les Églises

Couhé•   Le Dorat•

Bellac

Confolens•   16

Ruffec•   La Péruse   Lesterps

13   14–15   Limoges•

Moutonneau•   Rochechouart   *R. Vienne*

Tonnay   La Rochefoucauld•

Rochefort•   •Taillebourg

Saintes•   •Marthon

Cognac•   Angoulême•

Villebois-Lavalette•   •Quinsac

R. Dronne   Brantôme

Chalais•   St Aulaye   •Périgueux

Mussidan   7

•Blaye   St Antoine

Libourne•   St Émilion   Bergerac

Bordeaux   Ste Foy   4 Aug

2 Oct   •Rocamadour

R. Dordogne

0   25   50 miles

0   25   50   75 km

The Poitiers campaign, 1356

would simply return in greater strength to Languedoc, and, when he gathered his army at La Réole, thirty miles south-east of Bordeaux, in early July, Jean d'Armagnac summoned the feudal militia of Languedoc, and ordered that the countryside should be cleared and anything movable, particularly stores, should be taken to the nearest walled town. John II sent the count of Poitiers to Bourges to assemble another army, since he was tied down by Grosmont's activities in Normandy. The French had failed to second-guess the prince's intentions. Instead of moving south, he moved north-east to Bergerac on the Dordogne, and spent the last weeks of July and the beginning of August preparing to march into Périgord and Poitou, the old heartland of Eleanor of Aquitaine's territories. Firstly, however, he had to provide against the possibility that Jean d'Armagnac might use the defensive force he had just summoned to mount an attack on the southern border of English Gascony, and appointed Gascon lords to lead a force of 2,000 or 3,000 men in that direction.

The pressure on the French was increased by the news that Edward had given orders on 20 July for a third army to be gathered at Southampton, to invade Normandy. John II was still engaged in Brittany, even though Grosmont had retreated to his base near Cherbourg on 12 July, and the count of Poitiers had only managed to raise a small army at Bourges, which was still intended for the south. The prince of Wales moved quickly to the old border between English territory and lands which had always been French, at the river Vienne, which he crossed on 14 August to the east of Limoges, unfurling the standards of his army as he did so. The usual campaign of destruction now began, and the prince was heading towards Bourges; this was, he later wrote, 'where we expected to find the king's son, the count of Poitiers. The chief reason for our going there was that we expected to hear that the king had crossed . . .'[23]

The tactical situation was fast-moving: in the following week, the prince must have received news that the expedition planned by his father had been completely disrupted by the arrival of a fleet of galleys from Aragon which the French had hired, and which were preventing ships from reaching Sandwich: all shipping was ordered into port for fear of attacks. Also about this time, he probably learnt that John II was retreating from Brittany, and was likely to move down to Touraine to confront him. This was indeed the French plan, and the count of Poitiers was to join the king's army. The prince of Wales still hoped that Grosmont would be able to reinforce him. He therefore moved towards the Loire, where John Audley and John Chandos captured some French prisoners, who told him that the French were uncertain of his whereabouts, and that groups of French, under the lord of Craon, Jean Boucicaut, and the marshal of France Clermont, were searching for him. On 30 August the prince discovered that Craon and Boucicaut were in the castle at Romorantin: they were a tempting prize, and he attacked the fortress. It cost him five days to secure it and the two French commanders, and by that time the bridges over the Loire had been broken on John II's orders. The prince therefore marched to Tours, where the bridge was still intact, but it was too heavily defended, as both the count of Anjou and Clermont were in the city, and hasty repairs to the dilapidated walls combined with a fierce resistance were sufficient to hold off an assault force led by Bartholomew Burghersh the younger. The prince could not afford to commit his entire army to a siege, as he needed to maintain his mobility at all costs; he was far from his base, and living off the land, and was in jeopardy even if he had been able to join up with Grosmont, who was said to be on his way. There was a further adversary in play: the weather. The Loire, a sluggish and broad stream, was very variable in its flow: in a dry summer, it was possible to cross at a number of places, apart from the bridges, but continuous wet weather had made the river valley into a huge marsh, as Burghersh found when he tried to attack Tours. The only bridge available to Grosmont, at Ponts-de-Cé, south of Angers, had been broken; we know so little of his actual movements that it is not certain that he even advanced that far.

The prince of Wales left Tours on 10 September, heading back towards the safety of Gascony if all else failed. His prime objective was to engage the French in battle. He knew that John was now south of the Loire. John had had great difficulty in recruiting his forces, and there were a large number of relatively poorly equipped footsoldiers. He had paid many of them off in order to match the mobility of the prince's army, and, once he joined forces with the count of Poitiers and crossed the Loire at Blois, he moved swiftly. Furthermore, the dauphin Charles was now at Tours with another 1,000 men from Normandy, and joined the main French army soon after it reached the area. The prince was held up for a day at Montbazon by two cardinals, ambassadors from the pope: he told them bluntly that he was not empowered to make either truce or peace, and that anyway John was nearby and spoiling for a battle. He then spent two days halted at Châtellerault, hoping against hope that Grosmont was on his way, while his scouts failed to find the French, and the French army was ahead of him by 15 September. However, John had ridden ahead with the best-mounted men at arms, and now had to wait in turn for the rest of his army to catch up. The prince now outmarched him, and came to Chauvigny, ten miles to the east of Poitiers, on 17 September, having encountered part of the French rear-guard on the way. The French found an English detachment four miles from Poitiers, who retreated in the face of superior numbers, but the pursuit led them to the main English forces, where they were overcome and the counts of Auxerre and Joigny were captured. The prince had to halt at Chauvigny to allow the army to regroup. John had likewise halted to regroup, and, when the prince moved on the next day, he found the French army drawn up in battle order outside Poitiers, across his route southward to Bordeaux.

As the prince of Wales turned away in search of a suitable place in which to fight a defensive battle with the French, the two cardinals reappeared, urging a truce. The prince's reply was that it was not a time for sermons, but for a battle, and they had better be brief. Despite this, the cardinals did manage to secure a day's pause in hostilities. Both sides claimed that the other took advantage of this: the French were said to have brought up reinforcements, while the English were accused of fortifying their position. This position was on a hillside south of Poitiers, overlooking the abbey of Nouaillé; the valley of the small river Miosson was below. It was a site not unlike Crécy, but much more heavily wooded, and with substantial hedges. The negotiations on Sunday, 18 September came to nothing. When the cardinals returned to the prince's camp the next day, the prince was prepared to extend the truce, but the French, sure that they had their prey at their mercy, refused. The cardinals withdrew, and both sides prepared to fight.

This was an encounter on a much smaller scale than that at Crécy. John had an army composed mainly of noble retinues: if the count of eighty-seven banners said to have been reported by the English scouts is correct, there were fewer than 100 men at arms in each of these, as the best estimate of the total is around 8,000 in all, with 2,000 crossbow-men and an uncertain number of light infantry in moderate disorder. The English had a smaller force, of around 6,000 men, of whom half were men at arms and the rest were archers. John's army of reluctant lords, recalcitrant levies and professional crossbowmen had gathered less than a fortnight earlier; the English had been in the field for more than six weeks, and in any case the prince's army was battle-hardened from the previous autumn's campaigns. Many of them were veterans of the Crécy–Calais campaign of ten years earlier. But, as at Crécy, they were short of supplies and water, and had been in battle array all night.

Jonathan Sumption, in his masterly if somewhat indigestible account of the Hundred Years War, finds himself puzzled by one particular aspect of the battle:

> However, the most striking contrast between the two armies was at the level of command. Manoeuvring large bodies of men-at-arms who had never trained together was one of the perennial problems of medieval battlefields. Orders were generally transmitted to section commanders by trumpet, occasionally by messenger, and thence by shouting. Signals could be complex, and hard to hear inside a visored helmet. Yet the Prince and his adjutants had shown a remarkable ability to control the movements of their men in the midst of the fighting, far superior to anything that the King of France's staff had been able to achieve. The French divisional commanders had been given their orders before the battle, and they carried them out with grim persistence regardless of what was happening elsewhere. By contrast, the Prince had been able to improvise plans in the heat of the action and to communicate them quickly to those who had to act on them in the line.[24]

The answer to this, it seems to me, must lie in the interaction of the leaders of the two armies, both among themselves and between them and their men. This is something about which no historian and no set of documents can tell us, so I turned for advice to someone who had served in conditions which seem as near to this kind of warfare as possible in today's circumstances, a former officer in the British SAS. His comments were very interesting to a novice in such matters: he cited modern examples of manoeuvres with minimal communication. He explained the concept of a mission goal, where the point of departure and the ultimate objective were set, and logistics and support were provided, but the commander was left to achieve the desired result by his own means. He emphasized too the huge value of charisma in an officer, in terms of his relationship with his men: the officer in the Falklands War who could say to his men, 'Follow the black bobble hat if in doubt, and you'll be OK,' is very like the banneret with his group of men at arms: if the banneret was a knight renowned for his prowess in tournaments or war, his men would follow his banner with confidence.

The fact that the prince's men had been marching and fighting together for three months in the previous year, and had assembled again two months before the battle, meant that they knew each other and their commanders well. Medieval armies generally do not appear – as far as we can tell – to have had any kind of group training, and fighting on raids was an excellent substitute. By contrast, the French army had been thrown together scarcely more than a fortnight before. But there are two ways of training an army: my source of military wisdom suggested that the British way in modern times has been to train from the ranks up, and to spend much less time on co-ordinated training of the officer groups; the German approach has historically been the reverse, to concentrate on the brigade-level staff, and to ensure a tight and well-trained central commanding machine. I would argue that the prince's army had just such a coherent general staff, and that it was largely made up of the knights of the Garter.

In order to answer Jonathan Sumption's puzzle, let us try to look at the actions of the Garter knights leading the various divisions at Poitiers. Accounts of Poitiers are a great deal more consistent as to the sequence of events than the multiple and contradictory stories about Crécy. Geoffrey le Baker was writing within three years of the battle, and had undoubtedly spoken to the participants; the other accounts vary in details, and there are the usual problems of interpretation of the battle order, but the evidence gives far less scope for debate about what happened. Interpretation of the evidence is complicated by partisan views of French and English historians; as an extreme example, a classic French account of the battle published in 1940 offers us an engagement in which the course of events was largely determined by the prince's Gascon allies rather than the English forces or even the prince's advisers.[25] It is also worth reminding ourselves of the nature of a medieval army; H. J. Hewitt's vivid sketch is a good likeness:

> A feudal army had not a well-defined hierarchy of command . . . nor was it a military machine the parts or whole of which responded immediately

and unfailingly to the will of the commander-in-chief. It was an assembly of groups of men with their leaders whom they recognized by their shields or banners, and a 'battle' was nothing more than a temporary combination of small groups into a larger group.[26]

The leaders of these groups were therefore critical to the functioning of the army as a unit; if the leaders failed to co-operate or to understand each other's likely reaction in the face of unexpected problems, the army was likely to disintegrate into these smaller units.

King John, advised by the two marshals, Audrehem and Clermont, and by the Scottish knight William Douglas, who had long experience of fighting the English in his homeland, decided to start with a preliminary cavalry charge to destroy the English archers, followed by an attack on foot by the French knights. The cavalry would draw back as soon as the archers were in disarray, and there would be less risk of the slaughter of horses which had brought the French charges to a halt at Crécy. The French attack was to be led by the marshals, and this was to be followed by three divisions of knights under the dauphin Charles, the duke of Orléans (the king's brother) and the king himself.

The prince's position on the hillside was a strong one, and his archers were well entrenched, using hedges with ditches dug in front of them. The divisions of knights seem to have been drawn up with relatively little defensive work around them. The first division was under Thomas Beauchamp and John de Vere, both of whom had fought at Crécy. Beauchamp, at forty-two, had fought in all of Edward III's campaigns, and had a formidable reputation: in 1344 the abbot of Abingdon addressed him as a 'magnificent and powerful man and most energetic warrior'.[27] The central division was that of the prince, corresponding to the king's division at Crécy, with the prince's closest friends, Chandos, the younger Burghersh, Audley and Cobham. William Montagu the younger and Robert Ufford, more than thirty years older, were given the rearguard, the position in which Ufford had fought at Crécy.

We may know the sequence of events, but the very first move in the fighting is difficult to interpret, and the puzzle has never been clearly resolved. The best evidence is that of the prince of Wales himself, in his report home: 'Because we were short of supplies and for other reasons, it was agreed that we should take a path traversing their front, so that if they wanted to attack or to approach us in a position which was not in any way greatly to our disadvantage we would give battle.' The general consensus is that this manoeuvre, carried out by Thomas Beauchamp and the vanguard accompanying the baggage train, was a tentative attempt at a retreat, to see if the French would stay in their defensive position, because at that point the French 'refused to yield any advantage by being the first to attack'. If the prince could lure the French from their positions, and persuade them to pursue the vanguard, the battle would have opened as he wished; if the French remained immobile, he would be able to continue on his way southward. A retreat would not have solved his problems, as the French would have followed him closely, but the one thing he wanted to avoid was being manoeuvred into a position where he had to commit his troops to an attack.

The opening gambit, whatever its precise intention, worked far better than the prince of Wales could have hoped. Neither side, at this point, was sure what was going on in the enemy camp. The English sent out scouts under Eustace d'Auberchicourt, but he was captured. However, the French scouts quickly reported the movement of Thomas Beauchamp's troops to the marshals; Audrehem seems to have assumed that the retreat had begun, but Clermont was suspicious and advised caution. Audrehem insulted him, and led his men forward, while Clermont did not move. The result was a classic illustration of the point just made about the absolute necessity for understanding between the army's leaders. The narrow bridge at Nouaillé was blocked by carts, and the vanguard under Thomas Beauchamp were returning to report this by way of a ford a mile or so to the west. Audrehem's men charged, and at long range the archers were unable to make any impact on the horses, which were armoured on their heads and fronts. When Clermont at last moved forward, the next English commander came into play: Montagu, who was in charge of the third division, brought his men up to cover the flank of Beauchamp's men, now heavily engaged with Audrehem's men. This seems to have been both good fortune and quick thinking by Montagu, who found himself within striking distance of Clermont at the critical moment, and realized what was happening. At twenty-eight, only two years older than the Black Prince, Montagu had seen service at Crécy, in the sea-battle at Winchelsea and in Prussia. The expedition of 1355–6 was his first opportunity for major command. The combat was indecisive, until John de Vere took a body of archers to a position in the marshes of the river Miosson from which they could fire at the flanks and rumps of the horses. The effect was dramatic: the charge quickly turned into the same mass of injured horses and men that had marked the opening stages of Crécy. Clermont meanwhile had tried to mount a flank attack on William Montagu in the rearguard through a gap in the hedge, but Montagu moved the archers to cover the gap with their fire, with devastating effect: Clermont himself was killed, and a large number of his men died with him.

The first stage of the action had been decided by quick tactical thinking and an understanding of what would have appeared as a very confused struggle to the other English commanders. At this stage the prince of Wales was positioned higher up the hill so that he could get an overview of the action, again like Crécy, where Edward probably had the advantage of a windmill. His standard-bearer, Walter Woodland, and his bodyguard and war council were around him: Nigel Loring, William Trussell, Alan Cheyne and others from his household, and his friends Chandos, Audley and Burghersh. John de Vere was the senior figure present, with Baldwin Botetourt and Edmund Wauncy. The prince may have been able to send messengers with the necessary instructions; yet there was no guarantee that a messenger could reach any of the commanders in person. If no message was received, the prince and his advisers could rely on their friends to keep to the 'mission goal' while improvising their immediate responses.

There was now a pause, since the French battle plan had gone badly wrong: the charge which was meant to open the way for the dismounted knights had happened in the wrong place, and King John probably could not see what had befallen the marshals. The English had time to reposition themselves, and to improve their defensive position before the first division of knights reached them, and the vanguard under Thomas Beauchamp now joined the prince's battalion in the maze of hedges and vineyards. The prince, taking overall command in a battle for the first time, was evidently anxious to gather his forces and use the superior weight of numbers which this would give him. As the French climbed the hill – no easy task for a fully armed knight – the archers tried to pick them off. However, only a lucky shot which found a joint in the armour or a vizor slit would cause casualties, as plate armour was strong enough to deflect an arrow fired at long range. On they came, banners displayed, shouting their war cry 'St Denis', answered by the English 'St George'. This was an encounter in slow motion, as hundreds of individual hand combats were engaged and fought out along the length of the English position. The only English troops not yet committed were a reserve of some 400 horsemen.

As the prince of Wales and his companions watched, they saw the French attack falter, and then the French knights drifting away in ones and twos back to the main army; Geoffrey le Baker echoes the taunt thrown at Philip of Valois after Crécy, that he made a fair retreat, in describing the French withdrawal.[28] The dauphin's standard had been lost, and his standard-bearer, Tristan de Maignelay, captured. When they returned to the main army, the dauphin and the other royal princes left the field in search of a place of safety, since the outcome of the battle was now beginning to be in doubt. This was possibly on the king's orders; however politically advisable it was, it seems to have had an immediate and disastrous effect on French morale. No sooner was the dauphin on his way than the next division, led by the duke of Orléans, moved up to attack and a large part of it promptly retreated, without having struck a blow. The official line after the battle was that this was all done on purpose: 'Monsieur the duke of Normandy, messieurs of Anjou and Poitou, and the duke of Orléans retreated on the command of monsieur the king,'[29] wrote Jean d'Armagnac to the inhabitants of Nîmes a fortnight later. But the confusion it caused implies that Matteo Villani's scathing comments may have been at least in part deserved: he calls the dauphin and the duke of Orléans 'most vile and cowardly ... such fear had entered their timid and vile hearts that, although they could have retrieved the situation, they did not have the heart to face the enemy, and were not ashamed to abandon the king'.[30] The dauphin and his brothers left for Chauvigny in good order, with a strong escort, so Froissart tells us, and it may be that the removal of troops for the escort was the real problem. There is some suggestion that the remainder of Orléans' division may have made some sort of attack before retiring to join the remainder of the army, which was now regrouping round the king himself and preparing to charge the English.

John's assault might well have succeeded. He still had a contingent of crossbowmen, and the English archers were not only very tired, but running out of ammunition, even though they had been able to move forward during the lull and retrieve as many arrows as they could find. The English men at arms, short of water and sleep, had already fought for some hours. Geoffrey le Baker indicates that some of them were beginning to despair when King John launched his attack, blaming the prince for leaving so many men away from the army to defend the rest of Aquitaine. Although the remaining French contingent was smaller, they were fresh, well rested and fed. In terms of armament, the sides were equally matched. Matters were made worse by the fact that some of Beauchamp's men had set out in pursuit of the fleeing enemy, not realizing that the decisive action was yet to come. The prince and his commanders seem to have rallied their men successfully in this desperate situation.

The English, however, were battle-hardened in a way that few of the French troops were; and the prince of Wales and his advisers were much more experienced strategists. The French, although much of their battle plan had failed, stuck resolutely to it, while the prince and his commanders improvised brilliantly. One move, the dispatch of a small mounted reserve under Jean de Grailly, captal de Buch, to attack the French from the rear, was straight from the textbooks; but de Grailly, a Gascon who had fought with the prince for the last year, carried it out expertly. As few as sixty knights and a hundred archers left the English army, rode over the hill to the north and round the wood at Nouaillé: they were able to keep out of sight of the enemy until they reappeared behind them on the crest of the hill to the west of Nouaillé and charged down the valley of the Miosson. When they signalled their presence by unfurling their banners, the prince and a small number of men would mount and the French would be charged simultaneously from front and rear. The unexpected moves were those of the prince and Beauchamp: the prince, in face of the advancing French, ordered his banners to *advance* to meet the French, which both strengthened the morale and commitment of his men and surprised the enemy, who were expecting to attack a defensive line. Equally important was the improvised attack by Beauchamp, who succeeded in rallying enough of his scattered troops to mount an assault on the French flank before de Grailly was even in sight. This cannot have been a premeditated move on the prince's instructions, because the prince was in the thick of the fight, with other Garter knights such as Sir John Chandos and Sir James Audley. The double assault of Beauchamp and de Grailly, a classic if unplanned pincer movement, combined with the forward movement of the prince's division, was enough to decide the day.

The French, by now severely depleted, were driven towards the river: here, tradition has it, the final action took place in the *champ alexandre*, 'the field of Alexander', probably so called because of the heroic scenes that followed. John was as passionate about knighthood as his Plantagenet rivals, and he and his bodyguard made a last stand here. His standard-bearer, Geoffroy de Charny, was killed defending the *oriflamme*. John himself, and his youngest son, Philip, who had rejoined his father when his elder brothers departed, were taken prisoner. Philip, unarmed, had stood by his father in the last moments of the battle, warning him of assailants, crying 'Father, look to the right, and to the left' as they attacked.[31]

The English commanders had worked together with one aim in mind and had understood each other's tactics in an exemplary fashion. By contrast, the French had hampered each other: they had adhered rigidly to a battle plan, and had failed to co-operate. From the outset, when Clermont and Audrehem quarrelled, they were convinced of their ability to defeat the English easily, and therefore did not concentrate on what was actually happening, and what supporting action was needed. The departure of much of the second division was similarly due to poor co-ordination of the command, in that if John II did indeed order his sons to leave the battlefield, as he later claimed, he failed to get the message to his commanders, and they in turn failed to realize the purpose of what he was doing.

I would argue that the English success at Poitiers owes something – though by no means everything – to the spirit of teamwork reflected in Edward III's creation of the Company of the Garter. These were men who knew each other well, who had fought together, in real warfare and mock warfare, and who in a tight corner instinctively realized how the others might react. The prince may indeed have managed to convey his commands to them in the heat and confusion of battle: but he would not necessarily have known how matters stood with them. Much of what happened on the battlefield was like a 'mission goal': the commanders knew the objective, and were free to use any means they chose in order to achieve it, if orders did not reach them, or did not correspond to what was happening on the ground. The prince inevitably had to rely as much on their judgement as on his own, and he knew them well enough to trust them implicitly.

Describing the events of the evening after the battle, Baker tells us that, while the prince of Wales and his royal captive were at dinner, James Audley was found severely wounded on the battlefield. Baker gives a vivid picture of how the prince 'brought him back to life by his praiseworthy attention ... and comforted him by telling him that he had captured the king, which the wounded man would hardly have believed'. The prince then returned to dinner, where Audley's heroism was praised by John, and the king replied to the prince's efforts to comfort him by saying that at least he had been captured in fair fight. All this sounds plausible enough, but Baker dresses it up in rhetorical Latin, just as he invents a splendid speech for the prince before the battle, based on a classical model.[32] Le Bel, too, cannot resist a set piece for the prince: he tells us that the prince waited personally on his captive and indeed all the other diners, as a squire would wait on his lord, and in reply to the king's request that he would sit with him, declared:

> Don't feel humbled, sire, if God has chosen not to favour you today. I assure you, my father the king will treat you as honourably and as amicably as he can and will agree sensible terms: you will make a lasting friendship. It seems to me you should be of good cheer, even though the battle has gone against you, for you have earned a reputation for high prowess and surpassed the finest of your army in the way you fought today. I'm not saying this to flatter you! All your companions agree with me in awarding you the prize and the laurels if you'll accept them.[33]

And with that, King John was led into captivity in England by the prince of Wales.

For the moment, it seemed as if Edward and his son had the inheritance of France within their grasp. The history of King John's captivity, the long search for peace, the tortuous negotiations, the disastrous effects of the English victory on almost the whole of France, are not part of our subject. There were truces between France and England, but there were no truces and no mercy shown in the desperate civil war that now broke out in France, a war between ambitious great lords such as Charles king of Navarre, known to French history as Charles the Bad for his endless scheming, and at the same time a war between the peasantry, desperate from hunger and oppression by freebooters, and anyone with wealth or power. That France survived at all was due to the dauphin Charles, who succeeded in rebuilding the French state and re-establishing the order necessary if the threat from England was to be countered. Unlike his father and grandfather, his approach to war was political: it was not a theatre for military glory or high hopes of victory, but a question of patient defence and quiet diplomacy which would nullify the English predominance in military matters.

Even knights who had followed an orthodox military career until now found themselves unemployed. If, as in the case of Eustace d'Auberchicourt, they were younger sons, with little in the way of lands, they found that the truce signed in Bordeaux in 1357 had brought their military careers and hence their income to a temporary end. Eustace acted as a freebooter alongside other English captains in Champagne on his own account, but he and the other captains seem to have been acting in concert with Charles of Navarre: Peter Audley certainly attempted to take Chalons with Navarrese help,[34] and when the Navarrese stronghold of Melun was besieged by the French, 'Eustache d'Auberchicourt and Peter Audley were kept informed of the day [when the relief expedition was to set out] and were to be there with all their men'.[35] This seems to have been the first connection between Auberchicourt and the king of Navarre; he was later to spend a decade in his service.

There seems little doubt that Edward III covertly used the wayward king of Navarre – and was exploited in turn by him – during the truce of Bordeaux.[36] French chroniclers were convinced of this, and Matteo Villani, writing in Florence but with good contacts in the mercantile towns of eastern France, says repeatedly that the English and Navarrese acted in concert: the king of England 'concealed himself behind the shield of the king of Navarre, whose forces were all Englishmen'.[37] It was not a consistent policy. Edward had an interest in raising the huge ransom demanded for the release of John II, which required stable government and efficient tax-collection in France. Equally, a weak French state would be easier to conquer if he were to mount a new invasion. In effect, it was a 'dirty war', and like all such ventures was opportunistic and often muddled in its application. And it was hard to control the freebooters once they had been let loose; official denunciations by the English of their behaviour meant little to them. Jean le Bel sums up the situation neatly: the king 'let these brigands terrorise and wreck the whole kingdom . . . in the hope that it would either bring the war to a successful end or peace on his own terms'.[38]

Against this chaotic background, diplomatic efforts to find a solution continued. Edward negotiated with his prisoner, King John, in London; and John in turn negotiated with the government led by his son Charles in Paris. But it was impossible to get agreement between three parties with very different interests. In 1359 a treaty which was to provide for the release of John II and the re-establishment of the English presence in almost half of France was negotiated in London, subject to its acceptance in Paris by the dauphin and the estates-general of France. Ratification was intended to take place on 24 June. In return for Edward's renunciation of the French throne, it would have re-created an empire similar to that of Henry II, who had ruled from Scotland to Toulouse, and in whose time the kingdom of France was confined to the Paris basin and the eastern side of France. Not only Gascony, the inheritance of Eleanor of Aquitaine, was to be largely restored, but the lands of William the Conqueror, Normandy, Anjou, Maine, Touraine, as well as Brittany, were to be held by the English king again. For King John and his entourage, eager to return home after nearly four years in captivity, it seemed harsh but possible. For the dauphin and his advisers, it seemed an impossible folly, even if the alternative was a huge struggle to fund a war from an impoverished and disordered kingdom. They refused to put their names to the treaty, and on 24 June, instead of peace, the war was instantly renewed.

Edward's last great military adventure in France was also the most ambitious. He proposed to aim for the ultimate confirmation of his right to rule France: he was going to march on Reims, take the city and have himself crowned in the cathedral, where French kings had held their coronations (with one or two exceptions) since 1179. The archbishop of Reims was the senior member of the French clergy, and, like the archbishop of Canterbury in England, had the right to crown a new monarch: Edward had some reason to think he might be favourable to his cause. To achieve this, Edward would need a massive force, capable of besieging a large town; it was a bigger undertaking than the siege of Calais. Furthermore, he genuinely seems to have hoped that the French would accept the proposed treaty, because, although some degree of preparation and planning was in place by June, it was only on 24 June that the English war-machine swung into full action. The army that had taken Calais had gathered over a period of time, and had included the original expeditionary force and also many of those who had been fighting in Gascony under Henry of Grosmont, as well as reinforcements from England. Edward now proposed to raise 12,000 men, the largest single force ever to sail from England. But half the year had gone: the king reached Sandwich about 16 September, and did not sail until 27 October. He was hazarding everything on being able to fight a winter campaign. He had indeed carried out the siege of Calais through the winter, and Reims was well to the south: but the continental climate inland would be more extreme than that of the sea-coast. The preparations were thorough, and the result was an impressive but unwieldy mass which had to be moved slowly from Calais southwards to Reims. Jean le Bel describes it vividly:

> he set out from Calais next day, with the finest supply train ever seen: it was said there were 6,000 handsomely fitted wagons, all brought over from England. And he ordered his battalions so splendidly that they were a pleasure to behold: he commanded his Constable, whose title was the Earl of March [Roger Mortimer], to ride half a league ahead of him with 600 heavy cavalry, the most splendidly accoutred in the army, and 1,000 archers; next he formed his own battalion with 3,000 cavalry and 5,000 archers, and followed his marshal in battle array, ever ready to fight if the need arose; behind this great battalion came the baggage train, stretching fully four miles, carrying everything needed for camp or combat, including hand-mills and ovens for baking bread in case they found that all the ovens and mills in the country had been destroyed; and behind the train rode the Prince of Wales and his brother the Earl of Richmond [John of Gaunt] (recently married to the Duke of Lancaster's daughter): in their battalion they had 2,500 heavy cavalry, superbly mounted and richly armed, and 4,000 archers and as many brigandines forming the rearguard. They didn't allow a single fellow to fall behind: they'd wait for any straggler; so they couldn't cover more than three leagues in a day.[39]

Much of Le Bel's description is borne out by English records. The 1,000 carts requisitioned for the expedition were to carry everything from the portable boats for the king's fishermen and the portable mills and ovens which Le Bel describes to a mass of raw materials, lime for siegeworks, iron for horseshoes, and of course provisions. It was these last that were to be the Achilles heel of the unwieldy enterprise. In France, the harvest had been gathered and stored for the winter, and when the dauphin Charles, regent in place of his captive father, ordered these stores to be moved into the towns or destroyed, the task was relatively easy, particularly since the planned English incursion had been long expected.

The main invasion was preceded by two raids. The first, led by Henry of Grosmont, was formed of his own personal retinue and German mercenaries, recruited by Walter Mauny and led by the margrave of Meissen. Part of the reason for the raid foreshadowed the problem of provisioning: the mercenaries had been waiting so long in Calais that they had used up a significant part of the stores sent there for the main army, and Grosmont was effectively told to get them out of the town and take them on a raid down to Arras and along the Somme. He was followed by Roger Mortimer, who raided along the Channel coast, and met up with Grosmont as they returned to Calais. Apart from getting the German mercenaries out of Calais, the raids do not seem to have served any strategic purpose. It seems, reading Le Bel closely, as if they set out with minimal provisions: they took four days to reach the abbey of Mont-Saint-Éloi, near Arras, 'where they stayed for four days to rest and recover, for they found the place well provisioned and they certainly needed sustenance, having tasted neither bread nor wine for the previous four days'.[40] If this is true, their last square meal was in Calais itself. In order to get provisions, they had to attack towns; and they found almost everywhere that the townsmen, having suffered for years at the hands of the English and of freebooting companies in the lawlessness following the French defeat at Poitiers, had protected themselves by renewing their fortifications or raising new ones. Grosmont tried to take Bray-sur-Somme, probably to get provisions, and was driven off, and it was only after three weeks on the march that he succeeded in getting stores by storming Cerisy; at which point he was summoned back to Calais.

From the outset, therefore, the army that left Calais in mid-November was divided into three, specifically, according to John of Reading, 'on account of provisions'. At times they were as much as fifty miles apart, and communications were a further problem. If there was a broad swathe of devastation as a result, it was less as a matter of policy than a desperate search for the wherewithal to feed the men: the towns were not only well fortified, but well defended, with commanders whose instructions were in effect to batten down the hatches until the storm had passed. The chronicler at St Mary's abbey, York, seems to have had access to a detailed letter about the campaign; if his account reflects it accurately, there are no claims that serious economic damage has been inflicted on the French regime, as in the case of the prince's raid of 1355, but simply the endless repetition of the phrase 'destroying and wasting the country'. There was little engagement with the enemy, and no heroic actions worth reporting. Worse, if we are to believe Froissart, the weather was raw and rainy; the rain fell almost every day and every night, and, even though Edward had heard of the dearth of provisions in France, he had not been able to bring enough fodder for the horses with him: 'the horses got by as best they could', Froissart comments, stating the obvious.[41]

The three divisions were commanded by the king, the prince of Wales and Henry of Grosmont. The veteran leaders of Crécy and Poitiers were with the king – Thomas Beauchamp, Robert Ufford, William Montagu the younger and John de Vere, but there were also new faces: his sons Lionel of Clarence and Edmund of Cambridge were with him, as well as Jean, the young claimant to the dukedom of Brittany. The prince was accompanied by his old companions William Bohun and Richard Stafford, and by his brother John of Gaunt, who had already fought in three campaigns with the king. Edward's forces took the most easterly route, Grosmont was in the centre, and the prince took a longer path, first south-west to Montreuil, then back to the valley of the upper Somme before all three divisions met at a small village twenty miles from Laon and thirty miles north of Reims. They met apparently by chance, because 'one division did not know where the others were' until 28 November; and a council of war was held at which it was decided that, despite the problem with communications, they should continue in three separate divisions, but 'in such a way that each would know where the others were'.[42] The king went direct to Reims and set up camp there at the abbey of St Basle near Verzy; the prince, probably in search of a good store of provisions, marched away from Reims to Rethel, which he attacked unsuccessfully before rejoining the king and establishing himself at the monastery of St Thierry, north-west of the town; and Mortimer and Grosmont took up residence at Bétheny, to the north-east.

The siege of Reims was a largely non-military affair. What Edward seems to have hoped is that the show of force outside their walls, and the non-appearance of any relieving army, would persuade the citizens, and particularly their archbishop, Jean de Craon, said to favour the English cause, to open their gates and welcome him in. Villani says that he promised to make it 'the most magnificent and important town in France if he could be crowned there, and to treat the inhabitants kindly',[43] though there is no actual record of any English overtures to the city. Strict injunctions against any kind of harmful activity were issued, and the army settled in as best it could to blockade the town; the weather was poor, and provisions short. Edward could see that the fortifications were in excellent repair, but he probably did not know that the dauphin had warned the citizens of the English plans as early as 10 July. Furthermore, under the leadership of the captain appointed by the dauphin to guard the town, Gaucher de Châtillon, the archbishop had been treated as suspect, and had been forced to move to his palace in the heart of the city from his house near one of the city gates because he refused to allow defence works there; the low garden wall was replaced by a new enclosure, which joined the fortifications on either side. The archbishop had not made himself popular with the citizens, and in reality had little support. As elsewhere, all grain and other foodstuffs from the surrounding countryside had been brought into the city; anything which could not be removed had been spoiled. The citizens were armed and trained in organized bands, and the streets were equipped with chains which could be used to block the way in case the enemy penetrated the defences. Gaucher knew that he could hold out for a very long time against a blockade, and that the English would starve sooner than the inhabitants of Reims. Reims would not share the fate of Calais. The only alternative was a full-scale assault, and Edward knew that both politically and practically this would not succeed.[44]

At Christmas, Edward and his companions were said to have celebrated the festival in style: 'every lord made merry with others as though he were on his own estates in England.' The celebrations may have been improved if Froissart's information is correct. He says that soon after their arrival before the city, Eustace d'Auberchicourt, who had been operating as a freebooter in the area before they arrived, seized the nearby town of Attigny and found 3,000 barrels of wine there, much of which was sent as a present to the king and prince. Soon after the festival, chiefly because more supplies were urgently needed, but also to satisfy an increasingly bored army, a raiding party was sent out to the east, under Grosmont, John of Gaunt and James Audley. They took the town of Cernay, which was razed to the ground, and two smaller fortresses, which were entrusted to Eustace d'Auberchicourt; and

Bartholomew Burghersh the younger and his men scaled the walls of Cormicy. But this was only a diversion. The army could not stay in one place any longer, and on 11 January, after six weeks outside Reims, the English raised the siege. They left in good order during the night.

The problem now was where to go next. Edward does not seem to have had any real alternative master plan as to what his objective was. For the moment, his problem was still that of finding supplies, and the solution proposed was that the army should keep on the move, foraging for whatever it could recover from a countryside deliberately stripped of provisions, until a new supply fleet could be sent from England to Honfleur in Normandy. The timing of the arrival of supplies was uncertain, particularly in the depth of winter, when storms could keep ships in harbour for weeks at a time.

Edward could not return north the way he had come, because he had already exhausted any supplies there; so he headed southwards, and negotiated a large ransom from the men of the county of Bar to spare them from the passage of his troops. And less than a month later Edward presented a similar demand to the Burgundians if they wanted to prevent the English from entering their duchy, which was much less well defended than the countryside round Reims. The negotiations took a month, at Pontigny, where Thomas Becket had once been in exile two centuries before. While Edward negotiated, the prince of Wales rode south-westwards to Auxerre, where the freebooters were still active, and suffered the first real losses of the campaign, to nocturnal marauders who killed knights and squires in their quarters, and to attacks on his foraging parties. It was during this march from Reims that Geoffrey Chaucer was taken prisoner and ransomed; his friend the Italian poet Petrarch, travelling through the area later in the year, wrote to his friends at home that he did not recognize the thriving countryside he had seen on previous visits to Paris.

Edward now decided to threaten Paris, and to see what might happen as a result. He turned to the tactics of previous raids, and authorized burning and looting in a way that had not characterized the campaign until this point. Jean de Venette, who was in Paris at the time, has left vivid descriptions of what went on. For six days after the king's arrival, 'his troops, dispersed throughout the vicinity, wasted and burned everything so thoroughly that not a man nor a woman was left in any of the villages near Paris, from the Seine to Étampes'. On Good Friday, the smoke and flames rising from the towns to the heavens were visible at Paris in innumerable places. Thither a great part of the rural population had fled. It was lamentable to see men, women and children desolate. On Easter Day, I myself saw priests of ten country parishes communicating their people and keeping Easter in various chapels or any spot they could find in the monastery of the Carmelite friars at Paris. On the following day, the nobles and burgesses of Paris ordered the suburbs of Saint-Germain, Notre-Dame-des-Champs and Saint-Marceau to be burnt.[45]

Other mansions and manor houses near the city were destroyed to prevent their use by the English, while in some places the churches were fortified. At Châtres, a quarrel between the captain and leaders and the rest of the village led to the church being set alight by the captain's men, and the death of 1,200 people in the ensuing inferno. The mere presence of the English was enough to bring disaster on anyone living outside the city walls. As in the past, Edward hoped that the scale of the damage and the chaos within Paris would force the dauphin to act and bring his army out to drive off the enemy.

He had already met papal envoys who were seeking a peace settlement, and John had succeeded in tightening his grip on the Paris administration: he too was anxious to make peace and regain his liberty, while the dauphin was unwilling to pay the price that would be demanded in any peace treaty. A meeting of the peace negotiators was held on Good Friday, 3 April; the English were represented by Grosmont, William Bohun, Thomas Beauchamp, Chandos and Walter Mauny. Nothing came of it. The French blamed 'the excessive demands of the enemy'.[46] Although Paris was in turmoil and short of provisions, Edward could not afford to attempt a siege. Instead, he made one last attempt to draw out the dauphin by parading his army in battle array on the morning of 12 April, just outside the walls of Paris. But the dauphin made no move, and Edward gave orders for the army to move south-west towards Chartres in search of forage, setting out on the following day.

Natural disaster overwhelmed the army as it moved off. The persistent rain of the winter was followed by a huge hailstorm, which caught the army on the move and therefore at its most vulnerable. Jean de Venette says that 'the strength of the horses failed. They could not pull their loads, and the wagons, soaked with rain, remained stationary on the roads and highways. Many horses and their drivers were pitiably drowned by the hail and torrential rain.'[47] The English remembered it as Black Monday,[48] and it became a legend: a hundred years later, a London chronicler described it as 'a foul dark day of mist and of hail, and so bitter cold, that sitting on horseback men died'.[49] Henry Knighton claims that the army's supply train was almost entirely destroyed, with the loss of 6,000 horses, 'and they had to return to England'.[50]

Knighton was in a sense right: the losses were not dire enough to stop the campaign there and then, and supplies did reach them from Honfleur immediately after the disaster. Nonetheless Edward halted five days later near Orléans. Froissart reports that Henry of Grosmont argued that they should bring the fighting to an end. As so often, the chronicler presents his own summary of the situation as direct speech and attributes it to an appropriate figure. The choice before Edward was either to continue fighting with an uncertain outcome, much expenditure and the danger that he could lose all his gains, or to accept peace on honourable terms – though these would be much less favourable than they might have been a fortnight earlier. The king's choice was peace, a peace which, wrote Jean de Venette, eased 'the anguish of the French people, who had borne for twenty-four years and more the burdens and disasters of the wars waged by the English', and which was agreed upon 'by the inspiration of the Holy Spirit and to the joy of the angels'.[51] Terms were worked out at Brétigny, near Chartres, on 1 May. Edward was to have Aquitaine in full sovereignty, free of any French overlordship, but he had to give up his claim to the overlordship of Brittany and his more shadowy claims to Normandy and the provinces on its southern border. King John's ransom, originally set at four million gold florins, was reduced to three million. All this was to be worked out in detail at a conference at Calais beginning on 15 July. A preliminary agreement was ratified by both the prince of Wales and the dauphin by 15 May. Three days later Edward and his son were back in London, leaving the army to follow over the next few weeks. It had been an expensive seven months, not only in terms of cash, but also in terms of losses among the commanders: Roger Mortimer, earl of March, only two years older than Edward and his childhood friend, died of fever in February 1360 while the army was between Reims and Paris; the king 'mourned him greatly', according to Froissart, and his body was later brought back to England and buried at Wigmore. Other victims were Thomas Beauchamp's eldest son Guy, and Robert Morley, a highly experienced commander and administrator who had spent many years in charge of the English fleet.[52]

The dauphin continued his policy of defensive warfare when he came to the throne as Charles V in 1364, after John II's death in captivity in London. When the war had started, it had been the French whose tactics were outmoded, derived from an old-fashioned romantic view of the value of the mounted knight as chivalrous hero, descendant of the heavily armed warriors whom three centuries earlier the Byzantine princess Anna Comnena described as capable of piercing the walls of her city with their cavalry charge. Charles V, faced with the unquestioned superiority of English arms and English tactics on the battlefield, discarded the knightly idea that an army must be met by an army, if honour was to be preserved, and that battle was the decisive mode of warfare. Instead, his policy was to fortify, raise militias and target the enemy's sources of supply, the weakest point of any invading force, by withdrawing the provisions available into heavily defended towns and leaving the countryside empty of resources. It was a remedy which worked superbly against the English army: Charles had applied the English tactic of always trying to fight a battle from a defensive position to the strategy of the war as a whole.

The coming of peace with England had one consequence which Jean de Venette did not foresee in his celebration of the new order: the hordes of mercenaries who were let loose on the French countryside when their employment ceased in 1360 with the treaty of Brétigny. Both sides had employed them, officially and unofficially; now they were turned loose to find their own ways of making a living. This had happened in the years immediately after Poitiers, but not on a grand scale; individuals had held communities to ransom and fought private wars; after the treaty of Brétigny, the mercenaries worked out the advantages of co-operation, and fought as the so-called 'free companies'. When several of these companies collaborated, they could field a formidable army: at Brignais near Lyons in 1362, they annihilated a French royal army under Jean de Tancarville and Jacques de Bourbon, experienced commanders who totally failed to realize that they were faced by superior numbers and hardened fighters.

In November 1361, Edward actually sent commissioners to France to round up any English subjects who were engaged in this sort of warfare, order them to leave France within a limited time, and arrest them if they refused. The writ states that the king is taking this action because of a complaint by 'our brother of France' about the English depredations, and it is clearly a diplomatic attempt to satisfy John rather than a serious proposal for the removal of the English, as it begs all kinds of questions about how the two commissioners were going to enforce the king's demands.[53]

Edward III's attitude to these freelances was at best ambivalent, and there is some evidence that he covertly supported them: their operations were doing a great deal of harm to his opponents. A case in point is that of Eustace d'Auberchicourt. As a companion of the Garter, he was closely aligned with Edward, even though as a foreigner he was not technically one of the king's subjects. He had been one of the commissioners who confirmed the treaty of Brétigny at Calais on 4 October 1360. Five days earlier, he had made a prestigious marriage to the lady whose love affair with him Froissart describes, Queen Philippa's niece, the former countess of Kent, Elizabeth of Juliers. His military service for Edward had come to an end in 1363: he was supposed to go to Brittany that spring, but instead he took a substantial force, of 350 mounted soldiers, to Ireland.[54] However, in 1364, he contracted with Charles of Navarre to be 'guardian for my lord of Navarre of the lands which he holds in France, Normandy and Burgundy'.[55] His first recorded act was to sign a truce in respect of Normandy on 13 March, his co-signatory being the king's brother, Louis of Navarre.[56] On 7 June he sealed a charter of liege homage to Charles of Navarre: he was to serve in peace and war against everyone except the king of England and his children, most especially in the wars which that king had at present in the kingdom of France. He was specially charged with keeping the castle of Carentan.

One of his first actions in this capacity was also one of the most dramatic. Charles of Navarre believed that there was an opportunity to regain his lost lands in Normandy, and sent a force of about 400 men by sea from Bayonne under the command of Auberchicourt and a Navarrese knight to invade the duchy. They embarked at the end of July, and soon after their arrival news came that the long-standing civil war in Brittany between Jean de Montfort, backed by the English, and the French claimant, Charles de Blois, had flared up again. In September, Auberchicourt led his men to join an Anglo-Breton army led by John

Chandos[57] which was trying to prevent Charles de Blois from raising the siege of the town of Auray. The commanders on the French side were Charles de Blois himself, Jean de Chalon, whom Auberchicourt had fought in Champagne, and the young Breton captain Bertrand du Guesclin, who was later to prove the scourge of the English armies. The battle was fought entirely on foot: Chandos had a strong defensive position, on a hillside above a river. There were negotiations before the battle, and the Bretons with Charles de Blois were apparently ready to accept Jean de Montfort's terms. But the English soldiers and the French under du Guesclin were determined to fight: their livelihood depended on the spoils of war, whereas the Bretons had a vested interest in peace. As soon as negotiations failed, the Bretons on the French side began to desert, and in the opening moments Jean de Chalon was captured. The French formation broke, and more Bretons deserted Charles de Blois: his knights were overwhelmed, he himself was killed, and du Guesclin captured.[58] The latter was freed before the end of the year on promise of payment of a ransom of 100,000 francs to John Chandos.

Auberchicourt now returned to his original purpose, that of regaining the lands claimed by Charles of Navarre. He and his men joined the army under the command of Louis of Navarre, which invaded lower Normandy in mid-October: and it was at this point, on 14 November 1364, that Edward III addressed a fiercely worded writ to him and two other captains, Hugh Calveley and Robert Scot: he had recently heard, he declared, that, under colour of the war which the king of Navarre was waging on the king of France, they had invaded French territory with a large force and were waging open war, pillaging, robbing, burning, raping and causing much damage. This was in breach of the peace, and very damaging to the king's reputation; on receipt of the letters they were to cease their activities forthwith. These letters were also addressed to the prince of Wales, John Chandos and all French and English officials in France.[59] It was a public disavowal of the covert policies of the previous seven years: why Edward should have taken such action at this moment is obscure, because he had no obvious reason to wish to show favour to the king of France; it runs counter to his diplomatic attempts to outflank him by creating a major alliance with the count of Flanders. Whether Auberchicourt actually took much notice of the letter we do not know; but he remained in the king of Navarre's service.

*

By 1365, after much head-scratching by the French and by the pope, whose territories round Avignon had been subject to the raids of the companies, a scheme for getting them out of France had been devised. It hinged on the situation in Castile, where the autocratic rule of Pedro I, the son of Alfonso XI, was being challenged by a baronial revolt led by Henry of Trastamara, his illegitimate half-brother. Both the French and the Castilians' neighbours in Aragon were eager to see a change of regime, and, with the pope's connivance, an expedition to depose Pedro was launched in November 1365 under the guise of a crusade to drive the Muslims out of southern Spain. The leaders were to be Arnoul d'Audrehem, the marshal of France who had fought at Poitiers, and two younger commanders: Bertrand du Guesclin had made his name fighting against the companies in Brittany, while Hugh Calveley, a knight from the prince of Wales's lands in Cheshire, had been a leader of those same companies. This improbable plan was put into effect by the promise of huge sums to the mercenaries, and by September they were heading south. Alongside the French and English companies who had fought at Auray and elsewhere in Brittany were a much wider range of soldiers, freebooters from Burgundy and southern France and a variety of French knights seeking to retrieve their fortunes. This massive group of soldiers was quickly nicknamed the 'Great Company'.

The problem was that Pedro had recently signed a treaty with the prince of Wales in Aquitaine: part of the point of putting together the Great Company was to undermine English power there by transferring the allegiance of Castile from England to France. Pedro invoked the treaty; but all that he got in the way of support was a proclamation from Edward III on 6 December 1365 addressed to John Chandos as constable of Aquitaine, Hugh Calveley and two other captains who were actually part of the invading army. Edward instructed them to find any English forces intending to join the Great Company and to stop them; disobedience would be severely punished, and would extend to their friends and relatives.[60] Hugh Calveley ignored the letters, and continued as du Guesclin's second in command.

Auberchicourt played a more ambiguous role. He was in Navarre on 20–24 January 1366,[61] when he renewed his liege homage in the name of himself and his eldest son, excepting only his allegiance and duty to Edward III and his eldest son, in return for an annual pension of 1,000 livres tournois and a payment of 65,000 gold florins for past service, the price of loyalty in difficult times.[62] Records show him in Navarre at intervals until mid-March, and it is entirely possible that he had separated himself from the expedition and was working for Charles of Navarre instead.[63] An order was given to the castellan at St Jean Pied du Port, at the foot of the Pyrenees, who had detained Auberchicourt's siege engines; they were to be allowed through on 22 February, for the defence of the Navarrese town of Peña, as part of the defensive precautions taken by Charles before the invasion of Castile began. Intriguingly, a safe conduct was issued on the same date for Geoffrey Chaucer and three companions to travel freely through Navarre, and to talk to anyone they pleased.[64] It is not impossible that this was arranged by Auberchicourt, and was part of the covert English activities in Navarre.

On New Year's Day, the leaders of the companies feasted with Pere IV, king of Aragon, in Barcelona. They left for Castile a week later, and met little resistance, but then Calveley marched across the Navarrese border on his way to the Castilian capital at Burgos. His move was probably purely strategic, in that the main road to Burgos ran through Navarrese territory, and, although some towns were secured as a precaution, Calveley's troops recrossed into Castile a day or two later.[65] The campaign was very brief: Pedro's supporters deserted him when du Guesclin approached, and Henry was crowned king at Burgos on 29 March 1366. Pedro fled south to Seville, and then to Portugal. Five days earlier, du Guesclin and Auberchicourt had dined with the king of Navarre at San Vicente.[66] Following the unexpectedly sudden end to the expedition, Auberchicourt recruited a number of English knights who were with du Guesclin's expedition to Charles's service, and writs were issued in evidence of this: in one case, his own seal was used for a knight who did not have a seal of his own.[67] Stephen Cosington, one of the prince of Wales's household knights, was recruited on 6 April, and it seems clear that there was a broad strategy of placing men in Navarrese service in case of some future political development.

The prince of Wales and his advisers had not anticipated a swift victory by the companies. Their intelligence about Pedro seems to have been poor. Pedro's character was suspect: Thomas Gray has a long and highly inaccurate anti-Semitic story of how his love for his Jewish mistress led to his inclusion of Jews among the knights of the royal order of knighthood, the Order of the Sash. This, according to Gray, led many of his men to support Henry of Trastamara. Though the tale is not true, it indicates Pedro's poor reputation outside Spain.[68] Pedro's ambassadors at Westminster in November 1365 had had to work to counter such tales, and the prince's entourage at Bordeaux was also, according to Froissart, very reluctant to support this supposedly unchivalrous monarch. But the politics of the situation were now such that the prince had little choice in the matter: if Aquitaine was not to be threatened by a hostile power on its southern border, Pedro had to be supported. He consulted with his father in England, and seems to have been told firmly that diplomacy must take precedence over any hesitation about Pedro's character. An agreement was reached on 23 September 1366, and signed at a great meeting at Libourne near Bordeaux. The prince was to provide a great army for an invasion the following year, in return for the Basque province of Vizcaya, which would become part of Aquitaine, and the reimbursement of all his expenses. Pedro had only some valuable jewels, and no source of ready money until his kingdom was back in his hands, so the prince had to advance all the wages as well as a bribe to Charles of Navarre for free passage through his territory.

The stakes for the prince of Wales were therefore high: his five years as ruler of Aquitaine had shown that his skill on the battlefield was not matched by his skill as a ruler and diplomat. It may be that the scheme promised an attractive diversion from the everyday problems of administration and negotiation with dissident nobles, and that the lure of new military glory weighed heavily in his mind in favour of the expedition. Details such as the problems of obtaining the promised payments were a secondary question. From the outset, however, there was a degree of distrust between the prince and the ousted king of Castile.

Recruiting men for the army was not difficult: late in the proceedings, Froissart says, the prince of Wales tried to reduce the contingent to be provided by the Gascon lord of Albret, a noted leader of the companies, only to be told that these men had forgone opportunities for lucrative work elsewhere, and must be included. Under a leader of the prince's calibre, there were likely to be good opportunities for ransoms and other profits of war, and the largely mercenary army was quickly assembled. The core was the knights of the prince's household together with a contingent under John of Gaunt, who sailed from England to Cherbourg in December 1366 and marched down the west coast of

France, gathering on the way a force of Breton and English mercenaries recruited by Robert Knolles, another leader of the free companies. The bulk of the army was Gascon, with two or three other groups centred on commanders who had been freebooters in Brittany and eastern France such as John Cresswell and Robert Briquet. Auberchicourt returned to Gascony in early December with the other English members of the Great Company under the leadership of John Chandos to join the prince's army.[69] Only a handful of Castilians were present when the army marched from Dax at the foot of the Pyrenees at the end of January 1367.

Meanwhile, Henry of Trastamara, who had obtained the backing of Pere IV of Aragon, had also signed a treaty of alliance with Charles of Navarre, who was anxious to insure himself against the possibility of Henry's victory. This was a serious mistake, as Charles was notorious for duplicity, and Henry believed that he had genuinely achieved a diplomatic success. The king of Aragon thought the same, and even supposed that the prince of Wales had cancelled his plans because of this development.[70] In confident mood, Henry released du Guesclin and Calveley from his service, and allowed them to withdraw from Castile. But the prince, far from cancelling his plans, took advantage of his opponent's mistake, and promptly instructed Calveley – who had disobeyed specific instructions when he took Henry's side, and was probably anxious to make good his position – to invade Navarre immediately. This drove Charles to hasten to Gascony and reaffirm his commitment to the prince.

The journey into Spain was arduous, across the famous pass of Roncesvalles where, so the epic legend had it, Roland had lost his life fighting off an attack on the rearguard of Charlemagne's army. It was a daring move to take troops over the mountains in the winter snows; Henry's belief that the expedition would be abandoned offered the possibility of a tactical surprise which was too good an opportunity to miss. When the news of the prince's arrival in Navarre reached the Castilian capital, Burgos, there was indeed consternation, and a number of minor rebellions in favour of Pedro broke out. Henry was able to get word to du Guesclin, and to balance Calveley's defection to the prince's side by retaining his erstwhile French colleague. He set up his headquarters at Santo Domingo, near the border with Navarre, while the prince of Wales advanced through Navarre to the capital, Pamplona. Here he sent out a reconnaissance party under Thomas Felton, including Hugh Stafford and Thomas Ufford,[71] who were able to cross into Castile and meet supporters of Pedro at Logroño, which had never surrendered to Henry. They told him that the usurper's army was thirty miles to the west, and that his movements indicated that he was working on the assumption that the prince would cross the river Ebro into Castilian territory at Logroño; given that the city was in friendly hands, this was the obvious route. But the prince chose instead to take a more difficult and unexpected route, through the mountains to Salvatierra, entering Castile further to the north. If he had been able to do so quickly, he would have achieved a considerable tactical advantage, but the route proved harder than expected, and the army was short of provisions as it made its way through the difficult terrain. Six days' rest at Salvatierra were needed before the prince could move forward again, and the element of surprise was lost.

At this point there was a serious disagreement between Henry's Spanish advisers and their French allies. Du Guesclin and Audrehem argued strongly that all that was required was to guard the passes on the Salvatierra road that led to Miranda in Castile, and the prince's army would be so deprived of provisions that it would have to withdraw. Henry, on the other hand, instinctively wished to fight: his reputation as a chivalrous and heroic leader as against Pedro's calculating and cold approach was at stake, and furthermore there was news of increasing defections by his supporters now that the legitimate king was back in the region. But at first he heeded the advice he was given, which had been backed up by a letter from Charles V cautioning him against committing himself to a battle. Henry moved forward so that he was in a position to harry the English, particularly their foraging parties, using the light cavalry which were a Castilian speciality.

His success in doing this encouraged him to attempt a more serious action. Don Tello, Henry's second in command, and Audrehem were sent to make a dawn raid on the English encampment. Don Tello found Hugh Calveley's men just as they were getting up, and many of them were killed in their beds; their baggage train was badly damaged. Don Tello then attacked the encampment of the vanguard, but John of Gaunt, alerted by the noise of the attack on Calveley, gathered his forces in battle order and summoned help from the prince; the raiders were quickly driven off. Audrehem attacked an outpost manned by William

Felton on a nearby hill, some 400 men at arms and archers, including squires from the prince's household. Felton was killed, with many of his men, and the rest taken prisoner, after a fierce resistance: they were finally overcome by a combination of dismounted knights and cavalry, the tactic which had failed at Poitiers. Here, however, there were only a handful of archers to deal with the cavalry. It seems as if the prince of Wales had forgotten the standard precaution of keeping an adequate watch at night, perhaps because he did not think that an enemy assault was likely. And he also assumed that the whole enemy army was about to attack, and so did not immediately go to the help of Felton and his men.

The prince of Wales now retreated into Navarre, in order to take the alternative road into Castile by way of Logroño; the countryside was more welcoming, and forage would be easier to find, but the march back through the mountains was harsh, and Walter of Peterborough, one of Edward's clerks, describes in his history of the expedition how he spent the night sleeping in a small copse in the bitter cold. On 1 April the army at last reached Logroño and crossed the river Ebro. At this point the prince replied to a formal challenge to battle which Henry had sent a month before, by calling on him to give up the throne which he had usurped. Henry replied in an openly insulting and angry tone, accusing the prince of being much attached to vainglory (a comment not entirely wide of the mark) and suggesting that two or three knights from either side should choose a suitable battlefield. The prince curtly dismissed the idea.

The next day the prince of Wales advanced to Navarrete, a small fortress nearby, which Thomas Felton had reconnoitred the previous month. This was no longer the terrain for guerrilla warfare, and Henry was in any case more inclined to take up the challenge of a battle than to sit out a long campaign of attrition. The defections were continuing, and he and his council felt it was imperative to strike quickly. Henry had established a defensive position along the bank of a small tributary which fed the river at Najéra, and the prince's scouts had made him aware of this. The English were not prepared to attempt a frontal attack, so just before dawn they set out on a track which was concealed from the Castilians, leading behind a ridge which rose some 600 feet high to the north. Henry's scouts failed to find the prince's men, and their appearance from the north-east took the Castilians entirely by surprise.

They quickly attempted to realign their formation, but the defensive advantage had been lost.

The vanguard of Henry's army was largely made up of experienced troops under two war-hardened commanders, du Guesclin and Audrehem. But at both Crécy and Poitiers, the best commanders had been kept in the centre, where they could direct tactics. Here the two French knights were subordinate to Henry himself, and had little chance of influencing the course of the battle except as fighting men. The elite of the Castilian knights were also in the vanguard, among them the knights of the Sash, whose banner was carried by Pero López de Ayala, who later included an account of the battle in his *Chronicle of King Pedro*. They fought dismounted, since they had expected to be holding a defensive position. Henry commanded the central division, and there were two troops of light cavalry on the wings. The Castilian army seems to have lacked crossbowmen and archers.

Against them were ranged a force equal or possibly larger in size. The vanguard was commanded by John Chandos and John of Gaunt, with a large body of archers. The prince of Wales was in the next division, where the Castilians were placed for fear of possible defections; there were also Navarrese troops and Gascons under the command of Jean de Grailly, captal de Buch, and the lord of Albret. All these were dismounted; in the rear was a mounted division under Jaime of Majorca, Hugh Calveley and Jean d'Armagnac. This could be used as a highly mobile squadron if an encircling movement, as at Crécy and Poitiers, was called for.

The first defections occurred before the battle started. It was a bad omen for Henry of Trastamara, even though the group of light horse which changed sides was small. The actual fighting began with an English attack, John of Gaunt's men advancing with shortened spears shouting 'Guyenne, St George', to engage with du Guesclin's vanguard who answered with their war cry 'Castile, Santiago'. The hand-to-hand fighting was indecisive, and the prince of Wales engaged his main battalion, the centre of which was to support John of Gaunt. Two detachments were sent to deal with Don Tello and the count of Denia, who led the troops of light cavalry. However, on the approach of the English, all the light cavalry deserted, though the count of Denia himself entered the action and was captured fighting with the vanguard. The Castilian division was faced by the whole English army, and Henry called his main battalion forward. He himself rode into the thick of the fight, to the place where López de Ayala held the banner of the Order of the Sash. But very few of his men followed him into the fray, because the English clearly had the upper hand. Most of them fled, and the battle was effectively over. The English mounted knights pursued the fugitives, and many of the leaders were either killed or captured, mainly along the banks of the river Ebro as they attempted to cross. But Henry himself managed to escape.

The tally of captives was impressive, and included many of Henry's leading supporters, his brother among them. More important to the English was the capture of both du Guesclin and Audrehem, both familiar to the prince of Wales since they had previously been in English hands. Du Guesclin had been captured at Auray in 1364 by John Chandos's men, but had paid his ransom; Audrehem, on the other hand, still owed money to the prince for his ransom after Poitiers eleven years earlier. Worse, he had sworn not to fight against the prince until the ransom had been paid in full. The prince angrily reminded him of this, and is said to have threatened him with execution as a traitor.[72] Audrehem stood his ground, and pointed out that he was not fighting the prince, but Pedro, and both he and the prince were merely captains under the command of the Castilian rivals – both mercenaries, in effect. The prince pardoned him, though he was not forgiven the ransom due.

The victory was due to the prince of Wales's skill in manoeuvring his army rapidly in response to a changing situation: if his attempt to march into Castile by an unexpected route failed, the repositioning of his men at Nájera unseen by the enemy was a great success. Once the actual fighting began, his success was at least partly due to the defections from Henry of Trastamara's army. The failure of the usurper's division to engage with the enemy was very similar to the failure of the French second division to move forward at Poitiers. The tight-knit English command in the vanguard, combined with the use of archers, meant that the fighting was already strongly in their favour by the time enemy reinforcements came into play, and any hesitation that those reinforcements may have had – at Poitiers, the removal of the king's sons from the field, at Nájera the uncertain loyalty to the recently crowned Henry – was at once magnified. Morale once again was critical, and ultimately morale depended on loyalty, not only to comrades, but to those leading the army.

The aftermath of the battle was disastrous for the prince, both finan-
cially and personally. It rapidly became plain that Pedro could not meet
the costs of the campaign, which were almost as large as the ransom
paid by King John of France, because Castile was not a rich country,
and any attempt to raise such a sum would have simply alienated his
already dissatisfied subjects. The prince of Wales lingered in Castile in
the hope that his presence might pressure Pedro into action, but only a
fraction of the total due was ever paid: the most tangible part of it was
a great balas ruby[73] which still adorns the imperial state crown of England. Distrust quickly set in, and even grants of land were subtly
blocked: the prince was told firmly by the Basques that Vizcaya was not
Pedro's to give away, since they chose their own rulers, which was
indeed strictly true. At the end of August, the prince gave up and
returned to Gascony. By then he had contracted the unexplained mal-
ady which was to recur for the rest of his life, and to lead to his early
death. Military might had failed to outweigh French diplomacy, the
more so since Henry of Trastamara returned two years later, defeated
Pedro at the battle of Montiel, lured him to his tent afterwards, and
murdered him in cold blood with the connivance of Olivier Mauny,
Walter Mauny's cousin, and Bertrand du Guesclin. It was not the end of
English involvement in Spain: John of Gaunt married Pedro's daughter
Constanza in 1371, two years after her father's death, and became the
claimant to the throne of Castile, a position he maintained for the next
sixteen years. His efforts to establish himself in Castile were to end in
humiliation after a disastrous attempt to invade his kingdom with Por-
tuguese help in 1387. Henry of Trastamara's son Juan was recognized
as king in return for a payment to Gaunt which once again nearly bankrupted the kingdom.

An enduring victory in Castile would have had a considerable effect
on the war between France and England, as Castilian ships continued to
pose a serious threat to English shipping, and were responsible for the
critical defeat of the English fleet at La Rochelle in 1372, in which the
ships commanded by John Hastings, who had become a companion of
the Garter three years earlier, were trapped among the sandbanks of the
harbour entrance and overwhelmed. The Spaniards had no time for
chivalrous niceties, and Hastings was tied up like a dog on a leash in a
Spanish prison for the next two years, and died soon after he was
released. Even when there was peace in France, the Castilians were not

bound by it: three years later, they destroyed thirty-nine English merchant vessels off La Rochelle, seriously weakening the English naval resources, and the following summer they participated in the galley fleet that ravaged the south coast of England.

Ultimately, the leadership of the founding knights of the Company of the Garter was at its best on the battlefield. Their skills, which had evolved in the wars against the Scots, were essentially those of an attacking army in hostile territory, with the ability to win battles in difficult circumstances; but they were invaders, not conquerors. Both the logistics and the temperament for successful conquest were lacking; Edward III's own ability to weld together the lords of England into a loyal and effective high command was not shared by the prince, whose rule in Aquitaine was more of a precursor of his son's reign in England than a parallel to his father's. Haughty and insensitive to the concerns and local pride of the Gascon lords, his splendid court at Bordeaux failed to foster friendship and loyalty in the way that the festivities of Edward and Philippa had succeeded in doing. Yet England, regarded as almost irrelevant in terms of military power when Edward came to the throne, had enjoyed twenty years when its armies were the most consistent and most feared in Europe; and that triumph was due in large part to the companions of the Garter.

14

The Most Noble Order of the Garter

The closing decades of the fourteenth century saw a sharp decline in the military fortunes of the English in France, and the days of Edward III began to seem like a golden past, with the first companions of the Garter as heroic figures. This coincided with an increasing emphasis on knightly honour, of which Geoffroy de Charny was one of the first exponents, and which permeates the pages of Jean Froissart; his prologue declares his intention to record past deeds so that they can be 'viewed and known' now and in the future. Froissart's various introductions to the different versions of his work all return to the theme of great exploits and the glory to be gained from them.

The Company of the Garter at Edward III's death consisted of a core of members of the royal family by birth, a number of descendants of the original founders, knights chosen from the current military commanders (among them a group of courtiers including the chamberlain, William Latimer) and two men who held lands in both France and England, both sons-in-law of the late king. Clause 19 of the statutes provided that at an election each knight present 'shall nominate nine qualified persons, whom he shall believe to be free from all ignominy or shame, who shall be subjects of the sovereign of the order or others, foreigners not subject to him but who yet shall not favour or uphold any party opposed to the said sovereign'. Men like Walter Mauny, owning great estates in England and Hainault, would not have been troubled by this stipulation. But any foreigners and those who held lands from the king of France or one of his allies in the Low Countries could be in danger of a conflict of loyalties. There was no specific clause requiring allegiance to the king of England in the statutes of the Garter, and, during the period of English military ascendance, this requirement not to 'favour or uphold' the enemy had not been an issue.

But the increasing success of the French changed this. Within four months of Edward III's death, Enguerrand de Coucy, earl of Bedford and lord of Coucy, married to Edward's daughter Isabella, resigned from the Company of the Garter. He sent a letter to Richard II, which was carefully endorsed by one of the royal clerks to the effect that it was delivered by Jean Pieres to the king at Hatton Grange near Hounslow on 30 October 1377, and that Jean Pieres spoke in English. In it, Coucy declares that, since war has been renewed between his 'natural and sovereign lord the king of France' and the king of England, he feels obliged to resign from 'the company and order of the Garter' to which his father-in-law Edward III had appointed him.[1]

In more ways than one, this letter marks the end of the original company which Edward founded. In this case, the prospect of the coming war makes Coucy fear that he will be required to fight against Richard II, a fellow-companion of the Garter, which is forbidden by an article in the statutes: he is anticipating a position where he will be disqualified from the company. There is a similar concern in the dealings of Eustace d'Auberchicourt with Charles of Navarre, where he specifies in his contract that he shall not be required to fight against Edward III because he is his liege lord.[2]

Coucy's letter is the first occasion I can trace where the company is called an 'order'. Religious orders of knighthood were a familiar concept, and the alternative title is partly a reflection of the past history of groups of knights: it was easy to apply it to the Garter company, which had a strong religious element through its connection to the College of St George. However, it also reflects a parallel development of secular orders of knighthood, which, like the military religious orders, had statutes which prescribed elaborate rules for the knights' conduct and usually an oath of allegiance to the sovereign or prince. In contrast to these formal orders, we have seen that these fraternities, societies and companies of knights were usually more loosely regulated, and often very short-lived. Dozens of ephemeral knightly groups, usually called 'societies', appeared and disappeared in Germany during the late fourteenth and fifteenth centuries.

The first society of knights to call itself specifically an 'order' was that of the Sash in Spain, which did include an oath of loyalty to the sovereign and an elaborate set of rules. It stands alone in the period up to 1377, since the other early knightly organizations which call themselves 'orders' had a different purpose. The Order of the Collar founded by Amadeus of Savoy in 1364 and the shadowy Order of the Sword founded by Peter I of Cyprus in about 1347 were both intended to form the core of a crusading army, and are therefore not secular orders in the usual sense.

The next purely knightly society to be called an order is the Order of the Ship, established at Naples in 1381 by Charles of Durazzo, successor to Louis of Taranto. The original statutes survive in two copies evidently made for individual knights in the brief four-year existence of the order. It is specifically called an 'order of knighthood', the earliest instance of the usage in connection with a royal foundation of this kind, in the prologue to the statutes; but in the statutes themselves it is still called a 'company'.[3] Nine founder knights were named in the statutes, which are highly elaborate, and include detailed ceremonials for the admission of new members and for the holding of chapters of the order. The spiritual obligations of the companions are specified, and there are provisions for masses for deceased companions. However, the companions also undertook secular obligations to the prince, ranging from loyalty to the avenging of any offence against him and revealing anything which might tend to his harm or dishonour. An annual court was to be held at which such matters were to be discussed, and at which the companions' adventures during the year were to be recounted and set down in writing. The Order of the Ship never seems to have met after the founding ceremony and Charles was murdered in Hungary in 1386 shortly after he won that kingdom. Its regulations, and particularly those regarding the annual court, foreshadow those of the Order of the Golden Fleece.

By the end of the fourteenth century, therefore, there had been a number of attempts to set up confraternities, companies and even orders of knighthood, but none of them had survived for long, with the sole exception of the Company of the Garter. The reasons were diverse, but they were usually linked to the fate of the sovereign or prince who founded them. The Company of the Garter had survived into the next generation, but in 1399, with the deposition of Richard II, it might well have gone the way of the other institutions. However, partly because it had an established reputation and was seen as part of the English kingship, and partly because of the personal connections of Henry IV,

Richard's nemesis, the Garter was not suppressed: instead, it led the way for subsequent knightly orders, and showed how a relatively informal company could evolve into an institution with proper officers and records.

Henry IV was Edward III's grandson, and also grandson of his closest friend and cousin, Henry of Grosmont, who had played a large part in the formation of the Company of the Garter. Furthermore, he seems to have deliberately emulated his namesake in knightly exploits, going on crusade in Prussia in 1391, forty years after Henry of Grosmont. He himself had been made a knight of the company at the same time as Richard II, at the beginning of April 1377, two months before Edward III died. The complex story of Henry's overthrow of Richard is not our present subject. Suffice to say that Henry badly needed to show himself as a legitimate ruler, as, even if Richard freely resigned, Henry was not the nearest heir to the throne. His cousin, Edmund earl of March, was senior in descent from Edward III; and Henry's claim was distinctly dubious. By reinforcing the status of the Company of the Garter, with which he had such strong connections, he was also reinforcing, in a small way, his legitimacy as king. Furthermore, Richard had appointed his boon companions, 'new men', to the company, whereas Henry's supporters were the old aristocracy, in many cases descendants of the original Garter knights.

At Richard's accession, the companions of the order were still largely Edward's military commanders; even courtiers like the unpopular lord chamberlain, William Latimer, and the group associated with him, Richard Pembridge, Ralph Neville and Alan Buxhull, had reasonably distinguished careers as fighting men. Others were the sons of earlier holders, such as the younger Thomas Beauchamp and William Ufford, but again the military tradition was strong, and the household knights still provided the leaders of the English armies as well as most of the companions of the Garter. During Richard's minority, the new companions were for the most part men from his father's household. Richard seems to have been at Windsor quite frequently for St George's Day.[4] However, once he came to power in 1381, the Garter was one of the favours he bestowed on his close friends, the group of courtiers who came to represent everything that the older generation of nobles detested: Robert de Vere and Thomas Mowbray were his contemporaries and had very little military experience when they were elected in

1383-4. De Vere was the most notorious of Richard's favourites, and was impeached for treason when the lords had the upper hand over the king in 1387-8; he became the first Garter knight to be expelled from the company. Richard Fitzalan, son of the earl of the same name and elected immediately after de Vere, was one of these lords, and was charged with treason by the vengeful king ten years later. This was all of a piece with Richard's failure to understand the unspoken principle behind the Company of the Garter: that it represented the king in harmony with his great lords, working towards a common purpose. It was partly Richard's own character which brought about these dissensions, the other element being the withdrawal from the war with France, the common purpose which had until then brought the knights together.

The turbulence of Richard's last years meant that, when Henry IV became king, there were a large number of vacancies, partly due to the execution of four earls by the mob in the course of the so-called 'earls' rebellion' in January 1400. Ten new companions were therefore chosen within the first year of his reign: five of these were Henry's sons and brother-in-law, and among the others were one duke and three earls. Traditional appointments, such as that of the veteran campaigner Thomas Erpingham in 1401, continued to be made.

The real change under the new reign was the approach to the administration of the company. Apart from the activities of the College of St George relating to the Company of the Garter, largely to do with the St George's Day feast, no records from Windsor for the company from the fourteenth century survive, and it is fairly clear that even when Henry IV came to the throne there was a distinct lack of systematic documentation. It is just after his accession that the Windsor tables, evidently displayed in the Garter chapel or the knights' chapter house, were drawn up by John Page, which implies a determined attempt to record the company's past history.[5] The earliest records of chapter meetings and elections to survive date from the reign of Henry V; the 'Black Book' of the Garter compiled in the mid-sixteenth century notes for the reigns of Edward III and Richard II that there is nothing on record except items gleaned from other sources.

The company itself was evolving and slowly changing in character. Although tournaments had never been part of the feast of St George, the presence of so many knights famed for their skill in the lists among its members seems to have led to the idea that there was a link between the company and jousting. However, the first occasion on which we can document such a connection is at the Smithfield jousts of May 1390.[6] If only Geoffrey Chaucer, who was responsible for the building of the scaffolds for the onlookers, had put pen to paper;[7] but there is only a single witness, the author of the *Brut* chronicle for the period, writing thirty years later, who claims that the knights defending the lists in the king's name were the twenty-four knights of the Garter. He was perhaps confused into thinking this was a Garter festival because, at the end of the celebrations, Richard made the count of Ostrevant a knight of the Garter; the duke of Guelders may have been appointed at the same time.[8] These have sometimes been treated as the first elections of foreigners to the company for diplomatic reasons; in fact, like Jean IV of Brittany, Edward's son-in-law, they were relatives of the royal family. Guelders was Richard's second cousin through his great-aunt Eleanor, and William of Ostrevant was the son of the count of Holland and his second cousin once removed through his grandmother Philippa. However, their inclusion was probably more to do with their part in the jousts of St Inglevert, a celebrated tournament which had been held near Calais earlier in the year, and Richard's desire to outshine these with his Smithfield tournament.

The idea of the Garter as a company of knights who might be challenged as a group to a tournament makes its first documented appearance in 1408. In that year, Jean de Werchin, seneschal of Hainault, issued a general challenge to the Garter companions, couched in highly romantic terms, in which he recalled the deeds of the knights of the Round Table and Edward's foundation of the Garter, and challenged them, as successors to the knights of the Round Table, to meet him in single combat, on horseback and on foot, with lances, swords and axes. Since he was young and inexperienced, the companions of the Garter should look favourably on this knightly enterprise. Henry IV acknowledged that 'following the memory of the said order [of the Round Table] one of our predecessors as king ordained another order of knights which still exists and which is called the garter'; however, he politely pointed out that this one-sided challenge was 'very strange with regard to the said order [of the Garter], because we never read in the old histories of the round table that all the knights of that order went out to fight against one single foreign knight', and as sovereign of the order refused his request.[9] Instead, he offered John Cornwall as representative of the order; the affair dragged on, and it is not even clear whether the proposed encounter took place, although Werchin was granted a safe conduct in February 1410 to come to England with a large company of men. This seems to be the only example of a challenge to the knights of the Garter all together, and the surprise expressed by Henry IV is strong evidence that the company never regarded itself as a tourneying society.

The letter also tells us that, by 1408, the erroneous connection made by Froissart between Edward III's Arthurian Round Table and the Garter was widely accepted. The Round Table was never represented as an *order* of knights in any accepted sense of the word, and even Thomas Malory in the late fifteenth century does not depict it as such: when Arthur learns of Lancelot's rebellion at the end of *Le Morte Darthur*, he laments that he has 'lost the fairest fellowship of noble knights that ever a Christian king held together', not that the order that he has created has been broken apart.

The honorific element in Garter appointments, which began with Richard's appointment of de Vere and Mowbray, comes into play under Henry V. Although the original companions seem to have been chosen on the basis of their personal relationship to Edward III and the prince of Wales, they could for the most part be deemed to have merited their membership of the company by their military careers; and those of whom we know little probably qualified in this respect as well. When de Vere and Mowbray were elected, they had done nothing to merit election, and their membership therefore honoured them rather than rewarded them for past actions. This honorific element also applies in a different way with the election of Sigismund emperor of Germany in 1416, followed by that of Philip the Good of Burgundy in 1422. These were the first of a series of elections of foreign princes which gathered pace under Henry VI, and which spread the fame of the Garter throughout Europe. A dozen princes were members of the order during his reign, and a further nine were elected by Edward IV. Frequently, the election was a kind of reciprocal exchange of honours, and the English kings gathered the insignia of the corresponding foreign orders.

The reputation of the Garter in the later fourteenth and early fifteenth centuries outside the company itself and the court is hard to trace. In about 1400, Walter of Bibbesworth's little Anglo-French glossary was translated into English verse, and the author knew so little about 'garters' that he said rather vaguely 'from those men of the garters came the usage of the garters', i.e. garters were invented for the Company of the Garter.[10] There are no specific literary mentions of the Company of the Garter, even though Geoffrey Chaucer was clerk of the works at Windsor and responsible, however indirectly – he may have worked through a deputy – for the repair of St George's chapel: it was a separate and specific commission, and not a sinecure.[11] One great literary work has an apparent Garter connection, but the link is elusive. At the end of the unique manuscript of *Sir Gawain and the Green Knight*, the Garter motto has been written, as if to make this a comment on the poem itself. Scholars are still in two minds as to when the motto was written, but, even if it was not the work of the original scribe, it could be to do with ownership of the manuscript, and attempts have been made to link it to specific Garter knights, even to Henry of Grosmont, but these must remain speculative.[12] Alternatively, the writer may have felt that the content of the poem could reflect in some way on the Company of the Garter, and the more fantastic theories of this kind try to use it to authenticate the fifteenth-century stories of the foundation of the Garter and to link the 'shame' in the motto to the supposed rape of the countess of Salisbury by Edward III. It is a pity that we cannot define a link between the greatest knightly poem in English and what later came to be seen as the greatest English knightly institution. All we can say is that, if it is not an ownership inscription, it must date from a time when the memory of Edward's original confraternity was starting to fade, and it was beginning to be reinterpreted as a society with different ideals; but this would mean dating the inscription to the second quarter of the fifteenth century or later.

The emergence of the Garter as a 'knightly order' takes place in the reign of Henry V. In 1414, when the first St George's Day feast under the new king was held, Henry was much concerned with the threat posed by the Lollard heresy to the authority of the crown. Sir John Oldcastle, a leading Lollard, had rebelled in January, and, at the parliament at Leicester at the end of April, the chancellor, Henry Beaufort, who as bishop of Winchester was prelate of the Company of the Garter, made an impassioned attack on the Lollards. Probably to coincide with the Garter feast on 23 April, the poet Thomas Hoccleve addressed two poems to the king and the 'most honourable company of the Garter'.[13]

Men call them 'the flower of chivalry', but his appeal is not for any secular knightly prowess. Instead he praises Henry as the true upholder of the faith, and 'warrior against heresy's bitter gall', and asks that he should ban the kind of open discussion of matters of faith beloved of the Lollards. The 'company of the Garter' are by implication suitable champions to support such action, and the second poem speaks to them directly: their motto says 'that they are enemies of shame' – a free interpretation of the Garter motto – and 'you, my lords ... shall quench all this nuisance', a deed of high prowess, and suited to men 'of St George's livery'. He concludes with an appeal to both king and lords of the Garter to remember the Trinity, whose virtue gives them heart and strength 'in faithful unity'.

It is a surprising poem, until we remember Henry V's reputation as a devout monarch, and his opposition to the Lollards. Hoccleve seems to hope that the Garter knights, as a religious confraternity, might be persuaded to enlarge their commemorative role to the active defence of religion, and to the suppression of heresy. As one of the four clerks in the office of the privy seal and therefore a senior member of the administration, he was aware of Henry's strong views on heresy as a threat to the authority of the crown.[14] He certainly knew some of the Garter knights, but whether he is appealing to them as the king's closest companions or was aware of their personal views we cannot tell.

It is possible that Henry's undoubted enthusiasm for the Garter after Agincourt might have made it more rather than less of a religious institution, but he died before the renewal of the Company of the Garter was complete. Henry IV had called the Company of the Garter an 'order' in his response to the challenge from Jean de Werchin in 1408. Nonetheless, it was under Henry V that the company was formally transformed into an order, not perhaps as a deliberate act, but by a process of evolution. Henry added a number of new clauses to the statutes, and may have revised others; the earliest statutes of the company that we possess date from his reign. In 1415, at the trial of Henry, Lord Scrope, for treason, he is described as 'a knight of that distinguished and excellent knightly order of the Garter'.[15] A letter survives in which, the king being absent in France, his deputy requests one of the Garter knights to have masses said for two recently deceased fellow-companions. This probably dates from the autumn of 1420: Walter Hungerford and Lewis Robessart died in October and November of that year. In it, the writer speaks of 'the knightly order of Saint George the martyr of the company of the Garter', a designation which reconciles the new idea of the Garter as a knightly order with that of the original company.[16]

It was Henry who created the office of Garter king at arms, and installed his own personal herald, William Bruges, as its first holder. He had been appointed by letters patent from Richard II as Chester Herald in 1398 as part of the administration of his new principality of Chester. His father, Richard Bruges, had been Lancaster Herald, and William was the personal herald of Henry of Derby, before he became Henry V; he also held the title of Aquitaine king of arms. William's appointment in 1398 was one of the first to be made on a formal legal basis. He was appointed Garter king at arms between May 1417, when he is still referred to as Guyenne king of arms, and September 1417, when he is named as Garter king at arms for the first time.* This coincided with general regulations for the heralds of England.

Bruges' greatest work was the re-creation of the Company of the Garter to reflect the changing times. The old title of 'company' survived in the statutes, but it was now commonly referred to as an order. Bruges created two armorial records of the knights. One was a stained-glass window at Stamford in Lincolnshire, where he was buried in 1450; sadly, this is lost, but seventeenth-century drawings survive. The other is his Garter Book, which displays portraits of the knights in their robes and with their arms, the finest of the early armorials which gradually replaced the rolls of arms. These were the result of Bruges' considerable activity in tracing the history of the companions from the foundation, much of which seems to have been lost or forgotten. It was he who appears to have been responsible for the making of missing stall plates in the period after 1420. There are renewed references to provision for record-keeping and the updating of the tables in the accounts of the College of St George; we can only surmise that the records of the company had been kept by one of the clerks of the college, as a secondary duty. Now the organization and administration of the company were put in the hands of the company's own officer, a dramatic departure from earlier practice.

The appointment of Bruges, taken with the other reforms, was part of a movement towards the modern secular orders of knighthood, which

---

* His present-day successor ranks as the senior member of the College of Arms.

focus on honour rather than prowess, and in which heralds play a prominent part. Around 1400, the French heralds were formally organized, possibly the inspiration for the English College of Arms established in 1420. Until this point, there is very little evidence of a permanent official role for heralds, and the evolution of the 'king at arms' is even more obscure. What the early records reveal is that 'herald' in the thirteenth and fourteenth centuries means little more than a man expert in heraldic identification, who may well earn his living as a minstrel[17] or musician, or even as a barber.[18] The original role of these experts, back in the twelfth century, had been to do with tournaments, and the identification of knights' coats of arms as they fought in the confusion of the *mêlée*. They seem to have been commentators, announcing the names of the contestants to the audience, and perhaps adding comments, but they had no official status.

There is plenty of evidence that the public announcers at twelfth-century tournaments also doubled as minstrels and entertainers; in the biography of William Marshal, who rose to fame in the early thirteenth century through his prowess in tournaments, the waiting crowd at a tournament was entertained by 'a singer who was a new herald of arms', implying that there was some kind of recognition of his expertise in identifying the participants. Other references in the Marshal's biography suggest that heralds, although they might also be minstrels, did have a distinct function: we certainly find them as messengers at an early date. A satirical poem by Bertran de Born describes Eleanor of Aquitaine as sending a tax receipt on the torn-up tabard of a 'king of arms'; this is a joking reference, and cannot really be taken as evidence for such an official in her household. The point was that the queen's receipt was worthless, as if it had been written on any scrap of material to hand, and that it did not save the taxpayer from the knives of his creditors.[19] If such officials had existed, we would expect to meet them again in the succeeding years; but there is no sign of anything resembling an officially appointed herald for another two centuries.

There is, however, good evidence for kings of heralds. At the English court between 1272 and 1307, we have the names of at least fifteen possible kings of heralds. Typically, they appear to be in charge of a group of minstrels, or of all the minstrels at a particular occasion; 'king Baisescu' and 'king Caupeny' share out royal gifts between the minstrels at the great feast for the knighting of Edward II when he was prince of

Wales, in 1306. Such men are also called heralds, yet they are definitely minstrels, because in the same year 'king Caupenny' is paid with other minstrels 'for performing plays and making their minstrelsies in the presence of the Queen'.[20] 'Caupenny' was from Scotland, and is given the title 'king Caupenny of Scotland': we also hear of the 'king of Champagne', the leader of the minstrels from Champagne.[21] Interestingly, a king of heralds is paid for making a proclamation about the prohibition of tournaments in England at Northampton on Christmas Day 1300, underlining the idea that one of their functions was as public criers.[22] And from 1282 to 1320, two 'kings of heralds' appear on the royal payroll: Robert Little and Nicholas Morel. Andrew Norrois, apparently Nicholas Morel's successor, drew war wages in 1311–12, and was still at court in 1338.[23] They received summer and winter liveries with the rest of the court servants, presumably with a permanent responsibility for the minstrels at court. They were clearly minstrels themselves, as Robert is paid for 'making his minstrelsy' on New Year's Day 1303, and is probably the same as 'Robert the king's trumpeter' on the Scottish campaign of 1301.

There are traces of a tradition of heraldic titles which may stretch back into the late twelfth century. Bruiant appears as a herald in the Marshal's biography, in a poem about the tournament at Chauvency in 1285, and again in the accounts of Edward II; and 'bruyant' means loud or noisy: in modern French, 'un homme bruyant' is a loud talker. This, and the comment – again from the Marshal's biography – that knights have to have three or four heralds in tow, seems to suggest that heralds acted as cheerleaders. The Marshal himself was accused of creating a false reputation by having a certain Henry le Norrois with him, who cried 'God is with the Marshal' whenever he appeared in the lists.[24] It is possible that the name Norrois, like Bruiant, became a traditional one among heralds, and may have been handed down to Andrew Norrois a century later. His name is believed to be the origin of today's Norroy Herald at the College of Arms.[25]

Kings of arms are still grouped with minstrels in the statute regulating tournaments issued by Edward I in 1292, the *Statuta armorum*;[26] and it was only gradually, during the following century, that they began to acquire authority in questions of coats of arms. Visual collections of coats of arms began in the 1230s, and include the famous shields in Matthew Paris's great chronicle in the 1250s; the first known roll of arms, Glover's Roll, dates from about 1255. Many rolls of arms are clearly intended as a record of knights' arms which is to be used to identify shields, and the earliest examples – such as Glover's Roll – often survive only in copies, the originals presumably having been worn out with use. It is at the end of the thirteenth century that we find these rolls of arms being created as records of the knights present at a given military event: after the battle of Falkirk in 1298, a roll was created recording 'the great lords with banners who king Edward the first since the conquest had with him in Scotland in the twenty-sixth year of his reign at the battle of Falkirk on St Mary Magdalene's day'. Similar documents exist for the siege of Caerlaverock near Dumfries in 1300, for an expedition into Galloway in the same year, and the siege of Stirling in 1304. Only the Caerlaverock roll survives in the original, so we cannot tell whether these were all the work of the same herald travelling with the army or not.[27]

There is no doubt, however, that this is firm evidence that men with heraldic knowledge were now part of the real military world, as opposed to figures in the mock warfare of the tournament. But they were not employed as professional heralds, with a definite office: they were freelances who had other parts to play in the army. They probably performed multiple roles, like Robert Little at the court of Edward II. Little was certainly in Scotland in the year following Caerlaverock as one of the royal trumpeters. The correct identification of banners could be critical; Simon de Montfort's lookout (who doubled as his barber) wrongly identified the enemy's banners as those of Montfort's men at the battle of Evesham in 1265, with disastrous consequences.[28] Rolls of arms would help to avoid such errors, and it is possible that they were shown to the knights so that they could identify their friends in battle. But they are unlikely to have been the work of specialists whose sole job was to deal with heraldic matters: they are much more akin to the paintings done by the friar Walter atte More in the course of his diplomatic mission to Hungary in 1346. Walter atte More was not a herald, but he recognized the usefulness of the heraldic information and either painted it himself or, more probably, commissioned someone else to do it.

The status of the heralds is still unclear by the beginning of Edward III's reign. There are payments to William Volaunt, king of heralds, in 1354.[29] Andrew Clarenceux is entitled herald and king of arms in a wardrobe account of 1334, in his capacity as leader of a group of minstrels playing to the king on the day the king of Scotland did homage.[30] John Musshon, herald, was in the service of the prince of Wales in 1353, and appears several times in the prince's household records.[31] John Suffolk, herald, was in the service of Robert Ufford, earl of Suffolk, from at least 1340 to after 1359; his is the only testimony from a herald in the records of the Court of Chivalry.[32] After 1350, an increasing number of personal heralds appear, and even the *routier* captains had their own pursuivants. Heralds were sent out by Edward in their traditional role as criers of public events in January 1344 to announce the great tournament at Windsor. The accounts of the count of Holland show heralds coming and going in the 1330s, from the king of Cyprus or conveying invitations from neighbouring princes.[33]

The scattered mentions, taken together, seem to indicate that it was in the later 1340s that heralds acquired a more distinguished status and a definite place in royal and baronial households, but they were still largely messengers, conveying information by letters from their masters or by word of mouth. As such, they enjoyed immunity from war, in the same way as men in holy orders, and this immunity seems to have been invariably respected in the fourteenth century. One of the earliest pieces of firm evidence of their role in warfare is a letter from Henry of Grosmont describing his raid into Normandy in 1356: heralds were sent on 8 July by John II to challenge him to a battle at Verneuil.[34] They are still most in evidence at feasts, as masters of ceremonies organizing the entertainments and controlling the possibly unruly performers. Edward increased the number of his heralds in the 1350s for the long series of Garter feasts in the latter part of his reign.[35]

When it comes to written records, such as the list of the dead after Crécy, such items were far more likely to be the work of clerks in the army's administration; the freelance heralds were called in to help with the identification of arms, and indeed there is no reason why the clerks themselves would not have had some knowledge of heraldry. Le Bel tells us that Reginald Cobham was told by the king to take with him 'a herald who knew arms' to seek out the dead French nobles at Crécy, implying that not all heralds were expert in the subject.[36] The critical evidence for the heralds' lack of official recognition as authorities on coats of arms in the mid-fourteenth century comes from the proceedings of the Court of Chivalry which we discussed earlier. The evidence, carefully and laboriously assembled both in the court itself and by commissioners sent to obtain statements from outside the capital, who spent a good deal of time and energy on the process, never once involves a herald. If the court's proceedings had been informal and oral, we might argue that the records merely failed to mention the heralds' evidence. However, it is absolutely clear that only the evidence of fellow-knights and sometimes of clergy of similar standing is admissible, the sole exception being that of the earl of Suffolk's herald mentioned above. Written records such as the rolls of arms are never referred to, though painted heraldry in tombs, churches and great houses is endlessly cited. The knights themselves sometimes recall their training in heraldry, as in the case of Robert Laton, giving evidence in the Court of Chivalry in 1386, who testified that his father taught him to write down in a schedule (probably meaning a roll) all the arms that he had learnt from his ancestors.[37] Another knight, however, does remember a herald announcing the decision in an earlier case in the Court of Chivalry, presided over by Henry of Grosmont, at Calais in 1347; but the man in question was acting as Grosmont's public crier, rather than as an expert in arms.

Towards the end of the fourteenth century, Froissart could call heralds 'rightly the investigators and reporters of such affairs, and I believe that their honour is such that they would not dare to lie'.[38] He places a herald at the centre of the scene which is effectively the opening of the Hundred Years War: the much-travelled Carlisle Herald returns to Edward III's court at Westminster in April 1338 after five years wandering abroad, coming post-haste with letters from the Anglophile lords of Gascony that war had broken out with the French in their region, which he supplements with an oral report.[39] I would argue that Froissart is re-creating the scene as he thought it should have happened, looking back from the 1370s; heralds had gained considerably in stature in the intervening forty years. It is a neat way of outlining the beginning of hostilities to his audience, by creating a scene with which they would have been familiar. His declaration that he had got much of his information from heralds is certainly true, but that does not mean – particularly in the first book of the chronicle – that every scene containing a herald is genuine. Froissart often succumbs to the temptation to create a vision of heralds and heroes, history seen through a technicolor prism of shining deeds and brilliant colours.

In England, the heralds probably acquired their formal authority over the question of entitlement to arms and to the regulation of their use as a result of the increasing reluctance of men of knightly status to take up arms in the last quarter of the fourteenth century. If men who claimed a coat of arms were no longer seen on campaign, the proceedings in the Court of Chivalry, based on the testimony of their fellow-knights, could not be used as a method of establishing such a claim. Instead of the memory of fellow-knights, records were needed and written documents: and in respect of the Company of the Garter itself, such records were sadly lacking, as we have seen. Henry IV started the work of re-creating the lists of knights and may have amended the statutes in respect of holding the feast on alternative dates if St George's Day clashed with other religious festivals.

There are traces of some kind of territorial authority over heralds and minstrels which go back into the thirteenth century, and, although this evidence poses as many questions as it solves, there does seem to have been some kind of loose organization, whether founded on royal authority or simply by a mutual guild of performers choosing a spokesman. All we have to go on are titles; apart from the kings of arms whose names seem to recur – as in the examples already quoted of Bruiant and Norrois – there are records naming a minstrel or herald as king of a region. The name Norrois ('of the north') might link to 'Peter king of the heralds beyond the Trent on the northern side', who appears in a deed of 1276, or to William Morley, king's minstrel, called 'Roi de North' in 1322. The wording of Peter's deed complicates the issue, as it includes an extraordinary clause specifying that he is paying his creditor for his debts 'owed to him from the beginning of the world down to March 18 1276': is it another minstrel's joke? The document itself looks real enough.[40]

What seems to have happened in the first quarter of the fifteenth century is that all these informal traditions of the heralds, as well as their scattered records, were gradually brought together into a regulated and organized framework. The old reliance on the oral tradition and memory of knights was replaced by visual and written records, and the celebration of deeds of arms moved from the minstrels and poets to the chroniclers, Jean le Bel, Froissart and Pero López de Ayala, who believed that they should be held in writing. These new full-time heralds, appointed officially by kings and princes, seem to have appeared first in Froissart's home territory of the Low Countries; at the very beginning of the fifteenth century we have Claes Heynenzoon, king of heralds of the Rhine, who had begun as herald of the duke of Guelders and was later herald to the duke of Bavaria.[41] His activities were wide-ranging, and he left us two splendid armorials, *The Book of Arms of Guelders* and *The Book of Arms of Bavaria*, as well as his *Lobdichten*, poetic portraits of the great knights of his time. These volumes, as well as the extensive depictions of arms by skilled artists, include historical texts, among them two chronicles. The arms are arranged systematically by rank, beginning with the German emperor and working through the kings of Europe, each with the arms of those who owed allegiance to him. And while he was employed by the duke of Guelders, he was responsible for buying heraldic flags when the duke sailed to England. In the first quarter of the fifteenth century, the herald was increasingly the representative of the person whose name he bore: his status moved from that of a freelance whose skills were rewarded with the occasional gift to someone who had a definite diplomatic, legal and armorial function.

The appointment of William Bruges marks the starting point of the process by which the Company of the Garter, whose original members were Edward III's friends and comrades in arms, became the Order of the Garter, a symbol of honour. It was part of a wider transformation of knightly life in the fifteenth century, seen at its most striking in the rituals and festivals of the Burgundian court. Edward's court may have had its splendour of dress and its myriad tournaments; but these were only marginally political, and organized ritual played relatively little part. Under Richard II, ceremonial became much more central, and the handful of tournaments in the 1380s and 1390s were not held because of the king's enthusiasm for the sport but to enhance his prestige. The appearance of the heralds in regular positions of authority marked the point at which knighthood was institutionalized and absorbed into court rituals and ceremonies, and the royal orders of knighthood began to flourish.[42] And the fifteenth century was the moment when the modern concept of honour came to the fore, replacing the old emphasis on prowess, which was to survive in the ideals of the gentleman.

Furthermore, the English triumphs came to an end with Nájera, and the deaths of Edward III, Edward prince of Wales and John II mark the end of an era when the English and French rulers saw knighthood as a military virtue and a key element in their armies. Charles V's eminently practical approach to the defence of France and the gradual erosion of English power were perhaps another reason why Froissart chooses to emphasize great deeds of knighthood. Such deeds, he implies, are no longer as frequent as they should be: his task is to encourage such feats of arms by describing those of the past. There is a lull in knightly festivals after 1360, and they do not reappear until the last decade of the century. When they do, after the truce of Leulinghem in 1389, they are international gatherings of a kind that had not been seen for a century. The famous jousts at St Inglevert in 1390 are the first occasion when numbers of English and French knights had appeared in the lists together for as long as men could remember, and Froissart dwells on them in loving detail. The challenges of men like Jean Werchin led to the *pas d'armes* of the fifteenth century, where single knights offered to appear at a specified place and defend it against all comers, and the roster of combatants was again international. The heroes of these international events sought, as their predecessors had done in Prussia, honour and fame for their knightly achievements. Honour as an individual replaced the allegiance to the monarch which was at the heart of the Company of the Garter; and membership of the sovereign's personal order of knighthood likewise depended on individual honour rather than companionship in arms.

In the 1360s, Giovanni Boccaccio wrote his great poem on the lives and deaths of great princes, translated seventy years later by John Lydgate, a monk at Bury St Edmunds. One of the princes included was King Arthur, and Boccaccio tells us that the knights of the Round Table had 'laws and ordinances' which they had to obey. These prove to be the general principles of knighthood found in earlier writers, transformed into a formal code; but the idea that there was 'an especial law' for the companions of the Round Table, and that they should 'relate all that they had done, whether to their honour or shame, to those who were charged with keeping the history of the Round Table', is very much a concept of Boccaccio's own day, close to the rules of the Order of the Ship in Naples. Lydgate calls these 'laws and ordinances' 'statutes' and talks of the order's 'register', both of which echo the arrangements of the Garter in the 1430s. By this time, the translation of the religious confraternity of the Company of the Garter into the Order of the Garter is complete, and it has itself become the model for the Arthurian Round

that she was fairer or more genteel than others. She has a rather flirtatious way of dancing and talking, though she sings reasonably well, yet one might have found three hundred comelier and more gracious damsels present. All the same, there is no accounting for men's tastes and whims. One of the knights near the king said: 'Madresilva, you have lost your leg armour. You must have a bad page who failed to fasten it well.'

She blushed slightly and stooped to pick it up, but another knight rushed over and grabbed it. The king then summoned the knight and said: 'Fasten it to my left stocking below the knee.'[1]

The knight goes on to tell how the king wore the garter openly for more than four months; the queen never said anything, and it was only a favourite servant who eventually reproached him for his behaviour, saying that all the foreigners, the queen, her ladies and his subjects were amazed that he could honour 'such an insignificant damsel' in this way. 'The king replied: "So the queen is disgruntled and my guests are displeased!", and he said in French: "*Puni soit qui mal y pense.* [Let him be punished who thinks ill of it.] Now I swear before God that I shall found a new knightly order upon this incident: a fraternity that shall be remembered as long as the world endures."'[2] The narrator goes on to describe, reasonably accurately, the way in which the knights are seated in St George's chapel, with their swords and helmets displayed and their escutcheon fixed to the back of the stall, as well as the robes of the knights and the penalties for failing to wear the garter in public. The name 'Madresilva' is intriguing, since it is the Spanish for honeysuckle, called in English woodbine; and one of the mottoes embroidered on Edward's court garments was 'Sure as the woodbine'.[3] There must be a connection, but there is no evidence that will help us to explain the link.

The account is a mixture of reality and romance in the style of Froissart – whom Martorell may well have read. But its tone is also faintly disparaging: Madresilva is depicted as sexually attractive rather than as an ideal object of courtly love, and the whole episode turns on the king's whimsical and irrational fancy of wearing the dropped garter. The motto is distorted, and the image we are left with is of an arrogant ruler untroubled by any kind of ideals. Either Martorell invented the tale, and it passed into popular myth, or he himself heard a scurrilous tale of a kind which could be found in connection with other knightly orders. Elias Ashmole, the great seventeenth-century historian of the

Garter, writes of the Burgundian Order of the Golden Fleece, which has considerable parallels with the Garter:

> even that also hath met with the same fate; and the Institution reported to have risen from an effeminate ground: for it is said, that its Founder entering one morning into the chamber of a most beautiful lady of Bruges (generally esteemed his mistress) found upon her toilette, a fleece of Low Country wool; whence some of his followers taking occasion of sport, as at a thing unusually seen in a lady's chamber, he ... vowed that such as made it the subject of their derision should never be honoured with a collar of the order thereof, which he intended to establish to express the love he bore that lady.[4]

Likewise, the Order of the Collar in Savoy, which incorporated love-knots in its device, was rumoured to be based on a bracelet sent to the count of Savoy by his mistress. Neither of these stories is true – the Golden Fleece has its roots in classical mythology, and the Order of the Collar is unequivocally dedicated to the Virgin Mary.

A story of this kind was certainly current in England by 1463, when an Italian cleric, Mondonus Belvaleti, wrote a learned Latin treatise on the symbolism of the Order of the Garter for Edward IV. He reports the popular version discreetly, saying only that 'many assert that this order took its beginning from the feminine sex, from a lewd and forbidden affection'.[5] Another Catalan author, Roís de Corella, had probably heard of Martorell's story by 1480 when he spoke of 'the disorderly rule of the Garter'.[6] It is possible that the real context of Martorell's romance is not that of 1439–40, but that of the court of Edward IV in the 1460s. The character of the king in *Tirant the White* would fit Edward IV, impulsive and noted for his love affairs, much better than his great-grandfather. By the early sixteenth century, another Italian writing in England, Polydore Vergil, had picked up Martorell's story, and included a close paraphrase of it in his *English History* in 1534.

> But the reason for the founding of the order is utterly uncertain; popular tradition nowadays declares that Edward at some time picked up from the ground a garter from the stocking of his queen or mistress, which had become unloosed by some chance, and had fallen. As some of the knights began to laugh and jeer at this, he is reputed to have said that in a very little while the same garter would be held by them in the highest honour.

And not long after, he is said to have founded this order and given it the title by which he showed those knights who had laughed at him how to judge his actions. Such is popular tradition. English writers have been modestly superstitious, perhaps fearing to commit lèse-majesté, if they made known such unworthy things; and they have preferred to remain silent about them, whereas matters should really be seen otherwise: something that rises from a petty or sordid origin increases all the more in dignity.[7]

It is William Camden in 1607 who first names the lady of Martorell's and Vergil's romantic tradition as the countess of Salisbury. However, this is given only as a secondary possibility for the origin of the order: his first suggestion is quite different:

In this place [Windsor], king *Edward* the third, for to adorne martiall prowesse, with honors, the guerdon of vertue, ordained that most noble order and society of knights, whom (as some report) for his owne garter given forth as signall of a battaile that sped fortunately, hee called knights of the Garter: who weare on their left legge somewhat under the knee, a blew garter: carying this Empresse [motto] wrought with golden letters in French HONY SOIT QUI MAL Y PENSE, and fasten the same with a buckle of gold as with the bond of a most inward society, in token of concord and unity, that there might bee among them a certaine consociation and communion of vertues. But others there be, that doe attribute it unto the garter of the Queene or rather of *Joan* Countesse of Salisburie, a Lady of incomparable beauty, which fell from her as shee daunced, and the King tooke up from the floore: for, when a number of Nobles and Gentle men standing by laughed thereat, he made answere againe, that shortly it would come to passe that garter should bee in high honour and estimation. This is the common and most received report: Neither need this seeme to be a base originall thereof, considering how, as one saith

> *Nobilitas sub amore jacet*
> Nobility lies under love.[8]

Camden's preferred origin of the Garter as 'signal of a battle' is an interesting one, suggesting that it might have been an identifying badge of some sort; it is just possible that the Garter was such a badge at Crécy before its adoption for the company, but there is no firm evidence for the idea, nor are there any parallels for the use of a badge in this way. In his second story, which he has lifted from Polydore Vergil, he is quite clearly embellishing it by making a link with Joan of Kent, who was nominally countess of Salisbury after her then husband became earl in 1344 until the marriage was declared void in 1349.

It is Jean le Bel who recounts the story of Edward's rape of the countess of Salisbury. The countess is said to have been defending Wark Castle, a great fortress on the Scottish border which did indeed belong to the earl, and which was attacked in June 1340. At the time, William Montagu, her husband, was imprisoned in France after his capture at Lille in April 1340. He was released in September of that year, so the episode is firmly placed in the summer of 1340. Edward was in Flanders for most of 1340, but was in England from late February to late June, but did not go further north than Hertford. Edward is said to have gone to the countess's aid with his troops, and to have fallen in love with her, but was firmly put in his place by the countess. Two years later, he holds a great feast and jousts in London in August, and invites the countess, who comes reluctantly. Again, the king was indeed in London in August 1342, and held a feast at the time specified. The following year, while the earl and Robert d'Artois were in Brittany, according to the story, Edward went to Wark to see the countess again. Once more, the movements of the earl are accurately represented, but Edward himself returned from Brittany in March, and spent the rest of the year in the south of England. The rape is therefore supposed to have taken place in the summer of 1343, before the earl's return from Brittany. Le Bel does not pull his punches in describing the king's violence:

> that night, as he lay in the splendid bed provided for him, a bed befitting his station, and knew that the noble lady was in her chamber and the whole household and all his retainers except his privy chamberlains were asleep, he rose and ordered his chamberlains not to get in his way, no matter what he did, or they'd find themselves at the end of a noose. And he entered the lady's chamber, locked the door of the adjoining room so that her maids couldn't help her, and seized her and stopped her mouth – so hard that she uttered only two or three cries – and then forced himself upon her, so painfully, so punishingly, that no woman ever was so brutally abused. And he left her lying there, unconscious, bleeding from her nose and mouth and elsewhere: it was a distressing and a grievous wrong. Then he left next morning without saying a word, and returned to

London, deeply disturbed about what he'd done. From that day forth the good lady was never happy again; her heart was so troubled that she never again shared in festivities or mixed with worthy people.[9]

When the countess tells her husband what has happened, he goes abroad, and dies there: he did in fact leave for Algeciras in the autumn of 1343, but returned safely. He, and probably the countess, attended the Windsor feast of 1344 at which he played a prominent part, but he had been taken ill a few days earlier, performed poorly in the tournament, and died – 'of natural causes', says Murimuth – shortly afterwards.

Whoever concocted the story must have done so after the earl's departure for Algeciras, as all the historical details are correct up to that point. Overlaid on this historically accurate account is a tale which is obviously derived from Livy's account of the rape of Lucretia, well known throughout the middle ages, and used by writers from St Augustine onwards. There are a number of late fourteenth-century versions, including those by Chaucer, Christine de Pisan, Boccaccio and Gower. The central themes are the same in both: the infatuation of a king, Sextus Tarquinius/Edward, for the wife of one of his commanders; the heroine's beauty and chastity; the first encounter and return when the husband is absent; the invasion of her bedchamber; and the heroine's confession to her husband.[10] Jean le Bel, our only detailed authority for the episode, was convinced of its truth by the historical context in which it was set; it is unlikely, given his initial scepticism, that he was responsible for weaving in these details. The most probable source is someone in the French court well informed about the earl's movements, which were generally known to anyone with an interest in English affairs, who also had a literary background. It is reminiscent of the propaganda against the Knights Templar produced when Philip the Fair engineered their downfall in 1307. As such, it is no real reflection on Edward's character or the morals of his court, but is a rare historical survival of a piece of expert propaganda.[11] Its nearest parallel is the story of Joan of Kent artfully luring the prince of Wales into marriage, a much more innocent tale but one which also discredits the English royal family.[12]

Le Bel names the countess only casually, in a linking paragraph taking up the story after Edward's first visit to Wark; he calls her 'Alice', which is either a slip of the pen or an amendment by a copyist, thereby confusing generations of later historians into trying to unravel this puzzle.[13] Froissart himself has grave problems with the story, emasculating it and turning it into a love story in one version of his chronicles: he actually denies it directly, both on the grounds that the king would never commit such a crime, and also because he has tried to find supporting evidence: 'Now I declare that I know England well, where I have lived for long periods at the royal court and also with the great lords of the country. And I have never heard tell of this rape although I have asked people about it who must have known if it had ever happened.'[14] The story was in circulation in France in the late fourteenth century, since four French chronicles mention it, in almost identical wording which summarizes very briefly the events described by Le Bel. They are almost certainly copying each other, and one of them is from the abbey of St Denis, the centre where the official French royal chronicles were written. The story of the rape is a brief paragraph which attempts to explain the execution of Olivier Clisson and the exile of Godefroy d'Harcourt:

> After the king had returned home, the countess of Salisbury lamented to her husband that she had been raped by the king of England; the earl was very despondent and sad, and summoned his friends. He went with them to the court of the king of England where in the presence of the king and the peers of the kingdom, he surrendered all his lands and left them to his daughter, since he had no son, in such a way that his wife would be endowed with them during her lifetime.
>
> Then, leaving the court, he sent his defiance to King Edward and crossed to France to King Philip, and gave him letters about the alliance of Olivier Clisson and Godefroy d'Harcourt with the king of England. And soon afterwards he left France, and after that no one ever saw him.[15]

This is all sheer nonsense: William Montagu, first earl of Salisbury, had a son, remained in England and was loyal to Edward until his death. If we place the composition of the story in 1343, while Salisbury was still alive, it looks like an attempt to discredit both Edward and his closest friend, and also to implicate the latter in the summary execution of Clisson which had produced such a hostile reaction among the French nobility. Le Bel seems, unusually, to have fallen for this carefully composed piece of propaganda. It is almost certainly a deliberate fabrication commissioned by the French authorities to show that Edward was unprincipled and treacherous; its effect was not what they had hoped for.[16] It had little impact on contemporaries, yet it became embedded in later versions of Edward's history, and Froissart's sanitized version led Polydore Vergil to associate it with the founding of the Order of the Garter. What began as a denigration of Edward's character ended by casting him in the role of romantic lover.

Within a few years of Edward's death, an unknown writer penned a eulogy of the late king, which was later translated into English.[17] It is an idealized portrait of a king who was said to have outshone all his predecessors, and most of it is conventional – his devoutness, generosity, moderation and good governance of his realm – or rhetorical: 'there sprang and shone so much grace in him that anyone who had seen his face or had dreamed of him, was sure that anything that happened to him that day would be joyful and to his liking'. His fortunes in war are emphasized, for 'he was a man very bold of heart, who did not dread any mischance, harm or misfortune which might befall a noble warrior, and he was fortunate both by land and sea. And in all battles and encounters he always had the victory, and great glory and worship.'

Medieval writers did not like innovation; tradition was more important than 'newfangled things' and it is only with the distance of the centuries that we can perhaps see Edward's achievements more clearly. By positioning himself, like Arthur at the Round Table, as first among equals, a knight among knights, he gained the trust of the great lords who had brought down his father and troubled his grandfather's reign, and earned their respect by his willingness to fight alongside them. If caution prevented him from leading from the front, there were moments when he was prepared to throw himself into the fray, at Sluys, at Calais and at Winchelsea, or to strike boldly and unexpectedly, as in his dramatic crossing back to England in 1340. Swift action when the time was ripe was perhaps something he had learnt from William Montagu when he seized Mortimer in 1330; it was a lesson that he remembered throughout his military career. Likewise, he might play the part of the traditional knight on occasions, but he was also an innovator and an improviser. If the reading of the tactics at Crécy is correct, he used a combination of new technology – the longbow had only recently come to the fore, and cannons were entirely novel in battle – with a brilliant inventiveness, creating a strong position with the available resources in unfavourable terrain. And because of the strong mutual trust he had built between himself and his commanders, they both contributed to his tactical decisions and respected his judgement. It is this cohesion between Edward and his leading knights that is commemorated in the Company of the Garter.

Appendix 1
The English Battle Formation at Crécy: A Hypothetical Reconstruction

In chapter 7, it was argued that the account by Giovanni Villani of the English battle formation is the most reliable that has come down to us. This is a hypothetical reconstruction of that formation, which according to Villani was centred on a formation of carts. In the open chalk country of Crécy, such an artificial defensive structure would be very valuable. The only natural defences mentioned by the chroniclers are a wood on the left flank (anonymous Roman chronicle) and hedges (*Norman Chronicle*),[1] very different from the terrain of battles such as Halidon Hill, Morlaix and Poitiers, where the battle formation was determined by the substantial presence of woods and hedges. The contours of the landscape do present some features which were potentially useful. It is reasonably probable that Edward's position was above the modern village of Crécy, on the ridge which overlooks the valley of the river Maye; and he may well have placed his men so that the one obstacle on this hillside, the steep sixteen-foot-high bank of the Vallée des Clercs, forced the French to attack from a particular direction. No attacking army could cross this obstacle at speed.

In such circumstances, Villani's declaration that 'they enclosed the army with carts, of which they had plenty, both of their own and from the country' and his description of the creation of an artificial fortress of carts rings true, as we have argued. Diagram B shows a possible and highly tentative reconstruction of how this might have worked. The formation would probably have faced more or less due south, at the head of one of the valleys which run up to the ridge from the river. The carts

---

[1] *Istoire et croniques de Flandres*, 42, specifies that it was behind the army. Hedges: p. 227 above.

were probably drawn up in a roughly circular formation, and may have been two or more deep, chained wheel to wheel, judging from the evidence from Mons-en-Pévèle in 1304 and from the Hussite wars in the fifteenth century. Use of carts to provide a fortified encampment to protect the baggage is widely attested in the thirteenth and fourteenth centuries, and Philip Preston has suggested that the practice of surrounding the army with carts might also have been used when encamping for the night. Certainly there were men with the army who were practised in manoeuvring the four-wheeled carts into an array of some kind, and Edward had arrived at the battlefield two days before, according to the records of both the 'Kitchen Journal' and the itinerary in the Cottonian manuscript.[2] He had more than enough time to ride over the ground, select a suitable position and organize the creation of the array of carts. Furthermore, the evidence points to the availability of enough carts to create such a circle, though the anonymous Roman chronicler's assertion that he brought 3,000 carts with him on the expedition is definitely too high. As a working figure, let us take the recent estimate of a ratio of carts to men of 1:20,[3] giving 700 carts for an army of 14,000 men.

Let us assume a length for each cart of six feet when drawn up in formation, positioned lengthways around the perimeter with the shafts raised to close the gaps which would otherwise be left between the carts. If the carts were arranged in a double row, this would give a ring 700 yards in circumference, to which we have to add the gap of 100 yards at the entrance. This gives an enclosed area of about 20,000 square yards. Andrew Ayton estimates the total army at around 2,800 men at arms, 3,000 mounted archers and 8,000 infantry, about 14,000 men in all.[4] The suggested deployment is as follows: within the ring were about 3,000 men at arms and 8,000 infantry; the archers were deployed on the carts, or outside on the wings. Also within the ring were the horses for the men at arms, giving a total of about 11,000 men and 3,000 horses. The only available calculation for the space occupied by a medieval army drawn up in battle formation is for the Swiss army at the battle of Morat in 1476, where 10,000 men are thought to have occupied an area of 3,600 square yards (60 yards × 60 yards). If we allow an

[2] TNA E 101/390/11; BL MS Cotton Cleopatra D.VII. See Baker, *Chronicon*, 252, 254. For the 'Kitchen Journal', see p. 26.
[3] Harari, 'Strategy and Supply in Fourteenth-Century Campaigns', 318.
[4] Ayton and Preston, *Crécy*, 189.

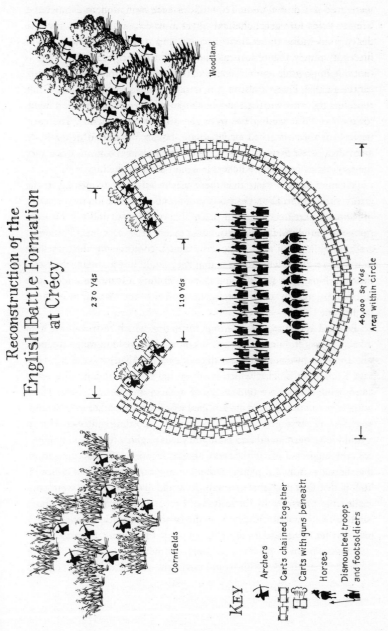

Reconstruction of the English Battle Formation at Crécy

230 Yds

110 Yds

40,000 Sq Yds
Area within circle

Woodland

Cornfields

ILLUSTRATOR - ANDREW FARMER

KEY

🏹 Archers

▢▢▢ Carts chained together

▢ Carts with guns beneath

🐎 Horses

Dismounted troops and footsoldiers

increased space of 0.5 square yards for each man, and an estimated 2 square yards for each horse, this gives a total of 11,500 square yards, leaving adequate room for formation and manoeuvre. These are of necessity purely theoretical calculations, but they indicate that there is nothing impossible about the idea of the cart fortification with the bulk of the English army inside it. The entrance of 100 yards or less, while open enough to invite the enemy to attempt an attack, would be a death trap given the covering fire from the archers on the carts. The carts were probably not in an exact square, but in a diamond or circle, to provide a better forward line of fire for the archers. Diagram B is a very tentative suggestion as to how this would have worked.

Villani makes it clear that there was a substantial opening in the array, sufficient to allow the passage of numbers of men at arms; equally, this opening created 'a narrow place'. This imitated artificially a feature found at Halidon Hill, and to a lesser extent at Morlaix and Poitiers, a valley which acted as a narrowing funnel, compressing the attacking force into a front which meant that they could not maintain their formation. Nor were superior numbers a striking advantage under such conditions, as only a relatively small number of men would be engaged at any one time.

Edward added to this defensive formation which restricted the area of action a skilful deployment of his most effective long-range weapon, the archers. If we are to believe the evidence of Villani and the anonymous Roman chronicler, which is supported in general terms by other chronicles, there were two wings of archers outside the circle. These were concealed, one in an unidentified wood, and the other in tall standing corn. The distance between these wings, according to Robert Hardy, should have been no greater than 500 yards to give proper covering fire, and the suggested size of the array of carts fits well with this calculation. Furthermore, Edward placed archers on the carts. Villani's evidence on this is detailed, and controversial. It would seem that they were concealed and protected by the canvas of the carts, which would have been supported on wooden hoops (as in the famous illustration from the Luttrell Psalter of an admittedly luxurious royal travelling wagon[5]). These carts were perhaps placed at an angle to the entrance to the array of carts, so that the crossfire would cover the gap to deadly effect; and

[5] Plate 24.

their supplies of arrows were in barrels on the carts, within easy reach. Furthermore – and this is admittedly a speculation – if the front row of carts were empty, it would be extremely difficult to reach the archers with a lance if a knight did penetrate to the carts themselves. Men on foot would have to clamber up the wheels to get at them; later Bohemian battle wagons carried ladders for the occupants to get up and down.

The guns were, according to Villani, positioned beneath the carts. They would have been relatively small, probably 'ribalds',[6] and such a placing would be perfectly possible. They would probably have been better at causing panic among the horses than actually inflicting serious injury, except at a relatively short range; it is unlikely that all 100 were in use.

Once the archers were in position, and the men at arms were drawn up in battle order within the array, the archers would conceal themselves. From the foot of the hill, the approaching French would have seen a small army standing in an array of carts which looked not unlike the traditional method of guarding the rear of a defensive position. The carts would have served to conceal the true numbers within the ring, and would have made the English army seem a tempting target.

As soon as the first French forces came within range, the archers on the wings would have stood up and begun their deadly volleys. This was what the Genoese crossbowmen encountered, and a commander with some control over his troops would have halted the attack to consider how to deal with the archers. Instead, the uncontrolled French cavalry rode over the crossbowmen, wasting their energy on attacking their own men, into the second trap, the archers concealed at the entrance under the canvas of the carts.

Even so, the sheer mass of the French cavalry enabled them to force their way into the 'narrow place', where the prince of Wales's men awaited them. It was in this 'small area' that, according to Edward himself, the real slaughter took place. The defensive array and the ambush had done their work, and the superior numbers of the French army were no longer an advantage. The battle was not won, however; but, in the struggle that ensued, the discipline and battle experience of the English were the decisive factors. It is possible that the manoeuvre used

[6] See p. 182 above.

at Poitiers, an encircling movement from the rear of the English army to attack the enemy from an unexpected quarter, may have been employed, and that this later became the story of the rescue of the prince of Wales. There would have been time to disengage a couple of dozen carts once it was clear that the main action was at the front of the array, so the existence of the circle would not have prevented such a manoeuvre.

If we are to accept this reconstruction as a possibility, it would mean that the emphasis of Edward's military thinking went beyond the creation of an army which was well organized and formed of men who had fought together, in some cases for two decades, to the deployment of the latest technology, and – as important as either of these factors – a genuine understanding of tactics and of the need for a specific type of site in order to make the most effective use of his archers. If he could not find the terrain that he needed, he was prepared to create by artificial means the necessary obstacles and constraints that would hinder the enemy.

Appendix 2
Eustace (Sauchet) d'Auberchicourt

The Auberchicourt family appear early in Edward III's life. Nicholas d'Auberchicourt[1] was lord of Buignicourt, on the borders of Hainault, where the young Edward stayed with his mother before their return to England in 1326. Among others at the castle at the time was the lord of Aisne and three of the Mauny brothers, among them Walter Mauny. The queen's escort from Buignicourt included Nicholas d'Auberchicourt, also called Nicholas but known as Colart. He sailed with her to England and was present at her landing at the Orwell estuary.[2] Five years later, Nicholas was knighted by Edward; he was given lands to maintain the estate of knighthood on 8 October 1331, and the grant specifies that this was as a reward for assistance at a crucial moment of the king's life: 'for good service while we were in foreign parts, and also when we came with Isabella queen of England, our dearest mother, to our kingdom'.[3]

Nicholas d'Auberchicourt returned to Hainault, and went on crusade to Prussia with William I of Hainault in 1336–7, after which we hear nothing more of him.[4] The castle of Auberchicourt was apparently burnt by the French garrisons of Douai and Lille in 1337.[5] It is his eldest son Nicholas (Colart) who appears in 1352 and 1355 as provost of Valenciennes,[6] and this gives added force to Froissart's account of the

---

[1] There are at least fifteen different spellings of the name in medieval records. I have standardized to the modern spelling of the place name, which is now in Ponthieu. For the genealogy of the family, see Feuchère, *Auberchicourt*, 53 ff.

[2] Froissart, *Chroniques*, Amiens version, 58, 62, 72.

[3] *Foedera*, ii.ii.824. He also fought in the 1327 campaign in Scotland: Froissart, *Chroniques*, Amiens version, 114.

[4] Paravicini, *Die Preussenreisen*, i.94.

[5] Lapierre, *La Guerre de cent ans dans l'Argonne*, 10; the author explains the brutality of Eustace's activities in 1358–9 as an act of revenge for this episode.

[6] Feuchère, *Auberchicourt*, 58.

Auberchicourts' involvement with Edward, as they would almost certainly have known each other. There were two or three younger brothers: we have clear records of Eustace and Gilles, the latter being bailiff of two estates near Cambrai in 1350.[7] It is possible that Eustace was employed by the count of Hainault, William II, as a squire in his household; Staes or Staesken, the Dutch for Eustace, appears in this role while the count went on pilgrimage to Jerusalem and then on crusade to Prussia. Given that this was a rare name in Dutch at this time, and that his father had accompanied William I on crusade, this seems a plausible identification; no other person named Staes occurs in these accounts. His activities during this period are very similar to those of Heinken Oem, who subsequently appears in the service of the prince of Wales as Henry Eam: indeed, in one instance, Staes and Heinken Oem appear in adjoining entries. The business which he is recorded as performing is very similar to that carried out by Heinken Oem, and he is called the count's 'kammerling' or member of his chamber.

If this identification is correct, his career and that of Oem run parallel: he moves to England on the death of William II at Staveren in September 1345, in which case his next appearance is an entry in the English patent rolls for 1345. On 20 October, Sausetus Daubrichecourt is given all the chattels of John Wardedieu, indicted for the death of Robert Poteman.[8] These lands were in Sussex, and included the future site of Bodiam Castle. But Wardedieu was then cleared of felony, and the grant to Sausetus never took effect. His daughter married Edward Dalyngrigge, who built Bodiam in 1385. In 1347, Froissart tells us that the six burghers of Calais pardoned at the request of Walter Mauny and Queen Philippa were escorted through the English lines by Sanse d'Aubrecicourt and Paon de Roet. The wife of Nicholas lord of Buignicourt was from the Roeux family and Paon de Roet or Roeux may have been his cousin (and later Chaucer's father-in-law).[9] This entry would place him firmly in the group of Hainaulters around the queen. A Dabrichcourt is next recorded in the accounts of the prince of Wales: Stacy Dabrichcourt brings him money to gamble with the queen on 18 September 1348, and appears again as Tassyn Dabrigcourt, recipient of a

[7] Ibid., 68.
[8] CPR 1343–1345, 557.
[9] Feuchère, Auberchicourt, 57; Froissart, Chroniques, Amiens version, 849.

gift of £6 13s. 4d. from the prince on 6 November, probably in 1353.[10] These are all Eustace, but both his Christian name or nickname and his surname are subject to the vagaries of fourteenth-century spelling: I have found at least fifteen variant versions of his surname.

Meanwhile, in the accounts of Margaret countess of Hainault, the prince's aunt, we find Nicholas d'Auberchicourt paid the substantial sum of £200 on 1 August 1353, which he is owed for wages to his brother Sausset d'Auberchicourt, who has served the duchess in the wars in Zeeland and on the Maas.[11] In 1355, we find an entry which connects Eustace d'Auberchicourt with both the prince of Wales and the countess of Hainault: on 4 May 1355, the prince arranges for his aunt's clerk, Stephen de Maulyons, to pay 100 crowns to Eustace out of a debt which Stephen owed to the prince, implying that Eustace was in Hainault at the time.

So we have Sausset, Sanse, Stacy and Tassin d'Auberchicourt in the English records for 1345 to 1355, and no records for Eustace during the period when these names appear. The only subsequent record relating to a man with a similar name to Sausset or Sanse is the early copies of the statutes of the Company of the Garter, which call him Sanchet. Now of these names, Sanchet is not found elsewhere. Stacy and Tassin are probably variations of Eustace (or Ustasse, as the name is frequently spelled in the chronicles). Could Sausset and Eustace be the same man?[12]

Sausset is a very rare name, apparently confined to a few families on the borders of Ponthieu and Hainault. There is a Sausset in the d'Aisne family: the lord of Aisne is mentioned as present at Buignicourt in 1326. This man's son is named Gerard, and Sausset is clearly a nickname. He first appears in the records under his real name. In 1339 he is Gerardo dicto Sausseto d'Enne,[13] but in 1342 he becomes simply Sausset d'Aisne, and as bailiff of Hainaut he is also referred to as Sausset without his real name.[14] Furthermore, Sanse de Biaureau and Sauses de Bousoit appear

[10] *RBP*, iv.76, 158.

[11] *Cartulaire de Hainaut*, 770: 'Par lettres medame, données à Caisnoit le mercredi nuit Saint Pière entrant aoust l'an dessusdit, payetà monsigneur Nicole d'Auberchicourt, lesquels medame le contesse pooit devoir à lui pour monsigneur Sausset d'Auberchicourt, sen frère, liquel servi ma dite dame en ses wières de Zélande et sur le Maize, si qu'il appert par chesle lettre ij^c l.'

[12] This suggestion has been made by a number of historians, notably Kervyn de Lettenhove in his edition of Froissart, xx.197, but usually without any supporting arguments.

[13] *Cartulaire de Hainaut*, 100.

[14] Ibid., 103, 211, 217, 241, 286.

in Isabella's entourage on her way to England in 1326 and among the Hainault knights who fought in the Scottish campaign in 1327.[15] Both of them are also known in the Hainault records as Sausse or Sausset.[16] Because of the difficulty of distinguishing 'n' and 'u' in Gothic script, the likely reading for 'Sanse' is 'Sause', a variation on Sausset and the mysterious Sanchet would become 'Sauchet', similarly a version of Sausset. It is noteworthy that the representation of Auberchicourt in the book compiled by William Bruges, the first Garter king at arms, one of the images for the windows he had made for St George's, Stamford, clearly reads Sausetus, as does Hollar's engraving of the images from the window.[17]

The meaning of this nickname has unfortunately been lost. The only modern writer to discuss the adoption of nicknames in Hainault at this period implies that it is in some way pejorative, but fails to give any justification for this idea: he suggests that it might mean red-faced or blotchy.[18] Subsequent dictionaries of names assume that it is related to 'sausse', sauce, and hence derives from the cook's red face. But this begs the question as to why there should be a group of men from the same small circle of families with the same disfigurement (though it could conceivably have been hereditary). It seems much more likely that it is some kind of private language whose meaning was soon forgotten.[19]

If Sausset is a nickname, and there are no documents that imply the existence of both Sausset and Eustace at the same time, it is strong evidence that the two are identical. All that is missing to complete the proof is an entry in the records like that for 'Gerard dit Sausset d'Aisne', which would read 'Eustace dit Sausset d'Auberchicourt'. I would argue that we should substitute Eustace's name for that of the mysterious 'Sanchet' in the list of Garter knights, particularly in view of the late date of the statutes and the problems involved in identifying the original members of the company. The next test of this hypothesis is to look at the career of Eustace d'Auberchicourt and to see how far it corresponds with the patterns we can detect in the careers of other Garter knights.

[15] Froissart, *Chroniques*, Rome version, 71, 114.

[16] For example, *Cartulaire de Hainaut*, 755: Sausse de Biauriu; 243: Sausset, sire de Boussoit.

[17] Hollar's engraving is in Ashmole, *Order of the Garter*, 643.

[18] Edouard Poncelet; see Hemricourt, *Œuvres*, ccxxvii–ccxxviii.

[19] Ibid., ccxxix, for examples from the later fourteenth and fifteenth centuries.

From 1355 onwards it is easy to trace Eustace d'Auberchicourt. The payment to him in May 1355 may have been a retainer, for in the autumn of 1355 he was in Aquitaine with the prince of Wales, and appears in the accounts kept by John Henxteworth from 20 September 1355 onwards. He probably travelled from England with the prince, and was with John Ghistels, possibly the son of Wulfart Ghistels.[20] Payments to them both appear on 1 October, on 10 December on the return from the raid to Narbonne that autumn, on 8 January 1356, and finally a gift of 40s. 6d. to each of them on 5 February.[21] After this Ghistels disappears from the accounts, and Auberchicourt's name appears alone: there are entries in February, March and April for his wages, and a final damaged entry on the last page apparently for wages to 30 June.[22] However, the partnership with John Ghistels continued, as in 1358 they owed one of the prince's officers £46 for money advanced to them, which the prince paid on their behalf.[23] Froissart also mentions them together in his lists of knights who fought in this campaign, and it is possible that they had entered into a partnership agreement whereby they shared the profits and expenses of the war.[24]

It is from the beginning of this raid by the prince of Wales that Auberchicourt appears regularly in Froissart's chronicle. As with the other Hainault knights, most of his exploits must have been told to Froissart by eyewitnesses or by Auberchicourt himself. Froissart says that, 'as I was afterwards told', the inhabitants of Carcassonne had tried to defend themselves by fixing chains across the streets, but Auberchicourt jumped over two or three of these and laid into the defenders with his sword, while elsewhere the English archers drove them back.[25] In the 1356 campaign he is mentioned as taking part in a skirmish at Romorantin.[26] The capture of the counts of Joigny and Auxerre is related in considerable detail by Froissart, and is again evidently based on an oral account, with

[20] Froissart, *Chroniques*, Rome version, 114, 440; Wulfart also served William II of Hainault in 1344: Hamaker, *De rekeningen der grafelijkheid van Holland*, xxvi.381, 395.

[21] Henxteworth, m. 1d, m. 4d, m. 9d, m. 13; a damaged entry on m. 5d for Auberchicourt might have included Ghistels' name.

[22] Ibid., m. 14, m. 15, m. 16, m. 17, m. 28.

[23] *RBP*, iv.264.

[24] Froissart, *Chroniques*, SHF, iv.136 (1355 raid); v.32 (battle of Poitiers); Froissart, *Chroniques*, ed. Lettenhove, v.378 (Poitiers campaign).

[25] Froissart, *Chroniques*, SHF, iv.166.

[26] Ibid., v.5.

some apparently authentic detail.[27] Auberchicourt was among a group of soldiers, including the captal de Buch, Bartholomew Burghersh the younger and Aimery de Pommiers, sent to reconnoitre the enemy positions; they encountered a French squadron which outnumbered them, and turned back, leading the enemy towards the prince and his army, who counter-attacked. In the ensuing encounter, the two counts were captured. The same fate befell Auberchicourt himself an hour or two later, when he was taken prisoner by a German knight; however, John Ghistels was able to rescue him.[28]

So far, Auberchicourt's activities – at least seen through Froissart's possibly rose-tinted lenses – had been entirely orthodox. But, like many other knights, he found the truce signed in Bordeaux in 1357 had brought his military career and hence his income to a temporary end. As a younger son, he had little in the way of lands, although he was well connected. Along with men of more humble birth who owed their knightly status entirely to their activities in the field, Eustace became a freebooter, one of the leaders of the dreaded companies, operating in Champagne on his own account in collaboration with a group of like-minded soldiers. He established himself in southern Champagne, a rich area with several royal castles, in the autumn of 1358, and spent the following year as one of the leaders of an army under the joint command of himself, Peter Audley (perhaps James Audley's younger brother) and Albrecht, a German mercenary with a brutal reputation who may be the same as Albert Sterz, a German captain executed in Italy eight years later. Eustace seized Nogent-sur-Seine, among a number of other towns and castles, and made it his headquarters.[29]

Froissart paints an idealized picture of Auberchicourt's behaviour during this period, emphasizing his success and his chivalric encounters, and dwelling particularly on his lady, Elizabeth of Juliers, niece of Queen Philippa. He represents Elizabeth as sending him letters, greetings and other signs, and Auberchicourt as inspired by the love of this

[27] Ibid., 14. The 'bushes and heather' leading up to the edge of the wood correspond closely to the terrain of the battlefield at Poitiers; but see Ainsworth, *Jean Froissart and the Fabric of History*, 219–53, for the literary element in Froissart's landscape descriptions.

[28] Froissart, *Chroniques*, SHF, v.16–17, 35, 41. This reinforces the idea that they were in partnership, as Ghistels would have been liable for Auberchicourt's ransom if he had remained in captivity.

[29] Le Bel, *Chronique*, ii.276–9 [243–5].

'young, fresh and pretty' beauty 'of the greatest blood in the kingdom'.[30] The reality of this campaign was very different. His men were responsible for a reign of terror which included an episode at Rosnay when they entered the church during mass, seized the chalice from the priest's hands and led him off as a prisoner. Elsewhere in France, the chaos after the capture of John II at Poitiers meant that such marauding went unpunished; but Eustace was unlucky in that the royal lieutenants in Champagne were well organized and prepared to act. They could raise troops from the towns, which, if not well trained, were plentiful, and could call on the local knights to serve in defence of their county. The freebooters would be outnumbered in any battle, and were not in a position to provision their strongholds to withstand a long siege. Eustace's response was to assemble his troops outside the town, and to fight a defensive battle, a tactic which had a reasonable chance of success, as at Crécy.[31] He succeeded, if we are to believe Froissart, in driving off the first two divisions of the French force, and in holding the third; but the arrival of the fresh troops in the French fourth division was too much for the small force at his command, and he himself was seriously wounded and captured. The French returned to Troyes, but the knight who had taken Auberchicourt prisoner knew that Eustace would be in danger of lynching because he was so hated for his behaviour, and took him elsewhere to recover.

Auberchicourt was able to raise his ransom of 22,000 *moutons* in a few months; on his release Elizabeth is said to have sent him a fine white courser.[32] He resumed his activities as a freebooter, and seized the town of Attigny on the Aisne as his base. His men found fifteen large tuns of wine there, and became very drunk: a house was burnt, and with it twenty of the English and forty horses.[33] Shortly afterwards, Edward III's army reached Reims, to begin their siege of that city, and Auberchicourt made contact with them: he is said to have sent them supplies from the stores he found at Attigny.[34] Early in 1360 he went on a foraging raid with Henry of Grosmont, but despite doing serious damage to towns and villages, they failed to return with enough supplies to prevent

[30] Froissart, *Chroniques*, SHF, v.159–60.
[31] Ibid., 165–73; *Chronique normande du XIVe siècle*, 140.
[32] Froissart, *Chroniques*, SHF, v.160.
[33] Ibid., 183.
[34] Ibid., 213.

Edward's lifting of the siege on 11 January.[35] After Edward's departure, he continued his ravages unabated; Jean le Bel believed that he was acting under Edward's orders, and bemoaned the fact that the French authorities in Champagne had failed 'up to the day when this was written' to do anything about Auberchicourt. In the end the local population seem to have bought him out: in May and June 1360 the count of Flanders ordered them to pay the 25,000 *deniers d'or* which they had promised on his surrender of Attigny and another castle.[36] The duke of Bar bought the fortress of Authey in June 1360 for 1,200 gold florins.[37]

Auberchicourt was certainly in Edward's service later in the year, as one of the commissioners who confirmed the treaty of Brétigny at Calais on 4 October 1360.[38] Five days earlier, he had made a prestigious marriage to the lady of Froissart's stories, Elizabeth of Juliers.[39] Her father, William of Juliers, was at one point very close to the king, who appointed him his 'private and very special sovereign secretary' in 1339, and created him earl of Cambridge in 1340.[40] On the death of her husband John earl of Kent in 1352, Elizabeth had become a nun at Waverley abbey, and the correspondence which Froissart depicts seems improbable. For Elizabeth it was a way out of the convent, for Auberchicourt it was a splendid opportunity for social and financial advancement. Both parties had to do penance for this illicit marriage, but they do not seem to have incurred any disfavour at court. Auberchicourt, as a second son, had relatively little in the way of lands, and his wife brought him a modest group of manors, her widow's portion from the estate of John of Kent. More important, however, he was now closely connected to the royal family: Elizabeth was sister-in-law to Joan of Kent, who was to become princess of Wales in 1361. Soon after the marriage, they sold the manors of Woking and Sutton to the prince of Wales.[41]

Auberchicourt continued in the king's service: he was supposed to go

[35] Sumption, *The Hundred Years War*, iii. 432.

[36] Orders printed from Archive du nord, B1596, fo. 174ʳ, in Lapierre, *La Guerre de cent ans dans l'Argonne*, 118.

[37] Froissart, *Chroniques*, ed. Lettenhove, xx.198.

[38] *Foedera*, iii.i.518.

[39] The Alice Dabrechicourt who appears as a damsel of Queen Philippa in 1358 (*CPR 1358–1361*, 131) could have been his first wife, or his sister; we have no further evidence.

[40] Ormrod, *Edward III*, 127.

[41] *RBP*, iv.500, 503, 524.

to Brittany in the spring of 1363. Instead he took a substantial force –
350 mounted soldiers – to Ireland in 1363; he had twenty horses for
himself and his retinue. However, the treaty of Brétigny meant that
there was little official military activity by the English, and the following year he entered the service of Charles of Navarre, whom he was to
serve for the remainder of his life. He took part in the battle of Auray in
1364 alongside John Chandos, but then returned to his earlier existence
as a freebooter, for which he was severely reprimanded by Edward III.

When du Guesclin was captured at Auray, it seems that he held the
castle of Carentan, of which Auberchicourt was nominally guardian. In
July 1365 Auberchicourt was party to a deal by which du Guesclin sold
it back to Charles of Navarre for 14,000 francs.[42] However, instead of
returning to Normandy, he spent the next eighteen months involved in
the French and English invasions of Castile, in the course of which he
played a very ambiguous role as a kind of English agent nominally in
the pay of Charles of Navarre.[43]

He did not remain to witness the disastrous outcome of the expedition
after the victory, with Pedro unable to meet his debts to the prince of
Wales and his army. Auberchicourt was by then in Tudela, where he
received 3,000 francs from Charles of Navarre, a gift which probably
marks his return to service with Navarre.[44] By the spring of the following year, he was back in Normandy, trying to eject Breton freebooters
from Charles of Navarre's castles in the region.[45] John Chandos evidently collaborated with him, as there is a writ for payments to both
Eustace and John for getting rid of the companies at this period.[46] He
was once again captain of Carentan, as in 1364; it is possible that he
had never surrendered this office.

Charles of Navarre came to Normandy in 1369, but the prince of
Wales summoned Auberchicourt to help to suppress the growing revolt
in Aquitaine. Charles was reluctant to let him go, but eventually relented.
Auberchicourt took ship to St Malo, and then rode to Nantes and
through Poitou to Angoulême.[47]

---

[42] Guesclin, *Letters*, 57, no. 152.
[43] See p. 454 above.
[44] *Archivo General de Navarra, Comptos*, vi.397, document 952.
[45] *Compte des recettes et dépenses du roi de Navarre*, 31, 33, 35–6, 42, 45.
[46] Ibid., 449.
[47] Froissart, *Chroniques*, SHF, vii.132–3.

John Chandos had preceded him to the prince's court, and Auber-chicourt joined his expedition that summer, fighting along the valley of the Garonne and at the siege of Domme. He seems to have stayed in Aquitaine for almost three years.[48] He and Walter Huet (an old col-league from the Spanish wars) were sent with 400 men to take over the castle of Rochechouart, but were driven off by Bertrand du Guesclin.[49] Late in 1370 he was at Belleperche when the mother of the duke of Bourbon was captured, and helped to arrange her exchange for Simon Burley, one of the prince's household knights.[50] He was also at the siege of Limoges in September 1370.[51] It was probably in the following year that, according to Froissart, he was captured at Pierre-Buffière near Limoges when he entered a castle which he believed to be in the hands of a lord friendly to the English and was taken prisoner by the Breton captain who was in fact holding it. His ransom was 12,000 francs; he could raise only part of it, but the duke of Bourbon, grateful for Auber-chicourt's help in releasing his mother, loaned him the rest. His son, whom Froissart calls François, remained with the duke as hostage for the repayment of the loan.[52] He returned to Normandy before the end of 1372, and died at Carentan, of which he had been captain since 1368, in December. His Navarrese squire Ferrant Martin de Merlo was with him.[53]

Auberchicourt was probably quite young when he died: if the Crécy–Calais campaign was his first experience of warfare, he would have been around forty-five in 1372. He seems to have had a remarkably varied and action-packed career.

He may have had two sons, François and William.[54] The eldest must

---

[48] Letters of protection for a year were issued for him, staying in Aquitaine with Edward prince of Wales. TNA C 61/83, m. 2 and m. 9; in October 1371 letters were issued for a year for Edmund de Munden, staying in his company in Aquitaine. These were repeated in November 1372 (TNA C 61/84, m. 2; C 61/85, m. 2).

[49] Froissart, *Chroniques*, ed. Lettenhove, xx.198.

[50] Froissart, *Chroniques*, SHF, vii.219, 224.

[51] Ibid., 244.

[52] Froissart, *Chroniques*, SHF, viii.ii.6.

[53] Froissart, *Chroniques*, ed. Lettenhove, xi.390.

[54] William's tomb was at St Mary's, Bridport in Dorset until the nineteenth century. John Leland notes the inscription in his *Itinerary*, i.245: 'Hic jacet Gulielmus, filius Elizabeth de Julers, Comitissae Cantiae, consanguinae Philippae quondam Reginae Angl.'

have been born before 1366, when his father swore liege homage to the king of Navarre on behalf of himself and his first-born son.

Auberchicourt's career corresponds for the most part to the pattern of similar Garter knights. He belongs to the entourage of the prince of Wales, but has also personal links to Edward III and Philippa, and is one of the Hainaulters in England associated with the queen. His service at Calais – we do not know whether he was at Crécy, but there is no reason why he should not have been – and at Poitiers is a common feature of the careers of the members of the company. Like Walter Mauny, he retained some interests in Hainault, but was less involved since he was a younger son, while Mauny had inherited the family estates there. His marriage makes him one of the knights with links by marriage to the royal house.

More problematic, and more interesting, is his time in the service of the king of Navarre. Charles the Bad's extraordinary political man-oeuvrings must have baffled and infuriated both the French and English kings in equal measure, but in general we find Auberchicourt in Navar-rese employ when Charles was either neutral or allied to the English. And his liege homage to Charles makes it clear that his prime loyalty is to Edward and the prince of Wales. It seems that he may have been act-ing with Edward's tacit approval, as a way of undermining the French, particularly during the period 1358–9 and again in 1365–6. This is similar to the tacit encouragement given to the English lords who had lost their Scottish lands in 1332. If Froissart is right about Elizabeth of Juliers's correspondence with him, he was clearly in touch with England in 1358–9, but it is equally plain that he failed to respect the normal conventions of warfare. Again, the career of Hugh Wrottesley offers a parallel for this lawlessness among the Garter knights.[55]

As to the convoluted politics of the Great Company's activities in Spain in 1366, Auberchicourt was clearly disobeying Edward's instruc-tions to return in December 1365, along with Hugh Calveley. It is just possible that he was in effect keeping an eye on Charles of Navarre for Edward, and that he spent his time in Navarrese service rather than as an active member of the Great Company, though, like Calveley, he only returned to Bordeaux when it was clear there was nothing more to be gained in Castile. Even after his participation in the battle of Nájera, his

[55] See pp. 319–22 above.

service was still divided between the prince of Wales and the king of Navarre. There were perhaps personal loyalties at work as well: in 1364, 1367 and 1368–9 we find him fighting under the leadership of John Chandos. The reality behind Froissart's portrait of 'a very valiant knight'[56] points to a man whose lifestyle was much more ruthless, devious and precarious.

Since the hardback edition of this book was published, Lisa Jefferson has offered a full account of her reservations about the identification of Eustace (Sauchet) d'Auberchicourt *in the following article:*

Jefferson, Lisa, 'A note on Sir Sanchet d'Abrichecourt, one of the first founders of the Order of the Garter', *Coat of Arms* 3rd ser. 9 (2013), 77–84

---

[56] Froissart, *Chroniques*, SHF, viii.ii.6.

Appendix 3
Sources for Biographical Material on the Companions of the Garter Elected before 1361

The following knights are not in *ODNB*; references are given to published material, and brief biographies are supplied for those knights for whom there is no printed biography apart from those in Beltz, *Memorials of the Garter*. Dates of admission to the Company of the Garter are approximate.

Eustace (Sanchet) d'Auberchicourt (KG 1349)   See Appendix 2.

John Beauchamp (KG 1349)   John Beauchamp was the younger brother of Thomas Beauchamp, earl of Warwick, and spent his life as a professional soldier. He first appears in the records at the Dunstable tournament of 1334, listed next to his brother.[1] He was part of his brother's retinue in 1337 in Scotland, and was in William Montagu's retinue in the following year in Flanders.[2] He appears as a household knight for the first time in this year.[3] He fought at Sluys in 1340,[4] and in Brittany in 1342, with his own retinue of three esquires.[5]

He was on the Crécy campaign of 1346 in the king's retinue, and served until Edward returned to England after the siege of Calais.[6] It was only after the campaign that he became a banneret; he appears at the tournament

---

[1] Long, 'Roll of the Arms of the Knights at the Tournament at Dunstable', 394.
[2] Ayton, *Knights and Warhorses*, 249–50.
[3] Shenton, 'The English Court', 255.
[4] *Complete Peerage*, ii.50.
[5] Ayton, *Knights and Warhorses*, 263.
[6] Wrottesley, *Crécy and Calais*, 176.

at Canterbury in 1348.[7] Shortly afterwards he was appointed captain of Calais, with responsibility for the ships stationed there.[8] In 1351 he was defeated in a battle at Ardres by a larger French force, and captured.[9] He may have been imprisoned for a year or two, as he was reappointed captain in January 1355, and a new indenture was drawn up for the same appointment in February 1356 for a year.[10] In June 1358 he was sent on an unsuccessful mission to negotiate an alliance with Brabant.[11] He served on the Reims campaign of 1359–60,[12] and in 1360 he was appointed constable of the Tower of London and of Dover Castle. He held these posts briefly, as he died unmarried on 2 December 1360. His tomb in St Paul's cathedral was later mistaken for that of Humphrey duke of Gloucester.[13]

Hugh Courtenay (KG 1349)   Hugh Courtenay was born in 1326, and was therefore four years older than the prince of Wales. He was heir to the earl of Devon; his father, also called Hugh, was incapacitated in some way, since he never appears in the records as a soldier after he became earl in 1340. In 1347 Hugh the younger and the earl's brother-in-law the earl of Northampton petitioned that he should be excused any military service overseas. Hugh fought in the king's division on the Crécy campaign with a small retinue.[14] He was at the Eltham tournament of 1348, where he was given a hood embroidered with dancing men; the other recipients were Henry of Grosmont, John Lisle and John Grey.[15] Hugh was the first of the Garter knights to die, almost certainly of the plague: Queen Philippa laid cloth of gold on his tomb at Forde abbey in Dorset on 2 September 1349.[16]

Henry Eam *see* **Henry Oem**

[7] Nicolas, 'Observations on the Garter', 43.

[8] *Complete Peerage*, ii.50; *Foedera*, iii.i.75.

[9] Baker, *Chronicon*, 116; *Chronique normande du XIVᵉ siècle*, 101.

[10] *Complete Peerage*, ii.50; *Foedera*, iii.i.324.

[11] Trautz, *Die Könige von England*, 379.

[12] Ayton, *Knights and Warhorses*, 205.

[13] Stow, *Survey of the cities of London and Westminster*, i.335.

[14] Wrottesley, *Crécy and Calais*, 199: two knights, eight esquires and eight archers.

[15] Nicolas, 'Observations on the Garter', 41.

[16] TNA E 36/205, fo. 6.

Richard Fitzsimon (KG 1349) Richard Fitzsimon first appears at the Dunstable tournament of 1334,[17] and then in Flanders in the service of Reginald Cobham.[18] He served with Henry of Grosmont in 1344 on his diplomatic mission to Castile, during which he attended the siege of the Moorish fortress at Algeciras, and again in 1345–6 in Aquitaine; he evidently returned home early in 1346.[19] He served on the Crécy campaign in the retinue of Robert Ufford, but is also named as being in the retinue of the king and of the prince.[20] He was the standard-bearer of Edward prince of Wales at the battle of Crécy, and was rewarded accordingly.[21] He appears to have died in 1358–9.[22]

William Fitzwarin (KG 1349) Sir William Fitzwarin was the second son of Fulk, second Baron Fitzwarin, and his wife Alianore de Beauchamp, daughter of John, Lord Beauchamp, of Somerset. Fulk had a distinguished career under Edward II, and was constable of the army during the civil wars of 1322. William's elder brother, Fulk the younger, was similarly an important figure in Edward III's campaigns, and was assumed to have been the founding member of the Order of the Garter when the stall plates at Windsor were first put up in the 1420s.

However, it was William who had a close connection with the royal household. We do not know when he was born, but it seems to have been in the period 1305–10. We find him in attendance on Queen Philippa at Windsor on 22 October 1330, in her chamber,[23] and it is in her service that he most frequently appears. He was appointed governor of Montgomery Castle in 1330, after the execution of Roger Mortimer, earl of March, the previous castellan; he held this position until 1355, when Roger's son was able to reclaim the family lands which had been forfeited because of his father's treason. By 1332 he had also been given the castellany of Knaresborough, which was held by Queen Philippa, and was the queen's chamberlain.[24] He was in the king's household in

---

[17] Long, 'Roll of the Arms of the Knights at the Tournament at Dunstable', 393.
[18] Beltz, *Memorials of the Garter*, 60.
[19] *Foedera*, iii.i.11, 40; Fowler, 'Henry of Grosmont', iv.250.
[20] Wrottesley, *Crécy and Calais*, 96, 118, 119, 160, 185.
[21] See p. 234 above.
[22] Wrottesley, *Crécy and Calais*, 189.
[23] Manchester, John Rylands, MS 235, fo. 10ᵛ.
[24] BL MS Cotton Galba E.III, fo. 184ʳ.

1333–4 as knight of the Marshalsea of the king's hall, and continued as a household knight until at least 1337. He was evidently a highly valued and trusted servant of both king and queen, as in 1335 he was granted the marriage of Elizabeth, widow of William Latimer, 'for long and gratuitous service to the king and queen Philippa', 'if she will marry him'; if not, he was to have the fee payable to the king on her remarriage. She chose not to marry him; he married Amicia, the daughter of a neighbour in Dorset, at some time before 1341. In 1336 he was promised an income of £30 per year 'for service to the king and queen Philippa', and received as part of this lands in Dorset.[25]

William first appears on a diplomatic mission in October 1330, when he is sent with two clerics to make an alliance with John duke of Brabant.[26] Over the next sixteen years he was regularly employed on diplomatic business, particularly where alliances were concerned. He was chosen to approach Alfonso XI of Castile in 1335 to explore the possibility of a match between his eldest son and Edward III's elder daughter Isabella, then aged three, though the alliance did not materialize. In August 1336 he went to Austria with a similar proposal, for the marriage of the eldest son of Duke Otto with Princess Joan, who was a year younger than Isabella. Again, the alliance did not materialize. He went to the count of Guelders in January 1338 for a conference of the local princes, returning via Hainault by 14 March. At the end of the year, five of his servants were accused of the murder at Antwerp of Oliver, son of Oliver Ingham, then seneschal of Aquitaine, and a very important figure in Edward's entourage. Once the war against France began, he was employed on military tasks such as gathering a force of Welsh footsoldiers in July 1338. When Edward III mounted his raid on France, and an encounter with the French army was expected at La Flamengrie, Fitzwarin appears as one of the nineteen named knights listed as being in the king's battalion. He had a modest retinue, and was paid £128 18s. 8d. in June 1340 and £140 in March 1341. In 1342 he served as a banneret in Brittany with one knight and eight esquires.

In the Crécy campaign, he fought, as would be expected, in the king's division, with a similar retinue to that in Brittany.[27] His retinue included men

---

[25] Marriage grant, CPR 1334–1338, 179; income grant, CPR 1334–1338, 320.

[26] CCR, Lists and Indexes II, 1900, 189.

[27] Ayton and Preston, Crécy, 246. The Acta Bellicosa (Acts of War) omits him from the list of bannerets in the king's division, but the St Omer chronicle names him, and he is on the

from Hereford and Somerset, as well as his brother John.[28] He was with the king throughout the siege of Calais, and accompanied him on his return to England. He then seems to have rejoined the queen's household, as he is paid as a knight of the queen's bodyguard in 1349–50. He was paid the substantial sum of £266 13s. 4d. in 1350 for services in Flanders and Germany, but this may be a question of wages in respect of his missions abroad over the previous twelve years or more; such belated settlements were far from uncommon. In the same year, he led a pilgrimage to Rome.[29]

He was back in England in 1351, when he was again paid as a member of the queen's household. But thereafter he disappears from the records of active knights, whether on campaign or as administrator at home. Apart from his surrender of Montgomery Castle in 1355, there is only a commission of inquiry in 1357. About the time of his return from Rome, in June 1351, he obtained a licence to give lands and rent to support three chaplains at Wantage to celebrate masses 'for the good estate of the king, queen Philippa and him, and for their souls when they are dead'.[30] Seven years later, because he had not yet made the grants, he asked for the licence to be applied to a grant he wished to make to the friars of Hounslow instead. Yet it was at Wantage that he was buried; his tomb is one of the two surviving memorials to the first Garter knights. The effigies of Sir William and his wife are much defaced by the ravages of iconoclasts and visitors scratching their names in the soft alabaster. The Garter is still visible over his armour, but any decoration or inscription has long since gone, and it is no more than a plain band.

Frank van Hale (KG 1359)   A Flemish knight, probably born in the 1320s, and brother of Simon Hale, a member of the king's household in 1328–30 who had come over with Philippa of Hainault and who lent Edward £400 in January 1339; he was said to have been better known as Simon de Mirabel.[31] Frank van Hale first appears in the English records in Flanders in 1341, receiving the substantial sum of £90 per annum as his retaining fee.[32] He served as a banneret in Henry of Grosmont's army

payrolls.
[28] Wrottesley, *Crécy and Calais*, 150, 173, 176.
[29] See pp. 330–33 above.
[30] *CPR 1350–1354*, 108.
[31] Note by Kervyn de Lettenhove in Froissart, *Chroniques*, ed. Lettenhove, ii.513.
[32] TNA E 101/389/8, m. 9.

in Gascony in 1345; Froissart says that he was at the siege of Bergerac, and he was certainly made keeper of the castle of Rochefort, guarding the mouth of the river Charente, in 1346. In 1349 he was appointed seneschal of the duchy, and accompanied Grosmont on his raid to Toulouse in November and December that year. He was in Grosmont's service in 1351, when he prepared the way, with Stephen de Cosington,[33] for talks between the duke and the count of Flanders. He served on the Reims expedition, probably in Grosmont's retinue, and was among the knights of the Garter named to negotiate the treaty of Brétigny, and was also a guarantor of it.[34] His connection with the house of Lancaster evidently continued after Grosmont's death, as he was paid an annuity in the 1370s through his attorney.[35] However, from 1363 onwards he appears in attendance on the count of Flanders as holding a fief from him as a witness to various acts, the last being in 1373. He was engaged again in peace negotiations in 1375,[36] and probably died shortly after that.

Otho Holland (KG 1349)   Otho, brother of Thomas Holland, is a shadowy figure. In 1342 he fought in Brittany with two esquires,[37] and was a household knight in 1343.[38] In 1350 he was given custody of Raoul count of Eu when Edward purchased him from Thomas, but guarded him so negligently that the count was seen armed and without an escort on the streets of Calais, for which Otho was imprisoned by the marshal of the king's court.[39] He may have fought alongside his brother for much of his career, and was with him in Brittany in 1355. The following year it was Otho who captured Castle Cornet on Jersey in his brother's name. He died in Normandy, presumably in the company of his brother, in September 1359. His lands were in Derbyshire[40] and in Staffordshire.

John, Lord Lisle (of Rougemont) (KG 1349)   See *Complete Peerage*, viii.73–6.

---

[33] Fowler, *The King's Lieutenant*, 101.

[34] *Foedera*, iii.i.531, 535.

[35] Beltz, *Memorials of the Garter*, 126.

[36] *Foedera*, iii.ii.1024–5.

[37] Ayton, *Knights and Warhorses*, 264.

[38] TNA E 36/204, fo. 86.

[39] Beltz, *Memorials of the Garter*, 85.

[40] BL Wolley Charter I.16, with his seal.

Henry Oem (KG 1349) For his career in service of William II, see pp. 324–5; for his service to the prince of Wales, see pp. 188–9, 325–6. Nothing else is known about him.

John Sully (KG 1353) For the career of John Sully, who very probably succeeded Henry Oem, we depend largely on his testimony in the Scrope–Grosvenor case in the Court of Chivalry.[41] He gave evidence in 1388, and stated his age as 102. If he was really born in 1276, he was 32 when he first fought in Scotland in 1315, and 84 when he fought at the battle of Nájera. A more realistic assessment would be that he was born about 1296. He said that he was at the first of Edward III's great victories, at Halidon Hill in 1333, and he is recorded at the Dunstable tournament in 1334.[42] He fought in Flanders in 1338 in William Montagu's retinue.[43] On the Crécy campaign, he transferred to the retinue of Richard Fitzalan, earl of Arundel.[44] He also claimed, probably correctly, to have fought at Winchelsea. He was certainly retained by the prince from 1353 onwards, and that year was given a handsome new year's gift by the prince of Wales of a silver cup and ewer.[45] He became one of his close associates: when the prince ordered five green hats in 1355, they were for himself, Roger Mortimer, Bartholomew Burghersh, Nigel Loring and Sully.[46] Sully went to Gascony in 1355, fought on that year's campaign and at Poitiers, and returned to Gascony with the prince in 1365.[47] After the battle of Nájera, he remained in Aquitaine, and the last mention of him is in 1370, until commissioners were sent to interview him for the Scrope–Grosvenor case in his retirement at Iddesleigh, where he was attended by his squire Richard Baker.

Thomas Ufford (KG 1360) Thomas Ufford was born sometime before 1334, the second son of Robert Ufford, first earl of Suffolk. He appears as a party to a transaction between his father and Edward Montagu in

---

[41] See p. 379 above.

[42] Long, 'Roll of the Arms of the Knights at the Tournament at Dunstable', 393.

[43] Ayton, *Knights and Warhorses*, 249.

[44] Wrottesley, *Crécy and Calais*, 97.

[45] *RBP*, iv.70, 80.

[46] *RBP*, iv.230.

[47] Henxteworth, m. 4; Nicolas, *Scrope–Grosvenor Controversy*, ii.240–43.

August 1352, possibly to do with a marriage.[48] He was listed as one of the knights going on Henry of Grosmont's abortive expedition to Normandy in 1355,[49] and three years later he was retained by Grosmont,[50] which implies that he fought in the Reims campaign of 1359–60. He was probably elected to the company in 1360 on the death of Roger Mortimer: at the time he was heir to the earldom of Suffolk. He was issued with Garter robes in 1362 and 1363,[51] and went abroad, probably with the prince of Wales, in 1364.[52] He fought on the Spanish campaign of 1366–7,[53] and presumably died there, as he predeceased his father, who died in 1368.

Richard de la Vache (KG 1355) Richard de la Vache served with Henry of Grosmont in Brittany in 1342–3,[54] and was a knight of the chamber by 1348: he fought in the tournament at Lichfield in that year.[55] His family were relatively modest knights from Buckinghamshire, and it is possible that his marriage to Amy de la Vache, who was connected in some way with Philippa's household, was his way into the royal circle.[56] He was one of the knights summoned back from England in May 1347 in anticipation of Philip of Valois's arrival before Calais with an army, and his presence in that list makes it likely that he was already a knight of the household, and therefore fought in the king's division at Crécy. He had been appointed to supervise the array of men at arms from Buckinghamshire and Bedfordshire in March 1346, and, as several of his fellow-arrayers for other counties were household knights, this would confirm that he too was one of them.[57] He does not seem to have served in any subsequent campaign, and was appointed constable of the Tower of London in 1361, a largely administrative post. He was issued

[48] Mutual recognizances for 2,500 marks, 26 August 1352: CCR 1349–1354, 503.
[49] Fowler, 'Henry of Grosmont', iv.261.
[50] CPR 1358–1361, 16.
[51] TNA E 361/4, rot. 7 and rot. 8d.
[52] CPR 1361–1364, 472.
[53] Chandos Herald, La Vie du Prince Noir, ll. 2247, 2461, 3231.
[54] Fowler, 'Henry of Grosmont', iv.262.
[55] Nicolas, 'Observations on the Garter', 26–9.
[56] Beltz, Memorials of the Garter, 106–7.
[57] Wrottesley, A History of the Family of Wrottesley of Wrottesley, 78–9.

with Garter robes in 1361–3.[58] He succeeded John Chandos as under-chamberlain in 1363 and died in 1366.

Thomas Wale (KG 1349)   Thomas Wale is another obscure figure, lord of a modest manor in Northamptonshire, born in 1303.[59] His first military record is a summons for the Scottish campaign in 1333.[60] He fought in Flanders in the retinue of William Montagu in 1338,[61] and under William Bohun, earl of Northampton, in Brittany in 1342. He went to Brittany with Richard Fitzalan in 1344.[62] There is a gift of a silver-gilt cup to him in the prince of Wales's register in the list drawn up in 1353, and he is described as 'the prince's bachelor'.[63] He died in Gascony on 26 October 1352, leaving no heir.[64]

Hugh Wrottesley (KG 1349)   See pp. 320–23. For a full account of his career, see George Wrottesley, *A History of the Family of Wrottesley of Wrottesley.*

[58] TNA E 361/4, rot. 4, rot. 7 and rot. 8d.
[59] Beltz, *Memorials of the Garter*, 63.
[60] *Foedera*, ii.ii.856.
[61] *Foedera*, ii.ii.1048.
[62] *Foedera*, iii.i.10.
[63] *RBP*, iv.73.
[64] Beltz, *Memorials of the Garter*, 63.

Appendix 4

Chronological List of
Royal Tournaments of Edward III

Most tournaments are discussed in the text, and references can be found in the relevant notes. References given below are only for those tournaments not referenced in the main text. Only the ninety-five tournaments where Edward himself is known or believed to have attended are included in the list; records of other tournaments held by individuals at which the king was not present are very sparse, and were probably infrequent. Likewise, records of attendance at the tournaments are erratic, and the names of knights known to have been present are not included here; where there is such information, the tournament is asterisked and the names can be traced in the sources referred to in the footnotes.

Dating has been done by cross-reference to the itinerary printed in Ormrod, *Edward III*, 610–31, and is inevitably tentative in many cases.

Year	Date	Place
1327	February	London[1]
1327	April[2]	
1327	23–7 December	Worcester
1328	9–14 January	Clipstone
1328	15 January	Blyth[3]
1328	17–18 January	Rothwell

[1] To celebrate coronation; TNA E 361/3, rot. 9 m. 2d, rot. 10 m. 1.
[2] Held by John Bohun, earl of Hereford; TNA DL 10/250.
[3] TNA DL 41/335; Smyth, *Lives of the Berkeleys*, i.235.

Year	Date	Place
1328	25–8 January	York
1328	24 May–23 June	Northampton[4]
1328	31 May	Hereford
1328	25 September	Thetford[5]
1328	31 October–31 December	Wigmore
1329	2 January	Coventry
1329	6–9 March	Guildford
1329	June	Amiens
1329	13–19 June	Canterbury
1329	25 June	Dartford
1329	2–3 July	Reigate
1329	12 August–4 September	Gloucester
1329	8–13 September	Hereford
1329	8–13 September	Wigmore
1329	28 September–7 October	Worcester
1329	8–12 October	Dunstable*
1330	?18 February	Westminster*
1330	c. 25 March	Winchester[6]
1330	22–7 July	Woodstock
1330	28 July	Northampton[7]
1330	16 September	Nottingham[8]
1330	13 November	Clarendon
1330	28 November	Westminster
1330	20 December	Guildford
1331	20 January	Westminster
1331	1–7 February	King's Langley[9]
1331	26 April	Dartford*
1331	1–21 May	Havering-atte-Bower*
1331	25 May–4 June	Newmarket*
1331	16–19 June	Stepney*
1331	during summer?	Lichfield*[10]

[4] Ibid., 235.

[5] TNA C 47/6/1, m. 5.

[6] Possibly Mortimer's celebration of the execution of Edmund earl of Kent; E 101/361/3, rot. 16d m. 1.

[7] London, Society of Antiquaries, MS 541, note sewn to m. 3, fair copy m. 3.

[8] Ibid.

[9] TNA E 361/3, rot. 19 m. 1d.

[10] TNA E 101/385/7, m. 1; E 361/3, rot. 19 m. 1d.

Year	Date	Place
1331	20 August	Bedford[11]
1331	22–5 September	Cheapside*
1332	16 June	Woodstock*
1334	16–26 January	Dunstable*
1334	?1–6 February	Woodstock[12]
1334	?9 February	Newmarket
1334	16–18 May	Burstwick[13]
1334	12–17 July	Nottingham
1334	?11–12 September	Guildford[14]
1334	13–30 September	Smithfield[15]
1337	?10 April	?[16]
1338	?	Windsor[17]
1339	1–31 January	Antwerp[18]
1339	1–6 November	Brussels[19]
1340	12–18 April	Windsor[20]
1340	1 October–27 November	Ghent[21]
1340	Between 9 and 15 December 1340	Le Bure[22]
1340	c. 25 December	Reading
1341	2 February	King's Langley
1341	20 February	Norwich
1341	1–10 June	King's Langley*
1341	4 October	Westminster[23]

[11] TNA E 361/3, rot. 19 m. 1d.

[12] For tournaments at Woodstock and Newmarket, see Ormrod, *Edward III*, 143 and note; and BL Add. MS 46350, rot. 7.

[13] TNA E 101/386/15; BL Add MS. 46350, rot. 7.

[14] TNA E 101/386/15.

[15] *Annales Paulini*, i.361; possibly celebration of military successes in Scotland.

[16] BL Add. MS 60584, fo. 38ᵛ.

[17] TNA E 361/3, m. 40a.

[18] TNA E 101/388/11; churching of Philippa, baptism of Lionel.

[19] TNA E 101/388/11; *Chronographia Regum Francorum*, ii.85.

[20] TNA E 101/388/11; E 361/3, m. 40a.

[21] TNA E 101/388/11.

[22] TNA DL /25/983; king may not have been present, jousts organized by Henry of Grosmont.

[23] TNA E 101/389/12.

Year	Date	Place
1342	?23–5 January	York
1342	January?	Hull
1342	11–12 February	Dunstable*
1342	10–14 April	Northampton*
1342	1–13 July	Eltham*
1343	24–7 June	Smithfield*[24]
1343	10 March onwards	Canterbury, Hereford[25]
1344	15–24 January	Windsor*
1344	15 November–30 December	Bungay*[26]
1344	30 November	Leicester*[27]
1344	21–7 December	Norwich[28]
1345	?	Winchester*[29]
1348	mid-February	Reading[30]
1348	February?	Bury St Edmunds*[31]
1348	20 April	Lincoln[32]
1348	4–12 May	Lichfield*
1348	14–19 May	Windsor*
1348	20 May	Eltham
1348	14 July	Canterbury*
1349	23 April	Windsor
1349	24 June	Windsor[33]
1350	25 November–8 December	Reading[34]
1350	6 December	Norwich[35]
1351	?	Bristol[36]

[24] TNA C 47/6/1, m. 16; *Murimuth*, 146, 230–31; *Annales Paulini*, ii.361.
[25] *Murimuth*, 146.
[26] TNA C 47/6/1, m. 4.
[27] Knighton, *Chronicle*, 50–51.
[28] Blomefield, *Norfolk*, iii.86.
[29] BL MS Harleian 4304, fo. 19ᵛ.
[30] Nicolas, 'Observations on the Garter', 38–9; TNA E 101/391/15, m. 10; E 372/207, m. 50; E 403/340.
[31] TNA E 372/207, m. 50; C 47/6/1, m. 4; *RBP*, iv.67.
[32] Baker, *Chronicon*, 97.
[33] Ibid., 101; TNA E 372/207, m. 50.
[34] TNA E 361/3, m. 49a.
[35] Blomefield, *Norfolk*, iii.94; Norfolk Record Office, Norwich bailiffs' account for 1349.
[36] TNA E 372/207, m. 50.

Year	Date	Place
1353	19–27 March	Smithfield[37]
1353	31 December	Eltham[38]
1355	22 February	Woodstock[39]
1357	?24 May	Smithfield*[40]
1358	1 January	Bristol
1358	23 April	Windsor
1359	27–9 May	Smithfield*[41]
1361	27 May	Smithfield[42]
1362	19 April	Smithfield[43]
1363	1 November	Smithfield[44]
1377	February	Smithfield[45]
1377	4 June	Smithfield[46]

[37] *Avesbury*, 419; in honour of Breton visitors.

[38] Ibid.

[39] Ibid., 422; *RBP*, iv.165; churching of Philippa, baptism of Thomas.

[40] John of Reading, *Chronica*, 129; Walsingham, *Historia Anglicana*, i.285, 296.

[41] John of Reading *Chronica*, 131; *RBP*, iv.323; *Brut*, ii.309; marriage of John of Gaunt and Blanche of Lancaster.

[42] TNA E 101/393/15 for date; *RBP*, iv.324; marriage of earl of Richmond.

[43] John of Reading, *Chronica*, 152–3; *RBP*, iv.475.

[44] TNA E 101/571/16, E 101/393/15, m. 13, E 101/394/16, mm. 5, 14, 17; Venette, *Chronicle*, 114. Four kings were present on this occasion: Edward, David II of Scotland, John II of France and Peter I of Cyprus.

[45] TNA E 101/397/20, mm. 18, 19, 21.

[46] TNA E 101/392/20, m. 6; planned but cancelled.

Appendix 5
The Statutes of the Garter

Translation into English of the earliest Latin text of the Statutes of the Order of the Garter, as recorded in the French Register with annotations for any significant difference between this text and the French text of Arundel 48 and other early manuscripts.[1]

By Lisa Jefferson

1. In honour of Almighty God, of Saint Mary the glorious Virgin, and of Saint George the martyr, our supreme lord, Edward III, King of England, in the twenty-third year of his reign ordained, established and founded a certain society or knightly order within his Castle of Windsor, in this manner: Firstly, he decreed himself to be the Sovereign of the said society or order, his eldest son the Prince of Wales, the Duke of Lancaster, the Earl of Warwick, the Captal de Buch, the Earl of Stafford, the Earl of Salisbury, Lord Mortimer, Sir John Lisle, Sir Bartholomew Bourghersh the younger, Sir John Beauchamp, Lord Mohun, Sir Hugh Courtenay, Sir Thomas Holland, Sir John Grey, Sir Richard Fitz-Simon, Sir Miles Stapleton, Sir Thomas Wale, Sir Hugh Wrottesley, Sir Nele (Nigel) Loring, Sir John Chandos, Sir James d'Audley, Sir Otto de Holland, Sir Henry Eam, Sir Sanchet d'Abridgecourt, Sir Walter Paveley.

2. It was agreed that the King of England, whoever it shall be at the time,[2] shall in perpetuity be the Sovereign of this Order of Saint George or Society of the Garter.

---

[1] The original of the earliest known Latin text is found in Oxford, Bodleian Library, MS Ashmole 1128, and is printed in Ashmole, *The Institution* ..., Appendix I. The earliest French text is found in a number of manuscripts and is edited by Lisa Jefferson in *EHR*, CIX (1994), 376–84.

[2] The French text says 'the King and his heirs, Kings of England' which is slightly different.

3. Item, it is agreed that none shall be elected as a member of the said Order unless he be of noble birth and a knight without reproach, since the institution of the Order does not admit those of low birth nor the reprobate.[3]

4. And the aforesaid twenty-six fellow knights and companions of this order shall wear the mantle and garter as ordained at the said castle as often as they shall be present there, that is to say each time that they enter the chapel of Saint George or the chapter house in order to hold a chapter or to regulate any matter pertaining to the Order. And in the same manner[4] they shall proceed on Saint George's Eve, moving as a procession with the Sovereign of the Order or his deputy from the King's great chamber as far as the chapel or the chapter house, and they shall return in the same manner. They shall then sit wearing their mantles and garters on the said eve at the time of supper, both those who wish to take supper and those who do not eat, until the usual time for departure from the said great chamber.[5] And thus robed also they shall proceed the next day towards the said chapel and return from there, as also at the time of dinner and thereafter, until the Sovereign or his deputy shall remove his own insignia of the order. Thus also when proceeding to the second vespers and returning therefrom, as also at the time of supper and thereafter, they shall be dressed as on the eve, until such time as the Sovereign of the Order shall decree it to be time for departure.[6]

5. And thirteen secular canons are ordained, who must be priests at the time of their induction or who must be preferred to the priesthood within the following year, and also thirteen vicars who shall be priests at the time of their admission or at the latest by the time of the next following ordinations, who shall celebrate continually for the souls of all the faithful deceased. These aforenamed canons shall be presented by the aforenamed founders of the Order, that is to say that each of the present founders shall present his canon to the Warden of the College.[7]

---

[3] The French text lacks the last phrase, has nothing more in this article after 'reproach'.

[4] The French text says that 'they shall likewise wear their mantles'.

[5] The French text says until 'la voydie' = 'the void, or voidee': the parting dish of wine with spiced delicacies, brought round to mark the end of a feast or ceremonial evening.

[6] Here again the French text says 'until the voidee'.

[7] This ruling has provoked a fair amount of discussion among modern scholars; it is clear that it does not date from the first institution of the Order, since it refers to 'quilibet

However, if one of the canons shall die, neither he who last presented him nor any other of the companions of the Order shall afterwards present, but only the Sovereign of the Order shall present to that canonry from that time forward in perpetuity. And thus it is unanimously agreed for the presentations of all other canons to be reserved to the Sovereign alone.

6. Item, it is agreed that the aforesaid canons shall each have a mantle of cloth of purple colour[8] with a roundel of the arms of Saint George.

7. Item, it is ordained that twenty-six veteran knights,[9] who have no means of sustenance, shall have there in the honour of God and of the blessed George a sufficient maintenance, that they may continually serve God in prayers. And for the election of those veteran knights it is ordained in the same manner as for the presentation of the aforesaid canons, thus that both the elections of the veterans as also the presentations of the canons are reserved to the Sovereign alone.

8. Item, it is agreed that the said veteran knights shall each have a mantle of red with an escutcheon of the arms of Saint George but without the garter.

9. Item, it is agreed that if the Sovereign of this Order or Society shall perchance be unable to attend the celebration of the feast of Saint George, [he shall nominate a deputy to hold][10] the chapter meeting at the hour of terce and the celebration of the feast on the next day, at the expenses of the Sovereign of the Order. But such a deputy shall not make new observances or ordinances. However, it shall be permitted to him to correct and redress those who transgress the statutes of the Order which follow.

10. Item, each year on Saint George's Eve shall be held a meeting of

---

fundatorum modernorum', or in French 'chacun des fondeurs qui sont a present', the Latin of 'modernorum' making it clear that these are not the original 26 First Founders. At what date this ordinance was issued has not been determined, but Peter Begent tentatively suggested that one should consider the period between 1352 and 1368 (Begent and Chesshyre, p. 27).

[8] The French text says 'murrey' = mulberry colour.

[9] The French text throughout calls them 'povres chevaliers' = poor knights, the title by which they came to be known in English until a much later date.

[10] There is clearly an omission of several words in the manuscript here, but the sense is clear and can also be supplied from the French version of the text, which in addition says that the nomination of a deputy should be 'par ses lettres' = by letter.

all the companions of the Order of Saint George, at the said Castle of Windsor, whether they be within the kingdom of England or outside it but that they may conveniently be able to come thither, and there they must attend the church service and shall wear their mantle at the time of the celebration of divine service, being each in their stalls in their respective places. And each of them shall have in the chapel above his stall his helmet and his sword which, in memory[11] of him and for the protection of the church, shall stay there for the period of his lifetime, in the manner that the noble and chivalrous order requires. But in the eventuality that the feast of Saint George shall fall within the fifteen days following Easter Day, the said feast of Saint George shall be postponed until the second Sunday after Easter Day, so that each of the companions of the Order may in due manner be able to come to that feast without having to ride on horseback on any of the three days that follow Easter Day.[12]

11. Item, that they shall gather together in the said place on Saint George's Eve, at the hour of terce, and if any do not come thus at the appointed time and have no excuse acceptable to the Sovereign of the Order or his deputy, they must be punished by the Sovereign of the Order and the Chapter,[13] in this manner that, because of this negligence, they shall not enter the chapter on this occasion, but shall wait outside at the door, and they shall have no voice in any matter that may be dealt with in the said chapter on that occasion. And if any do not come before the beginning of vespers, they shall not enter their stalls then, but shall stand down below in front of their stalls in the customary place for the candlebearers[14], for the duration of the said vespers at which they did not arrive on time. And a like penalty is ordained for those who do not arrive before the beginning of Solemn Mass[15] or of vespers on the following day. And whoever does not come to the celebration of the feast, having no excuse acceptable to the Sovereign of the Order, he shall be

---

[11] The French text says 'en signifiance' not in memory.

[12] The church maintained a ban on riding (the basis for which is Exodus 20.10) after vespers each Saturday and on Sundays and during feast days.

[13] The French text here refers to a preceding agreement as to the punishment, made in a chapter meeting : « auront leur penance selon l'accord du chapistre. Et l'accord est que ...'.

[14] Or candelabra or candlesticks. The French version says in the choristers' place.

[15] Or High Mass.

ordered in the name of penance that he shall not enter his stall at the next following feast but shall stand outside and in front of his stall in the aforementioned place during the time of first vespers, and at the time of the procession on the next day he shall walk in front of the three processional crosses, and coming into the choir again he shall stand in the aforementioned low place until the Offertory, when he shall be the last to offer. And when he has performed these penances thus, he shall come straightaway before the Sovereign's stall or that of his deputy to ask for pardon. And then the said Sovereign or his deputy shall restore him to his stall and to his former status. If he once more absent himself for a second time from the feast of Saint George held the next following year, without an excuse acceptable to the Sovereign or his deputy, and being within the kingdom of England, then he shall not from that time forward enter his stall until he has, within that said chapel upon the altar of Saint George, offered a jewel to the value of 20 English marks. And he shall double the fine each year from then onwards until he be reconciled.

12. Item, that all companions of the Order, wherever they may be, shall wear their mantle of bluet each year, inclusively from the hour of first vespers on Saint George's Eve until second vespers on the day following, in the same manner as they would if they were present in person with the Sovereign of the Order or his deputy, for the whole time that this feast is to be celebrated, provided yet that they be in a place wherein they enjoy their liberty.[16]

13. Item, it is agreed that if any one of the said society should appear publicly[17] without his garter, as soon as this shall be brought to attention or noted,[18] he shall pay to the Warden and College half a mark, in the same manner as others previously have paid who have been established to be guilty of the same fault.

14. Item, it is agreed that at the time of the Offertory at High Mass, the two companions who are opposite each other in their stalls shall always come forward together to make their offering. And if it happen that one of these be absent, then his companion who should be opposite to him shall come forward alone and shall make his offering on his

---

[16] The French version has additionally at the end of this article : 'Notwithstanding the prorogation of the feast'.

[17] The French text says 'should be found in public'.

[18] The French text says 'tentost aprés la chalenge' = straight after this is challenged.

own. And it is to be noted that the Sovereign of the Order at the time of a procession in the said chapel shall move forward behind the whole body of the companions.

15. Item, it is recorded that on each morrow of Saint George's Day, before the companions take leave of each other or depart, a requiem mass is to be celebrated for the souls of all the faithful departed,[19] and that the whole society should be there in its entirety, unless there be some reasonable hindrance for anyone, or unless he have the permission of the Sovereign of the Order or his deputy before he departs from there.

16. Item, it is agreed that each of the companions shall leave his mantle there, [ready] for unexpected visits and in order to observe the precepts and salutary admonitions of the aforesaid Sovereign.

17. Item, it is deemed appropriate that if it should happen that anyone of the said society or order shall travel through the said Castle of Windsor, he shall enter [there] in honour of the place, if he is conveniently able and is not hindered by any just and reasonable cause. And that before he enter the chapel he shall put on his mantle, for he should not enter except clothed in his mantle. And the canons present there at that time shall come to meet him, and shall lead him devoutly into the chapel. And if he shall happen to arrive at the time of mass, he shall wait there in the honour of God and Saint George and shall hear that same mass. But if he arrive after midday, he shall enter in the manner and form stated and shall then wait until the canons have once recited the psalm De Profundis for the souls of all the faithful departed,[20] and he shall make an offering once the psalm has been said. But if anyone of the said society shall ride through the midst of the town and not enter the chapel and make an offering according to this agreement, for each time that he has not done this, he shall for the virtue of obedience walk a mile[21] on foot towards the said chapel and shall offer one penny in the honour of Saint George.

18. Item, it is agreed that the Sovereign of the Order, immediately after the death of one of the companions has been made known

---

[19] The French text says the requiem mass is to be sung 'for the souls of companions who have died and for all christians'.

[20] The French text says for the souls of all christians.

[21] The French text lays down 'une lieue' = a league.

to him, shall see to it that a thousand masses are celebrated for the soul of him who has died, and each foreign king shall have 800 masses celebrated for the soul of him who has died, the Prince of Wales 700, each duke 600, each earl 300, each baron[22] 200 and each knight bachelor 100 masses.[23] And if the Sovereign of the Order or any other shall not have had this done within the quarter of the year after he has been notified of the death, he shall be obliged to double the number of masses in total of those to which his status or rank obliged him from the beginning, and if he be in arrears by half a year, then he must double them again in the same manner, and thus from time to time until the end of the year, and then he shall redouble the years in the same manner.

19. Item, it is agreed that as often as one of the companions of the order shall depart this life, the Sovereign of the Order or his deputy, having assured himself that the report be trustworthy, shall have all the companions who are within his kingdom of England and who are able to get there summoned by letter that they should meet together to elect a new companion, within six weeks after the notification of the death, in a convenient place which the Sovereign shall designate for this purpose. When all are thus met together, or six of them at least besides the Sovereign or his deputy, each one who shall be present at the election shall nominate nine qualified persons, whom he shall believe to be free from all ignominy or shame, who shall be subjects of the Sovereign of the Order or others, foreigners not subject to him but who yet shall not favour or uphold any party opposed to the said Sovereign, that is to say three earls or those of higher rank, three barons, and three knights bachelor, and these nominations shall be written down by the chief Prelate of the Order, that is to say the Bishop of Winchester whoever he be at the time, and in his absence the Dean of the College, or the registrar, and in their absence the oldest resident of the aforesaid college, and these nominations having been made by all the companions or at least six of them as said above, they shall be shown by him who has written them down to the Sovereign of the Order or his deputy, who shall choose from those nominated in this manner and shall admit the one

---

[22] The French gives a number of 200 for bannerets rather than barons.
[23] The text Ashmole was having copied had two interpolated additions, one for a marquess (450 masses) and one for a viscount (250 masses). These additions date from 1446.

who has obtained the greatest number of votes and who shall seem to him most fit to the honour of the Order and the usefulness of the kingdom and of the King.[24] And in the event that any of the companions shall not come to the election in the following manner, he shall be punished only if he was not prevented by just cause. But if he adduce just and demonstrable cause for his absence, this must be approved by the Sovereign or his deputy. But if the cause of his absence shall perchance be found insufficiently justified, and having been summoned he does not come to the election as is stated above, it is agreed that he shall pay one mark as a penalty to the Warden and college, and, when he is next in a chapter meeting, he shall sit in front of the Sovereign or his deputy and of the whole society, in the middle of the chapter house and on the ground, until he be reinstated by the Sovereign or his deputy.

20. Item, it is agreed that in the event that one of the knights of the said Society of the Garter shall die, and another be elected in his place, as soon after the election as he is elected he shall have the garter as a sign that he is one of the companions of the Garter, and he shall have the mantle as his livery of the Order at the time of his induction into his stall and not before. And in the event that he die before he has been installed, he shall not be named as one of the founders since he has not had full possession of his status, but he shall have half the number of the aforesaid masses since he had the livery of the garter and withal nothing more. And if one thus elected shall not come to the said place with all proper speed after he has received the garter, so that he may be installed, and certainly within the year after his election if he be living within the kingdom of England, and have no excuse acceptable to the Sovereign or his deputy and the society of the Garter, then his election shall be straightway declared invalid and void, and then the Sovereign of the Order or his deputy shall together with the society proceed to a new election. And neither the sword nor the helmet of any elected companion shall be affixed above his stall until he come to the Castle, but shall be placed outside and in front of his stall, this being so that if such an elected companion do not come to the Castle, as it is said above, his sword and his helmet shall not be taken down from above in unseemly fashion but shall be removed in

[24] The French text says 'the most profitable (or useful) to the crown and the kingdom'.

a manner befitting unimpaired knightly honour, and shall be taken out of the choir in courtly and honest fashion and shall remain from henceforward at the communal service and use of the aforesaid College.

21. Item, it is agreed that all foreigners who shall be elected to the society of the said Order of the Garter shall be notified of their election by the Sovereign of the Order, and the garter and mantle and the statutes of the Order under the common seal shall be sent to them with all proper speed but at the expenses of the Sovereign of the Order. And all foreigners shall be notified within four months following the time of their election, in order that they may be able to consider from the contents of the statutes whether they wish to accept such an election. And also that all foreigners elected thus, of whatever rank or dignity they may be, within the space of eight months after they have been notified of their election by the Sovereign or his deputy, and after reception of the garter, shall send a procurator who shall adequately be seen to be sufficient in status to the elected man. With the proviso however that such a procurator who is to be installed in his place shall be a knight free from all opprobrium, who at the time of his arrival for this purpose shall bring with him from him who has sent him a mantle of the Order of blue silk, and also a sword and his helmet[25] which are to remain in the College itself.[26] That this mantle shall be laid over the right arm of such a procurator by the Sovereign of the Order or his deputy at the time of his aforesaid installation, and he shall keep it there over his said right arm during the canonical hours next following the installation which he shall take in the name of his aforesaid lord or master. But the said procurator once installed shall not wear such a mantle afterwards, nor shall he enter the chapter meeting nor have any voice there by virtue of any powers that may have been attributed to him. And it is to be known that this favour of installation by proxy shall only be accorded to foreigners who for this reason are unable to come in person, so that they may participate in the masses and devout prayers of the Order, of

[25] The French text of Arundel 48 adds here the crest as well: 'son heaulme, son tymbre et son espee', which is interesting as the Latin text gives only the helmet and sword here, and both texts give only these for English-born companions, whereas here the crest is added for foreigners (Stranger Knights).

[26] The French text says they are to remain there 'pour tousjours' = for ever.

half of which they would be deprived if they were not installed before they died.

22. Item, it is agreed that if any earl, baron[27] or knight bachelor of the said Order shall die, he who shall succeed in his place, whether he be an earl, a baron or a knight bachelor, shall hold the same stall as his predecessor, whatever his rank may be. Nor shall any to be elected change this succession except the Prince of Wales, who shall always hold the stall opposite to that of the Sovereign after he has been elected. Thus it may happen that an earl can occupy the stall of a knight, and vice versa. And this is ordained so that it shall be known who were the First Founders of the Order.

23. Item, it is agreed that each companion of the Order at the time of his first entry, shall give a fixed sum of money according to the eminence of his rank, for the support of the canons and the poor veteran knights living there and also for the increase of alms perpetually ordained there: that is to say the Sovereign of the Order 40 marks, a foreign king 20 pounds, the Prince of Wales 20 marks, each duke 10 pounds, each earl 10 marks, each baron[28] 100 shillings and each knight bachelor 5 marks. And these pious gifts are thus established in order that each who enters this knightly order shall more worthily obtain the name, title and privilege of being one of the founders.[29] For it is judged worthy and suitable that he who is added to the number of the founders shall give generously for the sake of this benefit or name.[30] And until such sums have been paid in this manner in correct proportion as devised here at the time of his first entry, neither the sword nor the helmet of such an entrant shall be affixed above his stall. And it is to be known that the Sovereign of the Order shall be liable to pay the expenses of the entry of any foreigners who shall be elected, at the time of the installation of their procurators.

24. Item, it is agreed that whenever one of the First Founders of this society or order shall die, an escutcheon of metal of his arms, and his helmet shall be affixed to the back of his stall. And the other Founders who succeed later shall have their escutcheons and helmets placed in similar fashion but somewhat below those of the First Founders. And

---

[27] Here and below the French text refers to a banneret, rather than a baron.

[28] Here again the French text gives 'banneret'.

[29] The French text adds here 'of this same Order'.

[30] This sentence: 'For it is judged ... or name', does not appear at all in the French version.

their escutcheons and helmets shall not be of such great value[31] as those of the First Founders.

25. Item, that each upon entering shall promise and swear either in person or through a suitable and sufficient procurator to be installed in his name, that he will well and faithfully observe the statutes of the Order to the utmost of his ability. And it is to be observed that no one shall receive installation by procurator except only foreigners who for that reason are not conveniently able to attend in person.

26. Item, it is agreed that in the event that the Sovereign of the Order shall be outside his kingdom of England at the time of the installation of one of the companions of the Garter, or if perchance he is not able to perform in person those duties which pertain to him by virtue of his office, he may entrust his powers and full capacities in this matter to one of the companions of the same Order to carry out those appropriate duties which should pertain to his own office were he present.[32]

27. Item, it is agreed that a common seal shall be made, which shall be in the custody of him whom the Sovereign of the Order shall wish to appoint to this duty.

28. Item, that each of the companions of the aforesaid Order shall from henceforth have a copy of the statutes of the order under the aforesaid common seal, and the original copy of trhe statutes shall be sealed by the same seal and shall remain in perpetuity within the treasury of the said College,[33] and that after the death of each companion of the aforesaid Order, his executors shall be obliged to return those same statutes to the college, and to hand them over to the Warden of the College.

29. Item, it is agreed that none of the knights of the Order of Saint George and of the Society of the Garter shall leave the kingdom of England without the knowledge and permission of the said Sovereign. And it is therefore agreed that if some knightly expedition arise, or anything else which may be perceived to result in chivalric honour, the Sovereign of the Order shall be obliged to prefer by his grace the companions of the Order to all others in such knightly actions.

[31] The French text says that they shall not be as big as those of the First Founders. Neither injunction has been followed in practice.

[32] The French text says that this shall be done 'in his [the Sovereign's] name'.

[33] What follows here: 'and that after ... College', is, in the French text, allocated to a separate article.

30. Item, that no companion of the Order shall lift arms against another companion unless it be in the war of his liege lord or in his own just cause. And if it should happen that one of the companions of the Order be retained by a certain lord, or shall uphold the party and cause of a certain lord, and that later an adverse party should wish to retain any other companion of the Order to defend its opposing cause, then no such companion secondarily requested shall consent to this, but shall be obliged to excuse himself on the grounds that his companion has been previously retained or armed by the opposing party. And on this account each companion of the order, when he is retained by anyone, shall be obliged to make an exception and to stipulate that he shall be entirely and with full quittance excused from all service in advancing or waging a war if it shall be that one of his companions of the society of the Garter has been previously retained by the opposing side and armed in that cause. And if he who is secondarily retained has not known that one of his companions of the Garter had been previously retained by or had taken up arms for the opposing party, then as soon as this shall come to his notice he shall be obliged to relinquish completely all such service and totally to excuse himself.

31. Item, all licences to fellow knights of the said society granting leave to travel around to those who wish to gain honour through the exercise of knightly arts, and also all other written documents whether they be letters of certification or letters of instruction which shall be seen to concern the Order, must be issued[34] through the Sovereign of the Order under the common seal, which shall remain in the custody of one of the companions of the Order according to the wishes of the aforesaid Sovereign. And if he who has custody of the seal shall for reasonable cause move out of the Sovereign's presence, he shall hand over that same seal into the custody of another companion of the same Order who is present with the Sovereign and whom that same Sovereign shall designate to have custody of that same seal; thus that the common seal shall never be removed from the presence of the Sovereign while that same Sovereign be within his kingdom of England. And in similar fashion, in the absence of the Sovereign of the Order, his deputy shall see to it that this be done with the aforesaid seal.

---

[34] The French text states that this is 'doresenavant' = from henceforth.

32. Item, it is agreed that if any (other)[35] knight of the said society or Order, moved by a spirit of devotion, shall desire to make his residence permanently in the said Castle of Windsor, he shall be required to provide for the necessities of his life and of his dwelling from his own private means.

33. [Item,[36] that if any other knight who is not one of the said company shall, by devotion, wish to live there, then his living arrangements shall be made acccording to the agreement of the Sovereign and the company.]

34. Item, it is agreed that in the event that any knight who is not one of the said society of the Garter, or any other person,[37] shall wish to donate in any year ten pounds[38] or more to the said College, in order to participate in the support of the prayers to be said there, then the name of such a donor shall be recorded in the Calendar of Benefactors, so that the Canons and Veteran Knights shall be able to pray for him in perpetuity.

35. Item, it is agreed that if any of the canons shall die, and the Sovereign of the Order shall be outside his kingdom of England, then the Warden or Dean of the College, whoever he shall be at the time, shall send letters accordingly to the Sovereign of the Order, so that the Sovereign shall be able to present whom he wishes to enter that canonry.

36. Item, a registrar[39] shall be appointed by the Sovereign and the society of the Order, who shall be more learned than the others of the College, and he must be present at each chapter meeting that is held of the Order, for the registration and enactment of each and every election and the names of those elected, and the punishments imposed and the reasons for punishments that pertain to the said Order,[40] and this from

---

[35] The word 'alius' = 'other' is a scribal error in this text, caused by the similarity in wording of the next statute, which the scribe has omitted, again no doubt by eyeslip caused by the similarities of wording.

[36] Ashmole has annotated the text here to say 'The 33. Art. of E3 & H5 statts is here omitted.' I give the text above as translated from the French of Arundel 48.

[37] The French text gives 'Item, it is agreed that if any knight or any other person shall wish . . .'.

[38] The French text gives no monetary value, just 'any lands or rents'.

[39] By tradition in the Order he has always been called 'Register'.

[40] The French text has additionally here that he must record the reconciliations of those punished, and all other acts and the reasons for them that appertain to the said Order.

chapter to chapter annually. And the said registrar shall be sworn upon his receiving office that he shall faithfully keep the register, and that at the beginning of each chapter meeting held on Saint George's Eve each year, all matters registered the previous year shall there be publicly read out in the presence of the Sovereign and the society of the Order, so that if anything be badly described and worthy of correction, it may be amended in due form.

Abbreviations

Age of Edward III	*The Age of Edward III*, ed. J. S. Bothwell (Woodbridge, 2001)
Avesbury	*Chronicon Roberti de Avesbury*, in *Chronica Adae Murimuth et Roberti de Avesbury*, ed. E. M. Thompson, RS 93 (London, 1889)
Baker, *Chronicon*	*Chronicon Geoffrey le Baker de Swynebroke*, ed. Edward Maunde Thompson (Oxford, 1889)
BL	British Library
BN	Bibliothèque Nationale
CCR	*Calendar of Close Rolls* (London, 1900–63)
CPR	*Calendar of Patent Rolls* (London, 1891–1916)
EETS	Early English Text Society
EHR	*English Historical Review*
Froissart, *Chroniques*, Amiens version	Jean Froissart, *Chroniques Livre I: Le Manuscrit d'Amiens*, ed. George T. Diller, 5 vols. (Geneva, 1991–8)
Froissart, *Chroniques*, Besançon version	Jean Froissart, *Chroniques Livre III: Le Manuscrit Saint-Vincent de Besançon*, ed. Peter F. Ainsworth, 1 vol. to date (Geneva, 2007–)
Froissart, *Chroniques*, Rome version	Jean Froissart, *Chroniques: début du premier livre. Édition du manuscrit de Rome Reg. lat. 869*, ed. George T. Diller (Geneva, 1972)
Froissart, *Chroniques*, SHF	Jean Froissart, *Chroniques*, ed. Simeon Luce *et al.*, 13 vols. (in progress), SHF (Paris, 1869–)
Froissart, *Chroniques*, ed. Lettenhove	*Œuvres de Froissart: Chroniques*, ed. Kervyn de Lettenhove, 26 vols. (Paris, 1867–77)
Henxteworth	London, Duchy of Cornwall Office, Daybook of John Henxteworth
Historia Roffensis	(*Rochester History*) BL MS Cotton Faustina B.V
History of the King's Works	R. A. Brown, H. M. Colvin and A. J. Taylor, *The History of the King's Works: The Middle Ages*, 2 vols. (London, 1963)

Livre Charny	Michael Taylor (ed.), 'A Critical Edition of Geoffroy de Charny's *Livre Charny* and the *Demandes pour la Joute, les Tournois et la Guerre*', Ph.D. thesis, University of North Carolina at Chapel Hill, 1977
MED	*Middle English Dictionary*: http://quod.lib. umich.edu/m/med/lookup.html
Murimuth	*Chronicon Adae Murimuth*, in *Chronica Adae Murimuth et Roberti de Avesbury*, ed. E. M. Thompson, RS 93 (London, 1889)
ODNB	*Oxford Dictionary of National Biography*: www.oxforddnb.com
PROME	*The Parliament Rolls of Medieval England 1275–1504*, general editor Chris Given-Wilson (Woodbridge, 2005)
RBP	*Register of Edward the Black Prince*, 4 vols. (London, 1930–33)
RS	Rolls Series, London
SHF	Société de l'Histoire de France
TNA	The National Archives
TRHS	*Transactions of the Royal Historical Society*

Bibliography

PRIMARY SOURCES

A. Manuscripts

Cambridge, Corpus Christi College, MS 170
Eton College, MS 213
Heidelberg, Universitätsbibliothek, MS Cod. Pal. Germ. 848
London, British Library:

Add. MS 38823	MS Cotton Galba E.III
Add. MS 42130	MS Cotton Galba E.XIV
Add. MS 46350	MS Cotton Nero C.VIII
Add. MS 60584	MS Cotton Nero D.VII
MS Cotton Caligula D.III, item 76	MS Harleian 4304
MS Cotton Cleopatra D.VII	MS Harleian 5001
MS Cotton Faustina B.V	Wolley Charter I.16

London, Duchy of Cornwall Office, Daybook of John Henxteworth
London, The National Archives:

C 47/6/1	E 101/361/3
C 61/83	E 101/382/9
C 61/84	E 101/382/17
C 61/85	E 101/383/8
C 76/45	E 101/384/6
C 241/147	E 101/384/14
DL 10/250	E 101/385/4
DL 25/983	E 101/385/7
DL 40/1/11	E 101/386/2
DL 41/335	E 101/386/9
E 36/144	E 101/386/15
E 36/204	E 101/386/16
E 36/205	E 101/386/18
E 36/278	E 101/387/14
E 43/20	E 101/387/25

E 101/388/8	E 101/394/16
E 101/388/11	E 101/397/20
E 101/389/8	E 101/398/22
E 101/389/12	E 101/571/16
E 101/389/14	E 361/2
E 101/390/2	E 361/3
E 101/390/11	E 361/4
E 101/391/1	E 372/207
E 101/391/5	E 379/198
E 101/391/15	E 403/246
E 101/392/4	E 403/340
E 101/392/20	E 403/388
E 101/393/4	E 404/7/43
E 101/393/11	E 404/17/357-9
E 101/393/15	SC8/63/3125

London, Society of Antiquaries:
  MS 208
  MS 541
  MS 545
Manchester, John Rylands Library, MSS 234 and 235
Oxford, Bodleian Library:
  MS Ashmole 1128
  MS Douce 231
  MS Lat. Hist. a.2
Oxford, Corpus Christi College, MS 78
Pamplona, Archivio General de Navarra, Register 120, counter-roll for January 1365
Paris, Bibliothèque Nationale:
  MS français 693 (St Omer chronicle)
  MS français 5001
Windsor, St George's Chapel, Precentor's Rolls, XV.56.16, 22 and 23

B. Printed Sources

Accounts of the English Crown with Italian Merchant Societies, 1272–1345, ed. Adrian R. Bell, Chris Brooks and Tony K. Moore, List and Index Society 331 (London, 2009).

Actes et documents anciens intéressant la Belgique, ed. Henri Laurent (Brussels, 1933).

The Acts of War of Edward III (Acta Bellicosa), tr. in *Life and Campaigns of the Black Prince*, 26–40; the original is edited, with some omissions, in J. Moisant, *Le Prince Noir en Aquitaine, 1355–1356 – 1362–1370* (Paris, 1894), 157–74.

Alfonso X 'El Sabio', *Las siete partidas*, tr. S. Parsons Scott, ed. R. I. Burns, SJ, 5 vols. (Philadelphia, 2001).

[*Amadis de Gaule*] Nicolas de Herberay seigneur des Essars, *Le quatriesme livre de Amadis de Gaule* (Paris, 1555).

[Ambroise] *The History of the Holy War: Ambroise's Estoire de la Guerre Sainte*, ed. Marianne Ailes and Malcolm Barber, 2 vols. (Woodbridge, 2003).

Anglo-Scottish Relations 1174–1328, ed. and tr. E. L. G. Stones, Oxford Medieval Texts (Oxford, 1965).

Annales Gandenses, ed. and tr. Hilda Johnstone (Oxford, 1985).

Annales Paulini, in *Chronicles of the Reigns of Edward I and Edward II*, ed. William Stubbs, 2 vols., RS 76 (London, 1882).

The Anonimalle Chronicle 1333–1381, ed. V. H. Galbraith (Manchester, 1927).

Anonimo romano, *Cronica*, ed. Giuseppe Porta (Milan, 1979; abbreviated edn., Milan, 1981).

[Anonymus Cantuariensis] *Chronicon Anonymi Cantuariensis = The Chronicle of Anonymous of Canterbury, 1346–1365*, ed. and tr. Charity Scott-Stokes and Chris Given-Wilson, Oxford Medieval Texts (Oxford, 2008).

The Antient Kalendars and Inventories of the Treasury of His Majesty's Exchequer, ed. Sir Francis Palgrave, 3 vols. (London, 1836).

Archivo General de Navarra, Catálogo de la seccion de Comptos: Documentos, ed. José Rámon Castro (Pamplona, 1952–74).

Arnould, E. J. F., *Étude sur le Livre des saintes médécines du duc Henri de Lancastre* (Paris, 1948).

[Avesbury] *Chronicon Roberti de Avesbury*, in *Chronica Adae Murimuth et Roberti de Avesbury*, ed. E. M. Thompson, RS 93 (London, 1889).

[Baker, Geoffrey] *The chronicle of Geoffrey Le Baker*, tr. David Preest, intro. and notes by Richard Barber (Woodbridge, 2012).

Barbour, John, *The Bruce*, ed. and tr. A. A. M. Duncan (Edinburgh, 1997).

'Benedict of Peterborough', *Gesta Regis Henrici Secundi Benedicti Abbas*, ed. W. Stubbs, 2 vols., RS 49 (London, 1867).

Beneš z Weitmile, *Chronicon*, in *Fontes Rerum Bohemicarum*, vol. iv, ed. Josef Emler (Prague, 1884).

Boehmer, J. F., *Acta imperii selecta* (Innsbruck, 1870).

[Boucicaut] *Le Livre de fais du bon messire Jehan le Maingre, dit Bouciquaut*, ed. Denis Lalande (Geneva, 1985).

The Brut or The Chronicles of England, ed. Friedrich W. D. Brie, 2 vols., EETS OS 131, 136 (London, 1906–8).

Calendar of Charter Rolls, 1341–1417 (London, 1916).

Calendar of Inquisitions Miscellaneous (London, 1916).

Calendar of Liberate Rolls, 1240–1245 (London, 1931).

Calendar of Wills proved and enrolled in the court of Husting, London A.D. 1258–A.D.1688, ed. Reginald R. Sharpe, 3 vols. (London, 1890).

Cambridge Gild Records, ed. Mary Bateson, Cambridge Antiquarian Society, octavo series XXXIX (Cambridge, 1903).

Cartulaire des Comtes de Hainaut de l'avènement de Guillaume II à la mort de Jacqueline de Bavière, ed. Léopold Devillers, vol. i (Brussels, 1881).

Chandos Herald, *La Vie du Prince Noir*, ed. D. Tyson, Beihefte zur Zeitschrift für Romanische Philologie 147 (Tübingen, 1975).

Charny, Geoffroy de, *The* Book of Chivalry *of Geoffroi de Charny: Text, Context, and Translation*, ed. Richard W. Kaeuper and Elspeth Kennedy (Philadelphia, 1996).

Chevalier, Ulysse, *Choix de documents inédits sur le Dauphiné* (Lyons, 1874).

Chronica Monasterii de Melsa, ed. E. A. Bond, 3 vols., RS (London, 1868).

The Chronicle of Glastonbury: An Edition, Translation and Study of John of Glastonbury's Cronica sive Antiquitates Glastoniensis Ecclesie, ed. James Carley, tr. David Townsend (Woodbridge, 1985).

[*Chronicle of Lanercost*] *Chronicon de Lanercost: 1201–1346. E codice Cottoniano nunc primum typis mandate*, ed. Joseph Stevenson, Maitland Club (Edinburgh, 1839).

Chronicles of London, ed. C. L. Kingsford (Oxford, 1905).

Chronicon Adae Murimuth, in *Chronica Adae Murimuth et Roberti de Avesbury*, ed. E. M. Thompson, RS 93 (London, 1889).

Chronique artésienne (1295–1304) et chronique tournaisienne, ed. F. Funck-Brentano (Paris, 1899).

Chronique des quatre premiers Valois, ed. Simeon Luce, SHF (Paris, 1862).

Chronique des règnes de Jean II et Charles V, ed. R. Delachenal, 4 vols., SHF (Paris, 1910–20).

Chronique du religieux de Saint-Denis, ed. L. Bellaguet, 6 vols. (Paris, 1839–52).

Chronique latine de Guillaume de Nangis de 1113 à 1300, avec les continuations de 1300 à 1368, ed. H. Géraud, 2 vols., SHF (Paris, 1843).

Chronique normande du XIVᵉ siècle, ed. Auguste et Émile Molinier, SHF (Paris, 1882).

Chronique parisienne anonyme de 1316 à 1339, ed. A. Hellot, Mémoires de la Société de l'Histoire de Paris et de l'Île-de-France XI (1884).

Chroniques de Saint-Martial de Limoges, ed. H. Duplès-Agier, SHF (Paris, 1874).

Chronographia Regum Francorum, ed. H. Moranvillé, 3 vols., SHF (Paris, 1891–7).

Clement VI, *Lettres closes, patentes et curiales*, ed. Eugène Déprez, 2 vols., Bibliothèque des Écoles Françaises d'Athènes et Rome, 3rd ser. III (Paris, 1901).

Cochon, Pierre, *Chronique normande*, ed. Ch. de Robillard de Beaurepaire, Société de l'Histoire de Normandie (Rouen, 1870).

Le compte des recettes et dépenses du roi de Navarre en France et en Normandie de 1367 à 1370, ed. E. Izarn (Paris, 1885).

Crónicas de los reyes de Castilla, ed. Cayetano Rosell, 3 vols., Biblioteca de autores españoles 66, 68, 70 (Madrid, 1875–8).

Croniques de London depuis l'an 44 Hen. III jusqu'à l'an 17 Edw. III, ed. George J. Aungier, Camden Society XXVIII (London, 1844).

Delpit, Jules, *Collection générale des documents français qui se trouvent en Angleterre* (Paris, 1874).

Documents des archives de la chambre des comptes de Navarre (1196–1384), ed. Jean-Auguste Brutails, Bibliothèque de l'École des Hautes Études 84 (Paris, 1890).

Dugdale, William, *Monasticon anglicanum*, ed. John Caley, Henry Ellis and the Revd Bulkeley Bandinel, 6 vols. in 8 pts. (London, 1846).

Eulogium historiarum sive temporis, ed. F. S. Haydon, 3 vols., RS 9 (London, 1863).

Foedera, Conventiones, Literare et Cujuscunque Genera Acta Publica, ed. T. Rymer, 4 vols. in 7 parts (London, 1816–30).

Froissart, Jean, *Chroniques Livre I: Le Manuscrit d'Amiens*, ed. George T. Diller, 5 vols. (Geneva, 1991–8).

—— *Chroniques Livre III: Le Manuscrit Saint-Vincent de Besançon*, ed. Peter F. Ainsworth (Geneva, 2007–).

—— *Chroniques: début du premier livre. Édition du manuscrit de Rome Reg. lat. 869*, ed. George T. Diller (Geneva, 1972).

—— *Chroniques*, ed. Simeon Luce *et al.*, 13 vols. (in progress), SHF (Paris, 1869–).

—— *Œuvres de Froissart: Chroniques*, ed. Kervyn de Lettenhove, 26 vols. (Paris, 1867–77).

—— *Chronicles of England, France, Spain, and the adjoining countries*, tr. Thomas Johnes, 2 vols. (London, 1848).

'La Geste des Nobles François', ed. in [Denis-François Secousse,] *Recueil de pieces servant de preuves aux Mémoires sur les Troubles excites en France par Charles II, dit le mauvais, roi de Navarre et comte d'Evreux* (Paris, 1775), ii. 631–55.

Les Grandes chroniques de France, ed. J. Viard, 10 vols., SHF (Paris, 1920–53).

Les Grandes chroniques de France: Chronique des règnes de Jean II et de Charles V, ed. R. Delachenal, 10 vols., SHF (Paris, 1919).

Gray, Sir Thomas, *Scalacronica 1272–1363*, ed. and tr. Andy King, Publications of the Surtees Society ccix (Woodbridge, 2005).

[Guesclin] *Letters, Orders and Musters of Bertrand du Guesclin, 1357–1380*, ed. Michael Jones (Woodbridge, 2004).

Guiart, Guillaume, 'Branche des royaus lignages', in Natalis (Noël) de Wailly and Léopold Delisle (eds.), *Recueil des historiens des Gaules et de la France* XXII (Paris, 1865).

Hamaker, H. G. (ed.), *De rekeningen der grafelijkheid van Holland onder het Henegouwsche Huis*, Werken uitgegeven door het Historisch Genootschap gevestigd te Utrecht, new series xxi, xxiv, xxvi (1875, 1876, 1878).

Hemingburgh, Walter of, *De Gestis Regum Angliae*, ed. Hans Claude Hamilton, 2 vols., English Historical Society (London, 1848).

Hemricourt, Jacques d', *Le Miroir des Nobles de Hesbaye* (Brussels, 1673).

[Hemricourt] *Œuvres de Jacques de Hemricourt*, ed. C. de Borman, Alphonse Bayot and Edouard Poncelet (Brussels, 1931).

Histoire de Guillaume le Maréchal, ed. A. J. Holden and D. Crouch, tr. S. Gregory, Anglo-Norman Text Society Occasional Publications 4–6 (London, 2006–7).

Historiae Anglicanae Scriptores Decem, ed. Roger Twysden (London, 1652).

Hoccleve, Thomas, *The Minor Poems*, ed. Frederick J. Furnivall and I. Gollancz, rev. Jerome Mitchell and A. I. Doyle, EETS Extra Series 61 (London, 1970).

Hodenc, Raoul de, *Le roman des eles*, with the anonymous *Ordene de chevalerie*, ed. and tr. Keith Busby (Amsterdam, 1983).

Istoire et croniques de Flandre, d'après les textes de divers manuscrits, ed. Kervyn de Lettenhove, 2 vols. (Brussels, 1879–80).

John of Arderne, *Treatises of Fistula in Ano*, ed. D'Arcy Power, EETS OS 139 (London, 1910).

John of Gaunt's Register, ed. Sydney Armitage-Smith, Camden Society 3rd series 20, 21 (London, 1911).

The Kirkstall Abbey Chronicles, ed. John Taylor, Publications of the Thoresby Society XLII (Leeds, 1952).

[Knighton, Henry] *Chronicon Henrici Knighton vel Cnitthon, Monachi Leycestrensis*, ed. J. R. Lumby, 2 vols., RS (London, 1889–95).

—— *Knighton's Chronicle*, ed. and tr. G. H. Martin, Oxford Medieval Texts (Oxford, 1995).

Laborde, Leon de, *Notice des émaux, bijoux et objets divers, exposés dans les galleries du Musée du Louvre*, vol. ii (Paris, 1853).

Lancelot-Grail: The Old French Arthurian Vulgate and post-Vulgate in translation, general editor Norris J. Lacy, 10 vols. (Woodbridge and Rochester, NY, 2010); originally 5 vols. (New York, 1993–6). References are by part, chapter and section, and are identical in both editions.

The Lay of Mantel, ed. and tr. Glyn Burgess, and Leslie C. Brook, Arthurian Archives: French Arthurian Literature V (Woodbridge, 2013).

Le Bel, Jean, *Chronique de Jean le Bel*, ed. J. Viard and E. Déprez, 2 vols., SHF (Paris, 1904–5, repr. Geneva, 1977); numbers in square brackets refer to the English version, *Jean le Bel's True Chronicle*, tr. Nigel Bryant (Woodbridge, 2011).

The Life and Campaigns of the Black Prince, ed. and tr. Richard Barber (Woodbridge, 1986).

Le Livre de seyntz medicines: The Unpublished Devotional Treatise of Henry of Lancaster. Text, ed. E. T. Arnould, Anglo-Norman Texts 2 (Oxford, 1940).

[Li Muisit] *Chronique et annales de Gilles Le Muisis, Abbé de Saint-Martin de Tournai (1272–1352)*, ed. H. Lemaître, SHF (Paris, 1906).

Llull, Ramon, *Llibre de L'Orde de Cavalleria*, ed. Marina Gusta (Barcelona, 1980).

L[ong], C. E., 'Roll of the Arms of the Knights at the Tournament at Dunstable in 7 Edw. III', *Collectanea Topographica et Genealogica*, 4 (1837), 389–95.

López de Ayala, Pero, *Corónica del rey don Pedro*, ed. Constance L. and Heanon M. Wilkins (Madison, 1985).

[Malory, Sir Thomas] *The Works of Sir Thomas Malory*, ed. P. J. C. Field (Woodbridge, 2013).

Martin, Kurt (ed.), *Minnesänger: vierundzwanzig farbige Wiedergaben aus der Manessischen Liederhandschrift*, vol. 1 (Baden-Baden, 1966).

Martorell, Joanot, and Joan de Galba, Martí, *Tirant lo Blanc*, tr. David H. Rosenthal (London, 1984).

[Mathias von Nuewenburg] *Die Chronik des Mathias von Neuenburg*, ed. A. Hofmeister, Monumenta Germaniae Historica, Scriptores Rerum Germanicum, n.s. 4 (Leipzig, 1924–37).

Milemete, Walter de, *De nobilitatibus, sapientiis, et prudentiis regum*, ed. M. R. James, Roxburghe Club (London, 1913).

[*Morte Arthure*] *The Death of Arthur*, tr. Simon Armitage (London, 2012).

[Murimuth] *Adami Murimuthensis Chronica Sui Temporis*, ed. Thomas Hog, English Historical Society 20 (London, 1846).

Paris, Jean de, *Memoriale historiarum*, in Natalis (Noël) and Daniel Guigniaut (eds.), *Recueil des historiens des Gaules et de la France* XXI (Paris, 1855).

The Parliament Rolls of Medieval England 1275–1504, general editor Chris Given-Wilson (Woodbridge, 2005).

Perceforest, parts I–V, ed. Gilles Roussineau, Textes littéraires français (Geneva, 1987–2012; the original vol. 1 by Jane Taylor is replaced by Roussineau's edition of 2007).

Perceforest: The Prehistory of King Arthur's Britain, tr. Nigel Bryant, Arthurian Studies LXXVII (Woodbridge, 2011).

Political Thought in Early Fourteenth Century England: Treatises by Walter of Milemete, William of Pagula, and William of Ockham, ed. and tr. Cary J. Nederman, Medieval and Renaissance Texts and Studies 250 (Tempe, Ariz., 2002).

Prince, A. E., 'A Letter of Edward the Black Prince describing the Battle of Nájera in 1367', *EHR* 41 (1926), 416–18.

Reading, John of, *Chronica Johannis de Reading et Anonymi Cantuariensis 1346–1367*, ed. James Tait (Manchester, 1914).

Récits d'un bourgeois de Valenciennes, ed. Kervyn de Lettenhove (Louvain, 1877).

Registrum Simonis de Sudbiria, Diocesis Londoniensis, ed. R. C. Fowler, 2 vols., Canterbury and York Society xxxiv, xxxviii (Oxford, 1927–38).

Report from the Lords Committee for All Matters Touching the Dignity of a Peer, 5 vols. (London, 1820–29).

Riley, H. T., *Memorials of London and London Life in the XIIIth, XIVth, and XVth Centuries* (London, 1868).

Le Roman en prose de Tristan, ed. E. Löseth, Bibliothèque de l'École Pratique des Hautes Études 82 (Paris, 1890, repr. Geneva, 1974).

The Romance of Alexander: A Collotype Facsimile of MS. Bodley 264, ed. M. R. James (Oxford, 1933).

The Rule of the Templars, ed. and tr. Julie Upton-Ward (Woodbridge, 1992).

Secretum Secretorum: Nine English Versions, ed. M. A. Manzalaoui, EETS OS 276 (Oxford, 1977).

Sir Gawain and the Green Knight, tr. Brian Stone (Harmondsworth, 1974).

Smit, H. J. (ed.), *De rekeningen der graven en gravinnen uit het Henegouwsche Huis*, Werken uitgegeven door het Historisch Genootschap gevestigd te Utrecht, 3rd series, xlvi, liv, lxix (1924–39).

Storie pistoresi, ed. Silvio Ardastro Barbi, in L. A. Muratori (ed.), *Rerum Italicarum Scriptores*, XI, pt. v (Castello, 1927).

Taylor, Michael (ed.), 'A Critical Edition of Geoffroy de Charny's *Livre Charny* and the *Demandes pour la Joute, les Tournois et la Guerre*', Ph.D. thesis, University of North Carolina at Chapel Hill, 1977.

Vegetius, *Epitoma rei militaris*, ed. M. D. Reeve (Oxford, 2004).

[Venette] *The Chronicle of Jean de Venette*, tr. Jean Birdsall, ed. Richard A. Newhall, Records of Civilization, Sources and Studies L (New York, 1953).

Villani, Giovanni, *Nuova cronica*, ed. Giuseppe Porta, 3 vols. (Parma, 1990–91).

Villani, Matteo, *Cronica*, ed. Giuseppe Porta, 2 vols. (Parma, 1995).

Vita Edwardi Secundi, in *Chronicles of the Reigns of Edward I and Edward II*, ed. William Stubbs, 2 vols., RS 76 (London, 1882).

Voragine, Jacopo de, *Legenda Aurea*, ed. T. Graesse (Dresden and Leipzig, 1846).

The Vows of the Heron: A Middle French Vowing Poem, ed. J. L. Grigsby and Norris J. Lacy (New York, 1992).

[Walsingham, Thomas] *Chronicon Angliae ad anno domini 1328 usque ad annum 1388, auctore monacho quodam Sancti Albani*, ed. Edward Maunde Thompson, RS (London, 1874).

—— *Historia Anglicana*, ed. H. T. Riley, 2 vols., RS 28.i (London, 1863–4).

Walter of Peterborough, 'Prince Edward's Expedition into Spain, and the battle of Najara', in T. Wright (ed.), *Political Poems and Songs*, 2 vols., RS 14 (London, 1859–61),
i.97–122.

Wynnere and Wastoure, ed. Stephanie Trigg, EETS OS 297 (Oxford, 1990).

SECONDARY SOURCES

Ainsworth, Peter, *Jean Froissart and the Fabric of History: Truth, Myth, and Fiction in the* Chroniques (Oxford, 1990).

Alexander, Jonathan, and Binski, Paul, *Age of Chivalry: Art in Plantagenet England 1200–1400* (London, 1987).

Anstis, John, *The Register of the most noble Order of the Garter*, 2 vols. (London, 1724).

Antiquarian Repertory, ed. F. Grose, 4 vols. (London, 1807).

Archer, R., 'The Estates and Finances of Margaret of Brotherton', *Historical Research*, 60 (1987), 267–78.

Ashmole, Elias, *The Institution, Laws & Ceremonies of the most noble Order of the Garter* (London, 1672).

Ayton, Andrew, 'Edward III and the English Aristocracy at the Beginning of the Hundred Years' War', in Matthew Strickland (ed.), *Armies, Chivalry and Warfare in Medieval Britain and France*, Harlaxton Medieval Studies VII (Stamford, 1998).

—— 'The English Army and the Normandy Campaign of 1346', in D. Bates and Anne Curry (eds.), *England and Normandy in the Middle Ages* (London, 1994).

—— *Knights and Warhorses: Military Service and the English Aristocracy under Edward III* (Woodbridge, 1994).

—— 'Knights, Esquires and Military Service: The Evidence of the Court of Chivalry', in Andrew Ayton and J. L. Price (eds.), *The Medieval Military Revolution* (London, 1995), 81–4.

—— 'Sir Thomas Ughtred and the Edwardian Military Revolution', in *Age of Edward III*, 107–33.

—— and Preston, Sir Philip, *The Battle of Crécy, 1346*, Warfare in History (Woodbridge, 2005).

Barber, Richard, 'Edward III's Arthurian Enthusiasms Revisited: Perceforest in the Context of Philippa of Hainault and the Round Table Feast of 1344', *Arthurian Literature*, 30, forthcoming.

—— *Edward, Prince of Wales and Aquitaine* (London and New York, 1978).

—— and Barker, Juliet, *Tournaments: Jousts, Chivalry and Pageants in the Middle Ages* (Woodbridge, 1989).

Barker, Juliet, *The Tournament in England, 1100–1400* (Woodbridge, 1986).

Barnes, Joshua, *The History of that Most Victorious Monarch Edward III* (London, 1688).

Barnie, John, *War in Medieval Society: Social Values and the Hundred Years War, 1337–99* (London, 1974).

Bautier, R.-H., Sornay, J., and Muret, F. (eds.), *Les Sources de l'histoire économique ... des états de la maison de Bourgogne, i. Archives des principautés territoriale, ii. Les Principautés du nord* (Paris, 1984).

Begent, Peter J., and Chesshyre, Hubert, *The Most Noble Order of the Garter: 650 Years* (London, 1999).

Bell, Adrian R., 'Medieval Chroniclers as War Correspondents during the Hundred Years' War: The Earl of Arundel's Campaign of 1387', in Chris Given-Wilson (ed.), *Fourteenth Century England VI* (Woodbridge, 2010), 171–84.

—— *War and the Soldier in the Fourteenth Century* (Woodbridge, 2004).

Bellamy, J. G., 'The Coterel Gang: An Anatomy of a Band of Fourteenth-Century Criminals', *EHR* 79 (1964), 698–717.

Beltz, George Frederick, *Memorials of the Order of the Garter, from its founda-tion to the present time with Biographical Notices of the Knights in the reigns of Edward III. and Richard II.* (London, 1841).

Belvaletus, Mondonus, *Catechismus ordinis Equitum Perisc'lidis Anglicanae* ... (Cologne, 1631).

Benedictow, Ole, *The Black Death, 1346–1353: The Complete History* (Wood-bridge, 2004).

Bennett, Michael J., *Community, Class and Careerism: Cheshire and Lancashire Society in the Age of* Sir Gawain and the Green Knight (Cambridge, 1983).

Berard, Christopher, 'Edward III's Abandoned Order of the Round Table', *Arthurian Literature*, 29 (2012), 1–40.

Biddle, Martin, *King Arthur's Round Table: An Archaeological Investigation* (Woodbridge, 2000).

Billot, Claudine, *Les Saintes Chapelles royales et princières* (Paris, 1998).

—— 'Les Saintes Chapelles (XIIIᵉ siècle-XVIᵉ siècle): Approche comparée de fondations dynastiques', *Revue de l'histoire de l'église en France*, 73 (1987), 229–48.

Binski, Paul, *Westminster Abbey and the Plantagenets: Kingship and the Repre-sentation of Power* (London, 1995).

Birch, Debra J., *Pilgrimage to Rome in the Middle Ages* (Woodbridge, 1998).

Blatchly, John, and MacCulloch, Diarmaid, *Miracles in Lady Lane: The Ipswich Shrine at the Westgate* (Ipswich, 2013).

Bliese, John R. E., 'Rhetoric and Morale: A Study of Battle Orations from the Central Middle Ages', *Journal of Medieval History*, 15 (1989), 201–20.

Blomefield, Francis, *An Essay towards a Topographical History of the County of Norfolk*, 6 vols. (London, 1808).

Bock, Friedrich, *Das deutsch–englische Bündnis von 1335–42* (Munich, 1956).

—— 'Some New Documents Illustrating the Early Years of the Hundred Years War (1353–1356)', *Bulletin of the John Rylands Library*, 15 (1931), 60–83.

Bock, Nicolas, 'L'Ordre du Saint-Esprit au Droit Désir. Enluminure, cérémonial et idéologie monarchique au XIVᵉ siècle', in Nicolas Bock, Peter Kurmann, Serena Romano and Jean-Michel Spieser (eds.), *Art, cérémonial et liturgie au moyen-âge* (Rome, 2002).

Bond, Maurice, *The Inventories of St George's Chapel, Windsor Castle 1384–1667* (Windsor, 1947).

Booth, P. H. W., 'Taxation and Public Order: Cheshire in 1353', *Northern History*, 12 (1967), 16–31.

Bothwell, J. S. (ed.). *The Age of Edward III* (Woodbridge, 2001).

—— *Edward III and the English Peerage, Royal Patronage, Social Mobility and Political Control in 14th-Century England* (Woodbridge, 2004).

—— 'Edward III, the English Peerage and the 1337 Earls', in *Age of Edward III*, 35–52.

Boulton, D'Arcy Jonathan Dacre, *The Knights of the Crown: The Monarchical Orders of Knighthood in Later Medieval Europe 1325–1520*, 2nd edn. (Woodbridge, 2000).

—— 'The Middle French Statutes of the Monarchical Order of the Ship (Naples, 1381); A Critical Edition, with Introduction and Notes', *Mediaeval Studies*, 47 (1985), 176–271.

Bowers, Roger, 'The Music and Musical Establishment of St George's Chapel', in Colin Richmond and Eileen Scarff (eds.), *St George's Chapel, Windsor, in the Later Middle Ages* (Windsor, 2001), 171–90.

Brindle, Steven, 'The First St George's Chapel', in Nigel Saul and Tim Tatton-Brown (eds.), *St George's Chapel Windsor: History and Heritage* (Wimborne Minster, 2010), 36–44.

Brooke, Christopher, 'Chaucer's Parson and Edmund Gonville: Contrasting Roles of Fourteenth Century Incumbents', in David M. Smith (ed.), *Studies in Clergy and Ministry in Medieval England*, Borthwick Studies in History 1 (York, 1991), 1–16.

—— *A History of Gonville and Caius College* (Woodbridge, 1985).

Broome, Dorothy M., 'The Ransom of John II King of France 1360–70', Camden 3rd series XXXVII, *Camden Miscellany*, 14 (1926).

Brown, Elizabeth A. R., 'Diplomacy, Adultery and Domestic Politics at the Court of Philip the Fair: Queen Isabelle's Mission to France in 1314', in J. S. Hamilton and Patricia J. Bradley (eds.), *Documenting the Past* (Woodbridge, 1989), 53–84.

—— 'The King's Conundrum: Endowing Queens and Loyal Servants, Ensuring Salvation, and Protecting the Patrimony in Fourteenth Century France', in J. A. Burrow and Ian P. Wei (eds.), *Medieval Futures* (Woodbridge, 2000), 115–66.

Brown, Michelle, *The Luttrell Psalter Commentary* (London, 2006; issued with facsimile of the manuscript).

Brown, R. A., Colvin, H. M., and Taylor, A. J., *The History of the King's Works: The Middle Ages*, 2 vols. (London, 1963).

Bryant, Nigel (tr. and ed.), *Chrétien de Troyes: Perceval: The Story of the Grail* (Woodbridge, 1982).

Bullock-Davies, Constance, *Register of Royal and Baronial Domestic Minstrels 1272–1327* (Woodbridge, 1986).

Burne, A. H., 'The Battle of Poitiers', *EHR* 53 (1938), 21–52.

—— 'Cannons at Crécy', *Royal Artillery Journal*, 77 (1939), 335–44.

—— *The Crecy War: A Military History of the Hundred Years War from 1337 to the Peace of Bretigny, 1360* (London, 1955).

Burrow, J. A., *Thomas Hoccleve*, Authors of the Middle Ages 4 (Aldershot, 1994).

Burtscher, Michael, *The Fitzalans: Earls of Arundel and Surrey, Lords of the Welsh Marches (1267–1415)* (Little Logaston, 2008).

—— 'The Missing Earl: Richard Fitzalan, Earl of Arundel and the Order of the Garter', *Coat of Arms*, 3rd series, 3/1 (2007), 93–101.

Butterfield, Ardis, *The Familiar Enemy: Chaucer, Language, and Nation in the Hundred Years War* (Oxford, 2009).

Camden, William, *Britannia*, tr. Philemon Holland (London, 1610).

Campanelli, Maurizio, 'A New Account of the Battle of Crécy from Fourteenth-Century Rome', forthcoming.

Capra, Pierre, 'Les Bases sociales du pouvoir anglo-gascon au milieu du xive siècle', *Le Moyen Âge*, 81 (1975), 273–99, 447–73.

—— 'Le Séjour du Prince Noir, Lieutenant du Roi, à l'archevêché de Bordeaux', *Revue historique de Bordeaux*, 7 (1958), 241–52.

Carey, Richard J. (ed.), *Jean de le Mote, Le Parfait du Paon*, University of North Carolina Studies in the Romance Languages and Literatures 118 (Chapel Hill, NC, 1972).

Carolus Barré, M. L., 'Benoit XII et la mission charitable de Bernard Carit', *Mélanges d'archéologie et d'histoire, École française de Rome*, 62 (1950), 165–232.

Carpentier, Élisabeth, 'L'Historiographie de la bataille de Poitiers au quatorzième siècle', *Revue historique*, 263 (1980), 21–58.

Carruthers, Leo, 'The Duke of Clarence and the Earls of March: Garter Knights and *Sir Gawain and the Green Knight*', *Medium Aevum*, 70 (2001), 66–79.

Cavanaugh, Susan, 'A Study of Books Privately Owned in England: 1300–1450', Ph.D. thesis, University of Pennsylvania, 1980.

Cazelles, R., *La Société politique et la crise de la royauté sous Philippe de Valois* (Paris, 1958).

—— *Société politique, noblesse et couronne sous Jean le Bon et Charles V* (Paris, 1982).

Channel Pilot, vol. 2, 11th edn. [Hydrographic Department, Admiralty] (London, 1952).

Chaplais, Pierre, 'Règlement des conflits internationaux franco-anglais au XIVe siècle (1293–1377)', *Le Moyen Âge*, 57 (1951), 269–302.

Chareyron, Nicole, *Jean le Bel: Le Maître de Froissart, grand imagier de la guerre de cent ans*, Bibliothèque du Moyen Âge 7 (Brussels, 1996).

Cheetham, Francis, *Alabaster Images of Medieval England* (Woodbridge, 2003).

—— *English Medieval Alabasters* (Oxford, 1984).

Chettle, H. F., 'The *Boni Homines* of Ashridge and Edington', *Downside Review*, 62 (1944), 40–55.

Christensen, Eric, *The Northern Crusades: The Baltic and the Catholic Frontier 1100–1525* (London, 1980).

Collins, Hugh E. L., *The Order of the Garter 1348–1461: Chivalry and Politics in Late Medieval England* (Oxford, 2000).

Colón, Germán, 'Premiers échos de l'Ordre de la Jarretière', *Zeitschrift für Romanische Philologie*, 81 (1965), 441–53.

The Complete Peerage, by G. E. C[okayne], ed. Vicary Gibbs, 12 vols. in 13 parts (London, 1910–59).

Conrad, Klaus, 'Der dritte Litauerzug König Johanns von Böhmen und der Rücktritt des Hochmeisters Ludolf König', in *Festschrift für Hermann Heimpel*, Veröffentlichungen des Max-Planck-Instituts für Geschichte 36 (Göttingen, 1971), ii.382–401.

Contamine, Philippe, 'Geoffroy de Charny (début du XIVe siècle-1356)', in *Histoire et société: mélanges offerts à Georges Duby* (Aix-en-Provence, 1992), 107–21.

—— Giry-Deloison, Charles, and Keen, Maurice H. (eds.), *Guerre et société en France, en Angleterre et en Bourgogne XIVe-XVe siècle* (Villeneuve d'Ascq, 1991).

Cook, G. H., *English Collegiate Churches* (London, 1959).

Cooke, W. G. and Boulton, D'A. J. D., '*Sir Gawain and the Green Knight*: A Poem for Henry of Grosmont?', *Medium Aevum*, 68 (1999), 42–54.

Coote, Lesley A., *Prophecy and Public Affairs in Later Medieval England* (Woodbridge, 2000).

Coss, Peter, and Keen, Maurice (eds.), *Heraldry, Pageantry and Social Display in Medieval England* (Woodbridge, 2002).

Crouch, David, 'The Court of Henry II of England in the 1180s, and the Office of King of Arms', *Coat of Arms*, 3rd series, 6 (2010), 47–56.

—— *Tournament* (London, 2005).

—— Carpenter, D. A., and Coss, P. R., 'Bastard Feudalism Revisited', *Past and Present*, 131 (1991), 165–203.

Crow, M. M., and Olson, C. C. (eds.), *Chaucer Life-Records* (Oxford, 1966).

Crowfoot, Elisabeth, Pritchard, Frances, and Staniland, Kay, *Textiles and Clothing*, Medieval Finds from Excavations in London 4, 2nd edn. (Woodbridge, 2001).

Cruse, Mark, *Illuminating the* Roman d'Alexandre: *Oxford, Bodleian Library, MS Bodley 264* (Woodbridge, 2011).

Cunliffe, Tom, *The Shell Channel Pilot* (St Ives, 2010).

Curry, Anne, and Hughes, Michael (eds.), *Arms, Armies and Fortifications in the Hundred Years War* (Woodbridge, 1994).

Cushway, Graham, *Edward III and the War at Sea: The English Navy, 1327–1377* (Woodbridge, 2011).

Cuttino, G. P., 'Historical Revision: The Causes of the Hundred Years' War', *Speculum*, 31 (1956), 463–77.

Daly, L. J., 'The Conclusion of Walter Burley's Commentary on the *Politics*: Books I to IV', *Manuscripta*, 12 (1968), 163, 213.

Daumet, Georges, 'L'Ordre castillan de l'écharpe (Banda)', *Bulletin hispanique*, 25 (1923), 1–32.

de Graaf, Roland, *Oorlog om Holland 1000–1375* (Hilversum, 1996).

Delachenal, Roland, *Histoire de Charles V*, 5 vols. (Paris, 1909–31).

Delcorno Branco, Daniela, *Boccaccio e le storie di re Artù* (Bologna, 1991).

Delisle, Léopold, *Histoire du château et des sires de Saint-Sauveur-Le-Vicomte* (Valognes, 1867).

Denholm Young, N., 'Edward III and Bermondsey Priory', in his *Collected Papers* (Cardiff, 1969).

—— *History and Heraldry* (Oxford, 1965).

—— 'The Tournament in the Thirteenth Century', in R. W. Hunt *et al.* (eds.), *Studies Presented to F. M. Powicke* (Oxford, 1948).

Déprez, Eugène, 'La Bataille de Najéra: Le communiqué du Prince Noir', *Revue historique*, 136 (1921), 37–59.

De Santi, G., 'L'Expédition du prince noir en 1355 d'après le journal d'un de ses compagnons', *Mémoires de l'Académie des Sciences de Toulouse*, 10/5 (1904), 181–223.

Devon, Frederick, *Issues of the Exchequer* (London, 1837).

DeVries, Kelly, *Infantry Warfare in the Early Fourteenth Century* (Woodbridge, 1996).

—— 'The Use of the Pavise in the Hundred Years War', *Arms and Armour*, 4 (2007), 93–100.

Dictionary of British Arms, ed. Thomas Woodcock, Janet Grant and Ian Graham, 3 vols. in progress (London, 1996–).

Dictionary of Medieval Latin from British Sources, ed. D. R. Howlett (Oxford, 1975–).

Diller, G. T., 'Robert d'Artois et l'historicité des Chroniques de Froissart', *Le Moyen Âge*, 86 (1980), 217–31.

Doherty, P. C., 'Isabella, Queen of England 1308–1330', Oxford D.Phil. thesis, 1977.

Douch, R., 'The Career, Lands and Family of William Montagu, Earl of Salisbury', *Bulletin of the Institute of Historical Research*, 24 (1951), 85–8.

Du Cange, Charles Dufresne, sieur, *Dissertations sur l'histoire de Saint Louys, Du Cry d'Armes*, dissertation XI, in *Glossarium Mediae et Infimae Latinitatis*, VII (Paris, 1850), 28–35.

Durdík, Jan, *Hussitisches Heerwesen* (Berlin, 1961) (translated from the Czech).

Dygo, Marian, 'The Political Role of the Cult of the Virgin Mary in Teutonic Prussia in the Fourteenth and Fifteenth Centuries', *Journal of Medieval History*, 15 (1989), 63–80.

Ellmers, Detlev, 'The Cog as Cargo Carrier', in Robert Gardiner (ed.), *Cogs, Caravels and Galleons* (London, 1994), 29–46.

Engel, Pál, *The Realm of St Stephen: A History of Medieval Hungary, 895–1526*, ed. Andrew Ayton (London, 2001).

Feuchère, Pierre, *Les Vieilles Familles chevaleresques du nord de France*, 1.i: *Auberchicourt* (Fontenay-le-Comte, 1945).

Fleckenstein, Josef (ed.), *Das ritterliche Turnier im Mittelalter*, Veröffentlichungen des Max-Planck-Instituts für Geschichte 80 (Göttingen, 1985).

Foucard, C., *Lo statuto della Compagnia della Giarretiera istituta da Edoardo III, Re d'Inghilterra MCCCL* (Modena, 1878).

Fowler, Kenneth, 'Henry of Grosmont, First Duke of Lancaster, 1310–1361', Ph.D. thesis, University of Leeds, 1961 (contains documentary appendix not in printed version).

—— (ed.), *The Hundred Years War* (London, 1971).

—— *The King's Lieutenant: Henry of Grosmont, First Duke of Lancaster 1310–1361* (London, 1969).

—— *Medieval Mercenaries*, 1: *The Great Companies* (Oxford, 2001).

—— 'News from the Front: Letters and Dispatches of the Fourteenth Century', in Philippe Contamine, Maurice Keen *et al.* (eds.), *Guerre et Société en France, en Angleterre et en Bourgogne XIVᵉ–XVᵉ siècle* (Lille, 1991), 63–92.

Fügedi, Erik, 'Turniere im mittelalterlichen Ungarn', in Josef Fleckenstein (ed.), *Das ritterliche Turnier im Mittelalter*, Veröffentlichungen des Max-Planck-Instituts für Geschichte 80 (Göttingen, 1985), 390–400.

Galbraith, V. H., 'Extracts from the Historia Aurea and a French "Brut" (1317–1347)', *EHR* 43 (1928), 203–17.

Galway, Margaret, 'The Foundation of the Order of the Garter', *University of Birmingham Historical Journal*, 7 (1959), 18–35.

Gardiner, Robert (ed.), *Cogs, Caravels and Galleons* (London, 1994).

Geddes, Jane, 'Medieval Decorative Ironwork in St George's Chapel', in Nigel Saul and Tim Tatton-Brown (eds.), *St George's Chapel Windsor: History and Heritage* (Wimborne Minster, 2010), 63–8.

Gillespie, James L., 'Ladies of the Fraternity of Saint George and of the Society of the Garter', *Albion*, 17 (1985), 259–78.

Given-Wilson, Chris, *Chronicles: The Writing of History in Medieval England* (London, 2004).

—— 'The Exequies of Edward III and the Royal Funeral Ceremony in Late Medieval England', *EHR* 124 (2009), 257–82.

—— (ed.), *Fourteenth Century England II* (Woodbridge, 2002).

—— (ed.), *Fourteenth Century England VI* (Woodbridge, 2010).

—— 'Royal Charter Witness Lists 1327–1399', *Medieval Prosopography*, 12/2 (1991), 35–93.

—— *The Royal Household and the King's Affinity: Service, Politics and Finance in England 1360–1413* (New Haven and London, 1986).

—— 'Wealth and Credit, Public and Private: The Earls of Arundel, 1306–1397', *EHR* 106 (1991), 1–26.

—— and Bériac, Françoise, 'Edward III's Prisoners of War: The Battle of Poitiers and its Context', *EHR* 116 (2001), 802–33.

Good, Jonathan, *The Cult of Saint George in Medieval England* (Woodbridge, 2009).

Goodall, John A. A., 'The Aerary Porch and its Influence on Late Medieval English Vaulting', in Nigel Saul (ed.), *St George's Chapel Windsor in the Fourteenth Century* (Woodbridge, 2005), 165–202.

—— *The English Castle 1066–1650* (New Haven and London, 2011).

Goodman, Anthony, *John of Gaunt: The Exercise of Princely Power in Fourteenth-Century Europe* (Harlow, 1992).

Gransden, Antonia, 'The Alleged Rape by Edward III of the Countess of Salisbury', *EHR* 87 (1972), 333–44.

—— *Historical Writing in England II: c.1307 to the Early Sixteenth Century* (London, 1982).

Green, David, *The Black Prince* (Stroud, 2001).

Green, Richard Firth, 'King Richard II's Books Revisited', *The Library*, 5th series, 31 (1976), 235–9.

Greene, C., and Whittingham, A. B., 'Excavations at Walsingham Priory, Norfolk, 1961', *Archaeological Journal*, 125 (1968), 255–90.

Greene, R. L. (ed.), *A Selection of English Carols* (Oxford, 1962).

Greenstreet, James, 'Powell's Roll', *The Reliquary*, new series 3 (1889), 144–52.

—— '[Sixth] Nobility Roll', *Notes and Queries*, 6th series, 1 (1880), 351–2, 370–71.

—— 'Thomas Jenyns' Book', *The Antiquary*, 1 (1880), 205–9; 2 (1885–7), 97–101, 238–44; *Walfords Magazine and Bibliographer*, 8–12 [BL Add. MS 40851].

Grimsley, M., and Rogers, C. J., *Civilians in the Path of War* (Lincoln, Nebr., 2002).

Guenée, Bernard, *Between Church and State: The Lives of Four French Prelates in the Late Middle Ages*, tr. Arthur Goldhammer (Chicago, 1991).

Guesnon, A., 'Documents inédits sur l'invasion anglaise et les états au temps de Philippe VI et Jean le Bon', *Bulletin philologique et historique du Comité des Travaux historiques et scientifiques* (1897), 208–59.

Gumus, T. Tolga, 'A Tale of Two Codices: The Medieval Registers of the Order of the Garter', *Comitatus*, 37 (2006), 86–110.

Hanna, Ralph, *London Literature 1300–1380* (Cambridge, 2005).

Harari, Yuval Noah, 'Strategy and Supply in Fourteenth-Century Western European Invasion Campaigns', *Journal of Military History*, 64 (2000), 297–333.

Harriss, G. L., *King, Parliament and Public Finance in Medieval England to 1369* (Oxford, 1975).

Hay, Denis, 'The Division of the Spoils of War in Fourteenth Century England', *TRHS*, 5th series, 4 (1954), 91–109.

Hayez, M., 'Un exemple de culture historique au xve siècle: *La geste des nobles françois*', *École française de Rome: Mélanges d'archéologie et d'histoire*, 75 (1963), 127–78.

Hewitt, H. J., *The Black Prince's Expedition of 1355–1357* (Manchester, 1958).

—— *The Organization of War under Edward III, 1338–62* (Manchester, 1966).

Holmes, G. A., *The Estates of the Higher Nobility in Fourteenth-Century England* (Cambridge, 1957).

Hóman, Balínt, *Gli angioini di Napoli in Ungheria, 1290–1403* (Rome, 1938).

Hoskins, Peter, *In the Steps of the Black Prince: The Road to Poitiers, 1355–1356* (Woodbridge, 2011).

Howe, Emily, 'Divine Kingship and Dynastic Display: The Altar Wall Murals of St Stephen's Chapel, Westminster', *Antiquaries Journal*, 81 (2001), 259–303.

Huet, G., 'Les Traditions arthuriennes chez le chroniqueur Louis de Velthem', *Le Moyen Âge*, 36 (1913), 173, 197.

Huot, Sylvia, *Postcolonial Fictions in the 'Roman de Perceforest': Cultural Identities and Hybridities* (Cambridge, 2007).

Ingledew, Francis, *Sir Gawain and the Green Knight and the Order of the Garter* (Notre Dame, Ind., 2006).

Jaeger, C. Stephen, *Ennobling Love: In Search of a Lost Sensibility* (Philadelphia, 1999).

Janse, Antheun, *Ridderschap in Holland: portret van een Adellijke Elite in de late Middeleeuwen* (Hilversum, 2001).

—— 'Tourneyers and Spectators', in Steven Gunn and Antheun Janse (eds.), *The Court as Stage* (Woodbridge, 2006), 39–52.

Jeayes, I. H., *Catalogue of the Charters and Muniments at Berkeley Castle* (Bristol, 1892).

Jefferson, Lisa, 'MS Arundel 48 and the Earliest Statutes of the Order of the Garter', *EHR* 109 (1994), 356–84.

—— 'Two Fifteenth-Century Manuscripts of the Statutes of the Order of the Garter', *English Manuscript Studies*, 5 (1995), 18–35.

Johnstone, H., *Edward of Caernarvon* (Manchester, 1946).

Jones, Michael, *Ducal Brittany 1364–1399: Relations with England and France during the Reign of Duke John IV* (Oxford, 1970).

—— 'Edward III's Captains in Brittany', in W. M. Ormrod (ed.), *England in the Fourteenth Century: Proceedings of the 1985 Harlaxton Symposium* (Woodbridge, 1986), 99–118.

—— 'Sir John de Hardreshull, King's Lieutenant in Brittany', *Nottingham Medieval Studies*, 31 (1987), 76–95.

—— and Walker, Simon, 'Private Indentures for Life Service in Peace and War 1278–1476', *Camden Miscellany*, 32 (1994), 1–190.

Jones, Robert W., *Bloodied Banners: Martial Display on the Medieval Battlefield* (Woodbridge, 2010).

Kaeuper, Richard W., *Chivalry and Violence in Medieval Europe* (Oxford, 2001).

—— *Holy Warriors: The Religious Ideology of Chivalry* (Philadelphia, 2009).

—— *War, Justice and Public Order: England and France in the Later Middle Ages* (Oxford, 1988).

Keegan, John, *The Face of Battle* (London, 1977).

Keen, Lawrence, and Scarff, Eileen, *Windsor: Medieval Art, Archeology and Architecture in the Thames Valley*, BAA Transactions 25 (Leeds, 2002).

Keen, Maurice, 'Chivalry and the Aristocracy', in Michael Jones (ed.), *The New Cambridge Medieval History*, vol. 6: *c.1300–c.1415* (Cambridge, 2000), 209–21.

—— 'Chivalry, Heralds and History', in R. H. C. Davis and J. M. Wallace-Hadrill (eds.), *The Writing of History in the Middle Ages: Essays Presented to Richard William Southern* (Oxford, 1981), 393–414.

—— *The Laws of War in the Late Middle Ages* (London, 1968).

—— *Origins of the English Gentleman: Heraldry, Chivalry and Gentility in Medieval England, c.1300–c.1500* (Stroud, 2002).

Keeney, B. C., 'Military Service and the Development of Nationalism in England', *Speculum*, 22 (1947), 541–5.

Kerr, Jill, 'The East Window of Gloucester Cathedral', in *Medieval Art and Architecture at Gloucester and Tewkesbury*, British Archaeological Association Conference Transactions, VII (1985), 116–29.

Knowles, David, and Grimes, W. F., *Charterhouse: The Medieval Foundation in the Light of Recent Discoveries* (London, 1954).

—— and Hadcock, R. Neville, *Medieval Religious Houses: England and Wales* (London, 1971).

Krochalis, Jeanne, '*Magna tabula*: The Glastonbury Tablets', in James Carley (ed.), *Glastonbury and the Arthurian Tradition* (Woodbridge, 2001), 435–568.

Kruse, Holger, Paravicini, Werner, and Ranft, Andreas (eds.), *Ritterorden und Adelsgesellschaften in spätmittelalterlichen Deutschland* (Frankfurt, 1991).

Lachaud, Frédérique, 'Les Tentes et l'activité militaire: les guerres d'Édouard Ier Plantagenet (1272–1307)', *Mélanges de l'École française de Rome: Moyen-Âge*, 111/1 (1999), 443–61.

Lambert, Craig L., *Shipping the Medieval Military: English Military Logistics in the Fourteenth Century* (Woodbridge, 2011).

Lapierre, A., *La Guerre de cent ans dans l'Argonne et le Rethelois* (Sedan, 1900).

Le Patourel, J., 'Edward III and the Kingdom of France', *History*, 43 (1958).

—— 'The Treaty of Brétigny 1360', *TRHS*, 5th series, 10 (1960), 19–39.

Leland, John, *Itinerary through England and Wales*, ed. Lucy Toulmin Smith (London, 1964).

Leroux, Alfred, 'Le Sac de la cité de Limoges et son relèvement, 1370–1464', *Bulletin de la société archéologique et historique du Limousin*, 56 (1908), 175–9.

Lester, G. A., *Sir John Paston's Grete Boke* (Cambridge, 1984).

Lewis, N. B., 'The Organisation of Indentured Retinues in Fourteenth-Century England', *TRHS*, 4th series, 27 (1945), 29–39.

Liebnitz, Karl, 'Die Manuskripte des Walter de Milemete', *Waffen und Kostumkunde*, 34 (1992), 117–31.

Lindenbaum, Sheila, 'The Smithfield Tournament of 1390', *Journal of Medieval and Renaissance Studies*, 20 (1990), 1–20.

Livingstone, Marilyn, and Witzel, Morgen, *The Road to Crécy: The English Invasion of France 1346* (Harlow, 2005).

London, H. S., *The Life of William Bruges, the First Garter King of Arms*, Harleian Society, CXI/CXII (London, 1970).

Loomis, Laura Hibbard, 'Secular Dramatics in the Royal Palace, Paris, 1378, 1389, and Chaucer's "Tregetoures"', *Speculum*, 33 (1958), 242–55.

Loomis, R. S., 'Edward I, Arthurian Enthusiast', *Speculum*, 28 (1953), 114–27.

Lucas, H. S., 'Edward III and the Poet Chronicler John Boendale', *Speculum*, 12 (1937), 367–9.

—— *The Low Countries and the Hundred Years War, 1326–1347*, University of Michigan Publications, History and Political Science, VIII (Ann Arbor, 1929).

Luce, Simeon, 'Du Guesclin au siège de Rennes', *Bibliothèque de l'École des Chartes*, 53 (1891), 615–18.

Luxford, Julian, 'King Arthur's Tomb at Glastonbury: The Relocation of 1368 in Context', *Arthurian Literature*, 29 (2012), 41–52.

Luzzati, M., *Giovanni Villani e la compagnia dei Buonaccorsi* (Rome, 1971).

McDonald, Nicola, and Ormrod, W. M. (eds.), *Rites of Passage: Cultures of Transition in the Fourteenth Century* (Woodbridge, 2004).

McFarlane, K. B., 'Bastard Feudalism', *Bulletin of the Institute of Historical Research*, 20 (1943–5), 161–80.

—— *The Nobility of Later Medieval England* (Oxford, 1973).

McHardy, A. K., 'Some Reflections on Edward III's Use of Propaganda', in *Age of Edward III*, 171–83.

Mackinnon, James, *The History of Edward III (1327–1377)* (London, 1900).

Majláth, Béla, 'A Kolos Család Czímeres Levele', *Turul*, 5 (1887), 156–9.

Malderghem, Jean van, *La Bataille de Staveren* (Brussels, 1870).

Marks, Richard, 'Some Early Representations of the Garter in Stained Glass', *Report of the Society of Friends of St George's*, 5/4 (1972–3), 154–6.

May, Theresa, 'The Cobhams in Royal Administration 1200–1400', *Archaeologia Cantiana*, 82 (1967), 1–31.

Melchiori, G. (ed.), *King Edward III* (Cambridge, 1998).

Melville, Gert, 'Pourquoi des hérauts d'armes? Les raisons d'une institution', *Revue du Nord*, 88 (2006), 491–502.

Michael, M. A., 'A Manuscript Wedding Gift from Philippa of Hainault to Edward III', *Burlington Magazine*, 127 (1985), 582–98.

Michaud, Claude, 'The Kingdoms of Central Europe in the Fourteenth Century', in Michael Jones (ed.), *The New Cambridge Medieval History*, vol. 6: *c.1300–c.1415* (Cambridge, 2000), 735–63.

Moisant, J., *Le Prince Noir en Aquitaine, 1355–1356 – 1362–1370* (Paris, 1894).

Molinier, Émile, 'Étude sur la vie d'Arnoul d'Audrehem', *Mémoires présentés . . . à l'Académie des inscriptions et belles-lettres de l'Institut de France. Deuxième série: Antiquités de la France* VI (Paris, 1883).

Mooney, Linne R., 'Some New Light on Thomas Hoccleve', *Studies in the Age of Chaucer*, 29 (2007), 293–340.

Morgan, D. A. L., 'The Banner-Bearer of Christ: How God Became an Englishman Revisited', in Nigel Saul (ed.), *St George's Chapel Windsor in the Fourteenth Century* (Woodbridge, 2005), 51–62.

Morgan, Nigel, *Early Gothic Manuscripts [II] 1250–1285*, A Survey of Manuscripts Illuminated in the British Isles IV (London, 1988).

Morris, Marc, 'Edward I and the Knights of the Round Table', in Paul Brand and Sean Cunningham (eds.), *Foundations of Medieval Scholarship: Records Edited in Honour of David Crook* (York, 2008), 57–76.

Mortimer, Ian, *The Perfect King: The Life of Edward III, Father of the English Nation* (London, 2006).

Munby, Julian, Barber, Richard, and Brown, Richard, *Edward III's Round Table at Windsor: The House of the Round Table and the Windsor Festival of 1344* (Woodbridge, 2007).

Newton, Stella Mary, *Fashion in the Age of the Black Prince: A Study of the Years 1340–1345* (Woodbridge, 1980).

—— 'Queen Philippa's Squirrel Suit', in M. Flury-Lemberg and K. Stolleis (eds.), *Documenta Textilia: Festschrift für Sigrid Müller-Christensen* (Munich, 1981), 342–8.

Nicholson, Ranald, *Edward III and the Scots: The Formative Years of a Military Career* (Oxford, 1965).

Nicolas, Sir Nicolas Harris, *The controversy between Sir R. Scrope and Sir R. Grosvenor in the Court of Chivalry, A.D. MCCCLXXXV–MCCCXC*, 2 vols. (London, 1832).

—— *History of the Orders of Knighthood*, 3 vols. (London, 1841).

—— 'Observations on the Institution of the Most Noble Order of the Garter', *Archaeologia*, 31 (1846), 1–163.

—— *A Roll of Arms compiled in the Reign of Edward III* (London, 1829).

Oberman, Heiko A., and Weishepl, James A., 'The Sermo epinicius Ascribed to Thomas Bradwardine', *Archives d'histoire doctrinale et littéraire du moyen âge*, 25 (1958), 295–329.

Offler, H. S., 'Thomas Bradwardine's "Victory Sermon" in 1346', repr. in H. S. Offler, *Church and Crown in the Fourteenth Century* (Aldershot, 2000), item XIII.

Ormrod, W. Mark, *Edward III* (London, 2011).

—— 'Edward III and his Family', *Journal of British Studies*, 26 (1987), 398–442.

—— 'Edward III and the Recovery of Royal Authority in England 1340–1360', *History*, 72 (1987), 4–19.

—— (ed.), *England in the Fourteenth Century: Proceedings of the 1985 Harlaxton Symposium* (Woodbridge, 1986).

—— 'For Arthur and St George: Edward III, Windsor Castle and the Order of the Garter', in Nigel Saul (ed.), *St George's Chapel Windsor in the Fourteenth Century* (Woodbridge, 2005), 13–34.

—— (ed.), *Fourteenth Century England VII* (Woodbridge, 2012).

—— 'The Personal Religion of Edward III', *Speculum*, 64 (1989), 849–77.

—— *The Reign of Edward III* (Stroud, 2000).

Owen, A., *Le Traité de Walter de Bibbesworth sur la langue française* (Paris, 1929).

Owst, G. R., *Preaching in Medieval England*, Cambridge Studies in Medieval Life and Thought (Cambridge, 1926).

Palmer, John (ed.), *Froissart: Historian* (Woodbridge, 1981).

Pannier, Léopold, *La Noble-maison de Saint-Ouen: La villa Clippiacum et l'ordre de l'Étoile d'après les documents originaux* (Paris, 1872).

Pantin, W. A., 'A Medieval Treatise on Letter-Writing, with Examples, from the Rylands Latin MS. 394', *Bulletin of the John Rylands Library*, 13 (1929), 326–82.

Paravicini, Werner, 'Armoriaux et histoire culturelle: Le Rôle d'Armes des "Meilleurs Trois"', in Werner Paravicini, *Noblesse: Studien zum adeligen Leben im spätmittelalterlichen Europa* (Sigmaringen, 2012), 471–88.

—— 'L'Office d'armes: historiographie, sources, problématique', *Revue du Nord*, 88 (2006), 467–90 (special issue on *Le Héraut, figure européenne (XIVe–XVIe siècle)*).

—— *Die Preussenreisen des Europäischen Adels*, 2 vols. (in progress), Beihefte der Francia 17 (Sigmaringen, 1989–).

Parisse, Michel, 'Le Tournoi en France, des origines à la fin du XIIIe siècle', in Josef Fleckenstein (ed.), *Das ritterliche Turnier im Mittelalter*, Veröffentlichungen des Max-Planck-Instituts für Geschichte 80 (Göttingen, 1985), 174–211.

Pastoureau, Michel, *L'Armorial Bellenville* (Lathuile, 1974).

Pauli, Sebastiano, *Codice diplomatico del sacro militare ordine gerosolimitano oggi di Malta*, 2 vols. (Lucca, 1738).

Pépin, Guilhem, 'Towards a Rehabilitation of Froissart's Credibility: The Non Fictitious Bascot de Mauléon', in Adrian R. Bell, Anne Curry *et al.* (eds.), *The Soldier Experience in the Fourteenth Century* (Woodbridge, 2011), 175–90.

Perroy, E., 'France, England, and Navarre from 1359 to 1364', *Bulletin of the Institute of Historical Research*, 13 (1935–6), 152–3.

Phillips, Seymour, *Edward II* (New Haven and London, 2010).

Pór, Antal, 'Az Anjou ház és örökösei, 1301–1439', in S. Szilágyi (ed.), *A Magyar nemzet története*, Köt 3 (Budapest, 1895), 133–9.

Powicke, M. R., 'Edward II and Military Obligation', *Speculum*, 31 (1956), 92–119.

—— *Military Obligation in Medieval England: A Study in Liberty and Duty* (Oxford, 1962).

Prentout, Henri, 'La Prise de Caen par Édouard III – 1346', *Mémoires de l'académie nationale des sciences, arts et belles-lettres de Caen* (1904), 225–95.

Preston, Sir Philip, 'The Traditional Battlefield of Crécy', in Andrew Ayton and Preston, *The Battle of Crécy, 1346*, Warfare in History (Woodbridge, 2005), 109–37.

Prestwich, Michael, *Edward I* (London, 1988).

—— 'English Armies in the Early Stages of the Hundred Years War: A Scheme in 1341', *Bulletin of the Institute of Historical Research*, 56 (1983), 102–13.

—— 'The English at the Battle of Neville's Cross', in David Rollason and Michael Prestwich (eds.), *The Battle of Neville's Cross 1346*, Studies in North-Eastern History 2 (Stamford, 1998), 1–14.

—— *Plantagenet England, 1225–1360* (Oxford, 2005).

—— *The Three Edwards: War and State in England 1272–1377* (London, 1980).

Prince, A. E., 'The Indenture System under Edward III', in J. G. Edwards, V. H. Galbraith and E. F. Jacob (eds.), *Historical Essays in Honour of James Tait* (Manchester, 1933), 283–97.

—— 'A Letter of Edward the Black Prince Describing the Battle of Najéra in 1367', *EHR* 41 (1926), 415–18.

—— 'The Payment of Army Wages in Edward III's Reign', *Speculum*, 19 (1944), 137–60.

—— 'The Strength of English Armies in the Reign of Edward III', *EHR* 46 (1931), 353–71.

Pryor, J. H., 'Transportation of Horses by Sea during the Crusades', *Mariner's Mirror*, 68 (1982), 9–30, 103–25.

Ragone, Franca, *Giovanni Villani e i suoi continuatori: La scrittura delle cronache a Firenze nel trecento*, Istituto Storico Italiano per il medio evo, Nuovi studi storici 43 (Rome, 1998).

Rastall, Richard, 'Minstrels of the English Royal Households, 25 Edward I – 1 Henry VIII: An Inventory', *Royal Musical Association Research Chronicle*, 4 (1964), 7–20.

Renouard, Yves, 'L'Ordre de la jarretière et l'ordre de l'étoile', *Le Moyen Âge*, 55 (1949), 281–300.

Revard, Carter, 'Courtly Romances in the Privy Wardrobe', in Evelyn Mullally and John Thompson (eds.), *The Court and Cultural Diversity* (Woodbridge, 1997), 297–308.

Riches, Samantha, *St George: Hero, Martyr and Myth* (Stroud, 2000).

Richmond, Colin, and Scarff, Eileen, *St George's Chapel Windsor in the Late Middle Ages*, Windsor Historical Monographs 17 (Windsor, 2001).

Rigg, A. G., 'Propaganda of the Hundred Years War: Poems on the Battles of Crecy and Durham (1346). A Critical Edition', *Traditio*, 54 (1999), 169–211.

Riquer, Martí de, *L'Arnes del Cavaller* (Barcelona, 1968).

Robbins, R. H., *Historical Poems of the XIVth and XVth Centuries* (New York, 1959).

Roberts, A. K. B., *St George's Chapel, Windsor Castle, 1348–1416: a Study in Early Collegiate Administration* (Windsor, 1951).

Rogers, Clifford J., 'By Fire and Sword: *Bellum hostile* and "Civilians" in the Hundred Years' War', in M. Grimsley and C. J. Rogers, *Civilians in the Path of War* (Lincoln, Nebr., 2002), 33–78.

—— 'Edward III and the Dialectics of Strategy 1327–1360', *TRHS*, 6th series, 4 (1994), 83–101.

—— 'The Military Revolutions of the Hundred Years' War', *Journal of Military History*, 57 (1993), 241–78.

—— *War Cruel and Sharp: English Strategy under Edward III* (Woodbridge, 2000).

—— *The Wars of Edward III: Sources and Interpretations* (Woodbridge, 1999).

Rogers, Nicholas, *England in the Fourteenth Century: Proceedings of the 1991 Harlaxton Symposium*, Harlaxton Medieval Studies III (Stamford, 1993).

Rollason, David, and Prestwich, Michael (eds.), *The Battle of Neville's Cross 1346*, Studies in North-Eastern History 2 (Stamford, 1998).

Roy, É., *Études sur le théâtre français du XIVe et du XVe siècle: La comédie sans titre . . . et les Miracles de Notre-Dame* (Dijon, 1901).

Rubin, Miri, *The Hollow Crown: A History of Britain in the Later Middle Ages* (London, 2005).

Runyan, T. J., 'The Cog as Warship', in Robert Gardiner (ed.), *Cogs, Caravels and Galleons* (London, 1994), 47–58.

—— 'Ships and Mariners in Later Medieval England', *Journal of British Studies*, 16 (1977), 1–17.

Russell, P. E., *The English Intervention in Spain and Portugal in the Time of Edward III and Richard II* (Oxford, 1955).

Safford, E. W., 'An Account of the Expenses of Eleanor, Sister of Edward III, on the Occasion of her Marriage to Reynald, Count of Guelders', *Archaeologia*, 77 (1928), 111–40.

St John, Graham, 'Dying beyond the Seas: Testamentary Preparation for Campaigning during the Hundred Years War', in W. M. Ormrod (ed.), *Fourteenth Century England VII* (Woodbridge, 2012), 177–96.

—— 'War, the Church and English Men-at-Arms', in Chris Given-Wilson (ed.), *Fourteenth Century England VI* (Woodbridge, 2010), 73–93.

St John Hope, W. H., *The History of the London Charterhouse* (London, 1925).
—— *The Stall Plates of the Knights of the Order of the Garter, 1348–1485* (Westminster, 1901).
—— *Windsor Castle: An Architectural History*, 2 vols. (London, 1913).
Salter, Elizabeth, 'The Timeliness of *Wynnere and Wastoure*', *Medium Aevum*, 47 (1980), 40–65.
Sandberger, Dietrich, *Studien ueber das Rittertum in England, vornehmlich waehrend des 14 Jahrhunderts*, Historische Studien 310 (Berlin, 1937).
Sandler, Lucy Freeman, *Gothic Manuscripts 1285–1385*, 2 vols., A Survey of Manuscripts Illuminated in the British Isles V (London, 1985).
Saul, Nigel, *English Church Monuments in the Middle Ages* (Oxford, 2009).
—— 'The Growth of a Mausoleum: The Pre-1600 Tombs and Brasses of St George's Chapel, Windsor', *Antiquaries Journal*, 87 (2007), 220–58.
—— *For Honour and Fame: Chivalry in England 1066–1500* (London, 2011).
—— *Knights and Esquires: The Gloucestershire Gentry in the Fourteenth Century* (Oxford, 1981).
—— *Richard II* (New Haven and London, 1997).
—— 'Servants of God and Crown', in Saul (ed.), *St George's Chapel Windsor in the Fourteenth Century* (Woodbridge, 2005), 97–115.
—— and Tatton-Brown, Tim (eds.), *St George's Chapel Windsor: History and Heritage* (Wimborne Minster, 2010).
Saunders, Corinne, *Rape and Ravishment in the Literature of Medieval England* (Woodbridge, 2001).
Schmolke-Hasselmann, Beate, 'The Round Table: Ideal, Fiction, Reality', *Arthurian Literature*, 2 (1982), 41–75.
Schneider, Diethard, *Der englische Hosenbandorden: Beiträge zur Entstehung und Entwicklung des 'The Most Noble Order of the Garter' (1348–1702) mit einem Ausblick bis 1983*, 2 vols. (Bonn, 1988).
Selden, John, *Titles of Honor* (London, 1672).
Shenton, Caroline, 'The English Court and the Restoration of Royal Prestige', Oxford D.Phil., 1995.
—— 'Royal Interest in Glastonbury and Cadbury: Two Arthurian Itineraries, 1278 and 1331', *EHR* 114 (1999), 1249–55.
Sherborne, J. W., 'Indentured Retinues and English Expeditions to France', *EHR* 79 (1964), 718–46.
Shrewsbury, J. F. D., *The History of Bubonic Plague* (Cambridge, 1970).
Siddons, Michael, *Heraldic Badges in England and Wales*, 4 vols. (London, 2009).
Simpkin, David, *The English Aristocracy at War: From the Welsh Wars of Edward I to the Battle of Bannockburn* (Woodbridge, 2008).
Smith, J. T., *Antiquities of Westminster: The Old Palace; St Stephen's Chapel (now the House of Commons)* (London, 1807).

Smith, Kathryn A., *The Taymouth Hours: Stories and the Construction of Self in Late Medieval England* (London, 2012).

Smyth, John, *The Lives of the Berkeleys . . .*, ed. Sir John Maclean, 2 vols., Bristol and Gloucester Archaeological Society (Bristol, 1883–5).

Snead, G., 'The Careers of Four Fourteenth Century Military Commanders', MA thesis, UKC history, record id 440276, University of Kent, 1968.

Spencer, Brian, *Pilgrim Souvenirs and Secular Badges*, Medieval Finds from Excavations in London 7 (Woodbridge, 2010).

Spufford, Peter, *Money and its Use in Medieval Europe* (Cambridge, 1988).

—— *Power and Profit: The Merchant in Medieval Europe* (London, 2002).

Squibb, G. C., *The High Court of Chivalry* (Oxford, 1959).

Staniland, Kay, 'Clothing and Textiles at the Court of Edward III, 1342–1352', in Joanna Bird *et al.* (eds.), *Collectanea Londiniensa*, 223–34, Special Paper 2, London and Middlesex Archaeological Society (London, 1978).

—— 'Court Style, Painters, and the Great Wardrobe', in W. M. Ormrod (ed.), *England in the Fourteenth Century: Proceedings of the 1985 Harlaxton Symposium* (Woodbridge, 1986), 236–46.

—— 'The Great Wardrobe Accounts as a Source for Historians of Fourteenth-Century Clothing and Textiles', *Textile History*, 20 (1989), 275–81.

—— 'Medieval Courtly Splendour', *Costume*, 14 (1980), 7–23.

Stanley, Arthur P., *Historical Memorials of Canterbury* (London, 1912).

Stones, E. L. G., *Anglo-Scottish Relations 1174–1328* (Oxford, 1965).

—— 'The Folvilles of Ashby-Folville, Leicestershire, and their Associates in Crime, 1326–1347', *TRHS*, 5th series, 7 (1957), 117–36.

Stow, John, *A Survey of the cities of London and Westminster*, ed. John Strype, 6 vols. (London, 1720).

Stratford, Jenny, *Richard II and the English Royal Treasure* (Woodbridge, 2012).

Strickland, Matthew (ed.), *Armies, Chivalry and Warfare in Medieval Britain and France*, Harlaxton Medieval Studies VII (Stamford, 1998).

—— and Hardy, Robert, *The Great Warbow* (Stroud, 2005).

Strong, Roy, *Art and Power: Renaissance Festivals 1450–1650* (Woodbridge, 1984).

Sumption, Jonathan, *The Hundred Years War*, vol. i: *Trial by Battle* (London, 1990).

—— *The Hundred Years War*, vol. ii: *Trial by Fire* (London, 1999).

—— *The Hundred Years War*, vol. iii: *Divided Houses* (London, 2009).

Tatton-Brown, Tim, 'The Deanery, Windsor Castle', *Antiquaries Journal*, 78 (1998), 345–90.

Taylor, Craig, 'Edward III and the Plantagenet Claim to the French Throne', in *Age of Edward III*, 155–69.

—— 'English Writings on Chivalry and Warfare during the Hundred Years War', in Peter Coss and Christopher Tyerman (eds.), *Soldiers, Nobles and Gentlemen: Essays in Honour of Maurice Keen* (Woodbridge, 2009).

—— 'The Salic Law, French Queenship, and the Defense of Women in the Late Middle Ages', *French Historical Studies*, 29 (2006), 543–64.

Taylor, John, *English Historical Literature in the Fourteenth Century* (Oxford, 1987).

—— *The* Universal Chronicle *of Ranulf Higden* (Oxford, 1966).

Tobler, Adolf, *Altfranzösisches Wörterbuch*, ed. Erhard Lommatzsch (Stuttgart, 1915–).

Toman, H., *Husitské válečnictví za doby Žižkovy a Prokopovy* (Prague, 1898).

Topham, John, *Some Account of the Collegiate Chapel of St Stephen, Westminster* (London, 1795).

Tourneur-Aumont, J. M., *La Bataille de Poitiers (1356) et la construction de la France* (Paris, 1940).

Tout, T. F., *Chapters in the Administrative History of Mediaeval England*, 6 vols. (Manchester, 1920–33).

—— 'Firearms in England in the Fourteenth Century', *EHR* 26 (1911), 666–702.

—— 'The Household of the Chancery and its Disintegration', in H. W. C. Davis (ed.), *Essays in History Presented to Reginald Lane Poole* (Oxford, 1927).

—— *The Place of the Reign of Edward II in English History* (Manchester, 1914).

—— 'Some Neglected Fights between Crecy and Poitiers', *EHR* 20 (1905), 726–30.

—— 'The Tactics of the Battles of Boroughbridge and Morlaix', *EHR* 19 (1904), 711–15.

Tracy, Charles, *English Gothic Choirstalls 1200–1400* (Woodbridge, 1987).

Trautz, Fritz, *Die Könige von England und des Reich 1272–1377* (Heidelberg, 1961).

—— 'Die Reise eines Englischen Gesandten nach Ungarn im Jahre 1346', *Mitteilungen des Instituts für Österreichischen Geschichte*, 60 (1952), 359–68.

Trigg, Stephanie, 'The Vulgar History of the Order of the Garter', in G. McMullan and D. Matthews (eds.), *Reading the Medieval in Early Modern England* (Cambridge, 2007), 91–105.

Trowell, Brian, 'A Fourteenth Century Ceremonial Motet and its Composer', *Acta Musicologica*, 29 (1957), 65–75.

Tucoo-Chala, Pierre, 'Froissart dans le Midi pyrénéen', in J. J. N. Palmer (ed.), *Froissart: Historian* (Woodbridge, 1981).

Tudor-Craig, Pamela, 'The Fonts of St George's Chapel', in Nigel Saul (ed.), *St George's Chapel Windsor in the Fourteenth Century* (Woodbridge, 2005), 151–64.

Tyson, Diana B., 'Jean le Bel, Annalist or Artist? A Literary Appraisal', in Sally Burch North (ed.), *Studies in Medieval French Language and Literature Presented to Brian Woledge* (Geneva, 1988), 217–26.

—— 'Jean le Bel, Portrait of a Chronicler', *Journal of Medieval History*, 12 (1986), 315–32.

Vale, Juliet, 'Arthur in English Society', in W. R. J. Barron (ed.), *The Arthur of the English: The Arthurian Legend in Medieval English Life and Literature* (Cardiff, 2001), 185–96.

—— *Edward III and Chivalry: Chivalric Society and its Context 1270–1350* (Woodbridge, 1982).

—— 'Image and Identity in the Order of the Garter', in Nigel Saul (ed.), *St George's Chapel Windsor in the Fourteenth Century* (Woodbridge, 2005), 35–50.

Vale, Malcolm, *The Princely Court: Medieval Courts and Culture in North-West Europe 1270–1380* (Oxford, 2001).

van Buren, Anne H., *Illuminating Fashion: Dress in the Art of Medieval France and the Netherlands 1325–1515* (New York, 2011).

van Oostrom, Frits Pieter, *Court and Culture: Dutch Literature 1350–1450* (Berkeley, 1992).

Vattier, A., 'Fondation de l'Ordre de l'Étoile', *Comité archéologique de Senlis, Comptes-rendus et Mémoires*, 2nd series, 10 (1885), 32–47.

Verbruggen, J., *The Art of Warfare in Western Europe during the Middle Ages*, 2nd edn. (Woodbridge, 1997).

[Vergil, Polydore] *Polydori Vergili Historiae Anglicanae* ... (Basle, 1555, repr. Menston, 1972).

Viard, Jules, 'La Campagne de juillet-août 1346 et la bataille de Crécy', *Le Moyen Âge*, 2nd series, 27 (1926), 1–84.

—— 'Le Siège de Calais', *Le Moyen Âge*, 2nd series, 30 (1929), 129–89.

Villanueva, Lorenzo Tadeo de, 'Memoria sobre la Orden de Caballería de la Banda de Castilla', *Boletín de la Real Academia de Historia*, 72 (1918), 436–65, 552–75.

Wagner, Anthony R., *A Catalogue of English Mediaeval Rolls of Arms*, Aspilogia i (London, 1950), and corrections in *Rolls of Arms: Henry III*, Aspilogia ii (London, 1967).

—— *Heralds and Heraldry in the Middle Ages: An Inquiry into the Growth of the Armorial Function of Heralds*, 2nd edn. (Oxford, 1956).

—— and Mann, J. G., 'A Fifteenth-Century Description of the Brass of Sir Hugh Hastings at Elsing, Norfolk', *Antiquaries Journal*, 19 (1939), 421–8.

Walker, Simon, *The Lancastrian Affinity 1361–1399* (Oxford, 1990).

Walthey, Andrew, 'The Marriage of Edward III and the Transmission of French Motets to England', *Journal of the American Musicological Society*, 45 (1992), 1–29.

—— 'The Peace of 1360–1369 and Anglo-French Musical Relations', *Early Music History*, 9 (1990), 129–74.

Warner, Sir George, *Queen Mary's Psalter* (London, 1912).

Wentersdorf, Karl P., 'The Clandestine Marriages of the Fair Maid of Kent', *Journal of Medieval History*, 5 (1979), 203–31.

Wheatley, Abigail, *The Idea of the Castle* (Woodbridge, 2004).

Whiting, B. J., 'The Vows of the Heron', *Speculum*, 20 (1945), 261–78.

Willard, James F., Morris, William A., and Dunham, William H., Jr, *The English Government at Work, 1327–1336* (Cambridge, Mass., 1940–50).

Willement, T., *Willement's Roll: A Roll of Arms of the Reign of Richard II* (London, 1834).

[Wotton, Sir Henry] *The Life and Letters of Sir Henry Wotton*, ed. Logan Pearsall Smith, 2 vols. (Oxford, 1907).

Wright, Nicholas, *Knights and Peasants: The Hundred Years War in the French Countryside* (Woodbridge, 1998).

Wrottesley, George, *Crécy and Calais, from the Original Records in the Public Record Office* (London, 1898).

—— *A History of the Family of Wrottesley of Wrottesley*, William Salt Archaeological Society, Collections, new series vi.ii (London, 1903).

Notes

DIFFERENT VOICES: READING THE EVIDENCE

1. *Channel Pilot*, 358; Cunliffe, *Shell Channel Pilot*, 258–9, 283–5.
2. Sumption, *The Hundred Years War*, i.x.
3. Le Bel, *Chronique*, i.viii, quoting Jean d'Outremeuse.
4. Hemricourt, *Le Miroir des Nobles*, 157–8.
5. Tyson, 'Jean le Bel, Annalist or Artist? A Literary Appraisal', 218.
6. Tyson, 'Jean le Bel, Portrait of a Chronicler', 316. Sir Thomas Gray and Chandos Herald (see pp. 15–17 below) are the only other examples, and neither describes warfare in any detail.
7. Le Bel, *Chronique*, i.xvi.
8. Le Bel, *Chronique*, i.1–4 [21–2].
9. See pp. 489–90 below.
10. Le Bel, *Chronique*, ii.105 [181].
11. Froissart, *Chroniques*, Rome version, 217.
12. Le Bel, *Chronique*, i.212.
13. Chareyron, *Jean le Bel*, 60–65.
14. *Récits d'un bourgeois de Valenciennes*, 54–8.
15. Froissart, *Chroniques*, Amiens version, i.1.
16. Bell, 'Medieval Chroniclers as War Correspondents during the Hundred Years' War', 179–80, 183 (for his general conclusions on the value of chronicles as evidence).
17. Tucoo-Chala, 'Froissart dans le Midi pyrénéen', 130.
18. Ibid., 118–31.
19. Froissart, *Chroniques*, Besançon version, i.210–34; Pépin, 'Towards a Rehabilitation of Froissart's Credibility', 175–90.
20. Froissart, *Chroniques*, SHF, i.6.
21. Ainsworth, *Jean Froissart and the Fabric of History*, 254–302.
22. Ibid., 300.
23. Diller, 'Robert d'Artois et l'historicité', 229–31.
24. *Amadis de Gaule*, fo. a.iiij.
25. Li Muisit, *Chroniques et annales*, xiv.

26. Guenée, *Between Church and State*, 74.

27. Li Muisit, *Chroniques et annales*, 131.

28. Ibid., xv.

29. They are said to have cut off children's feet, hands or ears, saying 'This is to show that the king of England has been here': Li Muisit, *Chroniques et annales*, 118. The papal commissioners who visited the area in 1341 confirmed the destruction wrought in the area, as much by Tournai's neighbours from Hainault and Brabant as by the English, and record the inhabitants' complaints, but do not note such atrocities. See Carolus Barré, 'Benoit XII et la mission charitable de Bernard Carit', 165–232.

30. Venette, *Chronicle*.

31. Gray, *Scalacronica*, xxxi ff.

32. BL MS Harleian 4304, fo. 17ᵛ; if this is the case, the Thomas Gray who repulsed a Scottish raid in 1341 would have been his father.

33. See p. 21 below.

34. It survives in a summary made by John Leland in the mid-sixteenth century, printed in Gray, *Scalacronica*, 134–41.

35. We do not know his name, but it could well be Faucon herald at arms, who 'came with letters to the prince [of Wales] from Sir John de Chaundos, then beyond the seas' on 1 October 1354. *RBP*, iv.163.

36. Chandos Herald, *La Vie du Prince Noir*, 14–18.

37. *Life and Campaigns of the Black Prince*, 100.

38. Ibid., 85. For another poem on the campaign, this time with a view to praising John of Gaunt and in Latin, see Walter of Peterborough, 'Prince Edward's Expedition'. Walter's Latin verse does not help the author's rather confused account, though his details are sometimes accurate.

39. *Life and Campaigns of the Black Prince*, 89.

40. Ibid., 114–15.

41. Henry of Grosmont wrote a not dissimilar confessional, *Le Livre des seyntz medicines*; see p. 326 below.

42. López de Ayala, *Coronica del rey don Pedro*, 157. I am grateful to Elspeth Ferguson for the translation.

43. *Chronique des règnes de Jean II et Charles V*; Ainsworth, *Jean Froissart and the Fabric of History*, 64–9.

44. For the annals of St Paul's, Adam Murimuth, Robert of Avesbury and the French chronicle of London, see Gransden, *Historical Writing in England II: c.1307 to the Early Sixteenth Century*, 61–72.

45. For these three chronicles, see *Annales Paulini*, *Murimuth* and *Avesbury*.

46. See p. 24 below.

47. Munby *et al.*, *Edward III's Round Table at Windsor*, 182–7.

48. *Avesbury*, 279.

49. Ibid., 285.

50. Ibid., 408–10.
51. *Croniques de London*, 76.
52. Gransden, *Historical Writing in England II*, 73–6.
53. This is particularly true of the unpublished text in Corpus Christi College Oxford MS 78, on Edward prince of Wales in Aquitaine.
54. See introduction to English translation of Baker, *Chronicon*.
55. *Chronique des quatre premiers Valois*, ed. Simeon Luce, 230–31.
56. Ibid., 123–5. The marriage was said to be the reason why the prince went to Aquitaine in 1362.
57. *Chronique normande du XIVᵉ siècle*.
58. Kenneth Fowler, 'News from the Front', 67–76; for Rodez, see ibid., p. 68.
59. See *Foedera*, iii.i.1209; other examples are in *Foedera* iii.i.858, 910, 1025, 1089 and iii.ii.45, 70, 81, 87, 341, 442. For a similar letter sent by Edward I, see *Foedera*, i.ii.872. See also McHardy, 'Some Reflections on Edward III's Use of Propaganda'.
60. Fowler, 'News from the Front', 83–4. This was presumably the *cedula* enclosed with a letter to the towns and sheriffs of England on 3 August 1346 (*Foedera*, iii.ii.88).
61. *Foedera*, iii.i.1129.
62. For *The Acts of War of Edward III*, see *Life and Campaigns of the Black Prince*, 26–40.
63. Translated in Riley, *Memorials of London and London Life*, 285–8.
64. Prince, 'A Letter of Edward the Black Prince', trans. in *Life and Campaigns of the Black Prince*, 83.
65. *Murimuth*, 212–14, in Latin; *Avesbury*, 358–62 and 367–9, both in French.
66. *Avesbury*, 445–7; *Life and Campaigns of the Black Prince*, 55–6.
67. For what follows, see Spufford, *Power and Profit*, 25–7.
68. Giovanni Villani, *Nuova cronica*, ed. Giuseppe Porta.
69. Christa Hammerl, 'The Earthquake of January 25th, 1348, Discussion of Sources', 6–7, http://emidius.mi.ingv.it/RHISE/ii_2oham/ii_2oham.html, accessed 01/09/2010.
70. Some further details are recorded in a chronicle from Pistoia, but these could simply be elaborations of what Villani says, rather than independent evidence. *Storie pistoresi*, 223.
71. Matteo Villani, *Cronica*, ed. Giuseppe Porta.
72. Letter from Johann von Schönfeld to Gottfried bishop of Passau, in Boehmer, *Acta imperii*, 750.
73. Carpentier, 'L'Historiographie de la bataille de Poitiers au quatorzième siècle'.
74. Anonimo romano, *Cronica*, ed. Giuseppe Porta (Milan, 1979) is the first full edition of the text. For a full study of the section on Crécy, see Maurizio Campanelli, 'A New Account of the Battle of Crécy from Fourteenth-Century

Rome', forthcoming. I am most grateful to Dr Campanelli for allowing me to see his text in advance of publication.

75. The phrase is from Robert Macfarlane, *The Old Ways* (London, 2012), 311.
76. *Foedera*, iii.i.88–90.

PROLOGUE: THE POLITICAL BACKGROUND

1. Prestwich, *Edward I*, 406–10.
2. Phillips, *Edward II*, 441 and n.
3. Seymour Phillips, Edward's most recent biographer, is 'inclined to take the letter at face value', but points out that it could be an elaborate cover-up of a relationship with Mortimer. See *Historiae Anglicanae Scriptores Decem*, where it is quoted by the bishop of Hereford in 1334, defending himself against charges that he was behind Isabella's defection (cols. 2767–8).
4. It was part of Isabella's dowry in 1303.
5. Phillips, *Edward II*, 543.

CHAPTER 1. EDWARD, PHILIPPA AND THEIR COMRADES 1327–1330

1. Ormrod, *Edward III*, 19–24, for what follows.
2. Ibid., 20.
3. Denholm Young, 'Edward III and Bermondsey Priory', 213–20.
4. Shenton, 'The English Court', 115.
5. Ormrod, *Edward III*, 56. Some sources name Jean de Hainault; Le Bel, who may have been present, does not mention the knighting ceremony (*Chronique*, i.33 [33]).
6. *CPR 1327–1330*, 39; Chandos was granted £40 p.a. in revenue, less than Edward Bohun as son of the earl of Hereford, but much more than the other two knights named in the writ, who got 40s. each. This would support the idea that he was already a man of mature years. *CPR 1330–1334*, 173.
7. TNA E 101/383/8, m. 2.
8. Mortimer, *The Perfect King*, 60.
9. Ibid., 61–2, portrays Edward as eager to attack, and being restrained by Mortimer. The role played by Mortimer is ignored by Le Bel, but the English *Brut* chronicle portrays him as engaging in double-dealing with the Scots, preventing Thomas of Brotherton from ordering an attack and even disrupting the night-watch so that the Scots could withdraw unseen (ii.250–51).
10. Le Bel, *Chronique*, i.65 [45].
11. The dating of these in Mortimer, *The Perfect King*, 449, seems wrong: there are no dates in the accounts, the king was not at Worcester from 25 to 30

November, and the Clipstone and Rothwell dates make more sense after Christmas rather than before Edward II's funeral. For the entries for Worcester, Clipstone and Rothwell in the wardrobe accounts, see TNA E 101/382/9, mm. 15–16; E 101/383, mm. 2, 3; the York tournament is mentioned in Smyth, *Lives of the Berkeleys*, i.325.

12. Barker, *Tournament in England*, 56–8, 191–2.

13. Ibid., 50.

14. *Annales Paulini*, ii.264.

15. *RBP*, iii.59.

16. Munby *et al.*, *Edward III's Round Table at Windsor*, 135–6.

17. *Eulogium historiarum*, iii.227.

18. Denholm Young, 'The Tournament in the Thirteenth Century', 245.

19. *Murimuth*, 57; Baker, *Chronicon*, 42; Knighton, *Chronicon*, RS edn., i.449 (placed at Bedford in error).

20. Hemingburgh, *De Gestis*, ii.300.

21. *Avesbury*, 284; Dugdale, *Monasticon anglicanum*, vi, pt. 1, 352; TNA E 101/382/17; E 101/384, fo. 16ᵛ; E 101/398/22, m. 4.

22. Bryant, *Chrétien de Troyes: Perceval: The Story of the Grail*, 121.

23. Le Bel, *Chronique*, i.102 [59].

24. For a full account of the 'Craddok' material, see Barber, 'Edward III's Arthurian Enthusiasms Revisited', forthcoming.

25. Le Bel, *Chronique*, i.80 [51].

26. Edmund died in 1331, and Geoffrey inherited a lordship in France, so played no part in English affairs after the 1330s.

27. Walsingham, *Historia Anglicana*, i.304.

28. Baker, *Chronicon*, 48.

29. For example, in 1333 (*CPR 1330–1334*, 425) and in 1345 (*CPR 1343–1345*, 549); in both cases the offence was theft, and the convict was pregnant.

30. The counts of Hainault were also counts of Holland: William I of Hainault was also William III of Holland, and is often cited as William III as a result. Philippa's brother later became William II of Hainault and William IV of Holland.

31. *Accounts of the English Crown with Italian Merchant Societies*, ed. Bell *et al.*, 189.

32. Manchester, John Rylands, MS 235, fo. 11ᵛ.

33. See pp. 83, 156, 173 below on round table re-enactments.

34. Janse, *Ridderschap in Holland*, 339.

35. Smit, *De rekeningen der graven en gravinnen uit het Henegouwsche Huis*, xlvi.654.

36. Paravicini, *Die Preussenreisen*, i.57 for William II's Prussian journeys. His journey to Prussia explains his absence from Edward's Round Table feast in January 1344: see pp. 54–5 above.

37. Hamaker, *De rekeningen der grafelijkheid van Holland*, xxvi.85–88, 207, 333, 335, 338.

38. The Dutch pound was 20 shillings of silver, weighing 30 grams in all; Smit, *De rekeningen der graven en gravinnen uit het Henegouwsche Huis*, lxix.208.

39. Ibid., 129 for his armourer's journeys with horses for tournaments; several tournaments did not take place, and the count failed to appear on other occasions. Janse, 'Tourneyers and Spectators', 44, says that the count 'participated in at least ten tournaments in 1344 and 1345'.

40. For a survey of Philippa's possible commissioning of manuscripts, see Smith, *The Taymouth Hours*, 18.

41. See p. 181 below.

42. On this manuscript, see Sandler, *Gothic Manuscripts*, ii.103–5; Michael, 'A Manuscript Wedding Gift from Philippa of Hainaut to Edward III'; and Wathey, 'The Marriage of Edward III and the Transmission of French Motets to England'.

43. Coote, *Prophecy and Public Affairs*, 126.

44. Mortimer, *The Perfect King*, 182–5.

45. Ormrod, *Edward III*, 464–5, 534–7.

46. Coventry: Smyth, *Lives of the Berkeleys*, i.325; Guildford: ibid.; Nicolas, *Scrope–Grosvenor Controversy*, i.133; TNA E 361/3, m. 13a; E 101/384/6, rot. 2 m. 1; E 101/389/14, m. 2.

47. *Chronographia Regum Francorum*, ii.12; *Récits d'un bourgeois de Valenciennes*, 153.

48. *Croniques de London*, 62; TNA E 101/384/6, rot. 2 m. 1. There was a further tournament at Reigate, probably on 2–3 July: TNA E 101/384/6, rot. 2 m. 2.

49. TNA E 101/384/6, rot. 2 m. 4.

50. For all four tournaments, see TNA E 101/384/6, rot. 2 m. 1.

51. TNA C 47/6/1, mm. 2, 4; Nicolas, *Scrope–Grosvenor Controversy*, i.133; TNA E 101/384/6, rot. 2 m. 1; E 101/384/14; E 403/246.

52. All the details in this paragraph are from TNA E 101/384/6, rot. 2.

53. Vale, 'Image and Identity', 36; BL Add. MS 60584, m. 8^v; Stanley, *Historical Memorials*, 168.

54. Le Bel, *Chronique*, 51.

55. London, Society of Antiquaries, MS 541, m. 4.

56. *Brut*, i.267.

57. London, Society of Antiquaries, MS 541, m. 3, records armour issued in 1330 to the king for a tournament at Woodstock. He was there from 22 to 27 July, which covers the period forty days after the prince's birth, and this is the most likely explanation for the tournament there.

58. See Newton, 'Queen Philippa's Squirrel Suit'.

59. *CPR 1327–1330*, 516, 517, 520, 530.
60. *PROME*, iv.103.
61. Baker, *Chronicon*, 45.
62. See Shenton, 'The English Court', 25. The only contemporary evidence is slight: see Doherty, 'Isabella, Queen of England', 287, for documents where she names Mortimer her heir in 1329–30.
63. *Brut*, ii.269–71; Gray, *Scalacronica*, 104–7.
64. Shenton, 'The English Court', 18, 20, says that he was not present at the coup because he is not included in the pardons, and that the same applies to Humphrey Bohun and Ralph Stafford; but see *ODNB*, s.v. William Bohun, where W. M. Ormrod accepts the evidence of the *Brut*. They may not have been directly involved in the action, or their pardons may not have survived, but their subsequent careers would point to their being members of this fairly select group.
65. Gray, *Scalacronica*, 107.
66. *Brut*, ii.271.
67. Baker, *Chronicon*, 47f.
68. Thornham is obscure: all that we know is that he joined the Knights Hospitaller in 1331, and had to be pardoned for the murder at Nottingham in order to do so.
69. *Brut*, ii.271.
70. Baker, *Chronicon*, 46.
71. Ormrod, *Edward III*, 134–5.
72. Powicke, 'Edward II and Military Obligation', 103. This is earlier than any citation in *MED*.
73. *Murimuth*, 60.
74. Shenton, 'The English Court', 194–5.

CHAPTER 2. 'A JOLLY YOUNG LIFE': TOURNAMENTS, FESTIVALS, DISPLAY

1. Gray, *Scalacronica*, 106–7.
2. London, Society of Antiquaries, MS 541, note sewn to m. 3, fair copy m. 3.
3. Parisse, 'Le Tournoi en France', 182, explores the possible derivations. It had a generalized meaning of a battle on horseback by the late twelfth century, and it is often found as a synonym for *hastiludia*.
4. *Annales Paulini*, 352–3; *Murimuth*, 63. There is a problem with the dating of this tournament, which has been associated with Edward's homage of 1329. However, *Annales Paulini* places it after the coup of 1330, and gives a date of 2 May, while *Murimuth* dates it to the end of April 1331. This seems to me to indicate that it is the same event, and a deliberate public appearance by the king, as if he had not been abroad. Furthermore, he was

only at Dartford in 1329 at late as 25 June. Walsingham, *Historia Angli-cana*, i.193, says it was within a fortnight of his return from France in 1331.

5. *History of the King's Works*, ii.956–7.

6. TNA E 101/385/7, m. 2; E 361/3, rot. 10 m. 1d.

7. The entries in the accounts appear to be in chronological order, but this cannot be relied on. TNA E 101/385/7, m. 1; E361/3, rot. 19 m. 1d.

8. *Annales Paulini*, 353–4; TNA E 101/385/7, m. 1; Walsingham, *Historia Anglicana*, i.193.

9. *Annales Paulini*, 354–5.

10. Ibid.; TNA E101/385/7, m. 1; *Murimuth*, 63; Walsingham, *Historia Angli-cana*, i.193; *Avesbury*, 286; *Croniques de London*, 62.

11. TNA E 361/3, rot. 19 m. 1d. The entries in his account appear to be in chronological order, and largely correspond in this respect with TNA E 101/385/7. Apart from Lichfield, they can be dated with the help of the king's itinerary: Ormrod, *Edward III*, 613–14.

12. See Appendix 4, 'Chronological List of Royal Tournaments of Edward III' for details. The London tournaments are: 1331, Stepney, Cheapside; 1334, Smithfield; 1343, Smithfield; 1344, Windsor (citizens invited); 1353, Smith-field; 1357, Smithfield; 1359, Smithfield; 1361, Smithfield; 1362, Cheapside (planned), Smithfield; 1363, Smithfield.

13. Strong, *Art and Power*, 21–2.

14. Barber and Barker, *Tournaments*, 107.

15. Vale, *Edward III and Chivalry*, 35.

16. *Lancelot-Grail*, Lancelot 5, 155:387.

17. *Foedera*, iii.i.5; *CPR 1343–1345*, 196. Grosmont left England at the end of March 1344 for Spain, and was still away at midsummer; in the following years he was in Aquitaine in 1345–6 and at Calais in 1347. It was only in 1348 that the fraternity did indeed hold jousts, and even then we hear noth-ing further of it (Baker, *Chronicon*, 97).

18. See Appendix 4.

19. See Long, 'Roll of the Arms of the Knights at the Tournament at Dunstable'.

20. *Chronicle of Lanercost*, quoted in Gransden, *Historical Writing in England II*, 13.

21. Villanueva, 'Memoria sobre la Orden de Caballería de la Banda de Castilla', 570–73, chs. 22 and 23; Daumet, 'L'Ordre castillan de l'écharpe', 28–9.

22. See p. 310 below for the circumstances.

23. TNA E 101/384/6, rot. 2 mm. 1–2.

24. *Murimuth*, 173–5.

25. John of Reading, *Chronica*, 151; Anonymus Cantuariensis, *Chronicon*, 118–19.

26. Barber and Barker, *Tournaments*, 98.

27. TNA E 101/391/5.

28. TNA E372/207, m. 50. Vale, *Edward III and Chivalry*, 175, misreads the entry: there are no merchants involved.

29. BL Add. MS 60584, m. 57.

30. TNA E 101/388/8, m. 5; E 101/385/4, m. 79.

31. Newton, *Fashion in the Age of the Black Prince*, 77–8.

32. Knighton, *Chronicle*, 76–7.

33. Vale, *The Princely Court*, 25.

34. *Chronique du religieux de Saint-Denis*, ii.64–71; Froissart, *Chroniques*, ed. Lettenhove, xv.84–92.

35. TNA E 101/394/16, m. 6.

36. See p. 484 below for the transformation of this into the story of the damsel Madresilva (Honeysuckle) in a fifteenth-century Catalan romance.

37. TNA E101/390/1, m. 2; E101/389/14, m. 2; Vale, *Edward III and Chivalry*, 64.

38. Siddons, *Heraldic Badges*, ii.i.239–45.

39. Wotton, *Life and Letters*, ii.17.

40. See Loomis, 'Secular Dramatics in the Royal Palace ... and Chaucer's "Tregetoures"'.

41. *Sir Gawain and the Green Knight*, 22.

42. Ibid., 24.

43. Ibid., 31.

44. Heidelberg, Universitätsbibliothek, MS Cod. Pal. Germ. 848, fos. 42^v, 197^v, 237, 52^r and 229^v.

45. Martin, *Minnesänger*, 7.

46. There may be a connection with his nickname, 'the Black Prince', from his supposed habit of wearing black armour. *RBP*, iv.245–6. Plates covered with cloth of gold and with blue velvet are mentioned in another list: *RBP*, iv.323–4.

47. Newton, *Fashion in the Age of the Black Prince*, 62–3.

48. Tout, *Chapters*, vi.105.

49. Staniland, 'The Great Wardrobe Accounts', 276.

50. Crowfoot et al., *Textiles and Clothing*, 88. See also, for what follows, Staniland, 'Medieval Courtly Splendour' and 'Clothing and Textiles at the Court of Edward III'.

51. London, Society of Antiquaries, MS 208, fo. 9.

52. Nicolas, 'Observations on the Garter', 52.

53. Tout, *Chapters*, iv.390.

54. See p. 164 below.

55. For what follows, see Lachaud, 'Les Tentes et l'activité militaire'.

56. See Staniland, 'Court Style, Painters, and the Great Wardrobe'.

57. BL Add. MS 42130, fos. 181^v–182^r.

58. Safford, 'Expenses of Eleanor on her Marriage to Reynald, Count of Guelders', 114-15.

59. *Brut*, ii.297; John of Reading, *Chronica*, 88. Stella Newton points out (*Fashion in the Age of the Black Prince*, 9) that the *Brut* author misunderstands several terms in the Latin version. I have combined the two versions.

60. Newton, *Fashion in the Age of the Black Prince*, 8-11, 53-6.

61. Van Buren, *Illuminating Fashion*, 44-6.

62. Venette, *Chronicle*, 34.

63. Newton, *Fashion in the Age of the Black Prince*, 35, 36.

64. Cruse, *Illuminating the* Roman d'Alexandre, 183-94.

65. See Vale, *The Princely Court*, 212-13, on *The Vows of the Peacock* in court culture of the period.

66. *Récits d'un bourgeois de Valenciennes*, 48-9.

67. Quoted in Huot, *Postcolonial Fictions*, 2.

68. See *The Romance of Alexander: A Collotype Facsimile of MS. Bodley 264*; this is largely monochrome, but the five colour plates give some idea of its splendour.

69. Knighton, *Chronicle*, 93-5.

70. See Bothwell, 'Edward III, the English Peerage and the 1337 Earls'.

71. Although they were rarely together before the coup of 1330, Henry may have met Edward at the tournaments at Blyth and Hereford in 1328, and again at Northampton in July 1330; he was certainly at the Cheapside tournament in 1331, and at the queen's churching at Woodstock in 1332. See Fowler, *The King's Lieutenant*, 27-8.

72. *Antient Kalendars*, iii.164-5.

CHAPTER 3. APPRENTICESHIP IN WAR: SCOTLAND AND FLANDERS 1332-1340

1. Gray, *Scalacronica*, 106-7.

2. Strictly speaking, the Dunbars were earls of March, but I have used the alternative name to avoid confusion with the Mortimer earls of March in England.

3. Nicholson, *Edward III and the Scots*, 133.

4. *Chronicle of Lanercost*, 268.

5. The best account of the battle is in Rogers, *War Cruel and Sharp*, 39-46.

6. TNA E 361/3, rot. 19 m. 1d; DL 40/1/11, fo. 52ᵛ; BL Add. MS 46350, rot. 7; BL MS Cotton Galba E.III, fo. 183ᵛ.

7. TNA E 101/386/2, m. 7.

8. It is not clear if he actually served during the campaign; the writ for payment of his wages was cancelled. He did serve in 1334-5, but died during 1335. *CCR 1337-1339*, 7-8.

9. Rogers, *War Cruel and Sharp*, 69 n. 139. Documentation for this campaign is slight.

10. The date of Joan's birth is uncertain; if the normal forty days for Philippa's churching was observed, the feast for her churching on 8–10 March 1334 would give a date of 26–9 January 1334. See TNA E 101/386/16, m. 7, and Mortimer, *The Perfect King*, 433, 501.

11. TNA E 361/2, rot. 4 m. 13; TNA E 101/386/18, m. 23.

12. TNA E 101/389/14, m. 2.

13. *Lancelot-Grail*, Lancelot 1, 11:108; Lancelot 3, 86:215.

14. *Lancelot* is framed by King Claudas's dispossession of Lancelot, Lionel and Bors as children at the beginning of the story, and by the defeat of Claudas and restoration of their lands at the end. See index of proper names in *Lancelot-Grail* for full references.

15. Ormrod, *Edward III*, 99.

16. TNA E 361/3, rot. 24 m. 1d. See Tobler–Lommatzsch, *Altfranzösisches Wörterbuch*, 5.i, col. 501: the phrase 'escu lionel' occurs in the twelfth-century *chanson de geste Raoul de Cambrai* and elsewhere.

17. I am grateful to Thomas Woodcock, Garter King of Arms, for pointing out the identification of the shield. See *Dictionary of British Arms*, ii.223.

18. BL MS Cotton Nero C.VIII, fos. 233 ff.

19. *Historia Roffensis*, quoted in Rogers, *The Wars of Edward III*, 44.

20. Rogers, *War Cruel and Sharp*, 101.

21. *Historia Roffensis*, fo. 78.

22. Rogers, *War Cruel and Sharp*, 116 n. 181; Ayton, *Knights and Warhorses*, 257.

23. Gray, *Scalacronica*, 124–5.

24. Cazelles, *La Société politique*, 80–81.

25. *CPR 1330–1334*, 565. He was, however, sent again in 1337.

26. Baker, *Chronicon*, 56.

27. *Report on the Dignity of a Peer*, v.28–32.

28. Gray, *Scalacronica*, 123.

29. Edward of Woodstock, the king's eldest son, aged seven, succeeded John as earl of Cornwall; the earl of Norfolk had no heir.

30. *CPR 1338–1340*, 91, 95.

31. Ayton, 'Edward III and the English Aristocracy', 193.

32. Sumption, *The Hundred Years War*, i.51, estimates the magnate families at '150 to 200'.

33. McFarlane, *The Nobility of Later Medieval England*, 120.

34. Ayton, 'Edward III and the English Aristocracy', 184.

35. TNA E 101/388/8, m. 6.

36. Ibid.

37. TNA E 101/388/8, m. 1.

38. Not all of those who sealed were present in Flanders; for instance, Henry Percy was in the north of England in command of military activity on the Scottish border.
39. BL MS Cotton Caligula D.III, printed in Froissart, *Chroniques*, ed. Lettenhove, xviii.85–94.
40. Le Bel, *Chronique*, i.163 [81].
41. Rogers, *War Cruel and Sharp*, 173; TNA E 101/388/11.
42. See Rogers, *The Wars of Edward III*, 81–2.
43. TNA E 101/388/11; E 361/3, m. 40a.
44. *Avesbury*, 311.
45. I have followed the most recent account of the battle in Cushway, *Edward III and the War at Sea*, 92–100.
46. Philip's letter setting out the terms is in Fowler, 'Henry of Grosmont', appendix, 41.
47. *Croniques de London*, 84.
48. *Foedera*, ii.ii.1141.

CHAPTER 4. THE KINGDOM OF FRANCE

1. See Owen, *Le Traité de Walter de Bibbesworth*.
2. *Chronica Monasterii de Melsa*, iii.57. The abbey held lands at Nafferton.
3. Ponthieu had only been English since Edward's step-grandmother, Margaret of France, brought it as her dowry in 1299.
4. Baker, *Chronicon*, reflects this attitude in a more extreme form, calling Philip VI and John II 'the crowned one of France' rather than king of France, to emphasize that they were not the rightful occupants of the throne.
5. Taylor, 'The Salic Law', 550–52. The Roman *lex voconia*, in St Augustine's view, conflicted with the biblical tradition, which allowed women to inherit property. The crown, however, was not private property, but a public office, and a form of priestly office as well, from which women should be barred.
6. Cazelles, *La Société politique*, 53–7; see also Taylor, 'Edward III and the Plantagenet Claim to the French Throne'.
7. Cazelles, *La Société politique*, 72.
8. Ibid., 42–3.
9. *Chronique latine de Guillaume de Nangis*, ii.96–7.
10. John XXII mentions this in a letter congratulating him on his victory, quoted in DeVries, *Infantry Warfare*, 107.
11. The best account of the historical background is Whiting, 'The Vows of the Heron'. See also Butterfield, *The Familiar Enemy*, 115–16, and Vale, *The Princely Court*, 213–18. The most recent edition of *Vows of the Heron* is that of J. L. Grigsby and Norris J. Lacy.
12. Le Bel, *Chronique*, i.163 [81].

13. Sumption, *The Hundred Years War*, ii.412.

14. Eustace d'Auberchicourt until his death in 1368 (see Appendix 2), and then John Chandos.

15. *Grandes chroniques*, ed. Viard, ix.248.

16. *Historia Roffensis*, fo. 92.

17. See p. 234 below.

18. Anonimo romano, *Cronica*, abbreviated edn., 93.

19. Sumption, *The Hundred Years War*, i.562.

20. In fact he was beheaded in the courtyard of the Hôtel de Nesle on the morning of the 18th.

21. Le Bel, *Chronique*, i.198–200 [214–15].

22. Chareyron, *Jean le Bel*, 90–104, examines all the accounts in detail, and concludes that none can be said to solve the problem. Villani's version seems the most plausible.

23. *PROME*, v.35–6.

24. Cazelles, *Société politique, noblesse et couronne*, 40–43.

25. Delachenal, *Histoire de Charles V*, iii.553; although the writer requests that the letter be burnt immediately, a copy survives in a collection of documents relating to negotiations with France in BL MS Cotton Caligula D.III (item 76, not 170 as in Delachenal).

26. Cazelles, *Société politique, noblesse et couronne*, 309.

27. Luce, 'Du Guesclin au siège de Rennes'.

28. i.e. du Guesclin; Froissart, *Chroniques*, SHF, vi.117–19.

29. Sumption, *The Hundred Years War*, ii.215. For *regard* see p. 396 below.

30. *Récits d'un bourgeois de Valenciennes*, 220.

CHAPTER 5. 'AS IT WAS IN THE DAYS OF KING ARTHUR'

1. *History of the King's Works*, ii.950–54.

2. TNA E 101/388/11 (Norwich); *Foedera*, iii.ii.1145 (Ingham), 1146 (Norwich). *Murimuth*, 117 n. for series of tournaments, followed by Baker, *Chronicon*, 73.

3. TNA C 47/6/1, m. 18 ('the parson of Osmundeston', now Scole, near Diss).

4. TNA E 101/390/2, m. 4.

5. Ibid. m. 1.

6. There were jousts of war with the Scots at the end of December (*Murimuth*, 123) and tournaments on the return southwards at York and Hull (*Chronica Monasterii de Melsa*, iii.49).

7. *Murimuth*, 123–4, 223; Baker, *Chronicon*, 75; TNA C 47/6/1, mm. 2, 4; E 36/204, fo. 21ᵛ; E 101/389/14; *Chronica Monasterii de Melsa*, iii.49; *Brut*, ii.296.

8. *Murimuth*, 124, 223; *Chronica Monasterii de Melsa*, iii.49; TNA E 101/389/14. Froissart, *Chroniques*, Rome version, 563–4, has a garbled account confusing this tournament with that at Northampton, and incorporating a largely fictitious passage from Jean le Bel, *Chronique*, ii.2–4 [146–7], which is perhaps a distant echo of the Eltham occasion.

9. *Murimuth*, 121.

10. Jones, 'Edward III's Captains in Brittany', 107 n.

11. Cushway, *Edward III and the War at Sea*, 112.

12. Baker, *Chronicon*, 76.

13. *Murimuth*, 128.

14. *PROME*, iv.368.

15. Loomis, 'Edward I, Arthurian Enthusiast'.

16. Morris, 'Edward I and the Knights of the Round Table', 62.

17. *Chronicle of Glastonbury*, 245.

18. *Vita Edwardi Secundi*, in *Chronicles of the Reigns of Edward I and Edward II*, i.91.

19. Stones, *Anglo-Scottish Relations*, 197.

20. Shenton, 'Royal Interest in Glastonbury and Cadbury', 1254.

21. Luxford, 'King Arthur's Tomb at Glastonbury', 50.

22. Le Bel, *Chronique*, i.118–19 [65].

23. For an outline of Isabella's activities as a bibliophile, and a list of manuscripts possibly associated with her, see Smith, *The Taymouth Hours*, 16–17.

24. BL Add. MS 60584, m. 27ᵛ. See Revard, 'Courtly Romances in the Privy Wardrobe', 304–6, for details of all Isabella's borrowings.

25. TNA E 101/393/4, fo. 8; BL MS Cotton Galba E.XIV.

26. Cavanaugh, 'Books Privately Owned in England', 844–61.

27. The nature of John Flete's 'final account' is discussed in Revard, 'Courtly Romances in the Privy Wardrobe', 299, 303, 306–7.

28. *Dictionary of Medieval Latin*, s.v. 'romancia'.

29. BL Add. MS 60584, m. 26ᵛ.

30. Green, 'King Richard II's Books Revisited', 237; the list is printed in Cavanaugh, 'Books Privately Owned in England', 279.

31. This would identify it as a version of Chrétien de Troyes's *Perceval*, in which the two heroes figure with almost equal prominence.

32. *Antient Kalendars*, iii.265; Vale, *Edward III and Chivalry*, 45, 125.

33. Alfonso X, *Las siete partidas*, ii.428–9.

34. See p. 78 above.

35. 'Benedict of Peterborough', ii.159.

36. *Le Roman en prose de Tristan*, 424.

37. Johnstone, *Edward of Caernarvon*, 18.

38. Murimuth's chronicle exists in three versions: for full texts and translations, see Munby *et al.*, *Edward III's Round Table*, appendix C.

39. BN MS français 693, fo. 254.

40. The section of Gray's *Scalacronica* which described the event survives only in a sixteenth-century summary (135), which confuses the Round Table feast with the foundation of the Order of the Garter. Froissart's account (*Chroniques*, Rome version, 595-6), which makes the same mistake, was written many years later, after the early records of the Order of the Garter had been lost.

41. Newton, *Fashion in the Age of the Black Prince*, 18-20. The pawning seems to have been symbolic rather than related to the value of the crown. A list of crowns and circlets in BL Add. MS 60584, fo. 58ᵛ, shows the maximum value of any one of the crowns in Edward's possession in 1336 to have been £75.

42. Nicolas, 'Observations on the Garter', 6.

43. Walsingham, *Historia Anglicana*, i.263.

44. *Brut*, i.262.

45. Quoted in Schmolke-Hasselmann, 'The Round Table: Ideal, Fiction, Reality', 48.

46. The only exception is in the Merlin section of the *Lancelot-Grail*, where Merlin chooses fifty knights for Uther Pendragon when he establishes the table (Merlin 3:54); it is not at this point called the 'Round Table'. This passage is based on Robert de Boron's *Merlin*.

47. *Lancelot-Grail*, Merlin Continuation 60:16.

48. Ibid., Post-Vulgate Quest 107:359.

49. Ibid., 120:67.

50. Munby *et al.*, *Edward III's Round Table*, 238-39; *Chronicle of Lanercost*, 341, notes that 'excessive provisions' were used, 'as befitted the royal majesty'.

51. The expenditure listed by St John Hope, *Windsor Castle*, i.178-219, totals £6,868 8s. 4d. for sixty months, giving an average of £114 14s. 8d. per month.

52. *Morte Arthure*, ll. 16-22.

53. St John Hope, *Windsor Castle*, i.111.

54. *Antiquarian Repertory*, ed. F. Grose, i.324.

55. *CPR 1247-1258*, 157.

56. Munby *et al.*, *Edward III's Round Table*, 86; for the following discussion, see ibid., 84-99, 149-52.

57. *Perceforest*, ed. Roussineau, *Première partie*, ii.294; tr. Bryant, 258.

58. Barber, 'Edward III's Arthurian Enthusiasms Revisited'.

59. Wheatley, *The Idea of the Castle*, ch. 4, 'The Imperial Castle'.

60. Strong, *Art and Power*, 19.

61. Ormrod, *Edward III*, 261-2.

62. de Graaf, *Oorlog om Holland*, 285-97.

63. Giovanni Villani, *Nuova cronica*, iii.409: 'more than five thousand pounds sterling'.

CHAPTER 6. THE CRÉCY CAMPAIGN

1. For what follows, see Lambert, *Shipping the Medieval Military*, esp. ch. 3.
2. See below (p. 193) for the number of ships needed to transport 10,000 horses (500). This leaves 500 or more larger ships to transport 13,600 troops and a number of non-military personnel, as well as the provisions. The chroniclers, who all overestimate the strength of the army, are closer to the mark on the number of ships (Baker and Avesbury both give about 1,000; Murimuth gives 750 at the end of June, with further vessels still arriving before the departure a week later).
3. Cushway, *Edward III and the War at Sea*, appendix 2.
4. Livingstone and Witzel, *Road to Crécy*, 95.
5. Lambert, *Shipping the Medieval Military*, 136.
6. It is possible that the undated list of ships available to the king at the end of seventeenth-century copies of the army retinues (e.g. BL Add. MS 38823) may be related to the Crécy campaign.
7. Ayton and Preston, *Crécy*, 236.
8. Hewitt, *The Organization of War under Edward III*, 152.
9. Tout, 'Firearms in England', 689; further guns were supplied for the siege of Calais, but it is the use of guns in battle which is novel, as guns had not been employed at Berwick in 1333.
10. *Life and Campaigns of the Black Prince*, 30.
11. For numbers of carts, see Chapter 7.
12. TNA E 101/393/11, rot. 62.
13. e.g. TNA E 101/393/11, rot. 63.
14. Livingstone and Witzel, *Road to Crécy*, 89.
15. See p. 198 below on the policy of intimidation as against acceptance into the king's peace, i.e. changing sides.
16. Hewitt, *Organization of War under Edward III*, 53–6.
17. Wrottesley, *Crécy and Calais*, 193–4. The lower figure is for retinues with more than 300 men, the higher for retinues of more than 100 men; we do not know enough about the arrangements for feeding the army at large to do more than estimate.
18. TNA E 101/393/11, rot. 60.
19. It is described as 'salted' in the accounts; ibid., rot. 62.
20. Ibid., rot. 58d.
21. Ayton and Preston, *Crécy*, 181.
22. Ibid., 189.
23. The surviving lists are for the whole campaign up to 23 November 1347, when the bulk of the troops had returned from the siege of Calais: Wrottesley, *Crécy and Calais*, 193, 201. There are no accurate numbers for the actual battle.
24. *RBP*, i.14.

25. Ayton and Preston, *Crécy*, 207.
26. *RBP*, i.163.
27. *RBP*, ii.46.
28. Jones and Walker, 'Private Indentures for Life Service in Peace and War 1278–1476'.
29. Full text in Fowler, *The King's Lieutenant*, 234.
30. Prince, 'Indenture System', 293.
31. *Life and Campaigns of the Black Prince*, 29.
32. Nicholson, *Edward III and the Scots*, 17, 174.
33. Hay, 'The Division of the Spoils of War', 108–9.
34. Ibid., 101.
35. Ayton, *Knights and Warhorses*, 130–37.
36. *Life and Campaigns of the Black Prince*, 29.
37. Pryor, 'Transportation of Horses by Sea during the Crusades'. In the Sicilian ships, there is an item for the purchase of rings, evidently for securing their bridles as in a stable. Pryor interprets the rings as supports for slings which lifted the horses off their feet for the duration of the voyage; this is still found in modern veterinary practice, where a horse will be put in slings if it has a foot injury, so that it can stand comfortably for long periods on three legs.
38. Manchester, John Rylands, MS 234, fo. 50; fifteen grooms are listed as keepers of one destrier.
39. Henxteworth, m. 1, payment for windage at the start of the expedition to Gascony in 1355.
40. Ambroise, *History of the Holy War*, ii.53.
41. Printed in Le Bel, *Chronique*, ii.338.
42. *Life and Campaigns of the Black Prince*, 14. There is no supporting evidence that he had made arrangements for his arrival in Gascony, whereas he does seem to have made arrangements for a possible rendezvous with the Flemish army in Picardy before setting out.
43. Tidal information from Admiralty Easy Tide website, http://easytide.ukho. gov.uk.
44. Sumption, *The Hundred Years War*, i.494.
45. Ibid., 499.
46. *Life and Campaigns of the Black Prince*, 15.
47. The *Acts of War* lists many of the commanders, and others are named in the St Omer chronicle. I have excluded four clerks and the bishop of Durham.
48. For Hastings's campaign, which ended around 25 August, see Sumption, *The Hundred Years War*, i.498–9, 503, 512, 519, 524.
49. Viard, 'La Campagne de juillet-août 1346', 15. The French sources say that the castle was 'sold', but it seems more likely that the French commanders recognized Edward as king of France and were put on his payroll.
50. *Life and Campaigns of the Black Prince*, 30.
51. Viard, 'La Campagne de juillet-août 1346', 18.

52. *Chronique normande du XIVe siècle*, 76.

53. See pp. 308-9 below for the far-reaching consequences on Thomas Holland's career, and indeed on the succession to the English throne: without this money, Holland would not have regained Joan of Kent, and she would not have been free to marry the prince of Wales on Holland's death.

54. *Life and Campaigns of the Black Prince*, 34.

55. Papirius Masso and Thomas Warton, cited in Prentout, 'La Prise de Caen', 261.

56. Delpit, *Collection générale*, 72.

57. *Avesbury*, 364.

58. *Chronique normande du XIVe siècle*, 77 n. 1.

59. *Eulogium historiarum*, iii.206.

60. Edward III to his council, in Fowler, 'News from the Front', 84.

61. *Eulogium historiarum*, in *Life and Campaigns of the Black Prince*, 35.

62. *Eulogium historiarum* calls him 'du Bois'.

63. There is some confusion over the sequence of events at Gaillon and La Roche-Guyon: see Viard, 'La Campagne de juillet-août 1346', 41-3. However, Viard is mistaken in saying that La Roche-Guyon was not taken, as the *Acts of War* (Cambridge, Corpus Christi College, MS 170, fo. 102^r) specifically quotes a rhyme which says that 'the fleur-de-lis will lose its name when Rocheguyon is wounded', because the castle was reputedly impregnable. The same rhyme is quoted in *Chronica Monasterii de Melsa*, iii.56.

64. *Récits d'un bourgeois de Valenciennes*, 223.

65. *Grandes chroniques*, ed. Viard, ix.278.

66. *Life and Campaigns of the Black Prince*, 39.

67. Le Bel, *Chronique*, ii.92 [176-7].

68. *Life and Campaigns of the Black Prince*, 19.

69. Ibid., 22.

70. *Récits d'un bourgeois de Valenciennes*, 227.

71. BN MS français 693, fo. 260^v.

72. Le Bel, *Chronique*, ii.96 [178].

73. Knighton, *Chronicle*, 60-61.

74. Information from local noticeboards at St Valéry, September 2012.

75. *Chronica Monasterii de Melsa*, iii.57.

76. Data from http://easytide.ukho.gov.uk, adjusted back to the Julian calendar.

77. *Life and Campaigns of the Black Prince*, 22.

78. See the discussion in Preston, 'The Traditional Battlefield of Crécy': although he believes that the traditional battlefield is the most likely candidate, the problems and uncertainties are fully explored.

CHAPTER 7. THE BATTLE AT CRÉCY

1. See Keegan, 'The Personal Angle of Vision', in *The Face of Battle*, 128–33.
2. Li Muisit, *Chroniques et annales*, 161.
3. *Life and Campaigns of the Black Prince*, 22.
4. Ibid., 19–20.
5. *Acts of War*, 27.
6. *PROME*, iii.389–92.
7. Matteo Villani, *Cronica*, i.46, says that Edward 'arranged all his carts at the front *a modo d'una schiera*', in ranks or in a group, and that he put armed knights on top of the carts. The knights would not have been much use in that position, and his account seems to be entirely a garbled version of that of his brother.
8. Villani writes 'bombarde', but these were described as ribalds in the royal accounts, and were therefore smaller than the guns usually described as bombards. They would have been similar to that illustrated in Milemete's treatise of 1326.
9. 'pallottole di ferro', 'pellets of iron'. This is confirmed by a writ of 4 March 1346, referring to 'pellotis et pulvere' for the 100 'ribalds' shipped for the Crécy campaign: Tout, 'Firearms in England', 688.
10. 'dentro al carrino': I have translated 'carrino' as 'array of carts' below, as it does not specify the actual formation in which the carts were drawn up.
11. This corresponds to the 'small area' mentioned in Edward III's letter on the battle.
12. It was not unusual to give the prince of Wales his anticipated title, even during his father's lifetime.
13. Giovanni Villani, *Nuova cronica*, i.450–59.
14. Anonimo romano, *Cronica*, abbreviated edn., 5. In his introduction, the chronicler says that he has used oral sources, but this applies mainly to the section on Rome.
15. See Campanelli, 'A New Account of the Battle of Crécy from Fourteenth-Century Rome', forthcoming.
16. As at Waterloo, where the English identified the advancing Imperial Guard in the same way.
17. This would be 22 August by the modern Julian calendar, but still a late harvest.
18. The text reads 'crossbowmen' (*valestrieri*), but the English did not use crossbows.
19. 'soprastare', literally 'stand above'.
20. *Istoire et croniques de Flandre*, ii.42–3.
21. BN MS français 693, fo. 261ᵛ.
   Names are distorted throughout this text: I have normalized as follows:

Berinc = Warwick, Suatere = Fitzwalter, Werdon = Verdon, Stryvelyn = Stirling, Poinghe = Poynings, Frarin = Fitzwarin, Causmale = Carswell. I have not been able to identify the lords of 'Tringas' and 'Baruf'. Seventeen of the thirty-four names occur in the *Acts of War*. For a slightly different interpretation, and comments on St Omer's errors, see Ayton in Ayton and Preston, *Crécy*, 165–6, 242–4. The 'lord of Man' is Sir William Montagu, who became earl of Salisbury in 1349.

22. *Historia Roffensis*, fo. 92.
23. i.e. the *Grandes chroniques*, *Chronique des quatre premiers Valois*, and *Chronographia Regum Francorum*.
24. *Chronique normande du XIVᵉ siècle*, 81.
25. *Istoire et croniques de Flandre*, 42.
26. Mathias von Nuewenburg, *Chronik*, 398.
27. Le Bel and *Chronica Monasterii de Melsa* treat the carts as the usual wagon park to the rear of the army, found in most medieval battles (Froissart takes his account from Le Bel).
28. Baker, *Chronicon*, 67.
29. Vegetius, *Epitoma rei militaris*, 3.10.16–18.
30. Toman, *Husitské válečnictví za doby Žižkovy a Prokopovy*, 403–4.
31. Durdík, *Hussitisches Heerwesen*, 151–63.
32. The fullest account is in DeVries, *Infantry Warfare*, 32–48.
33. *Annales Gandenses*, 66; Paris, *Memoriale*, 643; *Chronique artésienne*, 84; Guiart, 'Branche des royaus lignages', 291.
34. Guiart, 'Branche des royaus lignages', ll. 20085–20110.
35. Harari, 'Strategy and Supply in Fourteenth-Century Campaigns', 318.
36. Anonimo romano, *Cronica*, abbreviated edn., 87.
37. Le Bel, *Chronique*, ii.299 [251].
38. See Ch. 6, n. 38 above.
39. Baker, *Chronicon*, 84.
40. Strickland and Hardy, *The Great Warbow*, 295–7.
41. Baker, *Chronicon*, 84.
42. Ayton, in Ayton and Preston, *Crécy*, 328, and *Dictionary of Medieval Latin*, s.v. 'ericius'. It is also used of siege machines, one of the group of such engines which even in classical times were named after animals, the best-known being the *testudo* or tortoise. It may seem a small point, but a great deal of ink has been spilt over the crucial question of the formation of the archers in this battle.
43. Mathias von Nuewenburg, *Chronik*, 398.
44. Baker, *Chronicon*, 84.
45. *lo conte Valentino*: Aymar VI de Poitiers, count of Diois and Valentinois.
46. The *catenelle* or small chains; not immediately identifiable as part of a suit of armour.
47. *Adoardetto*, literally 'little Edward', an insulting way of referring to the prince.

48. Anonimo romano, *Cronica*, abbreviated edn., 92–3.

49. *Chronique normande du XIVe siècle*, 81; the *Chronographia Regum Francorum*, ii.233, is the only other source to mention it: 'And in that battle the prince of Wales was captured by the count of Flanders, but later rescued.'

50. Thomas Daniel was specifically rewarded for raising the banner, but Fitzsimon may have taken charge of it again once the enemy had retreated.

51. Baker, *Chronicon*, 85.

52. Froissart, *Chronicles*, tr. Thomas Johnes, i.167; original in Froissart, *Chroniques*, SHF, i.281. Sir Thomas Norwich is not found in the official British records.

53. 'et fut honteux', literally 'and was ashamed'. *Récits d'un bourgeois de Valenciennes*, 234.

54. His name is given as 'Sir Haun di Tornello'; I have not been able to identify him.

55. Anonimo romano, *Cronica*, abbreviated edn., 95–7.

56. Beneš z Weitmile, *Chronicon*, iv.514.

57. BN MS français 693, fo. 262^v.

58. John of Arderne, *Treatises*, xxvii n.

59. Le Bel, *Chronique*, i.102 [180].

60. Technically, according to the Church, a day of truce; but the rule was rarely observed in the field.

61. *Récits d'un bourgeois de Valenciennes*, 230.

62. There is a modern viewing point where the mill is thought to have stood, though its precise position is not known.

63. Cochon, *Chronique normande*, 69.

64. *Murimuth*, 216; *Storie pistoresi*, 222; *Eulogium historiarum*, iii.210–11.

65. *Chronique des quatre premiers Valois*, 16.

66. BN MS français 693, fos. 262^v–263.

67. Le Bel, *Chroniques*, ii.108 [183].

68. A cloth attached to the helmet covering the neck which was usually blazoned with the owner's arms.

69. *Récits d'un bourgeois de Valenciennes*, 235.

70. Delisle, *Histoire de Saint-Sauveur*, 67–8, 88–9, 95–9.

71. BN MS français 693, fo. 263; this is confirmed by *Istoire et croniques de Flandre*, 44, but this information may have come from St Omer.

72. Anonimo romano, *Cronica*, abbreviated edn., 96.

73. Giovanni Villani, *Nuova cronica*, 458.

74. Baker, *Chronicon*, 85–6.

75. Facetiously named 'good day' (*goedendag*) from the warm welcome they gave to the enemy.

76. *Life and Campaigns of the Black Prince*, 23.

77. Ibid., 25.

78. *RBP*, i.14.

79. Prestwich, 'The English at the Battle of Neville's Cross', 1–14.
80. 2 Corinthians 2: 14.
81. Offler, 'Thomas Bradwardine's "Victory Sermon"', 4–6.
82. *Chronica Monasterii de Melsa*, iii.63–4.
83. Viard, 'Le Siège de Calais', 163.
84. BN MS français 693, fos. 272–3; Viard, 'Le Siège de Calais', 157.
85. *Avesbury*, 386.
86. Le Bel, *Chronique*, ii.113 [184]; Knighton, *Chronicle*, 78–80.
87. Le Bel, *Chronique*, ii. 157 [199].
88. Baker, *Chronicon*, 91.
89. 'runcino' – Chaucer's 'rouncy'.
90. Le Bel, *Chronique*, ii.161–7 [200–203].
91. 'Hay the Whit Swan', according to TNA E 372/207, m. 50.
92. See p. 79 above for full details.
93. See in particular the full-page images in Martin, *Minnesänger*, where pea-cock feathers are used.
94. Edward was at Lichfield only once in 1348, from 4 to 12 May; he was at Windsor in May, June and July, and at Eltham in May and July, so the dating is not certain. The dating of 9 April in the accounts for the Lichfield tournament (Nicolas, 'Observations on the Garter', 26) is clearly an error. Baker (*Chronicon*, 101) dates the Windsor tournament as being at midsummer 1349, but he gives the names of the French captives present, two of whom are known from the accounts to have been at Windsor in 1348. Baker's chronology is particularly difficult at this point: he still appears to be following Murimuth's curious habit of starting the year at Michaelmas, which suggests Murimuth's chronicle (or a continuation) may have covered these years. He goes on to say that the captives hunted at Clarendon: Edward was at Odiham, known for its hunting (*History of the King's Works*, ii.766), Woodstock and Clarendon in August and September. See Ormrod, 'For Arthur and St George', 19 n. 30. For other details of these tournaments, see Nicolas, 'Observations on the Garter', 26–30, 39, 40–42; TNA E 101/391/15, mm. 7, 9, 10; E 372/207, m. 50; *RBP*, iv.72–3.
95. Baker, *Chronicon*, 101.
96. Ormrod, *Edward III*, 306 n. 28. A date of 9 July seems unlikely, since the Canterbury jousts would almost certainly have been cancelled if this was the case.

CHAPTER 8. THE ROYAL CHAPELS AND THE COLLEGE OF ST GEORGE AT WINDSOR

1. *Foedera*, iii.i.167.
2. *Foedera*, iv.50.
3. See Cook, *English Collegiate Churches*, 12–17, and Knowles and Hadcock, *Medieval Religious Houses*, 420–44.

4. The canons of the great cathedrals also technically belonged to secular colleges, but these colleges had been set up after the foundation of the church to which they belonged.

5. Stow, *A Survey of the cities of London and Westminster*, vi.54.

6. Ormrod, 'The Personal Religion of Edward III', 857.

7. *Victoria County Histories, London*, i.461.

8. *Chronica Monasterii de Melsa*, iii.51–2.

9. *Eulogium historiarum*, iii.213.

10. See Howe, 'Divine Kingship and Dynastic Display'.

11. *Calendar of Charter Rolls 1341–1417*, p. 134.

12. *Wynnere and Wastoure*, l. 503.

13. Stratford, *Richard II and the English Royal Treasure*, 209, item R 706.

14. Howe, 'Divine Kingship and Dynastic Display', 262.

15. Tracy, *English Gothic Choirstalls*, 50.

16. Howe, 'Divine Kingship and Dynastic Display', 264.

17. Topham, *Some Account of the Collegiate Chapel of St Stephen*, 8 (note to plate VIII).

18. See Billot, *Les Saintes Chapelles*.

19. Edward I had begun to rebuild the chapel in 1297 in the style of the Sainte-Chapelle, but at that point there was no re-foundation of the chapel, and no claim to the kingdom of France, but simply a princely rivalry. See Alexander and Binski, *Age of Chivalry*, cat. no. 324.

20. Bowers, 'The Music and Musical Establishment of St George's Chapel', 174–5.

21. Ormrod, 'Edward III and his Family', 408, 413.

22. *Calendar of Liberate Rolls 1240–1245*, 205.

23. *History of the King's Works*, ii.1016.

24. Ibid., 862–3.

25. Biddle, *King Arthur's Round Table*, 78–80 (dating of woodwork), 398–402 (Windsor connection). Given Edward IV's known Arthurian enthusiasm and use of the rose en soleil, as well as Harding's mention of the Round Table as hanging there, a dating in the 1460s on cultural grounds seems much more probable.

26. See list in Good, *The Cult of Saint George in Medieval England*, 155–9; unfortunately, few dates can be given. However, only a handful are for monastic institutions, or for pre-Conquest churches: see Morgan, 'The Banner-Bearer of Christ', 56.

27. Good, *The Cult of Saint George in Medieval England*, 52–9.

28. *History of the King's Works*, i.481. The cost also included a similar figure of a pilgrim.

29. Oxford, Bodleian Library, MS Douce 231, fo. 1^r. See Sandler, *Gothic Manuscripts*, ii.95–6.

30. Milemete, *De nobilitatibus*, xxi. See also *Secretum Secretorum*, ed. Manzalaoui.

31. *Political Thought in Early Fourteenth Century England*, 21.

32. Voragine, *Legenda Aurea*, s.v. Julian, 145; Lambeth Apocalypse: illustrated in Good, *The Cult of Saint George in Medieval England*, pl. 2. For descriptions of the manuscripts, see Morgan, *Early Gothic Manuscripts*, ii.104; Warner, *Queen Mary's Psalter*, 45–6, pls. 223–4; Sandler, *Gothic Manuscripts*, ii.108.

33. Modernized from Greene, *Selection of English Carols*, 227.

34. BL MS Harleian 5001, fos. 24-24ᵛ; this is a seventeenth-century copy of the prince's wardrobe book for 1306–7. The garters and shoes are recorded as being 'for the Scottish wars', but this is probably an error and the comment should apply to the previous item, banners of St George and St Edward.

35. *Calendar of Inquisitions Miscellaneous*, ii.130, C87/25, goods of prisoners taken after the battle of Boroughbridge.

36. e.g. in Boulton, *Knights of the Crown*, 157–8.

37. TNA E 101/386/9, m. 12, and E 101/386/18, m. 58.

38. TNA E 101/387/25, m. 7.

39. *Calendar of Inquisitions Miscellaneous*, ii.434, C145/5, goods of the dean of Wolverhampton.

40. Arnould, *Étude sur le Livre des saintes médécines*, 72.

41. *Eulogium historiarum*, iii.231.

42. BL Add. MS 42130, fo. 158ᵛ; Brown, *The Luttrell Psalter Commentary*, 150.

43. *MED*, s.v. garter (2a), (1).

44. See p. 311 below.

45. TNA E 101/391/5; Rolleston's account roll is E 101/391/15; and the pipe roll is E 372/207, m. 50.

46. St Gregory is reputed to have said 'Non angli sed angeli' when he first encountered pale-skinned English boys at a slave market. See Bede, *Historia ecclesiastica*, ii.i.

47. TNA E 43/20 (1329–30); C 241/147/100 and C 241/147/130 (1367, 1368).

48. *RBP*, iv.66–77; Tout, *Chapters*, iv.434.

49. The first entries in the account go back to the time of Northwell's predecessor.

50. TNA E 101/388/8, m. 3.

51. Vale, *Edward III and Chivalry*, 149 n. 36, dates the streamers to 1346–7; Ormrod, *Edward III*, 303, suggests the dating of 1348–9. For other examples of streamers, see TNA E 101/387/14, m. 2, m. 23; E 101/388/8, m. 2; E 101/390/2, mm. 4–5; E 101/392/4, m. 2, m. 7; E 361/3, rot. 40d.

52. *Dictionary of Medieval Latin*, s.v. 'chlamys'.

53. TNA E 372/207, m. 50, m. 1/2.

54. See p. 255 above. Newton, *Fashion in the Age of the Black Prince*, 44, claims that *blu/bluettus*, the term used, is rare elsewhere, but see for example BL Add. MS 60584, fos. 9 ff.
55. TNA E 36/278, fo. 45.
56. *RBP*, iv.72–3.
57. TNA E 101/391/1, fo. 7.
58. Camden, *Britannia*, 278.
59. Vale, *Edward III and Chivalry*, 83–4.
60. *PROME*, iv.413, 447, 453–4; see also Harriss, *King, Parliament*, 372–3.
61. See p. 488 below.
62. Prince of Wales's accounts, TNA E 36/144, fo. 45^r (*de societate garter*); E 101/394/16, mm. 6, 7, 15, 18 (*societas* in all cases); accounts for 1383 and 1387 cited by Anstis, *Register*, i.10 n., 11 n. *Societas* is defined by the *Dictionary of Medieval Latin* as a 'company' in this context, with a secondary meaning of 'fellowship'; as *compaignie* is used by the French sources I have used 'company' throughout.
63. Accounts for 1399 and 1416, cited by Anstis, *Register*, i.13 n., 15 n. Baker is writing in the context of the foundation of the College of St George, and calls them both *fraternitas* and *comitiva*, a company.
64. Anstis, *Register*, ii.50 n.
65. See Jefferson, 'MS Arundel 48 and the Earliest Statutes of the Order of the Garter'.
66. See p. 528 below for the later clauses providing for a different feast day if St George's Day was too close to Easter.
67. St John, 'Dying beyond the Seas', 196. The calculation is taken from Boulton, *Knights of the Crown*, 140.
68. *John of Gaunt's Register*, ii.51.
69. Jefferson, 'MS Arundel 48 and the Earliest Statutes of the Order of the Garter', 379; see below, Appendix 5, notes 22 and 23.
70. Roberts, *St George's Chapel, Windsor Castle*, 8.
71. Saul, 'Servants of God and Crown', 98.
72. Roberts, *St George's Chapel, Windsor Castle*, 65.
73. St John Hope, *Windsor Castle*, i.152, 223.
74. *CPR 1361–1364*, 498.
75. *CCR 1343–1346*, 30 September 1343; *CPR 1361–1364*, 587; *CCR 1360–1364*, 30 September 1360; *CPR 1364–1367*, 342.
76. Tout, *Chapters*, iv.331.
77. *RBP*, iv.162, 456, 556.
78. *CPR 1361–1364*, 23; Roberts, *St George's Chapel, Windsor Castle*, 13.
79. TNA E 404/17/357–9.
80. Gray, *Scalacronica*, 150–51; on the event as a whole see Berard, 'Edward III's Abandoned Order of the Round Table', 35–8.

81. TNA E 403/388, 9 March and 12 March 1358.
82. Knighton, *Chronicle*, 158–9; *CCR 1354–1360*, 489; *RBP*, iv.252.
83. Anonymus Cantuariensis, *Chronicon*, 45.
84. Delachenal, *Histoire de Charles V*, ii.65–7.
85. Matteo Villani, *Cronica*, ii.182, 196–7; *Eulogium historiarum*, iii.227; John of Reading, *Chronica*, 130. See Ragone, *Giovanni Villani e i suoi continuatori*, 230–32, for Matteo Villani's connection to the court of Naples and to Niccolò Acciaioli, and hence to the chivalric world of the Company of the Knot.
86. John of Reading, *Chronica*, 131; *RBP*, iv.323; *Brut*, ii.309.
87. Vale, *Edward III and Chivalry*, 86.
88. Ibid., 88.
89. Mortimer, *The Perfect King*, 427–9.
90. TNA E 372/207, m. 50 (2).
91. See p. 346 below.
92. Antal Pór, 'Az Anjou ház és örökösei', including facsimile and edition of text of charter.
93. Statute X, in Daumet, 'L'Ordre castillan de l'écharpe', 25; not in second redaction of statutes.
94. Statute XXI, ibid., 27; statute XVI in Villanueva, 'Memoria sobre la Orden de Caballería de la Banda de Castilla', 567.
95. Clement VI, *Lettres closes*, ii.33.
96. For what follows, see Ormrod, *Edward III*, 320–21.
97. Ormrod's claim that 'The Black Prince took an extensive entourage ... in 1352' is a misreading of an account for 1348 entered belatedly in the records for 1352. *RBP*, iv.72–3.
98. *CPR 1354–1358*, 527; the entry for 21 April is entered as at Windsor.
99. 'Under Arthur's reign, the sheltered people ...'
100. Bowers, 'The Music and Musical Establishment of St George's Chapel', 178–9. *Sub Arcturo* is recorded on Herald HAVPCD 236 (1999).
101. See Brindle, 'The First St George's Chapel'.
102. Jane Geddes, 'Medieval Decorative Ironwork in St George's Chapel', 63–5.
103. St John Hope, *Windsor Castle*, i.143.
104. Kerr, 'The East Window of Gloucester Cathedral', 125–7.
105. Eton College MS 213; the figure for the height of the sills is from Brindle, 'The First St George's Chapel', 44.
106. Tracy, *English Gothic Choirstalls*, 53 and pl. 166.
107. Begent and Chesshyre, *The Most Noble Order of the Garter*, 25–6, 32; ordinances in 1431–2 imply that the canons only occupied the high stalls if the knights were absent, because if a knight was attending the service, the canon was to move to the lower stalls; but the 1522 statutes say specifically that, in the absence of any knights, the canons may sit 'in the high seats next unto the stalls of the said knights'.

108. St John Hope, *Windsor Castle*, ii.374.
109. Jefferson, 'MS Arundel 48 and the Earliest Statutes of the Order of the Garter', 378.
110. St John Hope, *Windsor Castle*, i.138, 139. Thirty-eight iron candlesticks were bought for the chapel, which were probably for the stalls, but this does not really help in working out the layout (forty-eight would be the expected number). They may have been positioned in front of the lower stalls.
111. Ibid., ii.374.
112. Bond, *The Inventories of St George's Chapel*, 59, 268–9.
113. St John Hope, *Windsor Castle*, i.133.
114. Ibid., 139.
115. Ibid., 162.
116. Tudor-Craig, 'The Fonts of St George's Chapel', 154.
117. St John Hope, *Windsor Castle*, i.131.
118. Cheetham, *English Medieval Alabasters*, 13.
119. Cheetham, *Alabaster Images of Medieval England*, 177.
120. Bond, *The Inventories of St George's Chapel*, 50–61.
121. Ibid., 4.
122. Ibid., 74–5.
123. Ibid., 41–7.
124. Given-Wilson, 'The Exequies of Edward III', 277–80.
125. I owe this observation to Karen Watts of the Royal Armouries, in response to an enquiry about pre-1350 examples of display of arms over tombs.
126. Goodall, 'The Aerary Porch', 169.
127. St John Hope, *Windsor Castle*, ii.506. The only entry which definitely implies a separate chapter house for the canons is that for glazing in 1430–31, so it is possible that in the fourteenth century it was shared with the canons. See also Tatton-Brown, 'The Deanery, Windsor Castle', 350, for the correct interpretation of the layout of the chapter house.
128. See p. 295 below for a discussion of the fate of the early records of the order.
129. Tatton-Brown, 'The Deanery, Windsor Castle', 350.

CHAPTER 9. 'THE COMPANY OF THE KNIGHTS OF SAINT GEORGE *DE LA GARTIERE*'

1. Jefferson, 'MS Arundel 48 and the Earliest Statutes of the Order of the Garter', 373–5.
2. As translated by Lisa Barber; see Appendix 5, 'The Statutes of the Garter'.
3. The data for 1351 is: Mortlake, 28 April, [ceremony (according to clause 10) 30 April], Westminster, 1–2 May; and for 1362: Windsor, 27–8 April, [ceremony (according to clause 10) 30 April], Westminster, 1–5 May.

4. Jefferson, 'MS Arundel 48 and the Earliest Statutes of the Order of the Garter', 374.
5. *Foedera*, iv.50.
6. Oxford, Bodleian Library, MS Lat. Hist. a.2; see Krochalis, '*Magna tabula*: The Glastonbury Tablets'.
7. Ibid., 519–21.
8. Windsor, St George's Chapel Precentor's Rolls, XV.56.16.
9. Ibid., 22 and 23. The latter roll ends on 29 September 1417; the feast of the Exaltation was on 14 September.
10. René d'Anjou, in the statutes of his Order of the Crescent, founded in 1448, imitated the Windsor tables, ordering that tables should be put up in Angers cathedral 'four feet high or thereabouts, on which were the arms, together with the helm and war cry, of each of the knights and squires of the order'. Du Cange, *Dissertations*, 46.
11. Ashmole, *Order of the Garter*, 191.
12. See St John Hope, *The Stall Plates of the Knights of the Order of the Garter*.
13. Baker, *Chronicon*, 109. He uses *fraternitas* and *comitiva*. The latter description only recurs in an entry on the issue rolls in 1401 to the 'officium virgarii comitive de Garteri', the office of verger of the Company of the Garter (TNA E 404/17/357).
14. He uses the word 'blueto', bluet, for blue, which corresponds to the entries in the wardrobe accounts (p. 273 and note above).
15. Nicolas, *History of the Orders of Knighthood*, ii.54. For example, Richard Fitzsimon, traditionally said to have died in 1348–9, seems to have died a decade later; see p. 513 and note.
16. See Appendix 2.
17. See p. 325 below.
18. See clause 19 of the statutes, p. 531 below.
19. Some of these deaths may have been due to causes other than the plague, but there is some doubt about both the nature and duration of the outbreak. Shrewsbury, *The History of Bubonic Plague*, 128, believes it may have started in the autumn of 1360, and may have been influenza.
20. TNA E 101/393/15, m. 14.
21. I owe this suggestion to Lisa Jefferson.
22. The king and the prince of Wales are excluded from the analysis which follows. John Sully is included, as he is likely to have been elected in 1353, not 1361; see p. 300 above.
23. Fowler, 'News from the Front', 85.
24. Devon, Warwick, Arundel, Lancaster, Hereford, Oxford. Kent and Pembroke were under age.
25. See *ODNB*, s.v. John de Vere, seventh earl of Oxford.

26. See above for the question of the date of the first meeting of the knights: he may have been chosen and not installed.

27. The fullest account of his career is in Burtscher, *The Fitzalans*, 33–68.

28. See p. 96 above for jewels as currency rather than display alone.

29. See p. 314 below.

30. The medieval text which uses this nickname has proved elusive: the earliest reference I can find is in *Complete Peerage*, i.242 in 1912, which does not quote a source.

31. Newton, *Fashion in the Age of the Black Prince*, 93–4.

32. Boulton, *Knights of the Crown*, 300.

33. Burtscher, *The Fitzalans*, 48, also thinks that the marriage was at the root of his exclusion.

34. *Life and Campaigns of the Black Prince*, 33–4.

35. Edward's four younger sons, and Sir Thomas Holland's younger brother Otho.

36. There were grants of revenue to William Montagu in December 1347 (*CPR 1345–1348*, 443–4) and a royal licence for him to raise money a year later by mortgaging estates he would inherit (*CPR 1348–1350*, 213).

37. Quoted in Wentersdorf, 'The Clandestine Marriages of the Fair Maid of Kent', 220.

38. Matteo Villani, *Cronica*, ii.544. He says that Joan was quite old, had already been married to two 'minor barons' and had several children.

39. *Chronique des quatre premiers Valois*, 123–5.

40. Possibly Sir Bernard Brocas, who had fought with him at Poitiers and was a leading Gascon lord, is intended.

41. One was probably a chantry chapel in the crypt at Canterbury cathedral. See Wentersdorf, 'The Clandestine Marriages of the Fair Maid of Kent', 217–19 and appendices C–G.

42. *RBP*, iv.428.

43. Chandos Herald, *La Vie du Prince Noir*, ll. 3771–2.

44. Two apparent instances in Edward's reign do not relate to Garter robes: in 1358 Philippa was given £500 for her clothes for the very lavish St George's Day feast of that year; the same applies to the issue of robes to Isabella, the king's eldest daughter, in 1361 (TNA E 101/393/15, m. 3, where the garment is a 'corset'). However, in 1376, when she was married to Enguerrand de Coucy, who was a companion of the Garter, she was issued with robes 'de secta militum de Garterio' (TNA E 101/397/20). For the entries in Richard II's reign, see Anstis, *Register*, i.10–15 nn.

45. Gillespie, 'Ladies of the Fraternity of Saint George and the Garter', exaggerates the formal element of these gifts, but has a useful coverage of the entries relating to them. Collins, *The Order of the Garter*, 79–83, rightly points out the fact that many ladies were part of the royal family or closely related to it.

46. Thomas of Woodstock, Edward's youngest son, became a knight in 1380.

47. Richard II and Henry of Derby, the future Henry IV, became knights in 1376-7.
48. *Complete Peerage*, i.344 n.
49. Jeanne was the wife of Philip V. See the accounts by Elizabeth A. R. Brown of this affair in 'The King's Conundrum' and 'Diplomacy, Adultery and Domestic Politics at the Court of Philip the Fair', especially pp. 74-7. A promised extended study by the same author never appeared.
50. Gray, *Scalacronica*, 66-7.
51. Archer, 'The Estates and Finances of Margaret of Brotherton', 269-70.
52. TNA SC8/63/3125.
53. Wrottesley, *Crécy and Calais*, 196 nn.
54. Goodall, *The English Castle 1066-1650*, 265.
55. *Croniques de London*, 90.
56. It was demolished during the Civil War; the modern castle is a nineteenth- and twentieth-century replica.
57. *Foedera*, iii.507.
58. See Wrottesley, *A History of the Family of Wrottesley of Wrottesley*.
59. Ibid., 147.
60. Booth, 'Taxation and Public Order', 25.
61. Bellamy, 'The Coterel Gang'; Stones, 'The Folvilles of Ashby-Folville'.
62. The case of Eustace d'Auberchicourt is even more complex than that of Henry Eam, and is explored in Appendix 2.
63. Hamaker, *De rekeningen der grafelijkheid van Holland*, xxi.246.
64. Janse, *Ridderschap in Holland*, 320.
65. Hamaker, *De rekeningen der grafelijkheid van Holland*, xxvi.81.
66. Ibid., 83.
67. Ibid., 103.
68. Conrad, 'Der dritte Litauerzug König Johanns von Böhmen', 383-4.
69. *Le Livre de seyntz medicines*.
70. Arnould, *Étude sur le Livre des saintes médécines*, 76.
71. TNA C 47/6/1, m. 1.
72. St John, 'War, the Church and English Men-at-Arms', 76.
73. Spencer, *Pilgrim Souvenirs and Secular Badges*, 272-6.
74. *RBP*, iv.73, 163.
75. TNA E 36/204, fo. 72ʳ. See also Blatchly and MacCulloch, *Miracles in Lady Lane*, 10-11.
76. See p. 262.
77. John of Reading, *Chronica*, 132-3. *Wynnere and Wastoure*, ll. 496-503, merely points to Edward's interest in Cologne, before the poem breaks off abruptly.
78. Including their attendants, the group was at least 361 people. *Foedera*, iii.ii.203.
79. Birch, *Pilgrimage to Rome in the Middle Ages*, 197-9.

80. Indulgences promised remission of punishment for sins in advance, which became one of the major abuses of the medieval Church.
81. Birch, *Pilgrimage to Rome in the Middle Ages*, 47. It may have been open earlier, but is not recorded until the thirteenth century.
82. Spufford, *Power and Profit*, 200.
83. See Chettle, 'The *Boni Homines*'.
84. Knowles and Grimes, *Charterhouse*, 49, 87–92.
85. Ibid., 6.
86. Brooke, 'Chaucer's Parson and Edmund Gonville', 6–8.
87. *Cambridge Gild Records*, 49–50. Tamworth can be identified as John Clement of Tamworth since his wife Alice is named in both the records of the guild and in his will (*Calendar of Wills in the court of Husting*, ii.167). He was the head of the royal chancery and seems to have run a small training school for chancery clerks: see Tout, 'The Household of the Chancery', 72.
88. BL MS Cotton Nero D.VII, fo. 105ᵛ.
89. Stanley, *Historical Memorials of Canterbury*, 164–71.
90. St John Hope, *The London Charterhouse*, 94–5, from the cartulary of the Charterhouse. The copy of the will in Archbishop Sudbury's register does not mention the effigy: *Registrum Simonis de Sudbiria*, i.1–3.
91. Froissart, *Chroniques*, SHF, viii.ii.287.
92. Ibid., vii.163.
93. Knowles and Grimes, *Charterhouse*, appendix C, 87–92. The report states that 'the cranial capacity is exceptionally large . . .'
94. Greene and Whittingham, 'Excavations at Walsingham Priory', 269.

CHAPTER 10. KNIGHTLY ASSOCIATIONS: ORDERS, COMPANIES, FRATERNITIES

1. Pauli, *Codice diplomatico del ordine di Malta*, ii.80.
2. Antal Pór, 'Az Anjou ház és örökösei', pp. 138–9; the Latin is 'societas fraternalis militie tytulo sancti Georgii insigniti'. Compare 'fratres militie Templi', in the Templars' own records.
3. The exact date is uncertain, as we only have a charter issued in April 1326 with amendments to the original statutes: Boulton, *Knights of the Crown*, 30.
4. Engel, *The Realm of St Stephen*, 130–34.
5. Ibid., 146.
6. Ibid., 183–4.
7. Tout, *Chapters*, ii.148.
8. Boulton, *Knights of the Crown*, 42.
9. Minorite chronicle, s.a.1342, translated from Latin and quoted in Fügedi, 'Turniere im mittelalterlichen Ungarn', 395.

10. Majláth, 'A Kolos Család Czímeres Levele'; Fügedi, 'Turniere im mittelalter-lichen Ungarn', 394.
11. Trautz, 'Die Reise eines Englischen Gesandten', 367.
12. They survive only in an eighteenth-century copy, printed in Chevalier, *Choix de documents inédits sur le Dauphiné*, ii.35–9.
13. Billot, *Les Saintes Chapelles*, 232.
14. Clement VI, *Lettres closes*, 32.
15. Billot, *Les Saintes Chapelles*, 232.
16. Clement VI, *Lettres closes*, 33.
17. French version of the Latin original in Vattier, 'Fondation de l'Ordre de l'Étoile', 42.
18. French original ibid., 37. Le Bel's figure of 300 is wrong; John's letter (Vattier, 'fondation de l'Ordre de L'Étoile', 39) clearly states 'cinq cens'.
19. Le Bel, *Chronique*, ii.204–7 [216–17].
20. 'four arpents' in the original. The *arpent* was a unit of length roughly equivalent, in medieval France, to 75 yards.
21. Modernized from *The Works of Sir Thomas Malory*, ed. Field, 786.
22. Alfonso X, *Las siete partidas*, ii.428.
23. Pannier, *La Noble-maison de Saint-Ouen*, 90.
24. The date of Epiphany is given in *Chroniques des quatres premiers Valois*, 23. For what follows, see Pannier, *La Noble-maison de Saint-Ouen*, 63 ff.
25. Ibid., 73–4.
26. The accounts (Pannier, 74) wrongly call him 'patriarch of Jerusalem'.
27. At Mauron, on 14 August 1352. Le Bel's phrase here is 'ilz firent sy soubtillement par une embusche qu'ilz firent', but there is no suggestion elsewhere that the French were exactly 'ambushed' at Mauron, and 'embusche' should probably be understood as a deft tactical ploy.
28. Le Bel, *Chronique*, ii.206 [217]. There is an account of the order in the long chronicle of Kirkstall, which says that the knights were 'moved rather by untamed courage than judgement', and claims that 140 were killed. *Kirkstall Chronicles*, 95.
29. Also called the Company of the Knot, from its device.
30. Matteo Villani, *Cronica*, ii.579.
31. Quoted in Boulton, *Knights of the Crown*, 236; for the full details of this order, see ibid., 211–40, and Bock, 'L'Ordre du Saint-Esprit au Droit Désir'.
32. The order is often referred to as the Order of the Band. Its Spanish name is *banda*, whose first meaning is 'sash', and all visual representations quite clearly show a sash worn diagonally over armour. See Riquer, *L'Arnes del Cavaller*, plate opposite p. 77, showing Henry of Trastamara and his son wearing the sash.
33. *Crónica de rey don Alfonso el Onceno*, in *Crónicas de los reyes de Castilla*, i.231–2.

34. Villanueva, 'Memoria sobre la Orden de Caballería de la Banda de Castilla', 436–65, 552–75.
35. Boulton, *Knights of the Crown*, 77–80.
36. This law code of the kingdom of Castile is at the foundation of modern Spanish law, and, through the former Spanish colonies of the southern United States, is a strong influence on the laws of Texas, California and Louisiana. The first translation was made by a lawyer in Chicago in the 1930s, and issued in looseleaf form for legal use.
37. This later became three times a year: see statute 15 in the version edited by Villanueva, 'Memoria sobre la Orden de Caballería de la Banda de Castilla', 566.
38. This was also a function of the Order of Santiago (St James); the first *casa de merced* for exchange of prisoners was established as early as 1170. The Trinitarians, founded in France in 1198, and the Order of Our Lady of Mercy, started in Barcelona in 1218, were orders wholly dedicated to ransoming Christian prisoners.
39. López de Ayala, *Corónica del rey don Pedro*, 164.

CHAPTER 11. KNIGHTS IN THEIR OWN WORDS

1. Llull, *Llibre de l'Orde de Cavalleria*, 35.
2. Ibid., 60.
3. Ibid., 50.
4. Kaeuper, *Chivalry and Violence in Medieval Europe*, 278.
5. See Charny, *The* Book of Chivalry, 3–17; Contamine, 'Geoffroy de Charny'.
6. *Murimuth*, 129.
7. The writ for the attorneys is dated October 1343: CPR 1343–1345, 130.
8. See pp. 415–16 below.
9. Baker, *Chronicon*, 103.
10. Wagner, *Heralds and Heraldry in the Middle Ages*, 21–3; Keen, *Origins of the English Gentleman*, ch. 2.
11. Charny, *The* Book of Chivalry, 85.
12. Ibid., 111.
13. Ibid., 115.
14. *Livre Charny*, ll. 548–600.
15. See Lester, *Sir John Paston's Grete Boke*, 34–57, on knightly miscellanies.
16. Taylor, 'English Writings on Chivalry and Warfare during the Hundred Years War', 74 ff.
17. See Squibb, *The High Court of Chivalry*, 2–3.
18. *PROME*, vii.148.
19. Reproduced in Keen, *Origins of the English Gentleman*, 40.

20. TNA C 47/6/1, m. 4.
21. For the Robert Laton case, see p. 478 below.
22. Keen, *Laws of War*, 55–6, 260–63.
23. See p. 381 below for chaucer's evidence on this.
24. Nicolas, *Scrope–Grosvenor Controversy*, i.124.
25. Ayton, 'Knights, Esquires and Military Service', 88.
26. Ibid., 95.
27. Nicolas, *Scrope–Grosvenor Controversy*, i.155–6.
28. Ibid., 178–9.
29. Ibid., 124–5.
30. Ayton, 'Knights, Esquires and Military Service', 87.
31. Keen, *Origins of the English Gentleman*, 51–2.
32. Paravicini, *Die Preussenreisen*, i.59, 94.
33. Quoted ibid., i.272, from *Scriptores rerum prussicarum* (Leipzig, 1861–), iii.599.
34. Paravicini, *Die Preussenreisen*, i.259, 263.
35. See p. 355 above
36. For what follows, see Paravicini, *Preussenreisen*, i.316–34, which quotes the original texts and gives a full discussion.
37. Ibid., 316–17. The account was written down some fifty years later.
38. Pannier, *La Noble-maison de Saint-Ouen*, 90.
39. Paravicini, *Preussenreisen*, i.337.
40. Ibid., ii.13 and tables 48–9.
41. Ibid., i.123. The document to which Paravicini refers is unfortunately in the unpublished third volume of his work, but appears to be the *Armorial Belleville*, ed. Pastoureau and Popoff, fos. 55ᵛ–57ᵛ. See also Paravicini, 'Armoriaux et histoire culturelle'.
42. Paravicini, *Preussenreisen*, i.123.
43. Gray, *Scalacronica*, 139 (John Leland's summary of lost text), confirmed by Baker, *Chronicon*, 119–20.
44. Paravicini, *Preussenreisen*, i.124.
45. Ibid., ii.28–9.
46. Boucicaut, *Le Livre de fais du bon messire Jehan le Maingre, dit Bouciquaut*, 42.
47. Paravicini, *Preussenreisen*, ii.24–5.

CHAPTER 12. LAWS OF WAR AND THE REALITY OF WARFARE

1. Le Bel, *Chronique*, i.69–70 [47].
2. Baker, *Chronicon*, 85.
3. *Récits d'un bourgeois de Valenciennes*, 234.

4. Ayton, *Knights and Warhorses*, 225, for average prices; pp. 59–60 for details on spare horses.
5. Henxteworth, m. 1, m. 1d, m. 3, m. 5d, m. 9, m. 10, m. 12, m. 13, m. 14, m. 14d.
6. Ayton, *Knights and Warhorses*, 239–41.
7. Prince, 'Indenture System', 291.
8. Keen, *Laws of War*, ch. IX, 139–55.
9. Ayton, *Knights and Warhorses*, 127–31.
10. 'Demandes pour la Joute', in *Livre Charny*, demande 52, 117.
11. Henxteworth, m. 24, 22 June 1356.
12. For what follows, see Keen, *Laws of War*, ch. X, 151–85.
13. *RBP*, iv.339.
14. i.e. with the shield point upwards.
15. See Broome, 'The Ransom of John II King of France 1360–70'.
16. 'Demandes pour la Joute', in *Livre Charny*, demande 74, 128.
17. Walthey, 'The Peace of 1360–1369', 142–3.
18. Laborde, *Notice des émaux du Musée du Louvre*, ii.112. I am grateful to Ronald Lightbown for pointing out this entry.
19. Baker, *Chronicon*, 152.
20. López de Ayala, *Corónica del rey don Pedro*, 165–6.
21. Keen, *Laws of War*, 53.
22. The highest ransom at Nájera was half as much again, for the count of Denia, and took twenty-three years to collect; the rights were sold on by the prince to the king, who resold them to the heirs of the captors. The sureties spent the intervening years in captivity in England.
23. Hayez, 'Un exemple de culture historique', 162.
24. 'La Geste des Nobles François', ii.634. The text and manuscript (BN MS français 5001, fo. 15ᵛ) read 'pour l'introduction des nobles': I have emended to 'instruction'.
25. Froissart, *Chroniques*, SHF, vi.119.
26. Keen, *Laws of War*, 197–206.
27. Le Bel, *Chronique*, ii.118–19 [186].
28. Ibid., ii.164–7 [202–3].
29. Froissart, *Chroniques*, SHF, iv.56–7.
30. Leroux, 'Le Sac de la cité de Limoges et son relèvement'; Walsingham, *Chronicon Angliae*, 67; *Chroniques de Saint-Martial*, 154.
31. Keen, *Laws of War*, 129–33.

CHAPTER 13. THE GARTER COMPANIONS AT WAR

1. Jean le Bel's figure: it is blank in Baker's account. Le Bel, *Chronique*, ii.177 [206]; Baker, *Chronicon*, 103.
2. *Avesbury* says that it was 'subtiliter elevatus', cunningly built, 409.

3. *Chronique normande du XIVᵉ siècle*, 104.

4. Baker, *Chronicon*, 109.

5. Froissart, *Chroniques*, SHF, iv.90, though his list is unreliable and adds some unlikely names; Sir John Lisle: *CPR 1350–1354*, 43.

6. TNA E 379/198, rot. 36 m. 1, and TNA E 372/207, rot. 51. I owe this reference to Dr Thom Richardson of the Royal Armouries, who discusses it in his forthcoming thesis on the armourers' accounts of Edward III's reign. For the use of pavises in England, see DeVries, 'The Use of the Pavise', 93–5.

7. *Wynnere and Wastoure*, ll. 295–8; the Garter motto is at l. 68.

8. Li Muisit, *Chroniques et annales*, 278.

9. Froissart, *Chronicles*, tr. Johnes, i.198. See also Froissart, *Chroniques*, SHF, iv.93–4.

10. *RBP*, ii.77.

11. *RBP*, iv.143–5.

12. Henxteworth, m. 23.

13. Ibid., m. 9, m. 10, m. 12; Baker, *Chronicon*, 128.

14. *Life and Campaigns of the Black Prince*, 50.

15. Baker, *Chronicon*, 131; echoed by Matteo Villani, *Cronica*, i.709: 'this country, where there was no memory among those living there at the time of war having disturbed it'.

16. *Life and Campaigns of the Black Prince*, 54.

17. Baker, *Chronicon*, 136.

18. The river Save, a tributary of the Garonne.

19. *Life and Campaigns of the Black Prince*, 54–5.

20. The quarrel is reported by Baker, *Chronicon*, 137–8, and in more detail by Matteo Villani, *Cronica*, i.709–10.

21. *Life and Campaigns of the Black Prince*, 52.

22. Matteo Villani, *Cronica*, i.709.

23. The main accounts of the campaign are those of Geoffrey le Baker and *Eulogium historiarum*. Matteo Villani, writing within a few years of the battle, gives an extensive account, but is better informed about the negotiations with the cardinals and about the French situation than he is about the English manoeuvres (*Cronica*, ii.21–41). See Carpentier, 'L'Historiographie de la bataille de Poitiers'.

24. Sumption, *The Hundred Years War*, ii.246.

25. Tourneur-Aumont, *La Bataille de Poitiers*.

26. Hewitt, *The Black Prince's Expedition*, 115.

27. Quoted in *ODNB*, s.v. 'Thomas Beauchamp, eleventh earl of Warwick (1313/14–1369)'.

28. Crécy (*Brut*, ii.298–9): 'And for al this, the same unglorious Philip withdrowe him ... wherfore it was seyd in commune among his owne peple "Nostre beall Retret", that is for to sey, "Our faire withdraweth hym".'

Poitiers (Baker, *Chronicon*, 149, my translation): 'what the invincible French would call "a fair retreat".'

29. Delachenal, *Histoire de Charles V*, i.237.

30. Matteo Villani, *Cronica*, ii.36.

31. Ibid., 38.

32. Baker, *Chronicon*, 142-5; Sallust, *Catiline Conspiracy*, 58. Catiline's speech to his troops before the battle in which he is killed was famous as a piece of rhetoric.

33. Le Bel, *Chronique*, ii.237 [228].

34. Froissart, *Chroniques*, SHF, v.153-4.

35. Ibid., 162.

36. Delachenal, *Histoire de Charles V*, ii.25-6.

37. Matteo Villani, *Cronica*, ii.295-6.

38. Le Bel, *Chronique*, ii.287 [247].

39. Ibid., 299 [251-2].

40. Ibid., 291-2 [249].

41. Froissart, *Chroniques*, SHF, v.202.

42. Knighton, *Chronicle*, 168-71.

43. Matteo Villani, *Cronica*, ii.383.

44. *Chronique des quatre premiers Valois*, 105-6, describes an assault on the city by the men of the prince of Wales, but the description of the attack, on the Paris gate, is very generalized, and unsupported by any other evidence. Delachenal, *Histoire de Charles V*, ii.159, dismisses it as fiction and is probably correct, even though Sumption, *The Hundred Years War*, ii.431, believes that it did take place. It seems out of line with the whole ethos of the campaign, unless it was a rather half-hearted attempt to test the strength of the defences. *Les Grandes chroniques*, ed. Viard, vi.167, say categorically that he left without ever attacking the city.

45. Venette, *Chronicle*, 98-9.

46. *Les Grandes chroniques de France*, ed. Delachenal, i.257.

47. Venette, *Chronicle*, 102.

48. *Anonimalle Chronicle*, 46. Black Monday was the traditional name for Easter Monday, which was in fact a week earlier.

49. *Chronicles of London*, 13.

50. Knighton, *Chronicle*, 179.

51. Venette, *Chronicle*, 103.

52. Knighton, *Chronicle*, 179.

53. *Foedera*, iii.ii.630.

54. Brittany: TNA C 76/45, m. 3 (I owe this reference to Professor Michael Jones). Ireland: CCR *1360-1364*, 450; Ayton, *Knights and Warhorses*, 77, 198 n. 10, 202, 203 n. 33.

55. *Archivo General de Navarra, Comptos*, v, document 202, 84.

56. Froissart, *Chroniques*, ed. Lettenhove, vii.497.

57. He seems to have fought alongside Chandos in 1362 or earlier: there is a payment to him for John Chandos's expenses on 13 April 1362. See TNA E 404/7/43.

58. There are several contemporary accounts of the battle, summarized in Sumption, *The Hundred Years War*, ii.518–20.

59. *Foedera*, iii.ii.754–5.

60. *Foedera*, iii.ii.779.

61. *Archivio General de Navarra*, register 120, counter-roll for January 1365–January 1366 (I owe this reference to Professor Michael Jones).

62. *Archivo General de Navarra*, *Comptos*, vi.28, documents 56 and 57.

63. However, Froissart says that in late March Henry of Trastamara kept Eustace d'Auberchicourt and Hugh Calveley with him, and said that he wanted them for a proposed crusade against Granada. Froissart, *Chroniques*, ed. Lettenhove, vii.95.

64. *Documents des archives de la chambre des comptes de Navarre*, 142; Fowler, *Medieval Mercenaries*, 175; Crow and Olson, *Chaucer Life-Records*, 65. Chaucer's wife Philippa was the daughter of Pain de Roet, a Hainault neighbour and possible companion in arms of Auberchicourt.

65. Fowler, *Medieval Mercenaries*, 173.

66. Guesclin, *Letters*, 57, no. 152.

67. *Archivo General de Navarra*, *Comptos*, vi.66–7, documents 151 and 153.

68. Gray, *Scalacronica*, 191.

69. Chandos Herald, *La Vie du Prince Noir*, ll. 1965–2000. Chandos had refused point-blank to join the Great Company: Froissart, *Chroniques*, ed. Lettenhove, vii.88.

70. Russell, *English Intervention in Spain and Portugal*, 78.

71. Sons of his old comrades Ralph Stafford and Robert Ufford; both became companions of the Garter.

72. See p. 402 above.

73. This would now be termed a spinel; it weighs thirty-four grams, is the size of a small egg and is the largest uncut example in the world.

CHAPTER 14. THE MOST NOBLE
ORDER OF THE GARTER

1. Beltz, *Memorials of the Garter*, 152, quotes Coucy as writing that it had been 'his honour and pride' to wear it; but this is not in the printed text. *Foedera*, iv.18.

2. See Appendix 2.

3. Boulton, *Knights of the Crown*, 294–7; see also Boulton, 'The Middle French Statutes of the Monarchical Order of the Ship'.

4. Saul, *Richard II*, 337, affirms that 'it was invariably his habit to return to Windsor for the annual Garter ceremonies', but the itinerary which he prints does not entirely bear this out, partly because we cannot be as sure of his whereabouts as in the case of Edward III. Anstis, *Register*, ii.55, can find records for only fourteen of the twenty-two years of his reign.

5. See pp. 296–7 above.

6. See Lindenbaum, 'The Smithfield Tournament of 1390'.

7. Crow and Olson, *Chaucer Life-Records*, 472.

8. *Brut*, ii.343. If Richard made the two foreigners knights of the order, there can have been only twenty-two Garter knights in the tournament, and the *Brut* evidence does seem to be unreliable.

9. Original in Beltz, *Memorials of the Garter*, appendix XV, 405–6.

10. *Femina* (Trinity College, Cambridge, MS B 14.40), ed. William Rothwell, The Anglo-Norman On-Line Hub 2005, http://www.anglo-norman.net/texts/.

11. Crow and Olson, *Chaucer Life-Records*, 412, 458–62.

12. See for example Cooke and Boulton, '*Sir Gawain and the Green Knight*: A Poem for Henry of Grosmont?' and Carruthers, 'The Duke of Clarence and the Earls of March'.

13. Hoccleve, *Minor Poems*, 41–3; Burrow, *Thomas Hoccleve*, 21–2.

14. Mooney, 'Some New Light on Thomas Hoccleve', 297–307.

15. 'unus militum de illo inclito et excellente ordine militaris de la gartour': *PROME*, ix.124, where the translation uses 'military order', instead of the more accurate 'knightly order'.

16. Pantin, 'Medieval Treatise on Letter-Writing', 382. The king's deputy was probably Humphrey duke of Gloucester, who presided on St George's Day of that year: Anstis, *Register*, ii.70.

17. Minstrels themselves were very ill-defined: the word has a wide range of meanings, and its origin seems to have been related to 'ministering' to someone, whether as a servant or a craftsman. Only later did it acquire the modern meaning of a musician or singer.

18. See Paravicini, 'L'Office d'armes'.

19. See Crouch, 'The Court of Henry II and the Office of King of Arms'.

20. Bullock-Davies, *Register of Royal and Baronial Domestic Minstrels*, 21–2.

21. Ibid., 24–5.

22. Ibid., 110.

23. Little (Parvus): ibid., 139–44; Morel: ibid., 123–5; Norris: ibid., 137.

24. The best general account is still Wagner, *Heralds and Heraldry in the Middle Ages*, 25–40. Henry le Norrois: *Histoire de Guillaume le Maréchal*, 266–7.

25. Bullock-Davies, *Register of Royal and Baronial Domestic Minstrels*, 123–5, 137. The last record for Nicholas Morel is in 1297; Robert Parvus appears until 1320.

26. 'No king of arms or minstrels may carry concealed weapons on them other than their blunted swords. The kings of arms should wear only their tabards'; translation in Crouch, *Tournament*, 202.

27. See Wagner, *A Catalogue of English Mediaeval Rolls of Arms*; the early rolls are discussed in Wagner, *Heralds and Heraldry in the Middle Ages*, 48–55; Denholm Young, *History and Heraldry*, 41–63; and most recently in Simpkin, *English Aristocracy at War*, 20–25.

28. Hemingburgh, *De Gestis*, i.323.

29. Wagner, *Heralds and Heraldry in the Middle Ages*, 35.

30. Ibid., 159.

31. *RBP*, iv.108, where he is listed next to the king's messenger; and iv.163, 168, twice given the substantial sum of 100s. in 1355; given 66s. 8d. in 1358. Other heralds appear in his accounts as early as 1348 (William Stafford, given a plate 'of the companionship of the Garter' on 18 December).

32. See his testimony in TNA C 47/6/1, m. 4. He had served with Ufford at Sluys and Calais, and on the Reims campaign.

33. van Oostrom, *Court and Culture*, 129.

34. *Avesbury*, 464.

35. Ormrod, *Edward III*, 320.

36. 'qu'il prist ung heroult congnoissant armes', Le Bel, *Chronique*, ii.108. Froissart describes the French and English heralds working together to identify the dead, but does not name individual heralds; the operation is directed by five English knights and recorded by four clerks. Froissart, *Chroniques*, Rome version, 737.

37. Nicolas, *Scrope–Grosvenor Controversy*, i.111, ii.300.

38. Froissart, *Chroniques*, Amiens version, i.i.1. Revising the text for the Rome version of his chronicle, he ends the sentence at '... reporters of such affairs'. Froissart, *Chroniques*, Rome version, 35.

39. Froissart, *Chroniques*, Rome version, i.197–8. For the likely date of composition see ibid., xxii.

40. Wagner, *Heralds and Heraldry in the Middle Ages*, 39–40.

41. See van Oostrom, *Court and Culture*, ch. iv.

42. See Melville, 'Pourquoi des hérauts d'armes?'.

EPILOGUE: THE LEGENDS

1. Martorell, *Tirant lo Blanc*, 121.

2. Ibid., 122.

3. See p. 81 above.

4. Ashmole, *Order of the Garter*, 181.

5. Belvaletus, *Catechismus*, 7.

6. Colón, 'Premiers échos', 448–53.

7. Vergil, *Polydori Vergili Historiae Anglicanae*, 379.
8. Camden, *Britannia*, 278.
9. Le Bel, *Chronique*, ii.31 [155].
10. Saunders, *Rape and Ravishment*, 174.
11. There are a number of modern discussions of the episode. The most authoritative is that of Gransden, 'The Alleged Rape by Edward III of the Countess of Salisbury'. See also Chareyron, *Jean le Bel*, 308–23, who suggests that Uther's rape of Ygerne in Arthurian legend may have been a model; but Uther is disguised as her husband, and the violence represented by Le Bel is absent. Ingeldew, *Sir Gawain and the Green Knight and the Order of the Garter*, 46–57, unconvincingly attempts to link this episode, as representative of the morals of the court, to the great alliterative poem.
12. See p. 310 above.
13. The beginning of ch. LXI reads: 'You have earlier heard how King Edward had had to conduct a series of mighty wars in many lands and marches, at vast cost and expense: in Picardy, Normandy, Gascony, Saintonge, Poitou, Brittany and Scotland. And you've also heard of his passionate love for the valiant lady of Salisbury, named Alice; he couldn't help himself, even though the Earl of Salisbury was one of his closest counsellors and most loyal servants. And so it was that, for love of that lady and in his longing to see her . . .' (Le Bel, *Chronique*, ii.1 [146]).
14. Froissart, *Chroniques*, Amiens version, ii.332.
15. *Chronographia Regum Francorum*, ii.204–5; see also *Chronique normande du XIVe siècle*, 54 and *Istoire et croniques de Flandre*, ii.9, which give even briefer accounts of the affair.
16. See Ormrod, 'For Arthur and St George', 29.
17. The origin of this piece is unknown, and it seems to have been added originally to a copy of Ralph Higden's encyclopaedic *Polychronicon*, possibly at St Albans. It is printed in Murimuth, *Adami Murimuthensis Chronica Sui Temporis*, 224–7; an addition critical of his taxations and exactions is printed from BL Add. MS 12118, fo. 157, in John of Reading, *Chronica*, 91. See Taylor, *The Universal Chronicle of Ranulf Higden*, 117–19, 122–3.

Index